D1599163

STUDIES ON THE HISTORY OF THE
CHURCH OF CYPRUS, 4th–20th CENTURIES

Published in association with

ΠΟΛΙΤΙΣΤΙΚΟ ΙΔΡΥΜΑ ΤΡΑΠΕΖΗΣ ΚΥΠΡΟΥ
BANK OF CYPRUS CULTURAL FOUNDATION

BENEDICT ENGLEZAKIS

Studies on the History of the Church of Cyprus, 4th–20th Centuries

Translated by
Norman Russell

Edited by
Silouan and Misael Ioannou

VARIORUM
1995

Published by   VARIORUM
Ashgate Publishing Limited
Gower House, Croft Road
Aldershot, Hampshire GU11 3HR
Great Britain

Ashgate Publishing Company
Old Post Road
Brookfield, Vermont 05036
USA

BX
450
. E54
1995

0-86078-486-X

British Library Cataloguing in Publication Data

Englezakis, Benedict
Studies on the History of the Church of Cyprus, 4th–20th Centuries
I. Title   II. Russell, Norman   III. Ioannou, Silouan
IV. Ioannou, Misael
275.693

US Library of Congress Cataloging in Publication Data

Englezakis, Benedict
Studies on the History of the Church of Cyprus, 4th–20th Centuries/
Benedict Englezakis; translated by Norman Russell.
    p. cm. Includes bibliographical references (pp.   ) and index.
ISBN 0-86078-486-X (hbk, alk. paper)
1. Cyprus (Archdiocese)—History. 2. Orthodox Easter Church—
Cyprus—History. 3. Cyprus—Church History. 4. Cyprus (Archdiocese)—
History—Sources. 5. Orthodox Eastern Church—Cyprus—History—
Sources. 6. Cyprus—Church History—Sources.   I. Title   II. Russell,
Norman   III. Ioannou, Silouan   IV. Ioannou, Misael.
BX450.E54   1995
281.9'5693–dc20   94–41962
        CIP

This book is printed on acid free paper

Typeset by Stanford DTP Services, Milton Keynes, MK17 9JP
Printed and bound in Great Britain by
Biddles Ltd, Guildford and King's Lynn

CONTENTS

LIST OF ILLUSTRATIONS

FOREWORD

Benedict (Archimandrite Paul) Englezakis died of cancer on November 13th 1992 aged forty-five, after a life that represented a human triumph over diverse types of adversity. His father had also died at a young age of the same disease, as did his beloved sister Chloe (Sister Ioanna) who in her last months was nursed by Father Paul, a year and a half before his own death.

He suffered a great deal mainly but not solely because of long periods of his own and his sister's poor health. He had also to bear the pain of the tragedy of Cyprus. I remember him describing how the Greek-Cypriot inhabitants of his own village, Petra, pleaded with their Turkish-Cypriot compatriots in 1964 not to leave the village. They left, he remembered, with regret and chiefly out of solidarity with members of their community who had suffered in villages where, unlike Petra, there had been conflict; but one couple spoke in a very different tone. They were leaving with the intention to return one day and evict their Greek-Cypriot neighbours. And so it occurred, in 1974. His family, like so many others, lost its property and he his library and home.

A third cause of concern was that historical and theological scholarship were not the qualities most appreciated in a Church of Cyprus which has, understandably to a certain degree, centred its attention in recent years on political and economic issues more than is customary. He felt his gifts were not fully used, although his wide knowledge of languages – he spoke English, French and Russian, read German and Italian and of the ancient languages, Greek, Hebrew, Latin and Slavonic – led to him frequently representing the Church of Cyprus at conferences outside the country.

A layman for much of his life, Benedict Englezakis was ordained deacon and priest by the then Metropolitan of Chalcedon, Bartholomew, in June 1990, and in October 1992 was given the honour of the office of Archimandrite on the personal initiative of the same hierarch, by then Patriarch of Constantinople.

Benedict Englezakis had the scholar's passion for the particular. He was always enthusiastic and engaged with the subject of his study. He was

meticulous in collecting and sifting evidence and skilled in the use of philological tools. The centre of his interests was biblical studies in which he had
obtained his doctorate at Cambridge University in 1976, and he was
considered one of the best biblical scholars in the Orthodox Church. His sense
of the living continuity of tradition was both more subtle and much broader
than that of many Orthodox, stretching from Old Testament times until today;
and was kept in balance with a sense of the development of tradition. He
often took pleasure in employing his historical erudition to point out that
some aspect of church custom which many Orthodox consider to date from
time immemorial in fact originated in, say, the seventeenth century. He had
a particular empathy for and understanding of the early centuries of the
Church.

Blessed with an irrepressible sense of humour, a quizzical and sometimes
ironical, but always penetrating, view of acts and actors in the Church and
the world at large, as well as encyclopaedic knowledge, he was a most pleasant
and interesting person to meet. His humanity burst scholarly and ecclesiastical barriers alike. Above all he had a gift for friendship and it was this which
supported him through his many difficulties. Amongst these friendships were
his relationship with the Leventis family as with many of his teachers and
fellow-scholars, and not least the deep bond with Yiannis (Father Silouan)
and Constantine (Deacon Misael) Ioannou, sons of a refugee priest from Cyprus
who died early. They became his spiritual children, followed him in theological studies and today serve the Patriarchate of Constantinople. As his
executors they have spared neither time nor energy nor expense in helping
to bring this volume to publication.

Father Paul has left behind him two published works with a third due to
appear. *New and Old in God's Revelation: Studies in Relations between Spirit and Tradition
in the Bible*, representing his doctoral dissertation, was published in Cambridge
and New York in 1982.

The present volume represents a collection of his articles on the history
of the Church of Cyprus: it was his unrealised hope one day to be able to
write a full history. His second doctoral dissertation, on the twelfth-century
Cypriot Saint Neophytos's use of the Bible, should appear in Greek within
the next two years. There remain a number of articles on biblical and theological themes in various publications and unpublished lectures given at the
seminary of St John of Damascus at Balament in the Lebanon in 1982 and
1984, or to many and various groups in Cyprus between 1976 and 1985,
especially on the Gospel of St John. These do not at present appear to exist
in a form that might permit publication.

I first met Benedict Englezakis after the tragic events in Cyprus in 1974
at the introduction and request of Archbishop Makarios and we have

remained friends ever since. I believe this volume, devotedly translated by Norman Russell, is a fitting continuation of the series of five books by Greek theologians that have appeared in English: this one covering the hitherto unrepresented area of church history. May it inspire others, as scholarly and as devoted as Father Paul, to continue his work.

COSTA CARRAS

London, 15th November 1994

TRANSLATOR'S NOTE

Father Paul (Benedict) Englezakis handed me the manuscript of his collected studies the day before he died in November 1992. I have made only minor changes, to bring uniformity to the system of notes and references. The bibliographies which accompanied some of the studies have been assembled at the end of the work and include the additional material mentioned in the Introduction. Fr Englezakis expressed the wish for the Greek originals of previously unpublished texts to be given and also of the nineteenth-century Greek epigrams of Chapter XIX as good examples of the genre. Where Greek texts have been given in the Latin alphabet they have been transliterated, while references to modern Greek works have been rendered phonetically. I hope this will not cause confusion. Turkish words are glossed in the index.

ABBREVIATIONS

AB	*Analecta Bollandiana*
BHG	*Bibliotheca Hagiographica Graeca*
BZ	*Byzantinische Zeitschrift*
CMH	*Cambridge Medieval History*
CPG	*Clavis Patrum Graecorum*
CSHB	*Corpus Scriptorum Historiae Byzantinae*
DACL	*Dictionnaire d'archéologie chrétienne et de liturgie*
DHGE	*Dictionnaire d'histoire et de géographie ecclésiastique*
DOP	*Dumbarton Oaks Papers*
DS	*Dictionnaire de spiritualité*
DTC	*Dictionnaire de théologie catholique*
ECQ	*Eastern Churches Quarterly*
EEBS	*Epetiris Etaireias Vyzantinon Spoudon*
EEThSA	*Epetiris Etaireias Theologikon Spoudon Athinon*
EEThSPTh	*Epetiris Etaireias Theologikon Spoudon Panepistimiou Thessalonikis*
EKEEK	*Epetiris tou Kentrou Epistimonikon Erevnon Kyprou,* Nicosia
EO	*Echos d'Orient*
GCS	*Die griechischen christlichen Schriftseller*
GOTR	*Greek Orthodox Theological Review*
ICC	*International Critical Commentaries*
JÖB	*Jahrbruch der Österreichischen Byzantinistik*
JTS	*Journal of Theological Studies*
KS	*Kypriakai Spoudai,* Nicosia
KX	*Kypriaka Chronika,* Nicosia
NE	*Neos Ellinomnimon*
OC	*Orientalia Christiana*
PG	*Patrologia Graeca*
PL	*Patrologia Latina*
PO	*Patrologia Orientalis*
RAC	*Reallexikon für Antike und Christentum*

REB	*Revue des études byzantines*
REG	*Revue des études grecques*
RHE	*Revue d'histoire ecclésiastique*
TM	*Travaux et mémoires*
TU	*Texte und Untersuchungen*
VV	*Vizantijskij Vremmenik*
ZKG	*Zeitschrift für kirchliche Geschichte*
ZNW	*Zeitschrift für die neutestamentliche Wissenschaft*

Reverend Dr Paul (Benedict) Englezakis

St Anne, Panagia Arakiotissa, Lagoudera, Cyprus, AD 1192

INTRODUCTION

"Perch' io non spero di tornar giammai"
(Guido Cavalcanti *Ballata*)

The ecclesiastical history of Cyprus has always been a subsidiary interest for me. I have nevertheless applied myself to it with pleasure and it has brought me considerable satisfaction. I came to it out of necessity and as a stranger; I leave it as a friend departing from the midst of friends. I have chosen twenty studies for a posthumous publication which in my humble judgment may help the tolerant reader, and even the new researcher, along the road towards the knowledge and understanding not only of the Cypriot Church but also, perhaps more importantly, of the modern methods and interests of general ecclesiastical history. In this sense I dare to hope that the present volume has a significance for the discipline of ecclesiastical history beyond the confines of Cyprus.

As a specialist in Biblical studies, I am particularly sorry that it has not been possible for me to leave a detailed study of the introduction of Christianity into the island and of the apostolic founders of its Church. With regard to Barnabas, the interested reader must consult chiefly the modern study of M. Hengel on pre-Pauline Christianity as a starting-point for further research. The methodology which will be followed for the proto-Christian period of the Church of Cyprus will be that of modern research – observing, of course, due proportions – on the early history of the Church of Alexandria, which is also shrouded in darkness, at least at first sight. The decisive moment or line of demarcation will be sought in the Jewish revolt of AD117, when, I believe, the Jewish Church of Cyprus was dissolved and the long and painful process of the rise and consolidation of the Gentile Cypriot Church began, a process which was only to reach completion under Constantine the Great.

In his letter *To Jovian* (*CPG* 2135) Athanasius the Great already refers in 363–4 to the Church of Cyprus as if to one of the more important Churches of his time, although if the interpretation of the Paphian mosaic of Dionysus given by W.A. Daszewski (which is also accepted by G.W. Bowersock) is true, the opposition of the pagan aristocracy did not diminish even in the fourth and fifth centuries. It would be a commonplace if I were to repeat that in many matters the historian must be attentive to the silent testimony of archaeological and epigraphic remains and other artistic monuments, which in all periods of Cypriot ecclesiastical history will be of essential assistance to him, especially, however, in this first period, which also remains the least studied. In this connection he should be mindful of the aphorism of Jörg Drews: "History says nothing; it only responds to questions." Everything depends on the questions which the historian know or does not know how to put. An atlas of the palaeo-Christian monuments of Cyprus would also be a welcome contribution.

With regard to the proto-Byzantine period, the fact that I am leaving my extensive studies over many years in a disjointed state, including those in my archive, causes me some pain. The first study which is published here on St Epiphanius of Salamis is a beginning. (On the subject of Cyprus J.F. Dechow, *Dogma and Mysticism in Early Christianity: Epiphanius of Cyprus and the Legacy of Origen*, Macon, GA, 1988, simply continues the confusions of C. Hanson.) Starting with St Epiphanius the student will move backwards in time to study from the beginning the relevant aspects of the Council of Ephesus, which halted the attack of Antioch on the metropolis of Cyprus and confirmed her autonomy, and only later will he go on to trace the controversies – both external and internal – that arose and, making use of critical editions of the texts (a new edition of the *Encomium* of the Apostle Barnabas by Alexander the Cypriot [*BHG* 226, *CPG* 7400] is being prepared by P. van Deum in the *Corpus Christianorum, Series Graeca*), will proceed to the appearance of the traditions concerning Barnabas, with his point of departure always being the studies of E. Morini. He will then continue with the various phases of the question in the Byzantine, Frankish, Turkish and modern periods, until the full dossier is published concerning the autocephaly, which constitutes one of the first requirements of the ecclesiastical history of Cyprus.

Here let me simply dwell on three points: (a) the question of the position of the signature of the archbishop of Cyprus in the episcopal lists of the Seventh Ecumenical Council; (b) that of his position after the archbishop of Bulgaria in the two Constantinopolitan councils of the second half of the twelfth century (*Regestes* 1041, 1109); (c) the ideas of Patriarch Dositheos of Jerusalem in the period of Turkish rule. Concerning this great man it is sufficient to note that he is unfortunately responsible for the distorted perspective on this period up to and including M.I. Gedeon (Ἐκκλησιαστικὴ Ἀλήθεια 24 [1900], pp. 86–8), on account of confusing the *proedros* of autocephalous Cyprus with the autocephalous archbishops of the Byzantine metropolises. A recognition of this error would resolve many problems with ease.

On the problem of Bulgaria the solution has already been implied in my second study. The problem presents itself in the form of Adrian, the *porphyrogennetos pansebastos sebastos* or "beloved uncle" (*PG* 140, 196C) of the Emperor Manuel Komnenos, known as John of Bulgaria (see L. Stiernon in *REB* 21 [1963], pp. 179–98; K. Varzos, Ἡ γενεαλογία τῶν Κομνηνῶν, I, Thessaloniki, 1984, s.n.), his ideas concerning his see of Ochrid as Justiniana Prima and his mistaken theories concerning Cyprus as Justiniana Secunda. The facts are known – especially after the recent excavations at Caričin Grad and the bibliography that these have inspired – and the student may begin with the studies of V.N. Zlatarski (dating from 1930, although the idea had been sown by H. Gelzer in 1902) or G. Prinzing (*Byzantino-Bulgarica* 5 [1978], pp. 269–87). The precedent, however, that is the subject of protest, set by the retreat of Archbishop John the Cretan before his princely namesake, caused an injustice to Cyprus that endured for centuries. (I draw attention here to the apparently rather inaccessible article of A. Tovar on the "note" in Codex Salamacensis 232 in *Emerita* 30 [1962], pp. 1–7. As to the twelfth century I suggest that a careful examination is needed of the passing reference of Michael the Syrian mentioned in my ninth study concerning the proclamation of the archbishop of Cyprus as patriarch by Isaac Komnenos, no doubt in the second period of his reign. (Cf. J. Hoffmann, *Rudimente von Territorialstaaten im byzantinischen Reich (1071–1210)*, Munich, 1974.)

I come now to the Seventh Ecumenical Council. I speak about this because the *Tacticon* of Parisinus gr. 1555A (*Notitia N. 3*, according to the definitive edition of J. Darrouzès) is no longer regarded by anyone as genuine. As the fourth study in this volume, I publish an undergraduate paper by my dear students, the Deacons Silouan and Misael Ioannou, which was written under my supervision in the department of General Ecclesiastical History of the University of Athens in 1987, and which I believe – in spite of its having the character of an academic exercise – is a sufficient beginning to the unfortunately (because of the lengthy passage of time) overdue reply which is required. To the bibliography of the brothers Ioannou I would add in passing the authoritative judgments of A. Bon, *Le Péloponnèse byzantin jusqu' en 1204*, Paris, 1951, pp. 22–4 and G. Ostrogorsky, *Zur byzantinischen Geschichte: Ausgewählte Kleine Schriften*, Darmstadt, 1973, pp. 53–4. And if there remained any doubt as to whether Cyprus was reduced to the status of a metropolis of Constantinople during the Iconoclast period, it is now dispelled by the witness to the contrary of an anonymous metropolitan of the ecumenical throne (10th century, between 960 and 969) in his work Περὶ προβολῆς καὶ ψήφου καὶ ἐκλογῆς καὶ καταστάσεως καὶ προνομίων μητροπολιτῶν καὶ ἀρχιεπισκόπων καὶ ἐπισκόπων καὶ τῆς καθόλου ἄνωθεν ἐκκλησιαστικῆς τάξεως καί συστάσεως, published by J. Darrouzès, *Documents inédits d'ecclési-ologie byzantine*, Paris, 1966, pp. 116–59. The statements made there about Cyprus were not contradicted even by Niketas of Amaseia, who a few years later wrote a polemical reply to the anonymous author (ibid., pp. 160–75).

My second study is the first lecture of the volume, which contains a total of three similar lectures without notes or bibliography. I decided to include them because they were asked for by my students, who wanted me to leave examples of the manner and style of my teaching. They perhaps add a broader horizon and a wider range of sympathies than the other studies. The first lecture is a very brief overview of the long centuries of the Byzantine era of the Church of Cyprus. Should I stress that here too I wish I could have left more extensive studies? It causes me particular sadness that there are no chapters on the liturgy, hagiology and monasticism of the Byzantine period, areas of study on which I have burnt much midnight oil. The student should give special attention (a) in the early Byzantine period to the role of the Church of Cyprus in the Monothelite controversy, as this appears elsewhere, particularly in the Syriac sources which S.P. Brock has published (see chiefly *AB* 91 [1973], pp. 299–346; cf. M. Albert in *PO* 39, 2, *N*.179; Turnhout, 1978; see also the important evidence of the Aethiopic *Chronicon* of John of Nikiu, ed. R.H. Charles, London/Oxford, 1916, p. 199, which is usually overlooked); (b) in the middle Byzantine period to the documents of the Iconoclast controversy, which (*me iudice*) likewise remain unexamined, although there has been some progress; (c) in the later Byzantine period to the editing of the written sources and especially the writings of St Neophytos the Recluse (1134–*c.*1220). That is to say, everything must be undertaken from the beginning, on the basis of the sources and either at the archaeological level or in the great libraries and collections where the sources are housed. Interpretations of interpretations and books about articles are pointless: it is the interpretation of real things which is needed, not of the opinions of others. This is addressed mainly to the local race of researchers.

In the lecture on Byzantine Cyprus have I perhaps given too much emphasis to the clash between Hellenism and the East on the island, something for which some classical historians and archaeologists of Cyprus have recently been criticised? I do not know. (See now also the work of G. Jehel, *La Méditerranée médievale de 350 à 1450*, Paris, 1992.) Prosopographically, apart from the urgent need to complete, as far as possible, the episcopal and archiepiscopal lists (and to publish their molybdobulls without further long delay), I point out the need for the more detailed study of just three out of the many Cypriot ecclesiastics of the Byzantine period: the monk Alexander, Saint Arkadios of Constantia and Anastasius of Sinai. Concerning the last named, much is promised by the researches which have been begun by B. Flusin, who – correctly in my opinion – tends to identify the two Anastasii with each other, which would give to Cyprus an important writer of the early Church (see *TM* 11 [1991], pp. 381–409). The second ecclesiastic will be of interest to the historian of the age of Heraclius (vital for Cyprus) and the Monothelite controversies. I have already noted that an edition of the *Encomium on Barnabas* of the first of my three ecclesiastics is already being prepared in the same series in which J. Noret also promises an edition of the life of St Auxibios of Soloi (*BHG* 204). I would draw attention to the decisive influence – which is often overlooked – of Alexander's address on the holy cross (*BHG* 410–410c, *CPG* 7398) on the later legends concerning St Helena in Cyprus (see, already, S. Menardos) and also to the importance of the Georgian translation of the address which has been published with an extremely interesting historical memoir by M.J. van Esbroeck in *Bedi Kartlisa* 37 (1979), pp. 102–32 (together with the equally valuable old Armenian translation of the Greek life of St Herakleidios [*BHG* 743] in *AB* 103 [1985], pp. 115–62).

The third study of the present volume, "Cyprus, Nea Justinianoupolis", is an address which was given in Nicosia as the Sixth Annual Lecture on History and Archaeology of the Cultural Foundation of the Bank of Cyprus, and was repeated in English at the University of London on 19 October 1990 as the First Lecture on Cyprus of the Department of Byzantine and Modern Greek Studies of King's College. As a cleric of the ecumenical patriarchate I feel a deep sense of satisfaction at the connection in this study of the ecclesiastical history of Cyprus with that of Asia Minor. (I have often stressed the debt which the Church of Cyprus has owed to the Great Church of Constantinople in every period of its eventful history.) The monograph of H. Ohme, *Das Concilium Quinisextum und seine Bischofsliste*, Berlin/New York, 1991, should now be included in the bibliography.

The fifth study is an early work of mine which I published as a post-graduate student at Cambridge but which had been written in Paris when I was twenty-one years old. It gives Cyprus another patriarch of the Holy City, the evidence for whom can certainly be augmented today. I leave that work to others. The Constantinopolitan council of 26 January 1156 (*Regestes*, 1038), which was attended by Patriarch Nicholas of Jerusalem, and the *Note* of 6 March 1166 (*Regestes*, 1059), which was signed by Patriarch Nikephoros, provide the chronological boundaries of the patriarchate of the Cypriot. The fact that Kinnamos (*Epitome*, Bonn, 1836, pp. 210–11) represents the marriage of the Emperor Manuel with Mary of Antioch in December 1161 as blessed by the patriarchs of Constantinople, Alexandria and Antioch, without mentioning the patriarch of Jerusalem, does not necessarily mean that John was no longer alive. This was related to a delicate diplomatic matter, since the Franks did not accept the Orthodox series of succession of the patriarchs of Jerusalem and Manuel, for reasons of wider policy did not want to press matters. I note that from the time of Symeon (†1099) the Orthodox patriarchs of Jerusalem were absent from their sees for the most part, in exile in Cyprus, and were only summoned to Constantinople in about 1150. Moreover, it is better now to attribute to Chrysostomites the *Treatise on the azymes written in Jerusalem in accordance with the discussion which was held with a Latin philosopher* by the most holy Patriarch John, which was published by Dositheos of Jerusalem, Τόμος Ἀγάπης, Jassy, 1698, pp. 527–38 (cf. H.-G. Beck, *Kirche u. theol. Litteratur*, p. 611, and the observations of J. Darrouzès in *REB* 21 [1963], p. 54). The character of the *Lives* written by John VIII Mercouropoulos, as well as reasons of chronology – which I cannot go into here – make the attribution of this text to him, in my opinion, almost impossible. I note too that Chrysostomites must also be the John who is commemorated as the predecessor of Patriarch Nikephoros in the Jerusalem diaconal diptychs of Sinaiticus gr. 1040, which were published by F.E. Brightman, *Liturgies Eastern and Western*, I, Oxford, 1896, pp. 501–3, esp. 501.18 and 502.6.

I should like to have returned to the history of the monastery of Koutzouvendi, if it had been possible, if only to correct the erroneous hypothesis (*pace viri doctissimi*) of C. Mango that it was a Maronite foundation (*Chypre carrefour du monde byzantin*, XVe Congrès International d'Études Byzantines, *Rapports*, Athens, 1976, p. 6). It is true that the monastery was from the beginning connected with Syria – not, however, with the Maronites but, quite the contrary, with the zealot "Roman", Nikon of the Black Mountain, whose letter *To kyrin George, abbot of Koutzouvendi* is preserved in Sinaiticus gr. 436. After his departure from the monastery of Metropolitan Luke, it is known that Nikon lived as a monk (see, conveniently, I. Doens in *Byzantion* 24 [1954] pp. 131–40) by the column of St Symeon of the Wonderful Mountain (†596) until 1084, when Antioch was captured by Suleiman, the monks of the Wonderful Mountain were scattered, and he himself fled to the Theotokos of Roidion. The founder George must also have been a refugee who came to Cyprus (together with so many of his fellow-countrymen) from Syria and especially from the Wonderful Mountain. Otherwise how should one explain not only the relationship with Nikon and the dedication of the monastery to golden Antioch, but also the fact, above all, that the founder of Koutzouvendi took as his "protector and great helper", according to his *Typicon* (Paris. gr. 402, fol. 153ᵛ), "our holy and God-bearing father Symeon the wonder-worker of the Wonderful Mountain"? This, together with the series of names of abbots of Koutzouvendi in the twelfth and early thirteenth centuries who are mentioned by St Neophytos the Recluse – a brother of the monastery and parecclesiarch from 1152 to 1158 (who in his writings

always refers to Symeon of the Wonderful Mountain before Symeon the Great
(†459), as, for example, when he is writing to Euthymios the Chrysostomite)
– the selection of members of the monastery and their establishment in
Constantinople as monks of the patriarch of Jerusalem in about 1156, the
appointment as steward of the monastery (in about 1176) and then as abbot
(in about 1209) of St Neophytos's brother, John, and the evidence for the
continual presence of Chrysostomite monks in Constantinople and Nicaea,
leaves no room for the appointment of abbots etc. by the Maronite patriarch
of Syria. The three Syriac manuscript marginal notes to which C. Mango
appeals must surely refer to a small Maronite community living near the
monastery – where until recently there were Maronite villages – or else
protected by the monastery for reasons concerned with the Byzantine army
(the Pentadaktylos was the headquarters of the Byzantine forces, the Duke
Eumathios Philokales was a military man, the Maronites made excellent
soldiers, the background of Nikon was military, and so on). It is perhaps superfluous to add that Koutzouvendi (from Katebates – Koutsobades) is a Greek
word which when transcribed into Syriac can have no possible etymology
in that language, nor can it be derived from Arabic or Armenian (Letter from
the Oriental Institute of Oxford in my archive). I note that the colonial
background of the old British school of Cypriot studies – the contribution
of which no one can deny and which the playful Oxford professor happily
copies even today – has recently been charted in an authoritative way by S.
Vryones, Βυζαντινή Κύπρος, Nicosia, 1990, who also stresses the need for
a more detailed study of the phenomenon and its later decorative elements.

There follows a series of five studies relating to St Neophytos the Recluse,
the greatest of the Cypriot monks. The first (VI) is philological, the second
(VII) introduces the publication of a previously unpublished text (*BHG* 932n),
which I edited in my inexperienced youth, sometimes emending unneces-
sarily. (Faults are not absent from any of my publications, as I hope I know
better than anyone.) A personal inspection of Coislinianus gr. 256 (fol. 219)
shows, moreover, that the interpretations of the number of the Antichrist are
not found in the scholia of this codex – as I had supposed – and therefore
Neophytos drew them from another source (homilies, for example, or
Byzantine apocalyptic texts). With regard to the type of biblical text, I find
that Coislinianus 256 is numbered by H.C. Hoskier as 140, and is discussed
by the British New Testament scholar on pp. 51–3 and 472–3 of the work
to which I refer. As for J. Schmid, he numbers the codex as 2048 (as do Gregory
and Aland) and analyses it on pp. 192–4 of his book. I also draw attention
to the older study of the same author, "Untersuchungen zur Geschichte des
griechischen Apokalypsetextes. Der K-Text", *Biblica* 17 (1936), pp. 11–44,

167–201, 273–93 and 429–60, where 2048 is set amongst the eleven genuine testimonies to type K.

During the many years I have been preparing an edition of the work of the Recluse entitled *On the Commandments of Christ* (Coisl. gr. 287) – which again I leave for posthumous publication – I have paid close attention to the matter of the type of Biblical text (or rather, the types of Biblical text, to be more exact), although here too everything remains uncompleted. I simply mention that the Matthaean text in that work of Neophytos belongs to H.F. von Soden's K^x type (dominant in Byzantium from the ninth to the eleventh centuries) with, however, an especially rich abundance of scriptural quotations. It suffices to say that in Neophytos even the – in von Soden's view – most critical pericope μ (woman taken in adultery) cannot be assigned to one of the 14 groups of that disputably great critic nor even, so far as I am aware, to the modern groups – although the Recluse, as a good monk, frequently alludes to the Scriptures, of course *ad mentem*. The interested reader can see the latest results of research on type K^x (between K^1 and K^r) in the theses of P.R. McReynolds, F. Nisse and R.L. Omanson presented at the Claremont Graduate School and the Southern Baptist Theological Seminary in the years 1968 and 1975. That Neophytos also knew the later Komnenian type K^r is evident, for example, from his autograph corrections to the *Eklogadion* of Parisinus gr. 318. The twelfth-century Gospel which is today in the possession of his monastery (Gregory-Aland 2791) cannot certainly be said to have belonged to the saint, and in any event it lacks the first twenty-five chapters of Matthew (1-25:17). I am dwelling on the typology of Neophytos's Biblical texts not as a Biblical scholar but as a student of ecclesiastical history. The former method, for those who are able to use it, is perhaps the surest way – or at least one of the surest ways – of ascertaining the circulation, transmission and publication of manuscripts and books in Cyprus in the twelfth and thirteenth centuries, an indispensable part of the history of the education and culture of the island and also of the development of its relations with the imperial capital. The history of culture belongs to the historian and not to the simple palaeographer or the specialist in the history of art, as latterly seems to have been thought. On certain recent theories supposedly concerning the bibliographical tradition of Cyprus around the time of Neophytos, which historically – as I have often stressed – have completely lost sight of the ridiculous, see conveniently H. Gamillscheg, "Fragen zur Lokalisierung der Handschriften der Gruppe 2400", *JÖB* 37 (1987), pp. 313–21.

Before leaving the seventh study I regret that I have to take issue again with C. Mango. In a study entitled "Le temps dans les commentaires byzantins de l'Apocalypse" published in the collection *Le temps chrétien de la fin de l'Antiquité au Moyen Age, IIIe – XIIIe siècles*, Paris, 1984 (= *Colloques inter-*

nationaux du CNRS No. 604), pp. 431–8, this distinguished writer refers to Neophytos's commentary on the Apocalypse, which he compares unsuitably to the monumental commentaries of Oikoumenios, Andrew and Arethas, and ends up insulting the saint and telling us – what else do we expect from Mango concerning Cyprus? – that his dates are not even Byzantine! If, however, he had read the study of G. Podskalsky, "Représentation du temps dans l'eschatologie impériale byzantine" on pp. 439–50 of the same volume, or knew of A. Strobel, *Ursprung und Geschichte des frühchristlichen Osterkalenders*, Berlin, 1977 (=*TU* 121), whom would he then have condemned "pour son ignorance et sa bêtise" (p. 431)?

The eighth study is also an edition of a small unpublished text (*BHG* 1996e). This too was written when I was an undergraduate and I have not of course remained so static as to still be satisfied with it today. Nevertheless I believe it can be included here as indicative of a noteworthy side of the saint's spirituality, which was the subject of my thesis in Paris in 1971. Neophytos does not represent a "lay spirituality". Monastic folklore is almost completely absent from him. His chief teachers are the Fathers and in particular the Three Hierarchs. There is an urgent need for a treatise devoted to the spirituality of the saint once his entire corpus has been published.

The ninth study is an exercise in the history of mental outlooks, which I now see already replies – if a reply is needed – to the later resonant titles of C. Galatariotou, whose thesis *The Making of a Saint*, Cambridge, 1991 (to confine myself to this alone) says more about the level of Cypriot studies in the university to which it was submitted than about Neophytos and the Cypriots of the Byzantine era, who are sometimes presented as Amazonian Indians and sometimes as bourgeois Viennese of the nineteenth century. A reliable and vital knowledge is the fruit of a long internal cultivation in its subject matter and this is an indispensable presupposition for all productive historical research. Otherwise we should deserve Paul Valéry's description of a well-known French polymath: "Il sait tout, mais rien de plus." I am sure that the author is already a much more mature historian.

Many bibliographical additions could be made to the ninth study, but I shall forego the opportunity and simply refer more generally to J. Spiteris, *La Critica Bizantina del Primato Romano nel secolo XII*, Rome, 1979, and R.-J. Lilie, *Byzanz und die Kreuzfahrerstaaten*, Munich, 1981; and especially with regard to item II.2.ix (*BHG* 2343m), to J.A. Munitiz, "Synoptic Byzantine Chronologies of the Councils", *REB* 36 (1978), pp. 193–218 (where, among other things – arising from the preceding discussion concerning the dating of Neophytos – an analysis is presented with references to both V. Grumel and J. Gouillard of the Byzantine monastic preference for placing the birth of Christ in 5500 ["idée mystique"] and not in 5507/8). I would also draw

attention to what I have written towards the end of the fourth study about
the supposed *metochia* of the Hermitage before 1204 because it seems to have
been overlooked by certain subsequent writers on the subject (who have indeed
confused the dating of Paris. gr. 301 with that of its marginal notes! See now
C. Astruc, ed., *Les manuscrits grecs datés des XIIIe et XIVe siècles, I. XIIIe siècle*, Paris,
1990, pp. 17–18 and pl. II ["début du XVe siècle"].) I note that item II. 2.
v, *Discourse against the Jews (BHG* 1919), should be taken as not belonging to
the period of Frankish rule but to the reign of the tyrant, Isaac Komnenos.
In two post-graduate seminars which I gave on 6 and 8 November 1989 at
King's College, London (Department of Byzantine and Modern Greek
Studies) and the School of Eastern Studies, Cambridge (Department of
Hebrew and Jewish Studies) respectively, I dated the composition of this
discourse precisely to Christmas 1186, on the grounds that it is connected
on the one hand with the Judaeo-Christian controversies which the Jewish
Messianic movement of that critical year provoked in Europe and Byzantium,
without on the other hand yet mentioning the battle of Hattin (4–5 July) or
the siege (September) or capture (2 October) of Jerusalem in the following
year of 1187. Again I express my regret that neither those seminars nor the
planned edition of the homily could be completed for later publication. Cf.
F. Baer, "Eine jüdische Messiasprophetie auf das Jahr 1186 und der dritte
Kreuzzug", *Monatsschrift für Geschichte und Wissenschaft des Judentums* 70 (1926),
pp. 113–22, 155–65; E. Ashtor-Strauss, "Saladin and the Jews", *Hebrew
Union College Annual* 27 (1956), pp. 305–26, esp. pp. 327ff; J. Prawer, *The History
of the Jews in the Latin Kingdom of Jerusalem*, Oxford, 1988.

   I have promised two other discourses of Neophytos for publication but
as the work is incomplete I am once again unable to include them here. The
first is the Ἐγκωμιαστικὸς λόγος εἰς τὴν παγκόσμιον ὕψωσιν τοῦ τιμίου
καὶ ζωοποιοῦ σταυροῦ, ἐν ᾧ ἐστι καὶ τρανὴ θεολογία (Paris. gr. 1189, fols.
39–57ᵛ = *BHG* 423), to which I refer at the conclusion of my ninth study
and which from fol. 44ᵛ onwards deals with the Byzantine controversies of
the twelfth century on the passage "My father is greater than I" (Jn 14:28).
A future editor will find that in his theology of the cross – and indeed in what
he says about the three crosses of the Crucifixion – the Recluse also uses as
a source, besides John Chrysostom and Andrew of Crete, Alexander the
Cypriot, whom he seems already to have known from 1176. It is sufficient
to compare the Greek title of Neophytos's discourse (Ἐγκωμιαστικὸς λόγος
εἰς τὴν παγκόσμιον ὕψωσιν τοῦ τιμίου καί ζωοποιοῦ σταυροῦ, ἐν ᾧ ἐστι
καὶ τρανὴ θεολογία) with Alexander's title in Ambrosianus 798: Λόγος
ἱστορικὸς περὶ τῆς εὑρέσεως τοῦ τιμίου σταυροῦ... ἐν ᾧ ἐστι θεολογία
ἀληθής...

The other homily the publication of which I promised in vain is the Ἐγκώμιον εἰς τὸν θεῖον ἀρχάγγελον Μιχαὴλ τὸν παμμέγιστον, Paris. gr. 1189, fols 7ᵛ-12 = BHG 1290. Let me dwell on this a little because it has significance for the understanding of the saint's personality. I refer to the well-known representation of Neophytos being raised from the tomb at the general Resurrection by the two archangels and which unfortunately has scandalised some people so much as well as the gaping onlookers who have applauded them. What the historian needs is the interpretation. For this the knowledge of the facts is indispensable. The correct path for the historian – because for the believer the outspokenness of the saints do not pose a problem – will be discovered if more account is taken of the following: (a) the typology of Byzantine representations of founders etc. which in another context G.H. Belting tried to assemble – without neglecting the more general typology of this kind in the history of art. For example, this wall-painting of the saint is not visible in the sanctuary of the Hermitage either to the celebrant or to those who serve him. What is its meaning? Is it a votive offering, a *deisis* or a funerary monument? Is it an icon expressing some idea (*Bildnis*) or a likeness representing a particular person (*Porträt*)?; (b) the date of its production. Are we not in the period which was so excellently described by C.M. Morris, *The Discovery of the Individual: 1050–1200*, London, 1972? (Cf. *Eccl. Hist.* 31 [1980], pp. 195–206, and for Byzantium the first items in T. Velmans, "Peinture et mentalité à Byzance dans la seconde moitié du XIIe siècle", *Cahiers de civilisation médiévale* 22 [1979], pp. 217–33.) Has this new phenomenon been studied in the writings of St Neophytos? And yet it is there, the primary element of his whole spirituality; and (c) perhaps the most important consideration: how did the saint himself view this wall-painting? The moralists might look at the unpublished discourse on the Archangel and abandon their analyses and psychologising concerning a person who lived eight centuries ago and whose way of life is so foreign to them. I reproduce the relevant passage from folios 11–12 of Parisinus gr. 1189:

Fol. 11   ...Χαίροις, ταξίαρχε, σαλπιγγόφωνε, θεόφθογγε παρουσίας δευτέρας Χριστοῦ τοῦ Θεοῦ ἡμῶν, διαδονῶν οὐρανόν τε καὶ γῆν καὶ τὰ καταχθόνια, καὶ ἀφυπνίζων νεκροὺς καθεύδοντας ἀπ' αἰῶνος ἐν τῷ λέγειν τρανῶς· Ἰδοὺ ὁ νυμφίος ἔρχεται, ἐξέρχεσθαι εἰς ἀπάντησιν αὐτοῦ [Matth. 25:6]. Τότε – φησὶν – ἀποστελεῖ ὁ

Fol. 11ᵛ   υἱὸς τοῦ ἀνθρώπου τοὺς ἀγγέλους αὐτοῦ / μετὰ σάλπιγγος φωνῆς μεγάλης καὶ συνάξουσι τοὺς ἐκλεκτοὺς αὐτοῦ ἀπὸ τῶν τεσσάρων ἀνέμων ἀπ' ἄκρων οὐρανῶν ἕως ἄκρων αὐτῶν [Matth. 24:31].

Τότε, παμμέγιστε Θεοῦ ἀρχάγγελε, μή μου ἐπιλάθῃ ἀντιβολῶ·
μή με τῆς συνάξεως ἀφορίσῃς ἐκείνης, εἰ καὶ μέγα ἐστὶ τὸ
ζητούμενον· μή σου τῆς πτήσεως τὸ ταχύτατον παραδράμῃ
με δέομαι.

Χαίροις, ταξίαρχε, ὁ κύκλῳ τοῦ Θεοῦ σὺν τοῖς μετόχοις
σου λειτουργικῶς παριστάμενος καὶ ὡς δῶρα προσάγων Θεῷ
κεκαθαρμένας δικαίων ψυχάς· π ά ν τ ε ς γάρ – φησίν – ο ἱ
κ ύ κ λ ῳ α ὐ τ ο ῦ ο ἴ σ ο υ σ ι δ ῶ ρ α [Ps. 75:12]. ᾿Ων
με, θεοπρόκριτε καὶ παμμέγιστε, τῆς κληρουχίας μεθέξειν
λιτάνευσον, ἔχων πρὸς τοῦτο συλλήπτορα μέγιστον καὶ τὸν
σὸν παμφαέστατον ἑταῖρον, τὸν τῆς νέας χάριτος
ἀξιεπαινετώτατον πρόδρομον, τὸν θειότατον ὄντως ἀπόστολον,
καὶ μυστολέκτην παρθενικοῦ μυστηρίου φανότατον, λέγω δὴ
τὸν σὸν συνταξίαρχον καὶ τῆς δόξης συμμέτοχον, Γαβριὴλ τὸν
θειότατόν τε καὶ παναγλαώτατον, καὶ τῆς ἡμῶν σωτηρίας
ἀρχιδιάκονον ἄριστον, καὶ σὸν μάρτυρα, διαπρύσιον ἄμα καὶ
ἀληθέσατατον, καὶ οὗ ἡ μαρτυρία· ο ὐ κ ἔ σ τ ι – φησί –
τ ι ς ἀ ν τ ε χ ό μ ε ν ο ς π ε ρ ὶ τ ο ύ τ ω ν, ἀ λ λ᾽ ἢ
Μ ι χ α ὴ λ ὁ ἄ ρ χ ω ν ἡ μ ῶ ν [Dan. 10:21].

᾿Ω θειότατον ἄρμα καὶ θεοσέβαστον, ὦ μακαριώτατον
ζεῦγος καὶ θεοτίμητον, ὦ καλλίστου γεωργοῦ, πανγεωργοῦ καὶ
σπορέως ζεῦγος πανοαοίδημον, δι᾽ οὗ καί πάλαι, καὶ νῦν
κατενεώθησαν ἄρουραι λογικαί, καὶ ἀντὶ μὲν ἀκανθηφόρων
σιτοφόροι γεγόνασιν, ἀντὶ δὲ ὑλοφόρων λεῖαι καὶ καθαραὶ
ἀνεδείχθησαν· ὧν τῆς μερίδος με, μακαριώτατον ζεῦγος Θεοῦ,
εὐμοιρῆσαι ἀξίωσον.

Fol. 12   Ὁρῶ γὰρ τὸ καινότατον σχῆμα, / πανένδοξοι, ὃ καὶ ὑμεῖς
τεθεωμένοι θεοδόξαστοι, καὶ ὑπερλίαν ὑπερβαίνειν με τοῦτο
λελόγισμαι, καὶ προύπτως πρὸς τοῦτο λέγειν οὐ βούλομαι. Ἀλλά
γε σύ, ὦ ἡγιασμένη μοι δυάς, ὡς φιλάνθρωπος εἰς ἔργον
ἀμεῖψαι δυσώπει τὸ πρόσχημα, κἂν καὶ λίαν ὑπὲρ ἐμὲ καὶ
ὑπερλίαν τὸ εἰκόνισμα.

["May you rejoice, O taxiarch, with your trumpet voice, inspired
messenger of the Second Coming of Christ our God, who shake heaven and
earth and the things under the earth and awaken the dead who have been
sleeping from the beginning of the age with your clear speech. 'Behold the
bridegroom comes, come out to meet him' (Matth. 25:6). Then – it says –
'the Son of Man will send out his angels with a loud trumpet call, and they
will gather his elect from the four winds, from one end of heaven to the other'
(Matth. 24:31). At that time, great archangel of God, do not forget me, I entreat
you. Do not exclude me from that gathering, even if what is sought for is great.
Do not pass me by in your swift flight I beseech you.

May you rejoice, O taxiarch, who stand in a circle liturgically around God with those who are sharers with you and offer as gifts to God purified souls of the just. 'For all around him' – it says – 'shall bring gifts' (Ps.75:12 [76:11]). Among them, O great prince chosen by God, pray for me that I may share in their lot, since you have as your great helper in this work your radiant companion, the most glorious forerunner of the new grace, most divine apostle and shining confidential messenger of the virginal mystery – I mean, of course, your syntaxiarch and fellow participant in glory, the most divine and most exultant Gabriel, the most excellent archdeacon of our salvation, and your most piercing and most true witness, whose role it is to bear witness. 'There is none' – it says – 'who contends concerning these except Michael our prince' (Dan. 10:21).

O most divine and most pious chariot, O most blessed and most divinely-honoured pair, O most renowned yoke of oxen of the best of husbandmen, the supreme farmer and sower, through which, now as in the past, spiritual fields are deeply ploughed, becoming wheat-bearing where there were once thorns and smooth and clear where there were once woods. O most blessed yoke of God, grant me a share of that portion.

For I see the very recent form, O most glorious ones – which you too who are to be glorified by God have gazed upon – and I consider that this transcends me exceedingly and I manifestly do not wish to speak about it. But you, O sanctified dyad, in your compassion intercede to turn this scene into reality, even though it is far beyond me and the image exceedingly far beyond me."]

This unpublished text speaks for itself. The first paragraph leaves no further doubt that the wall-painting on the western arch of the ceiling of the sanctuary of the Hermitage in front of the altar represents Neophytos being raised from the tomb at the general Resurrection by the archangels, and it is made clear in very beautiful apostrophes and images that this constitutes an entreaty and supplication.

The second paragraph introduces Gabriel, but primarily interprets in its opening lines the positioning of the wall-painting in front of the altar and opposite the four hierarchs making their offering to God. Neophytos is being brought forward liturgically by the angels who encircle the divine throne as a gift to God, and he himself – eternally a priest – offers his soul. "For the wrath of man will confess you and the residue of wrath will celebrate you", says the eleventh verse of the seventy-fifth (Mas. 76:10) psalm, to the twelfth verse of which there is a direct reference. The two themes are not mutually exclusive. The Lord's table is both a type of the heavenly altar and an image of the throne and of the Judgment.

The third paragraph confirms the corn-bearing/self-offering of the Recluse in the Sacrament (an essential element of patristic eucharistic teaching) and suggests, I believe, that the whole composition records the mystical vision which the young Neophytos had at the Holy Places in Jerusalem concerning his destiny: "I must go to another place where the king too – he says – will descend and there place his seal on bread" (*Typike Diataxis*, IV; cf. "the vocation in the desert prophesied to you", ibid., V). A recluse in the cave, and like a stylite on his cliff, Neophytos was offered, and wishes to be offered for ever, as an oblation and gift – bread stamped with the cross – on the altar of God "for the life of the world" (Jn 6:51). (The theme of the martyr [and later the monk] as "bread of Christ" goes right back to the second century.)

The fourth paragraph (a) dates the homily ("very recent form" [καινότατον σχῆμα]): we are therefore in the year 1183/4 – and if the splendid wonder-working church of the Archangel for which this was written (fols 8–9, 11ᵛ) was that of Lefkara, the birthplace of the Recluse, then the dating of the decoration of that church too is confirmed as belonging to the last quarter of the twelfth century); (b) interprets correctly the iambic distich of the wall-painting: σχῆμα = εἰκόνισμα, εἰς ἔργον ἐλθεῖν = εἰς ἔργον ἀμεῖψαι, though the Byzantine word-play is found not in the σχῆμα of the distich but in the homily's πρόσχημα = decoration, preliminary design, monastic habit, pretence.

This Byzantine wall-painting, which is unique in its form, represents Neophytos in prayer being raised from the tomb by the angels at the Second Coming to meet the approaching Bridegroom Judge. In the period of the decoration of the Hermitage intense discussions were taking place in Byzantium, under the influence of the new Western teaching on purgatory, on the lot and state of souls after death until the Resurrection and Judgment. These debates came to a climax in the thirteenth century and were reflected even in the iconography of churches (see for example R. Stichel, *Studien zum Verhältnis von Text und Bild spät- und nachbyzantinischer Vergänglichkeitsdarstellungen*, Vienna, 1971 and, as an introduction to the theology, J.A. Munitiz, ed., *Theognosti Thesaurus*, Turnhout/Leuven, 1979, pp. cxv–cxvii). The subject was of course much older and had always worried the simple believer. We find it in works with which Neophytos was certainly acquainted, as for example the *Erotapocriseis* pseudonymously attributed to Athanasius (*CPG* 2257). It is possible that the wall-painting of the Hermitage is not related to these anxieties and debates. If it is, however – which is also possible – then the only thing which that can mean, for those who know the history of Orthodox theology and piety, is that the Recluse not only did not regard himself as among the just, or much less, wanted to project himself as a saint or equal to the angels, but, quite the contrary, set himself among the non-saints, among those whose souls after death, having been tested at the toll-gates (he wrote about this – see *Typike Diataxis* XII), pass through a long night as it were, sleeping until the Resurrection of the body and the Last Judgment which will bring them finally to God or to Gehenna. What else would the hope and prayer of the believer be – "I supplicate with longing" – than of course to be taken by the angels and brought to God? This, I repeat, does not imply that like every great conception and work of art this incomparable wall-painting is not without more than one meaning.

I write with difficulty and it is impossible for me to expatiate. Here there remains nothing further for me to do than to recall – although it refers to a different matter – the judgment of E. Panofsky on Dürer's daring in concealing his famous self-portrait of 1500 in the Alte Pinakothek of Munich under the image of Christ: "It states not what the artist claims to be, but what he must humbly endeavour to become: a man entrusted with a gift which implies both the triumph and the tragedy of the 'eritis sicut Deus' " (*The Life and Art of Albert Dürer*, Princeton, N.J., 1971, p. 43).

With regard to the *hagiasterion* etc., the reply was already given a number of years ago by I.P. Tsiknopoullos (*KS* 32 [1968] pp. 227–33). I add, more generally, that the form of a "cell above a church" is known in the architecture of cave monasteries and especially of troglodytic monasteries built into cliffs from Meteora to Latrus, Cappadocia and Palestine. I referred somewhere in my ninth study to the article of G.P. Schiemenz. I would add the books of I. Peña, P. Castellana, R. Fernandez, *Les reclus syriens*, Milan, 1980, and J. Hirschfeld's *The Judean Desert Monasteries in the Byzantine Period*, New Haven/London, 1992, and stress that the roots even of the architectural reorganising of the Hermitage appear to be Palestinian transplanted to the soil of Cyprus. The geographical and intellectual contexts of the Recluse do not extend beyond the eastern part of the Empire (he does not even mention Athos). Without a sufficient knowledge of Eastern monasticism, both early and Byzantine, any judgment about Neophytos is pointless.

On the difficulties English-speaking scholars have with Neophytos, I would adapt a saying of De Gaulle with regard to politics: "La sainteté c'est autre chose!"

On 27 February 1989 I presented a paper at the Patristic Seminar of the Theological Faculty of Cambridge University entitled "A Byzantine Hermit's Use of the Fathers: St Neophytos the Recluse, *Homilies on the Sermon on the Mount*", which dealt at length with the patristic sources of the Recluse in his work *On the Commandments of Christ*, which I have already discussed. Since it has not been possible to prepare that work for publication either, I print here as the last item on St Neophytos a brief communication which I gave at the Tenth International Patristics Conference (Oxford 1987) dealing more generally with that work of the saint's, but also touching in passing on the subject of his sources and indeed on the more important subject of the way in which they were used by Neophytos and his whole hermeneutic theory and spiritual attitude.

I hope the tolerant reader will allow me two further observations: (a) apart from anything else there is a need for a new critical edition and detailed study of the saint's *Typike Diataxis* (*BHG* 1325m), which since Tsiknopoullos has usually, but wrongly, been called the *Typike Diatheke*. (Independently of this, it is often forgotten that the final *Diatheke* of Neophytos is a special document which constitutes an appendix to his *Typicon*. This should be dated, in my judgment, to 1211 from the reference to the Biblical passage "Let the unrighteous be smitten" [Is. 26:10 (LXX) and not Ps. 103:5 as is noted in the last edition] which I connect with the annihilation at the beginning of 1211 of the Sultan of Iconium (and politically also of Alexios III Angelos) by Theodore Lascaris at Antioch on the Maeander, and the subsequent messianic letters of the emperor sent out in June to all the Greek provinces in which he promised final victory over the "Latin dogs". See G. Prinzing, "Der Brief Kaiser Heinrichs von Konstantinopel vom 13 Januar 1212", *Byzantion* 43 [1973], pp. 395–431); (b) on the significance of Neophytos's texts for the history of Cyprus in the twelfth and thirteenth centuries, I would underline the importance of the methods and analyses of the Rezeptionästhetik school of H.R. Jauss: the "horizon of hope" of these texts is the Cyprus of the time in which they were written.

This completes what I have to say about the Hermit of Paphos, to whom I have dedicated periodically more than half my life – with such meagre results for the interested scholar or devout Cypriot. He was not as brilliant, subtle or witty as the Constantinopolitan intellectuals of his day, but neither was he as superficial, sterile or colourless as they were. He had something to say and to do and did not lack the spiritual strength to carry it out. His works are alive even today.

With the eleventh study we come to the period of Frankish rule. In spite of the notable progress which has been made in the study of the history of the Church of the subject people of the island (no doubt also because of the wealth of written sources), the history of the Church of Cyprus still remains little-known and is in need of further research. The sources are not lacking, but some escape the attention of scholars, many have been left unpublished, many cry out for attention. I mention by way of example the strange neglect of the publication of all the texts relating to the martyred monks of Kantara. I would set out three theses on this period: (a) It is utterly useless for the historian to try to justify the unionism which was the product of the *Constitutio Cypria*.

That regime constitutes and will continue to constitute an indelible stain not only on the Roman Church but also on the Church of Cyprus. All that it achieved was the widening of the gulf between East and West, the setting of a very bad precedent, and the poisoning, even to this day, of Cypriot piety and the Cypriot psyche; (b) Orthodoxy never disappeared but was maintained by the serfs who were the Church's laity and not by the clergy or the monks; (c) the correct line historically was that of Germanos II of Constantinople and, two centuries later, of Joseph Bryennios.

If the insignificant contribution of that Church to the Roman Catholic Church is limited to a few liturgical details (the introduction from Cyprus into the Latin calendar of the feast of the Presentation of the Virgin, the transmission of the form of the Theotokos Kykkiotissa to the West from as early as the thirteenth century, etc. – see P. Santa Maria Mannino, "La Vergine 'Kykkiotissa' in due icone del Duecento", A.M. Romanini, ed., *Roma anno 1300*, Rome, 1983, pp. 487–96, and V. Pace, "Presenze e influenze cipriote nella pittura duecentesca italiana", *XXXII Corso di Cultura sull' Arte ravennate e bizantina*, Ravenna, 1985, pp. 259–98 – its curious legacy to the Orthodox Church was not the sacramental theology of Lapithes or such terms as "transubstantiation" (μετουσίωσις), which seem to have originated from the schools of Nicosia, but the greater part of the current *Mega Euchologion*. One of the chief sources of J. Goar in 1647 was the famous Barberinianus gr. 390, the *Euchologion* of the Uniate bishop of Amathous, Germanos Kouskonares (see the description, history and bibliography in A. Jacob, "Les euchologes du fonds Barberini grec de la Bibliothèque Vaticane", *Didascalia* 4 [1974], pp. 131–222, esp. 169–73). The fact that the *Interpretation of the offices of the holy and great church* in the *Mega Euchologion*, which has caused so much trouble to the officials of the patriarchal court in every generation, describes – as J. Darrouzès has proved – the offices and dignities not of the Great Church of Constantinople but of the cathedral of the Greeks of Cyprus is a rather amusing episode. That the *Divine libelli of the orthodox faith* in the *Mega Euchologion*, however, which a candidate for episcopal ordination reads out loud, are the confessions of faith of the Cypriot bishops of the period of Frankish rule (as has been shown by O. Raquez, "Les confessions de foi de la chirotonie épiscopale des églises grecques", G. Farnesi, ed., *Traditio et progressio. Studi in onore del Prof. Adrien Nocent, OSB*, Rome, 1988, pp. 469–85, cf. fols 69v–79v of Barber. gr. 390) constitutes an irony of history. It is fortunate that the "interpretation" (διακριτική) of the theology of the Holy Spirit in these *libelli* (note the absence of any reference to the *Filioque*) is that of the great ecumenical patriarch, Gregory II the Cypriot. The legacy of the Cypriot Church of the Frankish period to the Churches of both East and West and also to scholarship is a series of sometimes exceptional manuscripts of works of the Greek

Fathers. I mention as an example the splendid codex, Ottobonianus gr. 25, which was copied in 1564/5 by the abbot of the Theotokos Arakiotissa for the Latin archbishop of Nicosia, Filippo Mocenigo, and on which the 1673 edition of St Neilos was based (see J. Gribomont, "L' édition romaine [1673] des Tractatus de S. Nil et l'*Ottobonianus gr.* 25", J. Dummer, ed., *Texte und Textkritik: Eine Aufsatzsammlung*, Berlin, 1987 [= *TU* 133], pp. 187–202).

The next seven articles of the present volume deal with the Turkish period. The work which still remains to be done by the historian of that age is similarly painstaking. It is sufficient to note that even the transition to the new period in 1571–72 has not yet been sufficiently elucidated, nor precisely how and when the autocephaly was restored, nor the circumstances surrounding the election and accession of the first archbishop of Cyprus after a lapse of three centuries, facts which are hidden in deep darkness – not, of course, by chance. For the connoisseur of historical coincidence, there can be little doubt about the truth of the information given by Angelo Calepio (December 1572) that the first archbishop was a Serb. Under the administration of arguably one of its most eminent grand viziers, Sokollu Mehmet Pasha (1565–79), the janissary son of a Bosnian priest, the Ottoman Empire at the time was "ruled by Serbs" in the sense that the highest posts, not only in the state but also in the Church, were given to the vizier's relations. (The vizier, it may be said, hated the Greek Cypriots for having provoked to a certain degree the expedition against their island, one of the aims of which had also been his fall from power.) What of the first Cypriot archbishop, Timothy, "un monacho de casa d'Acre gentilhuomo Ciprioto et amico del Patriarcha de Constantinopoli"? The patriarchate after the fall of Joasaph II (1555–65) was directed by Shaitanoglu, who favoured, according to Mavrogordato, Metrophanes III (first patriarchate 1565 – 4 May 1572) who had ordained Timothy and was the notoriously pro-papist former metropolitan of Caesarea and protégé of the ambassador of Venice. Our information on the Cypriots of Galata (one of whom was Timothy) has in the last few years been augmented significantly; the intrigues of the bailey of Galata and of Rome around the ecumenical throne have had fresh light thrown on them; the hopes which were pinned on Spain and the pope after Lepanto (7 October 1571) have become common knowledge since Braudel; an "amphibious" class of Greco-Latin Cypriots of the middle of the sixteenth century has been discovered; and letters of Timothy have been published from European archives – what have Cypriot scholars been doing?

The twelfth study turns to Archbishop Christodoulos (1606/7–1639, 1640/1) and the Church of Cyprus of his day, on the occasion of a letter of his to the tsar (which could be spurious?). To the bibliography should now be added the communication of Z.N. Tsirpanles, "Χριστόδουλος καί

Παρθένιος, Ἀρχιεπίσκοποι Κύπρου, καί οἱ σχέσεις τους μέ τό Βατικανό (1639–1641)", K.N. Constantinides, ed., Πρακτικά Συμποσίου κυπριακῆς ἱστορίας (Λευκωσία 2-3 Μαΐου 1983), Ioannina, 1984, pp. 85–109. I am not prepared to retract the last paragraph of my study, however, in spite of the objection of the respected professor. Christodoulos and the archbishops of Cyprus of the sixteenth and seventeenth centuries who were like him were not Orthodox insofar in the strict sense of the word. Since in the footnotes to the last few pages of this study I touched on the subject of the Cypriot bishops after 1571 – the number and the order of precedence of whom were not fixed – I note that in the document of Archbishop Timothy of May 1578 which has been published by A. Tselikas, "Ἑπτὰ ἐπίσημα κυπριακὰ ἐκκλησιαστικὰ ἔγγραφα (1578–1771)", Θησαυρίσματα 14 (1977), pp. 251–74, esp. 252–5, (a) the list of signatures in order of precedence (which is also apparent from plate 23) is: 31, 33a, 35, 32, 33b, 36, 38, 39; (b) Ambrosios of Paphos bears the title of bishop and is the second in order of precedence and not the protothrone bishop; (c) and what is even more noteworthy, the protothrone Makarios bears the title of metropolitan, a title which it is commonly believed Cypriot bishops only assumed in the seventeenth century.

A brief popular general view of the life of the Church of Cyprus in the Ottoman period is presented on the thirteenth study. As a convenient example of an exposition chiefly of "popular religion", I hope that it will remind the tyro scholar of the importance of this sector of contemporary historical research. The "religious sensibility" of Cyprus also needs its historian and I believe that an *histoire littéraire* of this sensibility could be written, just as a religious geography could be put together, in spite of the small extent of the island (and on the more local level, the differences between the maritime strip and the interior, the plain and the mountains, have not diminished).

There follow three items relating to Archbishop Kyprianos (1810–21). The fourteenth study attempts to bring to Cypriot ecclesiastical historiography the methods of the history of ideologies, the sixteenth publishes and analyses Kyprianos's last surviving encyclical, a monument to the nobility, pastoral capability and Christian dedication of his soul in the midst of a mass of worldly anxieties. In the course of my essay on the inkstand of the *ethnomartyr* archbishop I note another unexpected omission in the study before us: that relating to the so-called "privileges" of the Cypriot primate. I do not doubt that the key to the solution of the problem is indicated in the fourteenth study of the present volume. In spite of this, the wide ramifications of the matter (which is not tied to the autocephaly, or, of course, to the canonical privileges of the primate) demand the appearance of a special monograph at the earliest possible date.

Page from the manuscript of "Archbishop Kyprianos's Inkstand"
(see below ch. XIV, pp. 277–8)

The seventeenth and eighteenth items (the second a correction of the preceding one) contribute to the prosopography of the Cypriot events of 1821, which naturally also mark a watershed in the ecclesiastical history of the island. Some clerical martyrs are presented so that it should not be forgotten that the true glory of the Church of Cyprus also was always the cross of Christ, which it carried worthily. At the centre of that storm stands the conspicuous figure of Archbishop Kyprianos. An extensive study which I have made of his election, ordination and enthronement will remain unpublished because I have not been able to bring it to completion, as is also the case with the corpus of relevant documents.

As a brief taste of the surprises which await the researcher – even the ecclesiastical researcher – I offer the fifteenth item, as a kind of appendix, from *Codex* I of the palace of the archbishop of Cyprus (from a copy by "Hadji Nicholas acting as secretary"). It deals with the reply of the archbishop of Sinai, Konstantios Byzantios, dated 2 July 1810, from Larnaca, where he was staying, to the prelates and leading laymen in Nicosia on the matter of the election and ordination of the Great Oikonomos Kyprianos, for whom they had cast their votes. In this letter the distinguished archbishop, one of the more learned prelates of the nineteenth century and later ecumenical patriarch, amongst other things sets out and analyses in relation to the exiled Archbishop Chrysanthos the well-known principle laid down long before: that bishops – much less the archbishop of Cyprus – could not be deposed by a synod containing fewer than thirteen bishops and by implication not by a synod containing only three. This testimony, simple yet authoritative and indicative of a permanently valid ecclesiastical order, was not known either by Athens or by Nicosia in the crisis of the years 1971–1973.

I note the following in relation to the history of the Cypriot Church's autocephaly: (a) apart from the documents in *Codex* I of the Archiepiscopal Palace of Cyprus there is preserved in the Archive of the Archbishops of Cyprus, Book XXXVIII, 9 the original of a personal letter of Jeremias IV of Constantinople to Konstantios, which, according to an autograph note of Archbishop Sophronios, was given to him on 3 May 1872, having come from the Sinai *metochion* of Vasileia, where presumably the archbishop of Sinai had left it; (b) the documents referring to the matter before us which were released for publication in 1902 by the patriarchate of Constantinople or were published by K. Delikanes in his work Τὰ ἐν τοῖς κώδιξι τοῦ πατριαρχικοῦ ἀρχειοφυλακείου σωζόμενα... ἔγγραφα τὰ ἀφορῶντα εἰς τὰς σχέσεις τοῦ Οἰκουμενικοῦ Πατριαρχείου πρὸς τὰς ἐκκλησίας Ἀλεξανδρείας, Ἀντιοχείας Ἱεροσολύμων καὶ Κύπρου *(1574-1863)*, Constantinople, 1904, are spurious and were produced in order to justify the intervention of Joachim III in the Cypriot Archiepiscopal Question which aroused such passions in the years

following 1900; (c) in spite of the desire of Patriarch Jeremias IV – for interventionist reasons – that the archbishop of Sinai should also consecrate Meletios of Kition, Archbishop Kyprianos guarded the rights of his autocephaly and observed the canonical order (*Codex* I, p. 161. See the complete falsification of the documents by the circle of Joachim III in the Constantinopolitan *Tachydromos* of 8 April 1902, where the genuine text has been suppressed and an entire paragraph has been drawn up representing the patriarch's wish of 1810 as an order: "and if ... with the sovereign leave of His Beatitude it is permitted to Your Grace ... and His Beatitude consents for Your Holiness to carry out his ordination again, then, armed also with our ecclesiastical permission [συνηγορούσης καὶ τῆς ἡμετέρας ἐκκλησιαστικῆς ἀδείας] ... ". Cf. the unpublished original of the letter of Jeremias IV: "then on receiving the canonical judgment of His Beatitude and Holiness, the Archbishop of Cyprus, Lord Kyprianos, once he has been ordained will ordain also the most reverend candidate for the most holy metropolis of Kition ...".
Finally: "Having done all these things in this way, we have not the least doubt that Your All-Holiness in friendship to us will co-operate and also speak in a suitable fashion with His Beatitude and new colleague about that which concerns us, in which we are persuaded that His beloved Beatitude will consent to the requested honour and take notice of it [προθυμηθῇ σὺν τῇ δεούσῃ φιλοτιμίᾳ καὶ συνέσει της], for 'good things must be done well', as the saying goes ... "); (d) Archbishop Chrysanthos died at Euripos in Euboea on 1 September 1810, his death became known in Nicosia on 29 October (a note of the consul P. Angelatos, *KX* 2 (1924), p. 228), and in spite of the fact that a second *Ekdosis* had been given by the Patriarchal Synod on the 26 September 1810 for Kyprianos's ordination (*Codex* I, p. 159), Kyprianos was finally elected only on 29 October when the death of Chrysanthos became known (ibid., pp. 160–1), and was ordained on the following day, the 30 October 1810 (consular note already cited).

This is all I have to say about that crisis, which shook the Church of Cyprus to its foundations at that time on account of the bitter state of affairs in the secular sphere and the small number of Cypriot bishops, since unfortunately I am unable to prepare these documents for publication. With regard to the personal details of Archbishop Kyprianos, the unforgivably superficial statements which have been made recently in connection with his origins are shown to be mistaken (as if errors could not have been avoided even in this matter) by the document of 2 September 1854 recorded on p. 306 of *Codex* I of the Archbishop's Palace: Archbishop Kyrillos I, Kyprianos's nephew by his sister Maria, came from Kambia, not the *ethnomartyr*, who was born in Strovolos.

The nineteenth study brings us once again to the world of the Cypriot clerics of the ancient patriarchates which we last encountered in the fifth study. Their origin, their connection with the Church of Cyprus, and their influence on it and its influence on them cannot be ignored by the historian of the Cypriot Church. And there are many of them, seeing that Cyprus provided for centuries a vital support to the patriarchates and great monasteries of the East. To confine myself only to the Turkish period, special study is needed, for example, of the galaxy of prelates who were promoted – to the exasperation of Sergios Makraios – throughout the entire East and even in Italy by the Cypriot ecumenical patriarch, Gerasimos III (1794–97), both in his brief patriarchate in his old age and in the long and brilliant career which preceded it. The valuable inscribed offerings which he sent as ecumenical patriarch to his humble village near Paphos are testimony to his patriotism to this day. E. Kedourie's essay, "Religion and Politics", now printed in his book *The Chatham House Version and Other Middle-Eastern Studies*, London, 1984, pp. 317–50, 450–57, may be added to the bibliography of the nineteenth study, not because it is closely connected with my theme but because the journal of the zealous Arab patriot and Palestinian Orthodox, Khalil Sakakini (1878–1953), presents valuable comparisons with the journal of the young Greek, K.I. Myrianthopoulos.

The volume concludes with the twentieth study, a lecture on the Church of Cyprus in the period of British rule. Here I only observe, as the informed reader will immediately perceive, that some discussions are introduced which belong to the modern Latin-American school of ecclesiastical history, which also has some things to teach us about the true and hidden life of the Church of Christ. The more general philosophical and theological principles which I have followed as a historian can easily be extrapolated by the interested reader from the studies published here. First and foremost a Biblical scholar, I have always understood ecclesiastical history as an exegesis of the Holy Scriptures.

I should like to express my thanks to three libraries and their staff: the Bibliothèque Nationale of Paris, the University Library of Cambridge and the Library of the Centre for Byzantine Studies of Washington (Dumbarton Oaks, Harvard).

The financial burden of my research over many years which has resulted in these studies has been borne by the A.G. Leventis Foundation and its president C. Leventis. My gratitude to him is profound and is as unfailing as our friendship. I am also grateful to C. Carras for providing the funds for the English translation of this volume and to N. Russell for undertaking the laborious task of its translation.

I give what I have. May the reader not judge harshly. Time has been brief, the age unfavourable, the work a subsidiary interest. I have done what I could. I would have wished it myself to have been different. But what significance has that in the end? *One thing is needful, Lord!*

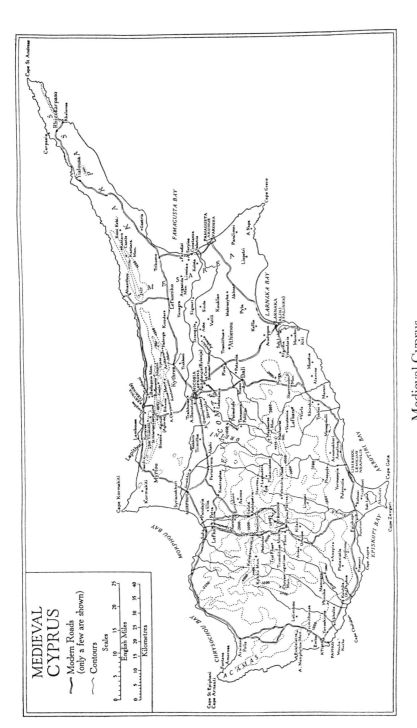

Medieval Cyprus

(*A History of Cyprus* I, G. Hill, Cambridge University Press, 1940.)

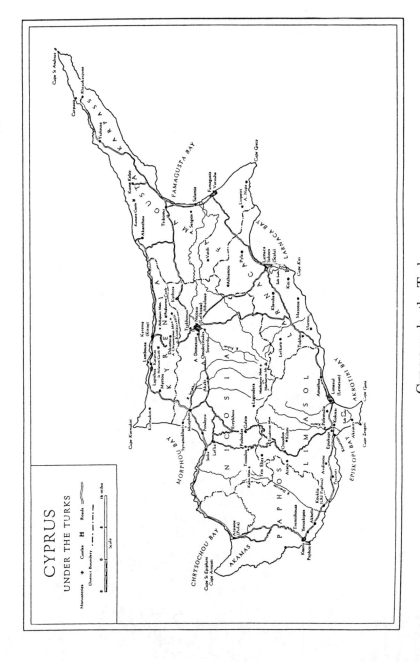

Cyprus under the Turks

(*A History of Cyprus* III, G. Hill, Cambridge University Press, 1948.)

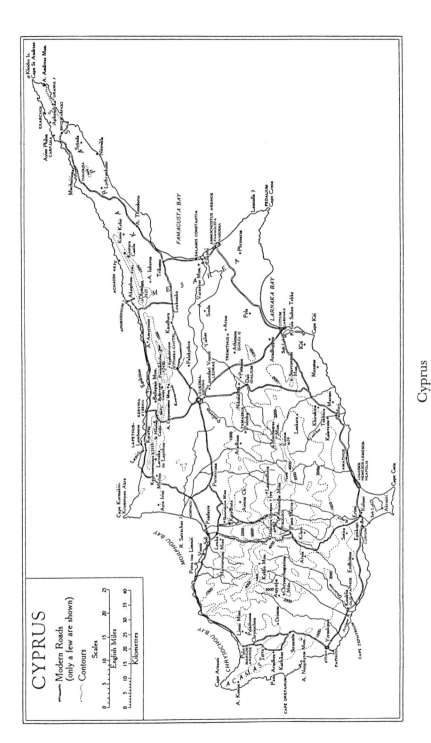

Cyprus

(*A History of Cyprus* IV, G. Hill, Cambridge University Press, 1952.)

I

EPIPHANIUS OF SALAMIS, THE FATHER OF THE CYPRIOT AUTOCEPHALY*

I

The oldest institution which has endured without a break in the history of Cyprus is its autocephalous Church. For twenty centuries this Church has provided the island's indigenous population not only with its rule of life and means of expression in the religious, family and cultural spheres but also, at various times, with the structures which contained and regulated its political and economic life. Anyone concerned with the Church as an institution is clearly dealing not so much with persons as with the spirit and traditions of a group. Can an individual, then, be called the father of such an institution, in the way that I have called St Epiphanius of Salamis the father of the Cypriot autocephaly?

The idea that the individual is the ultimate lever of historical change was one of the pillars of positivistic history as it used to be written until the appearance of modern theories. Without entering into the famous historiographical dispute of the twentieth century, I shall say at the outset that the title of my paper does not imply the acceptance of the Cypriot autocephaly as a creation of Epiphanius of Cyprus. In history, however, if an entity is to continue to be active and to make its progress through time, it is not sufficient for it simply to forge ahead. It needs in addition to be able to conserve what it has achieved, which is sometimes more difficult. If the indispensable presuppositions for this do not exist, the result sooner or later will be a return without any dramatic change to zero.

Cyprus did not receive its autocephaly at Ephesus in AD 431. It simply ensured that it retained its independence at a time when all the other met-

---

*Translated from "'Επιφάνιος Σαλαμῖνος, Πατὴρ τοῦ Κυπριακοῦ Αὐτοκεφάλου", B. Englezakis, ed., Πρακτικὰ Β΄ Διεθνοῦς Κυπριολογικοῦ Συνεδρίου, Β΄ Μεσαιωνικὸν Τμῆμα, Nicosia, 1986, pp. 303–12.

ropolitan sees were losing theirs. The reasons how and why Cyprus alone succeeded where others failed are various: the character of the island, its geographical position, the stance which it had adopted in the critical years of the Nicene struggle, and the skilful exploitation by the Cypriot bishops of the antagonism between Alexandria and Antioch on the one hand and Alexandria and Constantinople on the other. The policy of the Cypriots was nevertheless able to succeed precisely because of their alignment with Alexandria and Rome from as early as the time of the Council of Serdica – the Church of Cyprus was the only Eastern metropolitan see to sign its decisions – though principally after 367, when St Epiphanius, bishop of the island's metropolitan see of Salamis–Constantia, began his thirty-six-year episcopacy.

II

Few ecclesiastics enjoyed such fame and authority during their lifetime as Epiphanius of Cyprus, who represented in the second half of the fourth century the austere life, heroic self-denial, ardent faith and uncompromising attitude of the pre-Constantinian Church of the martyrs and confessors.[1]

From his birth in Palestine in about 315 right until his death in May 402 Epiphanius refused to conform to the mentality of the fourth century, which demanded a compromise between Christianity and Graeco-Roman antiquity. Jerome, who in an earlier period had maintained that apart from Athanasius only two men remained orthodox in the East, Epiphanius of Cyprus and Paulinus of Antioch, did not hesitate in 397 rightly to call the lion of Cyprus "a relic of the holiness of old and father of almost all the bishops".[2]

It is noteworthy that he seems to have acquired this reputation from his youth. The haughty Emperor Constantine II (337–361) did not dare to persecute Epiphanius when the latter, still at that time a monk in Palestine, was supporting his victims Athanasius, Eusebius of Vercelli and others. After

---

[1] See the excellent comprehensive studies of P. Nautin in *DHGE* XV, pp. 616–31, and W. Schneemelcher in *RAC* V, pp. 909–27. From the more recent literature the following are of note: *Epiphanius II. Panarion haer. 34–64*, hrsg. K. Holl, 2 bearbeitete Auflage hrsg. von J. Dummer, Berlin, 1980; L.A. Eldridge, *The Gospel Text of Epiphanius of Salamis*, Salt Lake City, 1969; I. Moutsoulas, Τὸ περὶ "μέτρων καὶ σταθμῶν" ἔργον Ἐπιφανίου τοῦ Σαλαμῖνος, Athens, 1971; J. Piilonen, *Hippolytus Romanus, Epiphanius Cypriensis and Anastasius Sinaita. A Study of the* διαμερισμὸς τῆς γῆς, Helsinki, 1974; and B.M. Weischer, "Die ursprüngliche nikänische Form des ersten Glaubenssymbols im Ankyrōtos des Epiphanios von Salamis", *Theologie und Philosophie* 53, 1978, pp. 407–14, and "Die Glaubenssymbole des Epiphanios von Salamis und des Gregorios Thaumaturgos im Qērellos", *Oriens Christianus* 61, 1977, pp. 20–40.

[2] Jerome, *c. Ioh. Hier.*, 12. On Jerome and his relations with Epiphanius see J.N.D. Kelly, *Jerome. His Life, Writings and Controversies*, London, 1975, pp. 195ff. and *passim*.

366 the Emperor Valens (364–78), who had no qualms about persecuting an Athanasius or a Basil, also avoided coming into conflict with Epiphanius, since he was anxious not to harm his cause by persecuting a man who enjoyed universal respect and whose holiness the whole world acknowledged and honoured.[3] According to Jerome the public appearances of Epiphanius were in themselves an event. Wherever he went crowds of people gathered to see him. They brought small children for him to bless, kissed his feet, which were always unshod, struggled to touch the hem of his garment and would not leave the church until he had consented to preach the word of God.[4]

Palladius of Helenopolis, who described Jerome as "malignant" and had every reason to vilify Epiphanius too, called him "holy".[5] The historian Socrates, who disagreed with Epiphanius with regard to Origen, referred to him as "renowned for his piety".[6] Theophilus of Alexandria, who had done him harm, regarded him as the most celebrated bishop of his time whose opinion many people declared themselves proud to follow.[7]

During the forty years of Epiphanius's episcopacy Cyprus for the first time in its history became one of the most sensitive centres of the Christian world. Crowned with the friendship of the renowned Athanasius and the discipleship of Hilary the Great (who, it seems, were the prime movers in his call to the throne of Cyprus), armed with a knowledge of five languages, supported by an iron constitution which allowed him to travel constantly even into extreme old age and already well-known in Egypt and Palestine, Epiphanius began on his arrival in Cyprus to exercise an influence which reached from one end of the Christian world to the other and played a decisive role in every ecclesiastical affair from Arabia and Persia to Africa and Rome.

In the last phase of his life nobody could match his authority. Approval by the old man of Cyprus implied agreement with ancient truth and rejection by him implied at least a suspicion of deviance. The name of Epiphanius stirred the imagination of his contemporaries as the last of the giants of a heroic age. Some modern scholars have criticised him as lacking in compassion or as a fanatic or reactionary. This, however, was not the opinion of the Christian people of his age, by whom he was regarded as a prodigy of love. That which moderns call fanaticism Epiphanius's contemporaries called divine zeal and a faith nourished under the desert sun.

---

[3] Jerome, op. cit., 4.

[4] Ibid., 12.

[5] Palladius, *Dialogue*, 17. Cf. the letter of Epiphanius to John of Jerusalem = Jerome, *Ep. LI*, 9. On Palladius's Origenism see R. Draguet, "L' 'Histoire Lausiaque': une oeuvre écrite dans l'esprit d'Évagre", *RHE* 41, 1946, pp. 321–64, 42, 1947, pp. 5–49.

[6] Socrates, *Eccles. Hist.*, 6, 10.

[7] Sozomen, *Eccles. Hist.*, 8, 14. Cf. 6, 32.

Epiphanius can only be understood first and foremost as a monk. His public life, his role as an ecclesiastical politician, his fame as a criterion of orthodoxy were the result not so much of his anti-heretical writings as of his pure and simple holiness. Certainly nobody would maintain that Epiphanius possessed the theological talent, the legislative genius or the broad outlook of, for example, Basil, but for the faithful who were his contemporaries Epiphanius surpassed Basil in holiness and pastoral gifts, since he was endowed even with the power to work miracles. Once again we meet with a situation in which scholarly theology encounters popular piety in the early Church.[8] Even though Epiphanius did not neglect to write, and indeed wrote at great length, he was nevertheless not a theologian.[9]

His first work as a bishop is considered today to be the letter *To Eusebius, Marcellus, Vivianus, Carpus and Egyptians on the date of Easter*,[10] in which, to the chagrin of Athanasius, he opposed the Alexandrian date for the celebration of Easter adopted by Nicaea and defended the traditional date observed in Syria and Cyprus (the first Sunday after the Jewish Passover instead of the first Sunday after the spring equinox).

A little later, at the request of the orthodox of Arabia "including priests, laymen and catechumens", Epiphanius wrote his epistolary treatise *Against the Antidikomarianitai*, in which he expounded the orthodox teaching on the perpetual virginity of the Theotokos and her correct veneration.

Epiphanius published the first of his great works, the *Ancoratus*, in 374 at the request of some priests and laymen of Pamphylia who had asked him about correct belief in the Holy Trinity and especially in the Holy Spirit.[11]

In 376 Epiphanius published the *Panarion* at the request of Paul and Acacius, the archimandrites of the monasteries of Coele Syria. In their prefatory letter these two presbyters (the second of whom was to become the celebrated bishop of Beroea) say that for a long time they wished to come and meet with Epiphanius face to face but were prevented from doing so by physical infirmity. They conclude with the following important words: "For not only we but all who hear you confess that the Saviour has raised you up in this generation as a new apostle and preacher for us, a new John, to

---

[8] Cf. for the 3rd century and extreme cases J. Lebreton, "Le désaccord de la foi populaire et de la théologie savante", *RHE* 19, 1923, pp. 481–506; 20, 1924, pp. 5–37.

[9] G. Florovskij, *Vostocnye otcy IV-go veka*, Paris, 1931, p. 200: "He was not a theologian, but he liked to pass judgments on matters of faith. He enters the history of theology precisely as a suspicious critic and heresy-hunter. Because of this characteristic he deserves our attention."

[10] On the works of Epiphanius generally see the studies of Nautin and Schneemelcher cited above in note 1.

[11] At the Council of Florence the pneumatological teaching of the "patriarch of orthodoxy", as Epiphanius was called, played a decisive role, even though it was badly interpreted.

proclaim the things that should be upheld by those who pursue this course."[12] According to contemporary evidence monks came and settled in Cyprus not only from Syria but from all over the world to see Epiphanius and put themselves under his spiritual guidance.[13] In 385 the patrician Paula, one of the richest and most famous women of the Empire, sailed from Rome to Salamis in order "to throw herself at the feet" of the apostolic man.[14] Moreover, another noblewoman, Olympias, sent economic assistance from New Rome for his monasteries in Cyprus. Olympias had become a deaconess of John Chrysostom, who much later was treated so unjustly by Epiphanius.[15]

In 392 Epiphanius published the treatise *On Weights and Measures* at the request of the Persian priest, Bardion. At about the same time he dedicated to Diodore of Tarsus his treatise *On the Twelve Precious Stones*.

The copious correspondence of St Epiphanius, unfortunately no longer extant, would have given us a still broader idea of his commanding presence on the world stage. It sufficient to say that apart from the letters to the Arabs and Egyptians already mentioned, the few surviving fragments include portions of a letter about Easter, and of letters to the priests of Pisidia, to the Emperor Theodosius (379–95) against icons (which had recently appeared in the Church and were regarded by Epiphanius as a threat to the struggle for the homoousion), to the Egyptian clerics, to Magnus, a Sabellian priest in Antioch, to Basilianos, to John of Jerusalem, to Jerome and to Basil. Basil writes that he received the letters of Epiphanius "as evidence of love that you remembered our humble and insignificant self and then sent brothers to visit us fit to be ministers of letters of peace." Further on he unites his voice with that of all Epiphanius's contemporaries, rendering the honour and recognition due to his love: "How then shall we not marvel at him who in these circumstances [he refers to the tragic quarrels between the orthodox bishops which he has just related] demonstrates a pure and guileless love for his neighbours."[16]

The journeys of Epiphanius are no less surprising from the point of view of their purpose and the distances which they covered, and testify, moreover, to the power of the man throughout the Christian world. Egypt, Asia Minor, Syria, Mesopotamia, Palestine, Alexandria, Antioch, Jerusalem, Constantinople and Rome were visited by Epiphanius, in some cases repeatedly. Of his famous contemporaries there seem to be very few whom he did not know

[12] Epiphanius, *Panarion*, Prologue, 1, 6.
[13] Jerome, *Ep.* CVIII, 7.
[14] Ibid.
[15] Palladius, *Dialogue*, 17.
[16] Basil, *Ep.* CCLVIII, 1.

personally. We have already seen that he was connected with four men who received from history the epithet "the Great": Athanasius, Hilary, Basil and Theodosius. Among Westerners he met Jerome through Paula and turned him from an admirer of Origen into his implacable enemy; he supported Lucifer of Sardinia and Eusebius of Vercelli at a critical time; he was admired by Augustine as a catholic doctor and, through his presence in person at the council held in 382 in Rome, he was largely the cause of Pope Damasus' (366–84) refusal to recognise the acts relating to Antioch of the Council of Constantinople of the preceding year which was later recognised as the Second Ecumenical Council. Among Easterners Epiphanius had from his youth known Athanasius, whom he followed faithfully to the end; he fought alongside his brother and successor, Peter, against Meletius of Antioch; and he set Cyril of Jerusalem amongst the heretics while judging Marcellus of Ancyra or Apollinarius, as old allies of Athanasius, to be blameless. With regard to the so called neo-Nicene theologians,[17] Epiphanius's position was not negative, as is sometimes said. By 377 he was already telling Basil that he regarded "it necessary to confess that there are three hypostases" (a formula which Athanasius had accepted in 362 as orthodox but superfluous),[18] while it appears that he did not hinder his subordinate Cypriot bishops from signing at least the dogmatic declaration of the Council of Constantinople of 381.[19]

Epiphanius's enemy was always the same: "Origen, maddened by God", the sublime theologian of the third century whom Epiphanius regarded as "the father of Arius and the root and parent of other heresies".[20] If his

---

[17] Cf. the critique of the theory of Jungnizäismus in A.M. Ritter, *Das Konzil von Konstantinopel und sein Symbol. Studien zur Geschichte und Theologie des II. ökumenischen Konzils*, Göttingen, 1965, pp. 270–93.

[18] Basil, op. cit., 3; Athanasius, *Tome to the People of Antioch*, 5.

[19] As is well known, the history of this council has many lacunae owing to the loss of the acta. Modern scholars, apart from G. Bardy, think that Epiphanius himself did not take part, and it is unanimously accepted that the creed of Constantinople was inserted into the archetype of the known manuscripts of the *Ancoratus*. This had already been demonstrated in Russia in 1902 in the work of A.P. Lebedev, *O simvole nasej pravoslavnoj cerkvi i vtorogo vselenskago sobora*. See the review in *JTS* 4, 1903, pp. 285–90, and A. Spasskij, *Istorija dogmaticeskih dvizenij v epohu vselenskih soborov*, I, Sergiev Posad, 1914, pp. 584–624. The study of the Ethiopian translation of the *Ancoratus* and of the "long version" of the creed in the Qērellos has confirmed the work of the Russian historians. See the two recent studies of B.M. Weischer cited above in note 1, and A. de Halleux, "La profession de l'Esprit-Saint dans le symbole de Constantinople", *Revue théologique de Louvain* 10, 1979, pp. 5–39. Such was also the opinion of Ritter (see note 17 above), and of the critical editor of the creed, G.L. Dossetti, *Il simbolo di Nicaea e di Constantinopoli*, Roma, 1967. The opposite opinion is held by V. Peri, "Risonanze storiche e contemporanee del secondo concilio ecumenico", *Annuarium Historiae Conciliorum* 14, 1982, pp. 13–57, esp. pp. 41ff.

[20] Epiphanius, *Letter to John of Jerusalem* = Jerome, *Ep.* LI, 3.

reverence for Athanasius led Epiphanius to support Paulinus and oppose Meletius,[21] his hatred of Origenist theology, with regard to both content and method, led him to harbour extreme suspicion of anyone who had dealings with Origenists, as the archbishop of Constantinople, John Chrysostom, undoubtedly had.[22] The terrible end of the story is well-known. At the most critical moment for John Chrysostom, Epiphanius of Salamis, the living legend, savagely attacked the golden preacher. Here let it only be stressed that Theophilus himself, called the Christian Pharaoh on account of his boundless power, needed the authority of Epiphanius in order to destroy John. In the midst of the imperial capital Epiphanius of Cyprus did not shrink from snubbing an archbishop beloved of the population and demanding his condemnation by the resident bishops.

III

Such power and decisive action of the metropolitan of Cyprus could not but influence the fate of the canonical constitution of his Church.

In the first place it should be noted that autocephaly was not understood in the fourth century as it came to be understood in the nineteenth and twentieth centuries. This significant definition did not exist in the Byzantine period,

---

[21] He tells us himself that he decided irrevocably to receive Paulinus into communion when the latter showed him a copy of the *Tome to the People of Antioch* written in Athanasius' own hand, and bearing at the end an autograph acceptance of the *Tome* by Paulinus (*Pan.*, 77, 21). On the Antiochene schism more generally see F. Cavallera, *Le schisme d'Antioche*, Paris, 1905, and W. Eltester, "Die Kirchen Antiochias im IV Jh", *ZNW* 36, 1937, pp. 251–86. The Eastern view of the matter is given by V.V. Bolotov, *Lekcii po istorii drevnej cercvi*, 4, Petrograd, 1918, ch. I, 1.

[22] See J.-M. Leroux, "Jean Chrysostome et la querelle origéniste", J. Fontaine et C. Kannengiesser, *Epéktasis. Mélanges patristiques offerts au cardinal Jean Daniélou*, Paris, 1972, pp. 335–41. The Evagrians, John Cassian, Palladius, Heracleides and Germanus, lived in Constantinople not far from John. Of these John consecrated Palladius bishop of Helenopolis and in 400 the Cypriot Heracleides, a disciple of Evagrius, metropolitan of Ephesus in place of the simoniacal Antoninus. There is nothing strange in the fact that the Tall Brothers came to Constantinople from Egypt and that a little while later Epiphanius naturally arrived there also. For Epiphanius's antagonism towards Chrysostom to be understood one must bear in mind not only his anti-Origenism but also his monastic character. Alexandria together with the monks of the capital (the same alliance that also destroyed Gregory the Theologian and later Flavian) formed a common front against John. On the special character of the early monasticism of Constantinople and the action of the monks against its bishops see G. Dagron, "Les moines et la ville. Le monachisme à Constantinople jusqu'au concile de Chalcédoine (451)", *Travaux et mémoires* 4, 1970, pp. 229–76, esp. pp. 261ff. The Bollandist priest and specialist on Chrysostom, F. van Ommeslaeghe, in his lecture "L'accusation d'Origénisme contre S. Jean Chrysostome" delivered at the Ninth International Conference on Patristic Studies (Oxford, 5–10 September 1983) denied the historicity of Epiphanius's opposition to Chrysostom, maintaining that we are dealing here with a confusion originating in secondary sources between John of Jerusalem and John of Constantinople.

the epithet simply indicating "not subject to anyone" or "self-governing" (*sui juris*).[23] In this sense, as Balsamon already informs us in the twelfth century, "in ancient times all the provincial metropolitans were autocephalous".[24] In speaking here, then, of the autocephaly of the Church of Cyprus we mean nothing other than, in relation to the period which concerns us, namely, the second half of the fourth century, the right of the "Cypriots to carry out their own ordinations"[25] – nothing more and nothing less than this.

In the preceding period, patriarchates in the sense of administrative entities covering one or more civil dioceses did not yet exist. The title of patriarch appeared officially only in the second half of the fifth century.[26] At the time when Epiphanius was the senior bishop in Cyprus the Church saw the patriarchal system taking shape and through its councils of bishops, especially those later recognised as ecumenical, attempted, in vain for the most part, to limit it, appealing to "ancient customs" and to "ancient traditions and practices".[27] Nevertheless, the new principle which was disseminated and imposed by every means by the metropolitans of the administrative centres of dioceses, was the "adaptation" of the ecclesiastical organisation to the political organisation of the state.[28]

For Cyprus the danger never appeared more threatening than in 367, in which year, at the moment when the autonomous provinces were disappearing one after the other, swallowed up by the voracity of the patriarchates then being set up, the Diocese of the East was divided into Oriens and Egypt,[29] the way thus being opened up for the ecclesiastical division of the East between Antioch and Alexandria. For Antioch the subordination of Cyprus was henceforth a logical consequence.

---

[23] Constantine Porphyrogenitus, *De administrando*, 29 (ed. G. Moravcsik, Washington, DC, 1967, p. 126). In what follows below I follow in general Peter, bishop of Kherson, "Problemy svjazannye s avtokefaliej", *Messager de l'Exarchat du patriarche russe en Europe occidentale* XCVII–C, 1978, pp. 71–97.

[24] Commentary on the 2nd canon of the Second Ecumenical Council in G.A. Rhalles and M. Potles, Σύνταγμα τῶν θείων καί ἱερῶν κανόνων, B', Athens, 1852, p. 171.

[25] Title of the 8th canon of the Third Ecumenical Council.

[26] Between 451 and 475. See E. Honigmann, "Juvenal of Jerusalem", *DOP* 5, 1950, pp. 209–79, esp. 271–75.

[27] See e.g. the 6th canon of the First Ecumenical Council, the 2nd canon of the Second Ecumenical Council and the 8th canon of the Third Ecumenical Council.

[28] See F. Dvornik, *The Idea of Apostolicity in Byzantium and the Legend of the Apostle Andrew*, Cambridge, Mass., 1958, pp. 3–38. For Cyprus especially see the very important study of E. Morini, "Apostolicità ed autocefalia in una chiesa orientale: La leggenda di S. Barnaba e l'autonomia dell'Arcivescovato di Cipro nelle fonti dei secoli V e VI", *Studi e ricerche sull' Oriente Cristiano* 2, 1979, pp. 23–45, supplemented by him in "Richiami alle tradizioni di apostolicità ed organizzazione ecclesiastica nelle sedi patriarcali d'Oriente", *Bulletino dell'Istituto Storico Italiano per il Medio Evo e Archivio Muratoriano* 89, 1980–1981, pp. 1–69.

[29] A.H.M. Jones, *The Later Roman Empire, 208–602*, II, Oxford, 1973, pp. 1095, note 9, 1460, note 12.

In 366, however, Epiphanius ascended the throne of Cyprus while in Jerusalem Cyril was at the height of his powers. The latter's policies, continued by famous successors, would lead finally to the detachment from Antioch not only of the Holy City but also of the three Palestines. In Antioch, by contrast, the schism was coming to a climax on account of the earlier consecration of Paulinus as bishop, the persecutions and exiles of Valens, and the repeated failures of the attempts at reconciliation. A Church which was shortly to be torn into four rival jurisdictions was not, of course, in a position to undertake further expansion, at least for the time being. Cyprus was thus on the one hand not alone in resisting the ambitions of Antioch in the East, as a result of the claims of the bishop of Jerusalem, and on the other hand secured a truce as a result of the Antiochene schism, while at the same time through the election of Epiphanius (which, as we have seen, was probably at the instigation of Alexandria) it greatly increased its defences in preparation for the imminent unavoidable conflict.

The resolute policy of Epiphanius in opposition to that of Antioch favoured the autonomy of Cyprus, since for thirty-two years (if we accept that in 398, four years before his death, he followed Rome and accepted Flavian) he neither recognised the official Church of Antioch, nor did he ever communicate with its bishop, but supported the small group "of the followers of Paulinus". Besides, while Epiphanius was alive what bishop would have dared even to dream of reducing him to obedience? Such a thing would have bordered on contempt if not sacrilege. The old man of Cyprus was never judged by anybody, but he himself judged all the official thrones of the East except that of Alexandria. Moreover, as the well-known *History of Egyptian Solitaries* records about the monks who had made themselves eunuchs, in the powerful religious circles of the Egyptian desert the charismatic authority of Epiphanius threatened sometimes to surpass the canonical authority of Alexandria and even that of the pentarchy, since the patriarchs "flatter each other in order to be esteemed in the councils" while the bishop of Cyprus "is a prophet and shows no favour to persons".[30]

The death of Epiphanius, far from diminishing his authority or that of Cyprus, augmented it further. The orthodoxy of the island now seemed permanent.[31] The Church of Cyprus proved to be the most faithful ally of

[30] *BHG* 3, n. 1448ᵘ, F. Nau, "Histoire des solitaires égyptiens", *Revue de l'Orient chrétien* 27, 1912, pp. 210–11.

[31] C. Hanson, "Epiphanius of Constantia and the Defense of the Cypriot Orthodoxy and Ecclesiastical Independence", *Seventh Annual Byzantine Studies Conference, November 13–15, Abstracts of Papers*, Boston, 1981, pp. 50–51, maintained as others have done before him that Cyprus in the fourth century was a nest of heresies. The evidence adduced for this is totally insufficient. The *Life of Epiphanius*, apart from the fact that it is not a trustworthy source on account of its fictional character, in no way gives such an extreme impression. *Pan.* 42.1.2 says simply

Alexandria and therefore of Rome in the East, constituting after 367 Egypt's wedge within the body of the Eastern Diocese.

When Cyprus denounced the insidious moves of the Antiochenes against the rights of her Church at the Third Ecumenical Council on 31 July 431, the Council, under the presidency of Cyril of Alexandria as the representative of Celestine of Rome, inquired first as to who those were who had consecrated the last three occupants of the metropolitan see of Cyprus, a start being made, characteristically, with "Epiphanius of blessed memory".[32] On the reply to this question the Council Fathers cast their vote "that the leaders of the holy churches in Cyprus may possess that which is unassailable and inviolable, having themselves carried out the consecrations of their reverend bishops according to the canons of the holy Fathers and ancient custom".[33]

With the end of the fifth century and the appearance in the East of the Roman theology on the apostolic sees, that is, with apostolicity now as a principle of ecclesiastical organisation,[34] the Cypriot bishops, who until then had made no mention of St Barnabas, remembered their apostle. The autocephaly, however, had already been assured in the fourth century by the work and person of Epiphanius of Salamis, especially by the route which he had charted for the Church of Cyprus as the permanent ally in the East of Alexandria and Rome. Cyprus was to remain aligned with Rome in the struggles against Monothelitism and Iconoclasm.

The memory of Epiphanius was to remain alive in Cyprus for centuries. His basilica and tomb are one of the great shrines of the island. His sacred name was given to a host of Cypriot villages. His likeness adorned the seals of many archbishops in the Byzantine period and was painted in the centre

---

that the heresy of the Marcionites is still found in Rome, Italy, Egypt, Palestine, Arabia, Syria, Cyprus, the Thebaid, Persia and other places. Where is the special position of Cyprus to be found? The well-known passage from Chrysostom's Letter 221 to Konstantios, a priest of Antioch (*PG* 52, 733), cannot possibly refer to Salamis in Cyprus, since it would then call the capital of the island a "village". It surely refers to Salamia in the Lebanon... The correct reading is: τοῦ Σαλαμίας ἕνεκεν χωρίου τοῦ κατὰ Τύρον (ἢ Κύρρον;) κειμένου. Cf. Theodoret of Cyrus, *Eccles. Hist.*, 5, 31 (32), 3, and F. Halkin, *Douze récits byzantins sur saint Jean Chrysostome*, Bruxelles, 1977, pp. 118, 136 (George of Alexandria: "in Antioch and the whole of its region in certain villages in the eastern parts"), pp. 452, 461 (Pseudo-Hesychius likewise). On Salamia or Salamias itself see E. Honigmann, *Évêques et évêchés monophysites d'Asie antérieure au VIe siècle*, Louvain, 1951, p. 31 (where he corrects A.H.M. Jones, *The Cities of the Eastern Roman Empire*, Oxford, 1937, p. 458, note 54), and the map facing p. 286. And finally, while Epiphanius was still alive what need had Chrysostom to enter the struggle against heresy in Cyprus?

[32] Minutes relating to the Cypriot bishops in E. Schwartz, *Acta conciliorum oecumenicorum*, I, 1, 7, pp. 118.17–122.22, esp. 121.39–41.

[33] Ibid., p. 122.8–9.

[34] See F. Dvornik, *The Idea of Apostolicity*, pp. 39–137.

of the apse of the bema in almost all the churches of the island, to the right of Barnabas, the two representing the twin foundations of the Church of Cyprus.[35] The Cypriots at that time remembered that they owed to Epiphanius above all the preservation of the freedom which was granted to them, in accordance with the famous vote of the Third Ecumenical Council, "by our Lord Jesus Christ, the redeemer of all men, through his own blood".[36]

---

[35] See e.g. V. Laurent, *Le corpus des sceaux de l'empire byzantin*, V, 2: *L'Église*, 1, Paris, 1965, n° 1484, 1485, and the churches of Asinou, Lagoudera and Pera Choriou.

[36] E. Schwartz, op. cit., p. 122.16-17. Cf. the first beatitude of the Synodicon of Cyprus (12th century): Βαρνάβα τοῦ πανευφήμου ἀποστόλου καὶ γενναιομάρτυρος καὶ Ἐπιφανίου τοῦ σοφωτάτου, τῶν μακαριωτάτων ἀρχιεπισκόπων Κύπρου, αἰωνία ἡ μνήμη. N. Cappuyns, "Le Synodicon de Chypre au XIIe siècle", *Byzantion* 10, 1935, pp. 489–504, esp. p. 492; and J. Gouillard, "Le Synodikon de l'Orthodoxie", *Travaux et mémoires* 2, 1967, pp. 1–316, esp. p. 111, note 376.

Barnabas (left) and Epiphanius (right), the two pillars of the Church of
Cyprus. Apse of the church of the Panagia Arakiotissa, Lagoudera,
Cyprus, AD 1192. (Cf. the sixth-century inscriptions from the school of
Salamis: "Barnabas the apostle our support, Epiphanius our great
champion", *Cahiers archéologiques* 13, 1962, pp. 66ff.)

II

THE CHURCH OF CYPRUS IN THE BYZANTINE EMPIRE (AD 330–1191)*

In this lecture we encounter Cypriot merchants permanently suspended between heaven, to which their charitable works raise them, and hell, into which their passions cast them. Bishops celebrate liturgies, write books, travel and constantly build. The paralysed are healed at the shrines. Monks guard beautiful churches filled with timeless art. The country people pray for rain. At the liturgy of the archbishop of Cyprus in the cathedral of Leucosia (Nicosia) the powerful of the land mix with drunkards smelling of garlic. From their hermitages saints threaten the laity for eating meat on Clean Monday. In contemplating these figures we find ourselves outside time. Past and present meet and merge together and only the future seems far off.

This is the picture which I should like to bring alive as far as possible in this paper. It is not a continuous picture but rather a series of heterogeneous elements at different stages in a continuum, which come together and are resynthesized into an astonishing unity, the unity of the Orthodox world of Cyprus. And that Cyprus which the historian loves, the living Cyprus, is essentially a country, a history and a Church – because that which defines the identity of Cyprus is precisely its geography, its history and its Church. I refer not to the individual, the fortuitous and the transient but to that which Solomos – following Dante – called "the common and the mainstream" (Τὸ κοινὸν καὶ τὸ κύριον).

I

I have entitled my address "The Church of Cyprus in the Byzantine Empire" because the Cypriot Church belongs to the Byzantine world not only before

---

* Translated from the unpublished lecture "Η Ἐκκλησία τῆς Κύπρου μέσα στήν Ὀρθόδοξη Αὐτοκρατορία, 330–1191 μ.Χ.".

330, the year of the foundation of Constantinople, but also after 1191, the year of the capture of Cyprus by the Crusaders, and even after 1453, when New Rome ceased to exist. The roots of the Byzantine world extend before 330 into the ancient Graeco-Roman world and Judaea (for centuries also part of that world). After 1191 the Church of Cyprus belongs in every respect to "Romania", even after the schism of 1260. After 1453 the Church of Cyprus remains Byzantine, to be placed, after 1571, in the enslaved "royal race of the Romans" –"Byzantium after Byzantium" in the well-known phrase of N. Jorga. Byzantine time, then, the time of the realities of Byzantium, transcends the chronological boundaries of the Empire, and the period 330–1191 is relative because it refers only to the external political history of Cyprus and not to the essential history of the island's intellectual outlook, culture and society.

It is clear, moreover, that this period, 330–1191, cannot be examined as a unified era. In reality it falls into three phases: (a) the *early Byzantine*, which extends from about – in history all things are approximate – 330 to 699, the year of the return of the archbishop of Cyprus from New Justinianoupolis (not Justiniane as it has wrongly been called since the period of Turkish rule); (b) the *middle Byzantine*, from 700 to 965, the year a decisive end was made to the payment of tribute to Islam; and lastly (c) the *later Byzantine* from 965 to 1191, given that the seven-year tyranny of Isaac Komnenos, so bitter for the Church of Cyprus, was only a brief episode in the history of Byzantine rule in Cyprus.

If clarity of thought is a necessary prerequisite to clarity of expression, I should indicate that the term "early Byzantine" is the only one which properly belongs to the history of the Roman Empire in the East, the term "later Empire", which is still used in Cyprus by some archaeologists, being justifiable only in relation to the West. Equally mistaken is the mention sometimes made of a period of Arab domination in the history of the Church of Cyprus – evidently from ignorance of the more recent research on the subject. I have called the period which for the Church begins in 700 (and not in 688/9, the year of the conclusion of a treaty between Justinian II and 'Abd-al-Malik) "middle Byzantine" in spite of the position of political neutrality which Cyprus maintained between the Empire and the Caliphate, since the Church of Cyprus in these centuries belonged to Byzantium, as did the culture and society of the Cypriots of the time. The third period, moreover, cannot in any way be called "Byzantine" in the proper sense for the simple reason that for Cyprus this period is later Byzantine, if the words are to have their exact meaning.

II

The factors which define the character of the history of Cyprus are its immutable geographical position on the one hand and its constantly changing political context on the other. Cyprus belongs to the eastern Mediterranean but is also situated on the line dividing the northern from the southern Mediterranean – and all these Mediterraneans are different from each other. In the period which we are examining, however, it was inhabited – and this is of great importance – by a people who belonged culturally to the central-western and northern Mediterranean, that is to say, to Europe, with their capital then at Constantinople. This cultural identity was threatened from two directions, from the entry of non-Greek-speaking Eastern Christian populations and from Islam, which from the seventh century had flooded over Syria, Palestine and North Africa: that is to say, from the eastern and southern Mediterranean.

The administrative arrangements of Justinian II, which endured for nearly three centuries, maintained the political neutrality and internal administrative autonomy of Cyprus. In other words they delivered the island fundamentally from Islam. At the same time the Church of Cyprus, by continuously acculturating the Eastern Christians who sought refuge in the island or came to live there, saved Cyprus from the "other Mediterranean", as F. Braudel has called it, the eastern Mediterranean which was Phoenician, Syrian, Egyptian or Armenian, and preserved it for that Mediterranean which in this period controlled the fortunes of Europe as a civilisation. The struggle between the Empire along with the Church on the one side and the East (both Christian and Muslim) on the other is characteristic of the nine centuries we are discussing and is a permanent feature of the Byzantine era in Cyprus. This structure collapsed with the arrival on the scene of the northerners, the English Crusaders. The hour of northern dominance, however, had not yet arrived, and with the appearance of the Lusignans and Venice Cyprus returned to the Mediterranean, to the western Mediterranean, however, which was now administering a death blow to its eastern part, Byzantium. The victors were Islam with regard to the political dimension and the Church with regard to the history of the island. For from 1191 to 1878, when England, which was to control all the Mediterraneans, reappeared, Cyprus was to remain Greek and Orthodox. The more recent events are well known. "What belongs to the future is known only to the gods ... ".

The ecclesiastical life as we encounter it in the relics of the Byzantine period, both written and archaeological, was ceaselessly influenced by the ebb and flow of these tides. The influence of Antioch, the hub of Asiatic Christianity, is discernible in the worship of the early Byzantine Cypriot Church. This was the great period of the Syriac liturgies and the new capital of Constantine itself constituted an ecclesiastical outpost of the city of Antioch. The rise of the patriarchal claims of the Antiochenes and the colossal figure of Epiphanius of Cyprus disrupted this tendency, which was replaced by the

Palestinian with its celebrated holy places and its own demands for inde-
pendence from the civil metropolis of the diocese of *Oriens*. The Cypriot basilicas
of the fourth and fifth centuries testify to this change, while a careful inter-
pretation of the written sources shows that behind these new alliances stood
Alexandria and, behind her, Rome. In the sixth century, while Egypt and
Syria were immersed in the ambiguous atmosphere of Monophysitism,
Cyprus was being subjected all the more intensely to the influence of
Constantinople. This influence reached its climax under Heraclius and his
dynasty despite the influx of Eastern Christians, who brought with them
Monophysitism and characteristic forms of Syrian piety such as stylite
monachism. The latter, however, does not seem to have flourished in Cyprus.

When inquiring about the fate after death of Philentolos, a rich merchant
of Constantia who "had distributed many alms to the poor and to orphans
and every other pious cause, and had founded a hospital, and in short [had
expended] all his income from land and sea and from trade and villages and
ships in pious works, and yet through the Enemy of good had suffered from
the passion of fornication", Archbishop Arkadios turned for prayers to "the
monasteries and stylites and recluses", and received from Abba Kaioumas,
a recluse of Ammochostos (Famagusta) who had been a monk for many years
at Klysma (Louez) on the Red Sea, the reply that the fornicating Cypriot
benefactor remained suspended between heaven and hell. Here in a single
scene are Constantia, Ammochostos, Syria, Egypt, the wealth of Cypriot
merchants of the seventh century and, as J. Le Goff would have said, the "birth
of Purgatory"!

III

Until the Arab invasions, however, the stronger influence was exercised by
the island's history rather than by its geographical environment. The Church
of Cyprus is one of the churches of late antiquity, of that world which has
been revealed to us so skilfully in the last few decades by such historians as
E. Stein, A.H.M. Jones, H.-I. Marrou and P. Brown. Archaeological
monuments, the basilica of Kourion with its peristyles, the basilicas of the
Drepano peninsula near Pegeia with their public baths, or the inscriptions
of Salamis, the works of episcopal authors such as St Epiphanius of Constantia,
the great heresiologue of the early Church, lives of the saints of the period,
Tychon of Amathous, for example, or John the Almsgiver – all these show
us the Cypriot Church living in an open society where life was lived publicly
in cities which were still cities and not villages or castles, as they were to become
in the period which followed. (A strange exaggeration – or weapon of
propaganda: the golden cup in the Metropolitan Museum of New York with

its repoussé busts of the four great cities of the sixth century: "Constantinople, City of Cyprus, City of Rome, City of Alexandria ... ". Cyprus has replaced Antioch!)

In the forty-ninth "edifying history" in F. Nau's series the description of the trial in Constantia in 638 of a "most wretched and impious sorcerer and presbyter" constitutes an astonishing scene from the society of late antiquity. "With every class present by rank" the eparch exercised judgment "presiding" at "the public proceedings" (*egressus publicus*) and putting his questions through "the most learned assessor", the assistant magistrate of the period, "in the hearing of all". The magus priest confessed:

> "'I swear by God ... that from the time I became a sorcerer (φαρμακὸς) I have not offered [the sacrament of the Eucharist] but whenever I came into the sanctuary an angel of God came down and bound me to a column with my arms behind my back, and he celebrated the Eucharist and gave communion to the people, and then when the service was completely finished he untied me so that I could come out.' The crowd cried out: 'Great is the God of the Christians', ... and when the crowd had shouted this, the lawless priest was condemned out of his own mouth and was burned on a pyre in the sight of all."

Hardly any element in the life and outlook of late antiquity is missing: the city, the magistrates, public life, miracles, the crowd, the pyre and also the great legacy of the period for all mankind: the code of Roman law, the hierarchical structure of the Church and monasticism. It may perhaps also be said that the pyre foreshadows the Middle Ages, but it would have been understood equally by Diocletian or Torquemada . And if the cry of the crowd: "God is great!" is reminiscent of the Muslim acclamation "*Allah Akhbar!*" let us not forget that many of the things which we now regard as Islamic customs were originally Byzantine. For example, the modern Cypriot πεύτζιν is nothing other than the Byzantine ἐπεύχι, that is to say, the prayer mat which our Byzantine forebears carried with them when they were travelling, their ἐπεύχιον. It is characteristic that this most Greek of words has survived in Cyprus for centuries after the Byzantine custom that it indicated had been forgotten and indeed is regarded as Arabic. Here is another survival: the clerical magus of 638 came from the village of Trachides, which must have been situated in the forested area called Trachones, near Famagusta. I do not know what the Turks call it at the present time.

I turn now to another unique scene from the life of the Church of Cyprus in late antiquity. Abba Anastasios, a Cypriot monk of Sinai with medical and scientific interests, when asked why Christians suffer more from diseases than non-believing nations, avoided any attempt at theodicy and ascribed the phenomenon to the Christians' overeating and profligacy (evidence of the wealth and higher culture of Byzantine society in relation to its neighbours, as we would say today). Here is another example: a few years previously (at the beginning of the seventh century), "a certain sophist philosopher and doctor was present at the *martyrium* of St Epiphanius, and observing the crowd of sick people said: 'You can with the help of God be healed through a dietary regime and through purgations and bleedings', and having embarked upon the task at the command of the archbishop, he healed the majority of them".

The archaeologist will observe that the basilica of St Epiphanius in Salamis is called a *martyrium*; the historian will note the ancient connection between medicine and philosophy; the doctor will mark the diet, the purgation and the constant bleedings, while the theologian will marvel at the liberal spirit of the abba and also of the archbishop of Cyprus, who orders the crowd of sick people who have approached the saint for healing to go to the doctor.

The fact is, however, that doctors do not always succeed, even when they are themselves the patient. In this connection a doctor from Lapithos called Theodore, "skilled in the art and therefore famous", travelled to Egypt – St Sophronios of Jerusalem tells us a little before 619 – in search of healing at the celebrated sanctuary of SS. Cosmas and Damian at the modern Aboukir, 25 kilometres north-east of Alexandria. The martyrs not only healed their colleague with a poultice of the roast lung of a pig on his paralysed feet but also revealed to him that his affliction sprang from the magic spells of a certain Jew at Lapithos.

The seas still belonged to the Byzantine fleet and the Cypriots were sailors with an island spirit. "I class them with the Rhodians", the same author writes elsewhere, "for I understand the islanders enjoy meeting each other more than they enjoy meeting people who are not islanders." Tireless travellers and tourists, they are to be encountered throughout the eastern Mediterranean, especially at the great sanctuaries. It is the age of pilgrimages, of the spirituality of the traveller and the visitor. You would have thought that all people from all classes were on the move. Archbishop Arkadios travelled to Lydda in Palestine to St George. Leontios of Neapolis went to Syria, to the cities which he describes so vividly in his *Life* of Symeon Salos. Theodore of Paphos also went to Alexandria to SS. Cosmas and Damian. A blind man "of a most noble and famous family" went to Seleucia to the holy spring of St Thecla. A poor man called George and his parents from the village of Phava, "situated near Limassol ... and lying fifty stades from the city and three and a half stades from the sea", also went to Abba Kyros because he had injured his leg while chasing a hare. Others went to Sinai to venerate the bush that had burned and had not been consumed. Crowds, "lovers of the cross and of Christ", flocked to Jerusalem "for the holy and glorious feast", and so on .

Cyprus herself, the "beloved of Christ" (φίλαινα τοῦ Χριστοῦ), was not lacking in places of pilgrimage. In the early Byzantine period the chief sites were the basilicas with the tombs and relics of St Barnabas and St Epiphanius at Salamis, of St Spyridon at Trimythous, of St Tychon and St John the Almsgiver at Amathous, of St Zeno at Kourion, of St Heracleidios at Tamassos, of St Triphyllios at what is today Leucosia, of St Auxibios at Soloi and of St Theodotos at Kyrenia. The most holy of all the shrines after the fifth century was the basilica of St Barnabas the Apostle, built by Archbishop Anthemios with gifts from the Emperor Zeno and other magnates of Constantinople, which was surrounded by stoas, gardens, cells, aqueducts and hostels "for refreshing foreign visitors". In extent and beauty the shrine resembled "a small and very pleasant city". To the right of the altar towards the south, in a special apsidal chamber decorated with silver and precious marbles, lay the casket containing the relics of the blessed apostle. And the monk Alexander's description concludes: "Watch over all your country, now and always, and guard her with your holy prayers from every evil … ".

Not long afterwards the Persian colossus, the age-old pandar of the eastern Mediterranean, appears on the stage once again. Cyprus was saved, only to be thronged with refugees from Syria, Palestine and Egypt. Her Church strove to assimilate them whether they were saints or heretics.

One of the saints was Artemon, whose relics were brought to Cyprus from Laodicea (Latakia) in Syria. His shrine – precisely where it was situated in Cyprus is not known today – contained a wonder-working baptistery which filled up with water on its own on the eve of Easter after the liturgy of the Resurrection. The Cypriots only baptized infants in this water.

When the refugees in question, however, were heretics, matters were more difficult, so much so that sometimes in order to be put right the help of the Cypriot saints was needed. In a *Plerophoria* (stories of miraculous proofs of the true faith – of the first importance for modern historians as sources for understanding ancient societies and mentalities) we read that St Epiphanius himself appeared twice to a Monophysite Egyptian refugee called John, encouraging him to make his communion in the Orthodox church of Constantia and abandon his fellow-heretics. When he failed to do this, the story tells us, remembering his parents in Egypt and his traditional confession of faith, the white-haired saint appeared to him the third time:

"I saw, then, as if in an ecstasy the same priest-like figure, very dignified in countenance and with a stern voice, who said to me: 'Why then have you disobeyed me the second time and did not communicate with the orthodox?' But out of fear I was unable to reply. Then he said to me: 'Did you not enter the metropolis of Constantia?' I said in terror, 'Yes, Master.' 'Did you not leave it and go to the church of Epiphanius?' And I said, 'I did, Lord.' He said: 'And what do you say of Epiphanius? Was he orthodox or a heretic?' And I said, 'Forgive me, Master, he is a servant of God and a saint and standard-bearer.' He replied: 'Epiphanius believes as the catholic Church does. Do not doubt but rise up and go to communion. For I am Epiphanius.' ... Understanding then my previous error and knowing the truth ... I went to the *kyriakon*, partook of the life-giving and holy mysteries and thanked God that he had included me, the unworthy, in his holy orthodox flock."

In spite of the strong presence of Monophysitism in Cyprus, the island, thanks to the alliance of the heavenly with the earthly, its ancient tradition and its able bishops, and in spite of the manoeuverings of the Empress Theodora, remained orthodox and Byzantine, only to succumb shortly afterwards to the blows of Islam.

IV

The "expedient arrangements" of Justinian II concerning the "refashioning of a policy" with the Arabs in Cyprus saved the island, as I have already mentioned, from Islam until its complete subjection in 965 "to the sceptres of the most Christian power" by Nikephoros II Phokas. Whenever the eastern Mediterranean Sea was not controlled by the Greeks, Cyprus, on account of its geographical position, could only survive through neutrality or autonomy. That is not to say that all the bishops or saints of Cyprus accepted these solutions. St Therapon, for example, whose "miracles were the talk of the whole of the East, while Cyprus, where there was even a sacred palace dedicated to the saint, boasted of his cures ... revelling in them immoder-ately ... " commanded his relics to be taken from Cyprus before the second capture of the island by the Arabs and so became an exile in Constantinople, "since the whole island is to be delivered into the hands of the murderous Hagarenes".

Yet in spite of the fact that Cyprus in the middle Byzantine period paid half its taxes to the Caliphate and was colonised by a number of Arabs, both soldiers and civilians, it continued not only to "belong to our parts" (τῶν καθ' ἡμᾶς μερῶν), as the famous *Life* of St Stephen the Younger calls it, but in reality even constituted a forward bastion of the Empire. Almost two centuries after the second Arab capture of Cyprus, Archbishop Sophronios I composed one of the most important works on the struggle between Byzantium and the Arabs, the *Diegesis,* for the forty-two elite soldiers who had met a martyr's death at Amorium – the home town of the imperial dynasty – after its capture by the Arabs in August 838.

In the Iconoclast period Cyprus became a refuge for the persecuted, both human beings and icons. And it was to remain the beloved place of pilgrimage of the monks of Byzantium even after the Triumph of Orthodoxy, amongst them St Peter of Atroa of the famous *Life* and St Athanasios the Athonite, the founder of the Great Lavra, who practised the ascetic life for a period at the monastery of St Eutyches, known as the monastery of the Priests, at Paphos.

The Cypriot saints themselves now pressed the Byzantines to visit their country, which maintained an existence "suspended between the Roman and the Saracen powers". Thus in the first half of the ninth century St Spyridon called on St Constantine the Jew to abandon his monastery on the Bithynian Olympus (then the monastic centre of the Empire) and to come to Cyprus, "and I will come to meet you there and stretch out my hand in turn". And when Constantine decided to remain in Attalia, "from which city," according to his biographer,

> "the majority of those who travelled to Cyprus were accustomed to depart, the great Spyridon, who had resolved to prepare the way for him from the monastery, appeared to him in a dream by some angelic power, threatening and reproaching him besides for cowardice and showing indignation at his disbelief and encouraging him to embark on the voyage to Cyprus."

Here was Cyprus once again under the mantle of her heavenly protectors, whose relics, icons and tangible blessings and memorials she had recently refused to abandon.

In 754 the Iconoclast council of Hiereia under Constantine V anathematised by name only three iconophiles: Germanos of Constantinople, George of Cyprus and John of Damascus. The second name is that of the Cypriot monk of the Taurus mountains in Cilicia who is the hero of the apology for the icons known as the *Nouthesia Gerontos.*

> "To the vacillating and wood-worshipping Germanos, anathema. To the like-minded George, falsifier of patristic teaching, anathema. To the infamous and Saracen-minded Mansur, anathema. ... The Trinity has condemned all three."

This event is indicative of the role of Cyprus – a province outside the control of the emperor – in the defence of the icons and traditional piety.

The Seventh Ecumenical Council was called on the initiative of the patriarch of Constantinople, Paul of Cyprus – of Salamis, as the *Synodicon Vetus* calls him – and in 787 one of its leaders was to be Constantine of Cyprus. From his interventions in the debates we learn that the aniconic tradition of St Epiphanius was not entirely forgotten in Constantia even in the eighth century. In this connection we are informed that the driver of a team of oxen from Constantia "entered the house of prayer of the Holy Theotokos in order to pray" in the city itself and put out the right eye of the icon of the Panagia with his ox-goad, with the result that he himself lost his right eye. The archbishop mentions later that at a council which took place in Cyprus on the question of icons the bishop of Kition deposited on oath the following statement which is interesting for the light it sheds on the liturgical life of the island and its painted churches:

"On the day of the holy Theotokos, the fifteenth of August, another man in the city known as Kition came into the church to decorate it with hangings. And taking a nail, he drove it into the wall through the forehead of the icon of St Peter. Then he stretched a rope and hung the curtain and in that hour felt an unbearable pain in his head and forehead. And for the two days of the feast he remained in his bed in agony. On becoming acquainted of this, the bishop of Kition censured him and ordered him to come and draw out the nail from the icon. He went and did this and as soon as he drew out the nail the pain subsided."

We are also told of the following incident which is interesting for the light it sheds on Cypriot life in this period. Thirty-two inhabitants of Kition went in 785 in two ships to Gabala in Syria "for the usual work" (unfortunately the archbishop does not tell us what the work was). There in one of the churches of the city they followed a furious debate between Hagarenes and Christians on the icons, at the end of which a Saracen put out the eye of a mosaic icon with his spear, whereupon the icon, of course, did not hesitate to put out his. I have to confess that this Muslim–Christian dialogue is not distinguished by any marked ecumenical spirit ... . The Seventh Ecumenical Council at all events beatified the memory of Germanos, John and George of Cyprus:

"Of the heralds of truth, eternal memory. ... The Trinity has glorified these three. May we be made worthy to follow their teaching."

In addition to the archbishop the following took part in the council: Spyridon of Kythroi, Eustathios of Soloi, Theodore of Kition, George of Trimythous and Alexander of Amathous.

After 806, when the archbishop of Cyprus himself was taken prisoner by Arab raiders and obliged to pay 1 000 denarii for his release (an exceedingly large sum which demonstrates the exalted position and the always-to-be-envied wealth of the primate of Cyprus), the activity of the Church seems to have enlarged its scope. During his second patriarchate (26 October 877 to 29 September 886) Photios the Great wrote to the spatharocandidatus Staurakios, "eparch of the island of the Cypriots", reproaching him for his exploitation of the island and for the burden of taxation which he had imposed upon it:

> "[since you have] violently [seized] human beings in this way in their entirety along with their property and swallowed them greedily in full view of their countrymen and browsed on them voraciously, what plea can you make in your defence?"

This was in spite of the fact that as long as Ignatios was alive the Church of Cyprus seems to have belonged to his camp, as one would unfortunately have expected, since Ignatios was supported by all the monastic zealots imbued with the Studite spirit. Cyprus remained faithful to her old allies during the Iconoclast period in spite of the fact that essentially the situation had changed completely in Constantinople, the genuine representative of the iconophiles and Orthodoxy now being Photios.

In 913/4 the Patriarch Nicholas Mystikos, "of the household" of Photios the Great, wrote in his role as regent to the Caliph al-Muqtadir mediating on behalf of the Cypriots, whose "land had been stained by atrocious massacres" by the Muslim general Damian (a renegade Syrian Christian) in retaliation for when the *patricius* Himerios in the course of an expedition against the Arab fleet passed by Cyprus and "took and killed Saracens in the island … although according to the treaty the Cypriots should have saved them from his hands and restored them to their own place". (Note that the guarantees for the security of each community by the "mother country" of the other were provided reciprocally by the two communities.) The regent patriarch sought a return to the *status quo ante* because the Cypriots "were not capable of resisting Himerios and saving the Saracens from his hand". The peace of Cyprus implies peace between the two superpowers, writes Nicholas, "because the two powers that have dominion over the whole earth, that of the Saracens and that of the Romans, transcend all others and shine forth like the two great luminaries in the firmament."

It is very likely that this letter (which should be required reading in schools of political science) was sent with the aim of supporting the mission of Bishop Demetrianos of Kythroi (Kythreas) to the court of Baghdad with the intention

of securing the release of the large number of Cypriots taken prisoner during
the invasion of Damian. In the *Life* of St Demetrianos, which was written a
few years later, we read that the saint, "although burdened with age …
himself followed the prisoners on foot" and on reaching distant Baghdad
appeared before the caliph "and recounted the violation of the treaties and
showed that the ferocity of the barbarians was out of all proportion to this".
The tears of the aged ethnarch of the Cypriots moved the Commander of
the Faithful (or, as the *Life* calls him, "the exarch of the barbarians" – the
Kythrean monastic writer evidently does not agree with the reciprocal
civilities of the two superpowers, since he calls the caliph a barbarian whereas
Mystikos had addressed him as celebrated, renowned, beloved friend and
luminary of the world!). At all events, the caliph was moved:

> " 'Be silent, man … and put a stop to your excessive grieving, for you
> will forfeit the fulfilment of the boon you desire.' When the said barbarian
> was informed of the cause, then, and of the inhuman cruelty of the per-
> secutors, he invited the blessed Demetrianos to appear before him after
> three days and delivered to him the booty and all the prisoners. … When
> he had arrived back with all the enslaved people and had given glory
> with them to God who had saved them, the blessed man sent them back
> rejoicing and exulting to their own homes."

The middle Byzantine period of the Church of Cyprus may lack brilliance
in comparison with the early Byzantine (which was the golden age of our
ecclesiastical history) but it is not lacking in struggles, sacrifices and holiness
– and therefore in glory.

V

In the later Byzantine period Cyprus participated in the general renaissance
which the Byzantine world experienced after the eighth century. It became
again an imperial province in the greatest era of Byzantium, the years of the
brilliant Macedonian dynasty. Then followed the era of the Komnenoi,
which was also great from the modern viewpoint, a period of changes, of
decentralisation, of the "powerful", of great landed estates and of the aristocratic ideal as represented in the epic of Digenis Akritas.

After 965 the archbishop of Cyprus is appointed by the emperor like all
the patriarchs, a fact which signifies that, usually at least, he is no longer a
Cypriot but belongs to the clerics who are connected in one way or another
with the court. Towards the end of the Byzantine period some of the bishops
are non-Cypriots, such as, probably, Basil Kinnamos of Paphos and certainly

Barnabas of Lapithos, who was a Cretan. Immediately afterwards the senior (*protothrone*) bishop of Cyprus, Neilos of Tamassos, was also a non-Cypriot. There were also non-Cypriot archbishops in the preceding periods, such as St Epiphanius in the fourth century, who came from Palestine, and Philoxenos, a Syrian from Doliche, in the sixth century. In this period Cyprus lies "in the midst of the land of the Romans", as the *Life* of St Leontios of Jerusalem emphasises, and that the Cypriots were not disturbed by a spirit of local patriotism is shown by the fact that after the abrogation of Byzantine authority in Cyprus, when the Cypriots acquired again the right to elect their archbishop, "the entire list of the clergy and as many as were monks and a host of the most learned from among the laity, and preceding them those set apart from the most holy episcopate as country bishops … all with a common mind" elected Isaias, archbishop of Lydda, a refugee from Palestine, which was now under Arab rule, by translating him "to the throne of the great Barnabas". Moreover, various Cypriots occupied other patriarchal thrones at different times, such as Paul of Constantinople, whom we have already met, Gregory of Constantinople in the thirteenth century, or, in the middle of the twelfth century, John Chrysostomites of Jerusalem, a monk of Koutzouvendi.

For later Byzantine Cypriot society, steeped like the Byzantine world as a whole in the new aristocratic ideal of the era, the series of aristocratic monastic archbishops of the period was not only natural but most appropriate for an autocephalous throne like that of Cyprus. It is characteristic that after Isaias and the establishment of the Empire of Nicaea the Cypriots did not wish to elect an archbishop again themselves. Fifty years after the abrogation of the authority of the emperor in Cyprus (1185), Archbishop Neophytos, writing a little after 1231 to John Vatatzes, says that he himself received his appointment "from that thrice-blessed Orthodox Lord and Emperor" Theodore Lascaris – we must assume before 1222 – "and your sacred majesty knows that this throne of Barnabas, the chief of the disciples and apostles of Christ, is not subject to the ecumenical throne but is an appointment of your sacred majesty and is autocephalous".

The first mention of the appointment of the archbishop of Cyprus by the emperor is found in the *Life* of Euthymios the Younger, where we read that Basil II (976–1025) had offered the holy Georgian prince the throne of Cyprus. He, however, refused it for the sake of Mount Athos, where he later founded the monastery of Iviron. At the beginning of the twelfth century Alexios Komnenos appointed Nicholas Mouzalon to Cyprus, who resigned in 1110 on account of his clash with the Katepan of Cyprus, Eumathios Philokales, the scandalous life of two bishops and certain abbots and monks, and his failure to alleviate the burden of taxation laid upon his flock. Thirty-seven years later the former elder of Cyprus was to be elected ecumenical

patriarch only to resign again on account of the opposition of certain metropolitans. In 1171 Manuel Komnenos offered the Cypriot see to Leontios,
the Oikonomos of the monastery of Patmos, who came from Stroumitza in
Macedonia. He refused the offer although four years later he was to become
by divine command patriarch of Jerusalem.

From 1152, moreover, until 1171 the archbishopric of Cyprus was
occupied by the "exceedingly wise" John of Crete, defender of the rights of
his see against John of Bulgaria (better known as Adrian Komnenos), who
was given precedence over Cyprus by his uncle, Manuel Komnenos, at the
council of 1157, no doubt because he was "of royal descent" and "born in
the purple", according to Nikephoros Basilakes. Between 1157 and 1169 the
Imperial Tribunal – the supreme court, we would say, of the Empire,
dependent on the Senate and the Holy Synod – declared invalid the sentence
of deposition which John of Crete imposed on John of Amathous because
the synod that condemned him was composed of eleven bishops, apart from
the presiding archbishop, instead of at least twelve in conformity with the
twelfth canon of Carthage. This is a decision which the Professor of Canon
Law at the University of Athens would have done well to have taken into
account on the 10 April 1972.

There are many references from the later Byzantine period to members
of the episcopate of Cyprus or to the names of archbishops about whom we
know almost nothing. From the tenth century Niketas of Ancyra refers to
"the famous Epiphanios, the late archbishop of the celebrated Church of the
Cypriots", who – unknown until then – resigned his throne without also
resigning his archiepiscopal rank. According to one witness the archbishop
of Cyprus took part in 1057/8 in the condemnation of the pope and the
removal of his name from the diptychs after the schism of 1054, but who he
was we do not know. In 1094 the archbishop and the bishops of Cyprus visited
Constantinople – we do not know why – and used the opportunity to take
part in the Council of Blachernae on the question of the veneration of icons,
which was held on the occasion of the confiscation of sacred vessels by
Alexios Komnenos for the purpose of expenditure on defence. In a manuscript
in Florence we encounter a certain Basil of Cyprus, who must have reigned
as archbishop at the end of the eleventh or the beginning of the twelfth century,
in any event before Mouzalon, according to the *Synodikon* of the Church of
Cyprus. In the time of John of Crete we hear again of a retired archbishop
of Cyprus, the "former archbishop of Cyprus, Rhoides", who is probably
the successor of Nicholas Mouzalon called Theodoret (it is also possible that
"the former" simply means "the preceding"), and so on. The archbishop after
John is called Barnabas, to whom I shall refer again. His successor was the
last in the series of archbishops of the Byzantine period, Sophronios II, who,

according to the information given by the contemporary Jacobite historian and patriarch of Antioch, Michael the Syrian, was proclaimed patriarch by the tyrant Isaac Komnenos, so that the latter could legally be crowned emperor. The lead seal of this archbishop is preserved today in Washington. It bears on one side the image of St Epiphanius and on the other the inscription: "Of the chief shepherd of the Cypriots, Sophronios".

This picture should not deceive us. The Church of Cyprus in the late Byzantine period is "cosmopolitan", especially in the twelfth century. It is no longer, however, a Church of seafaring islanders, as it once was for the most part in the early Byzantine era (consider the lovely marble ambo in the Museum of Paphos from Basilica A of Pegeia with the inscription "Dedicated as a thank-offering of sailors"). It is a Church of country people who exploit the sea. Having lost its seafaring tradition in the middle Byzantine period, Cyprus was now assimilated more to mainland Anatolia than to the commercial Mediterranean world, which was already dominated by Venice. Inevitably, the wealth of the region, which in the Mediterranean is always seaborne, also fell into Venetian hands. The island throughout this period served as a naval base and station for the Empire in the East and was permanently in the front line of hostilities between Byzantium, the Crusaders and Islam.

The Church of Cyprus similarly became a place of refuge and a base for the Orthodox of the Near East. As a refuge it received victims of persecution by the Arabs, the Seljuk Turks, the Kurds, the Latins and the Armenians. These were Orthodox of Asia Minor, Syria and above all Palestine – their patriarchs, their monks, their manuscripts, their arts, their wisdom. As a base it used its wealth to nourish Near Eastern Orthodoxy and especially the patriarchate of Jerusalem and its monasteries. The *metochia* and properties of these monasteries in Cyprus in this period were anything but negligible. The estates of the indigenous Church also seem to have been extremely extensive, as too were those of the island's magnates. The situation was similar throughout the Empire of the Komnenoi, and the Byzantine tax collector's power even extended to the administration of corporal punishment to clerics when the extraction of state revenues from the churches was at issue. In the end the tax collector became the terror of all the clergy from Archbishop Nicholas Mouzalon to St Neophytos the Recluse, and even to Patriarch Leontios of Jerusalem himself, who was pillaged by Kyriakos, "who was in charge of public revenues in Cyprus", and his assistant Triakontaphyllos.

A certain resistance on the part of the local clergy to this role of Cyprus as provisioner of Jerusalem is perhaps apparent in the *Life* of St Leontios from the behaviour of Theodoulos of Amathous. "Young in years, headlong in manner, rash and reckless in demeanour ... a low fellow among bishops", the bishop of Amathous appropriated sheep, oxen, horses and mules of the Holy Sepulchre in his diocese, refusing to return them until in attempting to cross a ravine he fell from his horse and "alas, repaid the debt in full, a spectacle to hear and to behold ... because our situation is fit for grief and lamentation".

This sentiment, that "our situation is fit for grief and lamentation" (θρήνου τὰ ἡμέτερα ἄξια), became common in the whole of Eastern Empire after the battle of Myriocephalon in 1176, when the Byzantine army, the largest and best-trained in the world, was annihilated. With the death of Manuel Komnenos four years later God seemed to have abandoned his servants. Cyprus was now overwhelmed by an endless agony. Already Constantine Manasses saw the island as a "solid fortress, an iron wall, a stone cage, a dark underworld admitting no escape, not having any means of exit", while Archbishop Mouzalon grieved for her as "formerly the land of Aphrodite, now of Hecate".

The heavy burden of taxation imposed on the people by the military administration, the merciless exploitation by the magnates, the economic privileges enjoyed by Venice from 1148, the almost complete absence of education, the moral laxity of corrupt bishops and abbots, whom the archbishop himself calls "tax-gathering hierarchs", conspired to reduce the population to misery and ruin. The incursion of Reynald, duke of Antioch, and the Armenian prince Thoros II in 1155/6, the raid by the Egyptian fleet in 1158, the piracy of the count of Tripoli, Raymond III, in 1161 and renewed Arab pillaging all made the situation worse. Even nature herself turned against the Cypriots. In 1175 there began a three-year drought which resulted in a great famine accompanied by a fearful plague and repeated earth-quakes. Not only were the flora and fauna of the island destroyed but, according to the evidence of St Neophytos, the human inhabitants grew savage and turned to crime. Only one third of the population survived these years. Entire villages disappeared, giving rise to irreparable gaps in local history. The eclipses of the sun in 1176 and 1178 wrapped the island in an atmosphere of apocalyptic doom. An unpropitious epilogue to the Byzantine era and an ominous prologue to the age of the Franks was provided by the bestial tyranny of Isaac Komnenos from 1185 to 1191.

An analysis which I made some time ago of the lexical characteristics of St Neophytos (1134–c.1220) before 1191 is indicative of the general sense of insecurity and anxiety which characterises this period and of the premo-nition of the approaching end. The saint constantly stresses that "the barbarous nations often arm themselves against us and we are defeated in wars and are unable to resist" and that "a turn for the worse has taken place". Words such as "affliction", "oppression", "damage", "wailing", "disaster", "blow", "danger", "grievous things", "difficulties", "want", "lack", "obstacles", "unbridled acts", "lawless deeds", "a world of transgressions" and "worthily chastised" recur frequently. The same is true of verbs such as "we suffer", "we experience tumults", "we have been cursed", "we endure", "we have been consumed", "we have been mown down", "we struggle", "we have been cut down", "we have been abandoned".

Surrounded by this moral, social, political and physical decay, the Recluse of Paphos, torn between anxiety and amazement, the two fundamental steps leading towards authentic existence, raised up his eyes towards the "refined and great" commonwealth of God. Time does not permit me to expatiate. Let me be permitted to add only this, that throughout his long life he was for his suffering country and people not only their voice but also a source of consolation, power, education and life for them. Within a physical space which was constantly being further constricted Neophytos raised up works of faith and culture which stir the emotions and provide religious and aesthetic inspiration to the present day. In a corrupt society he succeeded in consolidating a community of people imbued with the single ideal of struggling together for moral perfection. In his person the hard realities of life could no longer triumph over the profound truth of the Resurrection. Anyone who wishes to bring to life the Cypriot world of the twelfth and early thirteenth centuries, to analyse what people did and understand how they lived, must turn towards the Hermitage of Paphos, its caves, its iconography and the writings which were produced within it. For there is hidden there, with greater certainty than anywhere else, the collective consciousness of the people of Cyprus of that era. The response which the saint evoked in his people, in the lower orders of society as well as the higher, both clerical and lay, reveals that for his fellow-countrymen and fellow-believers he embodied in his person a common spiritual ideal. And to end more or less as I began, the cast of mind, the tastes, the patterns of thought, the assumptions and the spirit of a people are not encapsulated in – I repeat – the individual, the fortuitous and the transient but in "the common and the mainstream".

VI

It is now time to draw these various threads together. A variety of conclusions is possible, for we are dealing with a period of nine centuries of which I have simply attempted to give a fleeting taste. I should like to dwell on the problem of continuity.

First, the discontinuity separating the three phases of the period 330 to 1191 is obvious and I have hinted at it many times in the course of my lecture. This is connected with the discontinuity in the Byzantine world in general, which under a superficially static, if not stagnant, appearance was a dynamic, lively society which for a thousand years was constantly changing, not in a fortuitous and spasmodic manner, however, but in harmony with a comprehensive scheme defined by its classical and Christian roots.

The very seat of the archbishop changed – symbolically, I would say – three times. In the first few years it was at Paphos, the ancient city of Aphrodite on the western shore of the island, facing the elder Rome. Later it was moved to the new city of the son of the first Christian emperor, Constantia, also on the coast but facing Antioch, the metropolis of the diocese of the East. Finally after 965 it was transferred to the inland city of Leucosia, by this time a miniature version of Constantinople, with its Mese Street, its Hagia Sophia, its Odegetria, its Eleousa, its Mangana, its monastery of the Andreioi – characteristic features of the new age when the Byzantine dukes and the archbishops of Cyprus tried to console themselves for the Constantinople that they had lost, creating at least a humble copy of it in their distant posting of Cyprus. The unexpected glory of the city surprised the biographer of St Triphyllios, who does not know what to ascribe it to except to the saint's prayers: "and now larger and more beautiful than all the other cities of Cyprus, and presiding over them brilliantly, it has been enriched by him with his supplications". (How great would be his surprise today if he saw the ungrateful city which has completely forgotten its patron, whom Jerome placed among the most brilliant and most learned men of the fourth century.)

Let us turn next to the religious sensibility of the Cypriots. In the early Byzantine period the heroes of the Church of Cyprus are its holy pastors and bishops, in the middle Byzantine period the ideal is embodied by the holy monks, while the late Byzantine period has as its heroes the mounted military saints. If the early Byzantine is the era of splendid basilicas with stoas, baptisteries and public ceremonies, the middle Byzantine is the period of the contraction of the basilicas into smaller painted churches from which almost nothing has survived, while the late Byzantine is the age of the beautiful churches of monasteries built by local holy monks such as Neophytos, or foreigners such as Abbot George, founder of Koutzouvendi in 1090, and above all by the χαριστικάριοι (wealthy imperial officials). Such today are Asinou, a foundation of the Magister Nikephoros, who died in 1115 as the monk Nicholas; Arakas – the Byzantine Hierax – a foundation of Leo Authentes, and the Holy Trinity of Koutzouvendi, a foundation of Duke Eumathios Philokales, perhaps in reparation for the resignation of Archbishop Nicholas Mouzalon. Such would also have been the monastery of the Theotokos Alypou at Geri, a foundation of the Magister Epiphanios Paschales in imitation of the Theotokos Alypou of Nicaea, which has today become the

Panagia of Aloupou [fox]. Such would have also been the Eleousa of Kykkos, a foundation of Manuel Boutoumites, from which too nothing has survived apart from its ancient household icon, the face of which is no longer visible.

In its liturgical life the Church of Cyprus abandoned by stages from the early Byzantine period its paschal canon (which, in spite of Nicaea, it had retained for almost a century in preference to the Alexandrian), it lost its deaconesses, who are mentioned in the fourth century, and its liturgical forms retreated slowly before those of Palestine and the monastery of Studios. In this way it abandoned the archaic Anaphora of St Epiphanius, of which a small fragment was discovered in 1960 in a Sinai manuscript of the fourteenth century. Great sanctuaries, such as the basilica of Kampanopetra at Salamis, which housed perhaps a part of the stone of Golgotha, or, according to others, a part of the True Cross, are forgotten for ever. Venerable relics, such as those of SS. Therapon, Spyridon, Lazarus, Epiphanius and even those of Barnabas, leave Cyprus for the insatiable imperial capital. Local saints who are venerated in one period are forgotten in another. Such were Artemon, with his wonder-working baptistery, or Palamon, "renowned among the ascetics and martyrs", whose relics were venerated in the ninth century by St Constantine the Jew, who also read "the story of his life" and transferred his hand to the monastery of Hyakinthos at Nicaea. Monasteries such as that of Symboulos – "about 28 stades from the Christ-loving city of Kourion" – where Theodore of Paphos was given the tonsure at the beginning of the seventh century, have become nothing more than place-names (today Symvoulas at Akrotiri). In the *menologium* preserved in a gospel lectionary, MS n° 163 in the National Library of Greece, we read that on 4 October our twelfth-century forebears celebrated the memory "of the holy martyrs Dometios, Theoteknos and Diogenes and Gregory, new martyrs of Cyprus" – new martyrs created by the Arabs, no doubt. When? Who were they? Where did they suffer martyrdom? When were they forgotten? The questions are endless.

Yet you will also have sensed a striking continuity, not only from 330 to 1191 but even from 330 to the present day. In spite of the difference of detail, in spite of the interruptions, in spite of the yawning gaps we are still surrounded by the same atmosphere, the same place, the same climate, the same language, the same simple religious sensibility, humane spirit, avoidance of extremes and love of the saints, the same gentle temperament of the true people of Cyprus.

The same land, the same mentality. In the fourth century St Spyridon, while travelling from Trimythous to Kyrenia, "which was one of the cities in the island of Cyprus", arrived with his companion, the bishop of Kallinikiseoi, "or of the White Gods" (=Leucosia), at Kythrea and they

began to climb up "through the mountain called Pentadaktylos". The beauty
of the site of Parymni made Triphyllios desire to buy it, "since he considered
this advantageous to his own church", a temptation which was the occasion
of Spyridon's reproach and later of his gentle forgiveness. The land, the place-
names – all of them remain the same through the centuries. The only
difference is that the temptation of a modern bishop would have been to sell
Parymni rather than buy it. (Though how would he have sold it today if his
predecessor had not bought it in the fifth century?)

The same gentleness of temperament, simple religious sentiment and
witness to Christ. Now a scene taken from the middle Byzantine period: the
martyrdom of St Sozon from Plakountoudion, an old village near the Hagia
Moni of Paphos, the famous monastery of the Priests. I end my address with
Leontios Machairas: " ... St Sozon at Plakountoudion, was a shepherd boy
and he took to his heels when the Saracens burnt the icon of the Theotokos
at the monastery and tripped on the paving stones and is there to this day."
The child runs to save himself, he trips, however, breaks the jar, the milk is
spilt and he is given away. "And fleeing he fell and cracked the milk-jar and
dribbled the milk and all of them saw the place. And he went up to the cave
with the other children, and they came there and set it alight and burnt them."
I am glad that his native land has not forgotten the innocent shepherd boy,
the lamb of the Good Shepherd. At Chrysorogiatissa you can venerate his
ancient icon by the place of his martyrdom. He was betrayed by his milk!

The same people, the same sin, the same holiness. I come to the last
known scene from the Byzantine era of our Church: the concelebration of
Archbishop Barnabas and the bishops of Cyprus with St Leontios of Jerusalem
a little before 1180:

> "O thy divine judgments, O Master, and the richness of thy bounty! ...
> With all the episcopal company standing in order and the high priest
> himself [the archbishop of Cyprus] with the bishops around him, each
> occupying his own place, he [the patriarch of Jerusalem], the most
> senior of all present, seeing that he is the great high priest of God, cast
> his eye on the faces of those standing around, from the chief priest of
> Cyprus himself to Theophylact of Trimythous, and saw them shining
> more brightly than the sun ... and the rest in a row were also shining
> from the superabundance of the former, some of whose faces he saw turned
> to a gray colour, and some to a darker colour, and others to black, and,
> to be precise, the surface of their faces became leprous. One of them
> was ... the bishop ... of Lapithos called Barnabas like the archbishop."

I do not know of a more shocking scene from the whole history of the Church of Cyprus than this last patriarchal concelebration in the Byzantine church of Hagia Sophia in Leucosia. Before the altar of the Church of Cyprus a saint sees "serving the immortal King" a Barnabas "shining more brightly than the sun" and a black Barnabas with a face leprous with sin. Between them are all the shades and gradations of white to black. But has not this always been the Church of Christ on earth? "The whole Church is a Church of those who are repenting, the whole Church is a Church of those who are perishing", writes St Ephraim the Syrian.

As one looks at this liturgy one would have thought that the list of characters in the drama had been filled centuries ago. The appearance nevertheless after a brief interval of the bloodstained figure of Isaac Komnenos was to bring an abrupt and violent end to the scene. When the curtain rose again, the Church was to journey into the Babylonian captivity of the Franks.

Bust of Justinian II
(Grierson, p. 648)

III

CYPRUS, NEA JUSTINIANOUPOLIS[*]

I have written elsewhere that as far as it concerns the "common and the mainstream", leaving aside transient, fortuitous or individual instances, the identity of Cyprus is determined by its geography, its history and its Church. That is to say, the living Cyprus, the Cyprus that its inhabitants would die for, is a place, a history and a Church. The historic moment that I have chosen to examine in this paper – the transfer of the archbishop of Cyprus and his people to the Hellespont by the Emperor Justinian II in 691 – threatened to end the existence of the Church of Cyprus, to efface its geography, and divert the river-bed of its history. "A deranged page of history" is how the last student of the Arabic sources of the middle Byzantine period of Cypriot history described it, while the most recent researcher into the Greek sources termed it "a mysterious affair". I should be happy if this talk offers, as I hope it will, the outline of a solution to this historical enigma, which might have altered the future of Cyprus radically and irrevocably.

I

The ultimate question centres, of course, on the motives and intentions of Justinian II.[1] What were the emperor's reasons for transporting the Cypriot population to the Hellespont, on the one hand, and why did he transfer the ecclesiastical privileges of the archbishop of Cyprus from the church of Constantia to the church of New Justinianopolis, on the other?

A proper examination of the problem requires the elucidation of many other matters, some of which remain obscure because of the fragmentary nature of the sources or a complete lack of evidence. When exactly were the Cypriots displaced and when did they return? Was the whole of the population moved or only part of it, and which part? Did the archbishop leave alone or

---

[*] *Sixth Annual Lecture on History and Archaeology*, Nicosia, 1990.
[1] For the latest assessment see C. Head, *Justinian II of Byzantium*, Madison, Milwaukee & London, 1972.

was he accompanied by his bishops? Did he indeed leave of his own accord, or was he forced to do so by the emperor? Did he return because he wished it, or because he was expelled from New Justinianopolis? Did the transfer of the rights of Constantia to New Justinianopolis mean the abolition of the Church of Cyprus?

Ignorance has attributed the expatriation of the Cypriots to the so-called occupation of Cyprus by the Arabs; hostility to the Heraclian dynasty has ascribed it to the madness of the last member of the house. The first explanation is no longer taken seriously and so I shall not pursue it further. Not only can it not be substantiated, but it stands in direct contradiction to all the sources, Greek, Arabic and Syriac. As to the mental disturbance of Justinian II, the accusation relies on a hostile source from the time of the Isaurian dynasty which had every interest in blackening the dynasty which preceded it. The *Chronographia* of Theophanes, drawing on this hostile source, speaks as follows about the emigration of the Cypriots:

> "In this year [Annus Mundi 6183, i.e. AD 691/2], owing to a lack of good sense, Justinian broke the peace with 'Abd-al-Malik. He foolishly decided to evacuate the island of Cyprus. He would not accept the new money 'Abd-al-Malik sent as it was unprecedented that anyone else should mint their own gold coinage. In the course of the sea journey many Cypriots drowned or died of sickness; the rest returned to Cyprus."[2]

This tradition survives from Theophanes, through Paul the Deacon, to Archimandrite Kyprianos in the eighteenth century. Here is the paragraph which the national historian of the island devotes to the dramatic displacement of the Cypriots:

> "Wherefore another most sorry catastrophe befalls the island, which originates not with the Arabs, not with barbarians, but with the strange notions and the foolish inconsistent thoughts of our good Emperor Justinian. Using as a pretext the fact that 'Abd-al-Malik did not send him coins engraved with the figure used in Constantinople (because that is when the Hagarenes began to be arrogant and strike their own coins), he was shaken, and dissolved the peace treaty with 'Abd-al-Malik in the sixth year of his reign. He orders the people of Cyprus to move and emigrate to the lands under his charge, and abandons Cyprus unaided into the hands of the Hagarenes. What do you expect the poor Cypriots to do? They hurry to the ships. Women, men, children and old people

---

[2] *Theophanis Chronographia*, I, ed. C. de Boor, Leipzig, 1883, p. 365.

of every age and class are squeezed and crowded into them, some are drowned at sea, others fall ill and many die. A number, preferring the sweetness of life to the tyranny of the barbarians, return half-dead to their impoverished motherland. With great difficulty, I say, the bedraggled rabble disembarked in the straits of Gallipoli, where they settled in the region of Cyzicus."[3]

Naturally the modern historian does not agree. At the beginning of his account of the reign of Justinian II (685–95, 705–11), George Ostrogorsky writes:

"Like his father, he was scarcely sixteen years old on his accession. He possessed neither the astute circumspection nor the balanced judgment of the true statesman, for he was by nature passionate and impulsive, taking after his grandfather in disposition. He also had the autocratic spirit which was characteristic of all the Heraclians and, as in the case of Constans II, this took the form of a ruthless despotism which could brook no opposition. He bore a name which carried with it great responsibilities but also great temptations. With the example of Justinian I before him, filled with ideas of the magnificence of the imperial office, this young, immature, unbalanced ruler was often led astray by his burning ambition and his unquenchable longing for fame. His unrestrained despotism and his extreme irritability drove him to acts which stained his reputation in the eyes of his contemporaries and have blinded modern historians to the significance of his reign. For all his faults, Justinian II was a true representative of the Heraclian dynasty and a gifted ruler with a clear perception of the needs of the state."[4]

And the historian of seventh-century Byzantium, A.N. Stratos, without concealing the violence and brutality of Justinian II (which he attributes to unfortunate genetic characteristics which the children of Heraclius inherited from his first wife, Fabia Eudocia, who was an epileptic), calls him brave, courageous, pious, talented and able, and concludes: "A man endowed with excellent gifts, but lacking completely any sense of proportion."[5]

I have analysed elsewhere the geopolitical reasons that in 689 dictated the emperor's decision to make Cyprus neutral and share its dominion with

---

[3] Archimandrite Kyprianos, Ἱστορία χρονολογικὴ τῆς νήσου Κύπρου, Venice, 1788, pp. 108-9.
[4] G. Ostrogorsky, *History of the Byzantine State* (trans. Joan Hussey), Oxford, 1968, p. 129.
[5] A.N. Stratos, Τὸ Βυζάντιον στὸν Ζ΄ αἰῶνα, Athens, 1977.

the Caliphate.[6] This was done in the general context of the treaty between the emperor and 'Abd-al-Malik. Here I should add that I am convinced that despite the conclusive victory of his father, the great Constantine IV Pogonatos, over the Arab armies of Mu'awiya in 678 (which together with the victories of Leo III in 718 and of Charles Martel in 732 saved Europe from Muslim domination), and because of the mortal danger that Constantinople itself suffered for four years prior to the victory, the foremost priority of Justinian II's first reign was to remove all danger of siege to the capital. For this the necessary preconditions were: (a) to push back the western frontier beyond Thrace, which had been invaded by the Slavs; (b) to fortify the Straits; (c) to populate the capital's environs (Hellespont, Bithynia, Thrace) with military colonies. Imperial strategy focused on this aim; all the interests of the outlying regions came second, since the enemy had Constantinople as the final goal, as the naval campaigns of Mu'awiya and the sacking of the islands (beginning with Cyprus in 649) proved. The preservation of the capital meant to Justinian II, successor of Constantine Pogonatos, the preservation of the Empire and a guarantee of the eventual recovery of its dominions.

The expedition of 687/8, the reopening of the Via Egnatia and the liberation of Thessalonica reopened the western horizons of the Empire. The creation of the theme of Hellas meant for the victorious Justinian II the real-isation of his first goal, while the taming of the Slavs supplied him with the necessary human resources for the colonisation of the capital's environs. Curing the demographic weakness of the provinces around the Imperial City and strengthening the coastline of the Propontis went hand in hand. Internal and

---

[6] See Chapter II above. On relations between the Byzantines and the Arabs with regard to Cyprus see E.W. Brooks, "Byzantines and Arabs in the Time of the Early Abbasids", *English Historical Review* 15 (1900), pp. 728–47; R.J.H. Jenkins, "Cyprus between Byzantium and Islam. A.D. 688-965", *Studies Presented to D.M. Robinson* (eds. G.E. Mylonas & D. Raymond), St Louis, Mo, 1953, pp. 1006–14; A.I. Dikigoropoulos, *Cyprus "Betwixt Greeks and Saracens" A.D. 647–965*, D. Phil. Diss., Oxford, 1961; id., "The Political Status of Cyprus A.D. 648–965", *Report of the Department of Antiquities, Cyprus 1940–1948*, Nicosia, 1958, pp. 94–114; id., "The Church of Cyprus during the Period of the Arab Wars, A.D. 649–965", *GOTR* 11 (1965–66), pp. 237–79; A. Papageorgiou, "Les premières incursions arabes à Chypre et leurs con-séquences", 'Αφιέρωμα εἰς τὸν Κωνσταντῖνον Σπυριδάκιν, Nicosia, 1964, pp. 152–58; E. Eickhoff, *Seekrieg und Seepolitik zwischen Islam und Abendland. Das Mittelmeer unter byzantinischer und arabischer Hegemonie 650-1040)*, Berlin, 1966; Th. Papadopoullos, "Chypre: Frontière ethnique et socio-culturelle du monde byzantin" (*Rapport*. XVe Congrès International d'Etudes Byzantines), Athens, 1976; R. Browning, "Byzantium and Islam in Cyprus in the Early Middle Ages", 'Επετηρὶς τοῦ Κέντρου 'Επιστημονικῶν 'Ερευνῶν Κύπρου 9 (1977–79), pp. 101–16; N.E. Oikonomakis, "Η Κύπρος καὶ οἱ 'Άραβες (622-965 μ.Χ.)", Μελέται καὶ Ὑπομνήματα 1 (1984), pp. 217–374; and C.P. Kyrris, "The Nature of the Arab-Byzantine Relations in Cyprus from the Middle of the 7th to the Middle of the 10th Century", *Graeco-Arabica* 3 (1984), pp. 151–6.

external defence proved inextricably bound together both for the islands and the coastal zones, where the absence of infantry rendered naval operations futile and, conversely, the absence of naval forces rendered the infantry useless.

The enemy was approaching from the south. The defence of the southern straits and the southern coast of the Sea of Marmara therefore had first priority. In 684 the Arabs succeeded in penetrating the Straits of Abydus, showing that such an operation was possible for anyone who managed to defeat the fleet that guarded it. Cyzicus, the last major port before the capital, now became, paradoxically, the next great threat. The Arabs destroyed it and for four whole years could shelter peacefully in its port during winter and advance into battle every spring against Constantinople, which was only fifty or so nautical miles from their base. It was essential to eliminate this fatal weakness. If, contrary to expectation, a hostile force was again able to penetrate the Straits of Abydus, it should be possible to intercept it from another base, before it acquired control of the gulf of Cyzicus.

Events proved that Cyzicus itself was incapable of fulfilling this function, partly because after the earthquakes of 543 it was a town in irreversible decline, but mainly because it was too far inside its eponymous gulf, on the isthmus of the peninsula of Arctonnesos. What was needed was a new town, a fortress and naval arsenal in one, on the north-western side of the peninsula, to control both the gulf and the sea-route from the Dardanelles to Constantinople. At this juncture Cyprus enters the stage.

II

All the above observations have the appearance of common sense. They have not, however, been fully appreciated by anyone until now, and I would not have noticed them if I had not discovered, quite accidentally in a manuscript in Rome, the identity of New Justinianopolis, which has until now remained a mystery to all historians, Byzantine and modern alike. That all the pieces of the jigsaw puzzle fall into place so logically is for me proof of their truth. Reality is frequently simple, which is why it escapes notice.

In the course of a recent examination of Codex F10 of the Vallicellian Library of Rome[7] – a parchment manuscript from the first half of the tenth century, which gives the canonical collection known as *Sylloga XIV titulorum* – I read in the margin of the page that contains Canon XXXIX of the Council in Trullo, which mentions New Justinianopolis without further qualification,

---

[7] No 79 in vol. ii of E. Martini, *Catalogo di manoscritti greci esistenti nelle bibliotheche italiane*, Milan, 1902.

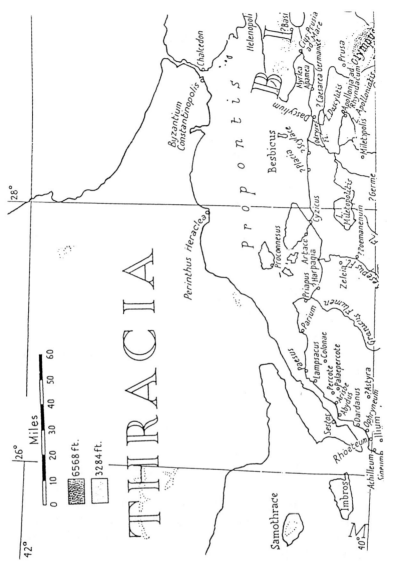

Propontis and the Straits
(Jones, pp. 28–9)

the following highly important explanation: Τὴν νῦν ἐν Κυζίκῳ Ἀρτάκην καλουμένην, "this is Artaki near Cyzicus".

The road to historical interpretation had been opened, once again, by geography – rather belatedly in this case, I should add, because, as I later discovered, this marginal scholion had been published already along with hundreds of others without comment in St Petersburg in 1905 in an obscure pamphlet which V.N. Beneševič circulated as a separate supplement of the Old Slavonic translation of the *Sylloga XIV titulorum* which he published in the same year.[8]

The bibliography on Artaki (Turkish Erdek) is not especially large.[9] The town is built on a slope on a triangular estuary, which extends to the sea towards the south-eastern shore of Arctonnesos on the Propontic coast of the Hellespont, about ten kilometres north-west of Cyzicus. It was in turn a sister Milesian colony, a suburb of Cyzicus and its eventual successor.

The island of Kyra Panagia, facing the town at a distance of 200 metres, rises on the seaward side of the deep harbour as a natural wall against the western winds. North-eastern winds do not reach it either, due to the peninsula of St Symeon on the south-east, but also due to the low point on which the town is built.

It was precisely this town that Justinian II decided to renovate and establish as the capital of the Hellespont (and perhaps later of the Opsikian theme in place of Nicaea), as a coastal fortress and naval port overlooking the Propontic sea-lanes to Constantinople, and perhaps a shipyard as well, since the surrounding forests provided an ideal source of timber. The fact that he graced it with his name demonstrates the ambitious plans he had in mind at the time. The imperial name was certainly not given to a refugee settlement, and the epithet "new" implied a whole programme.

I have stressed already (as Hélène Ahrweiler showed many years ago in her celebrated work on Byzantium and the sea)[10] that the Propontis is the

---

[8] V.N. Beneševič, *Kanoničveskij sbornik XIV titulov so vtoroj četverti VII veka do 883*, St Petersburg, 1905, pp. 45, 392.

[9] J. Marquardt, *Cyzicus und sein Gebiet*, Berlin, 1836 (Greek trans. K. Grigoriadis, Constantinople, 1879); S. Lambros, "Ἀνέκδοτον χειρόγραφον περὶ τῆς Κυζίκου μέχρι τῶν καθ' ἡμᾶς χρόνων", *NE* 1 (1904), pp. 72–88 (= George of Cyzicus, Ἀναγραφὴ τῆς Κυζίκου, 1825); F.W. Hasluck, *Cyzicus*, Cambridge, 1910; S. Amantos, "Ἄβυδος –Στενόν", Ἑλληνικά 1 (1928), pp. 402–4; P. Giannakopoulos, "Ἀρτάκη", Μεγάλη Ἑλληνικὴ Ἐγκυκλοπαιδεία 5 (1928), pp. 685–6; K.S. Makris, "Κυζικηνὴ χερσόνησος. Ἡ παροῦσα κατάστασίς της" Μικρασιατικὰ Χρονικά, 6 (1955), pp. 149–88 + maps (written in about 1900); V. Laurent, "Κύζικος", Θρησκευτικὴ καὶ ἠθικὴ ἐγκυκλοπαιδεία 7 (1965), pp. 1083–5; C. Mango & I. Sevcenko, "Some Churches and Monasteries on the Southern Shore of the Sea of Marmara", *DOP* 27 (1973), pp. 235–77; H. Ahrweiler, Λιμάνια στὸ Βυζάντιο (Διάλεξις Δήμου · Πειραιῶς), Peiraeus, 1990.

[10] H. Ahrweiler, *Byzance et la mer*, Paris, 1966.

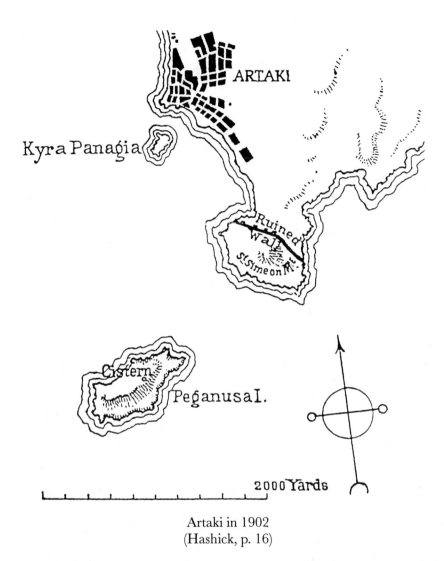

Artaki in 1902
(Hashick, p. 16)

sea of Constantinople, on which the security of the capital, the feeding of its population and the availability of commercial and industrial goods depend. One may well ask why the necessity of such a fortress was not appreciated earlier, and why it was not completed immediately after the reign of Justinian II. Everything depends on how the ruler of Constantinople viewed, or was forced to view, the Propontis. If he viewed it as a marine corridor linking the City and the Black Sea with the West, the need for Artaki was not obvious. But if he viewed the Propontis as a marine corridor linking Asia Minor with Europe (Rhaedestos and the Via Egnatia), the towns of the south and north coasts assumed considerable importance: Artaki and Pegae on the southern side, Madytos and Rhaedestos on the northern. The centre of the Empire in the seventh century was Asia Minor. But the expedition that liberated Thessalonica, the creation of the Helladic theme, the later adventures with Rome and Ravenna, all show that the imperial eye was trained west of Asia Minor, towards Europe, and not for the time being towards Syria (as in the case of the transfer of the Mardaites) or to Egypt. This line of strategy had been fixed, in any case, from the time of Justinian's father, Constantine IV, and grandfather, Constans II, who even wished to move the imperial capital to Sicily. For Justinian this was, in addition, part of the burden of his very name.

The descendants of Heraclius were all extremely ambitious, as is shown by their names: New Constantine, New Heraclius, New Justinian. For our Justinian was not called "the Second" during his reign (this distinction of names is a later, Western custom), and certainly not "Slit-Nose" (Rhinotmetos). His official name was "the New Justinian", which signified on the one hand a call to new responsibilities, but on the other, intensified temptations to mega-lomania. Imitation of his great predecessor is consistently shown in imperial portraiture, in legislation, in his building activities, in his turning towards the West, in his relations with Rome, in the convocation of the Quinisextum Council as supplementary to the Fifth and Sixth Ecumenical Councils, in the renaming of his second wife Theodora, in short in almost everything, even in the christening of cities with his name. In the Eastern Empire alone Justinian the Great had renamed about ten cities "Justinianoupolis". The "new" Justinian will rename Artaki in the Hellespont New Justinianopolis (perhaps to distinguish it from Justinianopolis Modrene – Nova Iustiniana Gordus – a little to the north, in the same Opsikian theme). His ultimate aim, in imitation of Justinian the Great, was to make his city not only a provincial capital but an auto-cephalous archbishopric. This bold venture had been achieved by Justinian the Great in 535, at Rome's expense, with the issue of Novel XI, *De privilegiis archiepiscopi primae Iustinianae*. But the new Justinian could not succeed so easily, since the new Justinianopolis was situated not in distant Illyria, but a few kilometres outside the seat of the ecumenical patriarchate.

III

The links between Cyprus and Heraclius and his dynasty are well-known. May I remind you only of the inscriptions of the Salamis aqueduct, the silver plates of David from Lambousa, St John the Almsgiver from Amathous, Arkadios of Cyprus, the *Ecthesis* and so on. The loyalty of Artaki to the house of Heraclius seems to have existed already, since this is where Heraclius was crowned for the first time in 610, on his way in fact from Cyprus to seize the throne in the Imperial City. It should be noted also that Cyprus belonged to the faction of the Greens, the main supporters of Heraclius and his descendants.

A Cypriot tradition, referred to by Constantine Porphyrogenitus in the tenth century, claims Justinian II as a native of Cyprus. The son of Constantine Pogonatos could not have been, of course, of Cypriot origin on the male side, but he was possibly so from the female side, through his mother or grandmother. However, we do not know the place of origin of Anastasia or Fausta, or indeed of Justinian's first wife Eudocia (the name of the unfortunate ancestress of the dynasty). At any rate, it would not have been strange if one of them had been from Cyprus. Take Eudocia for example: could such an origin lie behind the mistaken information of Nikephoros Kallistos that Theodora, the wife of Justinian the Great, was a Cypriot? And to whom did the imperial treasure hidden at Lambousa in the seventh century actually belong? Whatever the truth of this, the fact remains that Justinian II chose the Cypriots to colonise New Justinianopolis.

His reasons are likely to have been many and varied. The Slavs, with whom his father had colonised Thrace, and he Bithynia, were not seafaring people, and so they were unsuitable for his naval plans for New Justinianopolis. The emperor needed experienced sailors and shipbuilders. They could have been supplied by many provinces, but he chose Cyprus. The experience of Cypriots in shipbuilding was undisputed. A little earlier, the dockyards of Constantia had been the largest in the East.

Theophanes and those dependent on him say that the crisis that led to the dissolution of the peace treaty of 689 and to the transfer of the Cypriots to the Hellespont was caused by Justinian's refusal to accept the Arab tribute, which was sent in the form of the newly-minted gold coin of 'Abd-al-Malik. This is clearly a mistake, for this coin was first minted – as we now know – in the seventy-fourth year of the Islamic era, namely, in 693/4, three years after Justinian's decision to transfer the Cypriots.[11] It has also been claimed that Cyprus, or Constantia, was completely destroyed by the Arabs, hence

---

[11] See J. Walker, *A Catalogue of Arab-Byzantine and Post-Reform Umaiyad Coins in the British Museum*, London, 1956. See also J.D. Breckenridge, *The Numismatic Iconography of Justinian II*, New York, 1959; P. Grierson, *Catalogue of the Byzantine Coins in the Dumbarton Oaks Collection and in the Wittemore Collection, II. 2, Heraclius Constantine to Theodosius III* (641–717), Washington, DC, 1968.

the emperor's decision. All historians know, however, that this also is inaccurate. Cyprus did not belong to the Arabs in 691 (two years after the treaty of 689!) and Constantia was never wholly abandoned after 649. This is suggested by archaeological evidence, and is in any case proved by the fact that in the reign of Constantine Pogonatos (668–85), the father of Justinian II, the mint of Constantia countermarked the copper *follis* of Constans II, while in 680 the bishops of Cyprus took part in the Sixth Ecumenical Council in Constantinople during the archiepiscopate of Epiphanios II of Constantia. Cyprus was declared neutral in the treaty of 689 for the reasons I have already explained in another context, and in 691 there was no reason to transfer the population as far as the Arabs were concerned. Therefore the reasons for the removal must be sought elsewhere. I have hinted at them already.

First, it is unlikely that the whole population of Cyprus emigrated. It numbered at least 80 000 and was possibly 150 000 strong. The sole contemporary source, Canon XXXIX of the Quinisextum Council, does not mention a wholesale emigration of the Cypriots, an idea that clearly belongs to the realm of mythology. The transfer of populations in the Byzantine Empire was a common occurrence but has only recently been examined in sufficient depth.[12] In Cyprus itself it is said that in 578 Tiberios I had resettled 10 000 Armenians from the Persian frontier of Asia Minor for reasons which were not only military but also demographic and economic. Nevertheless, in 649 and 650 the first two Arab raids seem to have depleted the island's population again. According to an inscription of the basilica of Soloi, dated 655 and written by Bishop John (it can be read not only in the first edition of 1985 by T.T. Tinh, but now in the amended edition by D. Feissel),[13] the Arabs dragged off to slavery 120 000 Cypriots in 649, and in the next year 50 000 – apart from those whom they killed. These massive expulsions of the population of Cyprus, which were unknown to us until now, are surprising even if the numbers are regarded – as they must surely be – as grossly exaggerated. At any rate they prove that these raids were not simply "booty-hunting operations", especially since Mu'awiya settled 12 000 Arabs in Cyprus, who were later recalled by his son Yazid in 684, or perhaps by himself after the treaty of 678. For the rulers of Damascus Cyprus was not simply a base on the way to Constantinople, but was a natural extension of Syria, a necessary station between Syria and Egypt, and perhaps more importantly, a source

---

[12] P. Charanis, "Ethnic Changes in the Byzantine Empire in the Seventh Century", *DOP* 13, (1959), pp. 23–44; id., "The Transfer of Population as a Policy in the Byzantine Empire", *Comparative Studies in Society and History* 3 (1960–61), pp. 140–54.

[13] J. des Gagniers & T.T Tinh, *Soloi. Dix campagnes des fouilles (1964–1974)*, I, Sainte-Foy, 1985; D. Feissel, "Bulletin épigraphique n° 532", *REG* 100 (1987), pp. 380–1.

of timber and of experienced sailors for the newly constructed Muslim navy.[14]

Was this huge number of Cypriot captives repatriated or not? And if so, when? Today it is no longer possible to be certain. It is possible, however, to claim with a high degree of probability that it must have been repatriated, or a part of it, at some time between 650 and 689. According to Porphyrogenitus, when the Cypriots returned from New Justinianopolis in 699, as we shall see later, the caliph "sent to all Syria and gathered together all the Cypriots and carried them over to their own place".[15] Evidently the Empire and the Caliphate were disposed in the second half of the seventh century to repeated transfers of Cypriot population. It is in this context we must interpret the transportation of Cypriots to the Hellespont in 691.

At any rate, in the same chapter of his work *De Administrando Imperio* Constantine Porphyrogenitus speaks of Cypriots who were repatriated in 699 not only from Greater Syria or the Hellespont, but also from Thrace and southern Asia Minor. In 692, however, the Quinisextum Council does not refer to these latter, and so we have no idea why they came to be there, although Cypriots can only have been transported to Thrace upon the imperial initiative. The distances involved preclude a spontaneous move in search of peace and refuge.

That Justinian II transported some Cypriots to coastal provinces of naval significance – Hellespont, Thrace, Pamphylia – is easily explicable, as I have already said. The precise reasons, however, which impelled him to this decision in 690/91 remain entirely obscure. He cannot have intended to abandon Cyprus totally, since the treaty of the previous year had at least safeguarded the co-dominion of the island, and essentially a great deal more. It remained, if not a theme of the Empire, at least an *archontia*. Did he aim perhaps to force Damascus to repatriate its own Cypriots after common agreement, as finally happened in 699? Was he intending to deprive Damascus of the fiscal revenues of Cyprus, half of which from 689 was its legitimate share? The smaller the population of Cyprus, the lower the share of Damascus. This last solution is quite probable, and can be combined with Justinian's needs for defence, which I have summarised earlier. For Justinian a neutral Cyprus, whose revenues he was obliged to share with the Arabs, might very well have been left almost deserted. In any case, "Cyprus outside Cyprus" could offer him the ultimate gift "above monetary taxation", namely, the

---

[14] On this see M. Lombard, "Arsenaux et bois de marine dans la Méditerranée musulmane (VIIIe–XIe siècles)", *Le navire et l'économie maritime du moyen-âge au XVIIIe siècle principalement en Méditerranée* (ed. M. Mollat), Paris, 1958, pp. 53–99 (106).

[15] *Constantine Porphyrogenitus, De administrando imperio* (eds, G. Moravcsik & R.J.H. Jenkins), Washington, DC, 1967.

enriching of his city with an enviable and priceless autocephaly. Under the guise of salvaging the rights which the Third Ecumenical Council had recognised with regard to Cyprus, the Cypriot autocephaly, removed from the decapitated see of Cyprus, was translated to New Justinianopolis.

IV

The opportunity to fulfil his purpose in a most solemn and definitive way, a way capable of neutralising hostile reactions from New Rome or its fifth metropolitan, the bishop of Cyzicus, was given to the ambitious emperor by the new Ecumenical Council, the Quinisextum, which he himself convened in the Domed Hall (*Trullus*) of the Great Palace from the end of 691 to September 692. With it Justinian II codified ecclesiastical law, just as his great namesake had codified Roman law. Texts like the proem of Canon III show that his imitation extended to phraseology and style. To this day the Eastern Church is administered on the basis of the canonical code of Justinian II. The Council was the largest in history so far as the number of conciliar fathers is concerned. Most of them, however, were in fact titular bishops residing outside their provinces, which many were unable even to visit. The destructive effects of barbarian raids, Slav and Arab, were readily evident. Canon XXXV of the Quinisextum goes so far as to speak of bishops whose churches were totally bereft of clergy.

According to Canon XXXIX of the Council one of these "bishops who continue to reside outside their own province due to the barbarian incursions" appears to be the "bishop of the isle of the Cypriots", John, archbishop of Constantia. The Council knew, of course – hence the ambiguous reference – that Cyprus was a special case, for its archbishop had not been expelled by the barbarians but had been transferred from his diocese by the emperor himself.

"Whereas our brother and concelebrant John, president of the isle of the Cypriots, because of the barbarian assaults and to the end that they might be free from slavery to the infidel and be subject unfeignedly to the sceptre of his most Christian majesty, has with his own flock migrated from the said isle to the province of the Hellespont, by the providence and mercy of God and by the labour of our Christ-loving and pious emperor; we do resolve: that the privileges accorded unto the throne of the aforesaid by the fathers inspired of God at their sometime meeting in Ephesus shall be preserved uninjured; that the new Justinianoupolis shall have the right of the city of the Constantinians; and that the most pious bishop who is set over it shall preside over all the bishops of the province of the Hellespont, and shall be consecrated by his own bishops, according to the ancient custom (for our fathers inspired of God have resolved that the practices in each church are to be preserved), the bishop of the city of the Cyzicenes being subject to the president of the said Justinianoupolis in like manner as are all the rest of the bishops under the said most pious president John, by whom as need shall arise the bishop also of the same city of the Cyzicenes shall be consecrated."[16]

The canon, one of the most important monuments of the history of Cyprus and of the ecclesiology of Eastern canon law, deserves exhaustive comment, which in this context I must forgo. Its text is exceptionally diplomatic in expression and must be the result of many debates and compromises between the emperor on the one hand, whose will it expresses, and the conciliar fathers on the other, whose majority consented while still leaving open many doors. Incapable of justifying this unheard-of provision theologically, they justify it historically – thereby reducing it to the status of dispensation (*oikonomia*). For as Canon XXXVII – really a preamble to Canon XXXIX – said: "if the necessities of the moment prevent the exact observance of law, they shall not restrict the limits of condescension." The whole formulation, the convoluted syntax of the period, express a hesitation and a sense of provisionality so far as the archbishop of Cyprus is concerned but of permanent submission so far as the bishop of Cyzicus is concerned, with whom the conclusion of the canon deals. Justinian II knew that even if the archbishop of Cyprus returned at some time to his historical seat the principle laid down by the canon "that our fathers inspired by God have resolved that the practices in each church are to be preserved", could in conjunction with Canon XXXVIII ensure the perpetual primacy of his eponymous city over the see of Cyzicus, which at the time of the Council was either vacant or else its metropolitan refused to sign the Synodical Acts, for his signature is nowhere to be found. Perhaps the phrase "as need shall arise" is an implicit threat made to an outraged bishop of Cyzicus who has tendered his resignation, which, however, the Council hopes he will withdraw. To avoid unleashing the winds of Aeolus, the Council stresses that the primate of Cyprus emigrated together with his flock, so that titular bishops without a flock might nurture no misapprehension.

The way to Canon XXXIX is paved by the three previous canons. Indeed its full interpretation is impossible if we ignore them or the historical context which I have just analysed. The failure of Byzantine and modern historians

---

[16] P.-P. Ioannou, *Discipline générale antique*, I, 1, Rome, 1962 (Pontificia commissione per la redazione del codice di diritto canonico orientale, *Fonti*, IX), pp. 173–4 (Eng. trans. H.R. Percival).

and canonists lies precisely here. A guide to the correct interpretation was provided in 1913 by the Russian historian Platon P. Sokolov in the introduction of his book on the Greek metropolitans of Russia.[17] Sokolov, despite his positivistic and Erastian presuppositions, or perhaps because of them, gave full recognition to the situation-conditioned character of Byzantine ecclesiastical law in general, and of our canon in particular, which he expounded with perspicacity. But unfortunately he had no successors on this issue.

Canon XXXVI of the Quinisextum Council ratifies the *status quo* "On the rank and honour of the patriarchs", thus satisfying the Imperial City: it guarantees it equal rights with Old Rome, in exchange (among other things, of course) for the imminent detachment of its fifth metropolitan see, and the establishment of an autocephalous church before its very gates.

Canon XXXVII then ensures the authority of bishops who could not occupy their thrones because of barbarian raids, thus distinguishing between episcopal ordination and jurisdiction, and essentially allowing – unthinkable for the early Church – the existence of bishops without a flock (may I remind you that Canon XXXV has already mentioned bishops without clergy?).

Canon XXXVIII comes as an unexpected leap to the uninitiated, but was an absolutely necessary step for Justinian II. It refers to Canon XVII of the Fourth Ecumenical Council, which, strictly speaking, it misinterprets and lays down that ecclesiastical order must follow the civil order, so that "if any city be renewed by imperial authority ... let the order of things ecclesiastical follow the civil and public models". The case was won. The combination of Canon XXXVII with Canon XXXVIII now permits Canon XXXIX, whose title should be not "On the bishop of the isle of the Cypriots" but "On the bishop of the new Justinianoupolis".

John of Cyprus "with his own flock" had not abandoned his see (which would have called for his deposition), but "by the providence and mercy of God" had been transferred from his island to the province of the Hellespont by the Christ-loving and pious emperor. He can be regarded as having been covered by Canon XXXVII, since the move also took place (a) because of barbarian assaults – the Council knew that, strictly speaking, these had happened forty years previously but sought to save appearances – and (b) in order that the bishop and his flock might be set free from slavery to the infidel and submit "unfeignedly" to the sceptre of "his most Christian majesty". The co-dominion of Byzantium and Damascus over Cyprus is considered to be unworthy of the greatness of its archbishop, even though – this remains unspoken – three out of the five patriarchs already lived under Islam.

---

[17] P.P. Sokolov, *Russkij archierej iz Vizantii i pravo ego naznachenija do nachala XV veka*, Kiev, 1913.

The local church – "the throne" – is not an exclusively geographical concept, but a living reality: the bishop "with his own flock". And in this sense the local church is "sojourning in the world" to such a degree that it can, as it were, travel and survive not only through time, but also in space, even within the provinces and boundaries of other churches. Since, therefore, according to Canon XXXVII, the rights and authority of the archbishop of Cyprus, whose see is now at New Justinianopolis, are preserved, this city now has "the right of the city of the Constantinians" (this is the reading of all ancient manuscripts and of Porphyrogenitus; the reading "the right of Constantinople" is a corruption of the subsequent "vulgate" tradition which appears in the canonists of the twelfth century).

After these provisions, ecclesiastical order is an administrative matter. Canon XXXVIII imposes the new capital of the Hellespont, founded "by imperial authority", as the ecclesiastical metropolis of the self-same province in place of Cyzicus. The archbishop of New Justinianopolis, "according to the ancient custom" of Cyprus, which is now also his privilege, is consecrated "by his own bishops" who are no longer the twelve bishops of Cyprus (or at least not only these), but the twelve – and this is a coincidence – bishops of the Hellespont. And he in turn ordains them, even including the former metropolitan of Cyzicus, who – and the formula is repeated so that there should be no ambiguity – is now to be subject to the archbishop of New Justinianopolis.

We do not know the reasons today for the transfer of the Cypriots to Thrace and Bithynia. I am convinced, however, that with regard to the matter of New Justinianopolis, Justinian II transferred Archbishop John of Cyprus and the people of Constantia to Artaki, renamed New Justinianopolis, for the sole purpose of making the church of his eponymous city autocephalous, either by law of transfer (*jus translationis*), or, in the case of a return of the archbishop of Cyprus to his historical seat, by legal precedent and customary law.

But what happened to the bishops of the other Cypriot towns, apart from Constantia? Surely, as Ph. Georgiou correctly concluded as early as 1875, they must have remained in Cyprus together with their flocks.[18] Were they subject to the Hellespontian archbishop of New Justinianopolis? I would assume so, regardless of the distance involved. Did not Justinian the Great in 536 place Cyprus, the Cyclades, Caria, Moesia Secunda and Scythia under a *quaestor Justinianus*, whose seat was at Odessus? This collocation was even more peculiar than that of Cyprus with New Justinianopolis, and the inconvenience

---

[18] Ph. Georgiou, *Εἰδήσεις ἱστορικαὶ περὶ τῆς Ἐκκλησίας Κύπρου*, Athens, 1875, p. 31.

was greater not only for the twelve bishops but for all Cypriots, since in order to be judged at the appeal court they would have had to travel all the way to what is now Varna in Bulgaria.

The only problem in this elegant scenario could be the question of John's signature to the official acts of the Quinisextum. There the archbishop, all of whose surviving lead seals reiterate the title "archbishop of Cyprus",[19] signs immediately after the patriarchs as "John unworthy bishop of New Justinianopolis" – with nothing about Cyprus or Constantia. Perhaps the emperor (who signed first with cinnabar) would have been satisfied with nothing else. Since the patriarchs of Rome, Alexandria, Antioch and Jerusalem were not personally present, the former Cypriot monk (this is signified by the adjective "unworthy") was in reality the third to sign at the final session of the Council, after the emperor and Patriarch Paul of Constantinople. Are we to suppose that in such company Cyprus seemed too distant, unimportant, or semi-barbarian to mention? It was not Constantia which was the new Justinianoupolis (as it was thought later), but New Justinianopolis which was the new Constantia.

V

But "man proposes, God disposes". Three years later, towards the end of 695, Justinian II was deposed by the Blue *strategos* of Hellas, Leontios, had his nose slit and was exiled to Cherson. His great plans had collapsed for ever. When, ten years later, he returned to the throne for another six years, he would be no more than a vindictive ghost of his former self. The permission for election of a metropolitan of Cyzicus in 706 meant the final abandonment of the dream of New Justinianopolis. The emperor chose Germanos, the scholar priest of Hagia Sophia who was later to become the famous ecumenical patriarch. Many years earlier in 668 Justinian's father had castrated Germanos as the son of his relative, the patrician Justinian, who was suspected of having taken part in the assassination of the emperor's father, Constans II. Did Justinian II perhaps seek to atone for his father's crimes, which he believed continued to torment him? It cannot be accidental that he gave his son, who was born in exile, the name of his uncle Tiberios, whose nose Pogonatos had amputated in 681 in order to guarantee Justinian's own succession.

In 699, seven years before the election of Germanos, Apsimar, the *drungarios* (admiral) of the Cibyrrhaeot theme, who the year before had deposed Leontios, installed himself on the throne supported by the navy and the Greens. On his elevation he took the name of Justinian II's unfortunate

---

[19] G. Zacos & A. Veglery, *Byzantine Lead Seals*, I, Basle, 1972.

Lead seal of the Archbishop of Cyprus John I
(Zacos, Veglery, pp. 1679–80)

Lead seal of Justinian II and his son Tiberios
(Zacos, Veglery, pp. 27–28)

uncle Tiberios, who had also been chosen for the throne by the troops of the Anatolikon theme. Apsimar decided to repatriate the Cypriots. The whole defence policy of Justinian II was now reversed and the tension between Asia Minor and Greece made plain. This was to become all the more conspicuous in the Iconoclast period which followed (we should remember that Theodosios of Ephesus, the president of the Iconoclast Council of Hiereia in 754, was the son of Apsimar-Tiberios, just as the first opponent of the Iconoclast policies of Leo III was St Germanos, patriarch of Constantinople, the relative and appointee of Justinian II).

The witness of Constantine Porphyrogenitus that the Cypriots returned from New Justinianoupolis in 699 (seven years after the Quinisextum Council) should not be doubted – as it has been – especially as it is the sole source at our disposal. The action of Tiberios II perhaps had as its main object the removal from the neighbourhood of Constantinople of a possible foothold for Justinian II. The latter had taken refuge in Khazaria but remained constantly on the move, working to recover his throne. Alternatively, the restoration of the Cypriots may have proceeded from his wish to please the Cypriots themselves, who were his fellow Greens and perhaps wanted to return to their land. This is not to exclude the possibility that it was the Cypriots in Cyprus itself who wanted the return of their compatriots. It could also be that the repatriation of the Cypriots was meant to appease the Arabs, something the new emperor certainly needed. It signified a return to strict observance of the terms of the treaty of 689. The agreement for a simultaneous restoration of the Cypriots both from the Caliphate and the Empire speaks for itself.

What was the long-term consequence for the Cypriots of their transfer to the Hellespont, the aim of which was not primarily Cyprus but New Justinianopolis? Paradoxically, when the adventure that for a moment threatened to make a colony of the native Cypriot Church was over, the only thing that Canon XXXIX of the Quinisextum Council still continued to proclaim was its unequivocal and canonically final pronouncement that the autocephaly of Cyprus was indissoluble. Its privileges, recognised by the Third Ecumenical Council at Ephesus in 431, were "free from innovations" (ἀκαινοτόμητα), meaning that they were inalienable, precisely because they were recognised by an Ecumenical Council. Nine hundred years later the first Cypriot archbishop under Turkish rule would add to his title, gratefully and safely, the Latinized name *Nova Iustiniana*, having abandoned, in unison with the late Byzantines, the historically correct Greek form *Ioustinianoupolis*.

With the close of the seventh century the Church of Cyprus entered the middle Byzantine period of its history and Artaki returned to the old name which the Milesians had given it centuries earlier. The history of the coming centuries would vindicate the clear-sightedness of Justinian II. Artaki soon superseded Cyzicus, which from the eleventh century onwards was abandoned completely. The metropolitan of Cyzicus eventually established himself at Artaki, a possibility which Justinian had not allowed for. The town remained essentially Greek until 1922. The last metropolitan of Cyzicus was the well-known scholar and editor of the patriarchal acts, Kallinikos Delikanes, who later died as metropolitan of Caesarea. The inhabitants of Artaki themselves were transported to Euboea, where they live today seven kilometres from Chalkis in New Artaki. The Hellespontian town which was for seven years the seat of the archbishop of Cyprus and bore the illustrious name of Nea Justinianoupolis was given by Ankara to Turkish refugees from Benghazi and Crete. Its two most sacred treasures, the panel icons of Our Lady Phaneromene and Our Lady of Artaki, are now in the Patriarchal Cathedral of St George at the Phanar by the Golden Horn. Constantia, on the other hand, is today nothing more than pitiful ruins, shattered marbles, holy memories. The fate of mortal things. The archbishop of Cyprus, however, abides, now living in a new capital, a shepherd with his own flock, a symbol of endurance, continuity and resurrection and a reminder, like Our Lady of Artaki at the Phanar, of the "change undergone by the things being shaken, because they are created things", and of the existence of a heavenly Church and "Kingdom which cannot be shaken" (Heb. 12:27).

IV

THE POSITION OF CYPRUS IN THE EPISCOPAL LISTS OF THE SEVENTH ECUMENICAL COUNCIL*

Silouan and Misael Ioannou

The middle Byzantine period of the ecclesiastical history of Cyprus opens in spite of temporary local difficulties with a triumphant reaffirmation of the special character of the Cypriot autocephaly as confirmed by the *Psephos* of the Third Ecumenical Council and now again by a subsequent Ecumenical Council, the Quinisextum. With Canon XXXIX this council – the largest canonical council of the early Church – commanded that:

> "the privileges accorded to the throne [of Cyprus] by the fathers inspired by God formerly gathered at Ephesus [should be preserved] free from innovations, so that New Justinianopolis should have the right of the city of the Constantinians and that the most pious bishop who is set over it should preside over all [the bishops] of the province of the Hellespont and shall be consecrated by his own bishops, according to ancient custom."[1]

Accordingly, we see Archbishop John of Cyprus, proedrus of the first and oldest autocephalous Church, signing the acta at the end of the council immediately after the emperor and the patriarchs.[2] We must therefore stress at the

---

* Undergraduate paper which was written under the supervision of the author in the department of General Ecclesiastical History of the University of Athens in 1987.

[1] P.-P. Ioannou, *Discipline générale antique*, I, 1, Rome, 1962 (Pontificia commissione per la redazione del codice di diritto canonico orientale, *Fonti*, IX), pp. 173–4. Cf. also the scholia of the Byzantine commentators, Zonaras, Balsamon and Aristenos in G.A. Rhalles and M. Potles, Σύνταγμα τῶν θείων καὶ ἱερῶν κανόνων, Β', Athens, 1852, pp. 396–7.

[2] J.D. Mansi, *Sacrorum conciliorum nova et amplissima collectio*, XI, Florence, 1765, 989A.

outset that in accordance with the universal canon law of the early Church the archbishop of Cyprus was not an autocephalous archbishop but the president of an autocephalous Church, one of "the great autocephalous archbishops who did not belong *de jure* to the circle of the patriarchs but nevertheless constituted a kind of patriarch in themselves without the patriarchal title", according to the definition of H.-G. Beck.[3] A large part of the mistaken opinions which from time to time have been expressed on the archbishop and the Church of Cyprus from the time of Patriarch Dositheos of Jerusalem and earlier are due to the confusion of these two meanings and canonical realities.[4]

In 1934 G.I. Konidares, later Professor of General Ecclesiastical History in the Faculty of Theology of the University of Athens, formulated a theory concerning the abolition of the autocephaly of the Church of Cyprus in "the period of Arab domination", as he called the period in which the island occupied a position of neutrality between Byzantium and Islam.[5] He developed this theory in three publications up to 1976.[6] In its final form the theory is expressed thus:

"The comparative examination of the evidence of the seventh and eighth centuries enables us to discern more clearly (a) the external limitation of the autocephaly to 'the order of precedence of times', when circumstances and the care and supervision exercised by the first throne of the East – the ecumenical patriarch – made it a temporary necessity for the archbishop of Cyprus to be placed third in order of the metropolitans of the throne of Constantinople."[7]

---

[3] H.-G. Beck, *Kirche und theologische Literatur im byzantinische Reich*, Munich, 1959, p. 68.

[4] Cf. also the judgment of J.M. Hussey, *The Orthodox Church in the Byzantine Empire*, Oxford, 1986, p. 325: "This kind of [autocephalous] archbishop is found throughout the middle ages and is distinct from such as the autonomous archbishop of Cyprus who had suffragans and was virtually independent of the Patriarch of Constantinople." See also E. Chrysos, "Zur Enstehung der Institution der autokephalen Erzbistümer", *BZ* 62 (1969), pp. 263-86.

[5] G.I. Konidares, Αἱ μητροπόλεις καὶ ἀρχιεπισκοπαὶ τοῦ οἰκουμενικοῦ πατριαρχείου καὶ ἡ "τάξις" αὐτῶν, Athens, 1934 (Texte und Forschungen zur byzantinisch-neugriechischen Philologie, XIII), pp. 89–103.

[6] G.I. Konidares, "Ἡ θέσις τῆς Κύπρου ἔναντι τοῦ οἰκουμενικοῦ πατριαρχείου κατὰ τὸν Θ΄ καί Ι΄ αἰῶνα", Akadimia Athinon, Πρακτικά, XVIII, 1943, pp. 135-46. "Ἡ θέσις τῆς Ἐκκλησίας τῆς Κύπρου εἰς τὰ Ἐκκλησιαστικὰ Τακτικὰ (Notitia Episcopatuum) ἀπὸ τοῦ Η΄ μέχρι τοῦ ΙΓ΄ αἰῶνος (Συμβολὴ εἰς τὴν Ἱστορίαν τοῦ αὐτοκεφάλου)", University of Athens, Ἐπετηρὶς ἐπιστημονικῶν Ἐρευνῶν, II, Athens, 1970, pp. 139–72, also published in A. Papageorgiou (ed.), Πρακτικά Α΄ Διεθνοῦς Κυπριολογικοῦ Συνεδρίου, II, Nicosia, 1972, pp. 81-120. "Τὸ αὐτοκέφαλον τῆς Ἐκκλησίας τῆς Κύπρου", XVe Congrès International d'Études Byzantines, *Rapports et Co-Rapports*, V, ii, Athens, 1976, pp. 3–29.

[7] G.I. Konidares, "Τὸ αὐτοκέφαλον τῆς Ἐκκλησίας τῆς Κύπρου", XVe Congrès International d'Études Byzantines, *Rapports et Co-Rapports*, V, ii, Athens, 1976, p. 23.

(It should be noted that point (a) is not followed by a point (b) and that the word "of times" (χϱόνων) should of course be "of thrones" (θϱόνων). We shall call this "Konidares' theory" in this paper in spite of the fact that it had been enunciated three years previously by Sophronios Eustratiades, former bishop of Leontopolis, in his publication of the *Tacticon* of Codex Parisinus gr. 1555A in Νέα Σιών in September 1931 and had already received a reply in November 1931 in 'Απόστολος Βαϱνάβας from the learned Cypriot Archimandrite of the Holy Sepulchre, Hippolytos Michaelides,[8] who did not know, however, that the controversy had been initiated not by the former bishop of Leontopolis but by H. Gelzer, who had formulated the theory in 1900 in the *Transactions of the Imperial Academy of Sciences*, where we read the following peevish note, directed against Byzantium, arising from a *Tacticon* from the time of John Tzimisces: "It is characteristic of the ecclesiastico-political principles of the Eastern Romans that they did not flinch from subjecting this ancient auto-cephalous Church [of Cyprus] to the ecumenical patriarchate,"[9] a passage which, of course, Konidares would have known not only in 1970 (although he does not refer to the number of the page which he is nevertheless trans-lating)[10] but even in 1943 when he made his communication to the Academy of Athens.[11]

Leaving aside these strange matters (all the stranger since the former bishop of Leontopolis issued a *Tacticon* in 1931 which C. de Boor had already published in 1891[12] and L. Duchesne had shown to be fundamentally inau-thentic in 1892[13]), we come to Konidares' arguments, which may be summarised as follows:

1. On account of the Arab invasions the state of Cyprus was so lamentable that its entire economic and political life was totally dependent on Constantinople.

2. The wretched position in which Cyprus found herself made it unavoid-able that she should seek help from the Church of Constantinople and that the ecumenical patriarchate should exercise a higher and stricter supervision of the Church of the island. This was accomplished tacitly without abolishing the autocephaly by submitting it to three external

---

[8] See H. Michaelides, "Περὶ τὸ αὐτοκέφαλον τῆς 'Εκκλησίας Κύπρου", *Apostolos Barnabas*, Ser. II, 3, 1931, pp. 797–801.

[9] *Sitzungsberichte der bayerischen Akademie der Wissenschaften*, I, XXI, III, Munich, 1900, p. 572.

[10] G.I. Konidares, "Ή θέσις τῆς αὐτοκεφάλου 'Εκκλησίας τῆς Κύπρου", p. 183 (= Papageorgiou, p. 115).

[11] G.I. Konidares, "Ή θέσις τῆς αὐτοκεφάλου 'Εκκλησίας τῆς Κύπρου", p. 137.

[12] C. de Boor, "Analekten (I-III). Nachträge zu den Notitiae Episcopatuum", *ZKG* 12 (1891), pp. 520–34.

[13] L. Duchesne, "L'Illyricum Ecclésiastique", *BZ* 1 (1892), pp. 531–50.

restrictions, which were (a) the appointment of the archbishop of Cyprus
by the emperor, as was the case with the ecumenical patriarch; (b) the
positioning of Cyprus in the "order of precedence of thrones" and in
relation to the ecumenical patriarchate so that the Church of Cyprus
would rank as the third metropolis; and (c) the rare use of the right of
appeal to the ecumenical patriarch.

3. The *de facto* submission of the Church of Cyprus to that of Constantinople
    in the eighth century, which continued in the ninth and tenth centuries
    and even after the incorporation of Cyprus into the Empire in 965.

These arguments are based on the interpretation which Konidares gives
to the following:

1. To the fact that Constantine, archbishop of Cyprus, signed the acta of
    the Seventh Ecumenical Council as bishop of Constantia after the met-
    ropolitans of Caesarea and Ephesus.
2. To the assertion of Theophanes that Michael I (811–13) sent "a talent
    of gold" to the Christian refugees who had fled from Palestine to Cyprus
    in 813, a fact which shows, according to Konidares, that the Church of
    Cyprus had need of the Church of Constantinople.
3. To the letter of Archbishop Epiphanios to Patriarch Ignatios of
    Constantinople which addresses him as "Master" (δεσπότην).
4. To the *Tacticon* of Codex Parisinus gr. 1555A, which Konidares regards
    as a *Tacticon* from the age of Leo III and Constantine V and which ranks
    the archbishop of Cyprus after the metropolitans of Caesarea and
    Ephesus.

Various scholars have replied in detail to Konidares' theses, most notably
A.I. Dikigoropoulos. Already in 1929, before Michaelides had refuted the
arguments supporting this theory three years prior to its enunciation by
Konidares, Germanos, metropolitan of Sardis, had already refuted the idea
that the Church of Cyprus was ever subordinated to Constantinople in a study
published in Ὀρθοδοξία,[14] and in 1953 Gennadios, metropolitan of Heliopolis
and Thera, also refuted it in his well-known *History of the Ecumenical Patriarchate*.[15]

In the meantime V. Laurent in his series of studies proved the accuracy
of the judgments of L. Duchesne on the spuriousness of the Paris *Tacticon*,[16]

[14] Germanos, metropolitan of Sardis and Pisidia, "Ἱστορικὴ μελέτη περὶ τῆς Ἐκκλησίας
τῶν Σάρδεων καὶ τῶν Ἐπισκόπων αὐτῆς", *Orthodoxia* 4 (1929), pp. 16–18, n. 177.

[15] Gennadios, metropolitan of Heliopolis and Thera, Ἱστορία τοῦ Οἰκουμενικοῦ
Πατριαρχείου, I, Athens, 1953, p. 254.

[16] See especially V. Laurent, "L' érection de la métropole d'Athènes et le statut ecclésiastique de l'Illyricum au VIIIe siècle", *REB* 1 (1943), pp. 58–72, esp. p. 65.

and in 1959 H.-G. Beck summarised in an authoritative manner the general (with the exception of Konidares) scholarly consensus as follows: "Today – on account especially of the preliminary work of V. Laurent – [the *Tacticon* of Codex Parisinus gr. 1555A] should be rejected decisively. We leave it out of account, not seeing in it any official attempt … ".[17]

The recent critical study and publication of the *Tacticon* of Codex Parisinus gr. 1555A by J. Darrouzès within the framework of the general issue of critical texts of Byzantine ecclesiastical *Tactica* demolishes the chief support of Konidares' theory concerning the Church of Cyprus and renders any further discussion of this subject redundant.

We shall pass over Konidares' opinions on the political history of the Empire in general and on Byzantine Cyprus in particular since no scholar, as we have already shown in the first part of this study, any longer accepts the perspective Konidares represents. Moreover, in his two most recent publications he himself seems to have abandoned his long-held views. What relationship, for example, could there have been between an imperial financial subsidy for Orthodox Palestinian refugees in Cyprus and any supervision exercised by the Church of Constantinople over the Church of Cyprus? Or who is unaware that Eastern and Byzantine courtesy required the use of a hyperbole which only just fell short of the elaborate graciousness of the Chinese? If Archbishop Epiphanios calls Ignatios, the ecumenical patriarch and the son of an emperor, "Master", it cannot mean anything more than Cyril of Alexandria meant when he called John of Antioch his "Lord". Whether or not the archbishop of Cyprus was appointed by the emperor in the middle Byzantine period is revealed by the *Life* of St Demetrianos, of which Konidares is unaware. And if indeed he was appointed – as in the late Byzantine period – the only thing which this would prove would be that the autocephaly did not suffer any interruption, since only patriarchs were appointed. If appointment implies a suspension of the autocephaly, then the autocephaly of Constantinople and of all the other autocephalous churches was also suspended, and so on.

We come next to the detailed study and critical publication of *Tacticon* no. 3 by Darrouzès in 1981.[18] The following is a summary of his conclusions:

1. The text is transmitted by a single manuscript of the fifteenth century in Codex Parisinus gr. 1555A. Its content gives no indication of the provenance of the archetype.

---

[17] H.-G. Beck, *Kirche und theologische Literatur*, p. 150.

[18] J. Darrouzès, *Notitiae Episcopatuum Ecclesiae Constantinopolitanae*, Paris, 1981, pp. 20–33 and 229ff.

2.   The general title announces the usual subdivision into three parts in
      accordance with the three grades of the ecclesiastical hierarchy: patriarchs,
      metropolitans and autocephalous archbishops.
3.   The list of metropolitans as far as the metropolitan of Perge, who is the
      thirtieth in order, follows exactly one of the lists of signatures of the Seventh
      Ecumenical Council (787).
4.   The position of Cyprus in this *Tacticon* is analogous to its position at the
      Council of 787 at which the archbishop of Cyprus and five bishops were
      present. The *Tacticon*, like Hierokles, gives the names of fourteen sees,
      omitting Kirboia but adding Neapolis.
5.   In general we are dealing with a compilation drawn from ecclesiastical
      and civil lists. The critical study of the text has shown on the one hand
      that the compilation made use of dissimilar sources and on the other
      that these sources were used in a very special manner. The compilers
      used ecclesiastical lists such as those of the Seventh Ecumenical Council
      and civil lists such as the *Synecdemon* of Hierokles, conflating them and
      altering them in such a way so that the original sources can no longer
      be identified.
6.   Such total confusion cannot, of course, have come from an official
      secretum. The compilers did not have before them official lists and any
      chance "use of Tacticon no. 3 as an archival exemplar would have been
      contrary to the composition of the text".[19]
7.   Theoretically, this compilation, which was of a private nature, cannot
      have been put together before 787 or after the fifteenth century (the date
      of the unique manuscript). The scribal errors, however, – well-known
      in manuscripts of early *Tactica* – and the general context show clearly
      that the work belongs to the ninth century.

It is now evident that the theories on the ecclesiastical history of Cyprus
(and of Greece)[20] which Konidares based on this *Tacticon* rest on mistaken
assessments. The *Tacticon* belongs to the ninth and not to the eighth century;[21]

---

[19] Ibid., p. 33.
[20] Ibid., p. 29, n.1: "Au sujet des provinces d'Hellade et du Péloponnèse, il faut comparer
la notice avec Hiéroklès: Gelzer, *Geographie*, pp. 420–424; la distinction entre la liste civile et
la liste ecclésiastique doit être précisée, comme l'ont fait plusieurs auteurs avec diverses
nuances: Duchesne, *Grèce*, pp. 377–383; Dvornik, *Slaves*, pp. 240–243; Honigmann, *Synekdèmos*,
pp. 3–5; Jones, *Cities*, pp. 314–321. Au contraire, depuis son édition de la notice, G. Konidarès
n'a cessé de tenir à l'authenticité des listes de la notice comme listes épiscopales."
[21] Ibid., p. 21, n.3: "Le rapport avec un acte spécifique des empereurs Isauriens, reconnu
par Gelzer, devient une certitude pour Konidarès et son unique hypothèse de travail pour la
reconstitution de cet acte imaginaire. Au point de départ, la dépendence de diverses sources
repérées ruine cette méthode; voir à ce sujet les remarques de Honigmann, *Synekdèmos*, pp. 3–5."

it constitutes a compilation and not an original work; it bears an unofficial, not an official, character; it conflates civil and ecclesiastical lists; in the part which refers to Cyprus it copies the lists of the Seventh Ecumenical Council (as Archimandrite Hippolytos Michaelides had indicated in 1929).

Leaving *Tacticon* no. 3, then, out of account (as H.-G. Beck had already done in 1959) we are left basically with regard to Konidares' theory only with the series of signatures of the Seventh Ecumenical Council. On the basis of the critical axiom that "the evidence is not to be counted but weighed" we have here but a single witness, which is the source of the *Tacticon* in respect of that which concerns Cyprus, that is to say, the Seventh Ecumenical Council.

With regard to this problem we note here the following, which we have taken from an unpublished study by B. Englezakis:

1. The question of the series of signatures on the episcopal lists of the ecumenical councils is a broader, complicated problem which changes from council to council. In the most authoritative history of the councils itself, that of C.J. Hefele and H. Leclerq, a disagreement may be observed between these two eminent scholars since the latter, in contrast to the former, holds the view that the order of signatures in the councils does not always prove the order of precedence.[22]

2. A definitive scholarly opinion cannot be formulated before the existence of a critical edition and comparative study of all these lists. We cannot, of course, go into this difficult problem here. For the Seventh Ecumenical Council the foundations of research were laid by the study of J. Darrouzès on the episcopal lists.[23]

3. The position of the archbishop of Cyprus in the order of signatures at the Seventh Ecumenical Council was noticed already in 1715 by Patriarch Dositheos of Jerusalem in his book *On the patriarchs of Jerusalem*,[24] in which, however, as we have already indicated, he confused the archbishop of Cyprus with the autocephalous archbishops. The first reply to Dositheos was given in 1740 by Philotheos, archbishop of Cyprus (1734–59).[25] The exchange at that time, however, (a) belongs to the

---

[22] C.J. Hefele-H. Leclercq, *Histoire des conciles*, I, i, Paris, 1907, p. 92, n.2. A.N. Mitsides, "Τὸ αὐτοκέφαλον τῆς Ἐκκλησίας Κύπρου", XVe Congrès International d'Études Byzantines, *Rapports et Co-Rapports*, V, ii, Athens, 1976, p. 8, confuses matters, thinking that this is the opinion of both historians.

[23] J. Darrouzès, "Listes épiscopales au concile de Nicée II (787)", *REB* 33 (1975), pp. 5–76.

[24] Dositheos, patriarch of Jerusalem, *Περὶ τῶν ἐν Ἱεροσολύμοις πατριαρχευσάντων*, Venice, 1715, E΄, Κ΄, 11.

[25] See Archimandrite Kyprianos, *Ἱστορία χρονολογικὴ τῆς νήσου Κύπρου*, Venice, 1788, p. 381.

atmosphere of the Turkish period and (b) confuses the proedrus of the Church of Cyprus with the autocephalous archbishops.

4.   On the basis of Byzantine protocol, what must be examined is not only the order of the signatures but also their form, a matter as important if not more so than their order. In this regard a preliminary examination reveals the following:

(a) In the list of signatures to the speech after the reading of the letter of Patriarch Germanos of Constantinople to Thomas of Claudiopolis the order is:[26] Rome, Constantinople, Alexandria, Antioch, Jerusalem, Caesarea, Ephesus, Cyprus, Thessalonica, Ancyra (whose metropolitan, Basil, was a repentant heretic), Heracleia, Cyzicus, etc. All the metropolitans sign in an abbreviated form except for the patriarchs (or their representatives) and the archbishop of Cyprus. Thus the metropolitan of Caesarea signs: "[I,] Agapios, unworthy bishop of Caesarea of Cappadocia, having gladly accepted all the matters recorded above, have signed." The metropolitan of Ephesus signs: "[I,] John, bishop of Ephesus, having gladly accepted all the matters recorded above, have signed." Whereas the archbishop of Cyprus writes: "[I,] Constantine, bishop of Constantia of the Cypriots, in accordance with the orthodox faith referred to above and confessed by us, accept and kiss the sacred and holy icons and, venerating them with honour, have signed by my own hand." We would draw attention not only to the extended form of the signature of the primates but also to the formula "I accept and have signed" (δέχομαι καὶ ὑπέγραψα) in contrast with that of the metropolitans: "having accepted, I have signed" (δεξάμενος ὑπέγραψα).

(b) At the convocation[27] the order after the patriarchates is the same as above, that is, Caesarea, Ephesus, Cyprus, Thessalonica, Ancyra, Heracleia, Cyzicus – again not the "canonical" order not only with regard to the archbishop of Cyprus but also with regard to the metropolitans of Thessalonica, Ancyra and, indeed, Heracleia.

(c) At the signing of the definition[28] the preceding order is changed in accordance with the scheme: Caesarea, Ephesus, Cyprus, Heracleia, Ancyra, Cyzicus, Sardis, etc., that is to say, the metropolitan of Heracleia comes before the metropolitan of Ancyra and the metropolitan of Thessalonica goes out. The formulas used in the signatures are worth noting: the patriarchs or their representatives, together with the archbishop

[26] Mansi, *Sacrorum conciliorum collectio*, XIII, Florence, 1767, 133.
[27] Ibid., 365.
[28] Ibid., 380ff.

of Cyprus, sign: "by the grace of God" (ἐλέῳ Θεοῦ) and without the epithet "unworthy" (ἀνάξιος), while the metropolitans – including those of Caesarea and Ephesus – sign without the phrase "by the grace of God" and begin with "unworthy bishop".[29] Anyone who is surprised that the archbishop of Cyprus did not sign himself "archbishop" should note that even the metropolitans did not sign themselves "metropolitan", just as to this day the ecumenical patriarch has never signed himself anything but "of Constantinople". (We mention this since it is one of the "arguments" that the archbishop of Cyprus signed as bishop of Constantia a form which, however it is understood, was incorrect.) Thus the archbishop of Cyprus signs: "[I,] Constantine, by the grace of God bishop of the isle of the Cypriots, following the teachings of the Fathers and the tradition of the catholic Church, have agreed to the definition and have signed." Immediately afterwards, by a general exception and in a manner perfectly strange (if not comic), the metropolitan of Heracleia signs, beginning himself with the words "by the grace of God", a formula which neither the metropolitan of Caesarea nor the metropolitan of Ephesus had dared to use. It is evident that (a) the archbishop of Cyprus has the right of the presiding bishop of an autocephalous Church, which neither the metropolitan of Caesarea nor the metropolitan of Ephesus has dared to appropriate, and (b) the metropolitan of Heracleia is either inept, or angry, or suspicious and hostile – since twice previously he had come after even the metropolitan of Ancyra – or all of these together.

5. Instead of starting with the question: "Why was the archbishop of Cyprus demoted?" it would be more fruitful to begin with the other side of the problem: "Why were the metropolitans of Caesarea and Ephesus flattered but not the metropolitan of Heracleia?"

    Let us call to mind that the Iconoclast themes of the Empire were basically the Anatolikon and the Armeniakon, that is to say, the two large Asiatic themes, the armies of which constituted the backbone both of the heresy and of the threat to Irene and the Patriarch Tarasios in 787. In July 786 soldiers of these themes interrupted by force of arms the first attempt to hold an ecumenical council on behalf of the icons in the church of the Holy Apostles in Constantinople (the reason for the transfer of the council to Nicaea in 787). Caesarea and Ephesus were the capitals of these two themes.

---

[29] Ibid., 380.

The metropolitan of Heracleia, by contrast, had his seat in the European part of the Empire and indeed in Thrace, where Irene drew her support.

6. A matter which should be examined is the personal backgrounds of the monastic metropolitans of Caesarea and Ephesus and the metropolitan of Heracleia, when they were appointed to these sees and why.

7. In this context, and before we proceed to consider the disrupted order of the signatures after those of the patriarchs, let us note the disrupted order of the two signatures which precede those of the patriarchs, namely, the imperial signatures themselves. In spite of the fact that precedence with regard to her son Constantine VI was given legally to Irene only in the spring of 790, on 23 October 787 – thirty months or so previously – at the last session of the Seventh Ecumenical Council in the Magnaura palace in Constantinople Irene signed the *Horos* of the council first, before Constantine VI, in contrast to the *Sacra* convening the council, which both on 29 August 784 and in May 787 was issued in the name of Constantine and Irene, to whom, in that order, all the relevant letters of the pope were addressed and also all the speeches of the conciliar fathers after the signing itself ![30] Equally anomalously, in the final eighth session of the council Irene presided (a woman)[31] rather than Constantine VI. Let us recall that the title "Irene basileus" will be heard for the first time only ten years later, after the blinding of Constantine VI on 17 August 797.

8. In comparison with this unprecedented audacity the elevation of the "most necessary" metropolitans of Caesarea and Ephesus and the diminution of the archbishop of Cyprus and the metropolitan of Heracleia seem minor details.

9. Moreover, before the Seventh Ecumenical Council the order of the patriarchal signatures at the Quinisextum Council instead of the canonical one was Constantinople, Alexandria, Jerusalem, Antioch, while at the council held in Hagia Sophia in 869 against Photios (the Eighth Ecumenical for the Latins) the order is Rome, Antioch, Jerusalem, Alexandria.[32] Why then should anyone be so surprised at the position of Cyprus at the Seventh?

---

[30] Ibid., 416–17.
[31] Ibid., 413.
[32] Ibid., XVIIA, Venice, 1772, 508–12.

V

JOHN CHRYSOSTOMITES,
A TWELFTH-CENTURY PATRIARCH
OF JERUSALEM*

It is well-known that the chronology of the patriarchs of Jerusalem in the age of the Komnenoi presents a number of difficult problems.[1] None the less, it is indisputable that two patriarchs with the name of John presided over the Church of Sion in the twelfth century: the first at the beginning of the century (elected *c.* 1098), recognised at Constantinople in 1106/7 to before January 1122), the second in the third quarter of the century (after January 1156 but before 12 May 1157 to before February 1166).

The *curriculum vitae* of the first (John VIII, if we follow the number of Chrysostomos Papadopoulos) was excellently described by L. Petit in the *Dictionnarie de théologie catholique*.[2] His personality was sketched and his chronology deduced with a high degree of probability by V. Grumel.[3]

With regard to the second, John IX, almost all we know about him is that he was present at the second council which met to discuss the liturgical text, "*Thou art he who offers and is offered*" on 12 and 13 May 1157;[4] "of the monk John of Jerusalem";[5] "of the most holy patriarch of Jerusalem the monk Lord John";[6] "[I,] the humble monk John, by the grace of God patriarch of

---

* Translated from Ἰωάννης ὁ Χρυσοστομίτης, Πατριάρχης Ἱεροσολύμων κατὰ τὸν ΙΒ΄ αἰῶνα. An early work which was published when the author was a post-graduate student at Cambridge but which had been written in Paris when he was twenty-one years old. FT: "Jean le Chrysostomite, Patriarche de Jerusalem au XIIe siècle", *Byzantion* 43 (1973), pp. 506–8.

[1] See V. Grumel in *Recueil dédié à la mémoire du Professeur P. Nicov*, Sophia, 1940, pp. 109–114.
[2] *DTC* VIII, pp. 766–7.
[3] Grumel, art. cit., pp. 110–12. Cf. J. Darrouzès, *REB* 21 (1963), p. 54.
[4] *Regestes*, Nn. 1041–1043.
[5] *PG* 140, 180B.
[6] *PG* 140, 196C.

the holy city of Sion, Jerusalem, mother of all the churches, have defined and have signed."[7]

It should also be noted that one of these two patriarchs must be John Mercouropoulos, author of the *Life* of St John of Damascus[8] which was published by A. Papadopoulos-Kerameus in the Ἀνάλεκτα Ἱεροσολυμικῆς Σταχυολογίας from Codex Athen. 983, dated 1267.[9] If the Arabic archetype dates from 1085, the author of the ancient *Life* must be John VIII of Jerusalem and not John VI (died 969). Why, then, should we not return to the hypothesis of Papadopoulos-Kerameus[10] that John Mercouropoulos is the same person as John VIII and consequently the author of the two extant *Lives* of John of Damascus? What is certain, at any rate, is that John Mercouropoulos cannot be identified with John IX.

Some years ago when I was studying the *Typicon* of the Cypriot monastery of St John Chrysostom in Dmitrievekij's edition,[11] I was struck by the reading it gave for 24 April (fol. 145): "we celebrate the memorial of our holy father and master Lord John Chrysostom, who became patriarch of Jerusalem" (sic!). The error was quite implausible. I consulted the original manuscript, Parisinus gr. 402, where it may easily be seen that the true reading for 24 April is: "It should be known that on this day we celebrate the memorial of our holy father and master Lord John Chrysostomites, who became patriarch of Jerusalem."

The monastery of St John Chrysostom at Koutzouvendi was founded in 1090[12] by Abbot George, who died on 26 April in an unknown year.[13] Who, then, was John Chrysostomites, patriarch of Jerusalem? The *typicon* belongs to the thirteenth century, so the reference must be to one of the two

---

[7] *PG* 140, 197C.

[8] *BHG* 395.

[9] Ἀνάλεκτα Ἱεροσολυμικῆς Σταχυολογίας 4, pp. 303–50 (corrected 5, pp. 405–7). On the question of the *Lives* of John of Damascus, see M. Gordillo, *Damascenica*, *OC* 8, 2 (November 1926) and M. Jugie in *EO* 28 (1929), pp. 35–41.

[10] Papadopoulos-Kerameus, op. cit., p. x.

[11] A. Dmitrievskij, *Opišanie liturgičeskih rukopišej chranjaščichsja v bibliotekach pravoslavnago vostoka*, III: *Typica*, St Petersburg, 1917, pp. 121–7.

[12] Paris, gr. 402, fol. 56ʳ⁻ᵛ, inauguration of the saint's church on 9 December 1090.

[13] Paris. gr. 402, fol. 146ᵛ. On the history of the monastery see I.P. Tsiknopoullos, Ἡ ἱερὰ μονὴ τοῦ Χρυσοστόμου Κουτσουβένδη καὶ τὰ ἱερὰ αὐτῆς κτίσματα, Nicosia, 1959; C. Mango and E.J.W. Hawkins, *DOP* 18 (1964), pp. 333–9. May I be permitted to note that the *typicon* of the monastery mentions another two churches besides those of St John Chrysostom and the Holy Trinity (built by Duke Eumathios Philokales), namely, that of St Lazarus (fol. 228) and that "of the most holy Theotokos of the cemetery" (fol. 181, 264ᵛ), which must, I think, be identified with the Aphentrika or Panagia of Koutzouvendi. The hypothesis of M. Bardswell (*ECQ* 3, no. 5, pp. 304–8), based on information supplied by the mayor of the village that the church was "in the old days" Maronite, is irrelevant to our period even if not totally unfounded. The church's wonderful *Threnos*, or Deposition, (early 12th century) lends support to our hypothesis.

Johns of the twelfth century. The first, John VIII Mercouropoulos, must be excluded for the following reasons:

1. The monastery was founded in 1090, whereas Mercouropoulos was elected patriarch of Jerusalem in about 1098, when he was already, however, bishop of Tyre.[14]
2. He was never described as a monk.
3. His holy patron was John of Damascus, not John Chrysostom.[15]

Consequently, the hypothesis may be put forward with some confidence that the monk John, patriarch of Jerusalem, who attended the Council of Constantinople of 1157 was John Chrysostomites, a brother of the Cypriot monastery of St John Chrysostom at Koutzouvendi on Pentadaktylos.

This does not necessarily mean that he was a Cypriot. As J. Darrouzès reminds us,

> "The country with which Cyprus had the closest ties after the tenth century was Palestine. The movement of books which is represented by the number of Cypriot manuscripts in Jerusalem is due to the relations between orthodox monasteries: those of Jerusalem had dependencies on the island and recruited monks from the believing population. Cyprus was also the natural asylum of Christians in Syria and Cilicia who were threatened by Islam."[16]

And did not Symeon, the last patriarch of Jerusalem before the Latin occupation (1098), flee to Cyprus – where he was to die – during the Arab persecution of the Christians which preceded the arrival of the Crusaders? The probability nevertheless remains high that John Chrysostomites was one of the Cypriot patriarchs of the Holy City.

---

[14] Grumel, art. cit., p. 111.
[15] Papadopoulos-Kerameus, op. cit., p. 350.
[16] *REB* 15 (1957), p. 132.

VI

THE COMMENTARY OF ST NEOPHYTOS THE RECLUSE ON THE CANONS OF THE TWELVE DOMINICAL FEASTS*

Among the monastic authors of Cyprus the most eminent is undoubtedly St Neophytos the Recluse. Born in 1134,[1] at the age of eighteen[2] he entered the Monastery of St John Chrysostom[3] on the mountain of Koutzouvendi, where he remained for seven years. After a brief absence in Palestine in search of *hesychia*,[4] he established himself in 1159[5] in a precipitous cave near Paphos, where in 1170[6] he founded the troglodytic monastery of the Hermitage.[7] His life coincided with one of the more dramatic periods in the history of Cyprus when the tyranny of the despot Isaac Komnenos, "holy emperor of

---

* Translated from "Ἡ εἰς τοὺς κανόνας τῶν δεσποτικῶν ἑορτῶν ἑρμηνεία τοῦ ὁσίου Νεοφύτου τοῦ Ἐγκλείστου", Ἀπόστολος Βαρνάβας 39 (1978), pp. 367–75. The article was originally a communication entitled "La question du *Commentaire sur les canons des douze fêtes du Seigneur* par Néophyte le Reclus" given at the Fifteenth International Conference on Byzantine Studies at the University of Athens, Athens, 1976. A portion of the doctoral thesis of M.-H. Congourdeau referred to in the text was published by the author in French in *EKEE* 8 (Nicosia, 1975–1977), pp. 113–85.

[1] *Typicon*, V. The best edition of the *Typicon* is that of I.P. Tsiknopoullos in Κυπριακὰ Τυπικά, Nicosia, 1969, pp. 69–104.

[2] *Typicon*, III.

[3] Founded in 1090/1 by Abbot George Ktetor and enriched with an exceptional church dedicated to the Holy Trinity by the celebrated Eumathios Philokales, Duke of Cyprus, after 1092–1103 and about 1110 to before 1118. See C. Mango and E.J.W. Hawkins, *DOP* 18 (1964), pp. 333–9.

[4] *Typicon*, IV.

[5] Ibid., V.

[6] Ibid.

[7] See C. Mango and E.J.W. Hawkins, "The Hermitage of St. Neophytus and its Wall-Paintings", *DOP* 20 (1966), pp. 119–206 + plates.

Cyprus", was followed successively by the arrival of Richard Lionheart, the cession of the island to the Templars, its return again to Richard and finally its acquisition by the titular king of Jerusalem, Guy de Lusignan of the Lords of Poitiers, and the French knights. These were "years of captivity" in which the Cypriots, cut off at the outset from the Byzantine world, lived in servitude to the Franks, while the honour and autonomy of their Church were affronted and their ancestral faith humbled. But the Recluse of Paphos did not submit and continued his work without interruption until his death a little after 1214,[8] which according to tradition occurred on 12 April 1219. Fortunately he left a detailed catalogue in his own hand of his spiritual, hermeneutic, liturgical and other works in the twelfth chapter of the second and last edition of his founder's *Typicon*.

The seventh item of this catalogue is a *Commentary on the Canons of the Twelve Dominical Feasts*. In his fundamental study on the Recluse, L. Petit formulated the hypothesis that the nine homilies attributed to Neophytos in Codex Lesbianus 2 of the Monastery of Leimon belong to this work, which until then had been considered lost.[9] This hypothesis was judged to be probably true by H. Delehaye,[10] and from that time was accepted by everyone with the exception of A. Ehrhard, who expressed a different hypothesis, namely that the homilies of the Leimonian manuscript belong to the two lost tomes of Neophytos's *Panegyrike*.[11] In 1958 I.P. Tsiknopoullos proved Ehrhard's hypothesis to be without foundation for purely heortological reasons. The three tomes of Neophytos's *Panegyrike* assign the feasts of the annual cycle to three four-month periods, beginning with September. The nine homilies of the Leimonian manuscript, however, cover feasts which extend from November to August and the first two of these reduplicate the Paris *Panegyrike*. Clearly, then, the Lesbos homilies cannot belong to Neophytos's *Greater Panegyrike*.[12]

They cannot, however, even belong to the *Commentary On the Canons of the Twelve Dominical Feasts*. At this point it is necessary for us to recall that Petit had not read these homilies when he formulated his hypothesis. Neither had Delehaye. Ehrhard was the first, it seems, to see them and Tsiknopoullos the first to read them. Ehrhard understood at once that they could not belong to the *Commentary* because they did not contain the exegesis of any canon. Tsiknopoullos, however, bowed to the authority of Petit and indeed supplied

---

[8] See *Typicon*, end.

[9] "Vie et ouvrages de Néophyte le Reclus", *EO* 2 (1898-1899), pp. 257–68 + 372, esp. p. 265.

[10] "Saints de Chypre", *AB* 26 (1907), pp. 161–297, esp. p. 278.

[11] *Überlieferung und Bestand d. hagiogr. und homilet. Lt. d. griech. Kirche*, III. I, Leipzig, 1943, pp. 683–4.

[12] "Τὸ συγγραφικὸν ἔργον τοῦ ἁγίου Νοεφύτου", *KS* 22 (1953), pp. 67–214, esp. pp. 101ff and 151.

him with a detailed defence. (There is no commentary on the canons, but does Neophytos not explain the meaning of the feasts? Evidently Neophytos takes the epithet "dominical" in a broad sense,[13] and so on.) In the end Tsiknopoullos persuaded everyone and E.M. Toniolo in his critical edition of three mariological discourses of Codex Lesbianus 2 in *Marianum* says in 1974:

> "Neophytos speaks of 'feasts of the Lord' but the fact that feasts of the Virgin and the great saints are also included in this expression does not cause surprise, nor does it cause difficulties. He also mentions 'canons for the feasts' while his discourses do not refer to them. I believe, then, that Neophytos has given a name to this collection of his more to distinguish it from the books of the Panegyrics than to denote its content."[14]

The phenomenon is of course strange but it is not the first time that the authority (real or imagined) of a scholar has blinded those who come after him.

It is nevertheless sufficient only to have eyes to see that the nine discourses of Codex Lesbianus 2 are festal homilies, nothing more and nothing less. And it is sufficient to read them to see that they are heterogeneous discourses which do not constitute fragments of a unified work. This at least was seen by Toniolo: "I believe, then, that they are a collection of various sermons of the saint delivered at various times."[15]

In March 1976 Mme M.-H. Congourdeau, working in France under the direction of Mme H. Ahrweiler on a critical edition of Neophytos's *Discourse on the Epiphany*, informed me by letter about the results of her work on the homilies of Codex Lesbianus 2. Entirely independently of each other Mme Congourdeau and I had arrived at the same conclusions. In her own words,

> "The nine discourses of the Lesbos manuscript do not constitute a part either of the Commentary on the canons, as the tradition from Petit to Tsiknopoullos supposes, or of the two lost tomes of the *Greater Panegyrike*, as Ehrhard thought, or of another of Neophytos's works referred to in the *Typike Diatheke*, but in reality are festal homilies which were composed

---

[13] Ibid., pp. 147ff, and the same author's "Ἡ θαυμαστὴ προσωπικότης τοῦ Νεοφύτου πρεσβυτέρου, μοναχοῦ καὶ ἐγκλείστου", *Βυζάντιον* 37 (1967), pp. 311–413 + plates, esp. pp. 366ff.

[14] "Omelie e Catechesi mariane inedite di Neofito il Recluso (1134–1220c.)", *Marianum* 36 (1974), pp. 184–315, esp. pp. 189ff.

[15] Ibid., p. 190.

at various points in the life of Neophytos and were collected by the copyist of the composite work we find in the codex."

In a second letter dated 4 May, 1976, Mme Congourdeau wrote that in her opinion "Neophytos composed homilies throughout his life. From this mass he chose a few in order to put them in a collection (*Panegyrike*). Others were set aside and are not referred to in the *Typike Diatheke*." And she continues:

> "Eight of the discourses of Codex Lesbianus 2 are described as discourses 'of Neophytos, monk and recluse'. But Neophytos was a priest and we can suppose that this was neither an oversight nor a copyist's error (cf. codex Coislinianus 287). This therefore refers to discourses written before 1170. At that time Neophytos was already writing for the use of various monasteries (cf. the *Encomium on St Diomedes* in the *Greater Panegyrike*). His fame was so great that Basil Kinnamos urged him to found his own coenobium."

The only point on which I am unable to agree with Mme Congourdeau is on the chronology of the discourses of Codex Lesbianus 2.

With regard first to the title, the fact that Neophytos is called "monk and recluse" and not "presbyter, monk and recluse", as usual, cannot be decisive. The titles of Codex Coislinianus gr. 287 (*Commentaries on the Dominical Commandments*) are perhaps not due to a copyist's error. We may surmise that in 1176 (six years after his ordination) Neophytos was still not using the title "presbyter" for reasons of monastic humility. Besides, "monk and recluse" is all he calls himself even in what appears to be the last work which he has left us, the "bibliographical note" which was published recently by K. Hadjipsaltes from Codex Viennensis philosophicus gr. 330.[16]

That the Recluse had composed and delivered discourses before 1170 seems to me improbable. Mme Congourdeau is not the only scholar to believe this. Tsiknopoullos also believed that Neophytos began his career as an orator at the age of thirty, that is, in 1164.[17] But he offers no proof of this. With regard to the *Encomium on St Diomedes*,[18] it was not written before 1170, as Mme Congourdeau seems to say in her letter, but in 1176.[19]

The bishop of Paphos, Basil Kinnamos, ordained Neophytos priest in 1170.[20] There is no proof, however, that he did this on account of the

---

[16] *EKEE* 6 (Nicosia, 1973), pp. 125–32.

[17] "Τὸ συγγραφικὸν", p. 75.

[18] Paris gr. 1189, fol. 134ʳ–139ᵛ. Published by H. Delehaye, op. cit.

[19] See fol. 137ᵛ *et seq.* and Coisl. gr. 287, fol. 16ᵛ–17ʳ, 22ʳ–24ᵛ, 85ʳ, 193ʳ.

[20] *Typicon*, V.

hermit's reputation as an orator. Neophytos was undoubtedly revered by the surrounding country people[21] and we can surmise that the ecclesiastics of Paphos and Arsinoe knew him from his bibliographical and other researches.[22] Would it not therefore be better for us to guess that Neophytos's reputation with the new bishop of Paphos was that of a studious holy man of God rather than that of an orator? Finally, was it not only in 1176 that the scandal broke about Neophytos's literary endeavours? Only then in fact did some begin to ask themselves, "How has this man dared to write, seeing that the apostle said: 'If anyone preaches a version of the Gospel except the one that we have preached to you, let him be anathema' (Gal. 1:8)?"[23] 1170, the year of Neophytos's ordination to the priesthood and of the consolidation of his coenobium, remains the most probable moment for the beginning of his career as a preacher and author.

The results of the external criticism seem confirmed by the internal criticisms of the Lesbos homilies. Let us take the discourse on the Annunciation.[24] It begins with a defence of the preaching activity of the author. The first paragraphs have been lost but the question which the author is attempting to answer is, indicatively, "How is it that you are attempting to say things that are beyond you?" Neophytos replies, saying amongst other things that the ancient authors had encountered the same problem. Later in this apology[25] he says that in spite of the number of years of his residence in his hermitage, he does not possess a calendar of feasts of the Mother of God and the Lord – infallible proof that we are dealing with one of the first discourses of the Recluse. We hear a similar complaint expressed in 1176 in the *Commentaries on the Dominical Commandments*[26] and the prologue to the discourse also shows that it belongs to this period, that is to say, to the period of the scandal of 1176, of which we have already spoken. It is, besides, very likely that the mysterious reference in the same prologue to "the alpha item"[27] hints that the writer has marked this homily as the first of a series

---

[21] Paris. gr. 1189, fol. 133ʳ.

[22] Ἑξαήμερος, III, 169 in I. Hadjiioannou, Ἱστορία καὶ ἔργα Νεοφύτου πρεσβυτέρου μοναχοῦ καὶ ἐγκλείστου, Alexandria, 1914, Τυπικὸν, V: "Ζήτησις τιμίου".

[23] Paris. gr. 1189, fol. 137ᵛ (*Encomium on St Diomedes*).

[24] Cod. Lesb. Leimon. 2, fol. 298ʳ–306ᵛ, *BHG* 1076v. Published by E.M. Toniolo, O.S.M., op. cit., pp. 238–63. All the following references are made to this edition when they are cited by page and line.

[25] See fol. 298ʳ, p. 238, line 20: "πρὸς ἀπολογίαν τῆς σῆς ἐρωτήσεως" Coisl. gr. 287, fol. 16ᵛ: "προτάξαι ἀπολογίαν κτλ.".

[26] Coisl. gr. 287, fol. 22ᵛ: "οὐκ ἔχω ἐν τῇ Ἐγκλείστρα τὰς ἱερὰς δέλτους ἐκείνων (scil. τῶν πατέρων)".

[27] Fol. 298ᵛ, p. 240, lines 43–4. Cf. p. 241, n. 1.

(without implying, of course, that the first homily in a series is necessarily also the first chronologically).

The prologue of the discourse in this manuscript on the Dormition of the Theotokos[28] speaks again of the unworthiness of the author and of his desire to remain silent, which, in spite of his efforts, he has not been able to follow. It is evident that here again is a work belonging to the author's youth. A little later, speaking about the appearance of the Lord to His saints, the author hastens to add that his knowledge about such things derives from sacred books,[29] and begins a long aside on the fact that the appearances to the recent saints are in reality more wonderful events than the appearances of God to Abraham and the ancients, "since they have been brought close to me and are full of all truth and grace".[30] How can one avoid reading these lines as new hints of the controversy of 1176 on the later writings on God and the saints?

The beginning of the discourse on the Transfiguration[31] speaks once again of the unworthiness of the author. "A rhetorical convention", one could say. Nevertheless it is a convention which is not found in the instruction on the Transfiguration, written in about 1212.[32]

We come to the discourse on the Nativity of the Saviour.[33] The paragraphs on Jesus as "holy myrrh" are a parallel to a fragment of Discourse V of the *Commentaries on the Dominical Commandments*.[34] The parallel to the discourse before us is evidently the *versio brevior* and, without doubt, the original one: the text of the *Commentary on the Dominical Commandments* is disturbed[35] and the fragment under consideration displaced from its position. Given that the surviving *Commentaries* were written in 1176, the Lesbos discourse must be contemporary or rather must precede it a little, and this is the oldest of Neophytos's works which we are able to date with a certain degree of probability.[36]

---

[28] Fol. 325ᵛ–333ᵛ (*BHG* 1085 n), pp. 264–83.

[29] Fol. 327ʳ, p. 266, lines 54–5.

[30] Fol. 327ᵛ, p. 268.

[31] Fol. 318ᵛ–325 (*BHG* 1991 p).

[32] Paris. suppl. gr. 1317, fol. 98ʳ–100ᵛ. Published by B. Englezakis, "Ἀνέκδοτος κατήχησις τοῦ ὁσίου Νεοφύτου τοῦ Ἐγκλείστου εἰς τὴν ἁγίαν Μεταμόρφωσιν", Θεολογία, 44 (1973), pp. 699–701, and reproduced below, in Chapter IX.

[33] Fol. 260ʳ–273ʳ (*BHG* 1923).

[34] Coisl. gr. 287, fols. 49ʳ–51ʳ.

[35] See the reference to the woman who was a sinner (fol. 50ʳ), which destroys what follows.

[36] Tsiknopoullos, "Τὸ συγγραφικὸν", p. 89, is wrong in assigning the discourse *On various earthquakes* (Paris. gr. fols. 129ᵛ–134ʳ, ed. Delehaye, op. cit.) to 1170, since Neophytos refers in this discourse to the earthquake which destroyed Antioch in that year. Neophytos speaks of this event as belonging to the past.

In spite of this, as soon as we turn to the discourse on the Presentation of the Mother of God,[37] the atmosphere changes radically. The style and tone are those of Neophytos as an old man; everything is different – there is no prologue about unworthiness, no apology. The speaker is certain about his position and his authority. At the end of the discourse[38] he concludes with the words: "If[39] any relic of life is left to me, and the creditors lend to me again in my poverty, I have further things to write and say to you." The same phrase is found at the end of the instruction on the Presentation,[40] written, as is well-known, a little after 1209 and before 1214 when Neophytos reached his eightieth year. And this is not the only indication of old age. We should compare this discourse on the Presentation with that also of the *Panegyrike* on the same feast, written in about 1197.[41] The discourse of Codex Lesbianus Leimoniensis 2 not only lacks strength but also constitutes a composite text, the different parts of which are held together with difficulty. It addresses an assembly of monks,[42] but, as has already been observed, its last paragraph is directed towards a single person, whom the elder calls "beloved" and to whom he promises to send another homily within sixty days, that is to say, on the feast of the Purification – since he had promised the present discourse seventy-three days previously, on the feast of the Nativity of the Mother of the divine Son. Observe, then, that he kept his promise and paid his debt with the usual interest. "If you ask me interest on the discourse, as I previously promised you, let your interest be what you have read above from 'young virgins' to 'which I pray will never happen'."

If we examine the fragment which begins with the words: "Young virgins … approached their King and God",[43] and ends: " … need at any rate to be punished eternally, which I pray will never happen",[44] we shall see that it is a parallel to the text of fols. 96[b]–98[a] of the *Book of Instructions*.[45] In the nineteenth instruction the abbot speaks to his monks on St Marina with the sole purpose of comparing men with women and urging the former to show themselves at least as strong as the so-called "weak women". The full title of the instruction is "Compendious encomium on <the> holy and glorious great

---

[37] Fols. 248[r]–260[r] (*BHG* 1085 h), pp. 210–37.
[38] Fol. 259[v], p. 236.
[39] Εἰ correxi: εἰς Toniolo.
[40] Paris. suppl. gr. 1317, fol. 109[v]–112[r], published by E.M. Toniolo, op. cit., pp. 300–3, p. 302, lines 50–1: "εἴ μοι γένηται λείψανα ζωῆς καὶ λόγου δοθῇ μοι χάρις".
[41] Paris. gr. 1189, fol. 164[v]–169[r]:"τὴν Νέαν ταύτην Σιών, ἣν καὶ προσφάτως ἐδομησάμην ἐγὼ σθένει Θεοῦ".
[42] See fols. 254[r], 256[v], 257[v].
[43] Fol. 256[v].
[44] Fol. 258[r].
[45] Paris. suppl. gr. 1317, fols. 93[r]–98[r]: *Encomium on St Marina*.

martyr of Christ, Marina, and on the comparison of men with women on the day of judgment". The fragment which interests us is, then, in its natural place in the instruction, while in the discourse of the Lesbos manuscript 2 it constitutes a secondary element. As we have seen, the author himself suggests this, describing it as "interest on the discourse". It follows that our discourse on the Presentation of the Mother of God is later than the encomium on St Marina. As long as the final edition of the Presentation of the Mother of God is placed after 1209 and before 1214, 1209 is set as the *terminus post quem* of the discourse before us. A *terminus ante quem* is not possible.

I recapitulate my observations. The harvest is meagre. I had to wait for it and did so. The result of the entire study may be summarised in a few words:

1. The nine homilies of Codex Lesbianus 2 of the Monastery of Leimon do not belong to the *Commentary on the Canons of the Twelve Dominical Feasts*.
2. It is also impossible for them to be connected with the two lost tomes of the *Panegyrike*.
3. They are homilies with a different origin and not fragments of one of the known works of Neophytos.
4. The eight discourses, which are transmitted under the name of "Neophytos, monk and recluse", date from about 1176 and are the earliest written works of the Recluse which we possess today.
5. By contrast, the discourse on the Presentation of the Mother of God is the last discourse of Neophytos which is known to us and dates from after 1209, or perhaps even from after 1214.
6. The *Commentary on the Canons of the Twelve Dominical Feasts*, written, according to the catalogue of the twelfth chapter of the *Typike Diatheke*, between 1204 and 1209, has been lost or still remains to be discovered.

Can we perhaps surmise that the nine homilies of Codex Lesbianus 2 belong to the book which, according to the twelfth chapter of the *Typike Diatheke*, Neophytos prepared in 1214 and which he simply called "the so-called last"? I do not know.

VII

AN UNPUBLISHED COMMENTARY BY ST NEOPHYTOS THE RECLUSE ON THE APOCALYPSE*

The short work by St Neophytos which is published below for the first time is interesting from more than one point of view. Although a noteworthy example of a Cypriot contribution to biblical exegesis, a unique witness to the reaction of the Cypriot people to the events of 1204 and a monument from among the first works reflecting the local dialect and pronunciation, it fell into oblivion for a long time, a victim to the common fate of Neophytos's writings. There were also internal reasons, however, for the disappearance of the work: it does not have the breadth of the *Commentary on the Psalms* nor does it attain the expertise of the *Hexaemeron* or the exegetical skill of the *Song of Songs* and at least one of its interpretations cannot be exonerated from error and even from a suspicion of unorthodox opinion.

I. TITLE AND CONTENTS

The full title of the work, as given in the manuscript tradition, is Περὶ τῆς Ἀποκαλύψεως τοῦ ἁγίου Ἰωάννου τοῦ Θεολόγου σαφήνεια διὰ βραχέων. By the term σαφήνεια (exposition)[1] the saint means a special type of exegetical work lying formally between the fresh critical publication of the text and its editing with scholia and glosses. An outstanding example of a critical pub-

---

* Translated from Ἀνέκδοτον ὑπόμνημα τοῦ ὁσίου Νεοφύτου τοῦ Ἐγκλείστου εἰς τὴν Ἀπόκαλυψιν, Ἐπετηρὶς τοῦ Κέντρου Ἐπιστημονικῶν Ἐρευνῶν Κύπρου, 8 (1975–77), pp. 73–112.

[1] On the meaning of the word in the Fathers of the first eight centuries see G.W.H. Lampe, *A Patristic Greek Lexicon*, Oxford, 1961–68, *sub voce*. No example of the use of the word as a title is given by Lampe.

lication was given by Neophytos in the *Commentary on the Song of Songs*,[2] of a running commentary on the text in the *Commentary on the Psalms*,[3] and of interpretative homilies in the *Commentary on the Hexaemeron*.[4] In the present work on the Apocalypse of St John, however, Neophytos attempts simultaneously to give on the one hand "a clear, fitting and accessible" summary of the text of the book, and on the other a brief interpretation of some ill-understood points. To achieve this aim he divides the work into fourteen topics (ὑποθέσεις). After a brief prologue he begins by setting out the text of each topic in summary form, sometimes with the briefest explanatory notes appended to the text. At the head of each topic a title is given and at the end, separate from the text, is appended a brief commentary only a few paragraphs long. Sometimes the well-known technique of interpretation by questions (*quaestiones*) follows. The whole work concludes with an epilogue to which there is also added for good measure a paragraph of apology directed towards those who doubt the authenticity of the Apocalypse. Neophytos calls the work as a whole an "exposition". To which recognised hermeneutic form does this "exposition" belong? The first thing which is certain is that Neophytos was right to avoid calling his work an interpretation (ἑρμηνεία) or an exegesis (ἐξήγησις). With regard to John's text we are presented with an "arrangement" (διασκευή) or "emendation" (μεταγραφή), as the Alexandrians would have called it.[5] With regard to the rest, what we have is "a medieval, monastic gloss" on the Apocalypse.

The fourteen topics which Neophytos distinguishes in the Apocalypse are as follows:

i.   On the seven churches of Asia (Apoc. 1–3).
ii.   On the heavenly door and the ascent of the visionary (Apoc. 4).
iii. On the book sealed with seven seals (Apoc. 5:1–8:5).
iv.   On the seven angels bearing trumpets (Apoc. 8:6–11:19).
v.   On the angel and the scroll and Enoch and Elias (Apoc. 10: 1–11: 14).
vi.   On the great sign seen in heaven (Apoc. 12:1–13:10).
vii. On the evil beast and the number of his name (Apoc. 13:11–18).
viii. On the lamb and the undefiled and the voice (Apoc. 14:1–7).

---

[2] *KS* 25 (1961), pp. 223–44.

[3] I. Hadjiioannou, *Νεοφύτου πρεσβυτέρου μοναχοῦ καὶ ἐγκλείστου, Ἑρμηνεία εἰς τοὺς Ψαλμούς,* Athens, 1935.

[4] I. Hadjiioannou, *Ἱστορία καὶ ἔργα Νεοφύτου μοναχοῦ καὶ ἐγκλείστου,* Alexandria, 1914, pp. 157–213.

[5] See R. Pfeiffer, *History of Classical Scholarship. From the Beginnings to the End of the Hellenistic Age,* Oxford, 1971, pp. 114, 189.

ix.   On him who is seated on the cloud (Apoc. 14:14–16:1).
x.   On the seven angels and the seven plagues and the great war
      (Apoc. 16:2–21; 19:17–18; 19:11–21).
xi.   On the harlot city and its capture (Apoc. 17:1–19:11).
xii. On the binding of the devil for one thousand years (Apoc.
      20:1–10).
xiii. On the new heaven and earth and the heavenly Jerusalem above (Apoc.
      21).
xiv. On the life-giving river and on the tree which bears twelve crops a year
      (Apoc. 22).

II. DATE OF COMPOSITION

Until 11.19 no indication of chronology is given to the reader. At 11.19,
however, in the course of commenting on Apoc. 19:1–2, Neophytos protests
against those who do not wish to give glory to God for the righteous judgment
which has befallen "the great harlot" but instead are exasperated with the
divine retribution. The fall of the sinful city, says Neophytos, and our being
delivered "into the hands of our adversaries" is righteous and straightfor-
ward. Already in the title of the eleventh topic (11.1) there was mention of
"the harlot city and its capture (ἁλώσεως)" instead of the scriptural phrase
"its fall (πτώσεως)" (cf. Apoc. 18:2). These things are elucidated in the
Epilogue, where the author bases the credibility of the Apocalypse on the
prophecy of the capture of Constantinople, which, in his view, is contained
in the book (cf. Apoc. 17–18). Clearly we are in the period immediately after
the capture of Constantinople in 1204 by the Crusaders.

The strange thing is that Neophytos says at the beginning of his work
that he had "only just heard of the Apocalypse of St John the Theologian"
(*Prol.* 1). Should we then assume that from 1152, the approximate year in
which he began his monastic career at the monastery of Koutzouvendi,
until the last years of his life, after 1204, Neophytos had no access in Cyprus
to the text of the Apocalypse? One solution would be for us to surmise that
what is said in 11.19 and in the Epilogue about Constantinople are additions
made in the final transcription of the text in Parisinus gr. 1189, and that the
major part of the work belongs to an earlier period in Neophytos's life. In
the absence, however, of any other serious reasons for doubting the unity of
the text, we should not be hasty in accepting this conjecture.[6] However

---

[6] What is said by I. Tsiknopoullos, "Τὸ συγγραφικὸν ἔργον τοῦ ἁγίου Νεοφύτου",
KS 22 (1958), p. 89, namely, that the work was written by the saint at the age of 36 because
the orthography is very poor, cannot stand because it is the copyist who is responsible for the
orthography and not Neophytos, who in any case never spelled correctly throughout his life.

strange it may seem, we should accept that the text of the Apocalypse of St John – a book not read liturgically in the East – was in the twelfth and thirteenth centuries extremely rare in Cyprus. This fact is indicative not only of the production of books and the state of ecclesiastical libraries in Cyprus in the island's last years of Byzantine rule but also of the conservatism of an island Church and of the preservation there of a more ancient order, even in the matter of the canon itself of the New Testament.[7]

As is well-known, the Apocalypse was the last book to be received into the canon of the New Testament in the East. Thus although it is included in the table of the thirty-ninth Epistle of Athanasius (AD 367) and was accepted by Epiphanius of Cyprus (died AD 403), it was rejected by the great Antiochenes, Chrysostom and Theodoret, and by the three Cappadocians. The Quinisextum Council (AD 692) includes the Apocalypse in the first list of canonical books which it published but omits it from the second. The so-called *Stichometria of Nikephoros* in the ninth century does not yet refer clearly to the Apocalypse as canonical, and only a very small number of Byzantine manuscripts dating from before the eleventh century preserve the text of the book in its original state. According to Joseph Schmid,[8] the situation begins to change slowly from the tenth and eleventh centuries.[9] In Cyprus, however, we can see that in the second half of the twelfth century the dominant situation was still the older, early Byzantine one. As we shall see below, the text of the Apocalypse which Neophytos finally found and used was that which is preserved in the eleventh-century Codex Parisinus Coislinianus 256.

The fact that at the end of his "exposition" the Recluse thought it relevant to add "an apology for those who doubt" the apostolic origin of the book must be set within this wider context.

III. SOURCES

A reading of Neophytos's commentary on the Apocalypse leaves the student in a quandary: although in the vast majority of cases it is evident that the Recluse did not have in front of him any exegetical aid from an earlier age,

---

[7] The conservative character of the Church of Cyprus, which arose from its isolation, was already stressed by Norbert Cappuyns in his study, "Le Synodicon de Chypre au XIIe siècle", Βυζάντιον 10 (1935), pp. 487–504: "... l'indépendence ecclésiastique, qui depuis le cinquième siècle isolait l'île des autre chrétientés orientales" (p. 487), "... une église repliée sur elle-même et peu exposée à subir l' influence du dehors" (p. 504).

[8] *Studien zur Geschichte des griechischen Apocalypse-Textes, 2. Teil: Die alten Stämme*, Munich, 1955, pp. 31ff.

[9] Besides Schmid, see H.B. Stonehouse, *The Apocalypse in the Ancient Church*, London, 1929; H. von Campenhausen, *Die Entstehung der christlichen Bibel*, ch. vi; W.G. Kümmel, *Einleitung in das Neue Testament*, §. 36.

it nevertheless becomes obvious that in a number of other cases the author does draw his interpretations from older commentators. Thus already in 1.1, in his exposition of Apoc. 1:9, "I was on the island called Patmos", he writes: "that is … I was exiled by the Emperor Domitian to the island of Patmos".[10] And in his exposition in 7.2 of the number of the beast in Apoc. 13:8, he gives without attribution the ancient interpretation of Irenaeus, ΕΥΑΝΘΑΣ, ΛΑΤΕΙΝΟΣ, ΤΕΙΤΑΝ,[11] adding then a fourth also, the Byzantine ΒΕΝΕΔΙΚΤΟΣ, from the anti-Greek Pope Benedict VIII (1012–24), with whom, according to an Eastern tradition, the schism between Constantinople and Rome began during the patriarchate of Sergios II (1001–19).[12] Moreover, in 7.3, 10.12, 10.13 and 12.4, where he identifies Muhammad with the false prophet, he gives another common Byzantine folk interpretation. That Neophytos did not possess the old Greek commentaries of Andrew of Caesarea[13] and Arethas[14] or, very probably, of Oikoumenios[15] is beyond any doubt. Assuredly he would simply have possessed certain scholia on the Apocalypse.

As a matter of fact there survives today from the library of the Recluse, in fols. 207v–228 of the eleventh-century Coisl. gr. 256, a copy of the Apocalypse with scholia in the margin which, according to a note on fol. 228, belonged to the Recluse of Cyprus.[16] This, we must suppose, was the very copy of the Apocalypse which Neophytos discovered towards the end of his life and on which he based his own arrangement and scholia.

Unfortunately, it has not been possible for me to examine this manuscript personally. Mgr R. Devreesse, in the catalogue of the Coislinian codices compiled by him, notes concerning the text of the Apocalypse in his description of no. 256 that it is given "with certain marginal scholia; the last of these (fol. 226) bears the name of St Irenaeus (M. 7, 1222 B1–1223)" (this relates to the interpretation of Irenaeus mentioned above), but he informs us that the text is mutilated both at the beginning and at the end. I estimate that the surviving text does not go beyond Apoc. 15. In a letter to me dated 11 June 1977, Mme Gilberte Astruc-Morize of the Institut de Recherche et d'Histoire des Textes of the CNRS kindly informed me as follows:

---

[10] On the problem of the dating of the Apocalypse to the reign of Domitian or that of Nero see J.A.T. Robinson, *Relating the New Testament*, London, 1976, ch. viii.

[11] *Adv. Haereses* V, 30, 3.

[12] See *CMH* IV: I. *Byzantium and its Neighbours*, Cambridge, 1966, p. 458.

[13] *PG* 106 and J. Schmid, op. cit., *I. Teil: Der Apocalypse-Kommentar des Andreas von Kaisareia, Text*, Munich, 1955, *Einleitung*, Munich, 1956.

[14] *PG* 106 and J. Schmid, *Der Apocalypsetext des Arethas von Kaisareia und einiger anderer jüngerer Gruppen*, Athens, 1936.

[15] H.C. Hoskier, *The Complete Commentary of Oecumenius on the Apocalypse*, Michigan, 1928.

[16] See R. Devreesse, *Le Fonds Coislin*, Paris, 1945, p. 234.

"The number of scholia is not very important, and yet certain of them occupy a relatively large place in the margins (the text is unfortunately sometimes damaged where the leaves have been bumped together). With the exception of the scholion on folio 226, identified by Devreesse, the scholia are found essentially on folios 209ᵛ to 213 and the longer ones on folios 212ᵛ–213. I have easily been able to verify which part of the text was glossed in this way: Apocalypse 3:17 to 6:6 (in a discontinuous manner!). On folios 217ᵛ, 219ᵛ–220 one can make out in the margin some indications of the subject treated but these are no longer, properly speaking, scholia."

The evident difficulty which Neophytos had in interpreting his text is explained in this way.

For the New Testament scholar perhaps the most interesting question is that of the type of text exhibited by the Apocalypse of the Codex Coislinianus. I regret to say that under the present conditions in Cyprus this is another question to which I cannot reply in detail. Coisl. gr. 256 is placed by K. Aland under no. 2048.[17] Among the types of text distinguished by Joseph Schmid in the second volume of the work already mentioned, our text undoubtedly belongs to K (the common, or Alpha, text of Kenyon and Colwell).[18] We have here a manuscript of little value, one of the *plerique codices graeci* of the modern New Testament editions. In the third edition of the *Greek New Testament* of the United Bible Societies,[19] reference is made only once, I believe, to 2048, at Apoc. 13:10, where its singular reading is given: "ἀποκτενεῖ αὐτόν". If the strict approach of E.C. Colwell[20] were to be followed, not even this reference should have been made.

IV. ORIGINALITY AND VALUE

In the actual Prologue to the work the Recluse declares that his sole aim is to distinguish the fourteen topics into which the Apocalypse is divided, and secondly "to elucidate some of the difficulties with the help of the Spirit" (*Prol.* 1). He goes on to stress something often repeated by him, namely, that the sacred author "has condescended to write in a plain style" (*Prol.* 2) on account of the lower spiritual level of the faithful to whom he has addressed his book,

---

[17] *Kurzgefasste Liste der griechischen Handschriften des Neuen Testaments*, Berlin, 1963, p. 168.

[18] See also A. Merk (ed.), *Novum Testamentum*, Rome, 1964, p. 36*, where 2048 is marked as belonging to *recensio* K.

[19] Wurtemburg, 1975.

[20] 20. *Studies in Methodology in Textual Criticism of the New Testament*, Leiden, 1969, ch. viii: Method in Evaluating Scribal Habits, and ch. xi: 'Hort redivivus'.

and he concludes the Prologue with a prayer to Christ that he might be forgiven the fact that for the sake of achieving concision and clarity he will abbreviate and arrange some matters in the sacred text, adding that "I shall do as the Spirit illuminates the eye of my understanding" (*Prol.* 3) – a well-known topos of the prologues of theological works.

In the apologetic appendix at the end of the commentary Neophytos returns to the matters raised in the Prologue, giving a precise summary of the work he has completed:

> "and I too with supplication and fear have passed by what seems to be superfluous and with the help of God have opened up a little those things which are obscure to make them easier to understand. And you who read this with discretion, grant pardon, next after God, to my praise-worthy audacity" (*Apol.* 1).

Under the conditions of time and place in which Neophytos lived, this work can truly only be described as audacious. It is also well known that Neophytos's embarking on the composition of homilies and encomia provoked the scandal of 1176 which all but destroyed him:

> "How did this fellow dare to write, *asked the narrow-minded people around him,* seeing that the Apostle said that 'if anyone preaches a version of the Gospel to you different from the one I have preached to you, let him be anathema' (Gal.1:8)?"[21]

Now after 1204, towards the end of his life and his career as a writer, the undertaking of the Recluse is even more surprising because he dares to approach the inspired biblical text itself. His apology would have been the same as in 1176:

> "How is it that you are attempting to speak about those things which are beyond your powers? Pay heed, questioner, and understand my meaning. For I believe that not only I and those who like me are ignorant but also those to whom the grace of theology was given did not speak for this reason, so as to embellish that which transcends embellishment. For they know that they are proved to be unequal to the value of these things in great measure when they celebrate divine matters. Nevertheless,

---

[21] Paris. gr. 1189, fol. 137ᵛ (*Encomium on St Diomedes*): Πῶς οὗτος κατετόλμησε γράψαι, διηρωτῶντο οἱ περὶ αὐτὸν στενοκέφαλοι, τοῦ Ἀποστόλου εἰπόντος ὅτι, Εἴ τις ὑμᾶς εὐαγγελίσεται παρ᾽ ὃ ἡμεῖς εὐηγγελισάμεθα, ἀνάθεμα ἔστω; See H. Delehaye, "Saints de Chypre", *AB* 26 (1907), pp. 161–301, esp. pp. 217–8.

none of them shrank back from speaking that which he understood according to what he could attain ... . Which is a wonderful and great thing, that not to angels and archangels was such a grace given, but rather to men; for this is so that the lover of men might show how much honour he has granted to the human race; and this was so that he might worthily crown those who have been saved, and justly condemn those who have not been saved, since they are of the same nature but have no share in the same grace, either through lack of belief or through evil deeds."[22]

Throughout the long history of the Church the true monastic spirit has always sided with those given to bolder thought, greater incisiveness and more forceful argumentation, from Symeon the New Theologian to Gregory Palamas and the holy hesychasts of Mount Athos, and beyond them to Nil Sorski in fifteenth-century Russia and Nikodemos of the Holy Mountain and the *kollyvades* in Turkish-held, eighteenth-century Greece.

For all the "praiseworthy audacity" of the Elder, however, with regard to the division and arrangement of the Apocalypse, his work as a scholiast on account of his lack of essential aids cannot be said to be distinguished by originality or even to rise above mediocrity. Neophytos's intellectual powers were formidable and his judgment was always most lucid. The only thing he lacked was a grounding in systematic grammatical studies and a suitable library. For these weaknesses Neophytos himself can hardly be considered responsible. They are related to the more general weaknesses of Byzantine Cyprus if not of the whole of the later Byzantine system, when education was concentrated almost entirely in the Imperial City.[23] As for Neophytos himself, the student

---

[22] Cod. Lesb. Leimon. 2, fol. 298 (*On the Annunciation*): Πῶς δὲ σὺ τὰ ὑπὲρ σε λέγειν ἐπιχειρεῖς; Πρόσχες, ὁ ἐρωτῶν, καὶ μάνθανέ μου τὴν ἔννοιαν. Οἶμαι γὰρ ὅτι οὐκ ἐγώ γε μόνον καὶ οἱ κατ᾽ ἐμὲ ἀμαθεῖς, ἀλλὰ καὶ οἷς ἐδέδοτο τῆς θεολογίας χάρις οὐ διὰ τοῦτο ἐλάλησαν, ὥστε κοσμῆσαι τὰ ὑπερκόσμια: ἴσασι γὰρ ὅτι πολλῷ τῷ μέτρῳ τῆς ἀξίας τῶν πραγμάτων ἥττονες ἀποδείκνυνται εἰς τὸ ἀνυμνῆσαι τὰ θεῖα: ἀλλ᾽ ὅμως οὐ παρῃτήσατο ἕκαστος κατὰ τὸ αὐτοῦ ἐφικτὸν λαλῆσαι τὰ νοηθέντα. ... Ὅπερ ἐστίν ἀξιοθαύμαστον πρᾶγμα καὶ μέγιστον, ὅτι οὐκ ἀγγέλοις ἢ ἀρχαγγέλοις ἡ τοιαύτη δέδοται χάρις, ἀλλὰ μᾶλλον ἀνθρώποις: τοῦτο μὲν, ἵνα δείξῃ ὁ φιλάνθρωπος ὅσης τιμῆς τὸ τῶν ἀνθρώπων γένος ἠξίωσεν: τοῦτο δέ, ἵνα τοὺς μὲν σωζομένους στεφανώσῃ ἀξίως, τοὺς δὲ μὴ σωζομένους καταδικάσῃ δικαίως, ὡς τῆς αὐτῆς φύσεως ὄντας καὶ τῆς αὐτῆς ἀμοιρήσαντας χάριτος, εἴτε δι᾽ ἀπιστίαν εἴτε διὰ φαυλότητα ἔργων. See E.M. Toniolo, "Omelie e Catechesi mariane inedite di Neofito il Recluso (1134–1220 c.)", *Marianum* 36 (1974), pp. 184–315, esp. p. 238, and my study on the *Commentary on the Twelve Dominical Feasts* by Neophytos the Recluse, translated as Chapter VI above.

[23] See J.M. Hussey, *Church and Learning in the Byzantine Empire, 867–1185*, London, 1937, *passim;* P. Lemerle, *Le premier humanisme byzantin*, Paris, 1971, *passim.*

can only express unbounded admiration at his energetic efforts to achieve an education not only for himself but also later for the monks under his care, to create a library in his monastery through the copying of manuscripts in the Hermitage or their purchase from outside and, more generally, to promote the skills and aesthetic development of the company around him. The austere troglodytic Hermitage was under Neophytos a garden of culture and of the pursuit of learning. Works, however, of such breadth as the exposition of a whole book of the New Testament surpassed if not the powers at least the capabilities of the Cypriot abbot. Nevertheless, the sense of personal honour with which he undertook to render even this most difficult book of the New Testament accessible to his companions and the spirit of boldness and critical inquiry which he brought to the task compel the student to accept the work with respect, honouring its execution and praising its intention.

Neophytos's undertaking was extremely difficult from every aspect, but also for reasons inherent in the book which he undertook to interpret. I do not of course intend to enter here into the history of the interpretation of the Apocalypse in the early Church,[24] or into modern exegetical researches and commentaries.[25] I shall simply note that the problem of the interpretation of the Apocalypse was set out in all its acuteness for us moderns in the third century by Origen's pupil, Dionysius of Alexandria. This much may be said, that the fragment of Dionysius's work *On the Promises*[26] preserved by Eusebius is regarded by Werner Kümmel "as a genuine historical argument offering a fully convincing proof that the Apocalypse could not have been written by the author of the Gospel and Epistles of John."[27] Dionysius's argument is based mainly on criteria of language and style. Immediately on reading the book, Neophytos also noticed, according to his own testimony, "the verbosity and pedestrian vocabulary, the great confusion of words and unseemliness" of the Apocalypse ("whether the confusion and unseemliness was there from the beginning or came about through being copied over the centuries I cannot say" *Epil.* 1), but he did not have at his disposal either the philological education of the ancient Alexandrian bishop or, of course, the tools of modern commentators.[28] In this respect his work was one of popularisation rather than of philological criticism.

---

[24] Cf. n. 9 above.

[25] A full bibliography is given by W.G. Kümmel, op. cit., ss. 33, 34. The classic Modern Greek commentary is that of P.I. Bratsiotes, Ἡ Ἀποκάλυψις τοῦ Ἰωάννου, Athens, 1950.

[26] *Hist. Eccl.* VII, 25, ed. Schwartz, *GCS* 9, 2.

[27] *Das Neue Testament; Geschichte der Erforschung seiner Probleme*, Marburg, 1970, part I, ch. 1

[28] On the language of the Apocalypse see J. Schmid, op. cit., II, pp. 173ff; R.H. Charles, *The Revelation of St John, ICC*, I, Edinburgh, 1920, cxvii–clix: "A Short Grammar of the Apocalypse"; G. Mussies, *The morphology of Koine Greek as Used in the Apocalypse of St. John*, Leiden, 1971.

Also surprising is Neophytos's boldness in transposing passages and whole chapters from their accepted position with a view to restoring the original order and sequence as he conceived it – an entirely modern skill, in which R. Bultmann excelled, even to the point of excess, with regard to the Fourth Gospel and R.H. Charles with regard to the Apocalypse. Thus, for example, the tenth topic, "*On the seven angels*", has been put together from Apoc. 16:2–21, 19:17–18 and 19:11–21.

Neophytos's hermeneutic method, moreover, is the so-called eclectic, combining the eschatological, when the content of the Apocalypse refers to the last days, with the historical, as it seeks to find in the Apocalypse the history of the Church and of the world. An example of the application of the second method is the interpretation of Apoc. 17–18, already mentioned, as foretelling the fall of Constantinople to the Latins.

The most "original", not to say the strangest, interpretation, however, is that given by Neophytos of the twelfth chapter of the Apocalypse on the sign of the woman clothed with the sun. So far as I know, in all the early Greek commentators the woman symbolises either the Church (Hippolytus, Irenaeus, Methodius, Andrew) or the Theotokos (Epiphanius, Oikoumenios, Arethas). A difficulty for the second interpretation is that the heavenly woman is represented as "in labour, crying out in the pangs of childbirth" (Apoc. 12:2), whereas in the teaching of the Church the Virgin's childbirth was without pain. Oikoumenios sidestepped the problem in his commentary by saying that the woman's pangs should not be taken literally and other theologians explained them as constituting a hint of the eschatological and soteriological pangs to come. Neophytos, expressing at the outset his difficulty in laying bare "the hidden and obscure" sign of the woman, writes:

> "Let no one be deceived in thinking that this is the Theotokos; it is, rather, the corrupt antitheotokos, the mother of the antichrist. For the true Theotokos gave birth to Christ our true God in the flesh, not in pain as the present one does but glorified and with her virginity preserved" (6.4).

That is to say, in order to avoid attributing the painful childbirth of Apoc. 12:2 to the holy Theotokos, he regards the woman clothed in the sun and the moon as an Antitheotokos and consequently her son as the Antichrist. From this position he attempts, entirely unsuccessfully now, to justify the persecution of the woman by the dragon as arising from the ignorance of the devil, and the taking up of the child to the Lord as happening by economy: "not as a beloved child was he seized up to the Lord but in order that the Christ-hating and lawless people should be given a leader after their own heart" (6.5). Nowhere else does Neophytos fall into such a great error. Should we reckon that the Apocalypse of Coislin. gr. 256 did not contain any scholion on Apoc. 12? Or that Neophytos's extreme anxiety not to diminish the greatness of the Theotokos led him temporarily astray? Even the saints sometimes speak from themselves and not from the Spirit. An ancient reader of the *Greater Panegyrike* noted in the cropped right-hand margin of fol. 68 of cod. Paris. gr. 1189:

> "I do not accept, Father, this exegesis of yours since it does not fit. For below it says that 'the dragon was enraged with the woman and went away to make war on the rest of her children, that is, all who obey God's commandments and bear witness for Jesus' (Apoc. 12:17). For this reason the exegesis is not correct but in my opinion *** seems *** the church of the orthodox... ."

With regard to Neophytos's opinion that in spite of linguistic differences, the Apocalypse belongs to John "through the highest degree of contemplation" (16.2), let it be said in passing that, apart from modern conservative commentators, this opinion was also held by Harnack, Zahn, Lohmeyer, Preisker, Schlatter and Stauffer.

On the language and style of the Recluse I do not think there is any need to say anything here.[29] Let it simply be noted that in this work Neophytos offers new words of his own coinage, speaking of λευσχημονούντοι ἄνθρωποι, for example, and σαλπιφόροι ἄγγελοι.

With regard to Neophytos's attitude towards the Prophet of Islam, we have already noted that in 7.3, 10.12, 10.13 and 12.4 Muhammad is identified with the false prophet who is the servant of the Antichrist. This is because "he taught ... the broad and easy path of perdition" (7.3) – the classic Byzantine accusation against the prophet of the Arab people.[30] More than that Neophytos does not say, stressing only this, that the final defeat of Islam and the divine judgment on Muhammad have already been decreed by God (10.13, 12.4).[31]

Of special interest to us is the reaction which is portrayed in this commentary of the lay monastic classes in Cyprus to the fall of Constantinople

[29] See I.P. Tsiknopoullos, "Ὁ λεξιλογικὸς πλοῦτος τοῦ Ἐγκλείστου ἁγίου Νεοφύτου, *KS* 20 (1956), pp. 97–171, "Συγγραφικὴ τέχνη καὶ Γραφικὸς πλοῦτος τοῦ ἁγίου Νεοφύτου", *KS* 23 (1959), pp. 57–184.

[30] On the Byzantine attitude to Islam see Eu. Sdrakas, Ἡ κατὰ τοῦ Ἰσλὰμ πολεμικὴ τῶν βυζαντινῶν θεολόγων, Thessaloniki, 1961; A.-Th. Khoury, *Der theologische Streit der Byzantiner mit dem Islam*, Paderborn, 1969; id., *Les théologiens byzantins et l' Islam. Textes et auteurs (VIII–XIII s.)*, Louvain–Paris, 1969; S. Vryonis, *The Decline of Medieval Hellenism in Asia Minor and the Process of Islamization from the Eleventh Through the Fifteenth Century*, Berkeley-Los Angeles-London, 1971, pp. 421–36. A. Giannoulatos, *Islam*, Athens, 1975, pp. 27–30.

[31] On 10.13 see Dante, *Inferno*, xxviii.

to the Crusaders in 1204. As I have already said, Neophytos refers to this
shocking event clearly in paragraph 11.19 and in the Epilogue. He also refers
to it elsewhere in his writings,[32] treating it as a just retribution from God for
the lawless deeds of the capital City. In what is said in the present work, however,
apart from Neophytos's known anti-Latin sentiments and passion for
Orthodoxy, there may be discerned, I think, a certain provincial anti-
Constantinopolitan animus. This phenomenon is well-known[33] and does not
come as a surprise to us, although in relation to the Cypriot monk it is worth
noting that in spite of the apparent bitterness there is no trace of *schadenfreude*
or indifference – sentiments which Niketas Choniates attributes to the inhabitants of the provinces after the fall of the capital. Moreover, the rhetorical
question of 11.19 shows that the general sentiment in Cyprus at the time of
the capture of the City by the Latins was one of exasperation, while the ironical
remarks in *Epil.* 1 on the many monasteries, the gold- and silver-covered icons,
the psalmody and the orderliness of the City are expressive of the spirit of
Neophytos, who represents the tradition of hesychasm, with its love of poverty
and non-possessiveness, rather than that of the great coenobia, with its love
of acquisition.

A little before the "exposition" of the Apocalypse by Neophytos there
died in the West one of his greatest monastic contemporaries, the Cistercian
hermit, Joachim of Fiore (*c.*1132–1202).[34] His mystical teaching under the
name of the Eternal Gospel was expressed chiefly in his celebrated commentary,
Expositio in Apocalypsim. In this work the theory is put forward of the three
epochs in history: that of the Father (the period of the Law in the Old
Testament), that of the Son (the period of faith in the New Testament and
the Church) and that of the Spirit (the period of new inner illumination and
spiritual freedom). The greatest men of the age were entranced by the figure
of Joachim and his apocalyptic expectations. His commentary on the
Apocalypse exercised a decisive influence not only on the forerunners of the
Reformation but also on the reformers themselves and continues to influence
philosophical theory and religious sentiment in the West to the present day.[35]

The little work of our Recluse, of course, cannot be compared either in
profundity or in influence to the near-contemporary interpretation of the

---

[32] See e.g. cod. Paris. gr. 1189, fols 114 and 230.

[33] See Hélène Ahrweiler, *L' idéologie politique de l' empire byzantin*, Paris, 1975, pp. 87–102:
"Patriotisme provincial et attitude anticonstantinopolitaine".

[34] See F. Russo, *Bibliografia Gioachimita (Biblioteca di Bibliografia Italiana*, vol. 28), Florence,
1954; M.W. Bloomfield, "Joachim of Flora. A critical survey of his canon, teachings, sources,
biography and influence", *Tradition* 13 (1957), pp. 249–311.

[35] On the influence of Joachim on the "philosophy of history" in modern times see K. Löwith,
Meaning in History: The Theological Implications of the Philosophy of History, Cambridge, 1950, pp.
158–9 and Appendix I; E. Voeglin, *The New Science of Politics*, Chicago, 1952, pp. 110–21.

Apocalypse by Joachim. For even if Neophytos believed that from AD 1025 the world had entered into the last times and that the end would come in 1492, as we know from elsewhere[36] but can also see in 12.4, he never developed this belief into a historiological system – and this was in accordance with a common Byzantine tradition.[37]

V. MANUSCRIPT TRADITION

The text of Neophytos's Περὶ τῆς ᾽Αποκαλύψεως is preserved in a single manuscript: cod. Parisinus gr. 1189[38] (saec. XIII), fols. 57ᵛ–77ᵛ, which is the apograph,[39] bearing in the margin the autograph corrections of the author.

VI. THE EDITION

As long as we do not have before us cod. Coisl. gr. 256, which contains part of the text of the Apocalypse which Neophytos used for his work, the present edition, even though the *editio princeps* of the work, cannot be considered *sensu stricto* as definitive. (The same, however, may be said for all the old *editiones principes*!) For this reason I have not followed the already hallowed custom, in the case of a text preserved in a unique codex, of providing the entire orthography of the manuscript in the critical apparatus. As I. Tsiknopoullos has already observed,[40] the copyist of fols. 57–77ᵛ of the manuscript was evidently of low ability as far as orthography is concerned and it must be added that Neophytos was not distinguished as a careful corrector. Even though, as Alphonse Dain already informs us, "it goes without saying that the originals

---

[36] See cod. Coisl. gr. 287 (Commentary on the Dominical Commandments), fol. 85: ... καὶ ὁ παρὼν ἕβδομος αἰὼν τὰ τελευταῖα ἤδη βαδίζει, ἀδελφοί, ὡς ὁρᾶτε: ἒξ καί δέκα χρόνοι πρὸς τοῖς τριακοσίοις καταληφθέντες, ὡς ἄν εἴς τις καὶ σαφέστερον εἴποι. Παρῆλθεν ἡ ἐξάδα τῶν ἡμερῶν, καί εἰσῆλθεν ἡ ἑβδόμη, τουτέστι τὸ σάββατον: καί τοῦτο ἤδη παρῆλθε, τριῶν ὡρῶν καί στιγμῆς ἡμίσου καὶ μιᾶς καταλειφθείσης, καὶ νῦν ἐπιφώσκει ἡ ἐπιφανής καὶ μεγάλη ἐκείνη τοῦ κυρίου ἡμέρα. Cf. cod. Lesb. Leimon. 2, fol. 276.

[37] See Vasiliev, "Medieval Ideas of the End of the World", *Byzantion* 16 (1942–3), pp. 462–502; P.J. Alexander, "Historiens byzantins et croyances éschatologiques", *Actes du XIIe Congrès international d'Études Byzantines*, Belgrade, 1964, II, pp. 1–8.

[38] Analysis in: *Hagiographi Bollandiani* and H. Omont, *Catalogus codicum hagiographicorum in Bibl. Nation. Parisiensi*, Brussels, 1896, pp. 86–90; H. Delehaye in *AB* 26 (1907), pp. 279–97; A. Ehrhard, *Überlieferung und Bestand der hagiographischen und homiletischen Literatur der griechischen Kirche*, III, I Hälfte, Leipzig, 1943, pp. 681–2; I.P. Tsiknopoullos in *KS* 22 (1958), pp. 80–88; F. Halkin, *Manuscrits grecs de Paris, Inventaire hagiographique*, Paris, 1968, pp. 136–7.

[39] On this term see A. Dain, *Les manuscrits*, Paris, 1964, pp. 103–8, esp. p. 104.

[40] "Ἡ ὀρθογραφικὴ ἰδιομορφία τῶν συγγραφῶν τοῦ ᾽Εγκλείστου ᾽Αγίου Νεοφύτου", *KS* 19 (1955), pp. 43–72, esp. p. 57.

can be spoilt by the faults of every kind",[41] the fact nevertheless remains that
a serious deterioration of the text beyond the orthography (in which even
the Recluse does not excell[42]), is excluded at the outset. Only those variant
readings are given which are regarded as having critical value – that is, they
represent real changes – or are significant for the linguistic researcher of the
Cypriot dialect and pronunciation in the twelfth and thirteenth centuries.

Had I not been acquainted with Dain's notes,[43] I would have added that
I have respected for the great part the tradition of the Paris codex. I note
only that I have avoided, as far as possible, introducing corrections to make
the text more grammatical or more classical in expression, because I desired
to edit Neophytos, not to correct him. Conversely, I set myself the task not
of reproducing the manuscript but of editing the text of the codex.

With regard to the typographical presentation, the prevailing rules of
editing patristic commentaries of a continuous type are rendered inapplic-
able by the character of Neophytos's *Exposition*: the text of the Apocalypse
which Neophytos presents is not the biblical text which he had before him
but his own arrangement of it. This means that the modern editor is not
presented with biblical passages or allusions to biblical passages and therefore
cannot print these texts in a different fount. Nor is it reasonable for him to
do this: the biblical scholar who desires to examine the biblical text used by
Neophytos has only to turn to Coislinianus 256. Accordingly I have simply
enclosed the text of the fourteen topics within quotation marks, making an
exception only of those passages which begin explicitly with ἤτοι or δηλονότι.
For the remaining biblical references and allusions I have strictly observed
the prevailing custom.[44]

---

[41] Op. cit., p. 106.

[42] See I.P. Tsiknopoullos, "Η ὀρθογραφικὴ" – a study which must be used with extreme
caution.

[43] Op. cit., p. 173, "Respecter la tradition".

[44] I should like to express my gratitude above all to Mme Gilberte Astruc-Morize, of the
French National Centre for Scientific Research, for the information which she kindly sent
to me in respect of cod. Paris. gr. 1189 and Coisl. gr. 256.

ΝΕΟΦΥΤΟΥ ΠΡΕΣΒΥΤΕΡΟΥ ΜΟΝΑΧΟΥ ΚΑΙ ΕΓΚΛΕΙΣΤΟΥ

[Fol. 57ᵛ]ΠΕΡΙ ΤΗΣ ΑΠΟΚΑΛΥΨΕΩΣ ΤΟΥ ΑΓΙΟΥ ΙΩΑΝΝΟΥ ΤΟΥ
ΘΕΟΛΟΓΟΥ ΣΑΦΗΝΕΙΑ ΔΙΑ ΒΡΑΧΕΩΝ

<Prologus>

1. Μόλις περιτυχὼν ἦν εἶχον ἐξ ἀκοῆς Ἀποκάλυψιν τοῦ ἁγίου Ἰωάννου
τοῦ Θεολόγου, καὶ διελθὼν αὐτήν, ἐν ἑνὶ μὲν ὁρμαθῷ λόγου ἐφεῦρον
αὐτὴν συγκειμένην, ἔγνων δὲ αὐτὴν εἰς δεκατέσσαρας ὑποθέσεις
ὑποδιαιρουμένην, ἃς καὶ διακρῖναι σὺν Θεῷ προειλόμην, οὐ μὴν δέ, ἀλλὰ
5 καί τινα τῶν δυσλήπτων πνευματοδότως ἀνακαλῦψαι.
2. Οὗτος γοῦν ὁ τοῦ Χριστοῦ ἐπιστήθιος Ἰωάννης ὁ Θεολόγος, ὁ καὶ
τῆς Ἀποκαλύψεως ταύτης εἰσηγητής, ξένα μὲν καὶ οὐράνια ἤκουσε καὶ
εἶδεν ἐν τῇ Ἀποκαλύψει, πεζολογίαν δὲ εἰς τὰ πολλὰ κατεδέξατο λέγειν.
Εἰ δὲ αἰτία, ὡς ἔοικεν, <ζητεῖται,> ἡ τοῦ τότε λαοῦ ἀγροικία αἴτιος· ὁ
0 γὰρ λέγων, οὐ λέγει, πολλάκις, ὡς βούλεται, ἀλλὰ καθὼς ὁ ἀκούων δύναται
ἀκούειν· ἔνθεν καὶ πολλοὶ συμψελλίζουσι τοῖς νηπίοις, διὰ τὸ αὐτῶν
ἀτελές. Διὰ τοῦτο, οἶμαι, καὶ ὁ πυρίγλωσσος οὗτος ἐν τῇ ἀποκαλύψει
ταύτῃ πεζολογεῖν κατεδέξατο.
Fol. 58 **3.** Ἐμοὶ δὲ τῷ ἀμαθεῖ καὶ παντελῶς ἀπαιδεύτῳ, | Χριστέ
5 βασιλεῦ, λιταῖς τοῦ Θεολόγου καὶ ἀγαπητοῦ σου Ἰωάννου, μὴ ἔστω
ἔγκλημα, εἴ γε καταλείψω τι διὰ τὸ εὐσύνοπτον, ἢ παραμείψω τι πρὸς
τὸ εὔληπτον, ἢ σαφηνίσω τι πρὸς τὸ εὐδιάλυτον, ὅτι οὐχ ὡς ὑπέρφρων,
ἀλλ' ὡς τῶν τοῦ Ἁγίου σου Πνεύματος ῥήσεων ζηλωτής, δράσω καθὼς
μοι αὐτὸ δαδουχήσει τὸ ὄμμα τῆς διανοίας.

2, 8 πεζολογίαν scripsi : παιζολογίαν cum ε supra lin. m. sec. cod.   9 ζητεῖται suppleui
13 πεζολογεῖν scripsi παιζολογεῖν cum ε supra lin. m. sec. cod.

Apoc.1–3 **1.** Ὑπ(όθεσις) Α΄. Πε(ρὶ) τῶν ἐν τῇ Ἀσίᾳ ἑπτὰ ἐκκλησιῶν.

«Ἐγὼ Ἰωάννης, ὁ ἀδελφὸς ὑμῶν καὶ κοινωνὸς ἐν τῇ θλίψει καὶ βασιλείᾳ δι᾽ ὑπομονῆς ἐν Χριστῷ Ἰησοῦ, ὅς ἐστι τὸ Ἄλφα καὶ τὸ Ὦ, ἡ ἀρχή καὶ τὸ τέλος, ὃς ἔρχεται μετὰ τῶν νεφελῶν, καὶ ὄψεται αὐτὸν πᾶς ὀφθαλμός,

5 καὶ οἵτινες αὐτὸν ἐξεκέντησαν, καὶ κόψονται ἐπ᾽ αὐτὸν πᾶσαι αἱ φυλαὶ τῆς γῆς, ἐγενόμην ἐν τῇ νήσῳ τῇ καλουμένῃ Πάτμῳ,» ἤτοι διὰ τὸν λόγον τοῦ Θεοῦ ἐξωρίσθην ὑπὸ Δομετιανοῦ βασιλέως ἐν τῇ νήσῳ Πάτμῳ, «ἐν ᾗ καὶ ἐν ἡμέρᾳ κυριακῇ ἐγενόμην ἐν πνεύματι,» ἤτοι ἐν ἐκστάσει, «καὶ ἤκουσα ὀπίσω μου φωνὴν μεγάλην λέγουσαν, Γράψον ὃ βλέπεις καὶ πέμψον

10 ταῖς ἑπτὰ ἐκκλησίαις, εἰς Ἔφεσον καὶ εἰς τὰς λοιπάς. Κἀγὼ ἐπιστρέψας ἰδεῖν πόθεν ἡ φωνὴ καὶ τίς ὁ λαλῶν μετ᾽ ἐμοῦ, ἑπτὰ λυχνίας εἶδον χρυσᾶς, καὶ ἐν μέσῳ αὐτῶν υἱὸν ἀνθρώπου, ἐνδεδυμένον ποδήρη καὶ περιεζωσμένον πρὸς τοῖς μαζοῖς ζώνην χρυσῆν· αἱ δὲ τρίχες τῆς κεφαλῆς αὐτοῦ λευκαὶ ὡσεὶ χιών, καὶ οἱ ὀφθαλμοὶ αὐτοῦ ὡς φλὸξ πυρός, καὶ οἱ πόδες αὐτοῦ

15 ὥσπερ χαλκολιβάνῳ ἐν κα Fol. 58ᵛ| μίνῳ πεπυρωμένοι, καὶ ἡ φωνὴ αὐτοῦ ὡς φωνὴ ὑδάτων πολλῶν ἐν δὲ τῇ δεξιᾷ αὐτοῦ χειρὶ ἀστέρες ἑπτά, καὶ ἐκ τοῦ στόματος αὐτοῦ ῥομφαία δίστομος ὀξεῖα ἐκπορευομένη, καὶ ἡ ὄψις αὐτοῦ ὡς ἥλιος φαίνων ἐν τῇ δυνάμει αὐτοῦ.

2.»Καὶ ὅτε ταῦτα εἶδον, ἔπεσον πρὸς τοὺς πόδας αὐτοῦ ὡς νεκρός·

20 ὁ δέ, τὴν αὐτοῦ δεξιὰν ἐπιθεὶς ἐπ᾽ ἐμέ, λέγοι μοι, Μὴ φοβοῦ· ἐγώ εἰμι ὁ πρῶτος καὶ ὁ ἔσχατος καὶ ὁ ζῶν, ἐγενόμην δὲ νεκρὸς καὶ ἰδοὺ ζῶ εἰς τοὺς αἰῶνας, ἔχω δὲ τὰς κλεῖς τοῦ θανάτου καὶ τοῦ ᾅδου. Σὺ δὲ γράψον ἃ βλέπεις καὶ ἃ μετὰ ταῦτα μέλλει γενέσθαι. Τὸ δὲ μυστήριον ὃ εἶδες, ἑπτὰ λυχνίας χρυσᾶς, αἱ ἑπτὰ εἰσιν ἐκκλησίαι, οἱ δὲ ἑπτὰ ἀστέρες οἱ ἐν

25 τῇ δεξιᾷ μου οἱ ἑπτὰ εἰσιν ἄγγελοι τῶν ἐκκλησιῶν.

3.»Γράψον δὲ τῷ ἐν Ἐφέσῳ ἀγγέλῳ τῆς ἐκκλησίας·

Τάδε λέγει ὁ περιπατῶν ἐν μέσῳ τῶν ἑπτὰ λυχνιῶν καὶ τοὺς ἑπτὰ ἀστέρας κρατῶν ἐν τῇ δεξιᾷ αὐτοῦ· Οἶδα τὰ ἔργα σου καὶ τὴν ὑπομονήν σου καὶ τὸ κόπον σου, ὅτι ἐπείρασας τοὺς λέγοντας ἑαυτοὺς ἀποστόλους

30 καὶ εὗρες αὐτοὺς ψευδεῖς· καὶ ἔδειξας ὑπομονὴν διὰ τὸ ὄνομά μου, καί οὐκ ἐκοπίασας. Ἀλλά ἔχω τι κατὰ σοῦ, ὅτι τὴν ἀγάπην σου τὴν πρώτην ἀφῆκες. Ἀλλά μνημόνευσον πόθεν ἐκπέπτωκας, καὶ μετανόησον καὶ τὰ πρῶτα σου ἔργα ποίησον· εἰ δὲ μή, ἔρχομαί σοι ταχύ, ἐὰν μὴ μετανοήσῃς, καὶ κινήσω τὴν λυχνίαν σου ἐκ τοῦ τόπου αὐτῆς. Καλῶς δὲ ποιεῖς μισῶν

35 τὰ ἔργα τῶν Νικολαϊτῶν, ἃ κἀγώ Fol. 59| μισῶ» (cf. Apoc. 1,1–2,7).

4. Ἑρμ(ηνεία): Ἄγγελον λέγει τὸν ἐπίσκοπον τῆς ἐν Ἐφέσῳ ἐκκλησίας, ὃς τάχα ἐκ τῶν πρώτων ἔργων καὶ τῆς πίστεως χαυνωθείς. Ἀνάγει αὐτὸν μνημονεῦσαι πόθεν ἐκπέπτωκεν, καὶ ἐπαπειλεῖ αὐτὸν ἐξεῶσαι τῆς ἐκκλησίας, εἰ οὐ μετανοήσει.

40 **5.** «Καὶ τῷ ἀγγέλῳ,» ἤτοι τῷ ἐπισκόπῳ, «τῆς ἐν Σμύρνῃ ἐκκλησίας γράψον·

1, 13 τρίχες scripsi: τρίχαι cod.
2, 21 πρῶτος : ο supra lin. corr. recens
3, 26 α΄ in margine 33/34 ἐὰν—λυχνίαν in rasura μὴ [.αιχ] μετανοήσῃς καὶ [τοῦτ] κινήσω cod.
5, 40 β΄ in margine

Τάδε λέγει ὁ πρῶτος καὶ ὁ ἔσχατος καὶ ⟨ὁ⟩ νεκρὸς καὶ ζῶν· Οἶδα σου τὰ ἔργα καὶ τὴν θλῖψιν καὶ τὴν πτωχείαν, ἀλλὰ πλούσιος εἶ. Ἀπὸ δὲ τῶν λεγόντων εἶναι Ἰουδαίους, καὶ οὐκ εἰσὶν ἀλλὰ συναγωγὴ τοῦ Σατανᾶ, μηδὲν φοβηθῇς· μέλλουσι γὰρ τινὲς ἐξ ὑμῶν ἐκ διαβολικοῦ πειρασμοῦ βληθῆναι εἰς φυλακὴν ἡμέρας δέκα. Γίνου πιστὸς μέχρι θανάτου, καὶ δώσω σοι τὸν στέφανον τῆς ζωῆς» (cf. Apoc. 2,8-11).

6. Ἑρμηνεία: Προσεπήνεσε τῷ ἐπισκόπῳ τῆς ἐν Σμύρνῃ ἐκκλησίας, καὶ προδεδήλωκε τὴν ἐξ Ἰουδαίων κατ᾽ αὐτοῦ σκαιωρίαν, ἣν καὶ συναγωγὴν ἐκάλεσεν τοῦ Σατανᾶ.

7. «Γράψον δέ, φησί, καὶ τῷ ἀγγέλῳ τῆς ἐν Περγάμῳ ἐκκλησίας·
Οἶδα σου τὰ ἔργα, καὶ ὅτι κατοικεῖς ὅπου ἐστὶν ὁ θρόνος τοῦ Σατανᾶ, κρατεῖς δὲ τὸ ὄνομά μου καὶ οὐκ ἠρνήσω τὴν πίστιν μου. Ἔχω δὲ κατὰ σοῦ ὀλίγα τινά, ὅτι ἀνέχει τινῶν κρατούντων τὴν διδαχὴν τῶν Νικολαϊτῶν. Μετανοείτωσαν οὖν· εἰ δὲ μή, ἔρχομαι πολεμῆσαι αὐτοὺς ἐν τῇ ῥομφαίᾳ τοῦ στόματός μου. Τῷ δὲ νικῶντι,» δηλονότι τοὺς εἰδωλολάτρας, Fol. 59ᵛ| «δώσω αὐτῷ τοῦ μάννα τοῦ κεκρυμμένου, καὶ ψῆφον λευκὴν καὶ ἐν τῇ ψήφῳ ὄνομα καινὸν γεγραμμένον ὃ οὐδεὶς οἶδεν εἰ μὴ ὁ λαβὼν» (cf. Apoc. 2,12-17).

8. Ἑρμ(ηνεία): Τάχα ἐν τῇ ⟨ἐν⟩ Περγάμῳ ἐκκλησίᾳ ἔτι ἐπλεονέκτει εἰδωλικὸν θυσιαστήριον, διὸ καὶ θρόνος ἐκλήθη τοῦ Σατανᾶ. Τῷ δὲ ἐπισκόπῳ ἐπαινετὰ μὲν τὰ κατ᾽ αὐτόν, φαῦλα δὲ τὰ τῶν εἰδωλολατρῶν καὶ τὰ τῶν Νικολαϊτῶν· εἷς γὰρ τῶν ἐν ταῖς Πράξεσιν ἑπτὰ διακόνων ὁ Νικόλαος, ἐκπεσὼν τῆς ἑπτάδος, ὡς καὶ Ἰούδας τῆς δωδεκάδος, οἱ ⟨δὲ⟩ τῆς αὐτοῦ αἱρέσεως κοινωνοὶ Νικολαῗται καλοῦνται, οὓς ὁ νικῶν καὶ τὴν εἰς Χριστὸν πίστιν κρατῶν, καταξιωθῆναι ὑπισχνεῖται τοῦ μάννα τοῦ κεκρυμμένου καὶ τῆς λευκῆς ψήφου τῆς γεγραμμένης ὄνομα καινόν, ἃ ἐστι τεκμήρια τῆς γλυκύτητος ⟨τῆς⟩ τοῦ Ἁγίου Πνεύματος μετουσίας, καὶ τῆς ἀφράστου ζωῆς ἀπόλαυσις.

9. «Καὶ τῷ ἀγγέλῳ τῆς ἐν Θυατείροις ἐκκλησίας γράψον·
Τάδε λέγει ὁ Υἱὸς τοῦ Θεοῦ, ὁ τοὺς ὀφθαλμοὺς ἔχων ὡς φλόγα πυρός, καὶ τοὺς πόδας ὁμοίους χαλκολιβάνῳ· Οἶδα σου τὰ ἔργα καὶ τὴν πίστιν καὶ τὴν ἀγάπην, ἀλλ᾽ ἔχω τι κατὰ σοῦ, ὅτι ἀνέχει τῇ γυναικί σου Ἰεζάβελ προφήτιδα ἑαυτὴν ὀνομάζειν, τοὺς ἐμοὺς δούλους διδάσκουσα καὶ πλανῶσα τοῦ πορνεῦσαι καὶ φαγεῖν εἰδωλόθυτα. Καὶ μακροθυμῶ αὐτῇ ἵνα μετανοήσῃ. Καί, εἰ οὐ μετανοήσει, ἰδοὺ βάλλω αὐτὴν εἰς κλίνην, καὶ οὓς ἀπεπλάνησεν εἰς θλῖψιν μεγάλην. Καὶ τὰ τέκνα αὐτῆς ἀποκτενῶ ἐν θανάτῳ· καὶ γνώσονται πᾶσαι Fol. 60| ⟨αἱ⟩ ἐκκλησίαι ὅτι ἐγώ εἰμι ὁ ἐρευνῶν καρδίας καὶ νεφρούς, καὶ δώσω ὑμῖν κατὰ τὰ ἔργα ὑμῶν» (cf. Apoc. 2,18-29).

10. Ἑρμ(ηνεία): Οὗτος ὁ Θυατείρων ἐπίσκοπος ὑπογύναιος ἦν· ἡ δὲ γυνὴ αὐτοῦ ἐκέκλητο Ἰεζάβελ, τῆς τοῦ Ἀχαὰβ Ἰεζάβελ μηδὲν ἀποδέουσα

8, 63/64 cf. Act. 6,5
10, 81 cf. III Reg. 16, 31; cf. IV Reg. 22

5, 42 ὁ addidi   47 τὸν scripsi : τὸ cod.
7, 51 γ΄ in margine
8, 60 ἐν addidi   64 δὲ addidi   68 τῆς addidi
9, 70 δ΄ in margine   76 βάλλω scripsi : βάλω cod.   78 αἱ restitui
10, 80 ἑρμ(ηνεία) in marg. cod.

τῷ τρόπῳ καὶ τῇ κλήσει. Ἐκ διαβολικῆς δὲ ἐνεργουμένη γλώττης πολλοὺς
τῶν πιστῶν, ὡς προφῆτις δῆθεν, ἀπεπλάνα μοιχεύειν καὶ προσανέχειν
εἰδώλοις· πρὸς ἣν καὶ δεδήλωται ὅτι, εἰ οὐ μετανοήσει, αὐτήν τε καὶ τὰ
85   τέκνα αὐτῆς καὶ οὓς ἀπεπλάνησεν ὀλεθρίῳ παραδοθῆναι θανάτῳ.
    11. «Καὶ τῷ ἀγγέλῳ, φησί, τῆς ἐν Σάρδεσιν ἐκκλησίας γράψον·
Τάδε λέγει ὁ ἔχων τοὺς ἑπτὰ ἀστέρας καὶ τὰ ἑπτὰ πνεύματα τοῦ
Θεοῦ» (Apoc. 3,1).
    12. Ἑρμ(ηνεία): Ἐνυπόστατον καὶ τέλειόν ἐστι τὸ Πνεῦμα τὸ ἅγιον,
90   ὡς ὁ Πατὴρ καὶ ὁ Υἱός· πνεύματα δὲ ἑπτὰ εἰσι τὰ ἑπτὰ τοῦ Ἁγίου
Πνεύματος χαρίσματα, ἤτουν πνεῦμα σοφίας καὶ συνέσεως,
πνεῦμα βουλῆς καὶ ἰσχύος, πνεῦμα γνώσεως καὶ εὐσεβείας
καὶ πνεῦμα φόβου Θεοῦ, ἃ ἐπανεπαύθησαν εἰς Χριστόν, λαβόντα
τὴν τοῦ δούλου μορφήν, καθὼς καὶ νῦν λέγει ὁ «ἔχων τὰ ἑπτὰ πνεύματα
95   τοῦ Θεοῦ».
    13. «Οἶδα σου τὰ ἔργα, ὅτι ὄνομα μὲν ἔχεις καὶ ζῇς, νεκρὸς δὲ εἶ.
Γρηγόρησον οὖν καὶ μνημόνευσον τί εἴληφας, καὶ μετανόησον. Εἰ δὲ μή,
ἥξω πρὸς σὲ ὡς κλέπτης, καὶ οὐ μὴ γνῷς τὴν ὥραν ἐν ᾗ ἥξω ἐπὶ σέ.
Ἔχεις δὲ ἐν Σάρδεσιν ὀνόματα ὀλιγοστὰ ἃ οὐκ ἐμόλυναν τὰ ἱμάτια αὐτῶν,
100   καί, ἀξίως λευσχημονοῦντες, περιπατήσουσι μετ' ἐμοῦ, καὶ τὸ ὄνομα αὐτῶν
οὐ μὴ ἐξᾷ Fol. 60ᵛ‖ λειφθῇ ἐκ τῆς βίβλου τῆς ζωῆς» (cf. Apoc. 3,2–6).
    14. Ἑρμ(ηνεία): Οὗτος γὰρ ὁ τῆς Σαρδέων ἐκκλησίας ἐπίσκοπος, ὡς
τὰ λόγια προδηλοῦσιν, νεκρὸς ἦν τῇ πίστει καὶ τοῖς ἔργοις· διὸ καὶ
δεδήλωται αὐτῷ ὅτι, εἰ οὐ διορθωθῇ ἐξάπινα θνήσκει. Ὀλίγους δέ τινας
105   τῆς αὐτοῦ ἐκκλησίας, μὴ μολυνθέντας εἰς ἁμαρτίαν μετὰ τὸ βάπτισμα,
ἀλλὰ λευσχημονοῦντας τῇ καθαρότητι, ὁ ὑπερκάθαρος Χριστὸς ὑπισχνεῖται
σὺν αὐτῷ βηματίζειν. Ὄντως μακάριον χρῆμα ἡ καθαρότης, ὡς ἀγχίθεος
καὶ ἄφθαρτος.
    15. «Εἶτα καὶ τῷ ἀγγέλῳ τῆς ἐν Φιλαδελφείᾳ ἐκκλησίας γράψον·
110   Τάδε λέγει ὁ ἅγιος, ὁ ἀληθής, ὁ ἔχων τὴν κλεῖν Δαυίδ,» ἤτοι ὁ ἐκ
φυλῆς Δαυίδ καὶ μείζων Δαυίδ· «Οἶδα σου τὰ ἔργα καὶ ἀνέῳξά σοι θύραν,
ἣν οὐδεὶς δύναται κλεῖσαι, ὅτι ἐτήρησάς μου τὸν λόγον, καὶ οὐκ ἠρνήσω
μου τὸ ὄνομα. Ἐκ δὲ τῶν λεγόντων Ἰουδαίους εἶναι, καὶ οὐκ εἰσὶν ἀλλὰ
συναγωγὴ τοῦ Σατανᾶ, ποιήσω ἵνα ἥξουσι καὶ προσκυνήσουσιν ἐνώπιον
115   τῶν ποδῶν σου, καὶ γνώσονται ὅτι ἠγάπησά σε. Ὅτι ἐν ὑπομονῇ
ἐτήρησάς μου τὸν λόγον, κἀγώ σε τηρήσω ἐκ τῆς ὥρας τοῦ πειρασμοῦ

12, 91/93 Is. 11, 2–3

10, 84/85 αὐτήν τε …θανάτῳ: αὐτήν τε… ὀλέθριος εὑρήσει θάνατος uel quid
simile exspectes
11, 86 ε´ in margine
13, 100 λευσχημονοῦντες : λευχειμονοῦντες exspectes; cf. infra l. 106
14, 102 Σαρδέων : exspectes Σαρδιανῶν uel Σάρδεων   103 ἦν scripsi : εἶ cod. cum ν
m. sec. supra lin.   106 λευσχυμονοῦντας cod; cf. supra l. 100
15, 109 ς´ in margine   114 ἥξουσι καὶ προσκυνήσουσιν scripsi : ἥξωσι καὶ
προσκυνήσωσιν cod.

τοῦ μέλλοντος ἐλθεῖν ἐφ᾽ ὅλην τὴν οἰκουμένην. Διὸ κράτει ὃ ἔχεις, ἵνα
μηδεὶς λάβῃ τὸν στέφανόν σου» (cf. Apoc. 3,7–13).

16. Ἑρμ(ηνεία): Ἰδού, ὑπὲρ πάντας τοὺς ἐν τῇ Ἀσίᾳ ἐπισκόπους, ὁ
20 τῆς Φιλαδελφείας ἐπίσκοπος ὑπέρτερος καὶ καλὸς μεμαρτύρηται· διὸ καὶ
ἡ σατανικὴ τῶν Ἰουδαίων συναγωγὴ αὐτῷ προσκυνῆσαι Fol. 61 | δεδήλωται
καὶ ἐκ τοῦ καθολικοῦ πειρασμοῦ ἀπήμαντος τηρηθῆναι ἠξίωται.

17. «Καὶ τῷ ἀγγέλῳ, φησίν, τῆς ἐν Λαοδικείᾳ ἐκκλησίας γράψον·
Τάδε λέγει ὁ ἀμήν, ὁ μάρτυς ὁ ἀληθής, καὶ τῆς τοῦ Θεοῦ κτίσεως
25 δημιουργός· Οἶδα ὅτι οὔτε ψυχρὸς εἶ οὔτε ζεστός, ἀλλὰ χλιαρός, καὶ μέλλω
σε ἐμέσαι ἐκ τοῦ στόματός μου, διὰ τὸ λεγειν σε Πλούσιός εἰμι καὶ
πεπλούτηκα καὶ οὐδενὸς χρείαν ἔχω, σὺ δὲ εἶ ὁ ἐλεεινὸς καὶ ταλαίπωρος
καὶ πτωχὸς καὶ τυφλὸς καὶ γυμνός. Διὸ καὶ συμβουλεύω σοι ἀγοράσαι
παρ᾽ ἐμοὶ χρυσίον πεπυρωμένον ἵνα πλουτήσῃς καὶ λάβῃς παρ᾽ ἐμοὶ ἱμάτια
30 λευκὰ εἰς περιβολήν, πρὸ τοῦ φανερωθῆναι τὴν αἰσχύνην τῆς γυμνότητός
σου. Ἐγὼ γὰρ οὓς φιλῶ ἐλέγχω καὶ παιδεύω. Ζήλευσον οὖν καὶ μετανόησον.
Ἰδοὺ ἐπὶ τὴν θύραν ἔστηκα καὶ κρούω· ἐάν τις ἀνοίξῃ μοι, καὶ εἰσελθὼν
συνδειπνήσω αὐτῷ καὶ αὐτὸς μετ᾽ ἐμοῦ» (cf. Apoc. 3,14–21).

18. Ἑρμ(ηνεία): Οὗτος γὰρ ὁ τῆς Λαοδικείας ἐπίσκοπος, τυφλὸς καὶ
35 πτωχὸς καὶ γυμνὸς πάσης ἀρετῆς ὤν, ἐπὶ ματαίῳ καὶ φθαρτῷ πλούτῳ
ἐμεγαλαύχει καὶ ἐκόμπαζεν. Διὸ καὶ ἐδηλώθη αὐτῷ ὅτι, εἰ οὐ σπεύσει ἐκ
τοῦ πλούτου τῆς χρηστότητος τοῦ Θεοῦ κτήσασθαί τι, ὡς γυμνὸς μέλλει
ἀσχημονῆσαι καὶ τῇ κολάσει παραδοθῆναι. Τὸ δὲ «ἐπὶ τῆς θύρας ἔστηκα
κρούων» τὴν φιλοπτωχίαν δηλοῖ· καὶ «ἐάν τις μοι ἀνοίξῃ, καὶ συνδειπνήσω
0   αὐτῷ καὶ αὐτὸς μετ᾽ ἐμοῦ» Fol. 61ᵛ | δηλονότι ἐν τῇ βασιλείᾳ μου·
ἐ φ ᾽ ὅ σ ο ν , φησί, ἐ π ο ι ή σ α τ ε ἑ ν ὶ τ ο ύ τ ω ν τ ῶ ν ἀ δ ε λ φ ῶ ν
μ ο υ τ ῶ ν ἐ λ α χ ί σ τ ω ν , ἐ μ ο ὶ ἐ π ο ι ή σ α τ ε .

19. Ὁ δὲ μακάριος Ἰωάννης ἐφ᾽ ἑκάστης γραφῆς τῶν ἑπτὰ ἐκκλησιῶν
πρὸς τὸ τέλος γράφει λέγων· Ὁ ἔ χ ω ν ο ὖ ς , ἀ κ ο υ σ ά τ ω τ ί
5   τ ὸ Π ν ε ῦ μ α λ έ γ ε ι τ α ῖ ς ἐ κ κ λ η σ ί α ι ς , τουτέστιν Οὐκ ἐγώ,
ἀλλὰ Θεός λέγει πρὸς ὑμᾶς ταῦτα. Καὶ μ α κ ά ρ ι ο ς , φησίν, ὁ
ἀ ν α γ ι ν ώ σ κ ω ν κ α ὶ ο ἱ ἀ κ ο ύ ο ν τ ε ς τ ο ὺ ς γεγραμμένους
λ ό γ ο υ ς τ ῆ ς π ρ ο φ η τ ε ί α ς ταύτης.

18, 141–142 Mat. 25,40
19, 144–145 Apoc. 2,7,11,17,29; 3,6,13,22   146/148 Apoc. 1,3

15, 118 τὸν scripsi : τὸ cod.
17, 123 ζ in margine   129 παρ᾽ ἐμοί : παρ᾽ ἐμοῦ Scriptura   130 πρὸ τοῦ φανερωθῆναι
τὴν αἰσχύνην scripsi : προτοῦ φανερωθεῖναι ἡ αἰσχύνη cod.   131 ζήλευσον : ζήλωσον
exspectes

Apoc. 4   **1.** Ὑπ(όθεσις) Β΄. Πε(ρὶ) τῆς οὐρανίου θύρας καὶ ἀναβάσεως τοῦ θεωροῦ.

Ἀποπεράνας οὖν τὰ περὶ τῶν ἑπτὰ ἐκκλησιῶν αὐτῷ ἐντεταλμένα, «Εἶδον, φησίν, καὶ ἰδοὺ θύρα ἀνεῳγμένη ἐν τῷ οὐρανῷ, καὶ φωνὴ ἐκεῖθεν
5   μεγάλη κελεύουσά μοι, Ἀνάβηθι ὧδε, καὶ δείξω σοι ἃ δεῖ μετὰ ταῦτα γενέσθαι. Καὶ εὐθέως ἐγενόμην ἐν πνεύματι,» ἤτοι ἐν ἐκστάσει· «καὶ ἰδοὺ κείμενος θρόνος ἐν τῷ οὐρανῷ, καὶ ὁ καθήμενος ἐν αὐτῷ ὅμοιος λίθῳ ἰάσπιδι καὶ σαρδίῳ, καὶ κύκλωθεν τοῦ θρόνου ἶρις ὁμοία λίθῳ σμαραγδίνῳ, καὶ πάλιν τούτου κύκλωθεν εἰκοσιτέσσαρες θρόνοι, ἐν οἷς καὶ ἐκάθηντο
10   εἰκοσιτέσσαρες πρεσβύτεροι περιβεβλημένοι στολὰς λευκὰς καὶ ἐστεμμένοι τὰς κεφαλὰς στεφάνους χρυσοῦς. Ἐκ δὲ τοῦ μεγάλου θρόνου ἐξῆεσαν ἀστραπαὶ καὶ βρονταί· καὶ ἑπτὰ λαμπάδες πυρὸς καιόμεναι ἔμ Fol. 62|
προσθεν αὐτοῦ, καὶ θάλασσα ὁμοία κρυστάλλῳ κατέναντι τοῦ θρόνου· καὶ τέσσαρα ζῷα ἔσωθεν καὶ ἔξωθεν καὶ ἔμπροσθεν καὶ ὄπισθεν γέμοντα
15   ὀφθαλμούς, καὶ τὰ πρόσωπα αὐτῶν πρόσωπον λέοντος καὶ πρόσωπον μόσχου, πρόσωπον ἀνθρώπου, καὶ τὸ τέταρτον ὅμοιον ἀετῷ. Καὶ ἑκάστῳ τῶν τεσσάρων πτέρυγες ἕξ· ἃ καὶ βοῶσιν ἀκαταπαύστως, Ἅγιος, ἅγιος, ἅγιος Κύριος ὁ Θεὸς ὁ παντοκράτωρ» (cf. Apoc. 4,1–8).
2. Ἑρμ(ηνεία): Ἡ ἑτοιμασία τοῦ θρόνου τῆς κρίσεως ἀμυδρῶς πως
20   ἐνταῦθα δεδήλωται, καθὼς καὶ ἤκουσεν ἀνωτέρω, ὅτι «δείξω σοι ἃ μετὰ ταῦτα μέλλει γενέσθαι». Οἱ δὲ εἰκοσιτέσσαρες πρεσβύτεροι, οἱ δώδεκα μὲν εἰσὶν οἱ ἀπόστολοι, κατὰ τὴν ἀψευδῆ τοῦ Χριστοῦ ὑπόσχεσιν, οἱ δὲ ἕτεροι δώδεκα ἡ τῶν προπατόρων ἀκρότης, ἤτοι Ἀβραάμ, Ἰσαάκ, Ἰακώβ, καὶ οἱ λοιποὶ ἀκρέμονες τῶν προφητῶν καὶ δικαίων, τὰ δὲ τετράμορφα
25   ζῷα Χερουβίμ εἰσι· καὶ πρόδηλον τοῦτο ἐκ τοῦ εἶναι πολυόμματα καὶ ἑξαπτέρυγα καὶ κράζειν ἀκαταπαύστως τὸ Ἅγιον καὶ τὰ ἑξῆς.

2, 22 cf. Mat. 19, 28; cf Luc. 22,30

1, 8, 9 κύκλωθεν : melius κυκλόθεν   11 ἐξῆεσαν scripsi : ἐξήεασαν cod.
2, 21 εἰκοσιτέσσαρες : εἰκοσιτέσσαρε ς cod.

Apoc. 5,1-8,5 **1.** Ὑπ(όθεσις) Γ′. Περὶ τοῦ ἐσφραγισμένου βιβλίου σφραγῖσιν ἑπτὰ καὶ περὶ τοῦ ἀρνίου.

«Ὁ δὲ καθήμενος ἐπὶ τοῦ θρόνου κατεῖχε βιβλίον ἐν τῇ δεξιᾷ χειρί, ἑπτὰ σφραγῖσιν ἐσφραγισμένον. Καὶ εἶδον ἄγγελον ἐν φωνῇ μεγάλῃ κηρύσσοντα, Τίς ἱκανὸς λῦσαι τὰς σφραγῖδας καὶ ἀνοῖξαι τὸ βιβλίον; Κἀγὼ ἔκλαιον, βουλόμενος μαθεῖν τί ἄρα τὰ ἐσφρα Fol. 62ᵛ| γισμένα ἐν τῷ βιβλίῳ. Εἷς δὲ ἐκ τῶν πρεσβυτέρων λέγει μοι, Μὴ κλαῖε· ἰδοὺ ἐνίκησεν ὁ λέων ὁ ἐκ τῆς φυλῆς Ἰούδα, ἡ ῥίζα Δαυίδ, τοῦ λῦσαι τὰς σφραγῖδας καὶ ἀνοῖξαι τὸ βιβλίον. Καὶ εἶδον ἐν μέσῳ τῶν πρεσβυτέρων καὶ τῶν τεσσάρων ζῴων, ἔνθα καὶ ὁ θρόνος, ἀρνίον ἑστηκότα ὥσπερ ἐσφαγμένον, ἑπτὰ ἔχοντα ὀφθαλμοὺς καὶ κέρατα ἑπτά. Καὶ ἐλθὼν ἔλαβε τὸ βιβλίον ἐκ τῆς χειρὸς τοῦ καθημένου ἐπὶ τοῦ θρόνου. Καὶ εὐθέως οἱ πρεσβύτεροι καὶ τὰ τέσσαρα ζῷα, πεσόντες καὶ προσκυνήσαντες, ὕμνησαν λέγοντες, Σοὶ πρέπει λῦσαι τὰς σφραγῖδας καὶ ἀνοῖξαι τὸ βιβλίον, ὅτι ἐσφάγης καὶ ἐν τῷ αἵματί σου ἠγόρασας τῷ Θεῷ λαὸν ἐκ πάσης φυλῆς καὶ γλώσσης. **2.**»Εἶδον δὲ καὶ ἤκουσα κύκλῳ τοῦ θρόνου ἀγγέλων ὑμνούντων, ὧν ὁ ἀριθμὸς χιλιάδες χιλιάδων καὶ μυριάδες μυριάδων, Τῷ καθημένῳ ἐπὶ τοῦ θρόνου καὶ τῷ ἀρνίῳ, λέγοντες, ἡ εὐλογία καὶ ἡ τιμὴ καὶ ἡ δόξα καὶ τὸ κράτος εἰς τοὺς αἰῶνας. Τὰ δὲ τέσσαρα ζῷα καὶ ‹οἱ› εἰκοσιτέσσαρες πρεσβύτεροι, προσκυνοῦντες, ἔλεγον τὸ Ἀμήν. **3.**»Καὶ εἶδον ὅτε ἤνοιξε τὸ ἀρνίον τὴν πρώτην σφραγῖδα καὶ ἐμοὶ ἐπετράπη τοῦ βλέπειν, καὶ εἶδον ἵππον λευκόν, καὶ ὁ καθήμενος ἐπ᾽ αὐτὸν τόξον κατεῖχε, καὶ ἐδόθη αὐτῷ στέφος, καὶ ἐξῆλθεν ἵνα νικήσῃ. **4.**»Εἶτα ἤνοιξε τὴν δευτέραν σφραγῖδα, καὶ ἄλλος ἐξῆλθεν ἵππος πυρρός, καὶ τῷ καθημένῳ ἐπ᾽ αὐτῷ ἐδόθη μάχαιρα μεγάλη Fol. 63| καὶ ὁρισμὸς τοῦ λαβεῖν τὴν εἰρήνην ἀπὸ τῆς γῆς, ἵνα ἀλλήλους οἱ ἄνθρωποι κατασφάττουσι. **5.**»Ὅτε δὲ καὶ τὴν τρίτην σφραγῖδα ἤνοιξεν, ἰδοὺ ἵππος μέλας ἐφάνη, καὶ τῷ καθημένῳ ἐπ᾽ αὐτὸν ζυγὸς ἐπεδόθη ἐν τῇ χειρὶ αὐτοῦ καὶ ὁρισμός, Χοῖνιξ σίτου ἐν δηναρίῳ, καὶ κριθῶν τρεῖς χοίνικες ἐν δηναρίῳ· τὸ ἔλαιον δὲ καὶ τὸν οἶνον μὴ ἀδικήσῃς. **6.**»Εἶτα, καὶ τὴν τετάρτην ἀνοίξας σφραγῖδα, εἶδον ἵππον χλωρόν, καὶ ὄνομα τῷ καθημένῳ ἐπ᾽ αὐτὸν θάνατος, καὶ ὁ ᾅδης ἠκολούθει αὐτῷ· καὶ ἐδόθη αὐτοῖς ἐξουσία ἵνα ἐν ῥομφαίᾳ καὶ λιμῷ τὸ τέταρτον τῆς γῆς ἀποκτείνωσι. **7.**»Ὅτε δὲ καὶ τὴν πέμπτην σφραγῖδα ἤνοιξεν, εἶδον ὑποκάτω τοῦ θυσιαστηρίου τὰς ψυχὰς τῶν ἐσφαγμένων ἀνθρώπων διὰ τὸν λόγον τοῦ Θεοῦ, οἷς καὶ ἐπεδόθη στολὴ λευκὴ ἵνα ἀναπαύωνται ἄχρις ἂν καὶ οἱ σύνδουλοι αὐτῶν τελειωθῶσι. **8.**»Εἶτα, καὶ τὴν ἕκτην διανοίξας σφραγῖδα, σεισμὸς ἐγένετο μέγας, καὶ ὁ ἥλιος ἐγένετο ὥσπερ σάκκος τρίχινος μέλας, ἡ δὲ σελήνη μετεβλήθη

1, 4 σφραγῖσιν correxi : σφραγῖδας cod.
2, 19 οἱ addidi
4, 24 δευτέραν scripsi : δευτέρα cod.   25 πυρρὸς scripsi : πυρὸς cod.
5, 30 ἐν δυναρίῳ : legas δυναρίου
6, 32 ἀνοίξας : lege ἀνοίξαντος

εἰς αἷμα, καὶ οἱ ἀστέρες ὡς φύλλα καὶ ὄλυνθοι ἀπὸ συκῆς πεπτώκασιν ἐπὶ τὴν γῆν, καὶ ὁ οὐρανὸς καθάπερ βιβλίον εἰλίσσετο, καὶ πᾶν ὄρος καὶ νῆσος ἐκ τῶν τόπων αὐτῶν ἐκινήθησαν, οἱ δὲ βασιλεῖς τῆς γῆς καὶ οἱ
45 δυνάσται καὶ πάντες ἄνθρωποι κατέκρυπτον ἑαυτοὺς εἰς τά σπήλαια καὶ τὰς τρώγλας τῶν πετρῶν, λέγοντες, Πέσετε ἐφ' ἡμᾶς καὶ ἀποκρύψατε τῆς ὀργῆς τοῦ ἐπὶ τοῦ θρόνου καὶ τοῦ Fol. 63ᵛ | ἀρνίου, ὅτι ἦλθεν ⟨ἡ⟩ ἡμέρα τῆς ὀργῆς αὐτοῦ, καὶ τίς δύναται ὑποστῆναι;
9. »Μετὰ ταῦτα δὲ τέσσαρας ἀγγέλους εἶδον ἱσταμένους εἰς τὰς
50 τέσσαρας γωνίας τῆς γῆς καὶ κρατοῦντας τοὺς τέσσαρας ἀνέμους, ἵνα μὴ πνεύσωσιν ὅλως. Καὶ ἕτερος ἄγγελος ἦν ἀναβαίνων ἀπὸ ἀνατολῆς ἡλίου, σφραγῖδα κρατῶν Θεοῦ ζῶντος, καὶ ἔκραξεν λέγων τοῖς ἑτέροις ἀγγέλοις τοῦ μὴ ἀδικῆσαί τινα τῶν ἀνθρώπων, Ἕως ἂν σφραγίσω, φησί, τοὺς δούλους τοῦ Θεοῦ. Κἀγὼ ἤκουσα τὸν ἀριθμὸν τῶν ἐσφραγισμένων,
55 ἑκατὸν καὶ τεσσαράκοντα τέσσαρας χιλιάδας ἐκ τῶν δώδεκα φυλῶν τῶν υἱῶν Ἰσραήλ, ἤγουν ἐξ ἑκάστης φυλῆς δώδεκα χιλιάδας.
10. »Καὶ μετὰ ταῦτα εἶδον, καὶ ἰδοὺ ὄχλος πολύς, ὃν οὐδεὶς ἐδύνατο ἀριθμῆσαι, ἐκ παντὸς ἔθνους καὶ γλώσσης καὶ λαοῦ, περιβεβλημένους στολὰς λευκὰς καὶ ἐνώπιον τοῦ θρόνου καὶ τοῦ ἀρνίου παρισταμένους.
60 Εἷς δὲ τῶν πρεσβυτέρων λέγει μοι, Τίνες ἄρα καὶ πόθεν οἱ τὰς λευκὰς περιβεβλημένοι στολάς; Κἀγὼ εἶπον αὐτῷ, Κύριε μου, σὺ γινώσκεις. Καὶ ἀποκριθεὶς λέγει μοι, Οὗτοι εἰσιν οἱ ἐκ μεγάλων θλίψεων ὑπὲρ τοῦ ὀνόματος τοῦ ἀρνίου τὰς ἑαυτῶν στολὰς πλύναντες καὶ λευκάναντες, καὶ ἰδοὺ σὺν αὐτῷ ἀγάλλονται καὶ συνευφραίνονται.
65 11. »Ὅτε δὲ καὶ τὴν ἑβδόμην σφραγῖδα ἤνοιξε τὸ ἀρνίον, ὡς ἡμιώριον σιγὴ ἐγένετο ἐν τῷ οὐρανῷ. Καὶ εἶδον τοὺς παρισταμένους ἑπτὰ ἀγγέλους, ὅτι ἐδόθησαν αὐτοῖς ἑπτὰ σάλπιγγες, ἑτέρῳ δὲ ἀγγέλῳ Fol. 64 | ἐδόθη λιβανωτὸν ὥσπερ χρυσοῦν καὶ ἔτερα θυμιάματα πολλά. Καί, λαβὼν ἐκ τοῦ πυρὸς τοῦ θυσιαστηρίου τοῦ χρυσοῦ καὶ θυμιάσας ἐνώπιον
70 τοῦ θρόνου καὶ τοῦ χρυσοῦ θυσιαστηρίου, ἀνέβη ὁ καπνὸς τῶν θυμιαμάτων ἐκ χειρὸς τοῦ ἀγγέλου ἐνώπιον τοῦ Θεοῦ» (cf. Apoc. 5,1–8,5).
12. Ἑρμ(ηνεία): Τὸ ἐσφραγισμένον βιβλίον τοῦτο σημαίνει, τὴν ἄφατον καὶ πολλὴν τοῦ Θεοῦ μακροθυμίαν, ὅτι ὁ κόσμος, ἄξιος ὢν βασάνων καὶ τιμωριῶν πολλῶν διὰ τὴν ἀσέβειαν καὶ τὰς πράξεις τὰς πονηράς,
75 συγκαλύπτεται ἡ ὀργὴ κατ' ἐμφέρειαν βιβλίου ἐσφραγισμένου. Ὅτε δὲ ὁ τῆς συντελείας καιρὸς ἐπιστῇ, τότε τὸ ἀρνίον, ὁ ἀμνὸς τοῦ Θεοῦ, ὡς ἔχων ἐξουσίαν κρῖναι τὴν γῆν, ἀναπτύξει τὰ κεκρυμμένα καὶ ἄξια κατακρίσεως ἔργα, καθὼς καὶ ὁ θεῖος ἐξεῖπε Δανιήλ, Κ ρ ι τ ή ρ ι ο ν, φησί⟨ν⟩, ἐκάθησε, καὶ βίβλοι ἀνεῴχθησαν.

12, 78/79 Dan. 7,10

8, 47 ἡ suppleui
12, 75 κατεμφέρειαν cod.

13. Ἀρνίον δὲ εἴρηται διὰ τὸ ἄκακον καὶ ἄμωμον καὶ ‹ὡς ὑπὲρ ἄλλων› τυθέν, ὑπὲρ τῆς ἁμαρτίας τοῦ κόσμου· περὶ οὗ καὶ ὁ προφήτης προέφη Ἡσαΐας ὅτι ʽΩς πρόβατον καὶ ὡς ἀμνὸς εἰς σφαγὴν ἤχθη, ὁ δὲ Ἰωάννης ῎Ιδε, φησίν, ὁ ἀμνὸς τοῦ Θεοῦ ὁ αἴρων τὴν ἁμαρτίαν τοῦ κόσμου.

14. Οἱ δὲ ἑπτὰ ὀφθαλμοὶ τοῦ ἀρνίου τοῦτο παραδηλοῦσιν, ὅτι καθορᾷ πάντα καὶ λέληθεν αὐτῷ οὐδὲν τῶν γινομένων φαύλων τε καὶ χρηστῶν.

15. Τὰ δὲ ἑπτὰ κέρατα αὐτοῦ τὸ βασιλικώτατον αὐτοῦ ὑπεμφαίνουσι, ὅτι κερατίσει καὶ καταβαλεῖ πάσας τὰς βασιλείας τοῦ κόσμου καὶ τοῦ διαβόλου τὸ κράτος, καὶ αὐτὸς μόνος ὡς β α σ ι Fol. 64ᵛ| λ ε ὺ ς τ ῆ ς δ ό ξ η ς διαμένει βασιλεὺς ἀΐδιος ἐν μιᾷ βασιλείᾳ, σὺν τῷ Πατρὶ αὐτοῦ καὶ τῷ Πνεύματι.

16. Ὁ δὲ λευκὸς ἵππος καὶ ὁ πυρρὸς καὶ ὁ μέλας καὶ οἱ λοιποί, καὶ οἱ ἐπιβάται ἐπ᾽ αὐτοῖς ἄγγελοι, τὰς μελλούσας γενέσθαι θλίψεις ἐν τῷ κόσμῳ σημαίνουσι, καὶ τὸ ἰσχυρὸν καὶ ἀήττητον αὐτῶν καὶ πολεμικώτατον. Καὶ οὐκ ἡ πυρφλόγος καὶ ἀσώματος φύσις τῶν ἀγγέλων ἵππων καὶ ἐποχίας ἔχουσα χρείαν, ἀλλὰ ‹πρὸς τὸ› ἀπελθεῖν, καθὼς προσετάγησαν, καὶ ἆραι τὴν εἰρήνην καὶ πᾶν ἀγαθὸν ἀπὸ προσώπου τῆς γῆς, διὰ τὸ πληθυνθῆναι τὴν ἀνομίαν καὶ τὰ ἔργα τοῦ Σατανᾶ, ὅπως ἀναλωθῶσιν ἀλλήλοις, ὅτι ἀπέστησαν ἀπὸ τοῦ Θεοῦ καὶ ὁ Θεὸς ἀπ᾽ αὐτῶν.

17. Ἀπὸ δὲ τῶν ἀναριθμήτων μυριάδων τῶν δώδεκα φυλῶν τοῦ Ἰσραήλ, ἑκατὸν τεσσαράκοντα τέσσαρες χιλιάδες καὶ μόναι, λέγει, εὑρεθήσονται σωζομένων, ἐξ ἑκάστης φυλῆς τῶν δώδεκα χιλιάδες δώδεκα καὶ οὐδὲν πλέον· ἀλλὰ τοὺς προπάτορας δηλονότι καὶ τοὺς προφήτας καὶ τοὺς ὁμοίους αὐτῶν φιλοθέους. Οἱ δὲ ἐξ Ἰουδαίων καὶ ἐξ ἐθνῶν πιστεύσαντες καὶ βαπτισθέντες πλήθη πολλὰ καὶ ἀριθμοῦ κρείττω. Οἱ λευσχήμονες δὲ καὶ τῷ ἀρνίῳ συναγαλλόμενοι καὶ τῷ θείῳ παριστάμενοι θρόνῳ, οὗτοί εἰσιν οἱ δι᾽ αἵματος καὶ μαρτυρίας ἢ διὰ ἀσκήσεως καὶ καθαρᾶς πολιτείας πλύναντες καὶ λευκάναντες τὰς στολὰς τῶν ἰδίων ψυχῶν.

13, 82 cf. Is. 53,7   83/84 Ioh. 1,29
15, 91 Ps 23(24), 7ss

13, 80 < > suppleui : [...]λλ[..] cod.
15, 89 καταβάλει cod.   91 ἀΐδιος scripsi : ἀείδιος cod.
16, 93 πυρρὸς emendaui : πυρὸς cod.   96 πυρφλόγος : πυρίφλογος : exspectes
97 πρὸς τὸ conieci
17, 102 τεσσαράκοντα scripsi : σαράκοντα cod.   τέσσαρες scripsi : τέσσαρεις cod.
χιλιάδες καὶ μόναι correxi : χιλιάδας καὶ μόνας cod.   103 χιλιάδες correxi : χιλιάδας
cod.   106 κρείττω correxi : κρεῖττον cod.   107 λευσχήμονες : λευχείμονες exspectes

Apoc. 8,6-11,9 **1.** Ὑπ(όθεσις) Δ΄. Περὶ τῶν ἑπτὰ σαλπιφόρων ἀγγέλων.

«Οἱ δὲ λαβόντες τὰς ἑπτὰ σάλπιγγας ἄγγελοι, Fol. 65Ι ἰδοὺ ὁ πρῶτος ἐσάλπισε· καὶ ἐγένετο χάλαζα καὶ πῦρ μεμιγμένον αἵματι, καὶ ἐβλήθη εἰς τὴν γῆν, καὶ κατεκάη τὸ τρίτον τῆς γῆς καὶ τῶν δένδρων καὶ πᾶς
5 χόρτος ὁμοῦ.

2.» Ἐσάλπισε δὲ καὶ ὁ δεύτερος· καὶ ὡς ὄρος μέγα πυρὶ καιόμενον ἐβλήθη ἐν τῇ θαλάσσῃ, καὶ κατέκαυσε τὸ τρίτον αὐτῆς καὶ τὰ ἐν αὐτῇ.

3.»Εἶτα καὶ ὁ τρίτος ἐσάλπισεν ἄγγελος· καὶ ἀστὴρ μέγας πύρινος, ὁ λεγόμενος Ἄψινθος, πέπτωκεν ἐκ τοῦ οὐρανοῦ ἐπὶ πᾶν ὕδωρ ποταμῶν
10 καὶ πηγῶν καὶ ὡς ἄψινθος ἐπικράνθησαν, καὶ πολλοὶ τῶν ἀνθρώπων ἀπὸ τοῦ δίψους ἀπέθανον.

4.»Καὶ ὁ τέταρτος ἐσάλπισεν ἄγγελος, ἐπλήγη δὲ καὶ ἐσκοτίσθη τὸ τρίτον τοῦ ἡλίου καὶ τῆς σελήνης καὶ τῶν ἀστέρων, καὶ τὸ τρίτον τῆς ἡμέρας ἐγένετο σκότος. Εἶδον δὲ ὡς ἀετὸν ἐν τῷ ἀέρι, καὶ ἤκουσα αὐτοῦ λέγοντος μεγάλῃ τῇ φωνῇ, Οὐαὶ οὐαὶ τοῖς κατοικοῦσιν ἐπὶ προσώπου
15 πάσης τῆς γῆς ἐκ τῶν μελλόντων τριῶν ἀγγέλων σαλπίσαι.

5.»Τότε οὖν καὶ ὁ πέμπτος ἐσάλπισεν ἄγγελος· καὶ εἶδον ἀστέρα ἐκ τοῦ οὐρανοῦ πεπτωκότα εἰς τὴν γῆν, καὶ ἐδόθη αὐτῷ ἡ κλεὶς τοῦ φρέατος τῆς ἀβύσσου. Καὶ ἤνοιξεν αὐτό, καὶ ἀνέβη καπνὸς ἐκ τοῦ φρέατος, ὥσπερ ἀπὸ καμίνου μεγάλης, καὶ ἐσκότασε τὸν ἥλιον καὶ τὸν ἀέρα. Καὶ ἐκ τοῦ
20 καπνοῦ ἐξῆλθον ἀκρίδες ἐπὶ τῆς γῆς ὥσπερ σκορπίοι, ὧν τὸ μέγεθος ὥσπερ ἵπποι, καὶ αἱ οὐραὶ αὐτῶν ὡς κέντρον σκορπίου, αἱ κεφαλαὶ αὐτῶν ὡς ἐστεμμέναι χρυσίῳ· εἶχον δὲ πτέρυγας, καὶ πρόσωπα ἀνθρώπων, καὶ τρίχας Fol. 65ᵛΙ ὡς τρίχας γυναικῶν, καὶ ὥσπερ λέοντος οἱ ὀδόντες αὐτῶν, καὶ ὥσπερ σιδηροῦς θώρακας ἐφόρουν, καὶ ἡ φωνὴ τῶν πτερύγων αὐτῶν ὡς
25 φωνὴ ἁρμάτων καὶ πολλῶν ἵππων τρεχόντων εἰς πόλεμον. Βασιλεὺς δὲ αὐτῶν ⟨ὁ⟩ ἄγγελος τῆς ἀβύσσου, καὶ τὸ ὄνομα αὐτοῦ Ἑβραϊστὶ Ἀβαδδών, Ἑλληνιστὶ δὲ Ἀπολλύων. Εἴρηται δὲ αὐτοῖς χόρτον μὲν ἢ δένδρον μὴ βλάψαι, πλήττειν δὲ καὶ βασανίζειν τοὺς ἀνθρώπους μῆνας πέντε, ὅσοι ἐν τοῖς μετώποις αὐτῶν μὴ ἔχοντες τὴν σφραγίδα τοῦ Θεοῦ. Ἐν δὲ ταῖς
30 τοιαύταις ἡμέραις ἐπιθυμήσουσιν οἱ ἄνθρωποι τὸν θάνατον, καὶ αὐτὸς φεύξεται ἀπ᾽ αὐτῶν.

6.»Εἶτα καὶ ὁ ἕκτος ἐσάλπισεν ἄγγελος· καὶ φωνή, ἐκ τοῦ χρυσοῦ θυσιαστηρίου, αὐτῷ ἐπιτρέπουσα ἵνα, διὰ τριῶν πληγῶν, ἤτοι ἐκ πυρὸς καὶ θείου καὶ καπνοῦ, ἀποκτείνῃ τὸ τρίτον τῶν ἀνθρώπων, ὅτι οὐ
35 μετενόησαν ἀπὸ τῶν ἀσεβειῶν καὶ τῶν αἰσχρῶν πράξεων αὐτῶν, λήσῃ δὲ καὶ τοὺς δεδεμένους ἐν τῷ μεγάλῳ Εὐφράτῃ ποταμῷ τέσσαρας ἀγγέλους» (cf. Apoc. 8,6-9,15).

7. Ἑρμ(ηνεία): Λύσιν δεσμῶν τεσσάρων ἀγγέλων λέγει τὴν ἐκ τοῦ χρυσοῦ θυσιαστηρίου προτρεπτικὴν θείαν φωνὴν εἰς ὄλεθρον καὶ ἀπώλειαν
40 εἰδωλολάτρου λαοῦ.

7, 39/40 cf. Apoc. 9,20–21

1, 1 σαλπιφόρων : melius σαλπιγγοφόρων
2, 6 πυρὶ emendaui cf. Ier 28 (51), 25 : πῦρ cod.
5, 27 ὁ suppleui
6, 33 αὐτῷ scripsi : αὐτὸν cod. 34 ἀποκτείνῃ scripsi : ἀποκτενεῖ cod.

8. «Καὶ εἶδον στρατεύματα, μυριάδας μυριάδων ἔχοντας θώρακας πυρίνους, αἱ κεφαλαὶ δὲ τῶν ἵππων ὡς κεφαλαὶ λεόντων, ἐκ δὲ τῶν στομάτων αὐτῶν πῦρ ἐξήρχετο καὶ καπνὸς καὶ θεῖον· αἱ οὐραὶ δὲ αὐτῶν ὅμοιαι ὄφεσιν, ἔχουσαι κεφαλάς, καὶ ἐν αὐταῖς ἀδικοῦσι» (cf. Apoc. 9, 16–19).
45 **9.** Ἑρμ(ηνεία): Καὶ ταῦτα τὰ σρατεύματα ἐκ τῶν Fol. 66 | προρρηθέντων ἀκρίδων εἰσί.
10. «Εἶτα καὶ ὁ ἕβδομος ἐσάλπισεν ἄγγελος· καὶ ἐγένοντο φωναὶ μεγάλαι ἐν τῷ οὐρανῷ, ὑμνοῦσαι καὶ εὐλογοῦσαι τὸν Κύριον, ὅτι Ἦλθεν, φησίν, ὁ καιρὸς τῆς κρίσεως, ἐν ᾗ ἀποδώσῃς ἑκάστῳ κατὰ τὰς πράξεις αὐτοῦ.
50 Καὶ εἶδον ὅτι ἠνοίγη ὁ ναὸς τοῦ Θεοῦ ἐν τῷ οὐρανῷ, καὶ ὤφθη ἡ κιβωτὸς τῆς διαθήκης αὐτοῦ ἐν τῷ ναῷ αὐτοῦ· καὶ ἐγένοντο ἀστραπαὶ καὶ βρονταὶ καὶ χάλαζα μεγάλη καὶ σεισμός» (cf. Apoc. 11,15-19).
11. Ἑρμ(ηνεία): Αἱ παρὰ τῶν ἀγγέλων ἑπτὰ σάλπιγγες τὰ περὶ τῆς συντελείας παραδηλοῦσι δεινά, σύμφωνα δὲ καὶ τῷ θείῳ εὐαγγελίῳ. Τ ό τ ε ,
55 φ η σ ί ν , ἀ π ο σ τ ε λ ε ῖ ὁ Υ ἱ ὸ ς τ ο ῦ ἀ ν θ ρ ώ π ο υ τ ο ὺ ς ἀ γ γ έ λ ο υ ς α ὐ τ ο ῦ μ ε τ ὰ σ ά λ π ι γ γ ο ς φ ω ν ῆ ς μ ε γ ά λ η ς , κ α ὶ ὅ τ ι σ υ ν ά ξ ο υ σ ι τ ο ὺ ς ἐ κ λ ε κ τ ο ὺ ς α ὐ τ ο ῦ ἀ π ὸ τ ῶ ν τ ε σ σ ά ρ ω ν ἀ ν έ μ ω ν κ α ὶ τ ὰ ἑ ξ ῆ ς . Τούς ἐκλεκτοὺς μὲν συνάξουσι, τοὺς βδελυκτοὺς δὲ παρήσουσιν, ἵνα κατὰ τὴν βδελυγμίαν αὐτῶν ἀπολάβωσι. Διὰ τοῦτο καὶ οἱ τέσσαρες
60 πρῶτοι ἄγγελοι, σαλπίσαντες, τὸ τρίτον τῆς γῆς καὶ τῆς θαλάσσης καὶ τοῦ φωτὸς ἐξηφάνισαν, ὁ δὲ πέμπτος ἐκ τῆς ἀβύσσου καὶ τοῦ ᾅδου καπνὸν ἀνήγαγε σὺν ἀκρίδι. Ἀκρίδα, διὰ τὸ πλῆθος καὶ τὸ τετράπουν καὶ τὸ πτερόν, τῷ δὲ μεγέθει ὡς ἵπποι καὶ ὡς λέοντες, ὡς ἀνθρώπων πρόσωπα, καὶ τρίχες γυναικῶν· αἱ οὐραὶ αὐτῶν κολαστικαὶ ὡς ὄφεως καὶ σκορπίου,
65 καὶ τὰ λοιπὰ αὐτῶν εἴδη φοβερὰ καὶ φρικώδη. Ἐντέταλται δὲ αὐτοῖς μηδὲν τῶν ἐν τῇ γῇ παραβλάψαι, εἰμὴ τοὺς ἀνθρώπους τοὺς μὴ ἔχοντας τὴν σφραγῖδα τοῦ Θεοῦ βασανίσωσι μῆνας πέντε, πλήττοντες τοῖς Fol. 66ᵛ | κέντροις ἡμέρας καὶ νυκτός. Καὶ εἶθ᾽ οὕτως παραδοθῶσιν τῇ ἀπωλείᾳ· τοῦτο γὰρ καὶ τὸ ὄνομα τοῦ ἄρχοντος τῶν ἱπποακρίδων ἐκείνων
70 παραδηλοῖ, Ἀββαδὼν Ἀπολλύων. Ὁμοίως καὶ οἱ ἕτεροι τρεῖς ἄγγελοι τὰ περὶ τῆς συντελείας τοῦ κόσμου δεινὰ διαγορεύουσιν· περὶ ὧν λέγειν πλατυτέρως οὐ βούλομαι.

11, 54/57 Mat. 24,31

11, 53 ἑρμ(ηνεία) in margine   σάλπιγγες scripsi : σάλπιγγαι cod.   59 ἀπολάβωσι scripsi : ἀπολάβουσι cod.   62 ἀκρίδι correxi : ἀκρίδα cod.   69 τοῦτο scripsi : τούτῳ an recte?

Apoc. 10,1–11,14 **1.** Ὑπ(όθεσις) Ε'. Περὶ τοῦ ἀγγέλου καὶ τοῦ βιβλίου καὶ τοῦ Ἐνὼχ καὶ τοῦ Ἠλιοῦ.

«Καὶ εἶδον ἄγγελον ἐκ τοῦ οὐρανοῦ κατερχόμενον, περιβεβλημένον νεφέλην, καὶ ⟨ἡ⟩ ἴρις ἐπὶ τῆς κεφαλῆς αὐτοῦ, καὶ τὸ πρόσωπον ὡς ἥλιος,
5 οἱ πόδες αὐτοῦ ὥσπερ στῦλος πυρός, καὶ ἐκράτει ἐπὶ χεῖρας βιβλιδάριον ἀνεῳγμένον. Καὶ ἔθηκε τὸν πόδα αὐτοῦ τὸν δεξιὸν ἐπὶ τῆς θαλάσσης, τὸν δὲ εὐώνυμον ἐπὶ τῆς γῆς· καὶ ἤκουσα φωνὴν ἐκ τοῦ οὐρανοῦ λέγουσαν πρός με, Λάβε τὸ βιβλίον ἐκ τῆς χειρὸς τοῦ ἀγγέλου. Καί, ὡς ἦλθον τοῦ λαβεῖν αὐτό, λέγει μοι, Λάβε καὶ φάγε αὐτό. Καί λαβὼν ἔφαγον αὐτό,
10 ⟨καὶ⟩ ἐγλυκάνθη μὲν ὑπὲρ μέλι τὸ στόμα μου, ἐπικράνθη δὲ ἡ κοιλία μου. Καὶ λέγει μοι ὁ ἄγγελος ὅτι Δεῖ σε πάλιν προφητεῦσαι ἐπὶ βασιλεῖς καὶ ἔθνη καὶ λαούς, ὅτι ἐδόθη τοῖς ἔθνεσι τοῦ πατῆσαι τὴν πόλιν τὴν ἁγίαν μῆνας τεσσαράκοντα τέσσαρας. Καὶ δώσω λόγον τοῖς δυσὶ μάρτυσί μου, λέγει Κύριος, καὶ προφητεύσουσιν ἡμέρας χιλίας διακοσίας ἑξήκοντα,
15 περιβεβλημένοι σάκκους, καὶ οὐδεὶς δυνήσεται αὐτοὺς ἀδικῆσαι ἐν ἡμέραις τῆς προφητείας αὐτῶν, ἐξουσίαν δὲ ἔχουσι κλεῖσαι Fol. 67ᵛ τὸν οὐρανόν, τοῦ μὴ βρέξαι, καὶ τὰ ὕδατα μεταποιῆσαι εἰς αἷμα, καὶ πατάξαι τὴν γῆν ὁσάκις καὶ θέλουσι. Ὅτε δὲ τελέσωσι τὸ ἔργον τῆς προφητείας αὐτῶν, τότε συνάψει αὐτοῖς πόλεμον τὸ ἐκ τῆς ἀβύσσου θηρίον, καὶ
20 νικήσει καὶ ἀποκτενεῖ αὐτούς, καὶ τὸ πτῶμα αὐτῶν ἐπὶ τῆς πλατείας τῆς πόλεως ἐν ᾗ καὶ ὁ Κύριος αὐτῶν ἐσταυρώθη, καὶ παρὰ πάντων ὁρᾶται τὸ πτῶμα αὐτῶν κείμενον τρεῖς ἡμερας νεκρὸν ἄταφον. Καὶ μετὰ τρεῖς ἡμέρας ἔπνευσεν αὐτοῖς πνεῦμα ζωῆς, καί, κληθέντες, ἀνῆλθοσαν εἰς τὸν οὐρανόν, καὶ ἐπέπεσε φόβος μέγας τῇ πόλει, θεωροῦντες αὐτούς. Καὶ ἐν
25 ἐκείνῃ τῇ ὥρᾳ σεισμὸς ἐγένετο μέγας, ἐξ οὗ καὶ τὸ δέκατον τῆς πόλεως κατεπτώθη, καὶ ἀπεκτάνθησαν ἀνδρῶν χιλιάδες ἑπτά, ὁ δὲ λοιπὸς λαός, φόβῳ μεγάλῳ συσχεθείς, ἐδίδουν δόξαν τῷ Θεῷ τοῦ οὐρανοῦ» (cf. Apoc. 10,1–11,13)
 2. Ἑρμ(ηνεία): Εὔληπτα τὰ ῥηθέντα· ὅτι τὸ μὲν βιβλίον, ὃ κατέφαγεν
30 ὁ θεωρὸς οὗτος, τὴν χάριν ἐδήλου τῆς κατ᾽ αὐτὸν προφητείας, τὰ δὲ ἑξῆς περὶ τῆς ἐλεύσεως τῶν προφητῶν Ἐνὼχ καὶ Ἠλιοῦ. Καὶ οἱ δυνάμενοι κλεῖσαι οὐρανόν, καὶ γῆν καταπλῆξαι, ἡττήθησαν οἰκονομικῶς καὶ ἀνηρέθησαν ἐκ τοῦ θηρίου, ὅπως λάβωσι τὸ στέφος τῆς μαρτυρίας καὶ μὴ ἐλάττους φωραθῶσι τῶν προφητῶν καὶ τῶν λοιπῶν αὐτῶν θεοστεφῶν
35 ἀδελφῶν.

2, 31 cf. Gen. 5,21–24; cf. III Reg. 17–IV Reg. 2,12; cf. Mal. 3,22–23

1, 4 ἡ restitui 10 καὶ conieci 13 τεσσαράκοντα τέσσαρας scripsi : τεσσαρακοντατέσσαρας cod. 14 προφητεύσουσιν correxi : προφητεῦσωσιν cod. 15 δυνήσεται correxi : δυνήσηται cod. 24 θεωροῦντες : lege θεωρούσῃ uel θεωροῦσιν 26 κατεπτώθη : melius κατέπεσεν
2, 33 λάβωσι scripsi : λήψονται cod. 34 ἐλάττους scripsi : ἔλαττοι cod.

Apoc. 12,1-13,10   **1.** Ὑπ(όθεσις) ϛʹ. Περὶ τοῦ ὀφθέντος μεγάλου σημείου ἐν τῷ οὐρανῷ.

«Καὶ σημεῖον μέγα ὤφθη ἐν τῷ οὐρανῷ, γυνὴ γὰρ περιβεβλημένη τὸν ἥλιον, καὶ ἡ σελήνη περὶ τοὺς πόδας Fol. 67ᵛ| αὐτῆς, καὶ δώδεκα ἀστέρες
5 στεφανοειδῶς ἐπὶ τῆς κεφαλῆς αὐτῆς, καὶ ἐν γαστρὶ ἔχουσα, βασανιζομένη ἦν καὶ κράζουσα τοῦ τεκεῖν. Ὤφθη δὲ καὶ ἄλλο σημεῖον ἐν τῷ οὐρανῷ, δράκων γὰρ μέγας, πυρρός, ἑπτὰ κεφαλὰς ἔχων καὶ κέρατα δέκα, ἐλθὼν ἔστη ἐνώπιον τῆς γυναικός, ἵνα τὸ τικτόμενον καταφάγῃ παιδίον. Ἡ δὲ γυνὴ ἔτεκε παιδίον ἄρρεν· καὶ τὸ παιδίον ἡρπάγη πρὸς τὸν Θεόν, ἡ δὲ
10 γυνὴ ἔφυγεν εἰς τὴν ἔρημον ἐν τόπῳ ἡτοιμασμένῳ αὐτῇ, ἵνα ἐκεῖ τρέφεται ἡμέρας χιλίας διακοσίας ἑξήκοντα. Ὁ δὲ δράκων διάβολος, ὀργισθεὶς διὰ τὸ παιδίον καὶ τὴν μητέρα αὐτοῦ, ὥρμησε μετὰ τῶν ἀγγέλων αὐτοῦ συνάψαι πόλεμον μετὰ Μιχαὴλ καὶ τῶν ἀγγέλων αὐτοῦ. Καί, τούτου γενομένου, οὐχ εὑρέθη ἐν τῷ οὐρανῷ τόπος τῷ δράκοντι, ἀλλὰ ἀπερρίφη εἰς τὴν γῆν
15 μετὰ τῶν ἀγγέλων αὐτοῦ, κατεδίωξεν δὲ τὴν γυναῖκα ἐν τῇ ἐρήμῳ· ἀλλ’ οὐδὲ κατ’ αὐτῆς ἐδόθη αὐτῷ ἰσχῦσαι, ἀλλ’ ἑκατέρωθεν ἔμεινεν ἄπρακτος.
    2.»Εἶτα ἔστην ἐπὶ τὴν ἄμμον, καὶ εἶδον θηρίον ὅμοιον παρδάλει, καὶ οἱ πόδες αὐτοῦ ὡς ἄρκτου, κεφαλὰς ἔχον ἑπτὰ καὶ κέρατα δέκα, καὶ ἐπὶ τῶν δέκα κεράτων διαδήματα δέκα, καὶ ἐπὶ τὰς ἑπτὰ κεφαλὰς αὐτοῦ
20 ὀνόματα ἔγραφον βλασφημίας, τὸ δὲ στόμα αὐτοῦ ὡς στόμα λέοντος. Ἐδόθη δὲ αὐτῷ ἐξουσία μεγάλη καὶ θρόνος παρὰ τοῦ δράκοντος, καὶ ἐθαύμασε τὸ πλῆθος τοῦ λαοῦ ὅτι τὸ ἀρτιφανὲς θηρίον μεγάλην ἔλαβεν ἐξουσίαν παρὰ τοῦ δράκοντος, καὶ Fol. 68| προσεκύνησαν αὐτόν. Τῷ δὲ θηρίῳ ἐδόθη στόμα, καὶ ἐλάλει μεγάλα καὶ βλάσφημα, καὶ ἐδόθη αὐτῷ
25 ἐξουσία μῆνας τεσσαράκοντα δύο, πᾶσα δὲ φυλὴ καὶ γλῶσσα προσεκύνει αὐτό, ὧν οὐ γέγραπται τὰ ὀνόματα ἐν τῇ βίβλῳ τῆς ζωῆς. Ἀνοίξας δὲ τὸ στόμα αὐτοῦ ἐβλασφήμει πρὸς τὸν Θεόν, καὶ συνεχωρήθη αὐτῷ ποιῆσαι πόλεμον μετὰ τῶν ἁγίων καὶ νικῆσαι αὐτούς. Εἴ τις οὖν ἔχει οὖς ἀκουέτω» (cf. Apoc. 12,1–13,10).
30   **3.** Ἑρμ(ηνεία): Δύσληπτα καὶ δυσνόητα ὄντως καὶ δυσερμήνευτα τὰ ἐν τῇ ἕκτῃ ὑποθέσει ταύτῃ λαλούμενα, διὸ καὶ ὁ θεωρὸς καλῶς ἀπεφήνατο λέγων «Εἴς τις ἔχει οὖς ἀκουσάτω». Ἤδει γὰρ ὅτι πολλοὶ μὲν ἀκούσονται, ὀλίγοι δὲ μετὰ ὠτὸς γνωστικοῦ τὴν σύγκρισιν τοῦ μεγάλου τοῦδε σημείου διαγνώσονται· περὶ οὗ, κατατολμήσας ὁ ἄγροικος ἐγώ, λέξω, ὡς ἡ τοῦ
35 θείου Πνεύματος ἀποκαλύψει μοι χάρις.
    4. Ἐπειδὴ γὰρ ἡ ὁραθεῖσα γυνὴ τὸν ἥλιον περιεβέβλητο, καὶ τὴν σελήνην περὶ τοὺς πόδας εἶχεν αὐγάζουσαν, καὶ δωδεκὰς ἀστέρων τὴν

1, 7 πυρρὸς scripsi : πυρὸς cod.   ἔχων scripsi : ἔχωντα cod.   8 ἐνώπιον in rasura; ἐνώ πιον cod.   καταφάγῃ scripsi : κα ταφάγει cod.   9 ἡρπάγη scripsi : ἡρ πάγη cod.   θ(εὸ)ν corr., prius θ(εο)ῦ
2, 25 τεσσαράκοντα δύο scripsi : τεσσαρακονταδύο cod.
3, 35 ἀποκαλύψει corr. recens : ἀποκαλύψαι cod. ut uid.

κεφαλὴν αὐτῆς ἔστεφε, καὶ τὸ ἐξ αὐτῆς γεννηθὲν παιδίον ἡρπάγη πρὸς
Κύριον, μηδεὶς πλανηθήτω τὴν Θεοτόκον αὐτὴν εἶναι ⟨ὑπονοῶν⟩, ἀλλὰ
40 ἀντιθεοτόκον διεφθαρμένην καὶ τοῦ ἀντιχρίστου μητέρα. Ἡ γὰρ ἀληθὴς
Θεοτόκος Χριστὸν ἀληθινὸν Θεὸν ἔτεκεν ἐν σαρκί, οὐ βασανιζομένη ὡς
ἡ παροῦσα, ἀλλὰ δοξαζομένη καὶ ἐν παρθενίᾳ φυλαττομένη. Ὁ δὲ
διάβολος, ἰδὼν τὴν γυναῖκα οὕτω φαιδρῶς διακεκοσμημένην, ἠγνόησεν
ὅτι συνίστορα καὶ συμπράκτορα αὐτοῦ τέξεται ἡ γυνή, καί, ἐπειδὴ τὴν
45 αὐτοῦ βασιλείαν ἡ τοῦ Χριστοῦ γέννησις ἐκολόβωσεν ἐθαμβήθη μήπως
καὶ ὁ ἐκ τῆς γυναικὸς ταύτης τοιοῦτός τις Fol. 68ᵛ | λαχών, καθελεῖ παντελῶς
τὰ τοῦ ᾅδου βασίλεια· διὸ καί, ὡς κεχηνὼς δράκων καὶ πολυκέφαλος,
παρέστη τῇ γυναικὶ τοῦ φαγεῖν τὸ ἐξ αὐτῆς ἀποτικτόμενον βρέφος. Ὡς
δ' αὐτὸ ἡρπάγη πρὸς Κύριον, ὥρμησεν καταδιῶξαι ὄπισθεν αὐτοῦ,
50 κωλυθεὶς δὲ παρὰ τοῦ θείου Μιχαήλ, ἀνῃσχύντησε μετ' αὐτοῦ πολεμῆσαι.
Καὶ ἐπολέμησεν οἷα χύτρα πρὸς λέβητα, καί, συντριβείς, ἀπερρίφη μετὰ
τῆς αὐτοῦ συμμορίας.
  5. Τὸ δὲ παιδίον οὐχ ὡς φιλούμενον ἡρπάγη πρὸς Κύριον, ἀλλ' ἵνα
μισοχρίστου καὶ παρανόμου λαοῦ κατὰ τὰς καρδίας αὐτῶν δοθήσεται
55 ἀρχηγός· πρὸς οὓς καὶ ὁ Κύριος προαπεφήνατο λέγων, Ἐγὼ ἦλθον
ἐν τῷ ὀνόματι τοῦ πατρός μου, καὶ οὐ λαμβάνετέ με·
ἕτερος δὲ ἐλεύσεται ἐν τῷ ἰδίῳ ὀνόματι, κἀκεῖνον
λήψεσθε.
  6. Ὁ δὲ διάβολος λυττήσας καὶ κατὰ τῆς γυναικός, οὐδὲ κατ' αὐτῆς
60 ἐδόθη αὐτῷ ἰσχύς, ἀλλ' ἵνα ζήσῃ ἐν τῷ τέως· θνήξεται δὲ εὐκαίρως τὸν
ἄξιον αὐτῆς θάνατον.
  7. Τὸ δεκακέρατον δὲ καὶ ἑπτακέφαλον ἐκ τῆς θαλάσσης θηρίον
ἐπανελθόν, εὔδηλον ὅτι ὁ ἀντίχριστος ἦν, ὁ καὶ τὴν τοῦ πατρὸς αὐτοῦ
διαβόλου φαντασιώδη φέρων μορφήν. Ἐξ οὗ καὶ μεγάλην εἰληφὼς
65 ἐξουσίαν, τῶν ἁγίων μὲν ὤφθη πολέμιος, Ἐνὼχ δὲ καὶ Ἡλίαν ἀνεῖλε
κατὰ Θεοῦ συγχώρησιν, καί, στόμα διανοίξας παμμίαρον, τὸν ὑπεράγιον
ἐβλασφήμει Θεόν. Ὁ δὲ φύσει μακρόθυμος Κύριος οὐχ ἁπλῶς ἔφερε
μακροθύμως, ἀλλὰ καὶ σημεῖα μεγάλα ἐπιτελεῖν ἔδωκε τῷ ἐχθρῷ, οὐχ
ὅτι σημειοφόρου ἐκεῖνος ἐκέκτητο ἃ Fol. 69 | ξίαν, ἀλλὰ διὰ τὸν πλανώμενον
70 εἰς αὐτὸν παρανομώτατον λαόν. Ταῦτα δὲ νόμῳ προφητικῷ λέγονται ὡς
ἤδη γεγονότα τὰ μήπω γεγονότα· οὔπω γὰρ Ἐνὼχ καὶ Ἡλίας ἐφάνη οὐδὲ
ἀπεκτάνθησαν, ὁ δὲ προφητικὸς ὀφθαλμὸς ὡς ἤδη γεγονότα προβλέπει
τὰ μέλλοντα. Ὁ δὲ πλάνος ἀντίχριστος, καὶ ὁ εἰς αὐτὸν πλανώμενος λαός,
δύο καὶ μ′ μῆνας ἕξουσι μακροθυμίαν πρὸς Θεοῦ, ἤτουν ἔτη τρία καὶ
75 ἥμισυ, καί, εἶθ' οὕτως, οὐαὶ καὶ τῷ ἄρχοντι καὶ τῷ ἀρχομένῳ αὐτῷ
ἀσεβεστάτῳ λαῷ.

4, 51 cf. Sir. 13,2
5, 55/58 Ioh. 5,43

4, 39 ὑπονοῶν suppleui   47 δράκων scripsi : δράκαον cod.   50 ἀνῃσχύντησε scripsi :
ἀναισχύντησε cod.
7, 70 λέγονται corr., prius λέγοντι   71 Ἡλίας scripsi : Ἡλιοῦ cod.

Apoc. 13,11–18   **1.** Ὑπ(όθεσις) Ζ΄. Περὶ τοῦ κακωνύμου θηρίου καὶ τοῦ ἀριθμοῦ τοῦ ὀνόματος αὐτοῦ.

«Καὶ πάλιν εἶδον ἄλλο θηρίον ἐκ τῆς γῆς ἀνερχόμενον, ὃ εἶχεν ἀρνίου κέρατα, διὸ καὶ ὡς δράκων ἐλάλει. Καὶ ἔσπευδε τοῦ πεῖσαι πάντας
5 ἀνθρώπους πιστεῦσαι καὶ προσκυνῆσαι τῷ πρὸ αὐτοῦ ἐκ τῆς θαλάσσης ἀνενεχθέντι θηρίῳ, καὶ τὸ ὄνομα αὐτοῦ ἐνχαραχθῆναι ἐν τοῖς μετώποις αὐτῶν, καὶ τὴν εἰκόνα αὐτοῦ λαβεῖν ἐπὶ χεῖρας, καὶ τὸν ἀριθμὸν τοῦ ὀνόματος αὐτοῦ· τῷ δὲ ἀπειθοῦντι θάνατον προσηπείλει. Ὁ δὲ ἀριθμὸς τοῦ ὀνόματος τοῦ θηρίου ἀριθμὸς ἐστιν ἀνθρώπου, ἤτοι ἑξακόσια ξϛ΄·
10 καὶ ὁ ἔχων, φησί, νοῦν καὶ σοφίαν, ψηφισάτω τὸν ἀριθμὸν τοῦ θηρίου» (cf. Apoc. 13,11-18).

2. Ἑρμ(ηνεία): Εὐανθᾶς, τειτάν, λατεῖνος, Βενέδικτος· ἕκαστον τούτων τῶν ὀνομάτων ἀποσῴζει τὸ ψῆφος τῶν ἑξακοσίων ξϛ΄.

3. Τὸ δὲ ἐκ τῆς γῆς ἀναβὰν θηρίον καὶ λαλοῦν ὥσπερ δράκων, ἤτοι
15 ὡς ὄφις ὁ δόλιος, οὗτός ἐστιν ὁ Μαχάμετ, ὁ τοῦ διαβόλου καὶ τοῦ ἀντιχρίστου ἀ Fol. 69ᵛ|πόστολος καὶ προφήτης, ὁ διδάξας τοὺς υἱοὺς Ἄγαρ ὅσα μισεῖ ὁ Θεὸς καὶ φιλεῖ ὁ Σατανᾶς. Καὶ γὰρ ἐδίδαξεν αὐτοὺς τὴν πλατεῖαν καὶ εὐρύχωρον τῆς ἀπωλείας ὁδόν, καὶ ὑπέσχετο αὐτοῖς ἵνα μετὰ τὴν τοσαύτην ἀκαθαρσίαν εἰσάξῃ εἰς τὸν παράδεισον, ἵνα κἀκεῖ
20 μετὰ γυναικῶν συνευφραίνωνται. Αὐτοὶ δέ, τὴν εὐκολίαν τῆς διδαχῆς προσηκάμενοι, μετὰ προσθήκης αὐτὴν ἐκπληροῦσι, καί, ὡς ἐθελόκακοι καὶ ἐθελότυφλοι, οὐκ ἠθέλησαν ἀναβλέψαι καὶ γνῶναι τὴν οὕτω πρόδηλον καὶ ὀλέθριον ἀπάτην τῆς αὐτοῦ διδαχῆς, ἀλλ᾽ εἰς αὐτὸν ἔχουσι τὰς ἐλπίδας, ἵνα εἰσάξῃ αὐτοὺς εἰς τὸν παράδεισον.

25 **4.** Ὁ δὲ Θεός, οἷς οἶδε κρίμασι, στελεῖ αὐτὸν πρὸς αὐτοὺς ἐν τῇ ἐνδημίᾳ τοῦ ἀντιχρίστου, καὶ πείσει αὐτοὺς τοῦ πιστεῦσαι καὶ προσκυνῆσαι ὡς Χριστὸν τὸν ἀντίχριστον καὶ ἐν τοῖς μετώποις αὐτῶν διαγράψαι τὸ ὄνομα αὐτοῖς, τοῖς δὲ ἀπειθοῦσι προσαπειλεῖν θάνατον.

3, 19 εἰσάξῃ scripsi : εἰσάξαι cod.
4, 25 στελεῖ correxi : στείλει cod. 28 ἀπειθοῦσι correxi : ἀπηθοῦσιν cod. τ. δ. ἀπειθοῦσι προσαπειλεῖν θ. intellige 'filii Agar mortem non obedientibus intentabunt'

Apoc. 14,1–7   **1.** Ὑπ(όθεσις) Η΄. Περὶ τοῦ ἀρνίου καὶ τῶν ἀμώμων καὶ τῆς φωνῆς.

«Καὶ εἶδον τὸ ἀρνίον ἑστῶτα ἐπὶ τὸ ὄρος Σιών· καὶ σύν αὐτῷ ἑκατὸν τεσσαράκοντα τέσσαρας χιλιάδας ἀνδρῶν παρθένων καὶ ἀμώμων, οἳ οὐκ

5 ἐμολύνθησαν εἰς ἁμαρτίαν, καὶ ψεῦδος οὐχ εὑρέθη ἐν τῷ στόματι αὐτῶν, διὸ καί εἰσιν ἀπὸ τῶν ἀνθρώπων ἀπαρχὴ τῷ Θεῷ καὶ τῷ ἀρνίῳ. Καὶ φωνὰς μεγάλας ἤκουσα ἐν τῷ οὐρανῷ, ᾄδοντας ᾠδὴν τῷ Θεῷ ὥσπερ κιθάραις, καὶ οὐδεὶς ἠδύνατο γνῶναι τὴν ᾠδὴν εἰ μὴ οἱ σὺν τῷ ἀρνίῳ ἑκατὸν τεσσαράκοντα τέσσαρες χιλιάδες. Fol. 70| Καὶ ἰδοὺ ἕτερος ἄγγελος

10 ἐπεβόα μεγάλῃ τῇ φωνῇ πᾶσιν ἀνθρώποις λέγων, Φοβήθητε, ἄνθρωποι, καὶ δότε δόξαν τῷ Θεῷ· ἦλθε γὰρ ἡ τῆς κρίσεως ὥρα, ἐν ᾗ ἕκαστος λήψεται κατὰ τὰς πράξεις αὐτοῦ» (cf. Apoc. 14,1–7).

2. Ἑρμ(ηνεία): Σαφῆ τὰ ῥηθέντα· δηλοῦσι γὰρ ὅτι καθαρότης καὶ ἁγνεία καὶ ἄμωμος πολιτεία, συναυλία γίνεται τῷ παναμώμῳ Χριστῷ τῷ

15 Θεῷ ἡμῶν, καὶ περὶ τῆς τελευταίας ἡμέρας καὶ κρίσεως καὶ ἀνταποδόσεως.

2, 13 σαφῆ ||| τὰ ῥηθέντα cod.

Apoc. 14,14–16,1 **1.** Ὑπ(όθεσις) Θ΄. Περὶ τοῦ καθημένου ἐν τῇ νεφέλῃ.
«Καὶ εἶδον νεφέλην λευκὴν καὶ ἄνθρωπον καθήμενον ἐπ᾽ αὐτήν, καὶ
χρυσοῦν στέφανον ἐπὶ τῆς κεφαλῆς αὐτοῦ, καὶ ἐν τῇ χειρὶ αὐτοῦ
δρέπανον ὀξύ· καὶ ἔβαλεν αὐτὸ ἐπὶ τὴν γῆν καὶ ἐθέρισεν αὐτήν. Καὶ
5 ἕτερος ἄγγελος ἐκελεύσθη καὶ ἔβαλε δρέπανον ἐπὶ τὰς ἀμπέλους τῆς γῆς
καὶ ἐτρύγησεν αὐτάς, καὶ ἔβαλε τοὺς καρποὺς ἐν τῇ μεγάλῃ τοῦ Θεοῦ
ληνῷ ἔξωθεν τῆς πόλεως, καὶ ἐπατήθησαν, καὶ ἐξῆλθεν αἷμα ἐκ τῆς ληνοῦ
μέχρι σταδίων χιλίων ἑξακοσίων, ἕως καὶ χαλινοῦ τῶν ἵππων.
2.»Εἶτα καὶ ἄλλον εἶδον σημεῖον ἐν τῷ οὐρανῷ, ἀγγέλους ἑπτά, καὶ
10 τὰς ἐσχάτας ἑπτὰ πληγὰς φέροντας τοῦ θυμοῦ τοῦ Θεοῦ. Καὶ ἐξῆλθον
οἱ ἑπτὰ ἄγγελοι περιεζωσμένοι περὶ τὰ στήθη ζώνας χρυσᾶς, καὶ ἐν ταῖς
χερσὶν αὐτῶν φιάλας χρυσᾶς γεμούσας τοῦ θυμοῦ τοῦ Θεοῦ, ὅπως,
ἀπελθόντες, ἐκχέωσιν αὐτὰς ἐπὶ τὴν γῆν» (cf. Apoc. 14,14–16,1).
3. Ἑρμ(ηνεία): Ὁ ἐπὶ τῆς νεφέλης καθήμενος ὁ Υἱός ἐστι τοῦ Θεοῦ,
15 τὸ δὲ δι᾽ αὐτοῦ δρέπανον καὶ τὸ θέρος, τῆς Fol. 70ᵛ| γῆς παραδηλοῖ τέλος.
Ἄμπελος δὲ καὶ τρύγος οἱ ἄνθρωποι καὶ οἱ καρποὶ τῶν πονηρῶν ἔργων
αὐτῶν, ἅ, ὥσπερ σταφυλαί, ἐν τῇ ληνῷ συναχθῶσι τῆς μεγάλης τοῦ Θεοῦ
δικαιοκρισίας, ὅτι τὰ ἔργα τῶν ἀνθρώπων οὐκ εἰσιν ὡς σταφυλὴ οἴνου,
ἀλλ᾽ ὡς σάρκες αἱμάτων πολλῶν· ὅπερ δηλοῖ ἔξω τῆς πόλεως ποταμηδὸν
20 ἐκχυθῆναι καὶ ἔξω τῆς βασιλείας τοῦ Θεοῦ ἐναπομεῖναι. Αἱ δὲ ἑπτὰ φιάλαι,
παρὰ τῶν ἑπτὰ ἀγγέλων φερόμεναι, τὰς πολλὰς καὶ δεινὰς θλίψεις καὶ
πληγὰς εἰκονίζουσι τῆς συντελείας τῶν ἡμερῶν ἐκείνων.

1, 4 δρέπανον scripsi : δρεπάνη cod.

Apoc. 16,2–21; 19,17–18; 19,11–21   **1.** Ὑπ(όθεσις) Γ΄. Περὶ τῶν ἑπτὰ ἀγγέλων καὶ τῶν ἑπτὰ πληγῶν καὶ τοῦ μεγάλου πολέμου.

«Καὶ ἀπελθὼν ὁ πρῶτος ἐξέχεε τὴν φιάλην αὐτοῦ εἰς τὴν γῆν, καὶ ἐγένετο ἕλκος πονηρὸν καὶ κακὸν ἐπὶ τοὺς ἔχοντας τὸ χάραγμα τοῦ θηρίου

5 καὶ τὴν αὐτοῦ προσκυνοῦντας εἰκόνα.

2.»Καὶ ὁ δεύτερος ἐξέχεε τὴν φιάλην αὐτοῦ εἰς τὴν θάλασσαν καὶ μετήγαγεν αὐτὴν εἰς αἷμα, καὶ ἀπέθανε πᾶσα ψυχὴ ζῶσα ἐν αὐτῇ.

3.»Καὶ ὁ τρίτος ἐξέχεε τὴν φιάλην αὐτοῦ ἐπὶ τοὺς ποταμοὺς καὶ τὰς πηγὰς τῶν ὑδάτων, καὶ ἐγένοντο αἷμα.

10 **4.**»Καὶ ὁ τέταρτος ἐξέχεε τὴν φιάλην αὐτοῦ ἐπὶ τὸν ἥλιον, καὶ ἐκαυματίσθησαν οἱ ἄνθρωποι καύσωνι μεγάλῳ, ὥσπερ ἀπὸ πυρός, καὶ ἐβλασφήμουν τὸν Θεόν.

5.»Καὶ ὁ πέμπτος ἐξέχεε τὴν φιάλην αὐτοῦ ἐπὶ τὸν θρόνον τοῦ θηρίου, καὶ τὸ βασίλειον αὐτοῦ ἐγένετο σκότος.

15 **6.**»Καὶ ὁ ἕκτος ἐξέχεε τὴν φι Fol. 71|άλην αὐτοῦ ἐπὶ τὸν μέγαν ποταμόν, τὸν Εὐφράτην, καί ἐξηράνθη, ὁδοποιῶν τοὺς βασιλεῖς τοὺς ἀπὸ ἡλίου ἀνατολῆς.

7.»Καὶ ὁ ἕβδομος ἐξέχεε τὴν φιάλην αὐτοῦ ἐπὶ τὸν ἀέρα, καὶ ἐγένοντο ἀστραπαὶ καὶ βρονταὶ καὶ σεισμὸς παμμεγέθης, καὶ κατέπεσον

20 αἱ πόλεις τῶν ἐθνῶν, ἡ δὲ πόλις ἡ μεγάλη εἰς τρία μέρη διῃρέθη, καὶ οὐ μετενόησαν οἱ ἄνθρωποι ἀπὸ τῶν ἔργων αὐτῶν, ἀλλ᾽ ἔτι ἐβλασφήμουν τὸ ὄνομα τοῦ Θεοῦ.

8.»Καὶ εἶδον ὅτι τρία ἐξῆλθον ἀκάθαρτα πνεύματα δαιμονίων ἀπὸ τριῶν ἀκαθάρτων στομάτων, ἤγουν ἐκ τοῦ δράκοντος καὶ τοῦ θηρίου

25 καὶ τοῦ ψευδοπροφήτου, ἃ ἐστάλησαν τοῦ ποιεῖν σημεῖα ἐνώπιον τῶν βασιλέων πάσης τῆς γῆς, καὶ συναγαγεῖν αὐτοὺς εἰς ⟨τὸν⟩ πόλεμον τῆς μεγάλης ἡμέρας Θεοῦ τοῦ παντοκράτορος. Καὶ συνήχθησαν εἰς τόπον Ἑβραϊστὶ καλούμενον Ἀρμαγεδών.

Apoc. 19, 17–18   **9.**»Καὶ εἶδον ἄγγελον ἐν τῷ ἀέρι ἑστῶτα καὶ

30 καλοῦντα πάντα τὰ ὄρνεα, Δεῦτε, λέγων, συνάχθητε εἰς τὸν δεῖπνον τὸν μέγαν, ἵνα φάγητε σάρκας βασιλέων καὶ μεγιστάνων, ἵππων καὶ χιλιάρχων, δούλων καὶ ἐλευθέρων, καὶ ἀπὸ πάσης σαρκός.

Apoc. 19, 11–21   **10.**»Καὶ ἰδοὺ ἵππος λευκός, καὶ ὁ καθήμενος ἐπ᾽ αὐτὸν πιστὸς καὶ ἀληθινός, ἐν δικαιοσύνῃ κρίνων καὶ πολεμῶν. Καὶ ἐκ τοῦ

35 στόματος αὐτοῦ ῥομφαία δίστομος ὀξεῖα· οἱ ὀφθαλμοὶ αὐτοῦ ὡς φλὸξ πυρός· περιβεβλημένος ἱμάτιον ῥεραντισμένον αἵματι· τὸ δὲ ὄνομα αὐτοῦ Ὁ Λόγος τοῦ Θεοῦ, καὶ ἕτερον ὄνομα γεγραμμένον, ὃ οὐδεὶς εἶδεν εἰ μὴ αὐτὸς μόνος· καὶ ἐπὶ τὴν κεφαλὴν αὐτοῦ διαδήματα πολλά· καὶ Fol. 71ᵛ| τὰ στρατεύματα τοῦ οὐρανοῦ ἠκολούθει αὐτῷ ἐφ᾽ ἵπποις λευκοῖς καὶ

40 ἱματισμῷ λευκοβυσσίνῳ καθαρῷ. Καὶ συνεκρότησαν αὐτῷ πόλεμον τὸ ἀθροισθὲν πλῆθος τῶν βασιλέων τῆς γῆς καὶ τὰ σρατόπεδα αὐτῶν καὶ τὸ θηρίον καὶ ὁ ψευδοπροφήτης ὁ ποιήσας τὰ σημεῖα καὶ ἀπατήσας τοὺς βασιλεῖς. Καὶ τὰ μὲν πλήθη ἀπεκτάνθησαν διὰ τῆς ῥομφαίας τῆς ἐκπορευομένης ἐκ τοῦ στόματος τοῦ καθημένου ἐπὶ τοῦ ἵππου τοῦ λευκοῦ,

---

8, 26 τὸν suppleui

45 τὸ δὲ θηρίον καὶ ὁ ψευδοπροφήτης αὐτοῦ, κρατηθέντες, ἐβλήθησαν εἰς
τὴν λίμνην τοῦ πυρὸς καὶ τοῦ θείου, καὶ πάντα τὰ ὄρνεα ἐχορτάσθησαν
σάρκας ἀνθρώπων» (cf. Apoc. 19,11-21). **11.** Ἑρμ(ηνεία): Αἱ φιάλαι εἶδός ἐστι κρατήρων τῶν παρ' ἡμῶν
λεγομένων ποτήρια καὶ κοῦππαι, τὸ δὲ ἐν αὐταῖς κέρασμα ἄξιον τοῦ
50 ἀθεωτάτου ἐκείνου λαοῦ, ἕλκος καὶ αἷμα καὶ τὰ ἑξῆς τῶν ἑπτά. **12.** Ἀπὸ δὲ τοῦ δράκοντος διαβόλου καὶ τοῦ θηρίου ἀντιχρίστου
καὶ τοῦ ψευδοπροφήτου Μοχουμὲτ τρία πνεύματα ἐξῆλθον, καὶ διά τινων
σημείων ἀπατηλῶν ἀπεπλάνησαν καὶ συνήγαγον πάντας τοὺς βασιλεῖς
τῆς γῆς μετὰ τῶν στρατοπέδων αὐτῶν τοῦ πολεμῆσαι μετὰ τοῦ καθημένου
55 ἐπὶ τοῦ ἵππου τοῦ λευκοῦ, ὅς ἐστιν, ὡς εἴρηται, ὁ Λόγος τοῦ Θεοῦ, Χριστὸς
ὁ Θεὸς ἡμῶν· καὶ τοῦτο δηλοῦσι τὰ σήμαντρα, τό τε ὄνομα καὶ τὸ
ἡμαγμένον ἱμάτιον καὶ τὰ ἑξῆς. Ἡ δὲ ἐκ τοῦ στόματος αὐτοῦ ῥομφαία
ἡ ἀπόφασις αὐτοῦ ἐστι, ἀναιροῦσα τοὺς ἀντιπάλους. Ὦπται δὲ τῷ
θεωρῷ τοιαύτῃ κατασκευῇ νόμου πολέμου. 60 **13.** Καὶ οὐράνιαι ἀγγέλων στρατιαὶ καταδέχονται πολεμεῖν μετὰ τῶν
Fol. 72| ἀνθρώπων. Εἷς γὰρ ἄγγελος, ἐξελθών, ἑκατὸν ὀγδοήκοντα πέντε
χιλιάδας ἐν μιᾷ ῥοπῇ ἀνεῖλε τῶν Ἀσσυρίων, τὰ δὲ νῦν στρατόπεδα τῶν
μωρῶν βασιλέων, συγκροτήσαντες πόλεμον μετὰ τοῦ Β α σ ι λ έ ω ς τ ῆ ς
δ ό ξ η ς, ἐπολέμησαν ὡς στυπεῖον μετὰ πυρὸς, ὡς ὄστρακον μετὰ
65 σιδήρου, ὡς χύτρα πρὸς λέβητα, ὡς ὄνος μετὰ λέοντος, καὶ ὡς ἄνθρωπος
μετὰ ἀγγέλου. Διὸ καί, καθὼς ὁ ἄγγελος προαπεφήνατο, γεγόνασι δεῖπνος
μέγας παντὸς πετεινοῦ καὶ θηρίου τῆς γῆς, οἱ δὲ τούτων ἔξαρχοι καὶ
ἀπατεῶνες, ὅ τε ἀντίχριστος καὶ ὁ Μοχωμέτ, ἀπερρίφησαν εἰς τὴν λίμνην
τοῦ πυρὸς καὶ τοῦ θείου. Θεῖον δέ λέγεται ὁ δημοτικῶς λεγόμενος θείαφος,
70 ἱκανὸς κατακαίειν μετὰ πυρὸς λίθους καὶ σίδηρα, δι' ὧν καὶ ἐτεφρώθησαν
αἱ πόλεις τῶν Σοδόμων. Ἐγὼ δέ, πολλῆς συντομίας ἐπιμελούμενος,
συλλήβδην ταῦτα διὰ τὸ εὔληπτον φάσκω.

13, 61/62 cf. IV Reg. 19,35; cf. Is. 37, 36   63/64 Ps. 23(24), 7ss.   65 cf. Sir. 13,2
64/65 cf. Gen. 32,23 ss.

11, 49 κοῦππαι scripsi : κούπας cod.
12, 52 Μοχουμὲτ hic cod. scribit quoque Μαχάμετ, Μοχουμὲτ, Μοχωμὲτ
13, 62 μιᾷ correxi : μία cod.   63 συγκροτήσαντες scripsi : συνκροτήσαντες cod.

Apoc. 17,1–19,11 **1.** Ὑπ(όθεσις) ΙΑ΄. Περὶ τῆς πόρνης πόλεως καὶ τῆς ἁλώσεως αὐτῆς.

«Καὶ ἦλθε, φησί, πρός με εἷς ἐκ τῶν προρρηθέντων ἑπτὰ ἀγγέλων τῶν ἐχόντων τὰς φιάλας, καὶ ἐλάλησε πρός με, Δεῦρο καὶ δείξω σοι τὸ 5 κρῖμα τῆς πόρνης τῆς μεγάλης, τῆς καθημένης ἐπὶ τῶν ὑδάτων τῶν πολλῶν, μεθ᾽ ἧς ἐπόρνευσαν οἱ βασιλεῖς τῆς γῆς, καὶ ἐμεθύσθησαν ἐκ τοῦ οἴνου τῆς πορνείας αὐτῆς οἱ κατοικοῦντες ἐπ᾽ αὐτήν· καὶ ἀπήνεγκέ με εἰς τόπον ἔρημον Πνεύματος» (cf. Apoc. 17,1–3a).

2. Ἑρμ(ηνεία): Τάχα διὰ τὴν ἀκαθαρσίαν τῆς πόρνης οὐδὲ Πνεῦμα 10 ἦν ἐν τῷ τόπῳ.

3. «Καὶ εἶδον γυναῖκα ἐπὶ θηρίον κόκκινον καθημένην καὶ ὀνόματα γέμουσαν βλασφημίας, τὸ δὲ θηρίον ἑπτὰ Fol. 72ᵛ| κεφαλὰς εἶχε καὶ κέρατα δέκα. Ἦν δὲ ἡ γυνὴ περιβεβλημένη πορφύραν καὶ ὅλη κεκοσμημένη χρυσίῳ καὶ μαργάρῳ καὶ λίθῳ τιμίῳ, καὶ ἐν τῇ χειρὶ αὐτῆς ποτήριον χρυσοῦν 15 γέμον βδελυγμάτων καὶ ἀκαθαρσίαν πολλὴν ἐκ τῆς πορνείας αὐτῆς, ἐπὶ δὲ τοῦ μετώπου αὐτῆς ἔγραφε, Βαβυλὼν ἡ μεγάλη, ἡ μήτηρ τῶν πόρνων καὶ τῶν βδελυγμάτων τῆς γῆς. Καὶ εἶδον αὐτὴν μεθύουσαν ἐκ τοῦ αἵματος τῶν Χριστοῦ μαρτύρων» (cf. Apoc. 17,3b–6).

4. Ἑρμ(ηνεία): ἤτουν ἐκ βασιλέων τυράννων.

20 **5.** «Καὶ ταῦτα ἰδὼν καὶ θαυμάσας, λέγει μοι ὁ ἄγγελος, Διατὶ ἐθαύμασας; πρόσχες, κἀγώ σοι ἐρῶ τὸ μυστήριον· ἡ πόρνη γυνὴ ἡ πόλις ἡ μεγάλη, ἡ ἔχουσα βασιλείαν ὑπὲρ πάσας τὰς βασιλείας τῆς γῆς. Τὸ δὲ θηρίον ἐν ᾧ κάθηται ἔστι καὶ οὐκ ἔστιν· ἀναβήσεται γὰρ ἐκ τῆς ἀβύσσου καὶ ἀπελεύσεται εἰς ἀπώλειαν» (cf. Apoc. 17,3–8).

25 **6.** Ἑρμ(ηνεία): Τὴν ἐπ᾽ ἐσχάτων τοῦ διαβόλου ἠνίξατο ἔλευσιν καὶ ἀπώλειαν.

7. «Αἱ δὲ ἑπτὰ κεφαλαὶ τοῦ θηρίου ἐν ᾧ κάθηται ἡ πόρνη, τὰ ἑπτά εἰσιν ὄρη, τὰ δὲ δέκα κέρατα δέκα εἰσὶ βασιλεῖς, οἵτινες οὔπω ἔλαβον βασιλείαν, βασιλείας δὲ ἐξουσίαν μίαν ἕξουσιν ὥραν, καὶ μετὰ τοῦ 30 θηρίου μίαν ἕξουσι γνώμην, καὶ δώσει αὐτοῖς δύναμιν καὶ ἐξουσίαν, ἵνα μετὰ τοῦ ἀρνίου πολεμήσωσι, ἀλλὰ τὸ ἀρνίον νικήσει αὐτούς» (cf. Apoc. 17,9–14a).

8. Ἑρμ(ηνεία): Ἐν ταῖς ἡμέραις τοῦ ἀντιχρίστου οἱ δέκα οὗτοι φανήσονται βασιλεῖς, καὶ πολεμήσουσι τοὺς πιστεύοντας εἰς τὸν ἀμνὸν 35 τοῦ Θεοῦ, καί, ἡττηθέντες, βληθήσονται εἰς τὸ πῦρ σὺν τῷ ἐπιστάτῃ αὐτῶν, ὅτι τὸ ἀρνίον, φησί, «κύριος κυρίων Fol. 73| ἐστι καὶ βασιλεὺς βασιλέων» (cf. Apoc. 17,14b).

9. «Τὰ δὲ πολλὰ ὕδατα, ἐν οἷς κάθηται ἡ πόρνη, ὄχλοι εἰσὶν ἐθνῶν καὶ λαοὶ καὶ γλῶσσαι, οἵτινες κακώσουσιν αὐτὴν καὶ τὰς σάρκας αὐτῆς 40 φάγονται καὶ πυρὶ αὐτὴν κατακαύσουσι· ἔδωκε γὰρ ὁ Θεὸς ἐν ταῖς καρδίαις

1, 8 ἔρημον πνεύματος fuitne uar. lect. in exemplari Script. Inclusi?
3, 15 γέμον scripsi : γέμοντα cod. γ. βδελυγμάτων καὶ ἀκαθαρσίαν iude Apoc. 17,4 γ. β. καὶ τὰ ἀκάθαρτα   16 πόρνων cod. : an πορνῶν scribendum?
5, 20 anacolouthon
9, 40 ἔδωκε correxi : δοῦναι cod.

αὐτῶν τοῦ ποιῆσαι τὴν γνώμην αὐτοῦ, καὶ ἔδωκε τὴν βασιλείαν αὐτοῖς, ἄχρις ἂν τελεσθῶσιν οἱ λόγοι τοῦ Θεοῦ» (cf. Apoc. 17,15–17).

10. Ἑρμ(ηνεία)· Οὐκ ἔδωκε, φησίν, αὐτοῖς τὴν βασιλείαν εἰς τέλος, ἀλλὰ πρός τινα χρόνον, ἕως οὗ πληρωθῶσιν οἱ λόγοι τοῦ Θεοῦ, οὓς ἀπεφήνατο κατὰ τῆς πόρνης ἀγανακτήσας.

11. «Καὶ μετὰ ταῦτα εἶδον ἕτερον ἄγγελον καταβαίνοντα ἐκ τοῦ οὐρανοῦ, καὶ ἐφωτίσθη ἡ γῆ ἀπὸ τῆς δόξης αὐτοῦ. Καὶ ἐν φωνῇ μεγάλῃ ἐκραύγασε λέγων· Πέπτωκε Βαβυλὼν ἡ μεγάλη, καὶ γέγονε κατοικητήριον τῶν δαιμόνων καὶ φυλακὴ παντὸς πνεύματος ἀκαθάρτου» (cf. Apoc. 18,1–2).

12. Ἑρμ(ηνεία)· Οἱ τὴν πόλιν ἁλόντες, φησί, καὶ πορθήσαντες, ὡς δαίμονες καὶ ὡς ἀκάθαρτα πνεύματα ἐν αὐτῇ κατοικοῦσι, καὶ οὐχ ὡς ἀγαθοῖς ἀλλὰ διὰ τὴν πόρνην πρὸς αὐτοὺς παρεδόθη, ὅτι «ἐκ τοῦ οἴνου, φησί, καὶ τῆς μέθης τῆς πορνείας αὐτῆς πεπτώκασιν οἱ βασιλεῖς αὐτῆς οἱ πορνεύσαντες μετ᾽ αὐτῆς, καὶ οἱ ἔμποροι τῆς γῆς ἐπλούτησαν ἐκ τῆς δυνάμεως τοῦ στρήνους αὐτῆς» (cf. Apoc. 18,3).

13. «Οἱ δὲ βασιλεῖς ἑπτά εἰσιν· οἱ πέντε ἔπεσον καὶ ὁ εἷς ἔστι, καὶ ὁ ἕβδομος οὔπω ἦλθεν, καὶ ὅταν ἔλθῃ ὀλίγον δεῖ αὐτὸν μεῖναι. Καὶ τὸ θηρίον ὃ ἦν καὶ οὐκ ἔστι, καὶ οὗτος ὄγδοός ἐστι καὶ εἰς ἀπώλειαν ὑπάγει» (cf. Apoc. 17,9–11).

14. Ἑρμηνεία· Μετὰ τοὺς ἑπτὰ βασιλεῖς, φησί, φανήσεται ὄγδοος Fol. 73| εἴτε κυρίως ὁ ἀντίχριστος, εἴτε ὅμοιος αὐτοῦ θηριώδης, καὶ εἰς ἀπώλειαν ὑπάγει.

15. «Καὶ ἤκουσα ἐκ τοῦ οὐρανοῦ φωνὴν λέγουσαν, Ἔξελθε ἐξ αὐτῆς ὁ λαός μου, ἵνα μὴ συγκοινωνήσετε ταῖς ἁμαρτίαις αὐτῆς, καὶ ἐκ τῶν πληγῶν αὐτῆς ἵνα μὴ λάβητε» (cf. Apoc. 18,4)

16. Ἑρμ(ηνεία)· Οἱ ἐμοί, φησί, δοῦλοι καὶ τῆς ἁμαρτίας ἐχθροί, ἐξέλθετε καὶ διαχωρίσθητε τῆς πόλεως πόρνης, ὅπως μὴ γένησθε τῆς ἁμαρτίας αὐτῆς καὶ τῆς κακώσεως κοινωνοί.

17. «Ὅτι ἐκολλήθησαν αὐτῆς αἱ ἁμαρτίαι ἄχρι τοῦ οὐρανοῦ, καὶ ἐμνήσθη Κύριος τῶν ἀδικημάτων αὐτῆς καὶ εἶπεν· Ὡς αὐτὴ ἀπέδωκε τὰ διπλᾶ, οὕτως καὶ αὐτῇ ἀπόδοτε τὰ διπλᾶ κατὰ τὰ ἔργα αὐτῆς, καὶ ἐν ᾧ ἐκέρασε ποτηρίῳ διπλῷ κεράσατε αὐτὴν κατὰ τὸ μέτρον τοῦ στρήνους αὐτῆς, καὶ δότε αὐτῇ βασανισμὸν πένθους. Ὅτι εἶπεν ἐν τῇ καρδίᾳ αὐτῆς, Βασίλισσά εἰμι, οὐ χήρα, καὶ οὐ μὴ πένθος ἴδω ἐν ἐμοί· καὶ διὰ τοῦτο ἐν ἡμέρᾳ μιᾷ ἥξουσιν αἱ πληγαὶ αὐτῆς, θάνατος καὶ πένθος, καὶ ἐν πυρὶ αὐτὴν κατακαύσουσιν, ὅτι δίκαιος Κύριος ὁ κρίνων αὐτήν. Καὶ κλαύσουσι καὶ κόψονται οἱ στρηνιάσαντες καὶ πορνεύσαντες ἐν αὐτῇ βασιλεῖς, ἑστηκότες ἀπὸ μακρόθεν διὰ τὸν φόβον τοῦ βασανισμοῦ τῆς πυρώσεως αὐτῆς, κλαίοντες καὶ λέγοντες, Οὐαὶ οὐαί, Βαβυλὼν ἡ μεγάλη, καὶ πόλις

12, 55 μετ᾽ αὐτῆς scripsi : μὲ ταύτης cod.
15, 65 συγκοινωνήσητε scripsi : συγκοινωνήσεται cod.
16, 67 ἑρμ(ηνεία) in margine   68 ἁμαρ|||τίας cod.
17, 76 μιᾷ scripsi : μία cod.

ἡ ὀχυρά, ὅτι ἐν ὥρᾳ μιᾷ ἦλθεν ἡ κρίσις σου. Οἱ ἔμποροι δὲ καὶ πᾶς πλευστικός, ἀπὸ μακρόθεν ἑστῶτες καὶ χοῦν βαλόντες ἐπὶ τὰς κεφαλὰς αὐτῶν, ἔκραζον κλαίοντες καὶ λέγοντες, Οὐαὶ οὐαί, ἡ πόλις ἡ μεγάλη, ἐν ᾗ Fol. 74|

85 πάντες ἐπλούτουν οἱ ἔχοντες τὰ πλοῖα, καὶ νῦν τὸν γόμον αὐτῶν οὐδεὶς ὁ ἀγοράζων· ἀργύριον καὶ χρυσίον καὶ λίθους τιμίους, μάργαρον καὶ βύσσινον καὶ πορφύρα καὶ τὰ λοιπὰ πάντα ἀπῆλθον ἀπὸ σοῦ, ὅτι ἔκρινε Κύριος ἐπὶ σοί. Καὶ ἦρεν ὁ ἄγγελος λίθον ὡς μύλον μέγαν καὶ ἔρριψεν εἰς τὴν θάλασσαν λέγων, Οὕτως βληθήσεται Βαβυλὼν ἡ μεγάλη πόλις, καὶ οὐ μὴ εὑρεθῇ ἔτι.

90 **18.** »Καὶ μετὰ ταῦτα ἤκουσα ἐν τῷ οὐρανῷ ὄχλων φωνὰς μεγάλας, ὑμνούντων καὶ λεγόντων:

Ἀλληλούϊα, ἀλληλούϊα· ἡ σωτηρία καὶ ἡ δύναμις καὶ ἡ δόξα τοῦ Θεοῦ ἡμῶν, ὅτι ἔκρινε τὴν πόρνην τὴν μεγάλην, τὴν διαφθείρασαν τὴν γῆν ἐν τῇ πορνείᾳ αὐτῆς» (cf. Apoc. 18,5-19,2).

95 **19.** Ἑρμ(ηνεία): Ὕμνησαν ἄγγελοι κρίσιν ἰδόντες δικαίαν, καὶ σύ, ἄνθρωπε, ἀγανακτεῖς; Λέξον μᾶλλον καὶ αὐτός, Δ ί κ α ι ο ς ε ἶ , Κ ύ ρ ι ε , κ α ὶ ε ὐ θ ε ῖ ς α ἱ κ ρ ί σ ε ι ς σ ο υ · τί γὰρ ὤνησεν ἡμᾶς πλοῦτος καὶ τρυφὴ καὶ πόλεως εὐδαιμονία; μιᾷ ῥοπῇ καὶ ὡς ποτάμιον ῥεῦμα παρήλθοσαν πάντα, καὶ ἡμεῖς παρεδόθημεν εἰς χεῖρας ὑπεναντίων.

19, 96/97 Ps. 118(119), 137 sicut apud cod. Alexandrinum

17, 81 μιᾷ scripsi : μία cod.   87 μέγαν scripsi : μέγα cod. an μῆλον μέγα (lapidum quasi malum magnum) recte?

Apoc. 20,1–10   **1.** Ὑπ(όθεσις) ΙΒ′. Περὶ τῆς τῶν χιλίων ἐτῶν δεσμεύσεως τοῦ διαβόλου.

«Καὶ πάλιν εἶδον ἕτερον ἄγγελον καταβαίνοντα ἐκ τοῦ οὐρανοῦ, φέροντα ἐπὶ χεῖρας τὴν κλεῖν τῆς ἀβύσσου καὶ ἅλυσιν μεγάλην. Καὶ
5 κρατήσας τὸν δράκοντα, τὸν ὄφιν τὸν ἀρχαῖον, ὅς ἐστιν Διάβολος, ὁ πλανῶν πᾶσαν τὴν οἰκουμένην, καὶ δήσας αὐτόν, ἔβαλεν εἰς τὴν ἄβυσσον, καί, κλείσας αὐτήν, ἐσφράγισεν ἐπάνω αὐτοῦ ἕως χίλια ἔτη, ἵνα μὴ πλανᾷ τοὺς ἀνθρώπους· καὶ μετὰ χίλια ἔτη, δεῖ αὐτὸν ἀπολυθῆναι τῆς φυλακῆς χρόνῳ μικρῷ» (cf. Apoc. 20,1–3). Fol. 74ᵛ|
10 **2.** Ἑρμ(ηνεία): Παρεξετάσας γὰρ τοὺς παρελθόντας χρόνους τῶν αἰώνων πρὸς τοὺς καταλειφθέντας τελευταίους, «μικρῷ» ἐκάλεσε «χρόνῳ».
3. «Καὶ ἐξελεύσεται καὶ πλανήσει τὰ ἔθνη πάσης τῆς γῆς, καὶ τὸν Γὼγ καὶ τὸν Μαγώγ, ἐρεθίζων εἰς πόλεμον· καὶ κυκλώσουσι τὴν παρεμβολὴν τῶν ἁγίων, καὶ τὴν πόλιν τὴν ἠγαπημένην. Καὶ τότε καταβήσεται πῦρ
15 οὐράνιον παρὰ Θεοῦ καὶ καταφάγεται αὐτούς, καὶ ὁ διάβολος ὁ πλανήσας αὐτοὺς βληθήσεται εἰς τὴν λίμνην τοῦ πυρὸς καὶ τοῦ θείου, ὅπου τὸ θηρίον καὶ ὁ ψευδοπροφήτης ἐβλήθησαν» (cf. Apoc. 20,7–10).
4. Ἑρμ(ηνεία): Ὁ διάβολος καὶ ὁ ἀντίχριστος καὶ ὁ ὑπηρέτης αὐτῶν Μοχωμὲτ εἰς μίαν, ὡς λέγει βληθήσονται φλόγα καὶ κόλασιν αἰώνιον.
20 Εὔδηλον δὲ ὅτι ἐν τῷ ϛφλγ′ ἔτει ἐσταυρώθη ὁ Χριστός, καί, κατελθὼν εἰς τὸν ᾅδην, ἐδεσμεύθη ὁ τύραννος· καὶ ψήφισον ἀπὸ τοῦ ῥηθέντος ἔτους καὶ μέχρι ποίου ἔτους τὰ χίλια συνετελέσθησαν ἔτη, καὶ ἀπολυθεὶς ὁ πολέμιος ἐρεθίζει πολέμους.

1, 1 ante δεσμεύσεως τῆς deleui δεσμέσεως cum υ supra lin. m. sec. cod.   4 φέροντα scripsi : φέρων cod.

[Apoc. 21]   **1.** Ὑπ(όθεσις) ΙΓ΄. Περὶ τῆς οὐρανοῦ καὶ γῆς καινουργίας καὶ τῆς ἄνω Ἰερουσαλήμ.

«Καὶ εἶδον οὐρανὸν καινὸν καὶ γῆν καινήν· ὁ γὰρ πρῶτος οὐρανὸς καὶ ἡ γῆ καὶ ἡ θάλασσα συνεστάλησαν, ἡ δὲ ἁγία πόλις Ἰερουσαλὴμ 5 καινὴ κατῆλθεν ἐξ οὐρανοῦ, καὶ καινὴν εἶδον αὐτήν, ἡτοιμασμένην ὡς νύμφην κεκοσμημένην φαιδρῶς· ἔχουσα τεῖχος μέγα καὶ ὑψηλὸν καὶ δώδεκα πύλας, τρεῖς κατὰ ἀνατολάς, τρεῖς κατὰ βορρᾶ, τρεῖς κατὰ νότου, καὶ τρεῖς ἐπὶ δυσμάς· καὶ ἄγγελος ἐφ᾽ ἑκάστης, ὡς πυλωρὸς παρεστώς. Καὶ τὸ ὕψος τοῦ τείχους πηχῶν ἑκατὸν τεσσαράκοντα τε Fol. 75|σσάρων. 10 Καὶ ἡ ἐνδώμησις τοῦ τείχους δῶμοι δώδεκα διὰ τῶν δώδεκα λίθων· θεμέλιος ὁ πρῶτος ἴασπις, ὁ δεύτερος δῶμος σάπφιρος, ὁ τρίτος ὄρδινος χαλκηδών, ὁ τέταρτος σμάραγδος, ὁ πέμπτος σαρδόνυξ, ὁ ἕκτος σάρδιον, ὁ ἕβδομος χρυσόλιθος, ὁ ὄγδοος βήρυλλος, ὁ ἔνατος τοπάζιον, ὁ δέκατος χρυσόπρασος, ὁ ἐνδέκατος ὑάκινθος, ὁ δωδέκατος ἀμέθυστος· καὶ οἱ δώδεκα πυλῶνες 15 δώδεκα μαργαρῖται, καὶ ἡ πλατεῖα τῆς πόλεως χρυσίον καθαρόν. Ναὸν δὲ ἐν αὐτῇ οὐκ εἶδον, οὔτε σελήνην· ναὸς γὰρ αὐτῆς ὁ Θεός ἐστι, ἥλιος δὲ φωτίζων αὐτὴν τὸ ἀρνίον. Καὶ οὐ μὴ εἰσέλθῃ εἰς αὐτὴν πᾶν κοινὸν ἢ ἀκάθαρτον. Ὁ δὲ λαλῶν μετ᾽ ἐμοῦ ἦν κρατῶν μέτρον καλάμου χρυσοῦν, μεθ᾽ οὗ ἐμέτρησε τὸ μῆκος αὐτῆς, σταδίου δώδεκα χιλιάδων, 20 καὶ τὸ πλάτος τοσοῦτον, τὸ δὲ ὕψος τοῦ τείχους ἑκατὸν τεσσαράκοντα τεσσάρων πήχεων ἀγγέλου. Κεῖται δὲ τετράγωνος ἡ πόλις, καὶ ὅσον αὐτῆς τὸ μῆκος, τοσοῦτόν ἐστι καὶ τὸ πλάτος» (cf. Apoc. 21,1-21).

2. Ἑρμ(ηνεία): Διαρρήδην αἱ θεῖαι γραφαὶ εἰσηγοῦνται ‹...›, τὴν δὲ ἄνω Ἰερουσαλὴμ ἐλευθέραν καλοῦσι καὶ μητέρα τῶν πρωτοτόκων· 25 ἐλευθέραν, ἐπεὶ τὴν κάτω ἐδούλωσαν τῇ ἁμαρτίᾳ οἱ ἔποικοι αὐτῆς, τὴν δὲ ἄνω, ἐ λ ε υ θ έ ρ α ν καὶ καθαράν. Ἧς καὶ τὰ μέτρα καὶ τὴν εὐπρέπειαν ὁ θεωρὸς οὗτος ἡμῖν εἰσηγεῖται, ὡς νύμφην ὡραϊσμένην, καθὼς γέγραπται, ὅτι κ α ὶ ὡ ς ν ύ μ φ η ν κ α τ ε κ ό σ μ η σ έ μ ε κ ό σ μ ῳ. Fol. 75 ᵛ| Ἔνθεν, καὶ τὸ εὖρος αὐτῆς καὶ τὸ μῆκος παραδηλοῦσιν ἡμῖν 30 αἱ τῶν σταδίων δώδεκα χιλιάδες, τὸ δὲ ὕψος καθὼς εἴρηται ἀνωτέρω· τὸ δὲ κάλλος διὰ τῶν δώδεκα λίθων τῶν πολυτίμων, ὧν τὸ σύμπαχον καὶ τὸ μέγεθος ἐντεῦθεν δηλοῦται, ὅτι ὄρδινοι δώδεκα ἀνεβίβασαν αὐτὸ εἰς ἑκατὸν τεσσαράκοντα τέσσαρας πήχεις ἀγγέλου· οἱ δώδεκα δὲ πυλῶνες εἰς μονόβολος μαργαρίτης ἑκάστης θυρός. Ταῦτα δὲ καὶ διὰ Ἡσαΐου προεῖπε 35 Θ ε ό ς, ὅ τ ι θ ή σ ω τ ὰ ς π ύ λ α ς σ ο υ λ ί θ ο υ ς κ ρ υ σ τ ά λ λ ο υ, κ α ὶ τ ὸ ν π ε ρ ί β ο λ ό ν σ ο υ λ ί θ ο υ ς ἐ κ λ ε κ τ ο ύ ς.

3. Ὦ μακαρίου οἰκοδόμου ἔργον καὶ οἶκος ἀχειροποίητος, καὶ μ α κ ά ρ ι ο ι ο ἱ κ α τ ο ι κ ο ῦ ν τ ε ς· ἐ ν τ ῷ ο ἴ κ ῳ σ ο υ Κ ύ ρ ι ε· ε ἰ ς α ἰ ῶ ν α ς α ἰ ώ ν ω ν α ἰ ν έ σ ο υ σ ι κ α ὶ δ ο ξ ά σ ο υ σ ί σ ε.

2, 24/25 cf. Gal. 4,26; cf. Hebr. 12,22–23   28 Is. 61,10   35/36 Is. 54,12
3, 38/39 Ps. 83(84),5

1, 9 τεσσαράκοντα scripsi : σαράκοντα cod.   11 σάπφιρος scripsi : σάμφειρος cum π supra lin. m. sec. cod.   13 ἔνατος scripsi : ἔννατος cod.   χρυσόπρασος scripsi : χρυσόπρασσος cod.   17 δὲ supra lin.   20/21 τεσσαράκοντα τεσσάρων scripsi : τεσσαρακοντατεσσάρων cod.
2, 23 post εἰσηγοῦνται aliqua uerba om. cod. sed in marg. sup. paginae supplementum fuisse uid. a manu Inclusi quod iam margine rescisso deest praeter litterulas καιν. fortasse ‹καινὸν οὐρανὸν καὶ γῆν καινήν› 33 τέσσαρας scripsi : τέσσαρεις cod.

Apoc. 22   1. Ὑπ(όθεσις) ΙΔ´. Πε(ρὶ) τοῦ ζωτικοῦ ποταμοῦ, καὶ περὶ τοῦ ξύλου τοῦ ποιοῦντος δώδεκα καρποὺς τῷ ἔτει.

«Εἶτα ἔδειξέ μοι ὁ θεῖος ἄγγελος ποταμὸν ὕδατος ζωῆς ἐκβλύζοντα ἐκ τοῦ θρόνου τοῦ Θεοῦ καὶ τοῦ ἀρνίου, καὶ ἔρποντα διὰ μέσου τῆς
5   πλατείας τῆς πόλεως· τοῦ δὲ ποταμοῦ ἐντεῦθεν καὶ ἐντεῦθεν ξύλα ζωῆς ποιοῦντα καρποὺς δώδεκα, ἐφ᾽ἑκάστου μηνὸς ἀποδιδόντα καρπούς, ὧν καὶ τὰ φύλλα εἰς θεραπείαν λαοῦ. Καὶ μακάριος ὁ τηρῶν τοὺς λόγους τῆς προφητείας ταύτης» (cf. Apoc. 22,8–21).

2. »Κἀγὼ Ἰωάννης, ὅτε ταῦτα πάντα ἤκουσα καὶ εἶδον, ὥρμησα
0   προσκυνῆσαι κατέμπροσθεν τοῦ ἀγγέλου. Ὁ δὲ λέγει μοι, Τῷ Θεῷ προσκύνησον, ἐπεὶ κἀγὼ σύνδουλός σού εἰμι καὶ τῶν σῶν ἀδελφῶν. Ἡ δὲ χάρις τοῦ Κυρίου Fol. 76ǀ ἡμῶν Ἰησοῦ Χριστοῦ μετὰ πάντων ἁγίων. Ἀμὴν» (cf. Apoc. 22,8–21).

3. Ἑρμ(ηνεία) καὶ ἐρώ(τησις): Καὶ πῶς ὁ μὲν Δαυίδ π υ ρ ἐ ν ώ π ι ο ν
5   α ὐ τ ο ῦ, φησί, π ρ ο π ο ρ ε ύ σ ε τ α ι, κ α ὶ φ λ ο γ ι ε ῖ κ ύ κ λ ῳ τ ο ὺ ς ἐ χ θ ρ ο ὺ ς α ὐ τ ο ῦ, ὁ δὲ Δανιὴλ ὅτι π ο τ α μ ὸ ς π υ ρ ὸ ς ε ἷ λ κ ε ν ἔ μ π ρ ο σ θ ε ν α ὐ τ ο ῦ, αὐτὸς δὲ ποταμὸν ζωτικοῦ ὕδατος εἶδεν ἐκβλύζοντα ἐκ τοῦ θρόνου;

4. Ἀπ(όκρισις): Ὅτι περὶ τῆς κρίσεως καὶ τῶν ἐχθρῶν ἐκεῖνοι
0   προηγόρευσαν· κ ρ ι τ ή ρ ι ο ν, φησίν, ἐ κ ά θ ι σ ε, κ α ὶ β ί β λ ο ι ἠ ν ε ῴ χ θ η σ α ν· αὐτὸς δὲ μετὰ τὴν κρίσιν καὶ τὴν ἀποκατάστασιν τῶν δικαίων ἐν τῇ ἐπουρανίῳ Ἰερουσαλὴμ τὸ ζωτικὸν ἔφησεν ὕδωρ, ὥστε πρὸς μὲν τοὺς ἁμαρτωλοὺς καὶ ἀθέους ποταμὸς πυρὸς ἐκπορεύεται ἀναλίσκων αὐτούς, πρὸς δὲ τοὺς θεοφιλεῖς καὶ δικαίους ὕδωρ ζωτικὸν
5   ἀνακαινίζον αὐτούς. Τὰ δὲ ξύλα τὰ δωδεκάκαρπα τῷ ἐνιαυτῷ τὴν πολλὴν καὶ ποικίλην σημαίνουσι τοῦ παραδείσου τρυφήν. Τὸ δὲ τεῖχος τῆς πόλεως δώδεκα ὀρδίλους ἔχει ἐκ τῶν δώδεκα λίθων τῶν πολυτίμων, ὥσπερ δώδεκα ζώνας κυκλικῶς ἐν ὅλῳ τὸ τεῖχος· καὶ ἑκάστη ζώνη ἄλλην καὶ ἄλλην χροιὰν βεβαμμένη· τὸ δὲ ὕψος προλέλεκται ἑκατὸν τεσσαράκοντα
⊃   τέσσαρες πήχεις ἀγγέλου, σταδίους δὲ δώδεκα χιλιάδες τὸ μῆκος, καὶ τὸ εὖρος τοσοῦτον.

3, 14/16   Ps. 96(97),3   19/20 Dan. 7,10
4, 20/21   Dan. 7,10

1, 6 ἀποδιδόντα correxi : ἀποδιδοῦντα cod.
2, 10 κατέμπροσθεν scripsi : κατ᾽ ἔμπροσθεν cod.
4, 21 ἠνεῴχθησαν : ἀνεῴχθησαν cod.   28 ζώνας scripsi : ζώννας cod.   29/30 ἑκατὸν τεσσαράκοντα τέσσαρες scripsi : ἑκατὸν τεσσαρακοντατέσσαρας cod.

\<Epilogus\>

1. Ἐγὼ δὲ τὴν ἔννοιαν τῆς Ἀποκαλύψεως ταύτης παρείληφα, καὶ οὐδὲν ἄλλο ἐσπούδασα ἢ τὸ εὐσύνοπτον καὶ τὸ εὐάρμοστον, τὴν σαφήνειαν καὶ τὸ εὐδιάλυτον· ὁ δὲ βουλόμενος ἐντυχεῖν τὴν πολλὴν σύγχισιν τῶν λόγων αὐτῆς, ζητείτω τὴν βίβλον τοῦ κειμένου αὐτῆς. Ἡ
5 δὲ σύγχισις καὶ ἀναρ Fol. 76ᵛ | μοστία, εἴτε ἐξ ἀρχῆς εἴτε παρὰ τῶν κατὰ καιροὺς ἀντιγράφων ἐγένετο, λέγειν οὐκ ἔχω. Οὐράνια δὲ τὰ λεγόμενα καὶ ξένα, καὶ οὐ προσήκει ἡμᾶς παρέργως ἀκούειν τὰ ἐκ τοῦ Θεοῦ καὶ τῶν ἀγγέλων ἐκκαλυφθέντα ἐξ οὐρανοῦ· ἔχουσι γὰρ τὸ ἀξιόπιστον ἐκ τῶν ἤδη τετελεσμένων, πῶς τὴν πόλιν ἐνέπρησαν καὶ τὰς αὐτῆς σάρκας
10 κατέφαγον οἱ ἐχθροί, καὶ ἣν ἡμεῖς ὡς βασιλίδα μεγάλην ἐκλεΐζομεν, ὡς ἀκάθαρτον πόρνην προσανεῖχε Θεός, καὶ ἐν καιρῷ ἐπαγωγῆς ὁ πολὺς αὐτῆς πλοῦτος καὶ ἡ τρυφὴ καὶ ἡ δυναστεία ὤνησαν αὐτὴν οὐδέν. Ἔνθα γὰρ ἐπιπολάζει τὸ αἶσχος τῆς ἁμαρτίας, δόξα καὶ πλοῦτος λογίζεται εἰς οὐδέν, καί, ἀρετῆς μὴ παρούσης εἰκαῖα πάντα καὶ ἀτελῆ· ὥσπερ καὶ αὐτὴ
15 πολλὰ μὲν εἶχε μοναστήρια καὶ εἰκόνας κεκοσμημένας ἐν χρυσίῳ καὶ ἀργυρίῳ, καὶ ψαλμωδίας εὐήχους, καὶ αἰσθητὰς εὐταξίας, ἀλλ' ἐπειδὴ τὸ ποτήριον τῆς φύσεως αὐτῆς μεστὸν ἦν βδελυγμάτων καὶ πάσης ἀκαθαρσίας καθὼς ὁ βλέπων ἐμαρτύρησε περὶ αὐτῆς, οὐκ ἴσχυσεν αὐτῆς ἡ εὐδαιμονία ἐξαρπάσαι αὐτὴν ἐκ τῆς δικαίας ἀγανακτήσεως τοῦ Θεοῦ. Καὶ οἱ
20 πορνεύσαντες μετ' αὐτῆς βασιλεῖς, ἀπὸ μακρόθεν, φησίν, ἑστῶτες διὰ τὸν καπνὸν τοῦ βασανισμοῦ αὐτῆς, τὸ οὐαὶ οὐαὶ κράζουσι, καὶ πενθοῦσι καὶ κλαίουσιν. Εἰ οὖν ταῦτα τὴν Ἀποκάλυψιν ταύτην ἀληθεύουσαν ἔδειξαν, Fol. 77 | εὔδηλον ὅτι καὶ τὰ λοιπὰ ἀληθῆ τὴν ἀπόβασιν ἕξουσι.
2. Ἐμοὶ δὲ προσήκει ἐνταῦθα κατευνάσαι τὸν λόγον, καὶ ὁ βασιλεὺς
25 τῶν βασιλευόντων καὶ οἰκοδόμος τῆς πόλεως τῆς γλαφυρᾶς καὶ μεγάλης, περὶ ἧς καὶ ὁ λόγος διεξῄει πρὸ μικροῦ, δῴη ἡμῖν σύνεσιν καὶ ἰσχὺν ἔργα ἐπιτελεῖν ἄξια τῆς ἐν αὐτῇ κατοικίας, ὅτι, ὡς βασιλεῖ καὶ οἰκοδόμῳ τῆς πόλεως ἐκείνης καὶ πάντων τῶν γεγονότων, ὁ τρισάγιος ἐποφείλεται ὕμνος νῦν καὶ ἀεὶ καὶ εἰς τοὺς αἰῶνας τῶν αἰώνων. Ἀμήν.

1, 19/22 cf. Apoc. 18,9–10

1, 13/14 δ. καὶ π. λογίζεται εἰς οὐδὲν attractio numeri

1. Ἀπόλογος ἐν τοῖς ἀμφισβητοῦσιν.

Τάχα γάρ τινες οὐ κατεδέξαντο τοῦ Θεολόγου εἶναι τὴν Ἀποκάλυψιν ταύτην διὰ τὸ πολύλογον καὶ τὸ πεζόλεκτον. Ἐμοὶ δὲ τῷ ἀγροίκῳ δοκεῖ τοῦ Θεολόγου, διὰ τῆς θεωρίας τὸ ἀνώτατον, τὸ δὲ πολύλογον καὶ
5 πεζόλεκτον τοῖς τότε ἀκροαταῖς ἐπιγράφομαι τὴν αἰτίαν. Καὶ μαρτυρεῖ μου τῷ λόγῳ τὰ δηλωθέντα ταῖς ἐκκλησίαις τῆς Ἀσίας, ἀπειλούμενά τε καὶ παραινούμενα ἐκ τοῦ φανέντος Δεσπότου· ὅτι καὶ ἄγνοια καὶ ἀσέβεια ἔτι πρὸς αὐτοὺς ἐπεκράτει, οὐχ ἁπλῶς ἀγομένοις, ἀλλὰ καὶ ἡγουμένοις αὐτοῖς. Διὰ τοῦτο κἀγὼ τὰ δο Fol. 77ᵛ|κοῦντα περιττὰ εἶναι παρῆκα σὺν
0 ἱκεσίᾳ καὶ φόβῳ, τὰ δὲ δύσληπτα πρὸς τὸ εὔληπτον θεοσδότως παρήνοιξα. Ὑμεῖς δὲ οἱ νουνεχῶς ἐντυγχάνοντες ταῦτα, δότε μετὰ Θεὸν συγγνώμην τῇ ἐπαινετῇ τολμηρίᾳ.

1, 2 ἀπο κάλυψιν cod. ἀπο in rasura   3 πολύλογον scripsi : πολλύλογον cod.
11 συγγνώμην scripsi : συγνώμην cod.

VIII

AN UNPUBLISHED CATECHETICAL INSTRUCTION BY ST NEOPHYTOS THE RECLUSE ON THE TRANSFIGURATION*

The catechetical instruction of St Neophytos the Recluse (1134–c.1219) given below was transcribed by me in Paris some years ago from Paris. suppl. gr. 1317. This codex belongs to the first quarter of the thirteenth century and was described by Ch. Astruc in the third part of the catalogue of Greek manuscripts in the Bibliothèque Nationale published by him and M.-L. Concasty.[1] Written by Basil, a priest and notary of the diocese of Paphos who is also known to us from other sources, and containing the autograph corrections and additions of the saint himself, it is the protograph codex of his *Book of Catechetical Instructions* (Βίβλος τῶν Κατηχήσεων).

The *Catechetical Instructions* are a work of St Neophytos's old age and were addressed to his brother John when the latter was appointed abbot of the monastery of St John Chrysostom at Koutzouvendi (founded in 1090). I.P. Tsiknopoullos, doyen of Neophytos scholars, assigned their composition to 1211, but we should settle for a more approximate date at around that time, certainly after 1198 but before 1214.[2] It is possible, however, as Tsiknopoullos also rightly suspected,[3] that the saint included in the *Book* at least some instructions which he had delivered in the past to the brethren of his own monastery. It is impossible to give a precise date to the instruction published below. The fact that in lines 20–21 the saint refers to the "most faithful and

* Translated from " Ἀνέκδοτος κατήχησις τοῦ ὁσίου Νεοφύτου τοῦ Ἐγκλείστου εἰς τὴν ἁγίαν Μεταμόρφωσιν", *Theologia* 44 (1973), pp. 699–701.

[1] *Le Supplément Grec*, III, Paris, 1960, pp. 602–8.
[2] I.P. Tsiknopoullos, "Τὸ συγγραφικὸν ἔργον τοῦ Ἁγίου Νεοφύτου", *KS* 22 (1958), pp. 69–214, esp. p. 160.
[3] Ibid.

God-crowned emperors" of the Orthodox and uses the pronoun "our" in no way implies that the instruction was written before 1191, when Byzantine rule in Cyprus came to an end. The patriotic author of the work *Concerning the misfortunes of the land of Cyprus* never accepted the foreign domination of the island and still entrusted his monks to the "aristocracy" of the Byzantine emperor even in the second version of his *Typicon*, which was written in 1214 when the emperor himself was at Nicaea, far from the imperial capital. The reference to "tyrants" in line 19 points to a date after 1191. (The violence and cruelty of the Frankish King Amaury of Cyprus [1194–1205] against the Orthodox is well known but under his successor, Hugh I [1205–1218], things were not very much better.) Moreover, in the discourse *On the Cross* in his *Panegyrike* (Paris. gr. 1189), written in August 1196 (fol. 37ᵛ) the saint speaks again of "Christ-loving kings" and "Christ-hating tyrants" (fol. 38). The year 1198 must be set as the *terminus post quem*, for from the *Miracle* we know for certain that John was then still abbot, and the year 1214 as the *terminus ante quem*, for it is the year of the saint's last work, the *Typike Diatheke*, in which (fols 29–30) the *Catechetical Instructions* are mentioned.

The saint had earlier composed a beautiful *Discourse on the divine and glorious Transfiguration of our Lord and God and Saviour Jesus Christ*, which is contained in folios 309ᵛ–316ᵛ of Codex Lesbianus 2 of the Monastery of Leimon (inc. Μεταμόρφωσιν θείαν ἐξυμνεῖν ἐπεπόθησα). The text given here is the twentieth instruction of the *Book* and is contained in folios 98–100ᵛ of the Paris codex mentioned above. I decided to bring this small gem of Byzantine homiletics out of darkness specifically as a witness to *light*. Coming between the light-filled *Catechetical Instructions* and *Hymns* of Symeon the New Theologian (949–1022) and the light radiated by the holy hesychasts of the fourteenth century, it constitutes yet another testimony to the love which pious Eastern Christians have for the divine light. As an elder the Recluse of Cyprus never ceased singing the praises of this light; indeed one could put together a whole series of such hymnodies. Light, radiance, rays, the sun as the life in Christ are set against the darkness, the gloom, the blindness of the "unlit pitch blackness" (line 17) of life apart from and bereft of Christ. The Second Coming of Christ and the Judgment are also to be a descent and epiphany of the light of Tabor itself. Neophytos envisages them in a unique way as an "ineffable shedding of light" (lines 39–40) through which is renewed the "gloriously radiant kingdom of light of God in his greatness" (line 56).

I would not wish to conclude the present note without recalling that in his commentary on Psalm 103 (M 104)[4], in his exposition of the second verse,

---

[4] See I. Hadjiioannou, Νεοφύτου πρεσβυτέρου μοναχοῦ καὶ ἐγκλείστου Ἑρμηνεία εἰς τοὺς Ψαλμούς, Athens, 1935, p. 98.

"wrapped in a garment of light", the saint stresses that the light is not "servile or created but inaccessible yet naturally intempling" (ἐνναῖζον – a neologism of the saint). That is to say, he speaks of a supreme and uncreated light naturally (αὐτοφυῶς) flowing from itself yet remaining inaccessible. The terminology anticipates the Palamite themes of the fourteenth century.

Finally, I must thank Dr G. Christodoulou of Trinity College, Cambridge, for his friendly encouragement. An edition of the complete works of St Neophytos was announced some years ago by the Centre for Cypriot Studies. This little edition of a single catechetical instruction is only intended as a visible sign of welcome for the eagerly awaited great four-volume edition.

[Fol. 98ʳ]ΠΕΡΙ ΤΗΣ ΑΓΙΑΣ ΚΑΙ ΦΩΤΟΕΙΔΟΥΣ
ΜΕΤΑΜΟΡΦΩΣΕΩΣ ΤΟΥ ΘΕΟΥ ΚΑΙ ΣΩΤΗΡΟΣ ΗΜΩΝ

Εὐλόγησον.

Ἀδελφοὶ καὶ πατέρες, ἰδοὺ πάλιν ἡμῖν ἑορτὴ πνευματικὴ καὶ πανήγυρις· πάλιν τὸ φῶς τὸ ἀΐδιον τὸ ἐκ τοῦ φωτὸς τοῦ ἀϊδίου ἡμῖν ἐπέλαμψε σήμερον· πάλιν τὸ ἀπαύγασμα τῆς δόξης τοῦ πατρὸς καὶ ὁ χαρακτὴρ τῆς ὑποστάσεως αὐτοῦ ἡμᾶς καταυγάσαι εὐδόκησε· πάλιν ἡ φωταύγεια τοῦ ἀλήκτου φωτὸς καὶ εἰκὼν τῆς ἀγαθότητος τοῦ θεοῦ πρὸς ἡμᾶς ἐπεδήμησε· πάλιν τὸ ὑπὲρ ἥλιον φῶς τοῦ ἡλίου τῆς δικαιοσύνης ἡμᾶς κατεφώτισε· πάλιν τὸ φῶς τὸ ἀληθινὸν τὸ φωτίζον πάντα ἄνθρωπον ἐρχόμενον εἰς τὸν κόσμον πρὸς ἡμᾶς παρεγένετο· πάλιν τοῦ ἀρρήτου φωτὸς Fol. 98ᵛ| αἱ βολίδες καὶ τὸ φέγγος τῆς αὐτοῦ ἀστραπῆς τὰς τῶν πιστῶν ψυχὰς κατεφώτισε, καὶ τὸ σκότος τῆς πλάνης ἀπήλασε, καὶ τὸν ζόφον τῆς ἁμαρτίας ἠμαύρωσε, καὶ τὰ ἔργα τοῦ σκότους ἀπήλασε, καὶ τὰ ζοφώδη πνεύματα σὺν τῷ ἄρχοντι αὐτῶν παντελῶς ἐξετύφλωσε, καὶ τῇ ἀφεγγεῖ παννυξίᾳ τούτους παρέδωκε, καὶ τὰ νυκτώδη καὶ σκοτεινὰ δόγματα τῶν ἀθέων τελείως ἀπέσβεσε καὶ τῶν τυράννων τὸ θράσος ὡς κονιορτὸν διὰ λαίλαπος ἐξηφάνισε καὶ τῷ σκότει παρέδωκε· τῶν πιστοτάτων δὲ ἡμῶν καὶ θεοστεφῶν βασιλέων τὰ ψυχικὰ ὄμματα τῆς πίστεως κατεφώτισε καὶ τὸ κράτος τῆς ἀληθείας κραταιοτάτως ἐκράτυνε· καὶ τῶν αὐτοῦ ἀρχιερέων τῶν νῦν καὶ τῶν πάλαι τῆς ἀληθείας τὸν λόγον ὀρθοτομεῖν τὸν νοῦν κατεφώτισε· καὶ τῶν ἀρχόντων καὶ μεγιστάνων πρὸς [Fol. 99ʳ]| τὸ δικάζειν δικαίως καὶ κρίνειν τῇ ὑπεροχῇ τῇ μεγίστῃ ταύτῃ τετίμηκεν (ἐδόθη, φησί, παρὰ Κυρίου ἡ κράτησις ὑμῖν καὶ ἡ δυναστεία παρὰ ὑψίστου)· καὶ τῆς αὐτοῦ ἐκκλησίας τὰ θεῖα δόγματα ἐβεβαίωσε· καὶ τῷ φέγγει τῆς ἀληθείας κατηύγασε τῆς γῆς τὰ πληρώματα· καὶ φωτοειδῶς ἤδη αὐτοῦ τοῦ μεγάλου φωτὸς τὴν θείαν μεταμόρφωσιν γεγηθότες ἑορτάζομεν σήμερον ὅσοι φιλόχριστοι, ἵνα τὰ ἔργα τοῦ σκότους ἡμεῖς ἀποθέμενοι καὶ τὰ ὅπλα τοῦ φωτὸς περιθέμενοι ὡς ἐν ἡμέρᾳ

26–27 Σοφ. Σολ. στ′, 3.

εὐσχημόνως περιπατήσωμεν· διὰ γὰρ τοῦτο καὶ τοὺς ἱερούς μαθητὰς εἰς
ὄρος ὑψηλόν κατ᾽ ἰδίαν ἀνάγει καὶ μάρτυρας παριστᾷ τῆς τοιύτης
θεοσημείας· καὶ μεταμορφοῦται ἔμπροσθεν τούτων· καὶ τὰ ἱμάτια μὲν
35 ὡς τὸ φῶς, τὸ δὲ πρόσωπον ὡς ἥλιον ἀπαστράπτειν ὑπέδειξεν· ἵνα δεί
[Fol. 99ᵛ]‖ ξῃ ὅτι τὸν κόσμον ἀναφέρειν ἄνω ἀπὸ τῶν κάτω ἐλήλυθεν,
ἀνασῴζων τὸ ἀνθρώπινον πρὸς τὸ ἀρχέτυπον κάλλος καὶ ἀξίωμα καὶ μηδὲν
χαμερπῶς κατασύρεσθαι κάτω καὶ τῶν ἄνω ἀμνημονεῖν, ἀλλὰ ἀναβάσεις
ἐν τῇ καρδίᾳ θέμενοι τὰ ἄνω ἐπιζητεῖν καὶ τὴν ἡμέραν ἐννοεῖν τῆς
40 ἀνεκφράστου ἐκείνης καὶ δευτέρας αὐτοῦ παρουσίας· ὅτι πῶς οἱ ἁμαρτωλοὶ
ἐν αὐχμηροῖς ἐκ παθῶν ὀφθαλμοῖς δυνηθῶμεν ἰδεῖν τῆς ἀρρήτου ἐκείνης
φωτοχυσίας τὰς θείας μαρμαρυγάς, ὅπου γε οἱ θεῖοι μαθηταί, οἱ χρόνῳ
τοσούτῳ συνεπόμενοι τῷ Χριστῷ αὐγὴν ἀμυδρὰν τῆς τούτου
μεταμορφώσεως μὴ δυνάμενοι φέρειν, πρηνεῖς τῷ ἐδάφει κατέπιπτον; εἰ
45 οὖν ἐκεῖ οὐκ ἴσχυσαν ἐπὶ τοῦ ὄρους καθαρῶς ἐντρανίσαι τὴν αὐτοῦ
μεταμόρφωσιν, ἀλλ᾽ ἔπιπτον ἐπὶ πρόσωπον, ἐν ποίοις, εἰπέ μοι, ὀφθαλμοῖς
[Fol. 100ᵛ]‖ οἱ ἐν ἁμαρτίαις συζῶντες πρὸς αὐτὸν ἀτενίσωμεν τότε, ὅτε
οὐκ ἐπ᾽ ὄρους μεταμορφούμενον, ἀλλ᾽ ἐξ οὐρανοῦ μετὰ δόξης θεϊκῆς
κατερχόμενον καὶ οὐρανὸν καὶ γῆν, ὥσπερ γέγραπται, κατασείοντα; ἔτι
50 ἅπαξ, φησίν, ἐγὼ σείω τὸν οὐρανὸν καὶ τὴν γῆν· ὅτε μετὰ σαλπίγγων φωνῶν,
δυνάμεων οὐρανῶν, καὶ φωνῶν ἀγαλλιάσεων, καὶ ὕμνων τριαδικῶν καὶ
φωτὸς ἀνεκφράστου· ὅτε μετὰ χιλίων χιλιάδων καὶ μυρίων μυριάδων
ἀγλαϊφόρων ἀγγέλων καὶ θεαμάτων μεγάλων πρὸς ἡμᾶς ἀφικνουμένων
ἴδωμεν, πῶς ἄρα τότε τὴν δόξαν αὐτοῦ καὶ τὸ φῶς τὸ ἀπρόσιτον ἴδωμεν,
55 οὗ τὸ φῶς τῆς μεταμορφώσεως οὐκ ἴσχυσαν κατιδεῖν οἱ ἀπόστολοι, πῶς
οἱ ἁμαρτωλοὶ δυνηθείημεν ἰδεῖν τῆς δευτέρας αὐτοῦ παρουσίας τὴν δόξαν
τὴν ἀνεκλάλητον; οὐδεμία γάρ, φησίν, κοινωνία φωτὶ πρὸς σκότος· Fol.
100ᵛ‖ σκότος γὰρ ἡ ἁμαρτία καὶ σκότος ὁ διάβολος καὶ τὰ τούτου
εὐάρεστα· καὶ τῷ φωτὶ τῷ μεγάλῳ θεῷ καὶ τῇ παμφώτῳ αὐτοῦ βασιλείᾳ
60 τὸ ῥηθὲν σκότος κοινωνῆσαι ἀμήχανον. Ἐὰν δὲ οἱ ἁμαρτωλοὶ πρὸς Κύριον
ἐπιστρέψωμεν καὶ ποιήσωμεν αὐτῷ καρπὸν ἄξιον τῆς μετανοίας, πέπεισμαι,
κατὰ τὰ αὐτοῦ παναληθῆ ἐπαγγέλματα, ὅτι οὐ μόνον ἁπλῶς τὴν αὐτοῦ
θεασόμεθα δόξαν τὴν ἄρρητον, ἀλλὰ καὶ σὺν αὐτῷ, χάριτι αὐτοῦ, τῆς
αὐτοῦ βασιλείας ἐπαπολαύσομεν καὶ εἴποι πάντως ἐν τούτῳ ἀρτίως πᾶς
65 ὁ λαὸς τό, Ἀμήν, Γένοιτο, Γένοιτο.

31–32. Ρωμ. ιγʹ, 12-13.
38–39. Ψαλμ. ΠΓʹ 6.
49–50. Ἀγγ. βʹ, 6.
57. Βʹ Κορ. στʹ, 14.

IX

ST NEOPHYTOS THE RECLUSE AND THE BEGINNINGS OF FRANKISH RULE IN CYPRUS*

We can easily imagine how the Cypriots faced the terrible realities of the twelfth century if we take as our starting-point the historical accounts of the events and supplement them with the general knowledge which we have of the Byzantine world as a whole. It has, however, been established that the behaviour of individuals and communities is determined not only by the reality of the situation but also by the image of it which they form within themselves. This internal image of the Cypriots of the twelfth century cannot, of course, be revealed to us either by foreign or Byzantine historians, or by the aristocratic Constantinopolitan archbishop, Nicholas Mouzalon, who left the island a disappointed man, or by the boastful Manasses, who nearly fainted because a "scatophagous" (as he called him) Cypriot stank of "garlic and wine" during the liturgy at Nicosia.[1] The only witness to the collective imagination of Cyprus is Neophytos the Recluse (1134–c.1220).

Anyone who wishes to bring the Cypriot world of the twelfth and early thirteenth centuries vividly to life, to analyse its deeds and understand its conduct, must turn to the Hermitage of Paphos, to its caves and wall-paintings and to as many as survive of the works composed within it. For if the religious, political and educational ideal of the socio-economic ruling class is expressed in the iconographic programme of such churches as those of the Holy Trinity of Koutzouvendi, built by Duke Eumathios Philokales, of Asinou, built by the Magister Nikephoros, or of Arakas, built by Leo Authentes, the ideal of the lay Cypriot monk is expressed in the iconography of the

---

* Translated from "Ὁ ὅσιος Νεόφυτος ὁ Ἔγκλειστος καὶ αἱ ἀρχαὶ τῆς ἐν Κύπρῳ Φραγκοκρατίας", *EKEEK* 10 (1979–80), pp. 31–83.

[1] See K. Horna, "Das *Hodoiporikon* des Konstantin Manasses", *BZ* 13 (1904), pp. 313–55, esp. p. 344, v. 89ff.

Hermitage. In Neophytos's writings themselves, in their content but even more
so in their vocabulary, where old words appear with new significates and new
words as new signifiers, that is, on the lexical level, there is hidden more
assuredly than anywhere else the collective unconscious of the population
of Cyprus of his time.[2]

From this point of view the greatest loss from among those works of the
saint which have not yet been recovered or which have been lost irretriev-
ably is that of his two-volume spiritual correspondence and of his *Procheiron*,
a kind of diary of the fifty years from 1159 to 1209. Both of these are referred
to in the catalogue of the author's works in the twelfth chapter of his *Typike
Diatheke* but, sadly, are not known to us today. If we surmise, as basically we
may, that the wonderful little epistolary treatise, *Concerning the misfortunes of the
land of Cyprus*, would have belonged to one of these books, we can understand
the size of the void.

In my examination below of the beginnings of Frankish rule in Cyprus
as they appear in St Neophytos, my aim is not simply to look at the saint's
conceptual representation of Latin dogma and of the Crusader regime in
Cyprus, but to seek as far as possible to delineate the wider reaction of the
people as a whole. Of course I am far from believing that the mentality of
Neophytos was that of the average Cypriot. On the contrary, the saint was
a prominent figure from every aspect, naturally endowed beyond the usual
and spiritually purified and elevated above the common. The response,
however, which he found amongst his people, both in the lower orders of
society and in the higher, whether laymen or clerics, reveals that in his
person he embodied and represented for his fellow-countrymen and fellow-
believers a common spiritual ideal. Whether or not human beings ever
attain the living ideal archetypes within their souls does not belong to the
present work. What has significance here is that when these examples and
symbols appear, the ordinary members of a given society recognise them,
love them and reach out towards them. The outlook, the tastes, the manner
of thought, the convictions and the spirit of a people do not originate in the
individual, the fortuitous and the transient but in the "common and the
mainstream".

The period under examination, which begins with the arrival in the island
of the English king, Richard Lionheart, in 1191, when Neophytos was
already approaching his fifty-seventh year, and ends in 1220, when Neophytos

---

[2] This may be said on account of the extent of the corpus of Neophytos's work and
because with regard to indigenous ecclesiastical poetry and hagiography belonging to the twelfth
century nothing is certain, while with regard to epic poetry the akritic works were introduced
into Cyprus from outside and there is uncertainty about the precise chronology of native parallels.

died, covers a period of thirty years, that is to say, the first three decades of the four centuries of Frankish rule in Cyprus. This period is of exceptional interest both because it is the beginning of later developments and because it has been little-studied until now in the general histories of the island, or in the more specialised histories of the period of Frankish rule and of the relations between the Orthodox and Latin Churches during this time.[3]

I am not, of course, attempting to present here a general history of these three decades. What I am offering, however, is, I hope, a small but relatively important contribution towards such a history.

I. THE SOCIAL AND RELIGIOUS BACKGROUND

In spite of the administrative interest which the Byzantine central authority continued to show in Cyprus during the twelfth century on account of its strategic importance, that century was for the island, as it was for the whole of Roman East, a century of social decay. The reasons, however, for the final collapse and the change which took place are not so much internal as external, or even natural.

The internal state of disintegration is well portrayed by the long poem of Nicholas Mouzalon on his resignation from the archiepiscopal throne of Cyprus[4] and by the *Odoiporikon* of Constantine Manasses,[5] and also by certain, mainly hagiographical, texts, amongst which the *Life* of St Leontios, patriarch of Jerusalem, composed by the monk Theodosios of Constantinople, holds pride of place.[6] The external conditions are well-known from many sources.

The heavy taxation of the people under the military administration,[7] in conjunction with their inhuman exploitation by the powerful, the economic

---

[3] See esp. H.J. Magoulias, "A Study in Roman Catholic and Greek Orthodox Church Relations on the Island of Cyprus between the years A.D. 1196 and 1360", *GOTR* 10 (1964), pp. 75–106; J. Gill, "The Tribulations of the Greek Church in Cyprus 1196–c.1280", *Byzantinische Forschungen* 5 (1977), pp. 73–93; J. Darrouzès, "Textes synodaux chypriotes", *REB* 37 (1979), pp. 5–122.

4 S.I. Doanides, "Ἡ παραίτησις Νικολάου τοῦ Μουζάλωνος ἀπὸ τῆς ἀρχιεπισκοπῆς Κύπρου, ᾿Ανέκδοτον ἀπολογητικὸν ποίημα", ῾Ελληνικά, 7 (1934), pp. 109–50.

[5] See note 1 above.

[6] Monk Theodosios Constantinopolites, *Βίος τοῦ ὁσίου πατρὸς ἡμῶν Λεοντίου πατριάρχου ῾Ιεροσολήμων* in Makarios Chrysokephalos, *Λόγοι πανηγυρικοί*, Cosmopolis, 1793, pp. 380–434.

[7] See Doanides, "Ἡ παραίτησις Νικολάου τοῦ Μουζάλωνος, pp. 136–7, lines 889–912, pp. 132–3, lines 742–70, pp. 142–3; Theodosios, *Βίος Λεοντίου*, pp. 417–18 (the crimes of Kyriakos, who controlled the public taxes in Cyprus, and of Triakontaphyllos, who was in charge of levying them). Cf. K. Hadjipsaltes, "Συμβολαὶ εἰς τὴν ἱστορίαν τῆς ᾿Εκκλησίας τῆς Κύπρου κατὰ τὴν βυζαντινὴν περίοδον", *KS* 18 (1954), pp. xxvii–xlv, esp. p. xxxvi.

privileges granted to the Venetians after 1148,[8] the almost complete absence of education and the moral laxity of the clergy,[9] had as a result on the one hand the reduction of the population to misery and on the other its decimation by emigration. To hinder the latter a strict blockade was imposed on the harbours of the island, which, however, made the isolation of the place worse and exacerbated its social withdrawal. "A solid fortress, an iron wall, a stone cage, a dark underworld admitting no escape, not having any means of exit" is how Manasses describes Cyprus – "a land where words are scarce", which Mouzalon laments as "formerly the land of Aphrodite, now of Hecate".[10]

The plundering incursion of Reynald of Chatillon, duke of Antioch, and of the Armenian prince, Thoros II, in 1155–56, the raid by the Egyptian fleet in 1158, the piratical incursion of Raymond III, count of Tripoli, in 1161, the new (perhaps Arab) attacks which Neophytos apparently chronicles in the early 1170s,[11] all these certainly made the situation worse.

The three-year drought which gripped the island from 1175–76, the resultant famine, the succession of earthquakes and, above all, the fearful plague of 1174–75 not only denuded the island of its fauna and flora but, as Neophytos testifies, reduced the population to extreme savagery and left only a third of it alive.[12] The eclipses of the sun which occurred in 1176 and 1178 drove people to desperation and wrapped Cyprus in an atmosphere of apocalyptic doom. An unpropitious epilogue to the Byzantine era and an ominous prologue to the age of the Franks was provided by the bestial tyranny of Isaac Komnenos, which began in 1185.

The independent Cypriot kingdom of the seven years from 1185 to 1191 does not belong to the provincial states which were born from local patriotism when the centre of the Empire was weakened, or after the final capture of 1204. Such states were those of Armeno-Cilicia, founded by Thoros II (1145–68), or later the Despotate of Epirus and the Empire of Trebizond.

---

[8] Chrysobull of Manuel Komnenos of October 6656, ind. 11, i.e. 1148. See G. Hill, *A History of Cyprus*, I, Cambridge, 1972, p. 306, note 1.

[9] See Doanides, "Ἡ παραίτησις Νικολάου τοῦ Μουζάλωνος", pp. 120–8, lines 302–590; Theodosios, *Βίος Λεοντίου*, pp. 419–20.

[10] Horna, "Das *Hodoiporikon*", p. 346, lines 152–8, p. 337, line 98; Doanides, "Ἡ παραίτησις Νικολάου τοῦ Μουζάλωνος", p. 139, line 1000.

[11] Neophytos the Recluse, *Πεντηκοντακέφαλον* 31, codex 522 of the National Library of Greece, fol. 75. Cf. K. Dyovouniotes, "Νεοφύτου Ἐγκλείστου ἀνέκδοτα ἔργα", *EEBS* 13 (1937), pp. 40–49, esp. p. 45. For the rest see F. Chalandon, *Les Comnènes*, II, Paris, 1912, pp. 437–9; Hill, *A History of Cyprus*, pp. 306–8, 311.

[12] Neophytos the Recluse, Ἑρμηνεία δεσποτικῶν ἐντολῶν 10, Cod. Coisl. gr. 287, fols 187ᵛ–188; *Πεντηκοντακέφαλον* 32–5, codex 522, Nat. Lib. of Greece, fols 77ᵛ–81. Cf. I.P. Tsiknopoullos, "Κυπριακὰ τοῦ ἁγίου Νεοφύτου", *KS* 24 (1960), pp. 113–49, esp. pp. 138–41. The information given by Neophytos is confirmed by the Anglo-Norman annalist of the Crusades, Benedict of Peterborough; see N. Iorga, *France de Chypre*, Paris, 1966, p. 14.

The independent Cypriot state of 1185–91 was not such an expression of local sentiment but the product of the opportunism of Isaac and, more generally, of the callous individualism and moral indifference of the Byzantine patricians of the period, to whom the sources unanimously attribute the misfortunes and the collapse of the Byzantine world. The *protostrator* Manuel Kamytzes made a similar attempt, unsuccessfully, in Pelagonia in about 1198 when Alexios III Angelos refused to ransom him from his Bulgarian captivity. In Anatolia the phenomenon was commonplace in the period amongst the Byzantine landowning aristocracy.[13]

Neophytos did not of course belong by birth to the ruling class of the island, but neither did he belong to the lowest class. Those autobiographical details which he offers us concerning his life in the world suggest that his family occupied a middle position in rural society.[14] As a monk he was inspired by hesychastic asceticism, which, following the early tradition of the Pachomian and Basilian coenobia, preferred the brotherhood to be supported by its own labours and eschewed landed estates, serfdom and subsidies, and consequently every specifically political, economic, social and educational activity.[15] It is not known whether the allowance (σιτηρέσιον) which the bishop of Paphos, Basil Kinnamos, provided for the Recluse after his ordination[16] was later increased in accordance with the growth of the monastery. In any case, Neophytos never sought for his monastery the gift of land or tenants and annual financial subsidies, as the contemporary monastery of Machairas sought and obtained from the emperors Manuel Komnenos and Isaac and Alexios Angelos.[17] In the twentieth chapter of his *Diatheke* he expressly declares that he would receive "imperial or official aid" only for the building of a church and exhorts his monks to direct their affairs in such a way that "through the lack of any necessary thing you do not act as servants and disturb anyone."[18]

If it is borne in mind that these things were taking place in the thirteenth century whereas the movement towards worldliness in Eastern monasticism

---

[13] On Manuel Kamytzes see N.A. Veis, "Ἀναγνώσεις καὶ καταστάσεις βυζαντινῶν μολυβδοβούλλων", *Journ. Intern. d' Archéol.–Numism.* 11 (1911), pp. 1ff; Guilland in *REB* 7 (1950), pp. 162–3. On the situation in Asia Minor see S. Vryonis, *The Decline of Medieval Hellenism in Asia Minor and the Process of Islamization from the Eleventh through the Fifteenth Century,* Berkeley, 1971, esp. ch. I, II. Cf. H. Ahrweiler, *L'idéologie politique de l'Empire byzantin,* Paris, 1975, pp. 87–102.

[14] See *Typike Diatheke* 3, Cod. Edinburg. Univers. 224, fols. 9ᵛ, 11–11ᵛ; I.P. Tsiknopoullos, *Κυπριακὰ Τυπικά,* Nicosia, 1969, pp. 74–5.

[15] *Typike Diatheke* 9, *ibid.*, fol. 19; p. 80, x, pp. 80-81.

[16] *Ibid* 5; p. 78, 2–8.

[17] See *Τυπικὴν διάταξιν Νείλου,* 9, 22, 23 in Tsiknopoullos, *Κυπριακὰ Τυπικά,* pp. 11–12, 16–17.

[18] *Typike Diatheke* 20, fol. 50–50ᵛ; p. 90.

had already started in the tenth century, it becomes difficult to take Neophytos in his general judgments and outlook as a representative of the prevailing ecclesiastical order. This is certainly not to say that he does not represent the true ecclesiastical ideal, or that he was hostile in any way to the higher ecclesiastical or social hierarchy, or that he did not have relations with them, or, still less, that he dreamed of anything different from the existing political organisation.

The fact that in many places he censures the rich "who oppress the poor" and their love of money, rapaciousness and inhuman lack of compassion,[19] does not point to hostility towards society but to a religious censure of sin and indeed to the hypocritical piety that accompanies it. Here, for example, is what the saint has to say about these matters in 1176:

"... but you, rather, abound in injustice, stealing and carrying off and giving rein to greed and perhaps as a result you distribute small obols or adorn an icon or build a church dedicated to some saint and you imagine that you have achieved something impressive. And the holy icon which you have adorned as a result of greed you have polluted rather than adorned, having surrounded it with the proceeds of greed. And the saint whom you have supposedly adorned says to you, 'Why "have you entertained lawlessness that I should be like you"? For the approach of thieves and greedy people is loathsome to the Lord; "for they offer them in a way that transgresses the law". "Honour the Lord by your just labours and give him the first-fruits from your fruits of righteousness." For I dwell in the kingdom of heaven, but they whom you have treated unjustly because of your greed are oppressed by much poverty and have need of expenditure, that is, food, drink, clothing and blankets, and you must do good, then, to those who have been treated unjustly by you.' "[20]

---

[19] See e.g. Ἑρμηνεία δεσποτικῶν ἐντολῶν, Cod. Coisl. gr. 287, fols 130ᵛ–132.

[20] Ibid., fols 62–62ᵛ:

...σὺ δὲ μᾶλλον περισσεύεις ἀδικίαν, κλέπτων καὶ ἁρπάζων καὶ πλεονεκτῶν, καὶ ἴσως ἐκ τούτων διανέμεις μικροὺς ὀβολοὺς ἢ κοσμίζεις εἰκόνα ἢ ναὸν ἀνεγείρεις τοῦ ἁγίου τοῦ δεῖνος, καὶ φαντάζεσαι ὡς μέγα τι κατορθώσας. Καὶ τὴν ἁγίαν εἰκόνα, ἣν ἐκόσμησας ἐκ πλεονεξίας, ἐρρύπωσας μᾶλλον καὶ οὐκ ἐκόσμησας, περιθεὶς αὐτῇ τὰ ἐκ πλεονεξίας ἁρπάγματα. Καὶ λέγει πρὸς σὲ ὃν δῆθεν ἐκόσμησας ἅγιος: "Ἵνα τί «ὑπέλαβες ἀνομίαν, ὅτι ἔσομαί σοι ὅμοιος»; προσαγωγαὶ γὰρ κλεπτῶν καὶ πλεονεκτῶν βδέλυγμα Κυρίῳ· «καὶ γὰρ παρανόμως προσφέρουσιν αὐτάς». Τίμα δὲ τὸν Κύριον ἀπὸ τῶν σῶν δικαίων πόνων, καὶ ἀπάρχου αὐτῷ ἀπὸ σῶν καρπῶν δικαιοσύνης». Ἐγὼ γὰρ ἐν τῇ τῶν οὐρανῶν οἰκῶ βασιλείᾳ· ἐκεῖνοι δέ, οὓς σὺ πλεονεκτήσας ἠδίκησας, πιέζονται πτωχείᾳ πολλῇ καὶ χρείαν ἔχουσιν ἀναλωμάτων, δηλαδὴ βρωμάτων, πομάτων, ἐνδυμάτων καὶ σκεπασμάτων, καὶ δεῖ σὲ λοιπὸν ἐκείνους εὖ ποιεῖν ὡς ἀδικηθέντας ἐκ σοῦ.

The same is also true with regard to the censure passed by the saint on clerical dignitaries and bishops.[21] The bishops and the dignitaries are censured not as such but as worldly-minded and negligent clerics, although in at least one case the saint refused to acknowledge the true priesthood of bad bishops:

"... a bishop in the grip of perversity and folly is not a bishop but a counterfeit, called a bishop not by God but by men, like Ananias and Samaias in Jerusalem and Zedekias and Achias, the false prophets in Babylon."[22]

On the other hand, we know of his suitable relations with the respectable bishops of Paphos, Basil Kinnamos and Bacchos, as also with other ecclesiastical "archons"[23] and "learned men in the secular world".[24] It is also evident that among his spiritual children were numbered rich and respectable Cypriots, such as the *sebastos* to whom he addressed his epistle *Concerning the misfortunes of the land of Cyprus*. Nevertheless, it remains equally indicative that apart from two chance references to Archbishop John the Cretan (1152–71)[25] and the contemporary duke of Cyprus, Alexios Kassianos,[26] the name of no other archbishop, duke, king or other *archon* of the island is mentioned in any

---

[21] E.g. Πρὸς τοὺς ἀτακτοῦντας καὶ λύοντας τὰ τῆς νηστείας προοίμια in I.P. Tsiknopoullos, "Τὰ ἐλάσσονα τοῦ Νεοφύτου πρεσβυτέρου μοναχοῦ καὶ Ἐγκλείστου", Βυζάντιον 39 (1969), pp. 318–419, esp. pp. 404–7, 405.51-53, 406. 84–8, 407.97–9.

[22] Ἑρμηνεία δεσποτικῶν ἐντολῶν, Cod. Coisl. gr. 287, fol. 147ᵛ:
...οὐδ᾽ ἀρχιερεὺς κακονοίᾳ καὶ ἀνοίᾳ κεκρατημένος ἔστιν ἀρχιερεύς, ἀλλὰ ψευδώνυμος, οὐ παρὰ Θεοῦ, ἀλλ᾽ ἐξ ἀνθρώπων κληθεὶς ὡς Ἀνανίας καὶ Σαμαίας ἐν Ἱερουσαλήμ, καὶ Σεδεκίας καὶ Ἀχίας οἱ ἐν Βαβυλῶνι ψευδοπροφῆται.

[23] *Typike Diatheke* 5; pp 77–8.

[24] Ibid., 9, fol. 17; p. 79.

[25] On this archbishop see V. Laurent, "La succession épiscopale des derniers archevêques grecs de Chypre, de Jean le Crétois (1152) à Germain Pésimandros (1260)", REB 7 (1949), pp. 33–41, esp. pp. 33–5; K. Hadjipsaltes, "Συμβολαὶ εἰς τὴν ἱστορίαν τῆς Ἐκκλησίας τῆς Κύπρου", pp. xxix–xxxv. Misled by L. Petit, K. Hadjipsaltes thought that the death of the metropolitan of Russia, on which the dating of the death of John the Cretan depends, took place in 1174. In reality the metropolitan of Russia who died was not Clement but an unknown Michael, who in 1171 appears for a moment as a signatory of the synodical act of faith which was addressed to the house of Manuel Komnenos on 24 March 1171 in the patriarchate of Michael Anchiales. See E. Golubinskij, *Istorija russkoj Cerkvi*, I, Moscow, 1901, p. 288; A. B. Kartasev, *Ocerki po istorij russkoj cerkvi*, I, Paris, 1959, p. 177. The synodical act was published by A.S. Pavlov in VV 2 (1895), p. 383. Michael seems to have died immediately after the act of 24 March 1171, because he was unable to reach his see and therefore remained unknown to the Russian sources. Accordingly Archbishop John the Cretan of Cyprus died in 1171 and not in 1174.

[26] Duke of Cyprus in succession to Alexios Ducas Komnenos, i.e. after about 1161. See V. Laurent, "La succession épiscopale", pp. 33–4. On the two references to him by Neophytos see I.P.Tsiknopoullos, "Τὰ ἐλάσσονα τοῦ Νεοφύτου", p. 392. 51–2, p. 398.46–7.

of the extant works of Neophytos, a fact which shows that Neophytos was
not especially close to the island's ruling class and that his relations with it
were restricted to its local Paphian representatives. In this sense Neophytos
can be taken both socially and ecclesiastically to represent in the matter before
us the average Cypriot view of contemporary events and reaction towards
them, always, of course, as a man dedicated above all to the things of the
spirit.

On the political level, we noted on an earlier occasion an anti-
Constantinopolitan animus in a passage of the saint.[27] No trace, however,
of a schismatic spirit of local autonomy is found in him and he entrusted his
monks to the "aristocracy" of the Byzantine emperor even in the second version
of his *Typicon* in 1214, when the emperor was in exile at Nicaea, far from the
City. The Recluse not only never conceived of any other kind of political
organisation for the Empire but he never even criticised any contemporary
emperor by name, not even the tyrant Andronikos I himself, although he does
indeed refer without comment to the murder by him of his under-age nephew,
Alexios II.[28] Even in the case of Isaac Komnenos himself, however, the saint
never used an insulting epithet, even though he regarded his kingdom in Cyprus
as "rebellious".[29] This fact should be attributed largely to the monastic
virtue of the man and his renunciation of worldly affairs. It is consistent,
however, with his whole view of secular authority, in line with the apostolic
tradition, that such authority existed by the will and permission of God.
Nevertheless, it is worth noting again the entirely personal spiritual view of
St Neophytos even in this matter. In judging, for example, the authority of
the judiciary, he applies to it the dominical "Judge not, lest ye be judged",
saying amongst other things the following:

"... and you who are full of countless evils preside as supposedly unac-
countable and you mercilessly judge those who are ruled as people who
are accountable. And I do not in any way curtail your authority, nor do
I separate you from your presidency, but I exhort you as follows, since
I am concerned for your salvation: 'First take out the beam' of sin 'from
the eye' of your soul, 'and then you will see to take out the splinter', that

---

[27] B. Englezakis, "'Ανέκδοτον ὑπόμνημα τοῦ ὁσίου Νεοφύτου τοῦ 'Εγκλείστου
εἰς τὴν 'Αποκάλυψιν", *ΕΚΕΕΚ* 8 (1975–7), pp. 73–112, esp. pp. 83–4 (reproduced as Chapter
VII above, pp. 105–145).

[28] *Περὶ τῶν κατὰ χώραν Κύπρον σκαιῶν,* in I.P. Tsiknopoullos, "Τὰ ἐλάσσονα τοῦ
Νεοφύτου", p. 338.65–9.

[29] *'Εγκώμιον εἰς τὸν τίμιον καὶ ζωοποιὸν σταυρόν,* Cod. Paris. gr. 1189, fol. 37:
ἑπτὰ γὰρ ἔτη ἐκρατήθη ἡ χώρα αὕτη ἀνταρτικῶς καὶ ἐβασιλεύθη παρ' 'Ισαακίου
τοῦ Κομνηνοῦ καὶ ἐπικράνθη οὐ μετρίως.

is, the sickness of these lighter faults, 'from the eye of your brother', the people who are ruled. For you are their brother, even if you are more powerful than they and preside over them."[30]

Such "mystical anarchy" is a most rare phenomenon in the later Byzantine Empire.

The nature of the saint's monastic observance, as has already been said, is that of the spirituality of the early coenobium and is inspired by the hesychastic ideal. It is in this spirit that Neophytos judges both the monastic life[31] of his contemporaries and their empty forms of worship and love of ceremony.[32] Certain passages in his writings leave hints of mystical experiences but in his work generally the saint appears as an ascetic rather than a mystic. Living out like a true monk the real eschatological dimensions of his calling and character, Neophytos did not permit himself to fall into apocalyptic fantasies in spite of the hard historical reality that confronted him, even though, in keeping with the common Byzantine opinion, he believed that the life of the world, calculated at 7,000 years, was already in his time entering its last phase, which he expected to draw to a close in 1492.[33] These, however, are arithmetical calculations handed down from his predecessors rather than a genuine apocalyptic view of history.

The saint frequently stresses that "the barbarous nations often arm themselves against us and we are defeated in wars and are unable to resist" and that "a turn for the worse has taken place". Words and phrases such as "affliction", "apprehension", "damage", "wailing", "disaster", "blow",

---

[30] Ἑρμηνεία δεσποτικῶν ἐντολῶν 9, Cod. Coisl. gr. 287, fol. 146–146ᵛ:
... καὶ σὺ μὲν προκάθησαι ὡς ἀνεύθυνος δῆθεν ὁ μυρίων γέμων κακῶν, καὶ ὡς ὑπευθύνους ἀνηλεῶς κρίνεις τοὺς ἀρχομένους. Καὶ οὐδέν σου κωλύω τὴν ἐξουσίαν, οὐδέ σε τῆς προεδρίας διωστῶ, ἀλλὰ τοῦτο διακελεύομαί σοι τὴν σὴν σωτηρίαν πραγματευόμενος. «Ἔκβαλε πρῶτον τὴν δοκόν» ἁμαρτίαν «ἐκ τοῦ ὀφθαλμοῦ» τῆς ψυχῆς σου, «καὶ τότε διαβλέψεις ἐκβαλεῖν τὸ κάρφος», ἤγουν καὶ αὐτῶν τῶν λεπτοτέρων σφαλμάτων τὴν νόσον, «‹ἐκ› τοῦ ὀφθαλμοῦ τοῦ ἀδελφοῦ σου» ἀρχομένου λαοῦ. Καὶ γὰρ ἀδελφὸς αὐτοῦ εἶ, κἂν ὑπερέχεις αὐτοῦ καὶ προκάθησαι.

[31] E.g. Κατηχήσεων βίβλος 2, 12, Cod. Paris. suppl. gr. 1317, fols 153ᵛ–154ᵛ: ... ἀφ' ὅτου δὲ ἠμελήθη καὶ διελύθη ἡ καλὴ ταύτη καὶ ἀξιέπαινος εὐταξία, ἀπέστη καὶ ἡ τιμὴ τῶν γυναικείων μοναστηρίων καὶ εἰσῆλθεν ἀτιμία (fol. 154) etc.; Typike Diatheke 9, fols. 17ᵛ–18, p. 79: μεμάθηκα πείρᾳ, ἀπό τε τῶν κοινοβιακῶν συστημάτων, ..., ὅτι ἡ τῶν πολλῶν καὶ ἀπαιδεύτων καὶ μοχθηρῶν καὶ ἀνυποτάκτων καὶ μεμψιμοίρων συναυλία πολλοὺς θορύβους τίκτει καὶ σκάνδαλα.

[32] E.g. Περὶ τῆς Ἀποκαλύψεως, Epil. 1 in B. Englezakis, "Ἀνέκδοτον ὑπόμνημα" pp. 112.14–19 (p. 144. 14–19 above).

[33] To what I have written in B. Englezakis, "Ἀνέκδοτον ὑπόμνημα", pp. 84–5 (pp. 116–117 above) add D.M. Nicol, *Church and Society in the Last Centuries of Byzantium*, Cambridge, 1979, ch. 4 "The end of the world", esp. the bibliography on p. 105, note 23.

"danger", "grievous things", "difficulties", "want", "lack", "obstacles", "unbridled acts", "lawless deeds", "a world of transgressions and worthily chastised", and verbs such as "we suffer", "we experience tumults", "we have been cursed", "we endure", "we have been consumed", "we have been mown down", "we struggle", "we have been cut down", "we have been abandoned", recur constantly in those works of Neophytos written before 1191 and are surely a symptomatic sign of the general sense of insecurity and anxiety which characterises the period, as also of a premonition of the approaching end. The saint perceives with clarity the moral, social, political and physical decay and corruption around him. How does he react? Where does he place his hopes?

In the first place, we shall not be far from the truth if we say that in spite of his unwillingness to question authority openly, Neophytos does not give the impression of basing firm hopes on it, at least after the death of Manuel Komnenos. When describing in about 1179 the battle of Myriocephalon (17 September 1176) and the extreme danger to which Manuel was exposed in the course of it, Neophytos was able to write that "if the emperor is in danger ... the whole of Romania is in danger with him and Christian regimes everywhere".[34] Nevertheless, the bitter experience of the governments of Manuel's successors and of the Western "Christian regimes" together with his growing spiritual maturity taught him in a practical way that Christianity does not look to Caesar for its support but to the Cross.

It is clear, however, from the third chapter of the *Typike Diatheke* that from his childhood years Neophytos was already possessed by feelings of contempt for worldly things and a desire for their renunciation and his sanctification in the service of the transcendent:

"... almost from my first starting-point ... I felt these things and probably intended that I would at any rate obey these things myself, involved as I was in the life and finding it impossible to escape their harshness. If anyone is able to escape such difficulty and enjoy all the prosperity in the world, when death is imminent and, as I had heard, another world awaits us, what is the profit?

"I confess artlessly that these reflections and memories are not the work of my youth and rusticity, but of some divine grace and providence written and unwritten, and, 'As God is my witness, I speak the truth, I do not

---

[34] *Pentekontakephalon* 31, codex 522, Nat. Lib. of Greece, fols 75–77ᵛ: εἰ κινδυνεύσει ὁ βασιλεύς ..., συγκινδυνεύσει αὐτῷ ἅπασα ἡ Ῥωμανία καὶ πανταχοῦ τῶν χριστιανῶν τὰ συστήματα. Κ. Dyovouniotes, "Νεοφύτου Ἐγκλείστου ἀνέκδοτα ἔργα", p. 45.

lie.' For reflecting on what concerns me, I said that 'If in this life I do away with myself, in the life to come God will certainly make me appear, and I will exist again.' But what I shall say now in the Lord I shall say in truth: 'that if a poor vagabond dressed in rags came to my family home asking for bread, his life would be considered by me blessed and glorious and if it happened to me I would straightaway follow him.'"[35]

This passage reveals more clearly than any analysis of mine the "centrifugal" psychological and spiritual attitude of the saint. What is said in the forty-fourth chapter of the *Pentekontakephalon* about the *logismoi* which are provoked in the young Neophytos by the sudden deaths of monks in the monastery of Koutzouvendi and the chapters in the same book about mourning and the remembering of the true home in heaven,[36] and other relevant passages from his works, testify to this attitude and confirm it. The sociologist historian would perhaps judge it a personalist reaction to the prevailing moral and physical insecurity, salvific for the individual but unhealthy for the community, a reaction which was marginalising, eccentric and disjunctive. The philosopher, however, and the theologian recognise that the fundamental step towards authentic existence is *anxiety* (ἀγωνία) in conjunction with *amazement* (θάμβος) – a vibrant element also in the saint's whole work and personality.[37]

In the end the monastic outlook and way of life cannot be judged on the basis of secular criteria. The solitary search for spiritual perfection by the monk does not signify, as appears at first sight, an abandonment of the world and denial of practical service. It offers to man an ideal of perfection from which – at all times but especially in the hour of the greater crises – he can draw strength and inspiration. The spiritual level of a society cannot, as Arnold Toynbee correctly observed,

"be higher than the average level of the participants; the collective level can be raised only on the initiative of individuals; and, when an individual does rise above the level of his social environment, this is the fruit of a previous victory over himself in his own spiritual life."[38]

---

[35] *Typike Diatheke* 3, fols 7–11; pp. 74–5.

[36] Published in part in I.P. Tsiknopoullos, "Τρία ἀνώνυμα βυζαντινὰ ποιήματα ἐπανευρίσκουν τὸν ποιητὴν των ἅγιον Νεόφυτον", *KS* 7 (1963), pp. 75–117.

[37] See e.g. the amazement of the young Neophytos, not long after his admission into the monastery of Koutzouvendi, on his hearing the first verses of Genesis (ἠγάσθην ... ἐξεπλάγην ... θαῦμα): Ἑξαήμερος 3, I. Ch. Hadjioannou, Ἱστορία καὶ ἔργα Νεοφύτου πρεσβυτέρου μοναχοῦ καὶ ἐγκλείστου, Alexandria, 1914, pp. 168–9.

[38] A. Toynbee, *A Study of History*, new edition revised and abridged, London, 1972, p. 341.

Throughout his long life St Neophytos was for his suffering country and people not only their voice but also a source of consolation, strength, education and vitality. Within a physical space which was constantly being further constricted, Neophytos raised up works of culture which can stir the emotions even today. In a corrupt society he succeeded in consolidating a community of people imbued with the single ideal of struggling together for moral perfection. In a collapsing commonwealth he raised up his eyes towards the "refined and great" Commonwealth of God. If for Hellenism the rule is that "it is not fitting, being mortal, to think mortal thoughts, but so far as possible to become immortal"[39] and in Christianity the hard realities of life could not triumph over the profound truth of the Resurrection, Neophytos constitutes one of the rare examples of a Greek and Christian ethos in the period of the Komnenoi and Angeloi, when many wrote in better Atticising Greek than he did, yet remained without a share in an education which extended beyond that of linguistic form.

After this long but unavoidable introduction we can now proceed to the examination of how Neophytos dealt with the Frankish domination of Cyprus. We shall divide our study into three basic parts. In the first we shall examine the sources, in the second the attitude of the saint to the Latin Church and in the third his attitude towards the Frankish political authority. This is more logical than the reverse order because the attitude of Neophytos towards the Latin government was founded ideologically on his beliefs about the Church. Finally, I shall draw together some conclusions.

II. THE SOURCES

The evidence which we possess today on the subject of our study all comes exclusively from the writings of Neophytos himself and may be divided into direct and indirect evidence. It should be noted at the outset that even the direct sources are not only fragmentary but also circumstantial. The saint was not a historian. Even his treatise *Concerning the misfortunes of the land of Cyprus* arose primarily not from an interest in history but from a spiritual intention. As he himself testifies in the work, in its original form it was a letter addressed to one of his spiritual children. The only other works which refer directly to the Latins, his homilies *On the Seven Ecumenical Councils and on why and when the elder Rome and the new Rome grew apart from each other* and *On the high priesthood of Christ and the azymes*, have a didactic and polemical purpose rather than a purely historical one. Whenever Neophytos speaks elsewhere of the Latins in a direct way, he does so incidentally and almost impatiently, as if carried away

---

[39] Aristotle, *Nicomachean Ethics*, 1177α.12–1178α.8.

("I do not wish to say much about this; I have said even this out of respect for the Lord's condescension.")[40]

The indirect evidence may also be divided into two classes, the allusions and the silences. The argument from silence is, of course, a slippery one, but when in Neophytos's encomium on St Peter, for example, nothing is said about the papal primacy, it is evident that Neophytos is still unaware of the medieval Western understanding of the papal primacy.[41] On the other hand, the interpretation of Psalm 22, for example, may be considered to be allusive.[42] The ground here too, however, is dangerous. Are the "tyrant kings" who oppress the Church of Christ with "unspeakable afflictions" the ancient persecuting emperors or the Frankish occupiers or Isaac Komnenos?[43]

---

[40] Cod. Paris. gr. 1189, fol. 37: περὶ τούτων πολλὰ ἐγὼ λέγειν οὐ βούλομαι· ἔφην δὲ καὶ ταῦτα ὑπεραγάμενος τὴν δεσποτικὴν συγκατάβασιν.

[41] Cod. Lesb. Leimon. 2, fols 314–318. Cf. B. Englezakis "Ἡ εἰς τοὺς κανόνας τῶν Δεσποτικῶν ἑορτῶν ἑρμηνία τοῦ ὁσίου Νεοφύτου τοῦ Ἐγκλείστου", Ἀπόστολος Βαρνάβας 39 (1978) pp. 367–75 (translated as Chapter VI above, pp. 97–104). The East was in general slow in becoming aware of the ideological development in the medieval West on this point. See J. Darrouzès, "Les documents byzantins du XIIe siècle sur la primauté romaine" REB 23 (1965), pp. 42–88; J. Spiteris, La critica bizantina del primato romano nel saecolo XII Rome, 1979.

[42] I. Ch. Hadjiioannou, Νεοφύτου πρεσβυτέρου μοναχοῦ καὶ ἐγκλείστου, Ἑρμηνεία εἰς τοὺς Ψαλμούς, Athens, 1935, p. 30.

[43] There is ample evidence that Isaac caused distress to the Church of Cyprus. It is regrettable but typical of the man that Neophytos does not refer to Isaac's proclamation of the archbishop of Cyprus as patriarch anywhere in surviving works. This information, which derives from the Syrian historian, Michael the Great, Jacobite patriarch of Antioch (1166–99), is of the greatest significance both to the ecclesiastical history of Cyprus and to the history of the Byzantine imperial ideology of the period, and even to the struggle between Epirus and Nicaea (see A. Karpozilos, The Ecclesiastical Controversy Between the Kingdom of Nicaea and the Principality of Epirus (1217–1233), Thessaloniki, 1973; J. Meyendorff, "Ideological Crises 1071 to 1261", XVe Congrès International d' Études Byzantines, Rapports et co-rapports, Athens, 1976. G. Hill, A History of Cyprus, p. 313, note I, refers to the testimony of Michael the Syrian but does not realise its significance, nor does he give the text, which reads in translation as follows: "At that time there was in Cyprus, an island of the Greeks, a Greek leader called Komneneh. He rebelled against the emperor of Constantinople, called the Greek bishops together and ordered them to install a patriarch, who crowned this Komneneh emperor. They proclaimed this emperor and this patriarch in opposition to those of Constantinople, until the Frankish kings set sail from Rome, and the king of England came to capture Cyprus, and threw its Greek emperor into prison, and confined him in a castle near Antioch. The patriarch whom they had installed also died in Cyprus, and their empty plans failed" (J. B. Chabot, ed., Cronique de Michel le Syrien Patriarche Jacobite d'Antioche, III, Paris, 1905, p. 402). Michael terminates his narrative at the year 1195 and he himself died in 1199. The death of the "patriarch of Cyprus", then, occurred between the years 1194 and 1199. He seems to have been Sophronios II, whom witnesses mention as archbishop of Cyprus at the time of the arrival of the Franks in 1191. See V. Laurent, "La succession épiscopale", pp. 35–6; K. Hadjipsaltes, "Ἡ Ἐκκλησία Κύπρου καὶ τὸ ἐν Νικαίᾳ Οἰκουμενικὸν Πατριαρχεῖον ἀρχομένου τοῦ ΙΓ΄ μ.Χ. αἰῶνος", KS 28 (1964), pp. 137–68, esp. p. 142.17.

I offer here an analysis of only the major direct testimonies. The rest will be noted at the appropriate place.

1. *Concerning the misfortunes of the land of Cyprus* (Περὶ τῶν κατὰ χώραν Κύπρου σκαιῶν).

This small treatise is known from Cod. Marc. 575 (saec. XV) fols. 395ᵛ–396ᵛ and Paris. gr. 1335 (saec. XIV) fol. 6–6ᵛ. It was first published by J.B. Cotelier, *Ecclesiae graecae monumenta*, II, Paris, 1681, pp. 457–62. Since then it has frequently been reprinted. The relevant bibliography is given by I.P. Tsiknopoullos in *Byzantion* 37 (1967), pp. 410–11. To the editions mentioned there that of Bishop W. Stubbs in his prologue to the *Itinerarium peregrinorum et gesta regis Ricardi* should be added for the sake of completeness (Rolls Series 38, London, 1864, pp. clxxxv–clxxxix) and also that of Tsiknopoullos himself in *Byzantion* 39 (1969), pp. 336–9, 339–43. It is to this last edition that I refer below by page and line.

The reference to the twelve years of disaster (336.5 and 19) raises the question whether we should calculate the year of composition by adding twelve years to 1185, when the tyranny of Isaac Komnenos began, or to 1191, when the Frankish occupation began. F.E. Warren[44] chose 1203, while L. de Mas Latrie[45] preferred 1196, without, however, justifying his preference. Subsequent editors either date the work vaguely after 1191 or arbitrarily assign it to 1196, while Tsiknopoullos (340) suggested 1194, accepting – I do not know how – 1183 as the first year of Isaac's reign and 1189 as the year of Richard's arrival. The fragment, however, of the homily on the Cross (Cod. Paris. gr. 1189, fol. 37–37ᵛ), which I set out below at 2.ii, proves conclusively that Neophytos calculated the twelve years of disaster from 1185. Since the homily was written in August 1196, the treatise *Concerning the misfortunes* must have been composed a little before or afterwards, that is, in the second half at all events of 1196.

As I have already noted, in its present form the work is a historical lament adapted from an earlier letter of the saint to an important spiritual son who left the island after the French had installed themselves and fled to Constantinople, where the "Emperor Angelos" (=Isaac II) honoured him with the title of *sebastos*.[46]

---

[44] *Archaeologia* 47 (1882), p. 2.

[45] *Histoire de l'île de Chypre sous le règne de la Maison de Lusignan*, I, Paris, 1891, p. 125.

[46] The seventy-seventh rank in the Byzantine hierarchy. See H. Ahrweiler, "Le sébaste, chef de groupes ethniques", *Polychronion; Festschrift für F. Dölger*, Munich, 1966, pp. 34–8. It is worth noting that Niketas Choniates accuses Isaac Angelos (1185–95) in his *History* (*CSHB*, Bonn, 1835, p. 639) of offering high honours for money, such as the rank of *sebastos*, to anyone he met.

With regard to the content I shall only say here that although Neophytos deplores the plunder and seizure of Greek-Cypriot estates by the Franks and the reduction of his people's *archons* to humiliation and misery, he nevertheless makes no reference to any persecution of the Orthodox Church or to Latin interference in its internal affairs or at least seizure of its property. We know that the final arrangements for the imposition of a Latin hierarchy on the island and the endowment of Latin bishops with lands belonging to Orthodox dioceses took place on the 13 December 1196 at the insistence of Pope Celestine III.[47]

2. *The three greater Panegyrics* (Αἱ μειζότεραι τρεῖς Πανηγυρικαί).

A description of this work of the Recluse together with the relevant bibliography is given by I.P. Tsiknopoullos in *KS* 22 (1958), pp. 80–103.

i. "Discourse on the dedication of the Church of the Resurrection and on any church that is being dedicated" (Λόγος εἰς τὰ ἐγκαίνια τῆς ἁγίας Ἀναστάσεως, καὶ περὶ παντὸς ἱεροῦ ἐγκαινιζομένου ναοῦ) (Cod. Paris. gr. 1189, saec. XIII, fols 24ᵛ–29).

This discourse is still unpublished. The Eastern Church celebrates each year on 13 September the dedication of the Church of the Resurrection in Jerusalem which was carried out with great magnificence by Constantine the Great on 17 September 335. The beginning of Neophytos's discourse, however, creates a difficulty:

"The written sayings of the Spirit on various dedications are indeed elegant and infinite in number. But having selected a few of this large number as divine pearls and precious stones, I shall adorn them with the present crown of the discourse so as to preserve the honour not only of the church of the holy Resurrection of Christ alone, which had formerly been dedicated in a divine and beautiful way, but also the honour of every sacred church that is being dedicated, not with the precepts of our native discourses but gathering together testimonies from the divine utterances of the Holy Spirit."[48]

---

[47] See P. Jaffé, *Regesta Pontificum Romanorum*, II, Leipzig, 1888, p. 620, no. 17329; J.L. La Monte, "A Register of the Cartulary of the Cathedral of Santa Sophia of Nicosia", *Byzantion* 5 (1929–30), pp. 441–522, esp. p. 444, no. 2 (dated 13 December 1196).

[48] Ἄπειρα μέντοι καὶ γλαφυρὰ τὰ περὶ διαφόρων ἐγκαινισμῶν γραφικὰ τοῦ Πνεύματος ἀποφθέγματα· ἐγὼ δὲ ὀλίγα τινὰ ἐκ τῶν πολλῶν συλλεξάμενος, ὡς θείους μαργαρίτας καὶ λίθους πολυτελεῖς, τῷ παρόντι τοῦ λόγου κατακοσμήσω στεφάνῳ, ὥστε μὴ μόνον τὸν τῆς ἁγίας τοῦ Χριστοῦ Ἀναστάσεως νεὼν καὶ μόνον, τὸν πάλαι θείως καὶ καλῶς ἤδη ἐγκαινισθέντα, ἀλλά γε καὶ ἐπὶ παντὸς ἱεροῦ ἐγκαινιζομένου ναοῦ ἀποσῴζειν τὴν εὐφημίαν, οὐχ ὑποθήκαις λόγων ἡμεδαπῶν, ἀλλ᾿ ἐκ τῶν τοῦ Ἁγίου Πνεύματος θεηγοριῶν σαγηνεύων τὰς μαρτυρίας.

The phrase "which had formerly been dedicated in a divine and beautiful way" should be taken to imply a new dedication of the church of the Resurrection. But which one? Such a dedication is not mentioned explicitly in the documents of the twelfth century. It is not difficult for us, however, to conjecture what the Recluse means. It is known that on the capture of Jerusalem by Saladin on 2 October 1187 Isaac Angelos sought from him the restoration of the privileges enjoyed by the Orthodox of the Holy City under the Fatimids. Although he did not receive a perfect and exclusive sovereignty over the holy places, he nevertheless secured the Church of the Resurrection (except for some parts of it which were given to the Copts and Abyssinians) and the installation of the Orthodox patriarch of Jerusalem, Dositheos (1186–89),[49] appointed by him in place of the Latin patriarch, Heraclius, who fled to Ptolemais. The embassies exchanged between Constantinople and Jerusalem, and the agreement that was achieved along with the installation of Dositheos, would have taken place, we must suppose, in 1188, for in 1189 Isaac renewed the treaty which had been concluded between Saladin and Andronikos I in 1184.[50]

The Church of the Resurrection which the Orthodox received back in 1187 was no longer the circular building which Monomachos had completed in 1048. It was the Church of the Holy Sepulchre, under the single roof of which the Crusaders had taken in the Resurrection, Golgotha and the *katholikon*. Without doubt this new Latin building had to be rededicated in the Orthodox fashion, and according to the testimony of Neophytos this is what was done.[51]

But another passage on fol. 26 persuades us that this discourse was written during the Latin occupation of Cyprus. Comparing the fate of the Solomonic Temple with that of the Christian Church, the author writes:

---

[49] S. Runciman, *The Eastern Schism*, Oxford, 1971, p. 90, relying on M. Le Quien, *Oriens Christianus*, III, Paris, 1740, pp. 498–593, who follows Dositheos II, Ἱστορία περὶ τῶν ἐν Ἱεροσολύμοις πατριαρχευσάντων, Bucharest, 1715, p. 1243, accepts that Athanasios II returned to Jerusalem in 1187. This is proved to be incorrect by Dositheos I himself, who says on the occasion of his resignation from the throne of Constantinople in 1191: "... through the ineffable judgments and reckonings of God I was raised to the patriarchal throne of Jerusalem by my most mighty and holy emperor, equal to the angels (= Isaac Angelos, 1185–95) and afterwards in turn, after the capture of Jerusalem by the Hagarenes, I was translated to the patriarchal throne of Constantinople" etc (in Ch. Papadopoulos, Ἱστορία τῆς Ἐκκλησίας Ἱεροσολύμων, 2nd edn, Athens, 1970, pp. 444, 446–9 – the dates are constantly confused). The translation took place in February 1189.

[50] See F. Dölger, *Regesten der Kaiserurkunden des oströmischen Reiches*, II, nos 1584, 1591, 1593, 1608; S. Runciman, *The Eastern Schism*, p. 98; id., *A History of the Crusades*, II, London, 1965, pp. 467–8; J. M. Hussey, ed., *CMH*, vol. iv, pt. 1, Cambridge, 1966, p. 246.

[51] For the history of the church see C. Coüasnon, *The Church of the Holy Sepulchre in Jerusalem*, London, 1974.

"When the house of his rest and the present house together with every sacred house of God are gathered into one holy catholic and apostolic Church, and are based firmly on the unbreakable rock of faith, the gates of hell of the devil and of the tyranny of the unorthodox cannot prevail against it; for since it has its foundations in the holy mountains of the mercies of God through pure faith and good works, rain and the rivers of temptations and dangers are not strong enough to destroy it."[52]

This exegesis combines Matthew 16:18 ("you are Peter, and on this rock I will build my church, and the gates of hell shall not prevail against it") with Matthew 7:24–25 ("the house built on a rock, which did not fall as a result of the rain and the rivers") and Psalm 86:1 (LXX) ("His foundations are in his holy mountains"). It is worth noting that Neophytos follows an interpretation which sees the rock as "pure faith" founded on "good deeds", that is to say, he sees the rock as Orthodoxy and not as Peter.[53] On fol. 26ᵛ he defines the foundation of the Church as Christ himself with reference to I Corinthians 3:11. Especially worth noticing is the fact that by a figure of hendiadys he regards the gates of hell that threaten the catholic Church as the devil and the "tyranny of the unorthodox". This refers without doubt to the Frankish regime of Cyprus. "Unorthodoxy" (κακοδοξία) together with "wrong belief" (κακοπιστία) were in this period the chief terms which the Orthodox applied to the Latins. Neophytos himself in his prologue to his *Instructions*[54] speaks of impure rulers, of unbelieving and shameful rulers and of the unorthodox. The "tyranny of the unorthodox" cannot be anything other than Latin rule. As a further proof it will be sufficient to mention the exegesis of Matthew 7:24–5 which Neophytos gave in 1176, twenty-five years before the beginning of Frankish rule in Cyprus, in his *Commentary on the dominical commandments*. There we find a purely moral exegesis without the dogmatic overtones of orthodoxy–unorthodoxy.[55]

A point which should help us date the discourse more precisely is the fact that although in the course of it the saint develops his favourite theme

---

[52] Ὁ δὲ οἶκος τῆς αὐτοῦ ἀναπαύσεως καὶ ὁ παρὼν οἶκος, ἅμα Θεοῦ ἱερῷ οἴκῳ παντί, εἰς μίαν, ἁγίαν, καθολικὴν καὶ ἀποστολικὴν ἐκκλησίαν σαγηνευθείς, καὶ πρὸς τὴν ἀρραγῆ πέτραν τῆς πίστεως ἑδραωθείς, πύλαι ᾅδου διαβόλου καὶ τυραννὶς κακοδόξων οὐ κατισχύσουσιν αὐτῆς· ἔχουσα γὰρ τὰ θεμέλια ἐν τοῖς ὄρεσι τοῖς ἁγίοις τῶν οἰκτιρμῶν τοῦ Θεοῦ διὰ πίστεως καθαρᾶς καὶ ἔργων ἀγαθῶν, βροχή τε καὶ ποταμοὶ πειρασμῶν καὶ κινδύνων οὐκ ἰσχύουσιν αὐτὴν καταστρέψαι.

[53] See *Katecheseis*, Prologue, Cod. Paris. suppl. gr. 1317, fol. 8: ... καὶ "εἰ φιλεῖς με, Πέτρε", φησί, "ποίμαινε τὰ πρόβατά μου", δηλονότι καὶ ὅστις με ἄλλος φιλεῖ μετά σε, καλῶς ποιμανεῖ ἔχει τὰ πρόβατα μου καὶ τὰ ἀρνία μου.

[54] Ibid., fol. 9.

[55] Ἑρμηνεία δεσποτικῶν ἐντολῶν, 10, Cod. Coisl. gr. 287, fol. 178–178ᵛ.

of the foundation stones of the Church/Sion, he does not refer to the images of the twenty-first chapter of the Apocalypse but only to Isaiah 54. This had also been the case earlier in the discourse *Against the Jews*[56] and the ninth discourse of the *Commentary on the dominical commandments*,[57] both of which are unpublished, where he dwells at length on the twelve precious stones and the heavenly Sion. From his *Commentary on the Apocalypse* we know that Neophytos had not read the Apocalypse until the period immediately after 1204.[58] The discourse *On the Dedication*, then, belongs to the period before 1204. Whether 1191 or 1204 is to be preferred as the year of its delivery is impossible for us to say with any certainty. If the discourse was composed, however, on the occasion of the dedication of the Hermitage church, we should bear in mind that this church was decorated and furnished with an iconostasis in about 1197.[59]

ii. "Encomium on the precious and life-giving cross" (Ἐγκώμιον εἰς τὸν τίμιον καὶ ζωοποιὸν σταυρόν) (Cod. Paris. gr. 1189, saec. XIII, fols 29ᵛ–38ᵛ).

This discourse is still unpublished. The meaning of the passage printed here from fol. 37–37ᵛ is evident, since we can now for the first time establish a firm dating for the treatise *Concerning the misfortunes of the land of Cyprus*.

"He suffered pain for us and was humiliated and put to death and neither for His sake nor for our own did we undertake to renounce our bodily appetites. Therefore through our deeply sinful life and unrepentant ways we have been handed over to the nations 'and those who hate us persecute us' and we sow 'our seeds in vain and our adversaries enjoy the fruits of our labours and our strength has been spent for nothing' and we have become depleted and an alien people has multiplied in our land.

"All these things and more God threatened would be suffered by those who did not keep His divine laws. 'Because,' He says, 'you approached me from the side, I too will approach you in anger from the side.' For that is how things are. Unless someone is seriously ill the doctor will not resort to surgery with its sorrow and burning. And if we had not caused much sorrow to our wholly benevolent doctor and had not approached

---

[56] Paris. gr. 1189, fols 207–217ᵛ, esp. 210–211ᵛ·

[57] Coisl. gr. 287, fols 145–171, esp. 153–157ᵛ·

[58] See Englezakis, "'Ανέκδοτον ὑπόμνημα", pp. 87.1.1., 75–76 (pp. 119.1.1., 107–108 above). This supports what was said there.

[59] See C. Mango and E.J.W. Hawkins, "The Hermitage of St. Neophytus and its Wall-Paintings", *DOP* 20 (1966), pp. 119–206, esp. pp. 200–202.

Him from the side, He would not have approached us from the side and caused us saving sorrow for the last twelve years.

"For seven years this land has been held rebelliously and ruled over by Isaac Komnenos and has been made to feel sorrow in no small measure. When he was carried off the land was sold by the persecutor, Englinos, to the Franks for two hundred thousand measures of gold. They have held it in slavery and pillaged it for a further five years and nobody yet knows how long it will last. It is now the month of August of the year 6704, indiction 14, when the present discourse, with God's help, was composed. I have much to say on this subject but do not wish to do so; I have said these things out of respect for the condescension of the Lord, because He did not simply die for His unprofitable servants but 'was numbered among the transgressors'."[60]

It is evident that the treatise *Concerning the misfortunes of the land of Cyprus* is either a development of this passage or that the latter is a summary of the former. Even in its phraseology the second part of the first paragraph is a parallel to *Concerning the misfortunes*, p. 339.99–110.

iii. "A brief exposition on the Apocalypse of St John the Theologian" (Περὶ τῆς Ἀποκαλύψεως τοῦ ἁγίου Ἰωάννου τοῦ Θεολόγου σαφήνεια διὰ βραχέων) (Cod. Paris. gr. 1189, saec. XIII, fols 57ᵛ–77ᵛ).

---

[60] Ἐκεῖνος ὑπὲρ ἡμῶν ὠδυνήθη καὶ ἠτιμάσθη καὶ ἐτεθνήκει, ἡμεῖς δὲ οὔτε ὑπὲρ ἐκείνου οὔτε ὑπὲρ ἡμῶν αὐτῶν ἀνεχόμεθα τὰς ὀρέξεις ἀθετῆσαι τοῦ σώματος. Ἔνθεν καὶ διὰ τὸν πολυαμάρτητον βίον ἡμῶν καὶ ἀμετανόητον τρόπον παρεδόθημεν ἐν τοῖς ἔθνεσιν, "καὶ διώκουσιν ἡμᾶς οἱ μισοῦντες ἡμᾶς", καὶ σπέρομεν "διακενῆς τὰ σπέρματα ἡμῶν, καὶ ἔδονται τοὺς πόνους ἡμῶν οἱ ὑπεναντίοι ἡμῶν, καὶ ἡ ἰσχὺς ἡμῶν ἐγένετο εἰς κενόν", καὶ ἐγενόμεθα ὀλιγοστοί, καὶ λαὸς ἀλλότριος ἐπληθύνθη ἐν τῇ γῇ ἡμῶν.
Ταῦτα γὰρ πάντα καὶ τὰ αὐτῶν παραπλήσια προηπείλησε Θεὸς πάσχειν τοὺς μὴ τηροῦντας τοὺς θείους νόμους αὐτοῦ· "Ὅτι, φησίν, ἐπορεύθητε πρός με πλάγιοι, κἀγὼ πορεύσομαι πρὸς ὑμᾶς ἐν θυμῷ πλαγίῳ" καὶ γὰρ οὕτως ἔχει· εἰ μή που γὰρ δεινῶς τις ἀρρωστήσει, εὔδηλον ὅτι οὐδὲ ὁ ἰατρὸς ἐπάγει τομὴν μετὰ πικρίας καὶ καύσεως· καὶ ἡμεῖς εἰ μή που πολλὰ τὸν πανάγαθον ἡμῶν ἰατρὸν παρεπικράναμεν καὶ πλαγίως πρὸς αὐτὸν διετέθημεν, οὐκ ἂν διετέθη καὶ αὐτὸς πρὸς ἡμᾶς πλαγίως, σωτηριωδῶς παραπικραίνων ἡμᾶς ἰδοὺ δώδεκα ἔτη.
Ἑπτὰ γὰρ ἔτη ἐκρατήθη ἡ χώρα αὕτη ἀνταρτικῶς καὶ ἐβασιλεύθη παρ' Ἰσαακίου τοῦ Κομνηνοῦ καὶ ἐπικράνθη οὐ μετρίως· ἐκείνου δὲ ἀρθέντος, ἐπράθη ἡ χώρα παρ' Ἐγγλίνου διώκτου Φράγγοις χρυσίου χιλιάδων λυτρῶν διακοσίων, οἳ καὶ κρατοῦσιν αὐτὴν δουλικῶς καὶ λεηλατοῦσιν ἑτέρους χρόνους πέντε, καὶ ἕως πότε οὐδεὶς ἐν ἀνθρώποις τὴν ἀπόβασιν οἶδε. Ἔστι δὲ τόδε τὸ ἔτος, ˏςψδ', ἴνδικτος δὲ ιδ', καὶ Αὔγουστος μήν, ὁπηνίκα καὶ ὁ παρὼν σὺν Θεῷ συντέτακται λόγος. Ἀλλὰ περὶ τούτων πολλὰ ἐγὼ λέγειν οὐ βούλομαι· ἔφην δὲ καὶ ταῦτα ὑπεραγάμενος τὴν δεσποτικὴν συγκατάβασιν, ὅτι οὐχ ἁπλῶς ὑπὲρ δούλων ἀχρείων ἀπέθανεν, ἀλλ' ὅτι "καὶ ἐν τοῖς ἀνόμοις ἐλογίσθη".

This work was published for the first time by the present writer in *EKEE* 8 (1975–77), pp. 73–112 (pp. 105–145 above). In it the saint refers twice to the capture of Constantinople by the Latins in 1204. In the eleventh chapter there are two veiled allusions, while in the epilogue Neophytos speaks about the event openly. I refer the reader to the edition, especially pp. 75 and 83–4 (pp. 107 and 115–6 above).

The important passage in relation to our theme is what Neophytos says in his commentary on Apocalypse 13:18.[61] The explanations which he gives of the name of the beast (which he understands as the sea monster of 13:1ff.), ΕΥΑΝΘΑΣ, ΛΑΤΕΙΝΟΣ, ΤΕΙΤΑΝ and ΒΕΝΕΔΙΚΤΟΣ, he certainly found in the marginal scholia of Coisl. gr. 256 and perhaps did not recognise their provenance or their meaning.[62] But even if he did not appreciate the relevance of Benedict VIII, he certainly did not take Irenaeus's ancient interpretation, ΛΑΤΕΙΝΟΣ, as referring to the Rome of the Caesars but to papal Rome, the Latin occupiers in the East and their Church. Apart from this the saint does not comment on these opinions, nor does he choose any particular one, even though immediately afterwards he interprets the beast of Apocalypse 13:11 that arose out of the earth as prefiguring Muhammad, the apostle and false prophet of the Antichrist.[63] It is evident that Neophytos hesitates to equate the Latins with the beast that rose out of the sea in the thirteenth chapter of the Apocalypse even though he does not refrain from mentioning such an interpretation.

Also relevant is the fact that in commenting on Apocalypse 17:15–17[64] St Neophytos stresses that the dominion of the City has not been given to the nations for ever, "but for a while, until the words of God are fulfilled which he uttered in vexation".[65] The Recluse expects that Constantinople will one day recover her liberty. Prompted by Apocalypse 8:1–3, he writes with regard to the Crusader pillagers:

"Those who captured the city, it says, and sacked it live in it like demons and unclean spirits and it was handed over to them not as good men but because of the harlot, for 'the kings who committed fornication with her have drunk of the wine and of the drunkenness of her harlotry and the merchants of the earth have grown rich with the wealth of her wantonness'."

---

[61] Englezakis, "'Ανέκδοτον ὑπόμνημα", p. 102.2. 12-13 (p. 133.2.12–13 above).

[62] Ibid., pp. 77-8 (pp. 109–110 above).

[63] Ibid., p. 102.3 (p. 133.3 above). Cf. 105.12, 13; 109.4 (pp. 137.12,13; 141.4 above).

[64] Ibid., p. 106.9 (p. 138.9 above)

[65] Ibid., p. 106.10.43 (p. 139.10.43 above). (In the Greek text I have amended αὐτῆς to αὐτοῖς.)

Neophytos, then, sees the Latin Empire of Constantinople as demonic and unclean. By contrast, his feelings towards Nicaea can be conjectured from his exegesis of Apocalypse 18:4, which follows immediately:

> "You who are my servants and enemies of sin, come out and separate yourselves from the city of the harlot lest you become sharers in her sin and in her evil."

iv. "A brief encomium on our holy and God-bearing and wonderworking father Hilarion" (Εἰς τὸν ὅσιον καὶ θεοφόρον πατέρα ἡμῶν καὶ θαυματουργὸν Ἱλαρίωνα ἐγκώμιον διὰ βραχέων) (Cod. Paris. gr. 1189, saec. XIII, fols 105ᵛ–114ᵛ).

This discourse was first published by I.P. Tsiknopoullos in *KS* 30 (1966), pp. 138–47. Towards the end of the text is the following (fol. 114):

> "May you rejoice, holy father Hilarion, for you have been gathered into the Lord's net and have been brought into the royal vessels of your heavenly inheritance, joining the choirs of angels and the saints and the companies of the just, interceding with them for the whole world, which transgresses exceedingly and is rightly chastised. That is why the leading city which presides over all others, which is honoured by the precedence accorded to her, is now trodden underfoot by a foreign people and suffers grievously and by the just judgment of God is in a wretched state through her lawless deeds. But do not cease, God-bearing saint, to make supplication along with all who have a claim on you until the winter of our misery is alleviated by the consent of God."

The saint refers to a Constantinople under Latin rule after 1204. It should be noted that as in all the other instances the Franks are never called "barbarians" (as are the Muslims) but "a foreign people" (λαὸς ὀθνεῖος).

v. "Discourse against the Jews" (Λόγος ἀντιρρητικὸς πρὸς Ἰουδαίους) (Cod. Paris. gr. 1189, saec. XII, fols 206ᵛ–218).

An unpublished work. On fol. 209 we read in connection with Isaiah 11:7 ("and the lion shall eat straw like the ox") the following:

> "... the lion is a carnivorous beast and one would be amazed if one ever saw it eating straw. But we are amazed even more when we see persons of high degree humbled, either because they have been turned from unbelief to faith, or from pride and folly to a humility that exalts them, or else when we see a person humbled against his will by God's permission

and his lion-like, boastful power, which abounded in wealth and dominion, humbled like an ox about to eat straw.

"Perhaps our island of Cyprus has suffered something that somewhat resembles this at the present time and the majority of its great men sit bound, alas, in iron fetters. But I do not wish to expatiate on this because there is not sufficient time."[66]

The similarities in phraseology between this passage and the texts described in paragraphs 1 and 2.ii above lead me to assign the composition of this Christmas homily to the last quarter of 1196. In spite of his severe criticism of the "powerful" among his people, the saint is overcome by a deep sorrow for their wretched betrayal into the hands of foreigners.

vi. "Discourse on our father among the saints, John the Almsgiver" (Λόγος εἰς τὸν ἐν ἁγίοις πατέρα ἡμῶν Ἰωάννην τὸν Ἐλεήμονα) (Cod. Paris. gr. 1189, saec. XIII, fols 220–230ᵛ).

This too was first published by I.P. Tsiknopoullos in *KS* 30 (1966), pp. 148–59. On fol. 230 we read:

"Along with this [almsgiving] intercede also, O divinely inspired father, with the Lord who is merciful on behalf of the world, since you have free access to him, as a good shepherd, on behalf of all your spiritual flock, on behalf of City and Church and the most Christian emperors, on whom a foreign people make war and have attempted to 'move the immemorial boundaries' which the Lord and the ancient fathers have set, and to bring not simply house against house but countries against countries and cities against cities in a lawless way and to inherit woe by the just judgment of God."

The discourse is again about the capture of 1204.

---

[66] ... σαρκοβόρος γὰρ θὴρ ὁ λέων, καὶ ἐθαύμασεν ἄν τις, εἰ τοῦτον εἶδεν ἀχυροφάγον ποτέ. Ἀλλὰ θαυμάζομεν πλεῖον, ὁπηνίκα ὑψηλοὺς καὶ ἀρχικοὺς ἀνθρώπους ὁρῶμεν ταπεινωθέντας, εἴτε ἐξ ἀπιστίας πρὸς πίστιν ἐπιστραφέντας, εἴτε ἐκ τύφου καὶ ἀπονοίας πρὸς ὑφοποιὸν ταπείνωσιν, εἴτε καὶ παρὰ προαίρεσιν κατὰ θείαν συγχώρησιν ταπεινούμενον ἄνθρωπον, καὶ τὸν λεοντείαν ἐγκαυχώμενον δύναμιν, πλούτῳ καὶ δυναστείᾳ πλεονάζοντα, ταπεινωθέντα ὡς βοῦν πρὸς τὸ φαγεῖν ἄχυρα.
Τάχα οἷόν που παραπλησίως ἐν τῷ ἐνεστῶτι καιρῷ καὶ ἡ νῆσος ἡμῶν Κύπρος ἐπάσχησε, καὶ οἱ πλεῖστοι τῶν μεγάλων αὐτῆς κάθηνται, οἴμοι, σιδήρῳ πεπεδημένοι· περὶ ὧν πλατύτερον εἰπεῖν οὐκ ἀνέχομαι, ὅτι οὐκ ἄγει καιρός.

vii. "On the high priesthood of Christ and the *azymes* and the Last Supper" (Περὶ τῆς ἱεραρχίας Χριστοῦ καὶ τῶν ἀζύμων καὶ τοῦ δείπνου τοῦ μυστικοῦ) (Cod. Paris. gr. 395, saec. XV, fols 122–126).

This homily, prescribed to be delivered on Holy Thursday, belonged, as I.P. Tsiknopoullos proved, to the lost second tome of Neophytos's *Panegyrike.* It was published for the first time in a critical edition by Tsiknopoullos in *Byzantion* 39 (1969), pp. 344–8, 348–51.[67]

The passage which concerns us here is printed on pp. 344.17-345.35 and is a polemic against the Latin *azymes.*

The first writer on the Orthodox side against the Latin innovation of the *azymes* seems to have been Leo, the first Greek metropolitan of Russia († post 1004).[68] The chief critic of this custom in the Eastern Church, however, proved to be Michael Keroularios in his well-known letter to Peter of Antioch.[69] The dispute over the *azymes* remained at the heart of anti-Latin polemics throughout the eleventh century, but began to retreat at the beginning of the twelfth century on account of the outbreak of the new controversy over the papal primacy. The history of the various phases of the conflict over the *azymes* is well enough known today. The accusation of Judaising, which is the only one which Neophytos brings forward in the passage under review, can be assigned to the age of Keroularios and belongs to the lower levels of the polemic. Insofar as the following section proves that Neophytos knew at some time the more fully developed "theology" on the subject, we must suppose that the homily *On the high priesthood of Christ and the azymes* is chronologically prior to the little treatise *On why and when the elder Rome and new Rome grew apart from each other*, belonging, of course, to the period after 1191 and, as will be shown below, before 1204.

It should be noted that this anti-Latin discourse of Neophytos was included in the fifteenth-century Codex Parisinus 395 together with the polemical satire *Panagiotes' dialogue with an azymite.*[70]

---

[67] The "factual" scholia on p. 351 are mistaken. As J. Darrouzès noted in *REB* 8 (1950), p. 175, what is said about the high-priesthood of Christ derives from the narrative of Theodosios the Jew, on which see A. Vasiliev, *Anecdota Graeco-Byzantina*, Moscow, 1893, pp. xxv–xxvii, 58–60 ("Proof of how Christ became a priest"), 60–72 ("An account profitable to the soul of the ordination of our Lord Jesus Christ"), and F. Cumont in *Bulletin de l'Académie Royale de Belgique*, 1904, no. 3, pp. 81–96.

[68] See Leo, metropolitan of Preslav in Russia, Πρὸς Ῥωμαίους, ἤτοι Λατίνους, περὶ τῶν ἀζύμων, in A. S. Pavlov, *Ktiticeskie opyty po istorij drevnjesej grecoruskoj polemiki protiv Latinjam*, St Petersburg, 1878, appendix. Cf. E. Golubinskij, *Istorija russkoj Cerkvi*, I, pp. 853–4 and K.N. Sathas, Μεσαιωνικὴ Βιβλιοθήκη, I, Venice, 1872, p. 272.

[69] *PG* 120, coll. 781–96.

[70] On this see A. Argyriou, "Remarques sur quelques listes grecques énumérant les hérésies latines", *Byzantinische Forschungen* 4 (1972), pp. 9–30, esp. pp. 21–3.

viii. "Against those who neglect their duty and fail to keep the prelude to Lent" (Πρὸς τοὺς ἀτακτοῦντας καὶ λύοντας τὰ προοίμια τῆς νηστείας) (Cod. Marcianus III 4 (= Nanianus 228), saec. XV, fols 367ᵛ–368ᵛ; Lond. B.M. Burney. 54, saec. XVI, fols 212–215; Lond. B.M. Addit. 34060, saec. XVI, fol. 144; Bodleianus Holk. 57, saec. XVI, fols. 15ᵛ–18).

This epistolatory homily, prescribed for delivery on the first day of Lent (as the London Codex B.M. Addit. 34060 informs us), belonged, I believe, to the lost second tome of Neophytos's *Panegyrike*, which contained festal homilies for the second third of the ecclesiastical year (January-April). It was first published in a critical edition by I.P. Tsiknopoullos in *Byzantion* 39 (1969), pp. 404–7, 407–10 from the first three of the above codices, to which now should be added the Bodleian manuscript, which in many respects is superior to the two London codices.[71] On the basis of this manuscript and the passage from Parisinus Coislinianus 287, which is noted below, I give the last words of the title as Τὰ προοίμια τῆς νηστείας and not Τὰ τῆς νηστείας προοίμια, as did the first editor.

Through this "encyclical", which was written at a time when the see of Paphos was vacant, Neophytos places under canonical penalty those who break the fast of Clean Monday by outdoor amusements (a lack of discipline still prevalent in Cyprus). Which vacancy of the throne of Paphos is the one in question? Surely, as I.P. Tsiknopoullos has demonstrated, it is the one between Bacchos (?–1194–1198–?) and Sabas (?–1209–?).

It is indicative of the period that along with others the Recluse condemns those who break the ecclesiastical rules as "not Orthodox".[72] From the *Commentary on the dominical commandments* we can see that Neophytos had already noted as early as 1176 that the rules of fasting in Lent were not scrupulously observed: "those who eat meat on Wednesday or Friday of the second week before Lent (τῆς Ἀποκρέου), I say, are truly breaking the law to no purpose since they shamelessly fail to keep the prelude to the fast."[73] Why he did not censure these things more strongly at that time, whereas now he puts the transgressors under a heavy ecclesiastical penalty, a seven-year excommunication, is easy for us to conjecture: because of the Latins.

In his memorandum *On why and when the elder Rome and new Rome grew apart from each other* Neophytos noted as one of the Latin "acts of lawlessness"

---

[71] The existence of this manuscript was drawn to my attention by Dr A. Tillyrides, to whom I express my gratitude. For a description of the codex see R. Barbour, "Summary Description of the Greek Manuscripts from the Library at Holkham Hall", *The Bodleian Library Record* 6 (1960), pp. 591–613, esp. p. 603. The third part of the codex was written by Maximos Margounios.

[72] *Βυζάντιον* 39 (1969), p. 405.33.

[73] Cod. Coisl. gr. 287, fol. 44.

the eating of meat in the week preceding Quinquagesima (τὴν τυροφάγον ἑβδομάδα).[74] It is well-known that in his celebrated fourth epistle Photios already confirmed that the Latins "having cut out the first week of fasting from the rest of Lent, have descended to drinking milk and eating cheese and similar gluttony".[75] Keroularios repeats the charge[76] and the little eleventh-century work falsely attributed to Photios, *On the Franks and the rest of the Latins*, says clearly: "In Lent they begin to fast from the Wednesday of the first week".[77]

Thus the very severe and quite unexpected reaction of the Recluse to laxity on the first day of fasting for Lent becomes explicable: this practice tended to assimilate the Orthodox of the island to the Franks. For this reason draconian measures had to be taken to eradicate it forthwith.

ix. "Compendious record of the seven ecumenical and great holy councils and why and when the elder Rome and new Rome grew apart from each other" (Εὐσύνοπτος μνήμη περὶ τῶν ἑπτὰ οἰκουμενικῶν καὶ μεγάλων ἁγίων συνόδων καὶ ὅτου χάριν καὶ πότε ἡ πρεσβυτέρα Ῥώμη καὶ ἡ νέα Ῥώμη διεστήκασιν ἀπ᾽ ἀλλήλων) (Cod. Andriensis monast. Hagias 13, saec. XVII, fols 255–66).

This homily, prescribed to be delivered on the Sunday of the holy Fathers of the First Ecumenical Council, which falls between the feasts of the Ascension and Pentecost, belonged, as I.P. Tsiknopoullos showed, to the lost third tome of the *Panegyrike*. It was first published by Tsiknopoullos in *Byzantion* 39 (1969), pp. 352–7, 357–60.

This is one of the many *opuscula de origine schismatis*, a polemico-apologetic literary form which appeared after Photios and Keroularios and has been studied since the time of J. Hergenröther.[78] Neophytos's little work is of a unique form because it is incorporated into a festal homily *de synodis* and also refers to yet another form of anti-Latin literature, the lists of "falsified doctrines".

The saint says at the beginning that he often sought the cause of the schism but had only recently discovered it and hastened at once "to make it generally well-known". In consequence he presents a rapid survey of the seven Ecumenical Councils, after which he explains that he has called these to mind

---

[74] *Byzantion* 39 (1969), p. 355.136.

[75] I. Valettas, Φωτίου πατριάρχου Κωνσταντινουπόλεως ἐπιστολαί, London, 1864, pp. 168–71.

[76] *PG* 120, coll. 793A.

[77] J. Hergenröther, *Monumenta graeca ad Photium eijusque historiam pertinentia*, Regensburg, 1869, pp. 62–71, esp. p. 64, no. 5 (referring to Ash Wednesday).

[78] Ibid., pp. 154–81.

because when he saw that from the beginning the pope of the time always gave his assent to them, he went on to seek to learn precisely when and for what reason the schism had come about. Returning to what he had said at the beginning, he explains that now he has been informed of the relevant facts "from a certain book of the chroniclers that in an artless way gives an ample account of the emperors and the patriarchs". He gives a detailed narrative of the time of Charlemagne and his coronation as emperor by Pope Leo III, "who split both the Empire and the Church leading [the Romans] wrongly and contrary to the law into the customs of the Frankish state".

Referring next to eight such "violating" customs[79] he makes the following important remark, which unfortunately was omitted – either by an editorial oversight, I imagine, or by a typographical error – from the first edition: "But they also stumble on the Holy Spirit in no small way".[80] As will appear below, this is the only direct evidence that Neophytos knew of the existence of a doctrinal difference between East and West concerning the Holy Spirit.

After these nine "errors" Neophytos mentions that "the Latins transferred a large number of other falsified doctrines from the Frankish state to Rome, as many as twenty-seven, which are listed at the end of this discourse". The phrase is very vague, but certainly the author does not mean his own discourse, as the first editor supposed, but a list of Latin innovations which he had in front of him.

Before continuing the story of Charlemagne until the beheading of Nikephoros by Krum,[81] Neophytos lingers for a while on the subject of the azymes, which, as lines 182–3 show, he regarded as the greatest of the Latin unorthodoxies. His main argument against the use of unleavened bread in the Eucharist is the Byzantine argument that was current from the middle of the eleventh century (and was formulated originally against the Armenians)[82] that the azymes imply that the flesh of the Logos is without soul or mind and therefore constitute a revival of Apollinarianism. Neophytos, however, instead of Apollinarians, writes that "those who say that the place of his soul and his

---

[79] *Byzantion* 39 (1969), pp. 355.127–356.141.

[80] Ἀλλὰ καὶ εἰς τὸ Πνεῦμα τὸ Ἅγιον οὐ μετρίως προσπταίουσιν: Codex no. 13 of the monastery of Agia on Andros, fol. 262: after the words ἐν τῷ ὁμοιώματι δείκνυται καὶ τὸ ἀρχέτυπον ἐν τῇ εἰκόνι and before ταῦτα δὲ καὶ ἕτερα πλεῖστα, *Byzantion* 39 (1869), p. 356.140–142.

[81] In the first edition, p. 356.174, the word καθαρᾶς should be amended to κάρας. This is the result of dittography prompted by an anticipation of the following word ἐκκαθάραντες. The exegesis given by Tsiknopoullos on p. 359, that Neophytos is perhaps comparing the emperor's head to a cithara, is fanciful.

[82] Formulated first, it seems, by Niketas Stethatos. See Κατὰ Ἀρμενείων, ed. J. Hergenröther, *Monumenta graeca*, pp. 151–2. Cf. B. Leib, "Deux inédits byzantins sur les azymes, au début du XIIe siècle", *OCP* 2 (1924), p. 187; J. Darrouzès in *REB* 25 (1967), p. 290.

mind was taken by his divinity are called theopaschites, since what was suffered was suffered by the divinity and not by the form of the servant".[83]

At the end of the discourse Neophytos says that only a future Eighth Ecumenical Council could heal the schism. He praises the 318 fathers of the Council of Nicaea and concludes with an invocation of the Holy Spirit without mentioning anything about his procession.

The "book of the chroniclers" from which the saint drew his information is, I believe, the *Chronographia* of Theophanes.[84] With regard to the list of 27 "unorthodoxies" which he had in his hands, it must have belonged to the second half of the eleventh century, since the lists of that period included about 28 points, while those of the twelfth century had arrived at 32, and by the thirteenth century were to reach 104.[85] I have been unable, however, to locate among the few lists which have been published and are known the one which Neophytos had before him, on account of the number 27 and also because of the accusation about bending only one knee, which even the memorandum of Constantine Stilbes, metropolitan of Cyzicus, with its 104 accusations does not contain.

The dating of the discourse is not difficult. Since the capture of Constantinople and the atrocities of the Latins are not mentioned, the discourse must belong to the years before 1204 and after 1191, and as the arguments concerning the *azymes* prove, is later than the discourse *On the high priesthood of Christ*.

3. *Instructions* (Κατηχήσεις)

A description of this work of the Recluse together with the relevant bibliography was given by I.P. Tsiknopoullos in *KS* 22 (1958), pp. 159–70.[86] I

---

[83] Constantine Stilbes had accused the Latins of being theopaschites and compared them with the *Hadjidjarioi*. See J. Darrouzès, "Le mémoire de Constantin Stilbès contre les Latins", *REB* 21 (1963), pp. 50–100, esp. p. 89, nos 19, 102, 103, p. 99, nos. 101–102. It should also be said that this accusation against the azymites was also first formulated by Stethatos against the Armenians, on the basis of the Eastern interpretation of I John 5:8. See Stethatos, Περὶ τῶν ἀζύμων (under the name of John Damascene: cf. H.-G. Beck, *Kirche und theologische Literatur im byzantinischem Reich*, Munich, 1961, p. 536), *PG* 95, coll. 387–96, esp. 392.

[84] See C. de Boor, ed., *Theophanis Chronographia*, I, Leipzig, 1883, pp. 472.23–473.4 (cf. the phrase γενομένης τῆς Ῥώμης ἀπ' ἐκείνου καιροῦ ὑπὸ τὴν ἐξουσίαν τῶν Φράγγων, 472.30), 475.10–491.22.

[85] See A.S. Pavlov, *Ktitičeskie opyty po istorij drevnješej greco-ruskoj polemiki protiv Latinjam*, pp. 44–45, J. Darrouzès, "Le mémoire de Constantin Stilbès contre les Latins" (104 accusations).

[86] Cf. E.M. Toniolo in *Marianum* 36 (1974), pp. 191–2. Paris. suppl. gr. 1317 has been described by C. Astruc in C. Astruc and M.-L. Concasty, *Le Supplément grec*, III, Paris, 1960, pp. 602–8. What is said by J. Darrouzès in *REB* 8 (1950), pp. 185ff and I.P. Tsiknopoullos in *KS* 22 (1958), p. 160ff leaves no doubt that this codex, which came into the possession of the Bibliothèque Nationale in 1905, is the one described by A. Papadopoulos-Kerameus, Ἱεροσολυμιτικὴ Βιβλιοθήκη, IV, pp. 338ff. It would therefore be more correct to refer to this Codex as Paris. suppl. gr. 1317 olim Metoch. S.S. 370.

do not think, however, that we can accurately determine the year of composition, as Tsiknopoullos does in assigning it to 1211. From the place of the work in the list of the 12th chapter of the *Typike Diatheke*, although we cannot say anything about the date of composition of the individual instructions, the publications of the book may be placed somewhere between 1209 and 1213.

i. "On the holy fathers of Nicaea and on the orthodox faith which they defined and that correct belief requires a correct way of life" (Περὶ τῶν ἐν Νικαίᾳ ἁγίων πατέρων καὶ περὶ ἧς ἐδογμάτισαν ὀρθοδόξου πίστεως καὶ ὅτι ἡ πίστις ἡ ὀρθὴ χρήζει καὶ βίου ὀρθοῦ) (Cod. Paris. suppl. gr. 1317, fols 80–84).

An unpublished discourse containing on folio 81 a list of heretics in which the Latins do not appear.

Commenting in fols 83–84 on Isaiah 6:9–10, the saint writes as follows:

"'The heart of this people has grown fat', says God through Isaiah, 'and they have made their ears heavy and shut their eyes, lest they see with their eyes and hear with their ears and understand with their hearts and return and I heal them.' But they wish, He says, to remain in their sin in this way until 'cities lie waste without men and the land is utterly desolate'. That is what we see our island of Cyprus to have suffered, and many houses and almost all the villages are bereft of people and have remained uninhabited. 'Large and beautiful houses', He says, 'and there shall not be inhabitants in them and he who sows six artabes will get three measures back'. And this is what we have suffered in most years. But we have not thus recognised the fruit of our works, nor have we wondered in our hearts where such evil has come from and what manner of evil it is. We have not heard Him who has called us and said, 'Return to me, and I shall return to you'. But each person has set his own will as his own law and sins as he wishes being mindful neither of death nor of God nor of Judgment. We write these things not lightly or haphazardly but from a grieving heart that desires the saving return of each one of you ... ."[87]

---

[87] "'Ἀλλ' ἐπαχύνθη", φησὶν ὁ Θεὸς διὰ Ἡσαΐου, "ἡ καρδία τοῦ λαοῦ τούτου, καὶ τοῖς ὠσὶν αὐτῶν βαρέως ἤκουσαν καὶ τοῖς ὀφθαλμοῖς αὐτῶν ἐκάμμυσαν, μήποτε ἴδωσι τοῖς ὀφθαλμοῖς καὶ τοῖς ὠσὶν ἀκούσωσι καὶ τῇ καρδίᾳ συνιῶσι καὶ ἐπιστρέψωσι καὶ ἰάσωμαι αὐτούς". Ἀλλὰ βούλονται, φησίν, οὕτως ἐμμένειν τῇ ἁμαρτίᾳ ἄχρις ἂν "ἐρημωθῶσι πόλεις παρὰ τὸ μὴ εἶναι ἀνθρώπους καὶ ἡ γῆ καταλειφθήσεται ἔρημος". Ὅπερ ὁρῶμεν ὅτι καὶ ἡ νῆσος ἡμῶν ταύτη Κύπρος ἐπάσχησε, καὶ οἶκοι πολλοὶ καὶ αἱ κῶμαι σχεδὸν πᾶσαι ἔρημοι ἀνθρώπων καὶ ἄοικοι ἐναπέμειναν. "Οἰκίαι, φησί, μεγάλαι καὶ καλαί, καὶ οὐκ ἔσονται οἱ

We know from other sources the attempts of the first French king of Cyprus, Guy de Lusignan, to boost the declining population of the island.[88] From Neophytos's evidence we learn that twenty years after Guy's measures on behalf of the urban centres of the island, the Cypriot countryside still remained "deserted" and "without houses", and agriculture gave a poor return. Whatever rhetorical hyperbole there may be, the essence remains true.

ii. "On the holy and consubstantial and life-giving Trinity and on love and harmony and moreover on the Holy Spirit" (Περὶ τῆς ἁγίας καὶ ὁμοουσίου καὶ ζωαρχικῆς Τριάδος, καὶ περὶ ἀγάπης καὶ ὁμονοίας, καὶ αὖθις περὶ τοῦ Ἁγίου Πνεύματος) (Cod. Paris. suppl. gr. 1317, fols 84–88ᵛ).

Also an unpublished discourse in which, significantly, no reference is made to the pneumatological disagreement with the Latins.

Of interest to our theme is the theology of the instruction on the unity and fragmentation of mankind. The unity of human beings springs from their consubstantiality and has as its centre and expression the Orthodoxy of the Church. Satan, however, on the one hand separates from her countless numbers of people and on the other destroys the internal love and concord which binds the Orthodox.

Here is the passage verbatim (fols 86ᵛ–87):

"... And this suffices on the unity of the divine nature and divisions of its three holy hypostases. But it is necessary for us too, it is necessary for those who were made in the image and likeness of God, to have love and harmony and zeal for every good work, and not to be envious of others and bite and pull down one another. But just as all men are consubstantial through flesh and blood, and having come from the earth and advancing towards it, and nourished from it and returning to it, and having one father, God, believing in whom we have been baptised, so we should certainly love one another and support one another and be at peace and help one another as fellow soldiers perhaps and servants

ἐνοικοῦντες ἐν αὐταῖς, καὶ ὁ σπείρων ἀρτάβας ἓξ ποιήσει μέτρα τρία". Τοῦτο δὲ ἐν πλείστοις ἔτεσιν ἡμεῖς ἐπασχήσαμεν. Ἀλλ᾽ οὐδ᾽ οὕτως τὸν καρπὸν τῶν ἔργων ἡμῶν ἐπεγνώκαμεν, οὐδὲ συνήκαμεν τῇ καρδίᾳ πόθεν ἄρα καὶ τίς ὁ τρόπος τῆς τοσαύτης κακώσεως. Οὐδ᾽ ἠκούσαμεν τοῦ καλοῦντος ἡμᾶς καὶ λέγοντος· "Ἐπιστράφητε πρός με, καὶ ἐπιστραφήσομαι πρὸς ἡμᾶς". Ἀλλ᾽ ὡς ἴδιον νόμον ἔταξεν ἑαυτοῦ ἕκαστος τὸ ἴδιον θέλημα, καὶ ἁμαρτάνει ὡς βούλεται, μήτε θανάτου μήτε Θεοῦ μήτε κρίσεως μνήμην ποιούμενος.

Ταῦτα δὲ οὐχ ἁπλῶς καὶ ὡς ἔτυχε λέγοντες γράφομεν, ἀλλ᾽ ἐκ τεθλιμμένης καρδίας καὶ ἐπιποθούσης ἑκάστου ὑμῶν τὴν σωτηριώδη ἐπιστροφήν ...

[88] See Th. Papadopoullos, "Ἱστορικαὶ περὶ Κύπρου εἰδήσεις ἐκ τοῦ Χρονικοῦ τοῦ Ἐρνοὺλ καὶ Βερνάρδου τοῦ Θησαυροφύλακος", KS 28 (1964), pp. 39–114, esp. pp. 99ff.

of Christ the King. And just as the discourse has spoken about the unity
and harmony of the holy Trinity, so all men should be in harmony and
be drawn together, as all of one nature, towards the unity of our orthodox
faith. Since Satan has separated an infinite multitude of people from such
faith, it behoves us too, who are pious and Orthodox by the grace of
God, to have love and harmony towards the good. I say towards the good
because there is a wicked harmony and a satanic love. For robbers and
fellow thieves and fellow murderers and fornicators show harmony and
love one another. But God and good people hate such harmony and love
'for it is better to separate in a good way than to be in harmony in an
evil way'."[89]

That a bad peace was preferable to a good war was in Byzantium a basic
thesis of moderate ecclesiastical policy. That a good war was better than a
bad peace was the principle of hardliners who saw the struggle not only as
justified but as their duty.

iii. "On the Holy Spirit at Pentecost" (Περὶ τοῦ Ἁγίου Πνεύματος εἰς
τὴν ἁγίαν Πεντηκοστήν) (Cod. Paris. suppl. gr. 1317, fols 213–220ᵛ).
This second unpublished discourse on the Holy Spirit in the book of
Instructions is an additional one and outside the series. This is shown by an
autograph note of St Neophytos in the lower margin of fol. 84 which reads:

ζήτ(ει) εἰς τ(ὸ) τέλ(ος) τοῦ βιβλίου λόγ(ον) εἰς τ(ὴν) ἁγ(ίαν) ν′, κ(αὶ)
εἰς τ(ὸ) ἅγ(ιον) πν(εῦμ)α (see the discourse on Pentecost and on the Holy
Spirit at the end of the book).

---

[89] ... Καὶ ταῦτα μὲν ἀπόχρη περὶ ἐνώσεως θείας φύσεως καὶ διαιρέσεως τῶν
αὐτῆς παναγίων τριῶν ὑποστάσεων. Ἔδει δὲ καὶ ἡμᾶς, ἔδει τοὺς κατ᾽ εἰκόνα
καὶ ὁμοίωσιν Θεοῦ γεγενημένους, ἀγάπην καὶ ὁμόνοιαν καὶ σπουδὴν ἔχειν πρὸς
πᾶν ἔργον ἀγαθόν, καὶ μὴ φθονεῖν ἀλλήλους καὶ δάκνειν καὶ καταβάλλειν θάτερος
θατέρῳ. Ἀλλ᾽ ὥσπερ ὁμοούσιοι πάντες ἄνθρωποι διὰ σαρκὸς καὶ αἵματος, καὶ ἐκ
τῆς γῆς γεγονότες καὶ εἰς αὐτὴν βαδίζοντες καὶ ἐξ αὐτῆς τρεφόμενοι καὶ πρὸς
αὐτὴν ἐπιστρέφοντες, καὶ ἕνα πατέρα ἔχοντες, τὸν Θεόν, πρὸς ὃν καὶ πιστεύσαντες
ἐβαπίσθημεν, οὕτω πάντως ἔδει καὶ ἀλλήλους ἀγαπᾶν καὶ ἀλλήλων ἀνέχεσθαι,
καὶ εἰρηνεύειν καὶ συγκροτεῖσθαι ἀλλήλοις ὡς συστρατιῶται τάχα καὶ δοῦλοι
τοῦ βασιλέως Χριστοῦ. Καὶ ὥσπερ περὶ ἑνότητος καὶ ὁμονοίας τῆς ἁγίας Τριάδος
ὁ λόγος ἐδήλωσεν, οὕτως ἔδει καὶ πάντας ἀνθρώπους ὁμονοῆσαι καὶ συναχθῆναι,
ὡς ὁμοφυεῖς πάντας, πρὸς τῆς ὀρθῆς ἡμῶν πίστεως τὴν ἑνότητα. Ἐπεὶ δὲ ἄπειρα
πλήθη ἀνθρώπων ἐκ τῆς τοιαύτης πίστεως ἀπέσχισεν ὁ σατανᾶς, ἔδει κἂν ἡμᾶς,
τοὺς χάριτι Θεοῦ εὐσεβεῖς καὶ ὀρθοδόξους, ἀγάπην καὶ ὁμόνοιαν ἔχειν πρὸς τὸ
ἀγαθόν. Λέγω πρὸς τὸ ἀγαθόν, ἐπεὶ ἔστι καὶ ὁμόνοια πονηρὰ καὶ ἀγάπη σατανική.
Ὁμονοιάζουσι γὰρ καὶ λησταὶ καὶ συγκλέπται καὶ συμφονεῖς καὶ συμπόρνοι, καὶ
ἀγαπῶσιν ἀλλήλους, ὧν τὴν ὁμόνοιαν καὶ τὴν ἀγάπην μισεῖ Θεὸς καὶ ἄνθρωποι
καλοί· "κρεῖσσον γὰρ σχισθῆναι καλῶς ἢ ὁμονοῆσαι κακῶς".

Unfortunately the last 4 folios of the 33rd and last gathering of the Codex (that is, 8 pages) have disappeared and the homily is defective. The fact, however, is obvious enough that St Neophytos in spite of having written festal homilies on Pentecost and the Holy Spirit for his *Panegyrike* and for the book of his monastic *Instructions* – and certainly also having commented on the canon of the feast in his lost work, *Commentary on the canons of the twelve dominical feasts* – judged it necessary towards the end of his life to write a third discourse specifically on this theme, and to insert it for good measure in his last Sunday cycle.

We saw in the entry under 2.ix that St Neophytos had an imprecise knowledge of the fact that the Latins "stumble on the Holy Spirit in no small way". I believe that the special care the saint took to set out the Orthodox teaching on the Spirit is not irrelevant but is connected directly with his anti-Latin polemic. Even in the surviving portion of this last homily of his, although commenting on John 15:26, he does not omit to say in parentheses: "note that he is the Spirit of truth and that he proceeds from the Father" but he does not make any further reference or even allude to the controversy over the *Filioque*. On the contrary, both this homily and the instruction of fols 84–88^v, founded on the classic patristic teaching on the Spirit, aim at proving the Spirit's divinity as if he were fighting the ancient Pneumatomachoi. It remains possible that St Neophytos dealt with the *Filioque* in the remaining part of the homily but, for reasons which I shall explain below, I regard this as unlikely.

4. Τυπικὴ διαθήκη

On this work see I.P. Tsiknopoullos, *Kypriaka Typika*, Nicosia, 1969. Here I simply recall that it was written in 1214, is the last complete work of St Neophytos which is known to us, and is preserved in his protograph Codex, which today belongs to the University of Edinburgh, bearing the number Edenburg. Univers. 224 (Laing 811).[90] The first edition was published by Archimandrite Kyprianos, *Τυπικὴ σὺν Θεῷ Διάταξις καὶ λόγοι εἰς τὴν Ἑξαήμερον*, Venice, 1779, when fewer folios were missing from the Codex than is the case today. Of special interest for the problem before us are the following passages:

  i. Chapter VII "On *** of Cyprus and guardian of the present Hermitage" (Περὶ τοῦ τῆς Κύπρου ***γὸς καὶ ἐπιτρόπου τῆς παρούσης Ἐγκλείστρας) (from the edition of Kyprianos in Tsiknopoullos, pp. 78–79).

---

[90] Described by C.R. Borland, *A Descriptive Catalogue of the Western Mediaeval Manuscripts in Edinburgh University Library*, Edinburgh, 1916, p. 321.

The Recluse appoints as protector and guardian of his monastery a person who, in the event of the execution of his duties, he is ready to name "benefactor" and "brother". The two relevant folios are missing today from the manuscript: the first was already missing in the time of Kyprianos. We would nevertheless have been able to discover the identity of the guardian with absolute certainty from the table of contents, but unfortunately here too there are difficulties. Kyprianos omitted the title and the second editor, F.E. Warren, printed simply "περὶ τοῦ τῆς Κύπρου * καὶ ἐπιτρόπου ... ." Folio 1ᵛ is today worn and at the most critical point the title of the seventh chapter cannot be read with absolute certainty because of a hole. The ending -γός, however, is beyond doubt and I regard the reading ῥηγός, which was proposed by I.P. Tsiknopoullos in his edition, as correct.

In 1214 Neophytos appointed as guardian or *epitropos* of the Hermitage the twenty-year-old Frankish king of Cyprus, Hugh I (*regebat* 1205–18) and his successors after him. *Epitropos* has here the meaning not of the executor of the will (*Diatheke*), nor, as in some *Typica*, of the monastic steward, but of the secular person who defends the interests of the monastery against the authorities. Such a guardian, for example, was Nikephoros Ouranos, who was appointed in the *Typicon* of Athanasios the Athonite, or the emperor of Constantinople himself in the *Diataxis* of the monastery of Machairas. And it is true that St Neophytos beseeched the Frankish king to co-operate in the sending of monks to the emperor, when the need arises, and that, as we shall see below, he leaves the emperor as the final court of appeal and defender of the Hermitage, but it is, however, equally indicative of his attitude that he did not hesitate to appoint the Latin king of Cyprus as guardian. By contrast Neilos of Tamaseia in the *Diataxis* of Machairas does not consent even to name the king, being content to speak vaguely of those "who in the day-time shine in the government of this island", whom he does not "entreat" (παρακαλεῖ) as does St Neophytos but "adjures" (ἐνορκεῖ), although, in obedience to the apostolic commandment, he does not disdain to commemorate them in his monastery.[91]

ii. Chapter VIII "Memorandum to the emperor" (Ὑπόμνησις πρὸς τὸν Βασιλέα) (from the edition of Kyprianos in Tsiknopoullos, p. 79).

The saint submits an entreaty to the emperor of the Romans to fulfil every request which in the future the monks of the Hermitage might perhaps put before him and he prays that God might strengthen and preserve his divine power and grant many years to his reign.

---

[91] I.P. Tsiknopoullos, *Κυπριακὰ Τυπικά,* Nicosia, 1969, p. 61.

I.P. Tsiknopoullos[92] believed that the Recluse had a specific request of which we have no knowledge and surmised that perhaps it was "an imperial decree that the Hermitage should be made stavropegial by the bishop of Paphos." This is a misunderstanding. At the end of the seventh chapter the author had first sought from the king of Cyprus that if "through some pressing matter" the brethren be obliged to send a representation to the emperor, he should co-operate with them and be an advocate for them "for the favourable issue of the request". Immediately afterwards he submits, in the eighth chapter, a memorandum to the emperor that he should fulfil the petition of his monks "of whatever kind it might be". It is clear, I think, that St Neophytos is submitting a general and permanent founder's memorandum, and not a specific petition. "*Memorandum*" (Ὑπόμνησις) here means the legal petition to public authority, the ὑπόμνημα.

The style and the content of the chapter show clearly which authority St Neophytos regards as legal, in the sense of divine and God-protected. Note the readiness of the Recluse to submit to the jurisdiction of Nicaea, where in 1214 the empire of Constantinople was continuing its existence.

iii. Chapter X "On non-possessiveness and release from economic concerns" (Περὶ ἀκτημοσύνης καὶ λύσεως οἰκονομικῆς) (Cod. Edenburg. Univ. 224, fols 19–22, Tsiknopoullos pp. 80–81).

The first *Diataxis* of 1177 prescribed perfect nonpossessiveness for the monastery, a regulation which prevailed for the first 55 years of the life of the Hermitage (1159–1214). On account, however, of the Latin capture of the island and its economic collapse, and also of the increase in the number of visitors "through the fame of the Hermitage", the saint bowed to the will of the brothers so that the monastery could acquire a "small piece of land for some arable crops, a vineyard and a little pasture". He regarded himself, however, as not responsible "for instigating this", which contains dangers "harmful to the soul" and "causes dizziness".

Note the testimony of the saint that when, on account of the Latin capture, "all people were short of every necessity, it was wholly fitting that we too should go short".

iv. Chapter XII "On the ecclesiastical order of service and on the priest and sacred vessels and on the books of the Recluse" (Περὶ τῆς ἐκκλησιαστικῆς ἀκολουθίας καὶ τοῦ ἱερέως καὶ τῶν ἱερῶν σκευῶν, καὶ τῶν βιβλίων τοῦ Ἐγκλείστου) (Cod. Edenburg. Univers. 224, fols 26–30, Tsiknopoullos pp. 82–83).

---

[92] Ibid., p. 52*.

The Recluse prescribes extended daily prayers for, among others, *basileis* and *archons*. The *basileis* are of course the Byzantine emperors and the *archons* the authorities in the island, that is, in 1214, the Franks. Such a prescription does not indicate any political ideology because it is based on the Pauline commandment that the faithful are to pray "for all men, for kings and all who are in high positions, that we may lead a quiet and peaceable life, godly and respectful in every way" (I Tim. 2:1–2).

v. Chapter XXIII, Canon 8 "On bitter slavery" (Περὶ δουλείας δεινῆς) (Cod. Edenburg. Univers. 224, fols 62ᵛ–63, Tsiknopoullos pp. 95–96).

"With our land in bitter slavery to the Latin nation, and the divine solicitude having kept us free, we too, brothers, must keep ourselves with God's help free from sins and thank and glorify the Lord our benefactor as we are obliged to do so that we may attract to ourselves yet more divine solicitude."

The sense of the canon is not, as I.P. Tsiknopoullos wrote,[93] that the Recluse proclaims that "the Latin occupation was not able to enslave the spirit of the Cypriots". The Recluse confesses that until 1214, when he wrote this, his monastery was not disturbed by the Latins, but was left to continue its life in peace without any of its brothers being enslaved or its property confiscated. For this the brethren owe gratitude to God.

vi. Chapter XXIII "On the petition and memorandum for the release of those who have been excommunicated" (Περὶ λύσεως ἀφωρισμένων αἴτησις καὶ ὑπόμνησις) (Cod. Edenburg. Univers. 224, fol. 77ᵛ, Tsiknopoullos, p. 102).
This concerns a "memorandum to the Chrysostomite brethren in the imperial capital" at the request of Neophytos that they should attend to the lifting of the excommunication which, assuredly, the Recluse had imposed on certain people.[94] I surmise that this is to do with the excommunication which we examined above at 2.viii.

---

[93] Ibid., p. 51*.

[94] I.P. Tsiknopoullos, ibid., p. 121, wrote that we do not know which memorandum the saint sent to the Chrysostomites. This was repeated by K. Hadjipsaltes, "Νεοφύτου πρεσβυτέρου μοναχοῦ καὶ ἐγκλείστου βιβλιογραφικὸν σημείωμα", *EKEEK* 6 (1972–1973), pp. 125–32, esp. pp. 128–9. It is clear, however, that the content of the memorandum is given in the preceding line: † Εἶτα καὶ περὶ λύσεως ἀφωρισμένων αἴτησις καὶ ὑπόμνησις. In spite of this, in his works Ὁ ἅγιος Νεόφυτος πρεσβύτερος καὶ μοναχὸς καὶ ἔγκλειστος καὶ ἡ ἱερὰ αὐτοῦ μονή, Paphos, 1955, p. 41 and Ἡ ἱερὰ μονὴ τοῦ Χρυσοστόμου τοῦ Κουτζουβένδη, Nicosia, 1959, p. 34, Tsiknopoullos wrote that Neophytos sent the Chrysostomites "a warm memorandum about the concern they should have for the mother monastery, even though they were absent from her, as her loving spiritual children ..."

If we pursue the matter a little further, we may conjecture that the saint submitted this petition to the ecumenical patriarchate as the competent authority during the reorganisation of the ecclesiastical situation in Cyprus in the summer of 1209.[95] When the patriarch of Constantinople received into communion Isaias of Lydda, who had been installed as archbishop of Cyprus, contrary to the canons, by translation and without appointment by the emperor, he also received along with him those bishops who had been consecrated by him, amongst whom was Sabas of Paphos. Neophytos asked, then, that the Synod should lift the excommunication, we may surmise, which, at the time when the throne of Paphos was vacant before the election of Sabas, he himself as *locum tenens* had imposed on the transgressing Paphians.

Since "as many as were monks" had taken part, according to the *Synodical Note*[96] in the election of Isaias, it is possible that monks from Cyprus accompanied Sabas to Nicaea in June 1209, amongst whom were Chrysostomite brothers (under the leadership perhaps of their steward, John, a brother of St Neophytos[97]). It would have been to them that Neophytos, as a former Chrysostomite, entrusted the successful accomplishment of his petition. The old Recluse wished to include the relevant document in the canonical twenty-third chapter of his *Diatheke* for reasons of forgiveness.

Even if my hypothesis is shown to be mistaken, however, Neophytos's petition in the twenty-third chapter of the *Typike Diatheke* does not cease to be a clear testimony to the unshakeable attachment of the Recluse to the unity of the Orthodox in Cyprus, in matters of faith and order, with the Great Church.

From the above analysis certain conclusions may be drawn in the form of a postscript to the present section with regard to the more general political and theological contacts and the circulation of books in Cyprus in the years between 1191 and 1214.

It is plain that the written material which Neophytos collected was rather meagre and out of date. A *Weltfremdheit* of this kind was never absent

---

[95] See K. Hadjipsaltes, "Ἡ Ἐκκλησία Κύπρου καὶ τὸ ἐν Νικαίᾳ Οἰκουμενικὸν Πατριαρχεῖον", esp. 142.17 (the author has dated the act 4 June 1209 instead of 17 June 1209, reading δ΄ instead of ιζ΄. Cf. V. Laurent, *Les Regestes des actes du Patriarcat de Constantinople*, I, *Les actes des Patriarches*, IV, Paris, 1971, no. 1210).

[96] Ibid., p. 143.22–23.

[97] Cf. K. Hadjipsaltes, "Νεοφύτου πρεσβυτέρου μοναχοῦ καὶ ἐγκλείστου βιβλιογραφικὸν σημείωμα", p. 126. I regard the hypothesis formulated here as more probable than that of Hadjipsaltes, given that the monastery of Chrysostomos, according to the evidence of Vasilij Barskij, only became a *metochion* of Jerusalem in the 16th century (see I.P. Tsiknopoullos, *Ἡ ἱερὰ μονὴ τοῦ Χρυσοστόμου τοῦ Κουτζουβένδη*, Nicosia, 1959, p. 57), and its *typicon* of the 13th century (Cod. Paris. gr. 402) contains no indication of relations between the monastery and Jerusalem.

from Cypriot history. Isaac's coup and the change of constitution of 1191 evidently made the situation worse, the common fate of Mediterranean islands.[98] The saint, as one of his unpublished works shows, had earlier been informed of the controversy concerning the followers of Demetrios of Lampe over the interpretation of the text: "My father is greater than I" (Jn 14:28) – perhaps by Basil Kinnamos bishop of Paphos, since Archbishop John the Cretan had taken part in the relevant council in January 1170.[99] In about 1196 he was informed, doubtless by Bishop Bacchos of Paphos, who was one of the chief movers in the matter, of the dispute concerning Michael Glykas and he wrote again on this subject.[100] And yet – in spite of his manifestly theological interests – he did not succeed later in informing himself on the subject of the *Filioque*, which had nevertheless from the ninth century already appeared on the scene, let alone the fact that he seems to know nothing about the question of the papal primacy, which had been pressing sharply on the Byzantine consciousness since the eleventh century. If such an enquiring and learned Cypriot found himself in such provincial isolation, we can imagine the average condition of the inhabitants of the island.

At all events, after 1214 the hard realities of life were quick to inform even the Cypriot Church in a practical way about Carolingian pneumatology and the Hildebrandine ecclesiastical ideal.

III. ST NEOPHYTOS AND THE LATIN CHURCH

At what point the anti-Latin sentiment of later Byzantium ceases to be religious and becomes patriotic it is difficult to decide. It would be erroneous, however, to think that in Byzantium, a "medieval society", Church and State could not be distinguished clearly from one another. Byzantium was never the Western Empire of Charlemagne. The "civil aspect" (τὸ πολιτικόν) constituted in the East a sphere which had always been self-subsistent and independent and if not separated from the Church at least always clearly distinguished from it.

---

[98] F. Braudel, *La Méditerranée et le monde méditerranéen à l'époque de Philippe II*, Paris, 1949, pp. 117–23. Cf. B. Englezakis, "'Ανέκδοτον ὑπόμνημα", pp. 75–6 (pp. 107–108 above).

[99] See L. Petit, "Documents inédits sur le concile de 1166 et ses derniers aversaires", *VV* 11 (1904), pp. 465–93, esp. pp. 479, 480, 486, 487. Cf. S. Sakkos in Θεολογικὸν Συμπόσιον. Χαριστήριον εἰς τὸν Καθηγητὴν Π.Κ. Χρήστου, Thessaloniki, 1967, pp. 311–52. St. Neophytos takes up this theme in his homily Ἐγκωμιαστικὸς λόγος εἰς τὴν παγκόσμιον Ὕψωσιν τοῦ τιμίου καὶ ζωοποιοῦ σταυροῦ, ἐν ᾧ ἐστι καὶ τρανὴ θεολογία, Cod. Paris. gr. 1189, fols 39–57ᵛ, esp. 44ᵛ f.

[100] M. Jugie, "Un opuscule inédit de Néophyte le Reclus sur l'incorruptibilité du corps du Christ dans l'Eucharistie", *REB* 7 (1949), pp. 1–11; I.P. Tsiknopoullos in *Byzantion* 39 (1969), pp. 391–403.

It has been said that from the tenth century heresy had been regarded in the Byzantine world as a nationalist phenomenon and that anti-heretical theology tended with the passage of time to become a religious ethnology.[101] This is at the very least inexact. Official civil Byzantium never identified the Roman world with Orthodoxy, and its calculations remained even up to 1453 purely political. The Roman Empire of the East remained until the end a historic political unity, in contrast with the Western *respublica christiana*, which ideologically constituted from the beginning an ecclesiological unity.[102]

The traditional distinction in the East between Church and State was maintained unaltered by the last Byzantines, both in matters of theology and in ecclesiastical politics. I would not assert that patriarchs such as Germanos II, Gregory of Cyprus, Isidore, Kallistos I or Philotheos Kokkinos were not Byzantine patriots. But the life and works of these leave us in no doubt that they judged religious matters, such as heresy, or indeed national matters, such as the destiny of the empire, theologically and from a purely ecclesiastical standpoint. The nature of Byzantium's Orthodoxy is not defined by its attitude to the Crusader hordes and the racist Armenians but rather by its attitude to the peoples of Eastern Europe, an attitude supremely ecumenical, supra-national and friendly. Witness the warm reciprocal relations between the Orthodox communities of the Greek and Slav worlds which have endured to the present day.[103]

By contrast, the idea of heresy as a "racial distinction" was introduced into the Roman world by Carolingian policy and the court theology that grew out of this.[104] It is difficult to see how historians such as G. Dagron, for example, would have interpreted the refusal of the patriarch of Constantinople to accept the Cypriots as canonical Orthodox after 1260 or in 1404 and 1412.

---

[101] G. Dagron, "Minorités ethniques et religieuses dans l'Orient byzantin à la fin du Xe et au XIe siècle: l'immigration syrienne", *Travaux et mémoires* 6 (1976), pp. 177–216, esp. p. 214.

[102] See the various works of synthesis of W. Ullmann, esp. his *Principles of Government and Politics in the Middle Ages*, London, 1974, pp. 110–14.

[103] See conveniently D. Obolensky, *The Byzantine Commonwealth*, London, 1971; G.M. Prokhorov, "L'hesychasme et la pensée sociale en Europe orientale au XIVe siècle", *Contacts* 31 (1973), pp. 25–63 (French trans. from the Russian periodical of the Academy of Sciences of the USSR, *Trudi otdel'a srednivekovnoi filologii* 23 (1968), pp. 86–108).

[104] On the controversy concerning the Holy Spirit cf. R. Haugh, *Photius and the Carolingians*, Belmont, Mass., 1975. More generally W. Ullmann, *The Carolingian Renaissance and the Idea of Kingship*, London, 1969, esp. pp. 135–66, and esp. F. Dölger, *Byzanz und die europäische Staatenwelt*, Darmstadt, 1964 (p. 282: from the eighth and ninth centuries Europe excluded the *byzantinische Balkangebiet* since it did not follow the Roman faith); A.-D. van den Brincken, *Die "Nationes Christianorum Orientalium" im Verständnis der lateinischen Historiographie von der Mitte des 12. bis in die zweite Hälfte des 14. Jahrhunderts*, Köln–Wien, 1973.

This by no means implies that all Byzantines made a clear mental distinction between the Roman and the Orthodox elements in their consciousness or that they did not often confuse Latin and Frankish attitudes. They did not, however, as St Neophytos testifies, confuse Rome with the Frankish world, or the Franks with the English or the Germans.[105] The idea of "the West", as it developed later, does not appear to have been defined clearly in the Byzantine mentality of the twelfth century: Rome was still a part, although a devalued one, of the Byzantine political and ecclesiastical world. Things would change radically only after 1204.

In the Frankish-held Cyprus of the thirteenth century the situation would pass through various stages, the most important of which would be the arrangements of Celestine III in 1196 and Honorius III in 1221 and 1222, the burning of the monks of Kantara in 1231 and the Alexandrine settlement of 1260. Conflict between the two Churches was to begin, strictly speaking, in 1221, when the pope was to turn for the first time against the Orthodox bishops of the island. The witness of St Neophytos belongs specifically to that decisive period between 1191 and 1221 when the Latin Church established and consolidated its position in the island, without yet being able to penetrate the internal affairs of the Orthodox Church. It was a transitional state of symbiosis in which the Orthodox endured the pillaging of their ecclesiastical property, hoping for the preservation of their spiritual freedom, while the Latins prepared for the *reductio Graecorum*,[106] awaiting the appropriate moment when they would prevail over the Crown, which, of course, it tried not to provoke its Orthodox subjects beyond what was necessary.

The reaction of the native Orthodox is known only from St Neophytos. We have discussed above the social class from which the saint originated, the

---

[105] *On why and when the elder Rome and the new Rome grew apart from each other, Concerning the misfortunes of the land of Cyprus.*

[106] Cf. the letter of Innocent IV of 6 March 1254 to the legate Eudes de Chateauroux in T.T. Haluscynskij et M.M. Wojnar, eds, *Acta Innocentii P.P. IV (1243–1254)*, Vatican, 1962, pp. 171–5. In his analysis of the phrase *reductio Graecorum* J. Darrouzès, in "Textes synodaux chypriotes", p. 61, note 68, attempts to justify it and indeed eulogises Innocent, whom he compares with Bekkos. J. Gill, "The Tribulations of the Greek Church in Cyprus", expresses the same opinion on this pope. The truth is entirely different and must be sought not in the "ecumenical" and "broad" spirit of the pope but in his war against the Hohenstaufen emperor and in the fact that Henry I of Cyprus was Conrad's legal heir to the throne of Jerusalem. Few popes before Innocent IV, writes S. Runciman, *The Sicilian Vespers: A History of the Mediterranean in the Later Thirteenth Century*, Cambridge, p. 33, "had been so constant, so untiring and so courageous in battling for the papal cause; but few had been so unscrupulous, so treacherous and so ready to use spiritual weapons for a worldly end". See B. Englezakis, "Cyprus as a Stepping-stone Between West and East in the Age of the Crusades: The Two Churches", *XVe Congrès Internationale des Sciences Historiques, Rapports* II, Bucarest, 1980, pp. 216–21 (Chapter XI below).

particular cultural environment of Cyprus in which he lived and the spirituality which he embraced and cultivated. What he thought about the Latin Church and his reaction to it must be set within this context.

On the social level we do not expect from Neophytos any tendency, for example, to place reliance on the alien power. Such tendencies to seek support from foreigners are usually shown by the ruling classes in all periods and among all peoples. Such in the twelfth century was the grandiose aristocratic policy of Manuel Komnenos, which in the end only brought disaster to the East. The Recluse never hoped for anything from the Latin Crusaders, not even for protection from Islam. On the contrary, writing in 1196 on the failure of Richard to liberate Jerusalem, he notes with an element of satisfaction: "For providence was not disposed to drive out dogs only to bring in wolves instead."[107]

On the cultural level we do not expect from Neophytos a high anti-Latin theology. By "high" I mean that current of Byzantine theology which, beginning with Photios and running through Peter of Antioch and Theophylact of Bulgaria to Palamas and Mark Eugenikos, does not ascribe any special significance to the canonical and ceremonial differences between East and West but is interested mainly in the trinitarian differences, that is to say, the *Filioque*. This theology had as its policy of reconciliation common conciliar action to remove the addition from the Creed in return for which it would accept the *teaching* on the *Filioque* as a *theologoumenon*. Conversely, I shall call a "low" or lay-monastic anti-Latin theology that current of anti-Latin polemic which, beginning with Keroularios and Stethatos, attributes such significance to the canonical differences as to equate them with the trinitarian difference to the indisputable detriment of the truth, since it places faith, canons and ceremonies all on the same level. As a result, high anti-Latin theology produced dogmatic works in Byzantium which may be said to have an "integral" character, while the low version produced works of a "comprehensive" character which never tired of augmenting the differences, constantly discovering new ones, with a thirst for myths rather than history. This phenomenon, although incompatible with the evangelical spirit and harmful to the Church, does not seem strange to the historian, who certainly does not expect the populace to be concerned with the *Filioque* even though he is entitled to seek the latter in the hierarchy and in theology proper.

After the time of Epiphanius of Constantia Cyprus was never again an ecumenical Christian centre in spite of the important role which the island played in the Monothelite and Iconoclast controversies. The level of provincialism to which Cyprus fell in the twelfth century has already been noted.

---

[107] *Concerning the misfortunes of the land of Cyprus, Byzantion* 39 (1969), p. 336.18–19.

It would have been impossible for Neophytos to have followed the Photian line for the simple reason that he had no acquaintance with Photios's writings. It would have been easier for him to align himself with the lay anti-Latin movement, which was prevalent everywhere. Nevertheless, in spite of appearances, he did not allow himself to be led astray. The lack of a necessary cultural perspective pushed him in that direction but his high spirituality delivered him from it. Thus, although the historical and intellectual armoury of his polemic was that of the low current, its spirit was that of the Photian line. I do not know how many Byzantine monastic writers of the thirteenth century would have mentioned only ten errors of the Latin Church when they were able to refer to twenty-seven.

In his work *On the Seven Ecumenical Councils* Neophytos, as we have already said, regards the greatest error of the Latin Church as the *azymes*. For the average Byzantine the *azymes* were the chief characteristic – because they were visible – that distinguished the two Churches. If it is recalled that in the eleventh and twelfth centuries the *azymes* were the most serious obstacle to union with the Armenians – and thus predisposed the lay imagination to see them as a sign of insuperable heresy – the psychological reasons which caused the Byzantine populace to adopt an extreme position will be understood.[108] Neophytos's material on anti-*azyme* theology has already been discussed in paragraph 2.ix of the preceding section. The characterisation of new errors as a revival of old heresies already condemned by the Church is a stereotype theme often repeated in polemical literature. What is worth noting is that in Neophytos's source the Latins are described in summary form not as Apollinarians (a common anti-Latin accusation of later years) but by extension, since they were like the monophysites (in their Armenian form), as theopaschites. On the basis of a similar logic Cardinal Humbertus excommunicated Patriarch Keroularios and his followers in 1054 as Simoniacs, Valesians, Arians, Donatists, Nicolaitans, Severians and Manichaeans.[109]

The nine remaining anti-Latin accusations which the saint regards as worth mentioning are as follows:

1.   The beardlessness of the Latin priests;

---

[108] To the works mentioned in note 82 above may be added the information given by G. Dagron, "Minorités ethniques et religieuses", p. 214, note 185, and I. Karmiris, "Σχέσεις Ὀρθοδόξων καὶ Ἀρμενίων καὶ ἰδίως ὁ κατὰ τὸν ΙΒ´ αἰῶνα θεολογικὸς διάλογος μεταξὺ αὐτῶν", *EEThSA* 16 (1968), pp. 325–417. It should be noted that the *azymes* were also regarded as the first and chief reason for the disagreement between Orthodox and Latins by scholarly theologians such as the patriarch of Antioch, John V Oxites (1089–1100). See B. Leib, "Deux inédits byzantins sur les azymes", p. 113.

[109] *PL* 143, coll. 1002–4; *PG* 120, coll. 741–6. On the accusation that the Latins were theopaschites cf. note 83 above.

2. the wicked and licentious life of the Latin priests;
3. the sign of the cross with the open hand instead of with two fingers and the thumb;
4. the bending of one knee instead of two in prayer;
5. eating meat in Cheese Week;
6. fasting on Saturdays;
7. veneration of the ground;
8. refusal to venerate icons on the part of most of them;
9. the error concerning the Holy Spirit.

This information has been derived from a written source but it is not improbable that the saint observed some of these matters himself or that he heard about them from visitors to the Hermitage. We shall examine them not on account of the theological interest which they present but as indicative of Latin customs which could alienate the average Cypriot at the beginning of the Frankish period and provoke his resistance.

With regard to the first mark of difference, it is known that the controversy about beards had already started by the ninth century. The mutual recriminations have today an unintentionally comic character. The matter was included, however, in the *Libellus* of excommunication which Humbertus left on the altar of Hagia Sophia on 16 July 1054 and in the reply of Keroularios. The question was based theoretically by the Orthodox on Leviticus 19:27 and on the *Apostolic Constitutions* (I, III, 11) but the affair had broader dimensions: it came to constitute in time a symbol of cultural identity and political allegiance. Neophytos cannot properly be understood if it is not borne in mind that Richard compelled the Byzantine *archons* of Cyprus to shave their beards *tamquam in signum commutationis alterius domini*.[110] When precisely the Western clergy began to shave their beards is not known. The general practice of shaving was at any rate first imposed by Pope Gregory VII (1073–85) but the custom did not prevail before the fifteenth century.

The second accusation was thought by the first editor of the memorandum to have been inserted by a later copyist.[111] But there is no evidence for this. That the moral life of the Frankish clergy of Outremer was never particularly distinguished is well-known. In Cyprus the situation had come to such a head that already in March 1223 the papal legate of the East published with regret a whole series of orders concerning the Latin clergy of the island:

---

[110] *Itinerarium regis Ricardi*, ed., W. Stubbs in Rolls Series 38, London, 1864, p. 201. The similar order of Peter the Great in the Byzantine-minded Russia of the 17th century had the same significance.

[111] *Byzantion* 39 (1969), p. 360.

ut non cohabitent cum mulieribus, ut non eant ad moniales sine licentia, de pena clericorum de nocte euntium, etc.[112]

The third accusation is of very ancient origin, seeing that the first witness to the sign of the cross goes back to Tertullian, towards the end of the second and the beginning of the third century.[113] The original sign of the cross with one finger was changed by the Greeks in the course of the eighth and ninth centuries to the sign with two fingers (perhaps as an anti-monophysite emblem), and during the last quarter of the twelfth century the present Greek form was adopted through the introduction of the thumb as a third finger. The first witness to the sign of the cross with three fingers is usually considered to be the unknown author of the *Dialogue of Panagiotes with an azymite*, the composition of which is placed between 1274 and 1282.[114] Indeed, the suspicion has been expressed that the Greeks adopted the three-finger sign at Nicaea after 1204 with the intention of emphasising their difference from the Franks. So far as I have been able to discover, however, the first witness to the sign of the cross by the Greeks with three fingers is St Neophytos in the homily before us about the beginning of the schism, which was written after 1191 and before 1204. This custom must have been new at that time because the saint does not boldly write: "they do not make the sign of the cross with three fingers", but uses the more diplomatic form: "they do not make the sign of the cross with two fingers together with the thumb". Naturally the introduction of the three-finger sign caused controversy among the Orthodox, from whom arose that lay excommunication: "if anyone does not make the sign of the cross with two fingers, like Christ, let him be excommunicated", which was to have a similar history with the Russian *Raskolniki* in the seventeenth century.[115] Very probably the veiled phrase of St Neophytos suggests that the situation in Cyprus too was strained.

As has already been noted, the fourth of Neophytos's accusations is not found even in Stilbes' lengthy memorandum on the faults of the Latin Church. It is based on the description of the Lord's prayer in Gethsemane in Luke, who says in 22:41 that the Lord "bent his knees and prayed". The Latins in bending one knee in prayer do not follow Jesus. It is superfluous to say that the Latins by no means ignored the bending of both knees at prescribed points in their liturgy.

---

[112] See J. Hackett, *A History of the Orthodox Church of Cyprus*, London, 1901, pp. 510f.

[113] For the full history of the signing of the cross see E. Golubinskij, *Istorija russkoi Cerkvi*, IV, pp. 465–503.

[114] See A. Argyriou, "Remarques sur quelques listes grecques", pp. 21–3.

[115] See E. Golubinskij, *Istorija russkoj Cerkvi*, IV, p. 476 and note 2. Cf. A.A. Dmitrievskij, *Opišanie liturgičeskih rukopišej* ... II, *Euchologia*, Kiev, 1901, p. 424: Εἴ τις οὐ σφραγίζει τοῖς δυσὶ δακτύλοις, καθὼς καὶ ὁ Χριστός, ἀνάθεμα.

Points 5 and 6 have been examined in paragraph 2.viii of the preceding section.

The seventh accusation is understood better as formulated in *Opusculum contra Francos*, 9: "On entering the churches they fall to their faces on the ground and whisper, then they make the sign of the cross, kiss the finger and rise, and with that they finish their prayer."[116]

The eighth accusation was already formulated in the first letter of Michael Keroularios to Peter of Antioch and was rejected as of no substance in Peter's reply.[117] It is nevertheless true that in spite of Rome's support of the Seventh Ecumenical Council, Frankish theology remained semi-iconoclast.

With regard to the ninth accusation concerning the Holy Spirit, all that is necessary has already been said. I believe that the knowledge which Neophytos had of the subject was extremely vague and that he had never read the works of Photios or the Byzantine theologians who had written on the procession of the Holy Spirit. This was on account of the isolated character of the Cypriot Church and the absence of large libraries in the island.[118] Nevertheless, out of his concern for Orthodoxy, which he knew in a vague way to be threatened, the saint composed various homilies on the Holy Spirit, setting out in these the classic teaching of the Eastern Church on the Spirit along the lines that had already been formulated before the ninth century.[119]

It has also been noted above that Neophytos was unaware of the controversy concerning the papal primacy. He is on account of this a valuable witness to the "innocent" Eastern theological tradition concerning Peter. From the years immediately after 1176, when he wrote the *Discourse on the divine chief apostles Peter and Paul and on the rest of the apostles*,[120] which is still unpublished, until a few years before his death, when he issued the instruction *On the holy and wholly blessed apostles*,[121] which is also unpublished, no indication is found in his writings of an attribution to Peter of any supreme authority over the whole Church, much less a perpetual authority exercised by the bishops of Rome as his alleged successors. Thus, although on folio 313ᵛ of the first discourse Peter is called "most supreme" (κορυφαιότατος) and on folio 314 "chief apostle" (πρωτόθρονος) ("for God in His mercy did not simply bestow

---

[116] J. Hergenröther, *Monumenta graeca*, p. 65, no. 9.

[117] *PG* 120, coll. 781–96, 796–816.

[118] Cf. B. Englezakis, "'Ἀνέκδοτον ὑπόμνημα", pp. 75–6 (pp. 107–108 above) and "'Η εἰς τοὺς Κανόνας τῶν Δεσποτικῶν ἑορτῶν ἑρμηνεία", pp. 7–8, esp. notes 22, 26 (p. 101 above, notes 22, 26).

[119] See section II, paragraphs 3.ii and 3.iii of the present chapter.

[120] Cod. Lesb. Leimon. 2, fols 314–18. On the dating see B. Englezakis, "'Η εἰς τοὺς Κανόνας τῶν Δεσποτικῶν ἑορτῶν ἑρμηνεία", (Chapter VI above).

[121] Cod. Paris. suppl. gr. 1317, fols 88ᵛ–93.

forgiveness on him who had denied him but made Him first shepherd of the spiritual sheep; for 'if you love me', says Scripture, 'feed my sheep'"), on folios 314ᵛ and 317ᵛ Peter and Paul are nevertheless called πρωτόθρονοι and κορυφαῖοι together, which shows clearly how the saint understood these epithets. That the word "first" in the phrase "first shepherd of the spiritual sheep" has a chronological rather than a taxonomic significance is shown in the *Prologue* to the *Instructions*, where the saint explains:

"For this first work and token of love was given at the hand of the Good Shepherd to tend His spiritual sheep in a way conducive to their salvation, and 'if you love me, Peter', He says, 'feed my sheep', that is: whoever else loves me after you has the task of feeding my sheep well and my lambs too."[122]

In the Instruction *On the holy and wholly blessed apostles* nothing particular is said about Peter. We saw in paragraph 2.i of the preceding section that in the *Discourse on the dedication of the Church of the Resurrection* Neophytos regards the "rock" in Matthew 16:18 as "pure faith" and the foundation of the Church he defines as Christ. And narrating in the *Discourse on the synaxis of the divine taxiarchs Michael and Gabriel and the rest of the angels* the story recounted in Acts 12:4–11, he begins: "Peter, the most honourable excellence (ἀκρότης) of the apostles";[123] but in the *Encomium on our great bishop and father the divine Chrysostom* he names the most eminent (ἀκραίμονας) of the apostles Peter and Paul, saying:

"May you rejoice, father John Chrysostom, sweet in all things in name and in reality because, since you are equal to the apostles, the God of the apostles sent you the most eminent of these (ἀκραίμονας τούτων) to convey the Gospel of joy and the food of heaven; and before this, in your country of origin, the same blessed pair came, that Peter might give you the keys of the Kingdom, that just like him you too should build the Church on the rock of the confession of the name of Christ and the gates of hell, according to the judgment given to him, shall not prevail against it, and that your namesake, the beloved John, should provide you with

---

[122] Ibid., fol. 8: Τοῦτο γὰρ πρῶτον ἔργον καὶ ἀγάπης τεκμήριον πρὸς τοῦ καλοῦ ἐδόθη ποιμένος, τοῦ ποιμαίνειν σωτηριωδῶς τὰ ποίμνια τούτου τὰ λογικά, καὶ "Εἰ φιλεῖς με, Πέτρε", φησί, "ποίμαινε τὰ πρόβατά μου", δηλονότι· Καὶ ὅστις με ἄλλος φιλεῖ μετὰ σέ, καλῶς ποιμανεῖν ἔχει τὰ πρόβατά μου καὶ τὰ ἀρνία μου.
[123] Cod. Paris. gr. 1189, fol. 143ᵛ.

the grace of theology through the divine Gospel, which is what happened."[124]

This text is also worth studying because it provides the correct interpretation of the term ἀκρότης amongst the Byzantines, who often bestowed it on Peter, and because it clarifies Neophytos's understanding of Matthew 16:18: the rock is not Peter but the confession of Christ, who builds the Church on Himself through all its holy pastors who like Peter confess Him the Son of God. As for the grace of theology, this is not a function of Peter, but, as the vision of Chrysostom reveals, of the beloved disciple, John.

This is what the Cypriot monk professed in about 1200. On 13 November 1204, however, writing *To the bishops, abbots and other clergy with the army of the Crusaders at Constantinople*, Pope Innocent III declared that Peter symbolised the Latin Church and the New Testament, while John represented the Greek Church and the Old Testament, as they were in error over the Holy Trinity. "But soon they will become aware of it. Such is our faith and hope."[125]

Neophytos's view of the schism and the solution for which he hoped were in accord with his ecclesiological belief. He regarded the schism as a separation of Rome from the consensus of the seven ecumenical councils and the patriarchal pentarchy. "For since I saw in the said seven councils that the pope of the time joined in giving his consent to these and co-operated with them, I was puzzled and sought to discover when and for what reason the elder Rome had dissented from new Rome and had celebrated with *azymes* and adopted practices at variance with the conciliar traditions and given approval to them."[126]

That Neophytos, combined the narration of the beginning of the schism with the memorandum on the councils is no more fortuitous than his

---

[124] Ibid., fol. 163–163ᵛ: Χαίροις, πάτερ Ἰωάννη Χρυσόστομε, τὸ γλυκὺ κατὰ πάντα πρᾶγμα καὶ ὄνομα, ὅτι, ἰσαπόστολος ὤν, ὁ τῶν ἀποστόλων Θεὸς τοὺς ἀκραίμονας τούτων ἐξαπέσταλκέ σοι κομίσαι τὰ χαρᾶς εὐαγγέλια καὶ τροφὴν τὴν οὐράνιον· καὶ πρὸ τούτου, ἐν τῇ πατρίδι σου πάλαι, ἡ αὐτὴ εὐλογημένη δυάς, ἵνα ὁ μὲν Πέτρος τὰς κλεῖς σοι ἐπιδῷ τῆς βασιλείας τῶν οὐρανῶν, ἵνα ὡς ἐκεῖνος οὕτω καὶ αὐτὸς ἐν τῇ πέτρᾳ τῆς ὁμολογίας τοῦ ὀνόματος Χριστοῦ οἰκοδομήσῃς τὴν ἐκκλησίαν, καὶ πύλαι ᾅδου, κατὰ τὴν ἐκείνου ἀπόφασιν, οὐ κατισχύσουσιν αὐτῆς, ὁ δὲ συνώνυμος καὶ ἠγαπημένος Ἰωάννης διὰ τοῦ θείου εὐαγγελίου τῆς θεολογίας τὴν χάριν χορηγήσῃ σοι, ὅπερ καὶ ἐγένετο. Cf. K.I. Dyovouniotes, "Νεοφύτου Ἐγκλείστου ἀνέκδοτον ἐγκώμιον εἰς Ἰωάννην τὸν Χρυσόστομον", *EEThSA* 1 (1926), pp. 329–45, esp. p. 344.

[125] *Regesta Innocentii III*, VII.154, *PL* 215, col. 459 CD. Cf. J. Meyendorff, "St Peter in Byzantine Theology" in J. Meyendorff et al., *The Primacy of Peter in the Orthodox Church*, London, 1963, pp. 7–29.

[126] *On why and when the elder Rome and the new Rome grew apart from each other*, *Byzantion* 39 (1969), pp. 354.98–355.103.

reference to the patriarchs reigning at the time each council was called. These names have a symbolic rather than a practical significance. They do not imply the presence of these patriarchs at the councils but symbolise the five patriarchal thrones of the Church. The idea of the pentarchy presupposes that if one of the patriarchs is not in accord with the others, the rest can condemn him and can define or confirm the faith of the Church without him.[127] In accordance with this ecclesiological understanding, later Byzantine theology – and consequently St Neophytos – regarded as the only sure solution of the schism the calling of an ecumenical council which "will put an end to the breach of unity and the custom of the *azymes*."

In attributing the beginning of the schism to Frankish pressure on Rome the saint is not far from the truth. The coronation of Charlemagne in St Peter's by Leo III on Christmas Day 800 is symbolic of the alienation of Rome from the East Roman world and her orientation towards the Franks. For the Roman authority in Constantinople that act constituted a conspiracy and rebellion of the patriarch of Rome against the emperor in concert with the powerful northern barbarians.[128] The origins of the rift in the medieval Church, at all events, are to be found in Aachen rather than in Rome or Hippo.

Before concluding this section we should perhaps examine, by way of an appendix, the opinion concerning St Neophytos which M. Jugie expressed in 1919, that is, that the Recluse accepted the Immaculate Conception of the Theotokos.[129] I do not regard it as appropriate to expatiate on the theme, on the assumption that no modern Roman Catholic theologian would look for support for the papal dogma of 1854 from Neophytos. In rebuttal of Jugie's theory Neophytos's interpretation of Psalm 103:30 will suffice. Comparing the coming of the Holy Spirit to Mary, according to the Gospel, with the future renewal of creation by the Spirit, the saint writes as follows:

---

[127] Cf. C. Walter, "The Names of the Council Fathers at Saint Sozomenus, Cyprus", *REB* 28 (1970), pp. 189–206, esp. pp. 202–4. On the various lists of the councils see F. Dvornik, "Unpublished Anonymous Greek Treatises on the Councils", *The Photian Schism: History and Legend*, Cambridge, 1948, pp. 452–4. In his first edition of Neophytos's work (see note 126 above) I.P. Tsiknopoullos corrected the calculations of the years between each council (pp. 360ff.). On this phenomenon of the different calculations see V. Beneševič, "Monumenta vaticana ad ius canonicum pertinentia", *Studi Bizantini* 2 (1927), pp. 169ff.

[128] See W. Ullmann, *The Carolingian Renaissance*, esp. pp. 135–66; C.N. Tsirpanlis, "Byzantine Reactions to the Coronation of Charlemagne (780–813)", *Byzantina* 6 (1974), pp. 347–60; D.M. Nicol, "The Byzantine View of Western Europe", *Greek, Roman and Byzantine Studies* 8 (1967), pp. 315–39.

[129] M. Jugie, "Le témoignage de Néophyte le Reclus sur l'Immaculée Conception", *Bessarione* 35 (1919), pp. 17–20; "Néophyte le Reclus (1134–1220?), Homélies sur la Nativité de la Sainte Vierge et sa Présentation au Temple", *Homélies mariales byzantines* in *PO* 16, Paris, 1922, pp. 526–38, esp. pp. 526–8.

"'You will send out your Spirit and they will be created; and you will renew the face of the earth.' For just as the Holy Spirit anticipated the incarnation of the Logos and sanctified the Virgin for conception, so in the second coming of Christ the all-holy Spirit will in anticipation renew the face of an earth which has grown old and feeble as God, as Creator, and as consuming fire, equal to and consubstantial with the Father and the Son."[130]

If in the various rhetorical passages which Jugie has fished out Neophytos meant that which the great Assumptionist father said he did, he would certainly never have made such a comparison, nor would he have written that the Spirit descended on Mary at the Annunciation with the intention of the sanctification of the Virgin for conception.

In summary I would say that St Neophytos, in spite of the Latin crimes against his country, never permitted himself to descend to the level of the lay-monastic anti-Latin caricatures and lampoons of the time. He nevertheless opposed the sick spirit of that Christianity which brought forth the monster of the Crusades with a firm denial. In spite of its involuntary theological deficiencies, his resolute but sober attitude was worthy of the spirituality of Orthodox monasticism.

IV. ST NEOPHYTOS AND THE FRANKISH REGIME

The *Cosmic Struggle* enacted in Jerusalem was experienced by its contemporaries not as a momentary or fortuitous event but as a vast historical drama to which indeed they attributed dimensions which went beyond time and extended into eternity. One of the more enduring mental attitudes which that struggle created – "a prison of long duration" as Fernand Braudel would have said – was in the Byzantines a fear and mistrust of the Westerners. The blow which the Fourth Crusade succeeded in dealing to the Christian East was suffered by Cyprus at the hands of the Third Crusade. From that time until 1571 and beyond the Cypriot people would never again trust the Franks or regard them as brothers and members of the same family. The Franks would always remain for the average Cypriot, as for Neophytos, a "foreign people", "of another race", "alien", "lawless", "hostile", "persecuting", "criminal", "those who hate us". Their rule would be nothing but a "mad rage" and "perverse disposition", "bitterness and burning", "rough water", "a winter of wretchedness", "pillaging", "capture", "despoilment", "constriction", "tyranny of the unorthodox", "terrible slavery".

---

[130] I.Ch. Hadjioannou, Νεοφύτου ... Ἑρμηνεία εἰς τοὺς Ψαλμούς, p. 100.

If the Muslims were unbelieving dogs, the Franks were for Neophytos "wolves in sheep's clothing", "treacherous", "thievish", "rapacious". The first wrongdoer, the ungrateful Richard, was nothing short of "totally vile", "abominable" and "like the godless Saladin", epithets which the saint never applied to anyone else and which vividly reveal not only the despairing sentiments of hatred and cursing which the Byzantine Cypriots nursed against the Westerners who had enslaved them, but also the contempt with which they confronted the religious ideal of the Crusade and the myth of chivalry. "Having accomplished nothing against Saladin, whom he resembled, he sold the country to the Latins for two hundred thousand pounds of gold."[131] Such was the judgment passed by the Byzantine East on the most romantic knight of the medieval West. However much the conditions and the climate would change over the next four centuries, however much the chasm between "the oppressing classes and the subject classes" would widen, this profound reality would remain above all else for the population of Cyprus. "Cruelty and arrogance" were for the Byzantines the chief characteristics of the Western Christians from the time of Anna Komnena[132] to the age of the Patriarch Philotheos.[133] The historic saying by which the Recluse characterised the failure of the Third Crusade – "for providence was not disposed to drive out dogs only to bring in wolves instead" – prefigures the angry outburst of the last grand duke of Byzantium: "It is better to see the Turkish turban ruling in the midst of the city than the Latin tiara."[134]

This attitude of Neophytos is set, however, within a general Orthodox ethos, which, unlike the utopian dreams of the intellectuals or the fatalistic paralysis of the masses, kept the mind sober and furthered the interests of the Church, for it was in the Church that Neophytos saw a sure and certain future.[135] Orthodox and Roman, the saint belongs to the Eastern Europe of the thirteenth century, which rejected simultaneously the Islamic Near East, the Frankish West and the pre-Christian world of pagan Greece. He prefigures

---

[131] *Concerning the misfortunes of the land of Cyprus*, p. 336.7–8, 339.86–8. Cf. Cod. Paris. gr. 1189, fol. 209.

[132] Anna Komnena, *Alexiad* xiv, 2 (the chief meaning of ἀπανθρωπία here is "ingratitude". Cf. the modern Greek παλιανθρωπιά). See G. Buckler, *Anna Comnena. A Study*, Oxford, 1929, pp. 438–78: "The West".

[133] See the diatribe on the capture of Heracleia by the Latins, ed. K. Triantaphylles and A. Graputo, Συλλογὴ ἑλληνικῶν ἀνεκδότων, Α΄, Venice, 1874, pp. 1–33, esp. pp. 11–12. More generally, D.M. Nicol, *Church and Society in the Last Centuries of Byzantium*, ch. 3, "Byzantium between east and west: the two 'nations' ".

[134] Ducas, *Istoria Turco-Bizantina (1341–1462)*, ed. V. Grecu, Bucharest, 1958, p. 329.11–12. Cf. H. Evert-Kappesowa, "Le tiare ou le turban?", *Byzantinoslavica* 14 (1953), pp. 245–57.

[135] Cf. H. Ahrweiler, *L'idéologie politique de l'Empire byzantin*, pp. 119–28: "L'utopie intellectuelle, le fatalisme eschatologique et la certitude orthodoxe".

the monastic "politico-religious" current of Eastern European hesychasm of the fourteenth century.[136] If one were to set the correlative Latin view against this, it could be summarised in two words: *inobedientia* and *perfidia*.[137] "In their view the Greeks are white Hagarenes", George Pachymeres noted.[138]

St Neophytos regarded the Frankish tyranny, as we have already noted, as a temporary evil "permitted by God for our deeply sinful life and lack of repentance". The dialectic scheme sin–enslavement is a common topos in Byzantine historiography and ecclesiastical rhetoric.[139] It forms a vital thread which, originating in the Old Testament rather than the New Testament,[140] has dominated the lay Orthodox mind to the present day. The strange thing is that the Latins used the same theology to justify their crimes against the Orthodox. Thus, in defence of the sacrilegious Crusaders of 1204, Innocent III wrote to Theodore Lascaris on 17 March 1208:

"Although we accept that these men are not all without stain, we believe nevertheless that the Greeks have been punished by them through the just judgment of God because they have rent the seamless robe of Jesus Christ. For so long as the divine judgments are so hidden as to be called a deep abyss by the prophet, it often happens that through His hidden but always most just judgment evil is punished by evil."[141]

Through such a doctrine the Latins could justify any of their crimes, while the Orthodox were made able to bear the unbearable present.

The personal reply of the saint to the enslavement of his country is naturally determined by his monastic character and anchoritic environ-

---

[136] Cf. G.M. Prokhorov, "L'hesychasme et la pensée sociale en Europe orientale au XIVe siècle".

[137] Both these terms were used by Pope Alexander IV in his bull on Cyprus: T.T. Haluscynskij and M.M. Wojnar, *Acta Alexandri P.P. IV (1254–1271)*, Vatican, 1966, no. 46, 3 July 1260.

[138] George Pachymeres, *De Michaele et Andronico Palaeologis libri XIII*, ed. I. Bekker, *CSHB*, Bonn, 1835, I, p. 367.8–9.

[139] See Th. Papadopoullos, "Chypre: Frontière ethnique et socio-culturelle du monde byzantin", XVe Congrès International d'Études Byzantines, *Rapports et Co-rapports*, Athens, 1976, pp. 43–7 and the bibliography given there.

[140] See C.R. North, *The Old Testament Interpretation of History*, London, 1946; G. von Rad, *Theologie des Alten Testament*, Bd. I, *Die Theologie der geschichtlichen Überlieferungen Israels*, Munich, 1957, Bd. II, *Die Theologie der prophetischen Überlieferungen Israels*, Munich, 1960; J. Lindblom, *Prophecy in Ancient Israel*, Oxford, 1973, esp. pp. 311–75. G. von Rad showed how this scheme was perfectly realised in the Books of Chronicles in his classic work *Das Geschichtsbild des chronistischen Werkes*, Stuttgart, 1930. For the New Testament view see H.-I. Marrou, *Théologie de l'histoire*, Paris, 1968.

[141] *Regesta Innocentii III*, XI. 47, *PL* 215, col. 1272.

ment. The "natural course" of his spirituality advanced from the beginning on two fronts: inwardly towards the spiritual and upwards towards the heavenly. The saint was a recluse but, as H. Delehaye has already noted, regarded himself even as a stylite.[142] The Frankish capture intensified Neophytos's inward spiritual movement. In 1197 he abandoned his first cell and moved higher up the cliff-face to begin a second, more austere reclusion. To the new hermitage he gave the name "New Sion, which, by God's grace, will be a Godly watch-tower".[143] The higher position, the more austere reclusion, as well as the characteristic naming of the new cell are indicative of Neophytos's understanding of the external conditions of the world. Greater disturbance called for greater *hesychia*, more severe tribulations required more intense prayer, the collapse of the commonwealth below raised the eyes to the commonwealth of God. "For you have not come to a mountain that may be touched but you have come to Mount Sion and the city of the living God, the heavenly Jerusalem, and to innumerable angels in festal gathering and to the assembly of the first-born who are enrolled in heaven and to a judge who is God of all" (Heb. 12:18–23).

This is how Neophytos describes his decision to climb higher to a new cave:

> "Since a good stretch of my life has been granted to me in this Hermitage and I have lived here without anxieties for nearly forty years, and a constant stream of visitors, both welcome and unwelcome, has disturbed me, it seemed good, I think, first to God and then to me, that I should ascend to the upper rooms of the Hermitage and the higher parts of the cliff, with God's help, and there dig out for myself another small hole difficult of access for the multitudes so that I can have privacy there whenever I wish and can escape the disturbance of large numbers of frequent and importunate visitors and not fall away in the least from my beloved *anachoresis* and *hesychia* known only to God."[144]

---

[142] H. Delehaye, *Les saints stylites*, Bruxelles–Paris, 1923, p. cxxxviii, where there are parallel examples. Among more recent works see especially D.M. Nicol, *The Rock Monasteries of Thessaly*, London, 1963, esp. p. 92; G.P. Schiemenz, "Die Kapelle des Styliten Niketas in den Weinbergen von Ortahisar", *Jahrbuch der österreichischen Byzantinistik* 18 (1969), pp. 239–58, esp. pp. 254–6. That Neophytos considered the naturally-formed rocky platform of the Hermitage as a *stylos* is evident, amongst other things, from his blessing of his successor as a recluse in the fourteenth chapter of the *Typike Diatheke* (fol. 36, p. 85), where he prays that he should follow in his footsteps "καὶ τῶν ἐν τοῖς στύλοις διαλαμψάντων ὁσίων σου". Sadly, the modern irreligious buildings below the Hermitage have destroyed the topography of Neophytos's monastery together with its monastic ideology.

[143] *Typike Diatheke*, fol. 4, p. 53.

[144] *Theosemia*, ed. I. Ch. Hadjioannou, Ἱστορία καὶ ἔργα Νεοφύτου, p. 139.

From the "watch-tower of God"[145] the Cypriot countryside could be seen stretching out below; above there was nothing but the sky, the birds, the winds and the clouds. The Recluse in the end did not even go down to the church. He followed the liturgy unseen from the "cave of audience" which communicated with the church through a channel which had been specially opened. Sometimes he seemed forgotten even by his own monks.

"For I often desired just ten drops of water to be given to me during the public celebration of the feast of the Raising of the Precious Cross, but they were not given to me, nor was I thought of. But I judged that this did not happen out of contempt but because of the great throng of people and because I was hidden from sight and easily overlooked. And this did not happen once but at the times of the various festivals, so that I did not have enough fuel for a fire", he wrote in his *Diatheke,* exhorting his successor to be patient and watchful "against thoughts of grumbling and muttering, that you may not be found to be tiresome and troublesome".[146]

This perfect seclusion and self-denial, however, does not imply a withdrawal from all activity. The period from 1197 to 1214, in spite of the advanced age of the saint, proved to be the most productive of his whole life. The larger and more important part of his *oeuvre* was written in this period, when the buildings and decoration of the monastery were also completed, the library was enriched, the founder's *Typicon* was drawn up, a small property was bought and the manner of the succession and continuation of the sacred foundation was assured. That the saint began these projects and brought them all to a favourable conclusion after his second reclusion and between the ages of 60 and 80 is for his time a genuine achievement. It constitutes the greatest spiritual offering of Orthodox Cyprus during the whole of the Frankish era and also the greatest offering of Cyprus in general to Orthodox monasticism. Neophytos remains one of those rare cases of an individual's response to external circumstances which not only transcends the context provided by contemporary society but even manages to bring about a change in the cultural environment. Unfavourable conditions were never lacking in Cyprus but a corresponding number of men like Neophytos did not arise to meet them. This proves that true and permanent creation is always a spiritual feat, the roots of which are ultimately to be found in the religious elevation of the emotions.

---

[145] The etymology Sion = watch-tower came into patristic literature from Origen, *Com. on John XIII.* 13 (Σιών, ὅπερ ἐστὶν "σκοπευτήριον").

[146] *Typike Diatheke* 15, fols 39ᵛ–40ᵛ. For the first two words of the passage I read ἢ γάρ instead of εἰ γάρ of the manuscript and the critical edition.

A little after 1197, according to the latest research,[147] the church of the Hermitage was painted, the iconostasis was set up, the sanctuary was restored and the monastic refectory was decorated. The series and nature of the monastic buildings, as described in the twentieth chapter of the *Typicon*, suggest that building activity did not even diminish in the years of Frankish rule that followed. The "great building with many apses in the ravine" must have been built after 1200, when we would suppose that the stables and hay store were hollowed out of the rock, since the monastery only acquired animals a little before 1214.[148] The good taste of the Hermitage testifies to this day to the spiritual attitude of the Recluse to the problem of "the world".

The increase over the years in the number of pilgrims, on the other hand, must not necessarily be taken as a sign of economic recovery. The flow of visitors to small monasteries rather implies the contrary.[149] That which C. Mango and E.J.W. Hawkins have written about the existence of a *metochion* of the monastery from 1203/4 – which implies that the saint is lying when he asserts that the monastery had acquired no property until 1214 – is completely mistaken.[150] The note in Paris. gr. 301, fol. 315ᵛ, on which these two scholars relied, belongs to the fifteenth century and was published in its entirety by J. Darrouzès in 1959. The colophon of the manuscript belongs to 1 September 1204 but speaks of the Hermitage of St Epiphanius in the village of Souskiou near Kouklia,[151] and not of the Hermitage of St Neophytos. The foreign occupation was not as favourable towards Orthodox monasteries as these two writers are quick to surmise.

The ecclesiastical and other relations of Neophytos with Constantinople and Nicaea have been discussed in the second section, where his clear-sightedness was also observed in relation to the events which were enacted at the Holy Places in Palestine. Contact with them was never interrupted – until the end the only authority recognised by the Recluse as appointed by God and valid for all Orthodox was that of the emperor, even if he was in exile in Nicaea. His attitude towards the Frankish king of Cyprus, whom in his *Diatheke* he appointed guardian of his monastery, was dictated by the two classic

---

[147] C. Mango and E.J.W. Hawkins, "The Hermitage of St Neophytus and its Wall-Paintings", esp. pp. 200–202.

[148] *Typike Diatheke* 20, cf. 10.

[149] Cf. paragraph 4.iii of part II of the present chapter.

[150] C. Mango and E.J.W. Hawkins, "The Hermitage of St Neophytus and its Wall-Paintings", p. 127, referring to "J. Darrouzès in *REByz*, VIII (1951), pp. 172ff.".

[151] See G.A. Sotiriou, *Τὰ βυζαντινὰ μνημεῖα τῆς Κύπρου,* Athens, 1935, illustr. 46, pls. 57a, 74b, 76; J. Darrouzès, "Notes pour servir à l'histoire de Chypre (Quatrième article)", *KS* 23 (1959), pp. 27–56, esp. pp. 31–2. On the term *metochion*, rare in this period, A.P. Každan, *Agrarnye otnošenija v Vizantii XIII-XIV vv.,* Moscow, 1952, pp. 67ff. and his "Vizantijskij monastyr' XI-XIIvv. kak šocial'naya gruppa", *VV* 31 (1971), pp. 48–70, esp. p. 67.

Byzantine principles of government: "order" and "economy",[152] and probably also by considerations of protection of the monastery from the voracity of the Latin Church of the island, which usually only the king limited or was able to limit. Neophytos is neither inspired by the excessive episcopal suspicion of Neilos of Tamaseia, nor does he fall into the subservience of the contemporary clerics of Constantinople, as shown in their well-known letter to Pope Innocent III.[153] This letter clearly refers to individuals who, regarding the Latin occupation as permanent, began the pro-Latin policy which was to last until 1453 and which saw the salvation of the Christian East as lying in uniatism with Rome. The attitude of St Neophytos has been discussed sufficiently in the relevant paragraphs of the second section, with the result that there is no need for repetition. The Frankish states of the East were regarded by Neophytos not only as foreign, unlawful, unjust and oppressive but as spiritually sinful, unclean and demonic.[154]

V. EPILOGUE

Such in general terms was the encounter between Neophytos and the West in late twelfth-century and early thirteenth-century Cyprus. In summary the following conclusions may be drawn:

1. The attitude of Neophytos is purely religious and never exclusively patriotic, even though it always has political implications. The saint himself, however, is first and last always a monk, is interested primarily in the preservation of the Orthodox faith and remains until the end a heavenly-minded recluse who has renounced the world and transitory things for the sake of perfect devotion to the divine.

2. The knowledge which Neophytos was able to acquire about the Latins was small and, in comparison with the mainstream writers of his age, out of date. This is due almost entirely to the insularity of his environment.

3. The Latin Church was regarded by Neophytos as in schism, through the influence of the Franks, from the catholic ecclesiastical communion. Like others amongst his contemporaries – particularly those from a lay-monastic background – Neophytos took its chief error to be the liturgical custom of the *azymes*. In his polemic against it, however, he never followed the popular

---

[152] See H. Ahrweiler, *L'idéologie politique de l'Empire byzantin*, pp. 129–47: "Les principes fondamentaux de la pensée politique à Byzance".

[153] *PG* 140, 293–7. See A. Luchaire, *Innocent III: La question de l'Orient*, Paris, 1907, pp. 251–6; B.T. Gorjanov, "Religiozno-polemičeskaja literatura po voprosu ob otnosenii k Latinjanam v Vizantii XIII-XV vv.", *VV* 8 (1956), pp. 132–42, esp. p. 135.

[154] Cf. paras. 2.iii, 4.i, ii, iv, v, vi of the second part of the present chapter.

scurrilous lampoons but always wrote in a modest way in keeping with his monastic profession. In his last work before the *Diatheke*, the *Book of Instructions*, the saint described the unity of the Church in the true faith as a natural reflection on earth of the unity of the Holy Trinity, and the schism as a satanic work. The saint looks for the healing of the latter in a new ecumenical council held in accordance with the will of God.

4. For the Franks Neophytos has only contempt. He saw them as a foreign people, lawless and rapacious, who threatened the body and the soul of the Romans. If the Muslims were dogs, the Latins were wolves. But he never calls them "barbarians" or "heretics". His usual epithets were "unorthodox", "wrongly believing" and "a foreign people". Every tendency of the Cypriots to become assimilated to them must be fiercely resisted.

5. Neophytos regarded Frankish rule in Cyprus as the enslavement of his country. That humiliation, which had come upon them by divine permission as a trial and fatherly correction, would in time pass, retreating before the spiritual power of repentant prayer. The strongest and most sure resistance against the occupiers was a more intense spiritual life and struggle.

6. From the cultural viewpoint the life and work of Neophytos constitute one of the bright moments in the creation of Greek permanence and Orthodox continuity in Cyprus. In the first years of the period of hardship to come Neophytos actively demonstrated how to defend the inheritance of the past in a spiritual way and protect the security of the future, with the ancestral ideal of life becoming renewed and continuing to be recorded in its own homeland.

An effort has been made to describe the personal "destiny" of Neophytos within the psychological, intellectual, moral and spiritual world in which he evolved, to evoke the spiritual atmosphere of Cyprus in the first years of Frankish rule. The history of mental outlooks is, as Lucien Febvre noted many years ago, "à la fois extrêmement séduisante et affreusement difficile".[155] I leave to the specialist the judgment of the degree of my failure. The attempt, at any rate, was necessary, because the chapter which was begun then has not yet closed.

The events which followed directly afterwards are in their general lines well-known. The Latin tyranny became worse, reaching its nadir in 1231 in the burning of the thirteen monks of the Theotokos Kantariotissa. The positions on both sides had hardened to such a degree that the Orthodox on the one side were ready not only to die over the *azymes* but also to propose

[155] L. Febvre, *Combats pour l'histoire*, Paris, 1953, "Une vue d'ensemble. Histoire et psychologie", and "Comment reconstituer la vie affective d'autrefois? La sensibilité et l'histoire".

to the Latins a trial by fire (a Latin and Islamic custom rather than an Orthodox one), while the pope on the other justified the burning of the Orthodox by a written interpretation of the cutting off by Peter of the ear of the chief priest's servant.[156] What the reaction of Neophytos would have been to the Alexandrine Bull of 1261 is not difficult to guess. The Recluse would never have accepted the policy of cunning harmony of Pesimandros and his fellow bishops. "For it is better to be in good schism than in bad harmony." The only Cypriot who would continue in Byzantium the spirit and work of "high" anti-Latin theology would in future be Gregory II, the Cypriot ecumenical patriarch (1283–89),[157] who would preside over the official condemnation of the robber union of Lyons and would pave the way for the palamite spiritual synthesis.

---

[156] Th. Papadopoullos, "Μαρτύριον Κυπρίων", Ἀναμνηστικὸς τόμος ἐπὶ τῇ πεντηκονταετηρίδι τοῦ περιοδικοῦ Ἀπόστολος Βαρνάβας, Nicosia, 1975, pp. 307–38, esp. pp. 326 and 334 for the two proposals of an ordeal. The correspondence of Germanos II and Gregory IX is in K.N. Sathas, Μεσαιωνικὴ Βιβλιοθήκη, B, Venice, 1873, pp. 39–49. Cf. A.L. Tautu, Acta Honorii III (1216–1227) et Gregorii IX (1227–1241), Vatican, 1950, nos 179, 179a; V. Laurent and J. Darrouzès, Dossier grec de l'union de Lyon (1273–1277), Paris, 1976, pp. 576, 130 note 1, 505.

[157] The fullest description of Gregory's activities is still that of I.E. Troitskij in his studies on the schism of the Arsenites in Hristianskoe čtenie 50, 1 (1871), pp. 615–45; 6, pp. 1055–1119 (reprinted in I. E. Troitskij, Arsenij i Arsenity, London, 1973, pp. 231–327). For Gregory's theology the basic work is again still that of I.E. Troitskij, "K istorii sporov po voprosu ob ishoždenii Sviatago Duha", Hristianskoe čtenie 69 (1889), I, pp. 338–77, 2, pp. 280–352, 520–70. Among more modern studies see above all W. La Meere, La tradition manuscrite de la correspondance de Grégoire de Chypre, Bruxelles–Rome, 1937.

X

ST NEOPHYTOS THE RECLUSE, *HOMILIES ON THE SERMON ON THE MOUNT* (Coisl. Gr. 287)[*]

St Neophytos the Recluse, founder of the monastery of the Holy Cross, about six miles north-west of the city of Paphos in Cyprus, was born in 1134 at Lefkara, halfway between Larnaca and Limassol. Having received the monastic tonsure at the monastery of St John Chrysostom at Koutzouvendi in 1152, he became a recluse in Paphos in 1159, and in 1170 accepted the responsibility of guiding a small community that assembled in the caves around him. In 1183 the *Encleistra* complex was painted by Theodore Apseudes, a large part of his beautiful frescoes and two of his icons surviving up to the present day. In 1197, six years after the Latin occupation of Cyprus (first by Richard Lionheart, then by the Templars, and finally by the Lusignans of Jerusalem), Neophytos went to dwell in a cave, which he called the "New Sion", higher up on the cliff where his original hermitage was situated, and began a stricter seclusion, devoting himself entirely to writing. We find him still alive in 1214, when he signed the final *Ktetorikon Typicon* of his monastery (cod. Edenburg. Univers. 224), and we must suppose that he died some time before 1220.[1]

---

[*] "St Neophytos the Recluse, Homilies on the Sermon on the Mount (Coisl. gr. 287)", E.A. Livingstone, ed., *Studia Patristica XXIII, Papers Presented to the Tenth International Conference on Patristic Studies Held in Oxford 1987*, Leuven, 1989, pp. 13–16.

[1] See now D. Stiernon, 'Néophyte le Reclus', *DS* XI (Paris, 1981), cols 99–110. (The final 'jugement d'ensemble' to be used with caution.) The bibliography missed two of my publications: "'Ανέκδοτον ὑπόμνημα τοῦ 'Οσίου Νεοφύτου τοῦ 'Εγκλείστου εἰς τὴν 'Αποκάλυψιν", *ΕΚΕΕΚ* 8 (1978), pp. 73–112, (translated as Chapter VII above), and "'Ο ὅσιος Νεόφυτος ὁ "Εγκλειστος καὶ αἱ ἀρχαὶ τῆς ἐν Κύπρῳ Φραγκοκρατίας", *ΕΚΕΕΚ* 10 (1980), pp. 31–83, (translated as Chapter IX above).

According to the information given in the twelfth chapter of his *Typicon*, Neophytos wrote sixteen books, and, although less than half survive, he is certainly the greatest monastic author of Byzantine Cyprus. In 1681 J.B. Cotelier published for the first time a work of Neophytos, the small essay *De calamitatibus Cypri*, which won immediate fame among the medievalists. Since then the students and editors of the Recluse have included such scholars as the eighteenth-century historian of Cyprus Archimandrite Kyprianos (first editor of the *Typicon*, Venice 1779), W. Stubbs, F.E. Warren, L. Petit, P. Anrich, H. Delehaye, M. Jugie, R. Janin, J. Darrouzès, C. Mango, E.M. Toniolo, M.-H. Congourdeau, and above all the Cypriot I.P. Tsiknopoullos. The manuscripts of the works and of the library of the saint – mostly in the Bibliothèque Nationale of Paris – have received the attention not only of Montfaucon, the Bollandists, H. Omont and R. Devreesse, but recently also of C. Astruc, P. Turyn and P. Canart. Despite all this, a good part of Nephytos's literary production remains unpublished, to the detriment of our knowledge of Byzantine provincial monasticism and scriptural exegesis in the era of the Komnenoi, the Angeloi and the Empire of Nicaea.

I have been studying St Neophytos for the last twenty years and published several small texts and studies. Now I have completed my edition of one of the most important works of the saint, his book *On the Commandments of Christ* (*Ad Iohannem fratrem de mandatis Christi*), preserved only in the Parisian Codex Coislinianus graecus 287, which is the original manuscript bearing the autograph corrections of the author and dated 1176. From the *Typicon* we know that this work was complemented later in the life of the author in the form of a now lost commentary on the Old Testament Commandments. The whole was named Ἑρμηνεία δεσποτικῶν ἐντολῶν (and we can note Chrysostom's preferred adjective δεσποτικός).[2]

St Neophytos's commentary on the Sermon on the Mount (Matth. 5–7) – for this is really what he means by the "Commandments of Christ" – is made up of ten homilies, of which the first, and the beginning of the second, have been lost due to damage to the *codex unicus*, which is both *acephalus ac fine mutilus*. These ten homilies are followed by three supplements: (a) a discourse on Christ-like obedience (fols 198^r–201^v), (b) an extract from a letter to the superior of a monastery on the nature of governing according to Christ's example (fols 201^v–202^v), and (c) a letter to a certain monk Euthymios on how to combine *hesychia* with coenobitic life in imitation of Christ's life (fols 202^v–207^v). It is my opinion that folios 40^r–45^r are at present displaced, having formed originally a fourth supplement, being an extract from a letter on fasting and the fasting days of the Christian year.

---

[2] Cf. A. Wenger, ed., *Jean Chrysostome, Huit Catéchèses baptismales inédites* [2], Paris, 1970, p. 116, note 3.

From the third homily we learn that the subject of the first one was, quite appropriately, repentance. That of the second homily is the Kingdom of God and paradise (fols 1^r–4^r): the third homily deals with baptism, love and forgiveness (fols 4^r–16^r), the fourth with prayer (fols 16^v–35^v), and the fifth with the keeping of the five senses (fols 35^v–65^r). With the sixth homily (fols 65^r–83^r) the author concentrates on a more systematic exposition of the Sermon on the Mount from Mat. 5:25 onwards. The central theme of the eighth homily is Christ's Second Coming (fols 117^r–144^v), that of the ninth the Commandment "Judge not, that you be not judged" (Mat. 7:1), with a digressive excursus on the twelve precious stones (fols 145^r–171^v), and the last homily deals with the different parables of Christ concerning spiritual husbandry, and concludes with a discourse on perfection insisting that no man can achieve absolute perfection while on earth, and, thus, no one is really self-sufficient, but always reliant on his brethren and fellow-men (fols 172^r–197^v).

The Recluse is a lively person who can never slavishly copy another author, not even a Father of the Church. St John Chrysostom's homilies on Matthew – or rather the *catenae* and *eclogae* based on them – the *Asceticon* of St Basil, a text of Anastasius of Sinai based on St Epiphanius of Cyprus, St Maximus the Confessor, etc., are clearly behind a number of interpretations and other passages, in the same way that the *Apophthegmata Patrum*, the *Ladder* and the various *Vitae* of the saints are used as sources of illustration by way of edifying example. Our author is the contemporary, or near contemporary, of Theophylact of Bulgaria, Niketas of Heraclea, Euthymios Zigabenos and Nikon of the Black Mountain.[3] His exegetical work is small in comparison with their commentaries and compilations. But in reading Neophytos I, at least, have frequently the impression of hearing a more authentic voice.

Here is an example of the use that our Hermit makes of Chrysostom. What seems to have impressed Zigabenos from Chrysostom's interpretation of Mat. 5:48, "You, therefore, must be perfect, as your heavenly Father is perfect",[4] is not so much the greatness of man's calling in Christ, but the fact that we are only asked to forgive our fellow-servants, whereas God himself forgives His own ungrateful slaves. With regard to man's adoption by God the only thing that he notes is that we become sons of God not by nature, but by likeness.[5] Theophylact on the other hand underlines the profit which

---

[3] See H.-G. Beck, *Kirche und theologische Literatur im Byzantinischen Reich*, Munich, 1959, pp. 649–55.

[4] *PG* 57, 269; cf. *PG* 49, 407–408.

[5] *PG* 129, 225. On Zigabenos and scriptural exegesis in the twelfth century, see the pertinent remarks of A.P. Lebedev *Istoričeskie očerki sostojanija vizantino-vostočnoj cerkvi ot konca XIgo do poloviny XVgo veka*, Moscow, 1902, pp. 384–94.

we gain by forgiving our enemies: we obtain a lighter punishment of our sins.
And he continues by allegorising God's rain and sun (cf. Mat. 5:45) as
knowledge and teaching.[6] As for Neophytos, he insists that the reward from
loving our enemies and praying for them lies in our becoming brothers and
imitators of Christ "as far as this is possible". For love of one's enemies not
only brings calmness and peace to the soul, but makes the soul a vessel of
the Holy Spirit.[7] Chrysostom's influence does not really extend much further
than the old Platonic warning "as far as this is possible", applied not to man's
likeness to God, but to the imitation of Christ by man. And if someone asks
– Neophytos writes in another context to Euthymios – "Who are you to want
to imitate Christ?", then you should answer him with another question: "In
that case why did Christ become a man?"[8]

St Neophytos the Recluse was a self-taught man who remained untouched
by the great currents of the literary renaissance under the Komnenoi. The
secret of his freedom and liveliness lies in his authentic holiness. In con-
tradistinction to his more celebrated contempories, Neophytos, like the early
monks, was imbued with a genuine and ardent love for Scripture, and, like
the Fathers, considered the main duty of the spiritual guide in his capacity
as a writer to be exegesis. He was also convinced, like St Symeon the New
Theologian, that the same Holy Spirit that inspired the Fathers is still active
in the Church. This was his apology to those who, tempted by the devil, accused
him of despising the Fathers in daring to compose new interpretations of the
Scriptures.[9]

Thus, in *Homily Nine* he insists that by applying Jesus' Commandment
"Judge not, that you be not judged" (Mat. 7:1) to bishops, rulers and judges
who dare judge and condemn their fellow-men even to death, without first
correcting their own selves, he is not "contradicting the all-holy Fathers",
but applying their general interpretation to those men whose specific job it
is to judge.[10] In another place having called Christ's Commandments "real
pearls", the Recluse feels so much at one with the Fathers that he goes on to
say that, because of this, the book which contains his interpretation of Christ's
Commandments could be called *Margaritai* in the same way that St John
Chrysostom's well-known *florilegium* is called *Margaritai*. "And this is not
strange at all, for Chrysostom's words and mine both come from the same

---

[6] *PG* 123, 201. On Theophylact's use of Chrysostom, see E. Marsenger, *Der Matthäuskommentar des Theophylaktos von Achrida*, Schweidnitz, 1924.

[7] Cod. Coisl. gr. 287, fols 6ᵛ–8ᵛ.

[8] Ibid., fol. 207ʳ.

[9] Ibid., fols 16ᵛff., 193ʳ. Cf. *AB* 26 (1907), pp. 217–18, *Marianum* 36 (1974), p. 238 and my study in Ἀπόστολος Βαρνάβας 39 (1978), pp 367–75, (translated above as Chapter VI).

[10] Cod. Coisl. gr. 287, fols 145ʳ–148ᵛ.

and only Spirit. And just as many men have the same name, so each pearl can be called a pearl without rivalry between them, and books may bear the same title without competition among them."[11]

Similar voices are rare in later Byzantium. They can only come from those who know themselves to share the same life as the Fathers, Christ's own life. And this, according to the Orthodox Church, is the most authentic *Nachleben* of the Fathers. In recognising Neophytos as a saint, his Church saw in him a real successor to the Fathers, and indeed one of them.

I would like to finish on this note, without burdening you with more factual details on the Matthaean text of St Neophytos, the interesting form of his Greek, his manuscript and its prime importance for the history of Cypriot Byzantine handwriting and book production, and so forth, all of which will, I hope, appear, in due time, in the introduction to my edition of the work.

---

[11] Ibid., fols 161^r–161^v.

XI

CYPRUS AS A STEPPING-STONE BETWEEN WEST AND EAST IN THE AGE OF THE CRUSADES: THE TWO CHURCHES *

When Richard Lionheart captured Cyprus in 1191, the island left behind the uneasy isolation of its last years under Byzantine rule and entered, in Gibbon's famous phrase, "the World's Debate". The establishment of a Crusader kingdom in Cyprus offered a unique opportunity to the Roman Church to restore the unity of Christendom from below through working together with a relatively large Orthodox population. The subsequent story is well-known and need not be repeated here. As in every similar situation the popes subordinated the spiritual struggle to spiritual politics. Christian unity was conceived in terms of the conversion of the Greeks to the Roman faith, the realisation of which was thought to be only a matter of time. The highest priority was given to turning the Greek clergy into a reserve force which could be drawn upon to provide instruments for the papal machinery of goverment.

The Hildebrandine papacy approached the island as a good military base for the "sacred wars" of a Church mobilised for the Crusades, while the zeal of the Avignon Curia for the subjugation of the Greeks was compelled to retreat in the face of the tolerance required by state interests, and the Renaissance popes only remembered Cyprus when it intruded into their pre-

---

* This paper was originally published as a communication in English to the Fifteenth International Congress of Historical Sciences, Bucharest (*XVe Congrès international des sciences historiques, Rapports*, vol. II, Bucharest (Romanian Academy of Sciences), 1980, pp. 216-21). A Greek version was published by the author in Ἀπόστολος Βαρνάβας 41 (1980), pp. 438-43, from which the present English translation was made.

occupation with Italian politics. A little after the Council of Trent the reply of Bishop Logaras to the emissary the Latin archbishop had sent to him was:

> "My son, boundaries have been set between us Greeks and you Latins and jurisdictions have been drawn between us and our flocks, so that the care of my Greeks belongs to me and that of the Latins to your archbishop. The eighth and ninth councils were called to settle questions relevant only to you Latins and are of no concern to us."[1]

Florence and Trent were thus rejected completely and it is difficult to find a stronger denial of Christian unity even in sixteenth-century Istanbul. Rome was becoming a victim of her own divisive policy.

The Holy See's destructive course of conduct in Cyprus began in 1196 when Celestine III, in an act of flagrant violation of the canon law of the undivided Church, abolished the autocephaly of the Church of Cyprus and appointed a Latin hierarchy over the island. The arrangements of Honorius III in 1221 and 1222 made the situation worse. The number of Greek bishops was reduced to four, instead of fourteen; they were subordinated to the Latin bishops as their suffragans, "in accordance with the custom of the kingdom of Jerusalem"; they were driven out of the cities and ordered to reside in outlying villages of the Latin dioceses.

On 9 May 1231, in the face of the ever-increasing resistance of the Easterners, the pious companion of St Louis of France, Archbishop Eustorgius de Montaigu, reacted by burning thirteen Orthodox monks. The orders of Pope Gregory IX concerning these Greek monks who had denied the validity of the *azymes* were categorical: "as against heretics". His reply to the horrified protest of the patriarch of Constantinople, Germanos II, consisted of a graphic interpretation of Peter's cutting off the ear of the high priest's servant.[2]

Towards the end of the relentless papal wars against the emperors of the West, Innocent IV overturned the policy of his predecessors towards the

[1] Fra Angelo Calepio, *Vera et fidelissima Narratione del successo dell'espugnatione & defensione del Regno de Cipro*, in Estienne de Lusignan, *Chorograffia et breve historia universale dell'isola de Cipro ... per in sino al 1572*, Bologna, 1573. Cf. C.D. Cobham, *Excerpta Cypria*, Cambridge, 1908, p. 143.

[2] See Th. Papadopoullos, Μαρτύριον Κυπρίων, commemorative volume on the fiftieth anniversary of the periodical Ἀπόστολος Βαρνάβας, Nicosia, 1975, pp. 307–38. Letter of Gregory IX to Archbishop Eustorgius in L. de Mas Latrie, *Histoire de l'île de Chypre sous le règne de la Maison de Lusignan*, vol. III, Paris, 1855, pp. 629–30. Letter of Germanos II to Gregory IX and the papal reply in K.N. Sathas, Μεσαιωνικὴ Βιβλιοθήκη, vol. II, Venice, 1873, pp. 39–49. Cf. A.L. Tautu, *Acta Honorii III (1216–1227) et Gregorii IX (1227–1241)*, Vatican, 1950, nos 179, 179ᵃ; V. Laurent et J. Darrouzès, *Dossier grec de l'union de Lyon (1273–1277)*, Paris, 1976, pp. 576 and 130 note 1, 505.

Christian East and indeed Cyprus. From 1228 the ruler of the kingdom of Jerusalem was a viper of the house of Hohenstaufen, Conrad, son of Frederick II the Antichrist, whose immediate heir old enough to succeed according to hereditary right was the king of Cyprus, Henry I. From the beginning of his reign the pope was concerned that the archbishop of Nicosia and the bishops under him should not upset the king. In March 1247 the king was released from his oath of allegiance to his superior, the emperor, while the pope's flirtations with the Orthodox reached their climax. Few popes before him, writes Sir Steven Runciman, "had been so constant, so untiring and so courageous in battling for the papal cause; but few had been so unscrupulous, so treacherous and so ready to use spiritual weapons for a worldly end".[3] With the end of the war the tranquillity of the kingdom of Cyprus became a matter of indifference and the Cypriot Bull of Alexander IV stands as a monument not only to that pope's indecisiveness and mediocrity but also to the new fears of the Curia after the battle of Pelagonia (1259), which, as it rightly judged, signalled the end of the Latin Empire in the East. Unity between Latins and Orthodox in Cyprus would henceforth remain on the superficial level of the bull even after the Council of Nicosia of 1340, when the Greek bishops voluntarily consented to make a profession of the Roman faith. An eloquent witness to the interest, or lack of interest, of the popes in Cyprus is the fact that "in the sixty-nine years from 1291 to 1360, the archbishops were absent for something like thirty-six".[4] The situation never changed very much and in 1557 Pope Paul IV expressed surprise that his predecessors had left Cyprus for such a long time without an archbishop.[5]

For the Christian East Cyprus was a Western wedge within the body of Orthodoxy. For the West Cyprus was an outpost of Latin Christianity in the East. The stark reality, at all events, was that at the time when Boccaccio (1313–1375) was dedicating his "Genealogy of the Gods" to King Hugh IV of Cyprus the days had long since passed since Thomas Aquinas (1224–1274) had written his treatise "On Kingship" for the easternmost Catholic king, Hugh II. In 1350, when Archbishop Philippe de Chambarlhac felt obliged – to the great chagrin of the subjects of the pontiff in Cyprus[6] – to issue two

---

[3] S. Runciman, *The Sicilian Vespers: A History of the Mediterranean World in the Later Thirteenth Century*, Cambridge, 1958, p. 33. J. Gill ("The Tribulations of the Greek Church in Cyprus 1196–c.1280", *Byzantinische Forschungen* 5 (1977), pp. 73–93) is unaware of the historical reasons for the tolerance of Innocent IV towards the Greeks and presents him as "ecumenical and with a breadth of thought far in advance of his contemporaries".

[4] G.Hill, *A History of Cyprus*, vol. III, Cambridge, 1948, p. 1079.

[5] Ibid., p. 1096.

[6] A principle of the government of Clement VI (1342–1352) was that "the pontiff should make all his subjects happy" (G.Mollat, *The Popes at Avignon*, London, 1963, p. 38).

stern orders against mixed marriages on the island, it was already apparent
that Aphrodite, in keeping with her genealogy, had already begun her undermining work. While Ares was inspiring King Peter and his brave Order of
the Sword, the role of the chaste Artemis fell on the redoubtable Carmelite
saint, Peter de Thomas, apostolic legate in the East.

In 1359 this Holy Inquisitor decided to summon the Greek bishops of
the island – once again – "to the true faith and obedience to the Church of
Rome", and attempted to anoint them according to the Latin manner in
Nicosia's Cathedral of Hagia Sophia. Crying "Death to the legate", the
Greek populace came very near to burning him on the spot. "At which
time," notes his biographer Philippe de Mezières, "all the faithful ... regarded
the legate as a voluntary martyr."[7]

The patriarch of Constantinople, however, was of a different opinion.
"Repel the wolf of Arabia, who overturns the word of truth," wrote Kallistos
I to the Cypriots after this episode, "and in my view you will be called
genuine martyrs".[8]

A final attempt at the salvation of the degenerate noble feudal leaders
of Cyprus and their schismatic serfs was made by St Brigid of Sweden.

> "The Son of God says: This city is Gomorrah ... for this reason, people
> of Cyprus, I tell you that ... I will extirpate your seed from the kingdom
> of Cyprus ... . With regard to the Greeks ... they are unworthy to come
> to me after death ... until ... they submit devoutly to the Roman faith,
> conforming completely to the sacred requirements and forms of this
> Church."[9]

The totalitarian visions of the Swedish princess, however, were destined
to be dispelled not long afterwards by another holy prince, John VI
Kantakouzenos. On account of the Latin domination Cyprus became an
asylum for antipalamites such as Cyril Sides, Arsenios of Tyre, Ignatios of
Antioch, Antony Phoinikes, Atonemes, Gerasimos, John Kyparissiotes,
Antony Kolybas and others. Through the influence of these, and probably
of the Cypriot antipalamite metropolitan of Thessalonica, Hyakinthos, and
also on account of the presence in Cyprus of George Lapithes, a friend of
Gregoras and Irene Choumnaina, and other lesser humanists such as

---

[7] H.J. Magoulias, "A Study in Roman Catholic and Greek Orthodox Church Relations
on the Island of Cyprus between the Years A.D.1196 and 1360", *GOTR* 10 (1964), pp. 75–106,
esp p. 100.

[8] J. Darrouzès, *Les Regestes des Actes du Patriarcat de Constantinople*, vol. I, part 5, *Les Regestes de
1310 à 1376*, Paris, 1977, no. 2443.

[9] *Revelationes sanctae Brigittae*, vol. II, Rome, 1628, vii.16, vii.19.

Athanasios Lependrenos or Leo, the Greek bishops of Cyprus and their courts were drawn to the antipalamite camp, which – to the great joy of the vain Gregoras – received, it seems, the favour of King Hugh IV. The Latin theologians learned the little they knew of palamism through humanists such as Demetrios Kydones or the antipalamite refugees in Cyprus.[10]

On the other hand, relations between Cyprus and the hesychasts were not completely lacking. According to the *Life* of St Gregory of Sinai (*c.*1280–1346), written by the patriarch Kallistos I, the saint spent some time in Cyprus as a young man, was greatly loved by the Orthodox there and indeed received the monastic σχῆμα (habit) from a Cypriot monk.[11] Another member of the later circle of hesychasts, St Sabas the Younger, whose *Life* was written by the patriarch Philotheos Kokkinos, the biographer of St Gregory Palamas spent many years in Cyprus during the second decade of the fourteenth century, living as a fool for Christ's sake. The Latins took him for a lunatic, but among the Orthodox his fame became so great that he was finally forced to leave the island.[12] Joseph Kalothetos addressed a letter "To certain monks who have come from Cyprus and sought a simple explanation of both sides of the question".[13] Patriarch Kallistos I, in his letter mentioned above, wrote that he had first sent "frequent exhortations" to the clergy and the *archons* of the island, and indeed it should not be forgotten that in 1326 lay opposition to the Latins and the Unionist Greek hierarchy was so strong on the island that according to the evidence of Pope John XXII himself, the Greeks of Cyprus refused to receive communion at the divine Eucharist if it had not been brought from Constantinople.[14]

We know that between 1350 and 1360 the bishop of Solea was an antipalamite. It appears, however, that John of Karpasia belonged to the Orthodox side. Moreover, in about 1370 John Kantakouzenos sent a long letter defending St Gregory Palamas and his teaching. The imperial intervention was decisive. The current was deflected to such an extent that in 1401

[10] See J. Meyendorff, *Introduction à l'étude de Grégoire Palamas*, Paris, 1959, pp. 152 and note 123, 67, 126–7; E. Tsolakes, "Ὁ Γρηγόριος Λαπίθης καὶ ἡ ἡσυχαστικὴ ἔριδα", Ἑλληνικά 18 (1964), pp. 83–96; K.P. Kyrres, "Ὁ Κύπριος Ἀρχιεπίσκοπος Θεσσαλονίκης Ὑάκινθος (1345–56) καὶ ὁ ρόλος του εἰς τὸν ἀντιπαλαμιτικὸν ἀγῶνα", *KS* 25 (1961), pp. 89–122; ibid, "Ἡ Κύπρος καὶ τό ἡσυχαστικὸν ζήτημα κατὰ τὸν ΙΔ´ αἰῶνα", *KS* 26 (1962), pp. 19–31.

[11] N. Pomialovskij, *Zhitie izhe vo sviatyh otsa nashego Grigorija Sinaita*, St Petersburg, 1896, pp. 4–5.

[12] A. Papadopoulos-Kerameus, *Ἀνάλεκτα ἱεροσολυμιτικῆς σταχυολογίας*, vol. V, St Petersburg, 1898, pp. 190–359, esp. pp. 216–43.

[13] D. Tsames, "Ἰωσὴφ Καλοθέτου, Ἐπιστολαὶ καὶ βίος ὁσίου Γρηγορίου", *EEThSPTh* 19 (1974), pp. 47–129, letter no. 4.

[14] J. Hackett, *A History of the Orthodox Church of Cyprus*, London, 1901, p. 127.

Manuel Kalekas laments that the Greek community of Cyprus was pro-palamite.[15] So overwhelming was the victory that even George Lapithes himself has left no trace in the history of the Church of Cyprus apart from his Latinizing treatise on the seven sacraments, which survived anonymously and so altered and embellished with Byzantine elements as to be unrecognisable. The only Church which used Lapithes' diatribe without corrections was the Church of Constantinople. Patriarch Jeremias II incorporated it into his first reply to the Lutherans of Tübingen in 1576. This was also to be the revenge of the Church of Cyprus against the arrogant president of the Patriarchal Academy of Constantinople, Joseph Bryennios, who in 1412, for heterodox reasons, blocked the secret union of the Greek hierarchy with the ecumenical throne. By a striking historical irony the patriarchal letters of 1576 connect Joseph with Cyprus: after George Lapithes the second most important source for the letters is Joseph Bryennios himself.[16]

Writing in 1979, Jean Darrouzès described the relations between Greeks and Latins in Cyprus in the fourteenth century as follows: "The two communities lived alongside one another without real communication or exchanges."[17] In 1438, however, Aeneas Sylvius, later Pope Pius II, enumerated the various Churches represented at the Council of Basle and had this to say about the Latin representation from Cyprus: "I say nothing about the Cypriots, who are more Greek-minded than Latin."[18]

Four years later the island acquired a queen who was not only Greek-minded but Greek by birth. Helen Palaiologaina, daughter of the despot Theodore II of the Peloponnese, became the wife of John II of Cyprus on 3 February 1442. Until her death in 1458, this "most cunning Greek", who seems to have been a pupil of Gemistos Plethon, did everything she could to overturn the divisive Alexandrine Bull and secure the unity and survival of the kingdom with its indigenous faith and cultural tradition, namely, Greek Orthodoxy. If the marriage of Ivan III of Moscow with her cousin, Zoe-Sophia Palaiologaina, proved to be "the tsar's marrying in the Vatican", the appearance of Helen in the East in the years of Constantinople's death

---

[15] J. Darrouzès, "Lettre inédite de Jean Cantacuzène relative à la controverse palamite", *REB* 17 (1959), pp. 7–27.

[16] See J. Darrouzès, "Textes synodaux Chypriotes", *REB* 37 (1979), pp. 5–122, esp. pp. 37–55; G. Florovsky, "An Early Ecumenical Correspondence", *World Lutheranism of Today: A Tribute to Anders Nygren*, Stockholm–Lund, 1950, pp. 98–112 (the author is unaware of the patriarch's dependence on Lapithes).

[17] J. Darrouzès, "Textes synodaux", p. 73.

[18] J. Haller, *Concilium Basiliense: Studie und Dokumente zur Geschichte der Jahre 1431–1437*, vol. VII, Basle, 1926, p. 193. Cf. Th. Papadopoullos, "Chypre: frontière ethnique et socio-culturelle du monde byzantin", XVe Congrès International d'Études Byzantines, *Rapports et Co-Rapports*, Athens, 1976, esp. pp. 16–42.

agony was the epiphany of a new Cleopatra. Indeed, Helen called her first daughter, who died in infancy, Cleopatra – a whole political programme in a name.[19]

The attempt of Pope Callistus III Borgia to marry his nephew Peter Luis, commander-in-chief of the forces of the Church and brother of the future notorious Pope Alexander Borgia, to Helen's second daughter, Carlotta, met with failure. Nevertheless Cyprus was not backward in producing its own Borgia. James II, bastard son of John II by his Greek mistress, Marietta of Patras, was a typical "Renaissance prince", who would have pleased Nicolo Machiavelli no less than Cesare Borgia. During his brief reign James humbled the Lusignans and exalted his fellow-Greeks. He made the mistake, however, of trusting in Venice, "and in this way," wrote the humanist, Peter Bembo, a cardinal and friend of Lucretia Borgia, "the kingdom of Cyprus was reduced to the status of a province".[20]

Ten years before the end of Venetian rule we are informed that there were occasions when "the most noble Rectors of Cyprus" on their way to Hagia Sophia for a church service, had to hunt around for a priest to act as celebrant. At the same time, when they desired to celebrate in Greek churches they had to take portable altars with them, because the Greeks "did not allow any Latin to celebrate the liturgy on their own altars".[21] For the removal of these scandals and divisions between the two communities, the only solution, according to Bernardo Sagredo, was "the expulsion of the Greek bishops". The realisation of the wise counsel of this procurator of St Mark's was prevented by Selim the Sot.

The Crusader kingdom of Cyprus (1191–1571) failed to establish a bridge between Eastern and Western Christianity. Many reasons can be put forward in explanation of this: the island's lack of importance as a theological centre; the irrefutability of Byzantine propaganda: "the Greek hates to be governed by people of another race and another religion"; the later Byzantine conception of heresy as a racist phenomenon; Orthodoxy's role as ultimately the factor which defined East Roman Hellenism; the unhesitating ambiguity of the Greek bishops; the feudalistic and exploitative

---

[19] A. Vacalopoulos, "Une reine grecque de Chypre mal comprise par les historiens, Hélène Paléologine (1442–1458)" in A. Papageorgiou, ed., Πρακτικὰ τοῦ Πρώτου Διεθνοῦς Κυπριολογικοῦ Συνεδρίου, vol. II, Nicosia, 1972, pp. 277–80 (strangely, the author does not mention Cleopatra, on whom see E. de Lusignan, Chronograffia, fol. 60ᵛ. It should be noted that the mother of Helen was Cleope Malatesta).

[20] On the Borgia plans concerning Cyprus see G. Hill, A History of Cyprus, vol. III, pp. 541–3. On John II as a Renaissance prince see N. Iorga, France de Chypre, Paris, 1931, pp. 68–9.

[21] Bernardo Sagredo, Report to the Venetian Senate (1562), fragm. in de Mas Latrie, Histoire de l'île de Chypre, vol. III, pp. 540–66; Fra Angelo Calepio, Vera et fidelissima Narratione.

character of this Western colony, and so on. The greatest reason for failure, however, lay in the papal preference for emperors over the simple faithful, for spiritual politics rather than the struggle of the spiritual life. In the end the Frankish period was nothing other than the Latin captivity of the Church of Cyprus.

XII

AN UNPUBLISHED LETTER IN SLAVONIC FROM ARCHBISHOP CHRISTODOULOS I TO THE TSAR MICHAEL FEODOROVICH ROMANOV*

Archbishop Christodoulos (*archiepiscopico munere fungebatur* AD 1606/7–1639, 1640/1?), of hellenised French Lusignan(?) and Venetian Lucadelli stock, and at the same time a cousin of the Latin bishop of Paphos, Pietro Vespa, and of the Muslim brother-in-law of the Ottoman Pasha of Cyprus, Esseyit Mehmed, is one of the stranger figures of the period of Turkish rule in Cyprus. Consecrated by the Protestantising Patriarch Kyrillos Loukaris,[1] Christodoulos governed the Orthodox Church of Cyprus for thirty-three years, he himself being, at least from 1630, cryptocatholic. Although, according to Loukaris who consecrated him, "he was not learned and without a share in the wisdom of foreign peoples or of our own," he developed an unprecedented correspondence in the Italian, Spanish, Slavonic and Greek languages with leaders such as the duke of Savoy, the king of Spain, the pope and the Russian tsar. When in extreme old age he fell from office, his opponents gave out that he had died and he was lamented as such by the cardinals of the Roman Propaganda in their consistory of 19 August 1639, only for him to

---

* Translated from "Ἀνέκδοτος σλαβονικὴ ἐπιστολὴ τοῦ Ἀρχιεπισκόπου Χριστοδούλου Α΄ πρὸς τὸν Τσάρον Μιχαὴλ Φεοντώροβιτς Ρωμάνωφ", *KS* 41 (1977), pp. 7–21.

[1] That I should not seem to exaggerate and the reader gain the impression that Christodoulos was a uniquely paradoxical phenonenon in the period of Ottoman rule, I would remind the reader that Loukaris served as patriarch of Alexandria from 1601 to 1621, patriarch of Constantinople for six weeks in 1612 and continuously in six different sets of circumstances between 1621 and 1638. In the seventeenth century, however, in a period of seventy-three years there was a change of ecumenical patriarch forty-three times.

reappear on the stage, however, within a few months and live in harmony at first with his successor, Parthenios, later recovering his throne (the "Good Geron" according to the Latins) at the desire of the sultan and with the help of the Holy See and occupying it until his death a little before 14 July 1641.

As an ecclesiastical politician Christodoulos belonged to the period of Frankish rather than Ottoman rule, or rather, he provides a bridge from the Frankish to the Ottoman periods. This is not only because those who were archbishop before him from 1572 to 1606 are very little known to us and do not seem to have anything special about them, but also because his whole activity and conduct reveal a person who by blood but also psychologically belonged to the Frankish world and accepted Turkish rule as a temporary phenomenon which could shortly in the not too distant future go away. This is how we may explain, I believe, the "amphibious" character of his position between Orthodoxy and Catholicism (a phenomenon, as in the cases of Nikephoros and Hilarion Kigalas, which was sociological rather than religious), his correspondence and understanding with the duke of Savoy, Charles Emmanuel I (1580–1630)[2] and the king of Spain, Philip III (1598–1621)[3] and his optimistic expectations of these, as also his whole policy towards the Holy See and the Ottoman authorities in Cyprus.[4] His policy, the seeds of which he manifestly inherited from his predecessors, and especially from the learned Benjamin, put its stamp on the history of the Cypriot Church throughout the seventeenth century and opened wide the doors both to the cryptocatholicism of the archbishops who were his immediate successors and to the vain hopes of these and the *rayahs* that the West would one day move to help them. This futile policy (which, moreover, has its place within the framework and currents of the Greco-Latin seventeenth century[5]) was cut short in 1660 by the more formal recognition of the archbishops by the Divan and was changed definitely during the archiepiscopate of the great Philotheos (1734–1759), which coincided with the new era which began with the Venetian occupation of the Peloponnese (1685–1718), the coming to maturity of Orthodox counter-propaganda[6] in the person of

---

[2] See L. Philippou, Ἡ Ἐκκλησία τῆς Κύπρου ἐπὶ Τουρκοκρατίας, Nicosia, 1975, pp. 174ff.

[3] See I.K. Hasiotes, Ἰσπανικὰ ἔγγραφα τῆς Κυπριακῆς ἱστορίας, (16–17 αἰ.), Nicosia, 1972.

[4] See Zach. N. Tsirpanlis, Ἀνέκδοτα ἔγγραφα ἐκ τῶν ἀρχείων τοῦ Βατικανοῦ (1625–1667), Nicosia, 1973.

[5] See T. Ware, *Eustratios Argenti. A study of the Greek Church under Turkish Rule*, Oxford, 1964, ch. 1.

[6] To note 1 may be added that this great patriarch was ordained deacon at the age of 11, metropolitan at 25 and was elected patriarch at the age of 28.

Dositheos, patriarch of Jerusalem (*fungebatur* 1669–1707), and the Antiochene schism of 1724. Whatever the case, however, there can be no doubt about the sincere love of Christodoulos for the island, his assiduous indefatigability, his organisational abilities and his administrative gifts, the greatest of which appears to have been the decisiveness of his character. In spite of the obvious shortcomings of Christodoulos, the general impression one gains both from the older reports and from more recent information[7] confirms the opinion expressed by Loukaris about the goodness of the man who upon his election to the archiepiscopal throne of the island brought with him the calming of passions and peace.

The attitude of Christodoulos towards the end of his life, however, in his conflict with Parthenios is especially noteworthy. Whatever errors he fell into, he did not allow his personal struggle to result in harm to his Church and when he understood the hopelessness of his struggle, according to Giovanni Battista da Todi, "Il Vechio Arciuesco Christodulo, per non multiplicare scandali e per timore della uita e delli danari, ha ceduto il tutto e si è ritirato in un monasterio qui fuor di Nicosia e uiue in santa pace."[8]

This voluntary resignation and willing withdrawal of Christodoulos while "il Giouane proseguisca il suo offitio"[9] and his return after a few months, when the displeasure of the Porte with Parthenios became clear, show that Christodoulos was able until the end to place the "continuity of the office" of archbishop in the Church of his country above his own person. If Christodoulos was no Philotheos, he was still superior by far to the contemporary Cypriot bishops in moral character and zeal for the Church and he strived on behalf of the island no less, it seems, than the other "uneducated" archbishop of the period of Turkish rule, Chrysanthos. But in contrast to the latter, in his old age Christodoulos had the good fortune to find Parthenios his enemy and not the *oikonomos* Kyprianos.

According to Dr Olga A. Belobrova, in her book *The Cypriot Circle in Ancient Russian Literature*,[10] in the Central State Archive of Ancient Documents of the USSR in Moscow there must be at least four letters of Christodoulos, archbishop of Cyprus, to the Tsar Michael Feodorovich (*imperabat* 1613–1645). They are clearly systatic letters written by the archbishop on behalf of several missionary Cypriot monks who went to the tsar to ask for alms. The first,

---

[7] See K.P. Kyrres "Νέαι ἱστορικαὶ καὶ προσωπογραφικαὶ εἰδήσεις ἐξ ἄρτι ἐκδοθέντων Κυπριακῶν ἐγγράφων. Ἐπίμετρον περὶ τῶν Ἀρχιεπισκόπων Χριστοδούλου, Παρθενίου καὶ Νικηφόρου", *Κυπριακὸς Λόγος* 6 (1974), pp. 47–9, 96–9, 178–83.

[8] Zach. Tsirpanlis, Ἀνέκδοτα ἔγγραφα, p. 95, lines 52–56.

[9] Ibid. p. 87, lines 18–19.

[10] (in Russian) Leningrad, 1972. Cf. pp. 50, 86–87, 89–90.

written in Slavonic, accompanied the hieromonk Leontios and the monk
Gerasimos of the monastery of the Archangels Michael and Gabriel and is
given below in translation. The remaining three were written in Greek and
accompanied in turn:

(a) in 1628 Archimandrite Symeon and hieromonk Gerasimos of the island
"of Cyprus, city of Famagusta, of the monastery of the Archangels";[11]
(b) in 1629 the Archimandrite Joasaph and the monk Gerasimos of the
monastery of St Nicholas;[12]
(c) in 1632 the Archimandrite Nikephoros and the hieromonk Pachomios
and monk Matthew of the monastery of St Mamas.[13]

Since it is known that Abbot Sophronios also came to Russia to collect
funds with the deacon Joannikios and the monk Paisios of the monastery of
the Annunciation,[14] and also that in the years 1623–25 visits to Moscow of
Cypriot clergy are mentioned in the Russian archives, we must suppose that
Christodoulos sent other letters to the tsar which have been lost or not yet
discovered or not been referred to by Dr Belobrova.

There is no doubt at all that the surviving letters of Christodoulos must
contain precious information on Cypriot history from those years.
Unfortunately, however, the author gives us neither the text nor precise
details about their content. The only thing that may be concluded without
difficulty is that the monasteries referred to were successful in securing help
from the tsar and that the cause of their distress was the Turks.

I hope in the future to have the opportunity to study these letters of
Christodoulos at first hand and to publish them in their entirety. In the

---

[11] *Kipr'skoovo ostrova goroda Amogusta grechene, monstirja arhistratigov Mihaila i Gavriila* says the
title mentioned on p. 87. Until the publication of Christodoulos's systatic letter, and that of
Patriarch Kyrillos of Constantinople (Belobrova, p. 87, n. 5) and the relevant documents from
the Russian state archives, it is impossible for us to be absolutely sure that it concerns the
same monastery of the Archangels about which the first letter also speaks, even though I suspect
that the "city of Famagusta" may be a mistake in the Russian source, or simply indicates perhaps
the port of embarkation of the foreigners. At all events there is no evidence elsewhere of a
monastery of the Archangels in Famagusta itself, even though C. Enhart, *L'Art Gothique et la
Renaissance en Chypre*, I, Paris, 1899, p. 264, says that there is evidence in the fourteenth
century of a church of St Michael with a cemetery outside the walls of Famagusta.
[12] Of Stegi? Of the Priests? The first was restored, as is known, in 1638 under Nikephoros,
abbot of Kykkos; the second, to judge from the inscriptions in the north-east transept and
the western narthex, was restored perhaps in 1633.
[13] Of Morphou, I imagine. Only the publication of the letters will solve these problems.
According to a note of Dr Belobrova on p. 20 of her book the monastery is referred to as in
the last extremities on account of Turkish pillaging.
[14] Pallouriotissa?

meantime I have judged it useful to publish the first letter in translation from the Slavonic original of Christodoulos as edited by Dr Belobrova in the fourth appendix of her book, pp. 89–90. I should like to express my gratitude to Dr Olga Belobrova, member of the Institute of Russian Philology of the Academy of Sciences of the USSR, who had the kindness to send me this work of hers and to permit the use I have made of it in this study.[15]

The prototype of the Slavonic letter of Christodoulos is in the Central State Archives of the USSR, Cupboard 52, per. 4, year 1626, no. 11. It was written for Christodoulos by someone staying in Nicosia at that time who knew Russian and was signed by the archbishop in Greek. The editor observes that the writer of the letter was skilled in calligraphy and believes that he was an educated Slav who was influenced by south-Slav and Greek orthography.[16]

In plate V of her book, facing p. 32, the Russian author prints a photograph of the Greek signature and stamp of Archbishop Christodoulos. The signature is clearly legible and reads as follows:

† ὁ ταπεινὸς Χριστόδουλος ἀρχιεπίσκοπος Κύπρου, εὐχέτης τῆς ἁγίας σου βασιλείας†

It is certainly autograph and is given within a complicated monogram, according to the custom of the time. Strangely, there is no error in orthography.

The seal on the left, as far as I can see from the photograph, bears around the edge the inscription: ΧΡΙΣΤΟΔΟΥΛΟΣ ΑΡΧ(ΙΕΠΙΣΚΟΠΟΣ) ΚΥΠΡΟΥ [...] and in the centre an image reminiscent of that found by Zach. N. Tsirpanlis,[17] although we know from elsewhere that in 1628 Christodoulos's seal had a representation of the Theotokos in the middle.[18]

That the Archangel Michael was specially honoured in the East and in Cyprus there is widespread evidence.[19] But it seems that there was an entirely exceptional devotion to the Archangel in the Turkish period in the environs of Nicosia. Apart from the monastery of the Archangel of Lakatamia, we have in the region the monastery of the Destroying Archangel, the church of the Archangel of Trypiotes within the city and another church of the Archangel at Kaimakli. In the letter given below Christodoulos does not of course

---

[15] My thanks are also due to Messrs C.P. Kyrris, A. Papageorgiou and K. Hadjipsaltes.

[16] Op. cit., p. 22.

[17] Op. cit., p. 57.

[18] Ἐκκλησιαστικὴ Ἀλήθεια, 1904, no. 6, p. 71: in L. Philippou, Ἡ Ἐκκλησία Κύπρου, p. 261.

[19] See H. Delehaye, "Saints de Chypre", AB 26 (1907), p. 208.

specify for the tsar precisely which monastery is the one in question. I believe, however, that there can be little doubt that it is the monastery of Lakatamia (or Katalyon) since it may be deduced from what is said by Christodoulos that, formerly at least, the monastery belonged to the bishop of Tamaseia – therefore it was not in Nicosia but within the territory of the diocese of Tamassos (which is the case with the monastery of Lakatamia). This monastery, the date of foundation of which is unknown, was the seat of Archbishop Parthenios of Cyprus after 1640, and perhaps of Christodoulos himself in 1639 and imme-diately afterwards of Nikephoros (1640/1–1672/3). It is worth noting that in the document of Archbishop James II (1710–1718)[20] mention is made that the monastery of the Archangels was dedicated "in the most holy archdio-cese of all Cyprus" by Archbishop Nikephoros, which implies that previously it did not belong to the archdiocese, a fact now confirmed and clarified by our letter. The monastery fell later into the hands "of Latins and Hagarenes", was rebuilt by Archbishop Germanos, was given by him as a pledge to Ibrahim Aga, captain of the ceremonial guard of the imperial Palace, and at last to save it from destruction was ceded by James II to the monastery of Kykkos in 1713 for 1 500 piastres. It is a *metochion* of Kykkos to this day, now unforgiveably abandoned with even the church in ruins.[21]

From the Russian archives Dr Belobrova gives information in passing on pp. 15, 19 and 22 of her work about the mission of the monks of the monastery of the Archangels to Russia. It is mentioned in close connection with this that the bearer of the letter, the hieromonk Leontios, died on Turkish soil before he reached the borders of Russia and that the monk Gerasimos accompanied by the hieromonk Joseph and three lay servants, James Athanasiou, Philip Konstantinou and Demetrios Philippou, thus appeared without Leontios at the frontier town of Putivl. When the letter of introduction of Christodoulos was read, which only mentioned Leontios and Gerasimos, the explanation was given that after the death of Leontios, Gerasimos took with him his fellow-countryman Joseph from the monastery of St Sabbas in Jassy, and the laymen joined up with him later, "on the road". From Moscow the order was finally given that only Gerasimos should proceed to that city and all the rest should be sent back "to the place from which they had come"!

We are not told whether Gerasimos received all the help which he sought or only a portion of it, although it is mentioned explicitly that he met

---

[20] See G. Kargiotou, "Ἡ Μονὴ Παλλουριωτίσσης", *KS* 13 (1949), pp. 47–81, esp. p. 56.

[21] So far as I know, the best study on the monastery and the church is still I.K. Peristianes, "Μονογραφία τῆς Μονῆς Ἀρχαγγέλου Μιχαήλ", *Παγκύπριον Λεύκωμα*, 1925, pp. 159–73.

with generosity from the tsar (who therefore, in accordance with Christodoulos's promise, must be regarded as the "new founder" of the monastery of the Archangel). It is difficult to judge the contemporary value of the sum of 140000 Turkish piastres (ἄσπρα) which Christodoulos sought for the monastery.[22] In 1713 it is already mentioned that the monastery was sold for 1 500 piastres, although Germanos (1694–1705) had bought it for 2 500 piastres. It is known that in 1589 the church of St Lazaros of Larnaca was bought by the Greeks for 3 000 piastres.[23] These sums sound derisory and Sir George Hill regarded the cost of purchase of St Lazaros as symbolic. That a whole monastery should be given as a pledge for 1 500 piastres seems incredible. Surely the sum should be understood as referring to kurush (γρόσια), which would amount to 180000 piastres, which means that the price that Gerasimos had to pay was about 300000 piastres. Our sum of 140 000 piastres seems thus to fit in with the prices and values of the end of the seventeenth and the beginning of the eighteenth centuries.

It should in consequence be noted that document no. 30 of I.K. Hasiotes[24] also refers to the problems of the monastery of the Archangel Michael, which having suffered severely under the Turks had need of 3 000 scudi. The king of Spain, having received the representatives of the monastery who were sent to him, "fray Sofronio y su compañero," gives through this document, dated 4 August 1607, an instruction to the viceroy of Naples, Don Juan Alonso Pimentel de Herrera, that the necessary funds should be collected there by the monks. What is said about the disposal of the sacred vessels and other heirlooms of the monstery gives us the background to the content of Christodoulos's letter to the tsar of 1626. It seems that upon the death of James the Turks came to receive not only what was owed to them but the property of the deceased bishop and the whole monastery. I.K. Hasiotes correctly submitted in his notes that "Sophronios and his companion" must be identified with the similarly named two monks who on 21 August 1606 were recommended by the papal secretariat to the apostolic nuncio in Madrid, Antonio Caetani. Moreover, in the new light of Christodoulos's letter the possibility should not be excluded of the identification of these with the monks Leontios and Sophronios who in 1616 received letters of introduction from the same secretariat to the same nuncio for similar help.[25] This Leontios could be our Leontios the *diakonetes* of the monastery of the Archangel,

---

[22] On the value of the Turkish piastre about forty years later, in 1668, see Louis de Mas Latrie, *Histoire de l'île de Chypre sous le règne des princes de la Maison de Lusignan*, III, Paris, 1855, pp. 580ff.

[23] Sir George Hill, *A History of Cyprus*, IV, Cambridge, 1952, p. 306 and note 2.

[24] Ἰσπανικὰ ἔγγραφα, pp. 49–50.

[25] Ibid., p. 50.

for since in 1607/8 the two monks accomplished against their expectation the collection of funds in Naples instead of Madrid, it would not have been at all strange in 1616 for them to have attempted again to raise funds in Spain. Just as in 1626 the monastery also decided this time to make an appeal to Moscow, through the same able Leontios, who, however, now met his death in the service of the community thousands of miles away from his pictureque monastery of the Archangel. These are certainly only hypotheses – even though they seem very likely – and I leave the numismatic side of the question to more able specialists, even though I think that the sum of 3 000 Italian scudi which was asked for in 1606 is more than double the value of 140 000 Turkish piastres in 1626. One thing emerges clearly: that the monastery of the Archangel fell at the beginning of the seventeenth century into abject wretchedness and penury, that the work of saving it and refounding it was long and laborious, and was finally completed only in the archiepiscopate of Nikephoros. This confirms what is often testified by other sources, namely the poverty of the monks of the Church of Cyprus in the seventeenth century and indeed in the period immediately after the capture of the island by the Turks.

In general, while writing to the tsar Christodoulos was in one of his more Orthodox phases. He addressed himself to Michael, the first Romanov to be elected (1613), with the devotion appropriate to the Orthodox autocrat and calls him in a most Orthodox manner "supreme sovereign of all Christians", making before him the prescribed prostration before the Orthodox emperor, and twice praying for the augmentation of the Orthodox Empire. Always diplomatic and well-informed, he does not neglect to greet the powerful great prince, and father of the tsar, Patriarch Philaret Romanov (*pontificali munere fungebatur* 1619–1633),[26] whom, however, by a frightful blunder he calls "archbishop of all Russia" instead of the correct "patriarch of all the Russias". In the climate of the time the error was extremely serious and could have been fatal to the success of the mission. This fact, which Dr Belobrova does not seem to have noticed, is in my opinion proof that the translator of the letter in Nicosia was not a Russian but a south Slav or Greek who lived with south Slavs.

There only remains for me to mention a few matters concerning the last person whom we meet in this interesting letter: James, bishop of Tamassos. This refers without doubt to the figure noted by K. Hadjipsaltes as bishop

---

[26] On this great patriarch and ancestor of the last Russian dynasty, the Romanov, see, most conveniently, the article of I.S. Sabatin in Θρησκευτικὴ καὶ Ἠθικὴ Ἐγκυκλοπαιδεία, vol II, cols 1058–1061. The best short study is, in my opinion, that of Antony Kartasov in his work *Essay on the History of the Russian Church* (in Russian), II, Paris, 1959.

of Kyrenia in his article "Greek bishops of Paphos and Kyrenia in the period
of Turkish rule (sixteenth and seventeenth centuries)".[27] In a note in Paris.
gr. 1551 of the Bibliothèque Nationale, which was first studied by J.
Darrouzès,[28] James is referred to as the "most reverend bishop of Tamaseia
and Kyrenia"[29] in the time of Archbishop Athanasios (1592–1600). In 1598
this James took part in the local council held in Cyprus which under an exarch
of the throne of Constantinople examined the case against Athanasios.[30] In
1600, in the patriarchal and conciliar letter deposing Athanasios of Cyprus,
James is referred to first among the Cypriot bishops as "bishop of Tamassos
Lord James".[31] He is also referred to in 1607 by Kyrillos Loukaris as "James
bishop of Tamassos" or "Tamaseia". Since in the patriarchal letters from
Constantinople to the Church of Cyprus in 1600 and 1601 no bishop of
Kyrenia is mentioned, whereas in 1605 we have a witness to a Parthenios as
bishop of Kyrenia, we must suppose that the new archbishop, Benjamin,
restricted his leading bishop to the see of Tamaseia and gave the throne of
Kyrenia to Parthenios, who exercised his episcopate for only a short time,

---

[27] ""Ελληνες ἐπίσκοποι Πάφου καὶ Κερυνίας κατὰ τὴν περίοδον τῆς
Τουρκοκρατίας (16ος καὶ 17ος αἰών)", KS 24 (1960), pp. 63–71, esp. p. 67.

[28] "Evêques inconnus ou peu connus de Chypre", BZ 44 (1951), p. 98.

[29] The phrase "and of Kyrenia" excludes any idea that James might have been a chorepiscopus. The fact that both in the evidence of Loukaris referred to below and in the letters of
the ecumenical patriarch James is always mentioned first in the order of Cypriot bishops before
the bishop of Paphos, proves that upon the reuniting of the Church with the other Orthodox
Churches after the end of Latin rule in 1571, the privileges of the bishop of Paphos were
withdrawn and returned to the diocese of Tamaseia, which had occupied the first place according
to the tradition which prevailed immediately before the imposition of Latin rule (see e.g. the
signature of Neilos of Tamaseia on the *Typike Diataxis* of the monastery of Machairas). Only
after the death of James, the dissolution of the diocese of Tamaseia, and later of that of
Famagusta, and the definitive reorganisation of the sees under Nikephoros, did the bishop
of Paphos, on the retreat of the bishop of Nemesos, regain the precedence acquired under
Latin rule (in accordance, also, with the older, Komnenian tradition). The privileges of the
bishop of Paphos were finally codified in the *Praxis eklogis*, of Nektarios, Proedros of Paphos,
on 28 December 1676 in the archiepiscopate of Hilarion Kigalas (see K. Delikanes,
Πατριαρχικὰ ἔγγραφα, II, Constantinople, 1904, pp. 662–3 and Deacon Leontios S.
Leontiou, "Ὁ Ἀρχιεπίσκοπος πάσης Κύπρου καὶ Νέας Ἰουστινιανουπόλεως,
Πρόεδρος παντὸς Ἑλλησπόντου", *Παγκύπριον Λεύκωμα,* Nicosia, 1925, pp. 11–26,
esp. pp. 21–2).

[30] See L. Philippou, *Ἡ Ἐκκλησία Κύπρου,* pp. 41–53.

[31] See the letter in Ph. Georgiou, *Εἰδήσεις ἱστορικαὶ περὶ τῆς Ἐκκλησίας τῆς
Κύπρου,* Athens, 1875, p. 80, n. (a). Georgiou's reading "Ζαμάδου" is given by Delikanes
as "Ταμάνθου" and corrected by Zannetos to "Ταμασσοῦ". Hill, *A History of Cyprus,* p. 325,
n. 6, agrees with Zannetos. On whether Zannetos's correction is justified there can be no
doubt, since James of Tamassos is frequently mentioned and the confusion of T with Z and
Θ with σσ very common. Unfortunately when Georgiou was reissued in Nicosia in 1975, the
editor of the *General index,* M. Christodoulou, for some reason changed "Ζαμάδου" to
"Ἀμαθοῦντος".

since no mention of him is made in the crisis of 1606/7 and from 1609 the bishop of Kyrenia is known as Jeremias.[32] That at the council of 1598 and in the patriarchal letters of 1600/2 Benjamin is referred to as bishop of Solea is not an insuperable obstacle to this hypothesis, because there is not only no evidence that the sees of Solea and Kyrenia were united before Jeremias, but on the contrary there is evidence that Kyrenia under Athanasios was united with Tamassos.

The surprising thing is that in the patriarchal letters of Matthew II and Neophytos relating to Archbishop Benjamin (1601–1605), strangely no mention is made of the senior bishop of the Cypriot Church, James. This certainly was not due to ignorance of the situation in Cyprus, since Matthew II addresses the document of deposition of Athanasios (in June 1600) first to James, bishop of Tamassos. As a result of the deliberate thrusting aside of the bishop of Tamassos by the patriarch of Constantinople, the former did not take part in the consecration in Cyprus of the newly-elected Archbishop Benjamin, whom the witnesses say was consecrated by Bishops Philotheos of Paphos, Jeremias of Kition and Benjamin of Soloi.

The whole matter seems strange; it has not been given the careful attention it deserves by older scholars and gives us the right to conjecture that James had already embarked on the conduct which Loukaris darkly alludes to in 1606 after the deposition of Athanasios and perhaps had his eye on the archiepiscopal throne for himself, or for someone else favoured by him, and, as a result, he displeased Constantinople and was treated with disdain. The enmity of the bishop of Tamassos towards Benjamin thus becomes more intelligible.

If we continue our detective work (an indispensable part of the historian's task) we will surmise that confronted with this situation Benjamin created the see of Kyrenia around the flourishing town of that name and gave it to Parthenios in order on the one hand to weaken the bishop of Tamassos and on the other to acquire the goodwill of a powerful Cypriot family of the administrative class. For I do not think that this Parthenios, who was first brought to light by Jean Darrouzès, is as unknown as the distinguished French historian supposes. I believe that he is the "Father Parthenios", uncle of the famous renegades Mimis and Mustafa, whom in the "Charter" of Benjamin sent to the duke of Savoy the Cypriot primate seeks make a bishop (since his two nephews had been readmitted into the Orthodox Church and had received back their ancestral lands). All this was said in 1601, and in 1605 there is already evidence, as we have seen, that Parthenios was bishop of

---

[32] See his letter († Ἰερεμίας ἐπίσκοπος Σωλέας καὶ Κερινίας) dated 5 February 1609 to Philip III of Spain in Hasiotes, Ἰσπανικὰ ἔγγραφα, pp. 58–9.

Kyrenia.[33] Clearly in 1601 Benjamin already had him ready and was anxious lest the imminent liberation of Cyprus by Duke Charles Emmanuel would interfere with his election!

Unfortunately, neither did the duke come nor did the detachment of Kyrenia weaken the bishop of Tamassos. On the contrary, James grew even angrier, it seems, became emboldened and in the end succeeded through his polemic after the deposition of the former Archbishop Athanasios in bringing about in 1605 the resignation also of Archbishop Benjamin. In this task he

---

[33] See Darrouzès, "Evêques inconnus", p. 100; K. Hadjipsaltes, "Ἕλληνες ἐπίσκοποι Πάφου καὶ Κερυνίας" pp. 68–9. This being the case, the notion of Ph. Georgiou and H.T.F. Duckworth should not be repeated any longer, namely that since at the beginning of the seventeenth century the archbishop included the diocese of Famagusta within his jurisdiction, he carved out a portion of his jurisdiction in order to found the diocese of Kyrenia. The diocese of Kyrenia was carved out of the diocese of Tamassos before Famagusta was incorporated into the jurisdiction of the archdiocese.

On Timothy of Kyrenia, mentioned by K. Hadjipsaltes as coming between James and Parthenios ("Ἕλληνες ἐπίσκοποι Πάφου καὶ Κερυνίας", p. 68), see the correction of the error by the same author in *EKEEK* 6 (1973), pp. 157–62.

The text of Archbishop Benjamin's memorandum to Charles Emmanuel I of Savoy is given by Count de Mas Latrie, *Histoire de l'île de Chypre*, III, pp. 570–3.

The old hypothesis of Hadjipsaltes, *KS* 24 (1960), pp. 69–70, on the translation of Christodoulos in 1606 from the throne of Kyrenia to the archiepiscopate does not seem to me very strong both on account of the short space of time between 1605 and 1606 and because he would surely not have been elected bishop of Kyrenia when the archbishop had already lost his throne and withdrawn (the first letter of Loukaris, *To Christophes, logothete of Famagusta*, dated January 1606, already tells of the resignation of Benjamin and his departure from the island, the first visit of the patriarch to Cyprus and his return to Alexandria). Besides, Loukaris's letter of June 1607 *to the clerics of the ecumenical throne* excludes Hadjipsaltes' hypothesis. Kyrillos speaks about Christodoulos as someone unknown to him who has been elected by the Cypriots (doubtless under the influence of the logothete Christophes of Famagusta) and refers to him as: Χριστόδουλόν τινα Κύπριον ἄνδρα ἀμαθῆ μὲν καὶ σοφίας ἄμοιρον τῆς τε θύραθεν καὶ τῆς ἡμέρας, τὰ δ' ἄλλα καλὸν κ' ἀγαθόν. (See E. Legrand, *Bibliographie hellénique, XVII s.*, 4, Paris, 1896, pp. 230–1, 231–2, 235–7.) Certainly these words would not have been used if they were meant to refer to the bishop of Kyrenia, who would have been mentioned clearly to the ecumenical throne as "ἐπίσκοπος Κερυνίας" and not "Κύπριός τις ἀνήρ".

The list of the first bishops of Kyrenia under Turkish rule, then, on the basis of present knowledge is: James, Parthenios, Jeremias.

If it is ever proved that the dioceses of Solea and Kyrenia were united even before the time of Jeremias the list would be: James, Benjamin, Parthenios, Jeremias. This, however, is at present not at all clear, so far as I am myself aware.

This study had already gone to press when I learned that C. Kyrris had several years ago already identified Parthenios, bishop of Kyrenia, with the person mentioned in Benjamin's document (see C.P. Kyrris, "Symbiotic Elements in the History of the Two Communities of Cyprus", *International Symposium on Political Geography: Proceedings*, Nicosia, 1976, pp. 129–30, p. 154, n. 31). This gives me special pleasure as it supports the probability of the conjecture.

found allies, strangely enough, in two new bishops elected under Benjamin, Leontios of Paphos and Moyses of Famagusta.

These three bishops of Cyprus who had seceded from the archbishop were so malign and terrifying that on 31 January 1606 the great patriarch of Alexandria, Kyrillos Loukaris, could see no other salvation for the unfortunate island "unless God in His providence and extreme compassion caused them to be swallowed up by the earth like Dathan and Abiram, since they are the cause of all the troubles in the Church and even now do not cease to do even worse things!"[34]

> "Who has known, who has heard of bishops chosen by God, [lamented the great patriarch] who in the manner of unrighteous robbers lie in wait for those whom they should be shepherding, even the Christians, from whom an account will be demanded in the fearful judgment of the Lord, who ensnare them and have no mercy on them? ... I know these men not through being persuaded in any way by the words of others, but because I have observed the hypocrite James of Tamaseia with my own eyes and the accursed Leontios of Paphos, the enemies of truth, the destroyers of the Church, who hold the priesthood in contempt, who have extinguished every vestige of piety in Christians through their disgraceful deeds, who undertake every kind of lawlessness through love of money, who pull down church buildings, who betray our religion, and are willing doers of whatever one can say should be shunned."[35]

The fact that Christodoulos refers to James in his letter to the tsar, speaking about him with such respect, is another indication of his goodness. I wonder, however, if after ascending the archiepiscopal throne Christodoulos did not oblige James to retire to the monastery of the Archangels where, as he writes to the tsar, "he lived a long time into extreme old age". I am led to think this by the fact that the signature of the senior bishop of Tamassos, in contrast to that of his "friends" Leontios of Paphos and Moyses of Famagusta,[36] is not found in any of the surviving documents from

---

[34] Legrand, *Bibliographie*, p. 232.

[35] Ibid., p. 230.

[36] See, for example, the appeal of the Cypriot bishops to Philip III of Spain on 3 February 1609: after the archbishop and the bishop of Nemesos, there follow Leontios of "Pamphos" and Moyses of "Trimythous" (Hasiotes, Ἰσπανικὰ ἔγγραφα, p. 55 and plate III). In the appeal to the duke of Savoy of 5 October, 1609, Moyses signs as "Ἀμμοχώστου" immediately after the archbishop, and is followed by the bishop of Nemesos and then by Leontios, bishop of Paphos (L. Philippou, Ἡ Ἐκκλησία Κύπρου, pp. 179–80, K. Hadjipsaltes, "Οἱ μετὰ τὸν Γερμανὸν ἀκμάσαντες ἐπίσκοποι Ἀμαθοῦντος, Λεμεσοῦ ἢ Κιτίου μέχρι τῶν μέσων τοῦ ΙΖ΄ αἰῶνος", *KS* 29 (1965), pp. 69–76, esp. p. 69 and p. 70 – an important correction of the Sathas–Philippou text).

Christodoulos's archiepiscopate after 1607. Everything tends towards the view that the bishop of Tamassos was the leader both of the resistance to Athanasios and of the rebellion against Benjamin, and if indeed he settled in the monastery of the Archangels immediately after the accession of Christodoulos, we must suppose that James never accepted Christodoulos sincerely[37] or Christodoulos regarded James as dangerous beyond the point of toleration.

It is difficult to believe that the "bishop of blessed memory who gave up his spirit to God" is the occupant of the see of Tamassos described by Loukaris. But such was Christodoulos: "a man not learned and without a share in the wisdom of foreign peoples or of our own, but nevertheless a good and kind man".

It is precisely this indescribable quality – which older generations regarded as goodness and kindness but our contemporaries more sceptically call charm and attractiveness – that Christodoulos exhibited to the end of his life: a capacity which like no other helps one to survive, especially when it is united with intelligence. Christodoulos's secret renunciation of the faith of his people, whatever the motives were and whatever his disposition and mitigating circumstances, does not suggest a character of quality. But the historian neither condemns nor exonerates, neither censures nor praises: he presents what he sees. And truly he must be compassionate towards those who are led astray,[38] but he must also be sympathetic to those who are not led astray. Otherwise he would lose his right to wonder at the good.

---

[37] Characteristically in describing to "the clerics of the ecumenical throne" the excesses of the Cypriot crisis of 1605–1607 Loukaris says that of the chief perpetrators of the lawlessness ἕτεροι προσπίπτοντες ἤρχοντο, καὶ συγχωρήσεως ἠτοῦντο ἀξιωθῆναι, ἕτεροι τὸν χαλινὸν τῆς κακίας συστείλαντες μετάνοιαν ἐπηγγέλλοντο καὶ διορθοῦσθαι παρ' ἡμῶν παρεκάλουν (E. Legrand, *Bibliographie*, p. 236).

Beyond the rhetorical attempt there can be traced in the proposal a suspicion that some pretended to be repentant rather than were repentant in sincerity. We saw above that Kyrillos characterised the bishop of Tamassos as a "hypocrite" ...

[38] The last words of the monumental work of W. Stubbs, *Constitutional History of England*, vol III ch. 21, p. 639.

LETTER OF CHRISTODOULOS, ARCHBISHOP OF CYPRUS, TO THE TSAR MICHAEL FEODOROVICH,

28 JULY 1626.

Central State Archive of Ancient Documents of the USSR, Cupb. 52, per. 4, year 1626, No. 11.

(English translation)

To the pious and Christ-loving lord and king and great prince Michael Feodorovich, Vladimiric, Muscovite, Novgorodian emperor of all the Russias, king of Kazan, king of Astrakhan, lord of Pskov and great prince of Smolensk, of Tver, of Yugor, of Perem, of Viat, of Bulgaria, lord of other states, lord of the northern countries and supreme sovereign of all Christians perfect in all his virtues, crowned and set on the throne of his kingdom by an angelic hand from above, protected by the Holy Spirit, the sceptre of piety, the benefactor of the poor and protector of strangers, to the pious king we, the humble Christodoulos, archbishop of all the island of Cyprus, wish from Jesus Christ peace and blessing, health of body and salvation of soul, and increase of your kingdom, and victory and triumph over your enemies and for endless ages your kingdom to be kept unconquered, we wish you peace and blessing and we make deep prostration with knees and face to our mother earth before your pious and serene majesty together with the most sacred shepherd and teacher and preacher of the Gospel of Christ and illuminator of the Russian race, Philaret, archbishop of all Russia, together with the pious senate of your unshakeable kingdom. In addition to this we present to your pious majesty the present monks, named Hieromonk Leontios and Geron Gerasimos, who are from the monastery of the holy incorporeal and wonderworking archangels Michael and Gabriel and the rest of the incorporeal ones, having been received into this monastery by the Lord James, bishop of the diocese of Tamaseia, who having lived there into extreme old age, delivered his soul to God. After the decease of the bishop of blessed memory, the impious Ishmaelites came, taking the property of the departed and of the bishop[1] and seized all the property that was in the monastery, the sacred vessels and ecclesiastical vestments and took the monks prisoner and threw them all into chains.

---

[1] Clearly, the property of the diocese of Tamassos is meant as distinct from James's personal property.

With the property destroyed, they wished to turn the monastery to their accursed religion, on account of which some of the pious Christians who dwelt there intervened pleading that they should be allowed to buy the monastery from them, because it was very beautiful from its building and they valued it at 140 thousand Turkish piastres and borrowed the money from the merchants with interest. For this reason, not knowing where we can obtain such a sum but having our hope only in the Lord and His most holy Mother,[2] we have put all our expectations in your piety and sent these two monks whom we have mentioned to your pious majesty, beseeching that the Lord God will move you to divine mercy, that you may have pity on the sacred monastery: that you may liberate the holy monastery from dishonour and the monks from slavery, that your great piety might be named new founder of the holy church of the great, immaterial archangels Michael and Gabriel, that they might stand by Christ the Lord with all the incorporeal angels, interceding for your pious victory over your enemies and increase of your kingdom, health of body and salvation of soul for all ages, Amen. Written on the 28 July in the year 7134.[3]

In Greek: † *the humble Christodoulos archbishop of Cyprus, client of your majesty* †

(seal)

---

[2] Dr Belobrova prints "blagomater", but I believe that this is a mistaken reading of the sacred name b͞gmater = bogomater, Θεομήτωρ. Blagomater would mean "ἀγαθομήτωρ".

[3] In the surviving documents of Christodoulos addressed to the West the date is given from Christ in the manner prevailing there. The date from the creation of the word is above all Eastern Orthodox.

XIII

THE CHURCH OF CYPRUS IN THE EIGHTEENTH AND NINETEENTH CENTURIES*

The greatest and oldest continuous institution in the history of Cyprus is its Church. At the same time it is one of the most important channels of communication for the island with peoples and cultures overseas and is therefore one of the most important agents of change and enrichment. From the fourth until the eighteenth and nineteenth centuries this historically exciting institution has included without interruption the great majority of the population of the place and has exercised a decisive influence on, or at times even provided the framework for, the regulation of struggles for power (political institutions), the production and distribution of goods and services (economic institutions), artistic and literary activities and traditions (cultural institutions) and the regulation of matters concerning marriage, family life and the education of the young (social institutions).

It is clear, then, that there is a multitude of possibilities for the choice of a viewpoint for treating the subject of this lecture. Not being able, unfortunately, to know the preferences and interests of the particular audience whom I have the honour to address, I have made my own choice and have decided to treat the subject under the aspect of the religious sensibility of the period. I shall examine, basically, in due order the religion of ordinary people, the religion of the monasteries, and finally the religion of the great men of this world, the world of eighteenth- and nineteenth-century Cyprus. Generalisations and omissions are of course imposed by the nature and duration of our meeting.

* Translated from "Ἡ Ἐκκλησία τῆς Κύπρου τὸν 18. καὶ 19. αἰώνα", Διαλέξεις Λαϊκοῦ Πανεπιστημίου 1, Nicosia, 1984, pp. 309–26.

I

In order to succeed in his aim to investigate and analyse the religion of ordinary people – or, as it is sometimes called, "popular piety" – the ecclesiastical historian needs the contribution of three other sciences: (a) geography, (b) ethnography and (c) linguistics.

Geography is fundamental for the mapping out of the religious phenomenon. Is the religious belief of the inhabitant of the open plain of Mesaoria, for example, the same as that of the inhabitant of the remote villages of the Troodos? The zeal of the mountain dwellers in contrast to the indifference of the plains people can in the case of Cyprus be demonstrated statistically. The Church of Cyprus in the eighteenth and nineteenth centuries was governed from Marathasa, a stronghold of priests and monks. Comparisons must also be made between cities and the countryside, as between areas with a stable population and those with a more mobile one. In Cyprus in the eighteenth and nineteenth centuries the vigour of the Church came from the countryside, and especially from areas where people were not given to moving house or village or leaving the area very much. The sources do not record many clerics from Tillyria, for example, while it is known that the economic degradation of the region encouraged the erosion of any distinction between Christianity and Islam (known in Cyprus as λινοβαμβακισμός).

Ethnography lends the ecclesiastical historian its method, which is a method of interpreting the spoken word both of the suppressed culture and of the dominant culture. In our case the suppressed culture is of course that of paganism, of beliefs, of ceremonies, of the world of memories, which have been preserved from pre-Christian antiquity. It is remembered in popular laments, in the figure of Charon, for example, who, even if dressed in the clothes of the Archangel, betrays himself as an unbaptised pagan.

For the investigation of the place of religion in the dominant culture studies of the language are also indispensable, such as vocabulary, images and ceremonies both on the personal and the collective levels. Study joy in Cyprus in the eighteenth and nineteenth centuries and you will see how the whole vocabulary of joy is closely connected with the greatest religious festival of the people, Easter – Πάσχα or Λαμπρή. From the element of thanksgiving for a good meal, in which the fortunate fellow-diners "easter" – πασκάζουσιν – to an especially intense outbreak of joy, which used to be called κύριον πάσχα, to the foolish pursuit of permanent happiness, which was called in the proverbial phrase: Ἔν τζ᾽ ἔν πάντα πάσχα! (life is not a perpetual Easter). Even play itself in the popular mind belonged to Easter:

Θεὲ μου, νά᾽ ρτεν ἡ Λαμπρά, νὰ κρεμμαστοῦν οἱ σοῦσες ...
(My God, let Easter come so that the swings will be put up ...)

A deprivation of Easter meant at that time a deprivation of the joy of life itself. The Christian refused to turn Turk so as not to lose the festivities of Easter – τζαὶ τὸ κότσινον αὐκόν (and the red egg).

Quantitative history would find a field of research here, without our forgetting that the more life's experiences and emotions are internalised, the more numbers should be abandoned: religion is a phenomenon that transcends numbers, and anyone who relies exclusively on statistics for the essence of the religion of a people is on the wrong track.

I shall pursue my investigation of the religious sentiment of the people of Cyprus in the eighteenth and nineteenth centuries chiefly as it appears in the lexical and topographical fields.

It is well-known that the preservation of the Church's contact with the people, which is characteristic of Eastern Christianity, was achieved not thanks to the bishops but thanks to the monasteries and, above all, to the married parish clergy. While the bishop was always being restricted ever more narrowly to the margins of administration, the monastery ensured that the people received spiritual inspiration, while their liturgical needs and moral supervision were undertaken by the parish priest. It will perhaps sound strange but it must be said that the success of the priest in his leadership role was guaranteed by his poverty and lack of education, a lack which often touched on complete illiteracy. These two things enabled the people to feel that their priest was part of themselves, since they did not allow any barrier to be set up between them. The priest was a man like other men, and his parishioners did not have great expectations of him nor did they suffer great disappointments.

Various popular proverbs, stories, narratives and songs show that the people enjoyed a beautiful voice, a good bearing, a full beard and plaited hair in their priest and even the notoriety of some peccadillo. It was important that he should be a fair judge, but excessive continence and innocence, however, provoked suspicions and led to the teasing of his wife, who, together with his daughters, was always famous for her beauty. If the priest was not particularly distinguished for his chastity, the people do not seem to have got very upset, because it was the women who were responsible: Οἱ γεναῖτζες τζαὶ τὸν παπὰν ξηπαπαδεύκουν τον. In the song about the priest of Daliotes, who was killed by his mistress's husband, not the slightest degree of blame is expressed for the priest. On the contrary, his handsome appearance is praised:

εἶδεν στὴν τζεφαλούαν του ὁλόχρυσα μαλλούδκια
(he had a fine head of golden hair)

and his loss to the Church is lamented:

ποὺ δὰ χαμ᾽ ἔν σου μοιάζασιν᾽ π᾽ ἀνατολὴν τζ αἰ δύσιν,
νάιν φορεῖς τὰ ροῦχα σου τζ αἰ νάιν λουτουρκήσεις!
(who was like you in the east or the west
when you put on your robes and celebrated the liturgy!)

Pious priests were certainly in the majority. Invisible, they kept alive the flame
of faith and the ideal of virtue, they celebrated the divine liturgy, they made
copies of their books, they cultivated music and very often the art of painting,
they taught the psalter, they dispensed justice. An exceptional example of
this kind of priest was Papa-Christodoulos of Malounda Oreini who lived in
the middle of the nineteenth century. He wrote for his pupils an unpublished
anthology of sayings entitled: *A Mirror of Examples* (Βίβλος καλουμένη
καθρέφτης ὑποδειγμάτων) and from 1832 to 1857 copied in a calligraphic
hand a series of offices of Cypriot saints. In his last years he withdrew to a
place called Pervolia, half a mile from his village, and there lived an ascetic
life like a hermit. After his death, the country folk found that in the manner
of ancient monachism he had secretly girded himself with a heavy chain
weighting three okes (or about eight-and-a-half pounds). Unknown, he was
rescued from oblivion about two years ago.

The historian will not deny the superstition of the people and their
sometimes magical interpretation of religion, which hypocritical European
travellers never tire of recounting. The people, however, where they can still
speak to us, do not seem to be such as the foreigners saw them. On the contrary,
their deep feelings are revealed full of a refined religious sense and Christian
grace.

Listen to the prayer of a husband for his dead wife:

Ἁγιὰ Μαρίν᾽ ἀφταίννω σου τζ ερὶν πὄν καταλυέται
μάρανε τὸν Παράδεισον νὰ μὲν τὴν ποβαρκέται.
(Saint Marina, I light you a candle which will not be consumed
make Paradise wither so that it will not tire of her.)

Natural beauty retreats before conjugal love: a spiritualisation of Paradise
deeper than a superficial reading of the distich would allow.

Remember the miracles of which the people sang at that time: they express
all the most human feelings for the suffering, whether people, animals or plants.
Few verses are more evangelical than the last two of the *Song of Emines and
Christophes,* when two trees grow sadly from the graves of the two lovers.

Βλαστᾶ ἡ κόρη λεμονιὰν τζ ᾽ ὁ νέος κυπαρίσσιν

τζαὶ κάϑ' ἁγίαν Κεριακὴν ἐγέρναν τζ ' ἐφιλοῦσαν
(The girl's grave grew a lemon tree and the boy's a cypress
and every Sunday they would turn and kiss each other.)

Any comment could diminish the poetry of these two verses. I would remind you only that the union which merited such a blessing was a sinful union between a Christian and an unbaptised Turkish girl.

The Cypriot of that time began his humble life and ended it accompanied by his simple faith. At his baptism he would have become a member of his Church, which he was then to follow for ever, afraid in this life of her impartial punishments, but hoping always for her forgiveness and seeking her consolation or receiving her graces.

"Today, my child, today you have entered into the church and in the waters you have been baptised into the sacred institution. May your godparent live, may your parents both live, and you, my child, may you too live and find happiness and great felicity."

In a few years the little child would be ready for marriage.

῎Ω Παναγία Δέσποινα μὲ τὸν Μονογενῆ σου,
τ' ἀντρόγυνο π' ἀρμάσαμεν ἂς ἔχῃ τὴν εὐχὴν σου.
(O lady Panagia with your only-begotten Son,
may the couple we have joined together have your blessing.)

Notice how in their religious songs the people tried to preserve an educated form of Greek in spite of their dialect. The Church is something different – the believer does not want to bring it down to the level of everyday life. Religion is lived as a reaching up to something transcendent.

The greatest ambition of this life did not go beyond a visit to the Holy Places. At the entrance to his village the pilgrim would have been received on his return with the liturgical flabella, and until he closed his eyes would tell the story of all he had seen and venerated, when he would assume the great title *hadji*. He would descend into the grave wrapped in the shroud which he wore at the Jordan, holding in his hands the candles from the ceremony of the Holy Fire.

The popular poet, a true theologian, sweetly counsels:

Καὶ ἂν λάβῃς τοῦτον τὸ καλόν, φίλε ἠγαπημένε
χύννε κανέναν δάκρυον μὲ προσευχὴν ἁγίαν,

νὰ ἐπισκέψῃ ὁ Θεὸς ψυχὴν σου τὴν ἀθλίαν,
καὶ θάνατον τὸν ψυχικὸν ποτὲ νὰ μὴν γευθοῦμεν,
ἀλλὰ εἰς τὸν Παράδεισον ἀθάνατα νὰ ζοῦμεν.
(And if you receive this good thing, dear friend,
shed a tear with a holy prayer
that God may overshadow your wretched soul
and that we may never taste spiritual death
but live for ever in Paradise.)

Under the roughness of their perhaps uncultivated behaviour, the ordinary people practised a simple and sincere religion. In their devout churches, which they knew how to build, standing before their gilded iconostases, they contemplated like latter-day Platos the death which awaited them and, more than Plato, the resurrection which they hoped for.

Their God was of course an unimaginable king and dread judge. But he was also a loving Father who knew how to provide and how to forgive: Ἕν ἔσει ὁ φτωχός, μὰ ἔσει ὁ Θεός (the poor man has nothing but God provides). The patience of the Most High before the pettiness of man is infinite: Ὁ Θεὸς ἐβκῆκε ψηλὰ γιὰ νὰ βαστάχνει τὰ καμώματα (God mounted up high to bear the antics). One thing God cannot bear and that is pride, the ancient hubris. Ἀντὰν νὰ ὁρκιστεῖ ὁ Θεὸς τοῦ λίμπουρου, δκιᾶ του φτερὰ τζαὶ πετᾶ (when God decides to destroy the ant, He gives it wings and it flies), the people suppose.

Far from the "sadistic father" of a superficial view of things, the God of the people was full of understanding, and people did not hesitate to call on him even for their love affairs, those at least that were chaste.

Ἁγία Τριάδα βούθα μου τὴν κόρην ν᾽ ἀαπήσω
τζαὶ νὰ σοῦ κάμω λειτουρκὰν τζαὶ νὰ σοῦ λουτουρκήσω.
(Holy Trinity help me win the girl I love
and I will have a liturgy sung for you.)

The outlook of the ordinary Cypriot of the eighteenth and nineteenth centuries was imbued with the spirit of his faith. Whole books could be filled with the phrases which were of religious inspiration, either from the Gospel (Ἕν τὸ δεσμεῖν τζαὶ τὸ λύειν – it is not for us to bind and loose) or from worship (Ἔγινεν ἡ Ἁγία Βαρβαροῦ –it was a real feast of St Barbara– an ironical reference to the heavy and tasteless decoration of the cave of the saint at Louroutzina, which was full of multicoloured cloths of every size which were dedicated there against malaria). Even the magic spells of the people were Christianised (if that were possible):

῎Εγλεπα βούδκια τζι ἄλοα πάνω στὸ μεσομέριν,
στὸν ᾿Ιορδάνην ποταμὸν πάω νὰ τὰ ποτίσω.
᾿Επετάχτην ἡ κατσέλλα μου ἡ καλλύτερη
᾿πο τζεῖθθε στῆς Μαγδαληνῆς κτλ. κτλ.
(I was watching oxen and horses at midday,
I took them to the River Jordan to drink.
My best cow jumped over
onto the other side at Magdalene's etc.)

It is not the task of the historian to side with the contempt of modern man for the superstition of that time or to reject it. He knows, however, that although foolishness is a permanent characteristic of the human race there is a charming foolishness, like that above, and a stupid foolishness, like the readiness of modern people to believe in horoscopes or anything which is written in the morning newspaper.

Moreover, history will also note that although some of the ordinary people – just as some of the powerful – abjured their faith in order to preserve their material existence, the majority nevertheless endured great privations, very often even death, preserving the ultimate inalienable part of their freedom, the faith of their fathers and devotion to their Church. Among them two neomartyrs stand out, George and Polydore. The first was butchered on a visit to Acre in Palestine on 25 April 1752, because he refused to become a Muslim. St Polydore, having turned to Islam one day in Cairo when he was drunk, repented bitterly in various monasteries in the East until in the end he met the martyrdom he desired at New Ephesus on 3 September 1794.

The massacres of 1821 are well-known. Usually the names are commemorated of bishops and prominent men who were executed officially in Nicosia. The sacrifices of the people, however, were no less, especially of the parish clergy and the monks. Protomartyrdom was vouchsafed to the three priests of Yiolou, Protopappas George, Papa-Loizos and Papa-George, whom the Turks beheaded on 25 May of that memorable year, which was to reach its climax on 9 July. After that day the history of Cyprus would no longer be the same. I rather feel that the linking of the eighteenth and nineteenth centuries which we have made in this series of lectures is not justifiable.

II

It is now time to pass from the religion of ordinary people to the monasteries. The age of Christendom is not always the age of Christianity. For the period which we are studying a large part of the responsibility for this situation in Cyprus fell on the long servitude of the place and the misery which was suffered by the people. The only source of salvation could have been monasticism. But how was it possible historically for this institution, like others, not to have taken on the colouring of its environment?

Unfortunately, the monastic revival which may be observed in the Orthodox world in the eighteenth and nineteenth centuries with its centre on Mount Athos, in spite of having tried to flourish in Cyprus around the period of Ephraim the Athenian, did not finally bear fruit. It suffices to say that although the people gave to the Church in this period two official saints (the neomartyrs already mentioned) and the hierarchy gave one (St Panaretos of Paphos), the monasteries of Cyprus did not produce a single saint. This is not all. Although the celibate secular clergy provided learned men of the stature of Archimandrite Kyprianos, the monasteries did not produce a single man of letters of importance to Hellenism apart from Seraphim Pissidios, metropolitan of Ancyra and apostle of the Karamanli Greeks of Asia Minor, who in his youth had been a brother and *protosyngellos* of Kykkos.

Men of prayer, ascetics, saints adorned with the gifts of the Spirit – these are unknown in the history of the Cypriot monasteries of this period. Cyprus not only failed to produce a Kosmas of Aetolia, a Makarios Notaras or a Nikodemos of the Holy Mountain, but seems not even to have heard of them. The first edition of the *Philokalia ton ieron Niptikon* (1782) is found today, so far as I know, only in the Trooditissa, while the kind of works which predominate in the monastic libraries are the collections of canon law, musical works, and doctrinal handbooks. The catalogue of manuscripts of Kykkou reveals only two works with a spiritual content: the codex of Archimandrite Chrysanthos (end of the eighteenth century) with an anthology of various patristic texts and the *Imitation of Christ* of Thomas à Kempis in a copy of 1746 (a characteristic conjunction). If one compares the sterility of Cyprus with the wonderful fertility of other smaller Greek islands – Chios, Naxos or Skiathos, not to mention Patmos – one cannot avoid certain not very flattering conclusions. Let us say that Cyprus, as in all her monastic history, must be compared with Syria, Palestine and Sinai and not with the Aegean or Ionia. The broader socio-political and ecclesiastical changes of Cyprus in the first decade of the nineteenth century cut short the monastic revival which had been prepared for by the reforming efforts of Archbishops Philotheos and Chrysanthos and the twenty-year missionary work of Ephraim, to whom we owe an edition of the *Lausiac History* in the vulgar tongue and the first edition of Isaac the Syrian.

With regard to Philotheos I refer only to the encyclical which he issued in July 1735 in the common tongue with the aim of protecting the character of the monasteries as "houses of prayer". Thus he forbids not only "games" and "merrymaking" and "dances with musical instruments" at the monastic festivals, but threatens with excommunication and a scourge imitative of Christ all who dare again, as he says, to turn the house of God into a den of thieves, buying and selling anything whatsoever in a monastery. Christians should henceforth go to monasteries devoutly in order to pray with compunction. This was in 1735.

In 1775, under Chrysanthos, an austere *Synodical letter on the monks* was published in which we hear that there were still monks who went down to the villages, baptised the children of laypeople in order to have free access to ordinary homes, neglected their duties in order to engage in trade, swore oaths and false oaths in order to acquire money, borrowed funds, and bought cotton, silk and wine. This situation provoked the justifiable complaints of the people and had to cease immediately. For this reason all the above serious abuses were forbidden and those who did not repent were threatened with expulsion from the monasteries stripped of all they possessed.

In 1781 the Holy Synod published a new set of canons for the reformation of monastic life. The monks are forbidden to have married servants; workers in the monasteries are ordered to wear black and the monks to wear their habit at all times; superiors are required to fulfil their canonical duties to the Church punctiliously. The lay censure of the monks is justifiable, the Synod repeats, and to extinguish the evil lays down new penalties for those monasteries which dare to receive into their communities those monks who have been expelled for moral aberrations from other monasteries, a matter which the Synod regards as "self-defeating and disgraceful". The encyclical of 1775 was evidently applied and monks who were corrupt or given to commerce were stripped and thrown out. The opinion has been expressed that behind these encyclicals stands the figure of St Panaretos of Paphos, a hypothesis which I regard as highly probable.

Parallel with this the archbishops saw to the publication of a series of books which sought to restore monasticism to its patristic roots and the original desires of the Founders. Thus, under Philotheos, Ephraim puplished the celebrated *Description of the venerable and imperial monastery of Kykkos* (1751) and the *Typike diataxis ... of the venerable and imperial monastery of the Holy Theotokos, called Machairas* (1756). Under Chrysanthos, Archimandrite Kyprianos published the *Typike Diatheke* and other works of St Neophytos the Recluse (1779), and also services, intercessory canons, and other hymns for about fifteen Cypriot saints and monastic patrons. This liturgical cycle began in 1756 with the *Akolouthia of the holy and glorious apostle Barnabas ... thanksgivings on account of which Cyprus has through him enjoyed grace, autonomy and privileges. By the most Blessed and most learned Archbishop of Cyprus, Lord Philotheos.* Philotheos also attempted to enlarge the church of the Apostle Barnabas in his monastery but his work was interrupted by the Turkish authorities. He succeeded, however, in renewing the monastery of St Thecla and St Anastasios and in securing the rebuilding of Kykkos, which had been burned to the ground on 6 November 1751. Chrysanthos was fortunate enough to renew sixteen monasteries and seventy-six churches.

If the monasteries were backward under Turkish rule in the spiritual sphere, they made a lively contribution to the island in other ways. First in the cultural sphere, the monasteries of those years were oases where not only the land was cultivated but also the moral life, demotic literature and the arts. The Russian Barskij in the eighteenth century and the Englishman Baker in the nineteenth agree that the monks were more civilised in their manners and conduct than the rest of the population and even physically more healthy and handsome. Parthenios, the Arab abbot of Machairas (1721–66), was famous for his muscular strength. In 1735 Barskij refers to him as "the most virtuous amongst all the monks of Cyprus". It is known that the monasteries were also medical dispensaries for the people. The doyen of the practical doctor–monks of the time was the sacristan Mitrophanes of Machairas, who in 1894 wrote the celebrated *Iatrosophion, beginning in an orderly way with the hairs of the head and ending with the feet.* It was for his beauty that the national martyr, Laurentios, bishop of Kyrenia and former chorepiscopus of Lambousa, was proverbial. Women who had beautiful babies would caress them for years afterwards saying: Μάνα μου, τὸν Λαμπούσην μου, τὸν Λαμπούσην μου! With regard to the cultivation of the land the French geologist Gaudry already noted in 1854 the decisive significance of the monks in the preservation of the natural environment of Cyprus from its return to wilderness. "The monasteries", he writes, "appear at intervals like relics of civilisation. Around them the land presents a pleasant appearance of cultivation, fruit trees form orchards, and the traveller coming to them finds a warm welcome." At the end of the nineteenth century modern European farming methods were introduced not by the English but by the abbot of Kykkos, Gerasimos, who also brought to Cyprus the first threshing machine. This was in addition to translating from the French the fortifying book *Heavenly Father* and being elected a Deputy in 1896.

In the national sphere the contribution of the monasteries touches the very heart of the survival of Hellenism on this island. The monks were the most indomitable and revolutionary element. I refer only to the explosive "Monks' Revolt" of 1832 led by Joannikios of Machairas and his ally the Giaour Imam of Paphos, born of a Greek mother. The wealth of the monasteries was the capital of the nation in its hour of need, their land was the chief counterweight to the Turkish landholding and its extension automatically implied the extension of Greek ownership and the containment of Islamification and

Christian–Muslim syncretism. Around the monasteries and their *metochia* the material survival, at least, of the Christian population was secured and this was not a little thing. It was the most pressing priority of the time. The capital itself was saved from Turkish encirclement and secured for Greek supremacy by the bright idea of Abbot Sophronios of Kykkos to buy in the 1880s all the Turkish farms of the villages of Agios Dometios, Engomi and Kantartzi. Until then the *metochion* did not exceed 300 scalas of land. Without that extension the fate of the Greek community of Nicosia in the twentieth century would have been one of asphyxiation and decline. The region took on its present physical appearance when, after 1890, it was planted with thousands of olive trees by Abbot Gerasimos.

From the purely religious perspective the monasteries became the places of refuge where the wonder-working icons of the people and the liturgy and perpetual praise of God were preserved. The books of canon law in their libraries testify – the testimony is needed – that they were also the places of confession and therefore direction of the conscience of the people. There the oppressed population went on foot, barefoot, often making their way on their knees, to obtain divine grace. Before the evocatively decorated and unseen palladium which the Byzantine emperor had sent to them, they would have prostrated themsleves and their rough faces would have been streaked with tears. When they got up they would have turned to go sensing within them a new strength. They were given as a superb reward hope and consolation.

The wealth which the *rayah* now saw around him made him feel that he too was a proper human being, proud at last to be a Christian, a descendant of such emperors, a believer with the same faith as the tsars, whose gifts hung gleaming with gold all around. Fundamentally, what did Mehmet have comparable to Kykkos or to the property (μαλιῶν) of Machairas? In its poverty, in 1773, the monastery of the Panagia of Machairas was found to have 70 houses, 251 cooking pots, 1 bale of silk, 1 cart, 457 earthenware jars, 11 rooms of cheeses, 1 pool, 3 olive mills, 3 water-mills, 8 winepresses, 20 walnut trees, 108 cherry trees, 3470 fields, apiaries in 4 regions, 1020 goats, 1040 sheep and 62 books. It had also 303 ecclesiastical vessels of many various kinds "as many as there are" and 446 "things appertaining to the abbot's quarters" whatever they were. What, then, had Um Haram and her *tekke*?

III

It is usually said that the monasteries were the chief nurseries of the bishops of Cyprus. This judgment is true, but not absolutely so, for the archbishops. In the eighteenth century Archbishops Philotheos, Paisios and Chrysanthos did not come from the monasteries, nor did Kyrillos, Makarios and Sophronios in the nineteenth century. The archbishops, like some of the episcopate, were elected by the celibate clergy of the cathedrals and schools. From the fifteen archbishops of the eighteenth and nineteeth centuries only six were elected by translation from other sees, while nine were consecrated as deacons (three) or as priests (six).

This phenomenon of mobility within the ranks of the celibate clergy is worth noting because it shows (a) that in fact the best candidate was sought for the archiepiscopal throne; (b) that the ambition and power of the bishops was such that it hindered the election of the best of them for reasons of ecclesiastical politics; and (c) that youth was preferred to age or, alternatively, that the new was preferred to the old. One of the main reasons for this "progressiveness" was that the fundamental role in the archiepiscopal election was played by the clergy and the leading men of Nicosia. The most brilliant archbishops, with the exception of Chrysanthos, came from the ranks of the deacons: Philotheos, Makarios I and Sophronios. The class of presbyters supplied some figures too, such as Paisios, and the *ethnomartyr* Kyprianos. Another healthy sign is the absence of nepotism in the succession to the archiepiscopal throne.

On the other hand, discreditable signs are not lacking either. These usually arise from the tyranny of the political conditions. We have only one canonical deposition of an archbishop in these two centuries, that of Germanos in 1705, two attempts to seize the throne, in 1705 by Papa-James in the presidency of the former patriarch of Antioch, Athanasios, and again in 1730 by Nikephoros, metropolitan of Kyrenia under Silvester. The imposition of irregular candidates by the Turkish authorities is noted three times: in 1745 that of hieromonk Neophytos under Philotheos, in 1761 that of the deacon Kyprianos under Paisios, and in 1783 that of Joannikios of Machairas under Chrysanthos. The case of Joachim in 1821 could be considered a fourth, but his election and consecration were canonical, as was his resignation. We have two cases of the successful ejection of an archbishop with Ottoman help: that of Chrysanthos by his successor Kyprianos, and of Panaretos by his successor Joannikios.

Of these fifteen archbishops, apart from the above, the Turks put one to death and directly caused the death of a second, ill-treated a third to the point of bringing on apoplexy and paralysis, and imprisoned or exiled six more. Only nine archbishops died in office, among them Kyprianos, who was hanged, Kyrillos I, about whom there were suspicions that he was poisoned, and Makarios I, who died of cholera after refusing to abandon the poorer members of his flock in Nicosia, as did the other officials and the wealthier class.

Certainly the numbers give no satisfaction. On the one hand they show the readiness of the Church to do whatever was in its power for the good of the place, however innovative this was, such as the wholly unusual – for the time – election of able young deacons or hieromonks to the highest ecclesiastical office. On the other hand, these rough statistics show the insuperable difficulties which the external conditions of servitude and the moral degradation which followed put in the way of the Church in its upward progress. Fundamentally the numbers show how many, and what, exceptional figures graced the throne of Barnabas in those dark years, what inner strength they showed, what spiritual stature. They reveal, moreover, these numbers alone, how uninformed or deliberately misleading are those accusations which are sometimes made against the official Church as the collaborator with the Turks, especially in the economic exploitation of the people.

We shall see below the justification which the *ethnomartyr* Kyprianos gives on the question of taxes. The archbishops had a legal obligation towards the Porte and that is something which Cypriots tended and still tend to forget. It seems to me that the best analysis was made in 1788 by the historian, Kyprianos: "a people who have the bad habit of not attributing the unfavourable outcome of things where they ought and the increase of debts to the insatiable and merciless rapacity of the authorities set over us, but without discrimination holding responsible their Father superiors, not only today but always in the past".

It is not my task to justify what is unjustifiable, nor do I believe that the Church of the eighteenth and nineteenth centuries could be a model for the present or the future. As a historian I do not have many reasons for believing that anyone was ever taught a lesson by history. I recognise, however, that the greatest service which history can render is to liberate the mind from the tyranny of fashion and the opinion of the moment. This is not the occasion on which to expatiate. I would, however, with the greatest respect remind those who wish to write historical works that they must constantly read the history of historiography, that is to say, the history of history. Every generation in history has its own perspective, not our presuppositions, however good and just these may be. The hierarchy of the eighteenth and nineteenth centuries is an authority and therefore, in the necessary scheme of things, an organ of oppression. Only a fool would have expected the Church of the Ottoman Empire of the eighteenth century, as a historical institution, to follow the Beatitudes as a golden rule of political and economic administration. Historically this would have meant the end of history, a situation to which as a Christian I look forward, though far from any chiliastic ideas, whether religious or secular, that is to say, not on this earth and not as a mass movement.

The bishops of that period lived in their dioceses and behaved as prelates and pastors, but also as chief magistrates of the *rayahs* appointed by the

Caliph of Islam. One must not imagine, however, that their days rolled by in oriental luxury and an indolence like that of the *agas*. Underneath the surface their life remained apostolic. They were always on the move and spent much of the year on horseback. The "bishop's mule" (ἡ μούλα τοῦ Δεσπότη) is an expression still alive on the lips of Cypriots, though few know that that fabled beast was usually followed by a string of camels, for the bishops travelled with their whole household and staff. They constantly travelled between their sees and Nicosia where they frequently maintained their own residences near the Archiepiscopal Palace, and for several months each year toured their dioceses – the archbishop sometimes peregrinating the whole of Cyprus, as Kyprianos did in 1815. They frequently visited the "Most Holy" (Ἁγιωτάτη), as they called the archiepiscopal palace, the *Saray* and the *Konak*, or the consuls in Larnaca, they corresponded with every corner of the world, they collected taxes, they administered colossal properties, they sat in judgment, they received local and foreign visitors, they gave dinners, sent gifts, organised protests, attended to all the foundations from the schools to the leper hospitals, celebrated the liturgy and preached sermons.

The appeal of the Synod in person or by letter to Constantinople was the rule, on account of the presence there of the sultan's government and the ecumenical ethnarch of the Roman nation. In 1826 Archbishop Damaskenos, it is not known why, visited Paris, where he was received at the court of Charles X, while in 1889 Sophronios visited London, had an audience with Queen Victoria and was awarded an honorary doctorate of theology by the University of Oxford.

A customary ending in the correspondence of the bishops of those two centuries was the phrase "in haste" or "in the greatest haste". Chrysanthos, bishop of Kyrenia, writes on 30 September 1883: "After some days, if God wills, I shall go to the diocese of Morphou to visit some of its villages omitted because of my invitation in July from the inhabitants of Lapithos and Karavas to be present at their school examinations. After that I shall go to Marathasa. The labours and hardships are unbearable and the roads which I shall use are very dangerous. But what can I do!"

In 1854 Metropolitan Chariton of Paphos was in danger in extreme old age of being forced to retire because he did not travel round his diocese. Four months after his acquittal as "venerable and aged" he died, and thus the poor man found his rest. In 1878 it was the turn of Meletios of Kyrenia, who a little before had made a gift of 20 000 kurush (γρόσια) for the schools of Nicosia. He submitted his resignation and withdrew to his house in Nicosia. In his will he did not omit to leave £50 to the school of his birthplace of Lemythos.

I shall not refer here to the educational work of the bishops and their promotion of the national cause in the two centuries which we are examining.

I hope that it is better-known and believe that it makes them deserving of the gratitude of the island. Without them the socio-spiritual level of Cypriots today would not be higher than that of the neighbouring countries of the Middle East or Turkey. I shall give only a few examples of their purely spiritual pastoral activity.

What were their feelings about their flock? The references which they make in their correspondence are typical: "our poor brother native Christians", those "pitiable native poor", "the poor", "the long-suffering nation", "our spiritual children". Archbishop Chrysanthos even calls the people "friends of God and intercessors for us". Any comment is superfluous.

In 1812 when ordering the Christians of the *kadilik* of Lefkas to pay their taxes immediately, Kyprianos notes sadly: "that this is beyond the power of the poor I know. But if it is neglected," he continues, "the result will be worse: they will send you a crowd of tough gendarmes who will fall on you like thunderbolts and oppress you in every way and they will do you harm. And any pleading will not be heard by his honour [the *Muhasil*] to hold back his ferocity, which until now by the grace of God we have been able to restrain without bringing the slightest evil upon you ... receive my blessing, then, and try hard to pay your levies." And like a good pastor he concludes on a note of hope: "from now on in the current year we hope that the expenses will become fewer and more moderate and the *salgin* low". The same love and fatherly care is expressed in a document of 4 October 1820 to the *kadilik* of Mesaoria on the same theme. The archbishop imposes "a burden of indissoluble excommunication" on all who conceal the truth about their income, but explains that "there has not been any grace from the high *Devlet*" and announces a whole series of measures which he has taken so that no one should pay "either beyond his capability or less than his capability". So that "the poor should not be overburdened" he goes so far as to put a stop to the practice by which *rayahs*, Turks and Greeks, become "servants of monasteries, *tekkedes*, *tsiflikia*", something which had become, he says, "a traffic and an abuse", since good workmen were in this way freed from the obligation to pay tax, which then fell all the more heavily on the poor. I do not know of many similar instances in Western Churches at the beginning of the nineteenth century; in fact I know of none at all.

We have looked at the encyclical of Archbishop Philotheos of 1735 defending the atmosphere of compunction that should exist in the monasteries. In 1749 that learned archbishop, who conversed with his foreign visitors in Latin, issued in the vulgar tongue again a *Letter to be read in Holy Lent for the correction of Christians*. He advised the faithful "to cease from theft, fornication and pride", he exhorted them to go to confession and all to make their communion at Easter and he asked the priests to write down the names of those who did not go to confession "that they may be disciplined ecclesiastically as people who hold the sacraments in contempt".

In 1754 the attention of Philotheos was turned to popular superstition. He published a *Synodical letter of excommunication ... against magi,* in which he excommunicates all who consult magi or sorcerers and anathematises the magi themselves, who if they are clergy are to be deposed. The last point is revealing: it seems that some clergy sometimes overstepped the boundaries of practical medicine and the *Euchologion* and dabbled in magic.

Kyprianos's encyclical of 1820, on combatting locusts, turned to the subject of fatalistic beliefs. The archbishop does not neglect to furnish all the churches in the areas affected by locusts with icons of St Tryphon, which were painted in the iconographic workshop of the archiepiscopate. At the same time, however, he called upon the Cypriots to reject "the illusory and ridiculous superstition that the destruction and exterminations of the locust is a superhuman work". He goes on to explain methods of the systematic destruction of the locust, "as also happens in other places both in Europe and in the East", and calls them to a common struggle so that "each person should enjoy all the products of his work unharmed and intact".

Twice in 1775 and 1781 in encyclicals addressed to all the inhabitants of the island the Synod dealt with marriage. It stresses the sacramental character of the bond, which it regrets to say has become dishonoured, carnal and a game. It orders a stop to be put at once to "the invitations, the eating and drinking, the drunkenness, the violins, the gunshots, the dances, the drums, the songs and the insane expense". It decides, for the avoidance of scandal, that betrothals should be celebrated only eight days before the wedding, forbids the effusive welcomes and vulgar jokes of the progress of the wedding procession from village to village and advises that only relations and sponsors should be invited to the nuptials. Precisely the same advice was given a century later, in 1867, by Archbishop Sophronios. Another century further on this wise counsel remains a deadletter in Cyprus.

In November 1786 Archbishop Chrysanthos issued an encyclical on the occasion of the fast before Christmas. Since uninformed travellers and our contemporary authors who follow them speak uncritically of the religious feeling which the Church encouraged at that time as pure formalism, I would ask you to permit me to quote at some length so that the style and content of the teaching and pastoral care for the *rayahs* revealed in the encyclical might be better appreciated.

"Since the time has now come for the forty-day fast," writes the Archbishop, "we exhort you to eschew every sin and pollution and go all of you to the holy church, men and women together, and every day for the whole of Advent to hear the sacred Liturgy and the prayers for drought, and stand as in the house of God, leaving behind every worldly care and business concern and vain thought, so that you may not make the house of your heavenly Father a house of commerce and thieves, and pray before God and entreat God with all piety and contrition of heart to overlook your sins. First, however, you must be purified, you must abstain from your sins, because as long as the soul entertains such pollutions God in His holiness accepts neither hymns nor doxologies nor gifts from you but turns away from them as profane and abominable, because a hymn from an unclean mouth is not acceptable to God, but 'praise befits the upright' [Ps 33:1]. God must be glorified with pure words for them to be heard."

The "Master" returns in March 1798, in an encyclical for Easter, to the need for confession – a second baptism – and communion and also for love and mercy and for a devout life.

In a new document in April of the same year he goes so far, on account of the misery of that year, to commend to people that they should leave out even the "bread rolls and flagons of wine[φλαοῦνες]". He asks the people to take note that it would give him great satisfaction if they did not send him sanctified gifts for Easter that year.

A little later the Synod deals with the same subject in an encyclical. Again it asks for economies, the avoidance of gifts – especially to the heterodox – the curtailment of every vain and unprofitable expense, and even the giving of candles at weddings (with a loss, of course, to the churches). Anything surplus must be given to the poor, who were under unbearable pressure that year. "Gold-embroidered dresses and luxurious headscarves" are regarded by the Synod as unacceptable follies.

The spirituality of Chrysanthos and his Synod is liturgical, sacramental and ascetic, that is to say, purely Orthodox. In particular that prelate from the Three Olive Trees tried to reanimate the local Christian tradition of Cyprus, publishing in Venice, as I have already mentioned, the Offices of various Cypriot saints. In the prologue to the edition of 1799 his spiritual teaching is enriched with a new dimension, that of martyrdom, a theme supremely evangelical.

"The examples of their patience", he wrote, "will frequently console and soothe your hearts; whenever afflictions come upon you, misfortunes, heavy taxes, tortures, unjust damage and persecution, endure them with gratitude for love of the name of Christ, that you may be proved to be voluntary martyrs and therefore blessed. 'For all who desire to live a godly life in Christ will be persecuted' (2 Tim. 3:12)."

There does not remain time to discuss the religion of the powerful laymen of Cyprus in the eighteenth and nineteenth centuries. I simply note that the religion of the higher classes of the land-owning aristocracy (to the extent that we can speak about such a thing) did not differ very much from the religion of humble folk, with the addition of course of the corruption that power always brings to those who possess it. The situation appears to be different among the new urban classes of merchants which appear from the beginning of the nineteenth century, centred on the Levantine community of Larnaca and in the quarter where the Ionian islanders lived. An indication of the change is that already in 1815 Archbishop Kyprianos regarded it necessary to publish a *Letter of excommunication against the Freemasons* whom he calls "preachers of every evil, inciting and disturbing the people". The opinion has received support that the *ethnomartyr* did not really mean the masons but the *Philiki Etaireia*. This is a hypothesis which I find improbable. The document is a witness to the struggle which was beginning between Cypriot traditional ways and the introduction of foreign ideologies by the new classes. The only thing which Cyprus did not need of course in 1815 was masonic religious tolerance, in spite of the fact that on 22 May 1881 Chrysanthos of Kyrenia, in blackening the character of the young man who was to become Archbishop Kyrillos II, set religious tolerance amongst the Christian virtues. This aristocratic metropolitan, however, perhaps constitutes an exception. The word very shortly would be applied to Marathasa, given over now to the romantic nationalism of the period. Historically Cyprus could not stand aside from the path which the whole planet was following. The choice was restricted to that between a voluntary or an enforced Westernisation. In favouring education the Church favoured this path. It failed, however, to confront the new situation, for which it was unprepared, on the spiritual level.

This was the hierarchy of the eighteenth and nineteenth centuries. It included shadowy figures such as the irregular Archbishop Neophytos, who was imposed by the Turks in 1744, and whose principle was "Now it is not Christ who rules but Mehmet", and saints such as Panaretos of Paphos – from Peristeronopigi of Famagusta – who was recognised as a saint, only four years after his death, by the Cypriot ecumenical patriarch, Gerasimos III, in 1794. Those around him secretly observed "the godly Panaretos living ascetically in the city as if on the mountain, standing upright in prayer throughout the night". At Stavrovouni the two chains are preserved which were found round his body after his death. The contemporary historian, Kaisarios Dapontes, named him while he was still alive, "living virtue". He spent his life dedicated to his flock and to preaching and today rests, forgotten, under the bell-tower of St Theodore's at Ktima.

What is the final judgment of the historian? I leave the last word to the last archbishop of the period of Turkish rule, Sophronios. In a note in his own hand at the end of a biography of him he wrote: "Let others judge this. We only desire from God rest for our soul according to our works, which unfortunately bear the stamp of meanness, like everything human. It is enough for us to say simply that we did what we could, not what we would have wished."

Within a historically cruel atmosphere, which the Turkish tyranny created, the invasions of locusts, the epidemics of cholera and the frightening demographic decline of the island, divine grace continued its way, passing among sinful people – how could it do otherwise? – who acknowledged their unworthiness, however, and knew how to repent. This was a knowledge which the twentieth century would shake with an unprecedented crisis of spiritual identity.

XIV

ARCHBISHOP KYPRIANOS'S INKSTAND*

I. INTRODUCTION

The history of ways of acting has been succeeded today in many writers by the history of ways of thinking and of feeling.[1] Coming in this way to the third level – after the personal and the social – that of the soul, of the essential, of the conscious and intellectual, researchers can hope that in time they will be able to write the history of cultural systems. A part of this, beyond social history, is the history of ideologies, and one of the first objectives of that, in turn, is the charting of the different classes of dreams in the world, that is to say, the things that are wished for and desired.

Invaluable evidence of these classes of wished for things in a specific community is provided by etiquette, dress, wigs, insignia, seals, emblems, coats of arms, etc. To these symbolic objects, to all material endowed with special significance, which sculptured or painted representations provide, history must pay minute attention. Above all, in the matter of official ideals and dreams, the greatest attention is due to whatever belongs to princes, national leaders, and ecclesiastical primates, and indeed to the houses and institutions that these represent.[2]

The greatest and oldest institution with continuity and succession in the whole of Cypriot history is the Church of Cyprus, which has endured for twenty centuries on Cypriot soil, and, in human terms, seems destined to continue its activity and progress without interruption for the indefinite

---

*Translated from "Τὸ μελανοδοχεῖον τοῦ ἀρχιεπισκόπου Κυπριανοῦ", *KS* 45 (1981), pp. 143-60.

[1] See P. Chaunu, *Histoire, science sociale. La durée, l'espace et l'homme à l'époque moderne*, Paris, 1974, pp. 73–5, 371ff; J. Delumeau, "Leçon inaugurale au Collège de France (13 février 1975): Le prescrit et le vécu" in *Le Christianisme va-t-il mourir*, Paris, 1977, pp. 177–214.
[2] See G. Duby, "Histoire sociale et idéologies des sociétés" in J. Le Goff et P. Nora, éds, *Faire de l'histoire*, I, Paris, 1974, pp. 147–68, esp. p. 156.

future. Communities which can boast of institutions of such antiquity and continuity can be numbered today on the fingers of one hand. It is sufficient to note here that the Church of Cyprus is the oldest and most continuous institution in the contemporary Greek world.

This institution during the centuries of foreign rule on the island contained within itself the whole of the collective ideal of the Greek people of Cyprus and became the refuge and workshop of the common spirit of the Cypriot community, of its traditions, and of the personal ambitions and collective control of its members.[3] In times such as the period of Ottoman rule, then, the symbols, insignia and in general the heirlooms decorated with representational scenes of the archbishops and ethnarchs of Cyprus have a significance for the history of the ideology of Cypriot Hellenism and the outlook, pious desires and dreams of the Cypriot Church, since, beyond the personal perspectives of their owners, they embody the collective aims of the Church and community of Cyprus, at least in those classes whose self-consciousness rose above the level of the land and agriculture.

These emblems and scenes were in the face of external and internal enemies weapons of defence and attack, of education and propaganda. Through these were disseminated and analysed, in accordance with the particular circumstances, myths, ideas, meanings, representations of the present, programmes for the future, apologias for the past, advance notice to enemies and friends. The need for communication through these things was made all the more imperative by the fact that the ethnarch did not control the greatest instrument of mass communication before the press and the radio, namely, the coinage and the representations and inscriptions upon it.

Unfortunately, the fluctuations of history have not preserved many heirlooms of past archbishops, and little of what has survived has real historical significance. An exceptional place among these is occupied by the inkstand in the treasury of the Archiepiscopal Palace of Cyprus which belonged to the *ethnomartyr* Archbishop Kyprianos (30 October 1810– 9 July 1821). It is not an exaggeration to say that none of the documents or other relics of the great *ethnomartyr* affords us such a lively picture of him and the intellectual atmosphere of his time as this inkstand.

II. DESCRIPTION

The inkstand is of silver-gilt, of the oblong box type, without feet or handle, and dates from 1812. Its dimensions are $19 \times 5 \times 4.5$ cm.[4] This type of inkstand

---

[3] See the definition of the institutions given by P. Veyne, *Comment on écrit l'histoire*, Paris, 1971, p. 242.

[4] Plate I. A brief external description has been given by N. Evangelides, "Μελανοδοχεῖον τῆς Ἀρχιεπισκοπῆς Κύπρου", Ἐκκλησιαστικὸς Φάρος 4 (1912), pp. 58–61.

came into use in the sixteenth century, the oldest examples that we have today
dating from the seventeenth century. They were made of a variety of materials;
the fashion, however, at the end of the eighteenth and beginning of the
nineteenth centuries favoured silver. In comparison with other contemporary examples from outside Cyprus which contain bottles of ink and aromatic
substances, vessels of sand or sandarach dust and wax, boxes of paper discs
for seals, penknives, pens, candlesticks, hand-bells etc., the inkstand before
us seems rather humble. Its value, however, as will be shown below, does not
lie in its intrinsic worth but in the representations which decorate it.

The lid[5] is surrounded by a narrow border decorated with olive branches,
and has in the middle the incised representation of a two-headed eagle
within a raised field in the shape of a rounded oblong. At the extremities are
two similarly raised convex roundels in the form of medallions. All three silver
medallions are enriched with wreaths of laurel. The gilded ground of the cover
between them is covered by four open multipetalled roses in relief, surrounded
by formalised leaves of acanthus arranged in scrolls, of rather a Western or
classical Corinthian style.

The eagle incised lengthways in the elliptical panel is, like all the
engravings in the medallions of the cover, painted in a black colour. It has
its two heads crowned with mitre and diadem and holds on its shoulder a
large cross which sends out rays from the crossing of the arms. With its right
foot it holds vertically and leaning slightly outwards the royal sceptre of the
archbishops of Cyprus entwined with ribbons, and with its left foot, also
vertically but leaning to the left, it holds the serpent-headed archiepiscopal
staff without ribbons but with nodes. From the eagle's neck hangs by a chain
descending to the breast a sacred amulet inscribed with a cross such as
among the Byzantines was worn chiefly by the emperor and later by the
bishops.

The ancient Eastern symbol of the double-headed eagle was adopted,
as is well-known, as an emblem by later Byzantium, and continued to portray
under Turkish rule the Church's role of ethnarchic service and the ecumenical
nature of Orthodoxy. The very wide dissemination of this symbol deprived
it of almost all meaning. In the right place, however, as is appropriate, the
special meaning flowing from this contact will be examined.

The lower roundel bears engraved in the centre a glass vessel for ink in
the shape of a flower vase of the type which came into use from the middle
of the eighteenth century. Dipped into this are two quill pens, while in a circle
around the edge in beautiful Byzantine capitals is the anapaestic inscription:
Τοὺς πόλους ἀθρῶν τὰ παράσημα βλέπεις ("By observing the medallions

---

[5] Plate II.

you see the emblems.") The word παράσημον has here the sense of emblem, symbol or escutcheon. Clearly the beholder is invited to see engraved in the two medallions the forms of the signs of office of the archbishop of Cyprus. The glass inkwell with the two pens represents the privilege of signing in red ink.

In the upper roundel are represented the remaining privileges. Below is a folded purple *mandyas* and above this, upright and leaning to the right, the sceptre, which has an orb at its head and which in the middle, at the point at which it is held, is attached kerchief. Over all is represented an archiepiscopal mitre surmounted by a cross with a wreath and protruding decorations of plant form of the type which G. Soteriou regarded as coming from the head-dress of Byzantine *archons* because it does not bear the crossed bands of the imperial crown.[6]

The interior of the inkstand is divided into three parts.[7] At the extremities sit two square silver boxes ending in round mouths closed by silver stoppers attached by small silver chains. The one on the left has its mouth covered by a perforated silver plate in the form of a flower and was undoubtedly used as a vessel for the dust which was sprinkled on the paper to prevent the spread of ink. By oral tradition of the Archiepiscopal Palace the *ethnomartyr* used gold dust for this purpose, as a result of which even to this day, it is said, his red signature is tinged with gold. What the original purpose of the right-hand box was, it is difficult to say. It has an open mouth, and therefore was used neither for dust nor as a scent-bottle. It bears inside it today, however, traces of purple ink, which shows that at one time at least it was used as an inkwell.

In the middle oblong compartment, fastened with wax, stand two glass bottles of ink of elliptical shape with funnel-like mouths. The inkwells of this type were manufactured and arranged as pairs from the seventeenth century, as has already been said, from colourless, transparent, polished glass. They had at first a cylindrical shape, taking later hexagonal, stepped, elliptical, bell-shaped and vase-shaped forms. A metal inkwell of the stepped form is shown being held by Archbishop Kyprianos in the oil painting of him in the *synodicon* of the monastery of Machairas.[8] If the inkwells under examination belonged from the beginning, as I imagine they did, to the inkstand before us, it may be surmised that the one was used for the purple ink of the archiepiscopal signature (holograph or, earlier, by a cipher), and the other for the usual ink, of dark grey or black colour, with which the archbishop used to write.

---

[6] G.A. Soteriou, Κειμήλια τοῦ Οἰκουμενικοῦ Πατριαρχείου: Πατριαρχικὸς Ναὸς καὶ Σκευοφυλάκιον, Athens, 1937, pp. 53–4.

[7] Plate I.

[8] Plate IX. With his right hand the archbishop is writing on a piece of white paper the words of Psalm 39:4 (LXX 38:5): "Lord, let me know my end, and what is the measure of my days, what they are that I may know what I lack." A prophetic anxiety!

The sides of the inkstand are decorated with raised floral swags of semi-elliptical shape (*guirlandes en festons*), held together by rings from which hang strips of cloth.

There are eight such swags – three each on the front and back, and one on each left and right side. This decoration, originating from the ancient Greek sarcophagi, enjoyed a revival at the time of the Renaissance, and is met within Cyprus both in Romanesque sarcophagi, like that of the abbey of Bellapais, and in monuments such as the marble bowl of the fountain of the monastery of St Napa. As a decoration on precious silver objects it is also found on the reliquary which Archbishop Kyprianos's uncle, Archimandrite Charalambos, had made for the monastery of Machairas at Jassy in 1795.[9] The garland, however, of the archiepiscopal inkstand is lighter, with a baroque air.

On the lower part of the front panel[10] is incised in the same characters as on the lid the following iambic inscription: Οὐδὲ τὰ κλίτη κενεὰ ταῦτα βλέπεις ("Nor do you see these sides empty.") We may safely suppose that the author of this verse is the martyred archbishop, the inspirer of the whole of the inkstand.

Within the middle floral swag is the repoussé bust of a bishop which the inscription identifies: "The Apostle Barnabas". The holy patron of the Church of Cyprus has his head uncovered and surrounded by a nimbus, he wears a *sticharion, phelonion* and *omophorion* and has his right hand raised in blessing. In his left hand, which is veiled by the *phelonion* he holds a closed book of the Gospels. The iconographic type is that of St Nicholas (archetype of the good bishop), and is reminiscent of the representation above the door of the Bedestan in Nicosia. To the right of the founder of the Cypriot Church is raised the archiepiscopal sceptre, with a kerchief attached to its handle, and at its head a cross-surmounted globe studded with precious stones, without, however, the usual equator and southern half. This globe is preserved to this day in the treasury of the archbishop's palace and has been immortalised by the painter John Kornaros of Crete in his well-known painting of Kyprianos's predecessor, Archbishop Chrysanthos.[11] On the saint's left is raised the pastoral staff carried by Greeks since the sixteenth century, ending in two facing serpents (the so-called "shield"). Very near the head of the saint is the keyhole and around it the small silver nails by which the lock is held. Within the swag to the right of the saint is a hill covered with bushes and a chest under a tree. This is no doubt the tomb of the Apostle Barnabas, which was

---

[9] See the photograph in I.P. Tsiknopoullos, Ἡ ἱερὰ βασιλικὴ καὶ σταυροπηγιακὴ μονὴ τῆς ὑπεραγίας Θεοτόκου τοῦ Μαχαιρᾶ, Nicosia, 1968, p. 209.

[10] Plates I, III.

[11] See the photograph in I. K. Peristianes, Ἱστορία τῶν ἑλληνικῶν γραμμάτων ἀπὸ τῆς Τουρκικῆς καταστάσεως μέχρι τῆς Ἀγγλικῆς κατοχῆς (1571–1878), Nicosia, 1930, opposite p. 40.

found by Anthemios, archbishop of Cyprus, in 488 under a carob tree. In the left semi-circle there is a representation of a figure who is identified by the inscription: Ζήνων ὁ βασ(ιλεύς), the Emperor Zeno. The bearded sovereign is represented wearing a crown of the closed type, decorated at the summit with the so-called "orphan", and wearing a *sakkos* with a thong and torque. His arms are extended, offering to the Apostle Barnabas (and his successors) with his right hand the imperial sceptre, which in later centuries the archbishops of Cyprus carried, and with his left hand a quill pen and a piece of cloth which is surely not the consular *semicinctium* but the purple *mandyas* with which, according to tradition, the Isaurian emperor honoured the auto-cephalous archbishops of Cyprus.

The rear panel[12] is inscribed with an inscription recording the donor: "In the archiepiscopate of Kyprianos, 1812". Enclosed by the swag on the right is a repoussé decoration representing a closed codex bound in wooden boards with clasps, on which is inscribed "Matthew's Gospel". Within the swag on the left is a map of Cyprus in which may be read "Island of Cyprus". The book, of course, stands for the copy of St Matthew's Gospel which lay on Barnabas's breast bound in wooden boards – "ἔχον πτυχία θύϊνα"[13]; the map seems to have been inspired by French maps of the eighteenth century, such as the atlas of J. Roux.[14]

In the large central semi-elliptical space Archbishop Kyprianos is represented bearing a sceptre and attempting to raise with his left hand the supine figure of a young woman in the long Cypriot dress of the poor with flowing hair and bare arms. The archbishop wears on his head a *kalymmafkion* with a veil and is enveloped in a precious *rason*.[15] It is evident that since he holds the sceptre without being dressed in vestments, he is represented as Ethnarch of Cyprus and the wretched fallen girl whom he is attempting to raise symbolizes Cyprus herself. The synthesis is reminiscent of the Byzantine representation of the Resurrection of Adam as a result of the descent of the Lord Jesus into Hell.[16]

---

[12] Plate IV.

[13] *Souda* (commonly called Souidas) ed. A. Adler, II, Stuttgart, 1967, p. 733. *s.v.* Θύϊνα: ἐπὶ Ζήνωνος βασιλέως εὑρέθη ἐν Κύπρῳ τὸ λείψανον Βαρνάβα τοῦ ἀποστόλου, τοῦ συνεκδήμου Παύλου. ἔκειτο δὲ ἐπὶ τὸ στῆθος Βαρνάβα τὸ κατὰ Ματθαῖον εὐαγγέλιον, ἔχον πτυχία θύϊνα. This refers to the wood of the aromatic tree *Callitris quadrivalis*.

[14] A. and J.A. Stylianou, *The History of the Cartography of Cyprus*, Nicosia, 1980, pp. 398, 399. In a future edition of this monumental work the map described here should be included as the only old map of Cyprus of Cypriot origin.

[15] Kyprianos also wears a *rason* with a fur lining in the portrait belonging to the monastery of Machairas. Plate IX. Cf. note 28 below.

[16] See F. Cabrol, *DACL* IV, 682–93; A. Xingopoulos, "Ὁ ὑμνολογικὸς εἰκονογραφικὸς τύπος τῆς εἰς Ἅδου καθόδου", *EEBS* 17 (1941), pp. 113ff. From Cyprus see, for example, the icon of the church of St Cassian of Nicosia, from the sixteenth century (A. Papageorgiou, *Icons of Cyprus*. Paris–Geneva–Munich, 1969, p. 66).

On the right side of the inkstand there is a representation of a city beneath which is inscribed: Λευκοσία.[17] The scene seems to be inspired by the medieval seals of Western cities (in which, it may be noted, sigillographically the walls represent the freedom of the city communes). It is intended, I believe, to be an actual representation of the Paphos Gate (Porta di San Domenico), the Latin Church of the Precious Cross, St Catherine (the mosque of Haidar Pasha), Hagia Sophia (the mosque of Selimiye), the *Konak* of the Dragoman of Cyprus Hadjigeorgakis Kornesios and the archbishop's palace.

Within the swag on the left side – the bottom half cut away and crudely repaired – is represented, as the inscription Ἀμμόχουστος[18] testifies, Famagusta, the second city of the archdiocese and successor of the ancient Constantia, metropolis of Cyprus. I think it represents the Marine Gate (Porta del Mare) and within the walls and towers the cathedral of St Nicholas (the mosque of Lala Mustafa Pasha) and the Greek parish churches. Whether the domes here represent the domes of St Nicholas of the Greeks, at that time the Orthodox Cathedral of the city,[19] or that of St George, old cathedral of the Greeks, it is difficult to say. If the latter is the case, they have a symbolic significance, for the domes of this church appear to have been destroyed by an earthquake in about 1735.[20]

III. INTERPRETATION

It should be said at the outset that from the prosopographical point of view Archbishop Kyprianos's inkstand provides us with a reliable picture of the *ethnomartyr* during his years as archbishop. The oil painting in the monastery of Machairas, on which all the pictures and busts of the great man have been based until now, dates from his time in Moldavia and represents him almost as a young man.[21]

From the point of view of historical topography it should be said that in the representation of Nicosia we have the oldest – albeit in schematic form – portrayal of the original form of the palace of Venetian origin of the celebrated Intepreter of Cyprus, and the original form of the old Archiepiscopal

---

[17] Plate V.

[18] Plate VI.

[19] See. C.P. Kyrris, Ἱστορία τῆς μέσης ἐκπαιδεύσεως Ἀμμοχώστου 1191–1955, Nicosia, 1967, pp. 23, 224 illustr. 4.

[20] Ibid., pp. 15, 23, 223 illustr. 2.

[21] In the fire of 1892 the portrait of Prince Michael Soutsos, it seems, was destroyed, which bore the date 1796 (see A. Camariano-Cioran, "Contributions aux relations roumano-chypriotes", *Revue des études sud-est européennes* 15 (1977), pp. 493–508, esp. 507–8). The portraits of Kyprianos and his uncle, Archimandrite Charalambos, must date from about the same year.

Plate I   Archbishop Kyprianos's Inkstand

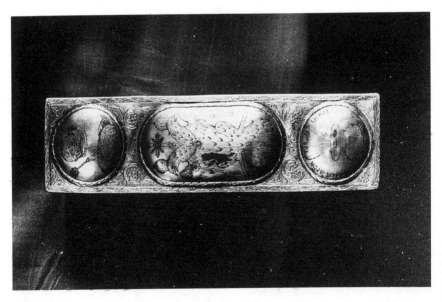

Plate II   Lid

Plate III   Front panel

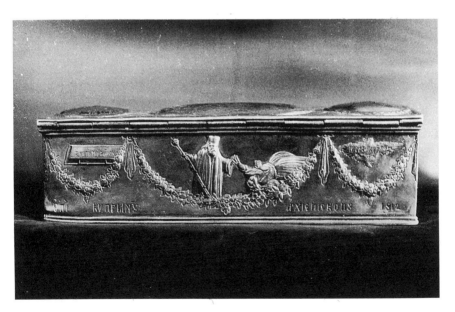

Plate IV   Rear panel

Plate V   Right side panel

Plate VI   Left side panel

Plate VII
Sketch of the portrait of Archbishop Kyprianos,
commissioned by the Archbishop for his birthplace at Strovolos

Plate VIII
Carved iconostasis of above sketch at the
church of Strovolos

Plate IX   Archbishop Kyprianos

Palace, as it appeared before the alterations of 1862–63,[22] which do not seem to have changed the facade very much.

The inkstand from the artistic viewpoint is a good example of the level of silversmithing in Cyprus at the beginning of the nineteenth century. It cannot, however, be compared with the silver-gilt heirlooms of the same period or of the last years of the eighteenth century at the monastery of Kykkos.[23] The style, a mixture of Byzantine, Renaissance and baroque elements, is typical of Cypriot art of all periods since the island was always a crossroads of many trends, fashions and aesthetic approaches harmoniously put together.

But here we are interested chiefly in the historical viewpoint. The inkstand we are examining is on the one hand a new moment in the development of the myth of the imperial privileges of the archbishop of Cyprus, and on the other an apologia of Archbishop Kyprianos for the manner in which he ascended the throne of Cyprus. With regard to the legend of the privileges bestowed by Zeno, here it is sufficient for us to note that the ancient sources make no reference to them – not even the Cypriot monk Alexander, from whom almost everything is drawn –[24] and the first written evidence of such a thing which we possess dates only from 1676.[25] Nevertheless

---

[22] Ph. Georgiou, *Εἰδήσεις ἱστορικαὶ περὶ τῆς ἐκκλησίας τῆς Κύπρου*, Athens, 1875, pp. 131–2.

[23] Cf. the silver-gilt covering of the icon of the Theotokos (1795), the ciborium of 1771, the artophorium of 1807, in Chrysostomos, abbot of Kykkos, *Ἡ ἱερὰ βασιλικὴ καὶ σταυροπηγιακὴ μονὴ τοῦ Κύκκου*, Nicosia, 1969, pp. 28, 53, 63. Of the same high artistic level is the reliquary of the head of St Neophytos in the monastery of that name (1797) and the covering of the Theotokos Trooditissa (1799).

[24] Alexander, monk of Cyprus, *Ἐγκώμιον εἰς τὸν ἅγιον ἀπόστολον Βαρνάβαν* in *Acta Sanctorum*, Junii, vol. II, ed. nov., Paris, 1867, pp. 431–47. Cf. S. Salaville, "Le moine Alexandre de Chypre (VIe siècle), *EO* 15 (1912), pp. 134–7; L. Duchesne, "Saint Barnabé", *Mélanges G.-B. de Rossi (Suppl. aux Mélanges d'Arch. et d'Hist. publiés par l'Ecole Française de Rome, XII)*, Rome, 1892, pp. 41–71; E.W. Brooks, "The Emperor Zenon and the Isaurians", *English Historical Review* 30 (1893), pp. 209–38; G. Downey, "The Claim of Antioch to Ecclesiastical Jurisdiction over Cyprus", *Proceedings of the American Philosophical Society* 102 (1958), pp. 224–8.

[25] Deed of election of Nektarios, Proedros of Paphos in K. Delikanes, *Τὰ ἐν τοῖς κώδιξι τοῦ Πατριαρχικοῦ Ἀρχειοφυλακίου σωζόμενα ἐπίσημα ἐκκλησιαστικὰ ἔγγραφα τὰ ἀφορῶντα εἰς τὰς σχέσεις τοῦ Οἰκουμενικοῦ Πατριαρχείου πρὸς τὰς Ἐκκλησίας Ἀλεξανδρείας, Ἀντιοχείας, Ἱεροσολύμων καὶ Κύπρου (1574–1863)*, Constantinople, 1904, pp. 662–5, esp. p. 663: "Ὧτινι ... φιλοδορούμεθα ..., πλὴν τῆς ὑποκλαπείσης λάθρα ματαίας τοῦ Βασιλικοῦ σκήπτρου καταχρήσεως, ὅπερ, ὡς μόνῳ τῷ Ἀποστολικῷ ἡμῶν Θρόνῳ πεφιλοτιμημένον ὑπὸ τῶν ἀοιδίμων πάλαι βασιλέων Ζήνωνος καὶ Ἰουστινιανοῦ τοῦ Μεγάλου μετὰ τῆς ἐρυθρᾶς ὑπογραφῆς, οὐδένα συγκοινωνὸν τοῦ μεγίστου τούτου προνομίου ἀποδεχόμεθα" (nothing is yet said about the *mandyas*). For the bibliography relating to Nektarios see A. Tillyrides, "'Ἄγνωστα κείμενα διὰ τοὺς μητροπολίτας Κυρηνείας Τιμόθεον (1625?–1647), Πάφου καὶ Τριμυθοῦντος Νεκτάριον (1677–1686) καὶ Ἀμαθοῦντος Γερμανὸν (1572–1600)", offprint from *Theologia*, Athens, 1976, pp. 14–16.

the signature in scarlet ink of the archbishop of Cyprus, although becoming permanent at the beginning of the seventeenth century, seems to have been already programmed by the Greek bishops of Cyprus in the period of Frankish rule.[26] This became the supreme symbol and emblem of the leader of the Cypriot Church in relation not only to fellow-Orthodox and Muslims but also to foreigners and indeed to the political authorities,[27] seeing that the

---

For another indication of the intense myth-making activity of seventeenth-century bishops of Western origin see letter 14 of Kosmas Mauroudes, metropolitan of Kition, to John Patrikios, *KS* 38-39 (1974–75), pp. 72–3 (on which the editor [p. 59] relies as "very significant and of incalculable importance"!).

[26] In the forged synodical deed of 1295, *Boundaries with God's help of the holy fathers who are bishops in Cyprus in the year 6803 from Adam*, it is said that the bishop of Karpasia and archbishop of Cyprus may have a seal "with red wax because he sits on the archiepiscopal throne". See J. Darrouzès, "Textes synodaux chypriotes", *REB* 37 (1979), pp. 5–122, esp. 87 and 22–30. It is known that neither did the bishop of Karpasia bear the title of archbishop, which belonged only to the Latin bishop of Nicosia, nor did archbishops seal with red wax in the East. This privilege belonged only to the emperor when he sealed with wax. The patriarchs issued documents with lead seals, documents of secondary importance being signed by them with a green wax seal (Du Cange, *Glossarium ad scriptores mediae et infimae graecitatis*, Lyons, 1688, *s.v.* Βούλλα, cols 218–19). The green colour was prescribed from the time of Philip Augustus (1180–1223) as the colour of the great seal of the French kings (Y. Metman, "Sigillographie" in C. Samaran, éd., *L' histoire et ses méthodes*, Paris, 1961, pp. 393–446, esp. p. 407). The false synod of 1295 bestowed it on the third-ranking bishop, in the synod's view, the bishop of Solea and Nicosia, the second-ranking bishop, the bishop of Paphos, having received the privilege of black wax. All these are inventions under Western influence. As is known, in the Byzantine period the archbishops of Cyprus sealed their more official documents with lead bulls. See e.g. A. Bryer, "A Seal of Epiphanius, Archbishop of Cyprus", *KS*, 34 (1970), pp. 19–24.

[27] On the pride of the Cypriots over this, see Archim. Kyprianos, Ἱστορία χρονολογικὴ τῆς νήσου Κύπρου, Venice, 1788, p. 314: "Proof of the attitude of the Porte is that it gives a favourable reception to the *arze* of the Cypriot episcopate, that is, their report on the public revenues and their lamentation, on every occasion when the *arze* is sent directly to the Porte with their seals, the name of the Archbishop being written in Turkish in cinnabar (whose seal is the only one stamped in red letters in the royal *Kaiti*, or Codex of seals, which includes those of the Patriarchs in black ink) and the names of the three Metropolitans in black ink. It may be concluded from this that the mighty kingdom of the Ottomans was informed after the fall, and no doubt this was confirmed by the Patriarch, that the Archbishop of Cyprus had an ancient privilege bestowed by the emperors for his obedience and faith and that of the Rayah, which has been maintained to this day, to sign his name in red letters and append his seal in red, and for this reason his cinnabar seal is accepted by the Porte and by all the Ottomans. I do not believe that any similar seal is to be found stamped in red in such Codices." Archbishop Philotheos also writes in his *Semioseis*, p. 386: "... and with regard to any reports sent by the Archbishop of Cyprus to the authorities outside the island until modern times, if these are not sealed in red letters they are not given credence by the recipients, who know by tradition the ancient insignia of Cyprus. Therefore the red signature and seal do not cause them any annoyance at all, just as the name of the sovereign was often written in red ..."

purple *mandyas* and the sceptre were only seen in Cyprus and even then only in church.[28]

There are many testimonies from before Kyprianos of the pride which the archbishops of Cyprus took in the supreme privilege of signing in red ink, such as, for example, the portrait painted by John Kornaros of Archbishop Chrysanthos in which he is not only shown writing his signature in porphyry letters, but his name, the word "Cyprus" and the whole acrostic inscription at the foot of the icon ("Ὁ Κύπρου Χρύσανθος") are rendered in red paint.[29] It seems, however, that Kyprianos wanted to leave a permanent visible token of this privilege in the inkstand before us. That he saw the role of the inkwell in this way is proved by his portrait which he commissioned for his birthplace, the village of Strovolos. Both in the surviving initial sketch[30] and in its carved execution on the church's iconostasis,[31] he is portrayed as wearing the gold

---

[28] Although the portraits of archbishops of Cyprus preserved in the cathedral and elsewhere show them wearing a black *rason* and head-dress, it seems that Kyprianos used to appear, at least on some occasions, dressed in purple. See the reminiscences of J.M. Kinneir of 14 January 1814 in C.D. Cobham, *Excerpta Cypria*, Cambridge, 1908, p. 416: "The Archbishop, dressed in a magnificent purple robe, with a long flowing beard, and a silk cap on his head, received me in the vestibule", etc. Black clothing was imposed on all Christians by Sultan Murat III (1574–95), a prescription of which Kyprianos reminded the Cypriots in his last encyclical of 16 May 1821: "Moreover, my children, your clothing should be sober and such as befits *rayahs*, your turbans and sashes and slippers should be black ..." (Archive of the holy Archiepiscopal Palace, Cyprus, Dossier of Archbishop Kyprianos, reproduced in Chapter XVI below). The beginnings of the red attire of the archbishop of Cyprus are to be sought, I believe, in the Frankish rather than the Byzantine period. By a special papal privilege the Latin archbishop of Cyprus, *legatus natus*, dressed in purple like the Cardinals. See Steffano Lusignano, *Chorograffia et breve historia universale de Cipro*, Bologna, 1573, fol. 32ᵛ ("... l' arcivescovo di Cipro, quando è alla residentia, va vestito tutto di rosso come li Cardinali ..."; J. Hackett, *A History of the Orthodox Church of Cyprus*, London, 1901, p. 476.

The staff was first used liturgically by Orthodox bishops at the end of the sixteenth and beginning of the seventeenth century. At all events, the form of the archiepiscopal sceptre of Cyprus is reminiscent of Western models or early Byzantine consular sceptres rather than those carried by the emperor, which in the East ended in a cross and not a sphere. See P.E. Schramm, *Sphaira, Globus, Reichsapfel*, Stuttgart, 1958, in which there are also many illustrations. The oldest representation known to me of the archiepiscopal sceptre of Cyprus is on the reliquary of the head of St John Lampadistes at Kalopanagiotes, dating from the archiepiscopate of Nikephoros (1641–74). See K. Myrantheus, *Ὁ ἅγιος Ἰωάννης ὁ Λαμπαδιστής*, Nicosia, 1969, illustr. 20.

[29] See the photograph in I.K. Peristianes, *Ἱστορία τῶν ἑλληνικῶν γραμμάτων* facing p. 40, and K.I. Myrianthopoulos, *Χατζηγεωργάκις Κορνέσιος, ὁ Διερμηνεὺς τῆς Κύπρου 1779–1809*, Nicosia, 1934, pp. 63–4.

[30] Plate VII. The sketch was in the possession of K. Myrantheus, formerly president of the council of the church of Chryseleousa in Strovolos, who now, however, asserts that he does not have it. He published an illustration in his work, *Κειμήλια τοῦ ἱεροῦ ναοῦ Χρυσελεούσης Στροβόλου*, Nicosia, 1949, Plate 8. The photograph reproduced here has kindly been supplied by the parish priest of the church, the Revd K. Koukos.

[31] Plate VIII.

and porphyry *mandyas* and carrying the archiepiscopal sceptre, and lying to his right, open and with two quill pens protruding from it, is a representation of our inkstand.[32] This silver-gilt box solved the problem of the representation and dissemination of the third of the archiepiscopal privileges in a plastic way and without the use of colour.

The question of an *archon's* signature was not a small matter for Byzantine politics and ecclesiastical diplomacy. It is known that from the fifth century the emperor signed in a reddish-purple ink called "the sacred encaustic". The first mention of this is in a law of Leo I from the year 470, incorporated later into the Justinianic code. That law forbade the practice of signing or the granting of the right of signing by encaustic on pain of confiscation of property and death (which excludes the granting of this right to Anthemios by Zeno, the heir and, through marriage to his daughter, son-in-law of Leo I).[33] From the ninth century the *archon* ἐπὶ τοῦ κανικλείου appears in the Byzantine court with the responsibility of keeping the imperial ink and inkstand. The marks which this official made on state documents on behalf of or for the emperor were made with a red ink different from the sacred encaustic called τοῦ κανικλώματος. Such importance was attached to the imperial ink that when there was a regency it was forbidden for the guardian of the imperial minor to sign documents with it, a special "frog" coloured, i.e. green, ink being supplied for the purpose.[34] Even the ecumenical patriarch, who signed in blue ink, entrusted his pen with the passage of time to the custody of an ecclesiastical official, the protonotary, of the first grade of the second pentad, who stood always to the right of the patriarch.[35]

Coming from the Danubian principalities, where the Byzantine tradition had been kept alive by the Roumanian princes and their Phanariot successors,[36]

---

[32] The only difference between the original and the representation is that the latter is shown with feet and two clasps, which is incorrect.

[33] *Codex Just.* I, 23:6–a.470: "... Hanc autem sacri encausti confectionem nulli sit licitum aut concessum habere aut quaerere aut a quoquam sperare: eo videlicet, qui hoc adgressus fuerit tyrannico spiritu post proscriptionem bonorum omnium capitali non immerito poena plectendo." See C.J. Carini, "Sulla porpora e sul' colore porporino nella diplomatica specialmente siciliana", *Nuove effemeridi siciliane*, ser. 3, vol. 10, Palermo, 1880; I.E. Karayannopoulos, *Βυζαντινὴ διπλωματική. Α΄. Αὐτοκρατορικὰ ἔγγραφα,* Thessaloniki, 1972, pp. 101–5.

[34] See B. de Montfaucon, *Palaeographia graeca*, Paris, 1708, p. 3.

[35] See e.g. the *Diataxis* of the patriarchal liturgy in I. Habert, *ARXIEPATIKON. Liber pontificalis ecclesiae graecae*, Paris, 1643, p. 27. Cf. J. Darrouzès, *Recherches sur les offikia de l' église byzantine*, Paris, 1970, pp. 446, 561 etc. With regard to the colour of the patriarchal signature, the first who seems to have used blue was John Glykys (1315–19, I. Kantakouzenos, 3.36), even though this was previously regarded as the patriarchal colour (see I. Habert, op. cit., p. 431, "καὶ θρόνου ἠερανέου τεθέντος κτλ.").

[36] See N. Jorga, *Byzance après Byzance*, Bucharest, 1971, and various relevant studies in the volume *Études byzantines et post-byzantines*, I, Bucharest, 1979.

Kyprianos could not but take steps to remedy his predecessors' lack of an inkstand commensurate with the exalted nature of the privilege of signing in red ink. Naturally he also had represented on it the other privileges, the emperor who by tradition had granted them, and the founding apostle of the Church of Cyprus, on whose account they had been granted. The privileges are interpreted in these representations not exclusively, or even primarily, as ecclesiastical, but, as the portrait of Archbishop Kyprianos clearly shows, as ethnarchic. Along with other things this helps us along the road towards the correct historical interpretation of the origin of the tradition about the privileges. In spite of the attempt of the seventeenth- and eighteenth-century sources to tie the archiepiscopal privileges to the time of the question of the Cypriot autocephaly under Zeno – or under Justinian I or Justinian II – the privileges have no direct relationship with autocephaly. They belong to the temporal power of the archbishops (urban, political or ethnarchic, according to the needs of the moment) and it is in that area that the creation and development of their myth must be sought.[37]

In the midst of the appalling Turkish oppression of the seventeenth century, the terrible evils of the eighteenth century and the indescribable agonies of the beginning of the nineteenth century, the dreams of a glorious historical past, the memories of the brilliant ancient struggles and victories of Cyprus, the knowledge that the archbishop stood in the midst of the ruins as a *rayah* yet invested with power and eminent throughout the entire Orthodox world, consoled the wretched Cypriots, restored their self-respect, fed their imagination, built up their morale, purified their character and uplifted their soul. There had been a past and therefore there could also be a future. Beyond

---

[37] The bishops begin to be considered *"defensores civitatis"* from the age of Constantine the Great. They were expected to defend the population from the high-handed action of governors and often to see to the appointment of civil servants, the supervision of economic matters and the maintenance of public buildings, or sometimes, especially in Egypt, even the administration of the army. See *Codex Just.* I, iv, 21, 31, 33, *Neara* 84, etc.; G. Bardy in A. Fliche and V. Martin, *Histoire de l'Église*, IV, Paris, 1945, pp. 539–40. With regard to Cyprus, we have from the fifth century the inscription of Illyrios, bishop (probably) of Lapithos, on the walls of that city, from the sixth century the episcopal inscription on the *apaneterion* (hotel) of Soloi, from the seventh century the builder's inscription of Archbishops Arkadios and Plutarchos on the aqueduct of Salamis, etc. (see T.B. Mitford, "Some New Inscriptions from Early Christian Cyprus", *REB* 20 [1950], pp. 105–75). For the urban authority of the Cypriot bishops in the years of Cypriot neutrality between the Empire and the Caliphate and the "ethnarchic" mission of St Demetrianos bishop of Kythroi to Baghdad, see R. Browning, "Byzantium and Islam in Cyprus in the Early Middle Ages", *EKEEK* 9 (1977–79), pp. 101–16. The role of the bishops in this respect in the Frankish and Ottoman periods is well-known.

On porphyry and the colour purple as a sign of social rank see the detailed study of M. Reinhold, "The History of Purple as Status Symbol in Antiquity", *Collection Latomus* 116, 1970.

the ugliness of servitude and the consequent corruption of character there existed the beauty of the Church of the poor of Christ.

A human being who has been enslaved consists of two persons: that which he was, which holds erect that which he is. If the idealized memory of the former is lost, it is impossible for the latter to hold himself erect. The greatest service which the Church in its ethnarchic role performed for the enslaved Cypriots, rather than provide practical benefits, which it certainly also did, was to preserve the memory of who they had once been. It gave them an idea of innate greatness and, in the face of the stubborn realities of everyday life, succeeded for centuries in keeping before people's eyes the enjoinder: "we do not agree with the multitude that the most precious thing in life is the bare preservation of existence. We hold, as I think we have said before, that it is better to become thoroughly good and to remain so as long as existence lasts."[38]

Within these dimensions, however, the inkstand which we are examining has the purpose of exalting and glorifying its owner, Archbishop Kyprianos, as saviour and restorer of Cyprus. His image on the inkstand represents Kyprianos as father of his country, proclaiming his archiepiscopate as a time of rebirth for Cyprus, a *saeculum Cyprianum*.

The conditions under which the *oikonomos* Kyprianos came to the throne in 1810 are in their broad lines well-known. His appearance on the Cypriot scene and his success personify in many ways the change which came upon both the Ottoman Empire and the Cypriot community in the first years of the nineteenth century. The extremely old Chrysanthos and the Dragoman of Cyprus, Hadjigeorgakis, already belonged to the eighteenth century that was past. With regard to the Divan, they represented the pro-Russian party which was protected in Constantinople by the Ypsilanti, who from 1806 had become completely powerless. With regard to Cyprus the two great old men represented the old landowning aristocracy, in contrast to the growing class of urban merchants. Having lived in Moldavia under the patronage of the Francophile Soutsoi and having spent twenty years amongst the "progressive" Greek merchants of the Diaspora, Kyprianos represented, by contrast, the "enlightened" new spirit, that is, the new era of the towns and of their culture.

For the Turks in Cyprus Kyprianos signified above all the end of the reign of the hated Chrysanthos and Hadjigeorgakis and their families, without their suspecting in any way that he represented at the same time the rise of a new kind of urban nationalism. For the consulates of Larnaca, the *oikonomos* symbolized a more cosmopolitan outlook, for the merchants of Scala he

---

[38] Plato, *Laws* 707d (trans. A.E. Taylor).

promised to be an archbishop with a Western education. For the ecclesiastics Kyprianos was identified with Machairas in opposition to the overweening
influence of Kykkos. For the people, finally, he meant hopes of lighter taxation
and at any rate a change. All things tended to favour him, apart, one should
say, from the decision of the centenarian Chrysanthos not to die, and the
canonical structures of the Church. In the end Chrysanthos was exiled and
the canons set aside. The new was imposed on the old, but his justification
and apologia was needed, especially in view of the fact that his imposition
brought about the death in exile of the indomitable Chrysanthos.[39]

See how Kyprianos himself describes the circumstances of his succession
to the throne one year later, in 1811: "After the departure to the Lord of our
blessed and ever-memorable predecessor, the Lord Archbishop Chrysanthos,
which took place in the year of salvation 1810 in the month of September
by the common vote and approval of all the celibate clergy of our island of
Cyprus, when we were promoted to the most holy throne of the
Archdiocese ..."[40] Six months later the tone becomes more assertive and aspires
to some grandeur: "Having become by the grace of God and the evangelical lamp, ephor of ecclesiastical and civil matters in this supreme office, of
this most holy Archdiocese, and having been entrusted with the spiritual flock
of our island of Cyprus ..."[41] Falling completely silent on the *how* of the
departure to the Lord of his sacred predecessor and of his own accession,
Kyprianos, a new "priest and king", thus speaks as absolute *archon* of the island
by the grace of God.[42] These are words which the dreadful days to come
would show to be exaggerated. We are in the area of pious desires and self-
deception rather than of hard reality.

---

[39] For events in the time of Chrysanthos see K.I. Myrianthopoulos, *Χατζηγεωργάκις Κορνέσιος,* esp. pp. 109–17, 119–26, 131–34. More generally on Kyprianos see K.D. Christophides (ed.), *Πανηγυρικὸν λεύκωμα ἐπὶ τῇ τελετῇ τῶν ἀποκαλυπτηρίων τῆς προτομῆς τοῦ ἐθνομάρτυρος Κυπριανοῦ ἐν τῇ γενετείρᾳ αὐτοῦ Στροβόλῳ,* Nicosia, 1929; K. Spyridakis, "Ὁ ἐθνομάρτυς ἀρχιεπίσκοπος Κύπρου Κυπριανὸς" in *Μελέται, διαλέξεις λόγοι, ἄρθρα,* A'a, Nicosia, 1972, pp. 297–317.

[40] K.I. Myrianthopoulos, *Χατζηγεωργάκις Κορνέσιος,* pp. 172–3.

[41] Foundation deed of the School of Nicosia in L. Philippou, *Τὰ ἑλληνικὰ γράμματα ἐν Κύπρῳ κατὰ τὴν περίοδον τῆς Τουρκοκρατίας (1571–1878),* Nicosia, 1930, pp. 93–6, esp. p. 94.

[42] "Since the most holy archiepiscopal throne remained vacant, its occupant having tendered his free and voluntary resignation ...". I regret to say that the *Memorandum* on the promotion of Archbishop Kyprianos recorded on p. 167 of the *Great Codex* of the Archiepiscopal Palace begins with such a lie. Matters were put on a proper canonical footing, as is known, by Konstantios, archbishop of Sinai, who refused to consecrate Kyprianos until the case had been judged by the Great Church or Chrysanthos had resigned in the canonical manner (*Great Codex,* pp. 156–7).

In the rest of the foundation document of the Greek School of Nicosia of 1 January 1812 the new archbishop, thanks to his self-justification and exaltation, and also seduced no doubt by the customary grandiloquent style of the period, is silent about the maintenance of such a school by Chrysanthos and Paisios and Philotheos, in which celebrated teachers specially brought from Greece had taught, such as Ephraim the Athenian and Prokopios the Peloponnesian.[43] In 1808 the Cypriot hieromonk Joannikios of the Holy Sepulchre and the Dragoman Hadjigeorgakis[44] were similarly silent about the documents making donations for the education of the place, but in that case it concerned private individuals. The archbishop should have put the honour of his throne above his own glory. This would also have been the best justification of his elevation to the archiepiscopate.

In 1813 the apologia does not sound different, even though when recalling the monastery of his profession he seems uneasy for a moment: "And as for us, from this starting-point of our life where we made our repentance and still maintain it and will keep it to the end of our life at the sacred and thrice-holy monastery of the all-holy Theotokos which is called Machairas, the momentum of things entangled us in the disturbance of the world, the administration, that is, of civil matters, in which we became involved, and having been snatched up into it, without warning, even though unworthy, we were promoted to the most holy and apostolic throne of the most holy Archdiocese of New Justiniani and all Cyprus ..."[45] "Administration of civil matters" is how the archbishop describes his service as *oikonomos* of the arch-diocese under Chrysanthos, something not very far from the truth, at least in the sphere of taxes, even though the expression "snatched up" strikes the ear painfully. Kyprianos's actions were motivated by ambition, which through a momentary inadvertance he was not able to conceal from history.

Referring in reality in the document of 1 January 1812 to the accusations brought against Cyprus which he had heard "in as many places and foreign dioceses as he had visited" that only this one of all the islands did not have "a common place of learning", he adds: "I repeat these accusations to those who have ears to hear, and from that time nourishing this zeal in the depths of my soul, when we became sovereign, with the help of God and we put our good aim into practice ..."[46] "From that time", then, the now "sovereign" had the "zeal" and "aim" for a good cause, which, however, he

[43] See K.N. Sathas, Νεοελληνικὴ φιλολογία, Athens, 1868, pp. 553–4; L. Philippou, Τὰ ἑλληνικὰ γράμματα, esp. pp. 130–58, 86–92.

[44] L. Philippou, pp. 88–92.

[45] Act of benefaction to the monastery of Machairas in S. Menardos, Ἡ ἐν Κύπρῳ ἱερὰ μονὴ τῆς Παναγίας τοῦ Μαχαιρᾶ, Peiraeus, 1929, pp. 142–9, esp. p. 146.

[46] Ibid., note 41, p. 95.

directed with the utmost ingratitude against his benefactor, Archbishop Chrysanthos.

Writing elsewhere about his monastery, the grandiose Machairiot uses an image reminiscent of the representation on the back of his inkstand:

> "Cities truly die like men, as one of the old philosophers said, and all-conquering time, which causes many things to decay and draws them away like a stream, gave them over to destruction ... Alas! the yoke of the barbarian tyranny, the lamentable disasters which have befallen our country and misfortunes and temporal circumstances have reduced her who was formerly conspicuous and eminent to a miserable sight and fallen state ... Therefore we, and in accordance with our archiepiscopal obligation and profession ... and looking to nothing else except to the restoration of things as they were ..."[47]

In spite of his personal ambitions, in spite of his diminution of heroic predecessors such as Chrysanthos and Philotheos, Archbishop Kyprianos did not exalt himself definitively above the institution which he served. As has been shown here, his desire was not to appear as an innovator but as a renewer and restorer of the original beautiful order of things. Such clearly was the ideology which his image on his inkstand expresses in accordance with the more general theory of leadership that prevailed until 1789, according to which every innovation leads unswervingly to backwardness, error and chaos. Certainly we are dealing here with stereotypes which often have no connection with reality. If they mean anything, it is simply the sensible moderation of the man and his conservative Byzantine outlook with regard to form, expression and moral matters.

No one can deny the contribution of Archbishop Kyprianos, even though it is still almost completely unknown. There was, however, the same continuity, within the new conditions, of the action of his famous predecessor, Archbishop Chrysanthos. This evidently did not satisfy Kyprianos, who as a simple follower of Chrysanthos could not easily have justified his position. He had to appear as one who renewed and restored; his archiepiscopate had to be seen as a renaissance of Cyprus. Only thus could the manner of his ascent of the throne of Cyprus be justified. Experienced as he was, Cyprian turned in this direction from the beginning. His policy was to be continued without change until 1821, when all these things, plans, concerns, dreams for himself, his family, his monastery, Cyprus, would crumble away before

---

[47] Second act of benefaction to the monastery of Machairas in Menardos, op. cit., pp. 149–53, esp. 149–52.

the gallows. A better end could not have been given. The busy ecclesiastic entered into history justified not by his life and works but by his sacrifice and death. The red cinnabar which justified him was his blood.

The historian, gazing today at the inkstand of Archbishop Kyprianos of blessed memory, recollects the human anxieties, the fears and ambitions, which were embodied here, and the costly, sudden and headlong outcome which the *ethnomartyr* did not foresee. Later he studies the intellectual instruments and the contents which provide meaning, the scale of values and the type of sensibility, the greatness and the trivialities of a whole era. The silver-gilt inkstand with the two bottles he imagines more as a symbol of the whole history of the Church on earth. The dark ink outlines the Church as authority, the ecclesiastical rather than the ecclesiological mentality, the material wealth, the prince bishops. The red ink records the Church as holiness, desire for the divine, the love of learning, the self-denial of service, the blood of martyrdom. In speaking about the Church the historian will show a preference either for the dark or the red, depending on what he is setting out. He is in a position, however, to know better than anyone else how much harm is usually caused by good dispositions of unclean hearts. "Avoir le coeur dégagé des passions et sur tout de celle de critiquer" was the advice to him of Jean Mabillon.[48]

It remains true that even the most ignorant of the feudal bishops of the Turkish period whenever they were called upon to do so, showed themselves able to offer their lives for their Faith and their Nation. The historian cannot deny this, independently of whether he can also borrow for the future on the security of the past.

The believer may know that to live truly in a Christian manner in the world is impossible; one can only die in a Christian manner. If faith and history come together in one person, the faithful historian will write as an epilogue that the contradictions of ecclesiastical history finally reveal nothing other than simply the innate contradiction between the Church of God and the history of this world.

---

[48] J. Mabillon, *Traité des études monastiques*, Paris, 1691, pp. 294–5: "Il faut avoir le coeur dégagé des passions, et sur tout de celle de critiquer, qui est une maladie assez commune à des jeunes gens qui font les suffisans, et qui ne peuvent souffrir la moindre faute, ni mesme la moindre apparence de faute, non seulement dans des auteurs du commun, mais dans les Pères mesmes, sans perdre le respect qui leur est dû. Il ne faut pas critiquer seulement pour critiquer, ce qui est une bassesse d'esprit, et l'effet d'une mauvaise humeur: mais il faut critiquer pour avancer dans les sciences, et pour en applanir les voyes. Il ne faut pas non plus se rendre trop difficile ni trop pointilleux, de crainte de tout gâter en voulant tout reformer."

XV

THE CANONICAL DECISION OF KONSTANTIOS, ARCHBISHOP OF SINAI, ON THE ELECTION AND DEPOSITION OF THE ARCHBISHOP OF CYPRUS*

Archbishop's Palace, *Codex* I, pages 156–7

Larnaca Scala, 2 July 1810

TEXT

|¹⁵⁶ Ἴσον τοῦ εἰς τὸ ἀνωτέρω συνοδικὸν Γράμμα ἀποκριτικοῦ τῆς Αὐτοῦ Σοφωτάτης Πανιερολογιότητος Γράμματος.

Πανιερώτατοι ἐν Χριστῷ ἀγαπητοὶ ἀδελφοὶ ἅγιε Πάφου καὶ ἅγιε Κυρηνείας, αἰδεσιμώτατε Μέγα Οἰκονόμε, μετὰ πάντων τῶν ἐν Λευκωσίᾳ ἱερέων, ἐνδοξώτατε Ἄρχων Διερμηνευτά, καὶ οἱ λοιποὶ ἐντιμώτατοι κληρικοὶ τῆς Ἁγιωτάτης Ἀρχιεπισκοπῆς Νέας Ἰουστινιανῆς καὶ πάσης Κύπρου.

Μετὰ χαρᾶς ὅσης πλείστης ἐδεξάμεθα τὴν ἀγαπητὴν ὑμῶν καὶ προσκλητικὴν συνοδικὴν ἐπιστολήν, ὅπως ἔλθωμεν εἰς Λευκωσίαν. Καὶ περὶ μὲν τῆς γενομένης καὶ ἐκ μέρους ὑμῶν ἐκλογῆς συνῳδὰ τῷ βασιλείῳ θεσπίσματι πρὸς τὸν Πανοσιολογιώτατον ἅγιον Οἰκονόμον Κὺρ Κυπριανόν, ἐπὶ τῷ ἀναδειχθῆναι τοὺς πνευματικοὺς οἴακας πάσης τῆς Κύπρου, ἐστὶν ἀρίστη καὶ φρονίμη, διότι μόνος αὐτός, ὡς εἰδὼς πάντα, δύναται ἐπὶ τοιούτων σφοδρῶν καὶ ἀλγεινῶν τῆς πατρίδος ὑμῶν περιστάσεων στῆναι πρὸς τὰ τοιαῦτα ῥαγδαῖα τῶν ἀλλεπαλλήλων καταιγίδων, καὶ κατευνάσαι

---

*Translated from the unpublished study "Κανονικὴ ἀπόκρισις Σιναίου Κωνσταντίου περὶ ἐκλογῆς καὶ καθαιρέσεως ἀρχιεπισκόπου Κύπρου."

τὴν τῶν πραγμάτων πικρὰν ταραχὴν καὶ ζάλην, ὡς ἐχέφρων τῷ ὄντι καὶ πολύπειρος κυβερνήτης. Περὶ δὲ τῆς διαδοχῆς αὐτοῦ τῆς γενομένης μόνον θύραθεν, καὶ οὐχὶ διὰ τῆς νομίμου καὶ κανονικῆς εἰσέτι, ἐφ' ᾧ προσκαλεῖται ἡμᾶς τοὺς παρεπιδημοῦντας ἐνταῦθα, ἵνα ἔλθωμεν καὶ συνδιασκεφθῶμεν περὶ τῆς ἐκκλησιαστικῆς ταύτης ὑποθέσεως, ἀποκρινόμενοι ὑμῖν λέγομεν, ὅτι τεκμειρόμενοι τὸ τῆς τοιαύτης διασκέψεως πρῶτον, καὶ πύματον, καὶ μέσον, ἀναγγέλλομεν ὑμῖν ἀποφατικῶς, ὅτι ἡ μόνη ὁδός, ἡ ἐν διαταγαῖς πρεσβυγενέσιν, ἱεραῖς τε καὶ ἀμετατρέπτοις, νομίμως μέλλουσα εἰσάξαι τοὺς ὑποψηφισθέντας εἰς τὴν τῶν προβάτων αὐλὴν ἐστίν αὕτη· ἢ ἡ διὰ παραιτήσεως τῶν ἐξορισθέντων, ἢ τέλος ἡ δι' ἀδείας τῆς Μεγάλης Μητρὸς ἡμῶν Ἐκκλησίας, δι' ἀναφορᾶς κοινῆς ὑμῶν ἐξιστορούντων πάντα τὰ αἴτια, καὶ ἐπιζητούντων τὰ τῆς χειροτονίας, ἥτις ἐπὶ τοιούτων ἐκκλησιαστικῶν ἀμφιβόλων ὑποθέσεων |¹⁵⁷ ἔχει πεπληρωμένην ἰσχὺν καὶ κράτος, καὶ ἄνευ παραιτήσεως, ἐπιτάξαι τὴν χειροτονίαν.

Τοῦτο δὲ οὐ βλάπτει τὸ τῆς Κύπρου αὐτόνομον, διότι ἀείποτε ἐπὶ τοιούτων κανονικῶν δυσεπιλύτων ὑποθέσεων, οὐ μόνον οἱ τῶν Ἀρχιεπισκόπων αὐτόνομοι, ἀλλὰ καὶ αὐτοὶ οἱ λοιποὶ τῶν τριῶν Πατριαρχῶν, μὴ δυνάμενοι παρ' ἑαυτῶν διαλῦσαι ἐκκλησιαστικάς τινας ἀμφιβολίας, κατέφυγον πρὸς τὸ κοινὸν καὶ ὑπέρτατον τῆς εὐαγοῦς ἡμῶν πίστεως τοῦτο κριτήριον, πειθαρχοῦντες τῇ τοῦ Ἀποστόλου ὑπὸ τοῦ Χρυσορρήμονος ὑπομνηματιζομένῃ ἐντολῇ ταύτῃ: «πᾶσα ψυχὴ ἐξουσίαις ὑπερεχούσαις ὑποτατέσθω· κἂν ἀπόστολος ᾖς, κἂν εὐαγγελιστής, κἂν προφήτης, κἂν ὁστισοῦν». Οἱ δ' ἄλλως ποιήσαντες, καὶ μόνοι αὐτοβούλως διορίσαντες, ἥμαρτον εἰς τὰ μάλιστα, καὶ σφοδρότατα κατεκρίθησαν, καὶ συνοδικῶς ἐπαιδεύθησαν. Μόνη γὰρ ἡ σύνοδος ἄπταιστος, διὸ καὶ τὰ παρ' αὐτῆς περὶ κανονικῶν διατυπώσεων ἀποφαινόμενα, ἱερὰ καὶ ἅγια, καὶ ἀναντίρρητα, οἷστισιν ὁ ἀνθιστάμενος, οἵας ἂν εἴη τάξεώς τε καὶ βαθμοῦ, ἐστίν ὑπόδικος καὶ ἀφορισμῷ καὶ καθαιρέσει.

Ἀλλὰ λέγουσι τυχὸν τινές, ὅτι ὑπ' ἀνάγκης παραβαίνεσθαι τοὺς ἐκκλησιαστικοὺς κανόνας συμβαίνει. Ἕπεται ναὶ τοῦτο, ὅταν πρὸς τὸ συμφέρον τῆς τοῦ Θεοῦ ἐκκλησίας, ὡς οἱ Πατέρες διακελεύουσι, ὁ τὴν ἐξουσίαν ἔχων τοῦτο οἰκονομήσῃ. Ἀλλὰ τίς ὁ ἔχων τὴν ἐξουσίαν ταύτην; Οὐδεὶς πάντως ἕτερος, εἰμὴ ἡ σύνοδος. Σύνοδος γὰρ ὡράθη σύνοδον λύσασα, διὰ τὴν τῆς ἐκκλησίας εἰρήνην, καὶ νηνεμίαν.

Πρὸς δὲ τοῖς πολλοῖς, παράδειγμα ἔστω ὑμῖν καὶ τὸ τῆς αὐτονομίας τουτοῖ ἀδύναμον, καὶ ὑποτεταγμένον ἀείποτε περὶ ἐκκλησιαστικῶν ἀποφάσεων τῇ τῆς Κωνσταντινουπόλεως Ἱερᾷ Συνόδῳ: ἐπὶ βασιλείας Μανουὴλ τοῦ Κομνηνοῦ, ὁ Πατριάρχης τῆς Κωνσταντίνου Λουκᾶς ἄκυρον ἡγήσατο καὶ παράνομον τὴν τοῦ ἐπισκόπου Ἀμαθοῦντος καθαίρεσιν, ἣν ὁ Ἀρχιεπίσκοπος ἐποιήσατο Κύπρου, ὅτι ἕνδεκα μόνοις συνῆν ἐπισκόποις, μὴ ἐπέκεινα, ὡς αὐτὸς τὸν δωδέκατον ἀριθμὸν ἐκπληρῶν. Καὶ ἐὰν τὸ ὑπὸ τῶν ἕνδεκα κατεκρίθη καὶ ἀνετράπη, πολλῷ μᾶλλον τὸ ὑπὸ τριῶν διορισθέν;

Ἡμεῖς δ᾽ ἐνταῦθα ξένοι ὄντες, καὶ ἕνεκα τῶν καιρικῶν ἀνωμαλιῶν παροδικῶς ἐπιχωριάζοντες, οὐ δυνάμεθα ὅλως, παραιτήσεως μὴ οὔσης, ἄνευ πατριαρχικῆς καὶ συνοδικῆς πρότερον ἀδείας, χειροτονίαν ἐπισκόπου ποιῆσαι, ἀπειργόμενοι ὑπό τε τῶν ἀποστολικῶν (κεφ. λε΄) κανόνων, καὶ τῶν λοιπῶν καθολικῶν καὶ τοπικῶν συνόδων, τῶν διακελευομένων, καὶ ἰσχυρῶς τὸ αὐτὸ προσφωνούντων· «ἐπίσκοπον μὴ τολμᾶν ἔξω τῶν ἑαυτοῦ ὁρίων χειροτονίας ποιεῖσθαι, εἰς τὰς μὴ ὑπαγομένας αὐτῷ πόλεις· εἰ δὲ ἐλεγχθείη αὐτοβούλως τοῦτο ποιήσας, καθαιρείσθω αὐτός τε, καὶ οὓς ἐχειροτόνησεν».

Εἰδότες οὖν τὰ μέγιστα κατὰ κανόνας κωλύματα ταῦτα, ἐσμὲν βέβαιοι, ὅτι οὐ μόνον σύμψηφοι τούτων φανῆτε ἅπαντες σὺν τῷ ἁγίῳ ὑποψηφίῳ Κυρίῳ Κυπριανῷ, ἀλλὰ καὶ οὐδεμίαν ἄλλην ἑτέραν ἀξίωσιν, ἢ (ὅ, μὴ γένοιτο) βίαν κοσμικὴν περὶ τῆς πρὸ ὥρας ἐλεύσεως ἡμῶν ἐν Λευκωσίᾳ ἐπάξετε. τότε δέ ἐλευσόμεθα ἐν χαρᾷ καὶ ἀγαλλιάσει, ὅτε ἢ ἡ παραίτησις, ἢ ἡ τῆς Κωνσταντινουπόλεως, τῆς μόνης ἰσχυούσης διαλῦσαι τὸ τοιοῦτον, ἄδεια κατὰ κανόνας ἥξει. Διὸ καὶ σπεύσατε ὡς οἷον τε τάχιστα καταπράξαι τὸ δυοῖν θάτερον καὶ ἄφευκτον τοῦτο.

Ταῦτα δὲ οὐ κυρεύοντες ὑμῶν, οὐδὲ δεσποτικῶς, γράφομεν, ἀλλ᾽, εἰς διδασκαλίαν λόγου προχειρισθέντες ὑπὸ τοῦ Δεσπότου Χριστοῦ, συμβούλων τάξιν ἐπέχομεν παραινούντων. Ὁ συμβουλεύων τὰ παρ᾽ ἑαυτοῦ οὐκ ἀναγκάζει τὸν ἀκροατήν, ἀλλ᾽ αὐτὸν ἀφίησι ἐπὶ τῶν λεγομένων αἱρέσεων κριτήν. Ἐν τούτοις κριθήσεται ὑπεύθυνος μόνον, ἂν τὴν ἀλήθειαν μὴ εἴποι. Τὰ δ᾽ ἄλλα ἐσμὲν καὶ ἐσόμεθα.

αωῖῳ, Ἰουλίου β΄ α
Ταπεινοὶ ὑπὲρ ὑμῶν παρακλήτορες πρὸς Κύριον

† Ἀρχιεπίσκοπος Σιναίου Κωνστάντιος

TRANSLATION

|156 Copy of the reply of His most learned All-holiness to the above synodical letter.[1]

All-holy beloved brethren in Christ, holy bishops of Paphos and Kyrenia, most reverend Great Oikonomos, together with all the priests in Nicosia, most renowned Dragoman of the Archons, and the rest of the most honourable clerics of the most holy Archdiocese of Nea Justiniani and all Cyprus.

We received with the greatest joy your affectionate synodical letter inviting us to Nicosia. With regard to the election held by you, in conformity with the imperial constitution, of the most holy Oikonomos the Lord

---

[1] The reference is to the immediately prior entry: "Copy of a synodical letter sent to His most learned All-holiness Archbishop Lord Konstantios, temporarily resident at Larnaca Scala, with the ejection and exile of His Beatitude Lord Chrysanthos, Archbishop of Cyprus and Metropolitan of Kition, by imperial edict, and succession to the most holy archdiocese of all Cyprus of the Most Reverend bishop-elect, Lord Kyprianos" (*Codex* I, p. 156).

Kyprianos to take up the spiritual helm of all Cyprus, your letter is good and prudent, because only he, since he has full knowledge of everything, is able in the exceedingly painful circumstances of your country to stand against these successive violent storms and calm the bitter disturbance and dizziness of things like a truly prudent and experienced helmsman. With regard to his succession, which was imposed only from outside, and is not yet legal and canonical, seeing that you invite us who sojourn here to come and examine this ecclesiastical matter, we say to you in reply that in forming a judgment about the beginning, middle and end of this question we announce to you negatively that the only path in conformity with ancient, sacred and unalterable ordinances which will bring the candidates lawfully into the sheepfold is this: either through the resignation of the exiled persons or finally through the permission of our Great Mother Church by a common report in which you set out all the causes and request consecration, which permission in matters of such ecclesiastical doubt|[157] has full power and authority, without appeal, of sanctioning the consecration.

This does not harm the autonomy[2] of Cyprus, for always in such complicated ecclesiastical matters not only autonomous archbishops but even the other three patriarchs themselves, when unable to resolve certain ecclesiastical doubts by themselves, resorted to that common and supreme tribunal of our pure faith, in obedience to the command of the Apostle as commented on by Chrysostom: "Every soul should be submissive to supreme authorities; even if you are an apostle or an evangelist or a prophet or anything whatever".[3] Those who have done differently and have determined things according to their own will have sinned greatly and have been condemned severely and have been disciplined synodically. For only the synod is without fault because its declarations on the canonical regulations are sacred and holy and incontrovertible, and whoever resists them, of whatever rank and degree, is subject to excommunication and deposition.

But perhaps some say that it happens that the ecclesiastical canons are violated out of necessity. This indeed happens when, for the good of God's Church, as the Fathers direct, he who has the authority makes such a disposition. But who is it who has this authority? Certainly nobody except for the synod. For a synod has been known to dissolve a synod for the peace and calm of the Church.

In addition to these general considerations, let the weakness of the autonomy and its subjection at all times in the past in matters of ecclesiastical decisions to the Holy Synod of Constantinople be a precedent for you: in the reign of Manuel Komnenos, Luke, the patriarch of the city of

---

[2] In the terminology of the time this of course means autocephaly.

[3] *PG* 60, 615.

Constantine, declared invalid and abusive the deposition of the bishop of Amathous, which the archbishop of Cyprus had done, because he had held a meeting with only eleven bishops, not more, since he himself supplied the twelfth member.[4] And if what was decided by the eleven could be judged negatively and overturned, how much more what was commanded by three?[5]

Since we are a foreigner here and on account of the anomalies of the times are a transient visitor, we cannot in any way, in the absence of a resignation, without previous patriarchal and synodical permission consecrate a bishop, being prevented by the apostolic canon (ch. 35), and the other catholic and local councils which have commanded and strongly endorsed the same: "Let a bishop not dare to carry out ordinations outside his own jurisdiction, in cities which are not subject to him; if he is convicted of doing this of his own volition, let him be deposed together with those whom he has ordained."[6]

Knowing therefore these very great impediments according to the canons, we are sure that you should not only appear all of you ratifiers of these along with the holy bishop-elect Lord Kyprianos, but you should bring no other petition or (God forbid) secular pressure to bear on our coming prematurely to Nicosia. We shall come with joy and exultation when either the resignation arrives or the permission in accordance with the canons comes from Constantinople, which alone has the authority to resolve this matter. Therefore make all speed to effect one of these, for one or the other is unavoidable.

We write this not in a domineering or despotic spirit, but for the sake of the teaching delivered by Christ the Master, adopting the role of offering consolatory advice. He who advises what comes from within does not force the hearer but lets him judge among the choices described. In any case he will only be held responsible as to whether he told the truth. As for the rest, I am and will be

1810, July 2,

a humble intercessor with the Lord for you

† Konstantios, Archbishop of Sinai

---

[4] *Regestes*, 1097. Cf. G.A. Rhalles – M. Potles III, pp. 322–5, esp. p. 324 (memorandum of Balsamon on the twelfth canon of Carthage = *PG* 138, 60–1). On the number of Cypriot bishops in the twelfth century see A. Poppe, "Soobscenie russkogo palomnika cerkovnoj organizakii Kipra v nacale XII beka", *EKEEK* 7, 1975–1977, pp. 53–69, with Greek summary by B. Englezakis, "Εἰδήσεις ῥώσου προσκυνητοῦ περὶ τῆς ἐν Κύπρῳ ἐκκλησιαστικῆς ὀργανώσεως κατὰ τὰς ἀρχὰς τοῦ ΙΒ΄ αἰῶνος", ibid., pp. 70–72.

[5] This refers to the supposed metropolitans Chrysanthos of Paphos and Eugenios of Kyrenia, together with Kyprianos, or perhaps the chorepiscopus of the archdiocese, Laurentios (and not Spyridon as Hackett sometimes calls him) of Trimythous.

[6] In the second part the canon is abbreviated.

XVI

THE LAST KNOWN DOCUMENT OF THE *ETHNOMARTYR*, ARCHBISHOP KYPRIANOS, 16 MAY 1821*

The document edited below is not unknown as it was first published anonymously by K. Myrianthopoulos in 1930 in the official journal of the Church of Cyprus, *Ἀπόστολος Βαρνάβας*.[1] That edition, however, neither corresponds to modern scientific rules nor is it free from erroneous readings and, above all, has not yet been submitted to historical examination. A document does not become a piece of historical evidence simply by its material existence: it becomes such only in the measure in which the historian can know and *comprehend* something from it.[2]

The present document is a pastoral letter which, at the direction of the Ottoman government of the island, the *ethnomartyr*, Archbishop Kyprianos (1810–1821), addressed to the inhabitants of the administrative district of Kythrea. So far as we are aware, this letter is the last known document of the archbishop of blessed memory. It is not known how it survived. It came later into the possession of Archbishop Sophronios (1865–1900) and was given subsequently to the Archiepiscopal Palace when in 1930 the nephew of Archbishop Sophronios, Aristodemas D. Phoinieus donated the personal archive of his uncle to the Church.[3]

---

* Translated from "Τὸ τελευταῖον γνωστὸν ἔγγραφον τοῦ ἐθνομάρτυρος ἀρχιεπισκόπου Κυπριανοῦ – 1821, Μαΐου 16," *KS* 46 (1982), pp. 103–18.

[1] K. Myrianthopoulos, "Σπουδαῖον ἔγγραφον τοῦ ἐθνομάρτυρος ἀρχιεπισκόπου Κυπριανοῦ", *Ἀπόστολος Βαρνάβας* 2, per. II (1930), pp. 440–1. A full page photograph without annotation or mention in the text was published in the *Μεγάλη Ἑλληνικὴ Ἐγκυκλοπαιδεία* 15, p. 431.

[2] H-I. Marrou, *De la connaissance historique*, Paris, 1975, p. 79: "Le document ... est un document dans la mesure où l'historien peut et sait y *comprendre* quelque chose."

[3] K. Myrianthopoulos "Σπουδαῖον ἔγγραφον", p. 440; ibid, *Ἀρχεῖον τῆς Ἀρχιεπισκοπῆς Κύπρου. Ἀναγραφὴ ἐγγράφων ἀπὸ τοῦ 1767–1853* (MS), Nicosia, 1941, p. 17. *Ἀρχεῖον τῆς Ἀρχιεπισκοπῆς Κύπρου. Βιβλίον Μ΄* (MS), Nicosia, 1948/9, p. 4, n. 4.

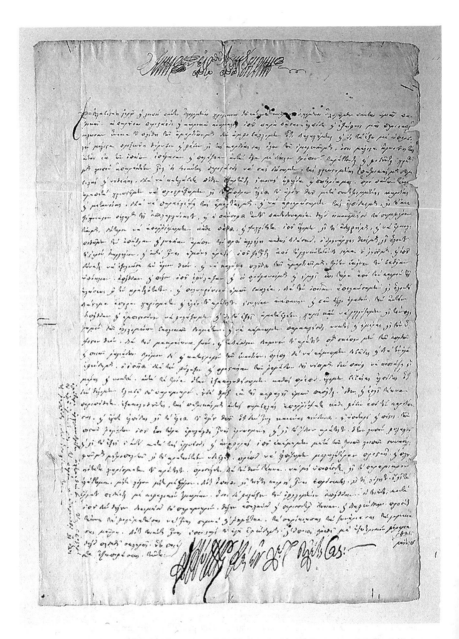

The last known document of the *ethnomartyr* Archbishop Kyprianos,
16 May 1821 (Treasury of the Archiepiscopal Palace.)

Some years ago, on instructions from Archbishop Makarios III, the document was removed from the Archive of the Archdiocese of Cyprus, framed and installed in the Treasury of the Archiepiscopal Palace, where it is kept under close security.[4]

Summary: The archbishop regards it as his obligation to calm the hearts of his fellow Greeks agitated by the latest events and rumours. He advises them in a fatherly way first to resort to God and repentance, secondly to forgive one another in order to blot out their sins which had brought about the ordeal, and thirdly to be obedient to the sultan, the benefactor of the Christians, fulfilling all their duties towards him and offering extended prayers for his majesty.

Similarly prayers should be said for the governor of the island, the protector of the subjects of the empire. The archbishop himself and the three metropolitans have already sent reports and guarantees to the government, the protection of which is sure. Christians must in all things watch their language and their deeds, and on pain of death appear and behave in a humble way as befits those who live in servitude.

In a postscript note addressed to the recipient archimandrite of the throne, it is stressed that the letter is given out at the order of the governor and must be read out to quieten the people.

Original: Yellowish paper with a light sheen, dimensions: 565 × 395 mm. A simple leaf preserved in good condition and having six folds, five of which are horizontal and one vertical. Originally, it seems, there was only one horizontal fold and the vertical one.

The text is written in black ink on 39 lines; dimensions: 450 × 340 mm. The writing, slanting to the right (except for the letter 'τ' which leans to the left), is light and well-spaced, with some ligatures and monograms but with very few abbreviations. Capital letters are not used, the orthography is almost perfect, the accentuation is careful, the punctuation rhythmical, with faults. The archbishop signs in red ink, in accordance with his privilege, and in the same ink writes a note of three lines at the foot of the left margin.[5]

In the upper part of the page the President of the Cypriot people writes his name and title in the customary fashion without lifting pen from paper and at the beginning of the text adds his cypher.

---

[4] For permission to publish it I warmly thank His Beatitude Archbishop Chrysostomos. I also owe thanks to the archivist of the Archdiocese, Mr Ch. Theodotou.

[5] See photocopy.

Κυπριανὸς ἐλέῳ Θεοῦ ἀρχιεπίσκοπος
Νέας Ἰουστινιανῆς καὶ πάσης Κύπρου

|²† εὐλαβέστατοι ἱερεῖς κ(αὶ) λοιποὶ πάντες εὐλογημένοι χριστιανοὶ τοῦ κατηλλικίου κυθραίας εὐχόμενοι εὐλογοῦμεν πάντας ὑμᾶς πα|³τρικῶς. αἱ παροῦσαι περιστάσεις κ(αὶ) καιρικαὶ ἀνωμαλίαι ὁποῦ παρὰ πᾶσαν ἐλπίδα καὶ ἐξαίφνης μᾶς περιεκύ|⁴κλωσαν ἕνεκα τοῦ πλήθους τῶν ἁμαρτιῶν μας δὲν ἀμφιβάλλομεν ὅτι διαλαλούμεναι κ(αὶ) εἰς τὰ ἔξω μὲ ὑπερβο|⁵λὴν μάλιστα προξενοῦσι θόρυβον κ(αὶ) φόβον εἰς τὰς καρδίας σας ὅλων τῶν ὁμογενῶν μας, ὅσοι μάλιστα ἀγνοοῦσι τὰς |⁶ αἰτίας ἐκ τῶν ὁποίων ἐπήγασαν κ(αὶ) πηγάζουσιν αὐτὰ ὅλα μὲ δίκαιον τρόπον. ταράττονται κ(αὶ) φοβοῦνται χρέος |⁷ μας λοιπὸν ἀπαραίτητον εἶναι εἰς τοιαύτας περιστάσεις νὰ σᾶς δώσωμεν, τὰς χρεωστουμένας πατρικάς μας συμ|⁸βουλὰς κ(αὶ) νουθεσίας, διὰ νὰ καταλάβετε πόθεν ἐξαρτᾶται ἡ κοινὴ ὠφέλεια κ(αὶ) σωτηρία μας. πρὸ πάντων τέκνα|⁹ ἀγαπητὰ χρεωστοῦμεν νὰ προστρέξωμεν εἰς τὸ ἄπειρον ἔλεος τοῦ ἁγίου θεοῦ μετὰ συντετριμμένης καρδίας |¹⁰ κ(αὶ) μετανοίας, διὰ νὰ παραβλέψῃ τὰς ἁμαρτίας μας, κ(αὶ) νὰ ἀφιερώσωμεν τὰς ἐλπίδας μας, εἰς τό ἀνε|¹¹ξιχνίαστον πέλαγος τῆς εὐσπλαχνίας του, κ(αὶ) ἡ πάνσοφος αὐτοῦ παντοδυναμία θέλει οἰκονομήσει τὰ συμφέρον|¹²τά μας, δεύτερον νὰ ἀπορρίψωμεν κάθε πάθος, κ(αὶ) ψυχρότητα ὁποῦ ἔχομεν εἰς τοὺς ἀδελφούς μας, κ(αὶ) νὰ ἐγκολ|¹³πωθῶμεν τὴν ἀπάθειαν καὶ γνησίαν ἀγάπην τὴν πρὸς ἀλλήλους καθὼς διδάσκει, ὁ εἰρηνάρχης θεός μας εἰς ὅλον του |¹⁴ τὸ ἱερὸν εὐαγγέλιον, καὶ αὐτὴ εἶναι ἡ μόνη ἀρετὴ ὁποῦ ζητεῖται ἀπὸ τὸ γλυκύτατόν του στόμα, τοῦ ἰησοῦ μας, κ(αὶ) ὁποῦ|¹⁵ δύναται νὰ ἐξιλεώσῃ τὸν ἅγιον θεόν, κ(αὶ) νὰ καλύψῃ πλῆθος τῶν ἁμαρτιῶν μας. τρίτον ἐκείνην τὴν βαθεῖαν|¹⁶ ὑπόκλισιν, εὐπείθιαν, κ(αὶ) πίστιν ὁποῦ ἐφύλαξαν κ(αὶ) οἱ πρόγονοί μας, κ(αὶ) ἡμεῖς ἕως τώρα ἀπὸ τὸν καιρὸν τῆς |¹⁷ ἁλώσεως εἰς τὸν κραταιότατον, κ(αὶ) πολυχρόνιον ἡμῶν βασιλέα, διὰ τὴν ὁποίαν ἀπηλαύσαμεν εἰς ὅλον τὸ |¹⁸ διάστημα ἄπειρα χαρίσματα κ(αὶ) ἐλέη τοῦ κράτους του, ἡσυχίαν ἀνάπαυσιν κ(αὶ) πᾶν ἄλλο ἀγαθόν, τὴν αὐτὴν|¹⁹ εὐπείθειαν κ(αὶ) ἐμπιστοσύνην νὰ φυλάξωμεν κ(αὶ) εἰς τὸ ἐξῆς ἀμετάβλητον, χωρὶς κἂν νὰ γογγύζωμεν εἰς τὴν πλη|²⁰ρωμὴν τῶν ὀφειλομένων βασιλικῶν δοσιμάτων, κ(αὶ) νὰ κάμνωμεν παρακλήσεις νυκτὸς κ(αὶ) ἡμέρας εἰς τὸν ὕ|²¹ψιστον θεόν, διὰ τὴν μακραίωνα ζωήν, κ(αὶ) ἀδιάσειστον διαμονὴν τοῦ κράτους του πρὸς σκέπην μὲν τῶν εὐπειθῶν|²²κ(αὶ) πιστῶν ῥαγιάδων τρόμον δὲ κ(αὶ) καταστροφὴν τῶν ἐναντίων, πρέπει δὲ νὰ κάμνωμεν τοβάδες κ(αὶ) διὰ τὸν ἀγα|²³ἐφένδη μας ὁ ὁποῖος διὰ τὴν φύλαξιν κ(αὶ) προστασίαν τῶν ῥαγιάδων τῆς νήσου μας δὲν παύει νά κοπιάζῃ ἡ|²⁴μέρας κ(αὶ) νυκτός. αὐτὰ τὰ τρία ὅταν ἐξακολουθήσωμεν καθὼς πρέπει, ἔχομεν βεβαίας ἐλπίδας ὅτι|²⁵ δὲν θέλομεν βλαβῆ τὸ παραμικρόν, οὐδὲ θρὶξ ἐκ τῆς κεφαλῆς ἡμῶν πεσεῖται. ὅθεν κ(αὶ) ἐσεῖς τέκνα,|²⁶περιπόθητα, ἐξακολουθοῦντες, τὰς πατρικάς μας αὐτὰς συμβουλὰς ἀπορρίψατε κάθε φόβον ἀπὸ τὴν καρδίαν|²⁷ σας, κ(αὶ) ἔχετε ἐλπίδας εἰς τὸ ἔλεος τοῦ ἁγίου θεοῦ ὅτι δὲν

εἶναι κανένας κύνδυνος. ἡ ὑποταγὴ κ(αὶ) πίστις, τῶν|²⁸ πιστῶν ῥαγιάδων
ὅπου ἕως τώρα ἐφυλάχθη εἶναι ἐγνωσμένη κ(αὶ) εἰς τὸ ἴδιον κράτος του.
ὅταν λοιπὸν φυλαχθῇ|²⁹ κ(αὶ) εἰς τὸ ἐξῆς ἡ αὐτὴ κατὰ τὰς ἐγγυήσεις
κ(αὶ) ἀναφορὰς ὁποῦ ἐκάμαμεν μετὰ τῶν τριῶν λοιπῶν συναδελ|³⁰φῶν
μας μητροπολιτῶν εἰς τὸ κραταιότατον νδεβλέτι, πρέπει νὰ ἐλπίζωμεν
μεγαλητέραν προστασίαν, κ(αὶ) πλου|³¹σιότατα χαρίσματα τοῦ κράτους
του. προσέχετε διὰ τὸν θεὸν τέκνα, νὰ μὴ ὑποπέσητε εἰς τὸ παραμικρὸν|³²
ἐλάττομα, μήτε λόγον μήτε μὲ ἔργον, διότι ὅποιος εἰς τοιούτους καιροὺς
εἶναι ἀπρόσεκτος, εἰς τοὺς λόγους του, ἢ εἰς τὰ |³³ ἔργα του παιδεύεται
μὲ κεφαλικὴν τιμωρίαν. ὅσοι δὲ φυλάξουν τὴν ὀφειλομένην εὐπείθειαν,
οἱ τοιοῦτοι, κοντὰ|³⁴ ὁποῦ δὲν θέλουν δοκιμάσει τὸ παραμικρόν, θέλουν
ἀπολαύσει κ(αὶ) περισσοτέραν εὔνοιαν, κ(αὶ) διαφένδευσιν. προσέτι|³⁵ τέκνα
τὰ φορέματά σας νὰ εἶναι σεμνὰ κ(αὶ) ῥαγιάτικα, τὰ σαρίκια σας τὰ ζωνάρια
σας τὰ γεμενιὰ|³⁶ σας μαῦρα. διότι τοιαύτη εἶναι ἡ προσταγὴ τοῦ ἀγᾶ
ἐφένδη μας, κ(αὶ) ὅποιος εὑρεθῇ μὲ ἐξωτερικὸν φόρεμα|³⁷ θέλει παιδευθῇ
σκληρῶς. οὕτω ποιή|³⁸σατε ἐξαποφάσεως. ταῦτα:-

|³⁶⁻³⁷ 1821

|³⁷ μαΐου:16

|³⁹† ὁ Κύπρου καὶ ἐν Χ(ριστ)ῷ εὐχέτης σας:-

Ὑστερόγραφος σημείωσις ἐν τῇ ἀριστερᾷ ᾦα:

|¹ ἡμέτερε ἀρχιμανδρῖτα εὐχόμεθά σοι. εἶναι προσταγὴ|² τοῦ ἀγᾶ
ἐφένδη μας, τὸ παρὸν νὰ ἀναγνωσθῇ εἰς ὅλους|³ τοὺς ῥαγιάδες, διὰ ἡσυχίαν
των-

|⁴† Κ

Kyprianos by the grace of God
archbishop of New Justiniani and all Cyprus

† Most devout priests and all other blessed Christians of the *kadilik* of Kythrea,
having prayed we bless you all in a fatherly way. The present circumstances
and disturbances of the times which against all hope have suddenly surrounded
us on account of the multitude of our sins are no doubt passed on by word
of mouth in an undeniably exaggerated way and cause disturbance and fear
in the hearts of all our fellow-Greeks, as many of course as are unaware of
the causes from which all these things sprang and still spring in a just way.
They are shaken and in fear and it is therefore our indispensable duty in such
circumstances to give you the fatherly advice and encouragement that we
owe you so that you can understand on what our common benefit and
salvation depends. Above all, my beloved children, we must run towards the
infinite mercy of holy God with a contrite heart and with repentance so that
He should overlook our sins and we should entrust our hopes to the trackless
ocean of His mercy, and His supreme power and wisdom will look after our

interests. Secondly, we must reject every passion and coldness which we have towards our brothers, and embrace dispassion and true love for one another, as our God, who is prince of peace, teaches us in all His sacred Gospel, and this is the only virtue which is sought by His sweetest mouth, our Jesus, and which can propitiate holy God, and cover a host of our sins. Thirdly, that deep submission, obedience and faith which our ancestors also preserved, and which we from the time of the capture until now owe to our most powerful and long-lived emperor, and through which we have enjoyed throughout the interval infinite gifts and mercies of his power, calm, rest and every other good, that same obedience and trust should be preserved by us unaltered in the future without our groaning at the level of the imperial taxes owed by us and we should make intercessions night and day to the highest God for the long life and unshaken duration of his power, for the protection of the obedient and faithful *rayahs* and for the frightening and destruction of his opponents, and we must make *davas*, also for our *aga effendi* who does not cease to work night and day for the maintenance and protection of the *rayahs* of our island. When we follow these three things as we should we can depend on it that we shall not experience the slightest harm, neither will a hair fall from our head. And so you, too, my dear children, following this fatherly advice of ours, put every fear out of your hearts and place your hope in the mercy of holy God because there is no danger. The submission and faith of faithful *rayahs* which until now has been observed is known even to his majesty. When in the future, then, the same is kept in accordance with the guarantees and reports which we have made with our three brother metro-politans to the most powerful *devlet*, we hope for greater protection and richer graces of its power. Take care for God's sake, my children, that you do not fall into the slightest fault, either in word or in deed, because whoever is careless in such times in his words or his deeds is liable to capital punishment. Those who maintain the required obedience, such people, who will not experience the slightest tribulation, will enjoy greater goodwill and protection. Moreover, my children, your clothing should be sober and such as befits *rayahs*, your turbans and sashes and slippers should be black. For this is the command of our *aga effendi* and whoever is found in foreign dress will be punished severely. Make a firm decision to do this. That is all.

1821

May 16

† Archbishop of Cyprus, your intercessor in Christ.

Postscript note in the left margin

To our archimandrite, our blessing. This is ordered by our *aga effendi* to be read to them. † K

COMMENTARY

The document shows the dire situation which the national Church of the Romans faced in the Ottoman Empire after the founding of the *Philiki Etaireia*, the Society of Friends, in 1814 and after the crossing of the Danube on 22 February 1821 by Alexander Ypsilanti and the declaring of the hierarchy of the Peloponnese for the revolution.

From the beginning resistance was varied. Thus to restrict ourselves to the two presiding *ethnomartyrs,* the patriarch of Constantinople, Gregory V, refused to be enrolled into the Society, because as a bishop he thought that no one should promise blind obedience and he was bound in any case by the oath of obedience which he had given to the sultan, while Archbishop Kyprianos of Cyprus is known not to have refused initiation into the Friends.[6]

The conditions are also known which prevailed both in Constantinople and in Cyprus from March to July of that year. The ecumenical ethnarch was obliged on 4 April to make a proclamation against the revolution and to excommunicate Michael Soutsos and Alexander Ypsilanti, and on Holy Saturday, 10 April, he was hanged.[7] The archbishop of Cyprus, seeing the reign of terror which was being intensfied daily, foresaw the coming destruction and tried by every means to avert the holocaust.[8]

Events unfolded quickly. In April the Turks armed themselves while a decree of the sultan ordered the disarming of the Christian subjects of the Empire in Cyprus. To this end, on 21 April/3 May about four thousand soldiers set sail from Acre[9], while on 20 April news was already arriving in Cyprus of the execution of the patriarch and other leading Greeks in Constantinople.[10]

---

[6] T. Kandiloros, Ἱστορία τοῦ ἐθνομάρτυρος Γρηγορίου τοῦ Ε΄, Athens, 1909, pp. 123–34; E. Protopsaltes, Ἡ Κύπρος εἰς τὸν ἀγῶνα τοῦ 1821, Athens, 1971, pp. 11–15.

[7] In accordance with official British sources and witnesses, see C.A. Frazee, *The Orthodox Church and Independent Greece 1821–1852,* Cambridge, 1969, pp. 30–31 (archives of the British Ambassador, Lord Strangford, and memoirs of R. Walsh).

[8] A detailed chronological ordering of events is today impossible. The more successful attempts are those of G. Hill, *A History of Cyprus,* IV, Cambridge, 1952, pp. 122–34 and J. Koumoulides, *Cyprus and the War of Greek Independence 1821–1829,* London, 1974, pp. 40–65.

[9] The date is given according to the Roman newspaper *Notizie del Giorno,* Thursday 25 October and Friday 2 November 1821, Greek trans. by N.G. Kyriazes, *KX* 13 (1937), pp. 250–9. Cf. C.D. Cobham, *Excerpta Cypria,* Cambridge, 1908, pp. 450–3. They draw the date from there, as do S. Tricoupes (1853) and I. Philemon (1860), who do not translate it into Old Style, which is the cause of the confusion that has prevailed in the modern bibliography. The Roman newspaper, however, uses the New Style throughout, giving, for example, the date of the hanging of the archbishop as 21 July. The correspondence of the French consul at Larnaca (see below) speaks vaguely of the "beginning of May", that is, Old Style, the end of April.

[10] Letter of the French consul Edmond Méchain of 2 May/20 April 1821, *KX* 7 (1930), p. 49, trans. N.G. Kyriazes.

The ferment was such that for the reassurance of the people an archiepiscopal letter was read out on 22 April to all the inhabitants of Nicosia, who were reassured about the good intentions of the administration and were called upon to hand over their weapons in peace and obedience to the authorities.[11]

The sources are unanimous. "The island of Cyprus, which would have been very quiet and peaceful if they left it undisturbed, is today in a state of disturbance from the day of the arrival of a great number of soldiers ..."[12] "From the arrival of the soldiers, sent to Cyprus by His Excellency the Pasha of Acre, various acts of indiscipline, insults, thefts trom the shops, and daily threats" alarm not only the Greek Christians but also the European inhabitants of Larnaca.[13] The concentration of these undisciplined and fierce, for the most part Arab, forces could not have had any other results than the provocation of greater harm. The consular documents speak more about the attacks which were made on Europeans, but this does not mean, of course, that they were the chief victims. The Eastern hurricane was borne in the first place by the Greeks, and especially the country people. The report of the French consul on 21 May/2 June that the soldiers from Syria had declared that "they had only come to fight the French"[14] should not distract us. In a calmer moment the same writer on 22 June/4 July confesses that the acts of violence against Europeans had happened because the Easterners had confused them "with the unfortunate Greeks".[15]

The main thing to be noted here is the attack which was made on the French consulate on 15/27 May 1821. The event is well-known and does not need to be discussed here in detail.[16] At about 10am on that Sunday morning, a detachment of Albanians fired repeatedly at the national flags flying over the Larnaca consulates, especially the French, which was displayed at three places. The French community, which had gathered that afternoon for a general meeting, reacted so strongly that the other European consuls together with Cypriot Turkish leaders had to intervene to restrain the French. The governor, who until that day had not hurried to fulfil his obligations to ensure the security of the Europeans, ostentatiously consented at last to

---

[11] G. Papacharalambous, "Ἐγκύκλιος τοῦ ἀρχιεπισκόπου Κυπριανοῦ ἀναφερομένη εἰς τὰ ἐν Κύπρῳ γεγονότα τοῦ 1821", KS 28 (1964), pp. 175–81.

[12] Letter of the French consul of 2 June/21 May 1821, KX 7 (1930), p. 50.

[13] Letter 28/16 May 1821 by the same, KX 13 (1937), pp. 213–15, esp. p. 213. It should be noted that this most important (as will be shown below) letter was written the same day on which the present document of Archbishop Kyprianos was published.

[14] Letter of French consul of 2 June/21 May 1821, KX 7 (1930), p. 50.

[15] Ibid., p. 52.

[16] See N.G. Kyriazes, "Ἀγωνιώδεις ἡμέραι τῆς ἐν Λάρνακι εὐρωπαϊκῆς παροικίας", KX 13 (1937), pp. 210–27, esp. the first four documents. Cf. three other letters of Méchain in KX 7 (1930), pp. 49–50, the letter of 4 July on pp. 52–4 and that of 17 August on pp. 57–9.

some satisfaction of French honour. "The king's flag was taken down, raised again and saluted by the guns of the garrison. This mark of honour made an impression on the soldiers, whose spirits were somewhat quietened."[17]

Exactly when this happened we do not know, but it is unlikely that it took place on the same day. Another letter of the consul mentions the movement of soldiers away from Larnaca,[18] and for the satisfaction of French demands we would expect negotiations to be carried out by intermediaries. "My intervention with the local authorities", the consul Méchain reports to the French Minister of Marine, "almost resulted in an occasion and signal for a general insurrection. The Consuls of the Powers and the leading Turks begged me not to insist and I contented myself with a relative satisfaction."[19] All these things, of course, could hardly have taken place and been agreed after the afternoon meeting of the French. The depth of the crisis which suddenly broke out on the island on 15 May 1821 can, however, be appreciated.

On Monday 16 May, Archbishop Kyprianos issued the document before us, at the command, as he himself says, of the Governor of Cyprus Mehmed Silahşor, known as Küçük Mehmed. The explicit recipients of the document are "the most pious priests and all other blessed Christians of the *kadilik* of Kythrea" although all the scholars who have referred to it have understood that it was addressed to the entire Christian population of the island.[20] They regarded it as a copy of a general encyclical. No shred of evidence has been put forward in support of this hypothesis even though such evidence is certainly not lacking.

In spite of this, let us begin with what is known for certain. A *kadilik* or *kaza* was the popular name for the administrative subdivision of a province known officially as a *nahiye*. In 1821 Cyprus was divided into 16 such districts, that of Kythrea (Degirmenlik = Mills) helping to make up, along with that of the Mountain (Dag) and the independent regime of the capital, the province of Nicosia (Lefkoşa).[21] The district under the *kadi* of Kythrea contained at the beginning of the nineteenth century about 38 villages,

---

[17] Letter of 4 July/22 June 1821, *KX* 7 (1930), pp. 52–3.

[18] Letter of 2 June/21 May 1821, *KX* 7 (1930), p. 50.

[19] Letter of 4 July/22 June 1821, *KX* 7 (1930), p. 52.

[20] K. Myrianthopoulos "Σπουδαῖον ἔγγραφον", p. 440; G. Hill, *A History of Cyprus*, p. 128, n. 2; J. Koumoulides, *Cyprus and the War of Greek Independence*, p. 48; and K. Spyridakis, "Ὁ ἐθνομάρτυς ἀρχιεπίσκοπος Κύπρου Κυπριανός", *Μελέται, διαλέξεις, λόγοι, ἄρθρα,* A', A', Nicosia, 1972, pp. 297–317, esp. 313.

[21] Archim. Kyprianos, *Ἱστορία Χρονολογικὴ τῆς νήσου Κύπρου,* Venice, 1788, p. 303; G. Hill, *A History of Cyprus,* pp. 5–8.

which were spread out along the trunk roads which connected Nicosia with Larnaca and Famagusta.[22]

In 1821 the secretary, or tax-collector, of this district must have been, as we are informed by an unpublished letter of Kyprianos, *Kyr* Giannakos Frangous.[23] Officials from among the leading Greeks were Hadji Jonas and Hadji Atallas,[24] who were beheaded on 13 July, and above all Tselepi Hadji Petrakis, son of the famous *oikonomos* of Kythrea, Papa Christodoulos, who was famous for his wealth.[25]

If our encyclical was addressed exclusively to the inhabitants of the district of Kythrea, various reasons, drawn principally from geography, could be put forward to explain this.

The *kadilik*, extending over the roads connecting Nicosia, Larnaca and Famagusta, was burdened by the movements of the soldiers who had arrived some ten days previously, as indeed were other districts. A more acute crisis in this area, sensitive on account of the communications and economy of the island, Küçük Mehmed, enraged but powerless (since he was still awaiting the sultan's reply to his proposals) could not have desired – and especially at the period of harvest, which is May in Cyprus. Let us not forget that the food supplies of Nicosia came from Kythrea, and the rebellion of 1765 attempted to starve the capital by changing the direction of the waters which turned the mills of Kythrea, bringing them to a stop, and then by preventing through force of arms the transportation of flour to the capital.[26] In the present case, panic or despair on the part of the inhabitants of the *kadilik* of Kythrea would have meant the abandonment of the harvest and delay or interruption in the milling, in other words threatened famine at the moment when the government had to feed thousands of additional military mouths and a general sense of disturbance and danger of insurrection prevailed in the capital, both on the side of the *rayahs* and, even more so, on the side of the security forces. This is something that in the end was not avoided, for in the mutiny

---

[22] Th. Papadopoullos, *Social and Historical Data on Population (1570–1881)*, Nicosia, 1965, pp. 128–9; map in H.C. Luke, *Cyprus Under the Turks 1571–1878*, London, 1921.

[23] Archive of the Archdiocese of Cyprus, dossier Arch. Kyprianos, n. 6: note 21 April 1820. Names of earlier secretaries of Kythrea in C.P. Kyrris in *EKEEK* 6 (1972–3), pp. 374 (viii), 393 (xv).

[24] G.I. Kepiades, Ἀπομνημονεύματα τῶν κατὰ τὸ 1821 ἐν τῇ νήσῳ Κύπρῳ τραγικῶν σκηνῶν, Alexandria, 1888, p. 20.

[25] N.G. Kyriazes, "Τσελεπῆς Χατζηπετράκης Κυθέριος", *KX* 1 (1923), pp. 320–3; 2 (1924), pp. 35–40, 93–7, 131–8, 185–7, 206–10.

[26] G. Mariti, *Viaggi per l'isola di Cipro*, Lucca, 1769, ch. 20; Eng. trans. in C.D. Cobham, *Travels in the Island of Cyprus. Translated from the Italian of Giovanni Mariti*, Cambridge, 1909, pp. 98–9; Archim. Kyprianos, Ἱστορία Χρονολογική, pp. 321–2. The revolt of Mehmed Ağa in Nicosia was put down by the same method in about 1680, Ibid., p. 310. Cf. G. Hill, *A History of Cyprus*, pp. 72–3, 84–5.

of the foreign soldiers on the 20 June/2 July Küçük himself only just escaped with his life.[27] In the middle of May 1821 Kythrea was valuable to the administration, as indeed it had been at other times.

The relationship between the encyclical and the events that had taken place in Larnaca the previous day, although not noticed by anyone until now, is striking. What is the aim of the encyclical? The reassurance of the Greeks (whether of the district of Kythrea or of the whole of the island is irrelevant) over exaggerated rumours (?) and the bolstering of their confidence in their Turkish masters. If in the text the archbishop asserts that he is acting in this address on his own initiative and out of pastoral duty, in the note he reveals that he is acting under the orders of the governor. What is the purpose of this pressure on the part of the governor?

If the conviction prevailed among the people that the administration had come into conflict with the representatives of the European Powers, that could only have been to the detriment of the Turks. For two things could have happened. If the consuls were defeated the panic of the people could have paralysed life on the island, and we have seen that the rulers were not only not yet ready or empowered for the worst but had every interest in securing the harvest. If, on the other hand, the consuls imposed their will and Ottoman power was humbled through providing the satisfaction sought, the Greeks would gain courage, hoping for more from a powerful Christian Europe. In view of both these possibilities, the Greeks, first, should not give credence to what was being said and secondly, should believe in the supposedly good disposition of the administration towards them. At all events it would be good for them to be kept in line by fear. "Whoever is careless in such times in his words or his deeds is liable to capital punishment."

For a better understanding of the historical context of the document Turkish fears in the period under examination should not be underestimated. Greek warships encircled the island keeping the Turks in a state of permanent anxiety.[28] Native-born Muslims knew from the history of the previous two decades that the mainland armies threatened them no less than the Greeks.[29] The governor had not until the middle of May shown his particular abilities; he was young and regarded in the island as "little used to the business of government".[30]

---

[27] Letters of the French consul of 3, 4 and 6 July 1821, *KX* 7 (1930), pp. 52–4.

[28] *KX* 7 (1930), pp.15–37, 53, 60 and *passim; Notizie del Giorno,* 25 Oct. and 2 Nov. 1821, Greek trans. N.G. Kyriazes, *KX* 13 (1937), pp. 250-9; T. Gordon, *History of the Greek Revolution,* I, Edinburgh, 1832, p. 193 (in C.D. Cobham, *Excerpta Cypria,* p. 459; G.I. Kepiades, Ἀπομνημονεύματα, p. 13.

[29] Cf. Mariti, *Viaggi* in Cobham, *Travels,* pp. 98–9; Archim. Kyprianos, Ἱστορία, pp. 321–2; and the disturbances of the first decade of the 19th century, G.H. Hill, *A History of Cyprus,* pp. 100ff.

[30] Letter of the French consul of 28/16 May 1821, *KX* 13 (1937), p. 213. Cf. note 12.

The tested power of the archbishop was still unplumbed, the disposition of the Porte towards him unforeseeable – the grand vizier having taken office only one month previously – and rumours of an imminent invasion of Turkey by Russia provided a climax to the feeling of uneasy expectation.[31]

We come now to the content of the archbishop's letter. Independently of the aims of the governor who had requested it, the archbishop does not of course restrict himself to these alone. Like a true pastor he first invites his people to seek refuge where they can find help. Convinced of the "ocean of his mercy" and the "supreme power and wisdom" of God, he seeks harmony and love among Christians, using the terminology peculiar to Orthodox spirituality. He speaks of "dispassion", "genuine love", "God of peace", "sweetest Jesus". In spite of his desperate attempt in what follows to hide the sword of Damocles that hangs over him, the archbishop, by issuing a call to general repentance and forgiveness, betrays his fears and, as if against his will, prepares the people for Christian martyrdom. Nevertheless the hope that the cup would still pass him by did not abandon him. Perhaps God would have mercy, perhaps the sins would be covered. It is difficult to decide whether the archbishop was preparing himself for martyrdom or whether he was attempting to avert what was coming. Probably both of these. Within a month the Englishman John Carne would meet another Kyprianos, totally dedicated now to the idea of martyrdom.[32]

The appeals for obedience and prayers for the rule of Sultan Mahmut II (1785–1839) and the destruction of those who opposed him are reminiscent of the similar appeals of the martyr, Gregory V.[33] And although the first had biblical support (Rom. 13:1–7; I Tim. 2:1–4), the second ("frightening ... and destruction of his opponents") if they prove anything it is not the condemnation of the revolution – to which the archbishop gave substantial financial help – but the fearful nature of Ottoman military absolutism on the one hand and the unavoidable necessity of keeping up appearances on the other to avert greater evils for the sorely afflicted Greeks. The last warnings speak for themselves: carelessness even in word is punishable by death. It is the command of the governor that the Christians should wear mourning and dress in black clothes, shoes and headgear.

The popular *Song on the beheading of the bishops* attributes the wearing of mourning by the Greek–Cypriots to the arrival of news about the Greek

---

[31] Letter of 19/7 May 1821 from Constantinople to the English consul, referred to in a letter of Méchain of 2 June/21 May, *KX* 7 (1930), p. 51. Cf. note of codex H–8 of the Cathedral of Paphos, published by I.P. Tsiknopoullos, *KS* 31 (1967), p. 118: "... ἀμάχη ... ἀναμεταξὴ τουρκῶν καὶ ρώσσων" (see n. 52 below).

[32] J.Carne, *Letters from the East*,[3] II, London, 1830, pp. 162–79.

[33] T.Ch. Kandeloros, Ἱστορία τοῦ ἐθνομάρτυρος, pp. 214–19.

victories in the Peloponnese.[34] The permanent wearing of black by the Roman subjects of the Ottoman Empire had nevertheless been ordered – even if the order was not always applied with the same strictness – from the sixteenth century, through a decree of the Sultan Murat III (1574–95) which no doubt repeated older orders.[35]

The assertion that the Greeks had never from the time the island was captured in 1571 risen in revolt was not quite accurate, even though it was also believed by the Porte, as appears from a passage from the disarmanent order which was preserved by I. Philemon.[36] Also known from elsewhere is the information that the archbishop, as legally guarantor of the *rayahs* (*râya vekil*), had before the disarmanent along with his fellow bishops sent to the *Devlet* reports and guarantees that the Greeks would abide by the law.[37] The exhortation that the taxes should be paid uncomplainingly must be set within the context of the more general calls for obedience and care and also of the pressing economic needs of the time.[38]

Finally, who was the archimandrite to whom the archbishop entrusted the circulation of the pastoral letter? From the address "our archimandrite" we would be inclined to suppose that he was the archimandrite of the archdiocese, and not one belonging to a monastery or some church. In that case, however, what need would there be for a written communication between him and the archbishop? As is known, the archimandrite usually had his seat in the archbishop's palace, the exarch being responsible for all external affairs.[39] If the reference, however, is not to the archimandrite of the archdiocese, we encounter difficulties not only in the interpretation of the pronoun

---

[34] Th. Papadopoullos, "Τὸ Ἄσμα τῶν Ἀρχιερέων", *KS* 35 (1971), pp. 1–50, esp. p. 22, lines 128–41. Cf. ibid., *Δημώδη κυπριακὰ ᾄσματα ἐξ ἀνεκδότων συλλογῶν τοῦ ΙΘ´ αἰῶνος,* Nicosia, 1975, p. 147, lines 126–39.

[35] Archbishop Ch. Papadopoulos, *Ἡ ἐξωτερικὴ κατάστασις τῆς Ἐκκλησίας Κωνσταντινουπόλεως ἀπὸ τῆς ἁλώσεως μέχρι τοῦ ΙΗ´ αἰῶνος,* Athens, l950, p. 15, cf. p. 32; Ibid., *Ἡ Ἐκκλησία Κωνσταντινουπόλεως καὶ ἡ μεγάλη ἐπανάστασις τοῦ 1821,* Athens, 1950, p. 5. For Cyprus in 1605 see P. Texeira in *KX* I (1923), pp. 41–2.

[36] I. Philemon, *Δοκίμιον ἱστορικὸν περὶ τῆς ἑλληνικῆς ἐπαναστάσεως,* III, Athens, 1860, p. 259. This is the source for Ph. Georgiou, *Εἰδήσεις ἱστορικαὶ περὶ τῆς ἐκκλησίας τῆς Κύπρου,* Athens, 1875, p. 119. Cf. the encyclical of 22 April in G. Papacharalambous, *KS* 28 (l964), pp. 175–81.

[37] See e.g. the *Ἄσμα τῶν Ἀρχιερέων,* pp.145–6, lines 64–9.

[38] The Trappist monk, Fr. Marie-Joseph de Géramb, *Pèlerinage à Jerusalem et au Mont-Sinai en 1831, 1832, 1833,* Paris, 1839, pp. 48–51, mentions that according to the Divan, which was summoned after the arrival of the soldiers from Acre, the bishops gave a gift to the governor of 100 000 kurush. The giving of bribes was a necessary policy in the Ottoman Empire, especially in times of danger. That the clergy tried in the period before 9 July to propitiate the Turks with money and gifts is mentioned by various sources.

[39] Letter of Archbishop Sophronios of 12/24 January 1895, in J. Hackett, *History of the Orthodox Church of Cyprus,* Greek trans., p. 241.

"our" but even more in the identification of the archimandrite of another foundation whom the archbishop would have entrusted with the publication of his encyclical to the district of Kythrea. For the rank of archimandrite was not then a mere title but always implied the office of administrator of a diocese or of one of the stavropegial monasteries.

The last mention of an archimandrite of the archdiocese prior to 16 May 1821 is in 1815 by the English diplomat William Turner, where the anonymous archimandrite is presented as a deaf old man.[40]

On 23 November 1820 Archbishop Kyprianos speaks of the absence from Cyprus of his cousin's son, Theophylact Theseus, as if he were an archimandrite without, however, calling him explicitly his archimandrite or the archimandrite of the diocese.[41]

On 6 December 1821 Theophylact Theseus signed the well-known document of Cypriot refugees in Europe as "the Archimandrite Theophilos of the martyred Archbishop of Cyprus of blessed memory",[42] and from this L. Philippou concluded that Theseus had before 1821 (and after 1815, we must add) received from his uncle the office of archimandrite of the archdiocese.[43] Although this complex man did not hesitate at times to resort to the inflation of his titles, we should probably accept that he is telling the truth in 1821 in spite of the fact that before this he was temporarily resident in Marseilles with his brother Nicholas.[44] The title could have been given to him in 1817, for example, when the Theseis were celebrating in Cyprus the betrothal of Nicholas to Katherine Havvas.[45]

Was it possible, however, for the Archimandrite Theophylact Theseus to have been in Cyprus on 16 May 1821? We know that immediately before 9 July the Archimandrite Theophylact was distributing revolutionary proclamations in Cyprus, arousing through that foolish act the worst suspicions of the governor against the archbishop and the leading Greeks. The oldest written

---

[40] In C.D. Cobham, *Excerpta Cypria*, pp. 428, 429, 432.

[41] O.I. Iasonides, "Ἀνεύρεσις αὐτογράφου ἐθνομάρτυρος Κυπριανοῦ", Ἑλικών Ι, fasc. 20, Limassol, 1910, p. 2. Cf. *KS* 42, (1978), p. 70.

[42] I.K. Peristianes, Γενικὴ ἱστορία τῆς νήσου Κύπρου, Nicosia, 1910, pp. 779–82, with a reproduction. It was first published in the Ἐφημερίδα τοῦ λαοῦ of 15 January 1910, and not in the *Notizie* of Rome, as G. Hill, *A History of Cyprus*, p. 137, note 1, mistakenly records. This and the document referred to in note 40 belonged to O.I. Iasonides, who, through his mother, inherited them from his great-uncle Nicholas Theseus, about whom more below.

[43] L. Philippou, "Νικόλαος καὶ Θεόφιλος Θησεῖς", Πάφος 1 (1935), pp. 81–5.

[44] Ibid.; P. Echinard, *Grecs et Philhellènes à Marseille de la révolution française à l'independence de la Grèce*, Aix-en-Provence, 1970, *passim*; E. Protopsaltes, Ἡ Κύπρος εἰς τὸν ἀγῶνα τοῦ 1821, pp. 38–42. On the deceits of the archimandrite the chief witness is Archbishop Joannikios (1840–9), one-time exarch of Archbishop Kyprianos.

[45] Register XIV of Archbishop's Palace, 4 January, 1817, No. 95 in C.P. Kyrris, *EKEEK* 6 (1972–3), p. 378.

evidence which we have of this is in the first volume of S. Tricoupes' *History of the Greek Revolution* which was published in London in 1853, that is, 32 years after the event, and which places it before 21 April/3 May, when Theophylact is thought not even to have disembarked from the ship which had brought him.[46]

Other sources, however, closer to the events, consider that he had disembarked and indeed visited Nicosia, from which he later fled.[47] When the latter took place, however, it is difficult to determine. The evidence of John Carne, which belongs to the end of June, speaks of the recent escape from Nicosia of a nephew of the archbishop called Theseus. It might, however, be referring to the escape of Theophylact's older brother, Kyprianos Theseus, who nevertheless was a resident of Larnaca (though it is not impossible, of course, that he was at that moment at Nicosia).[48] What is sure is that on 3 July Theophylact and Kyprianos Theseus were in Kastellorizo or Symi, from where Kyprianos sent Theophylact in haste to Hydra for consultations with Demetrios Ypsilanti and the Hydriot community leaders. The style and content of the letter addressed to these leave no doubt that the author at least had only just arrived in Greece.[49] Before September Theophylact took part in the siege of Tripolis,[50] and in November or early December he met the Cypriot refugees who had fled to Marseilles as an emissary of his brother Nicholas, who was probably already in the Peloponnese.[51]

If the archimandrite of the present document was Theophylact Theseus, we would have to suppose in consequence that arriving in Cyprus some months before 21 April 1821, he distributed revolutionary proclamations, which provides the first grounds for Turkish legal action. He did not arouse the suspicions of the *vali* at once, however, and having stayed in the island until the middle or end of June when, with a warrant out for his arrest, he escaped

---

[46] S. Trikoupes, Ἱστορία τῆς ἑλληνικῆς ἐπαναστάσεως, I, London, 1853, p. 255.

[47] *Notizie del Giorno*, 25 Oct. and 2 Nov. 1821, Greek trans. by N.G. Kyriazes in *KX* 13 (1937), pp. 255–6; Ἄσμα τῶν ἀρχιερέων, *KS* 35 (1971), p. 28, lines 82–4; cf. line 86, where Kyprianos is his brother, about whom more below. The variant B2 repeats the same information (pp. 33–4, lines 82–4, 86), but B3 refers to *the archimandrite* as having been executed (p. 38, line 56). This variant, however, is of lower historical value (p. 13) and is especially prone to dealing out death, since it asserts that the governor killed all the consuls of Larnaca (p. 39, lines 92–3).

[48] J. Carne, *Letters from the East*,[3] II, pp.176–7. Cf. the official documents on the confiscation and sale of Kyprianos's property in *KX* 5 (1927), pp. 1–4; I (1923), pp. 98–100 (Cf. pp. 25–6, 69–70 on the villa of Kontea which he acquired from the archdiocese).

[49] In E. Protopsaltes, Ἡ Κύπρος εἰς τὸν ἀγῶνα τοῦ 1821, p. 43.

[50] Ibid., p. 45, Ἀποδεικτικὸν 9049.

[51] According to the autograph note of Archbishop Joannikios mentioned by L. Philippou in "Νικόλαος καὶ Θεόφιλος Θησεῖς". See notes 43, 44 above.

from Cyprus with his exceedingly rich brother Kyprianos, a great merchant in Larnaca.

Such a theory would explain in some way the written instruction–apology of the archbishop towards his archimandrite and nephew, a patriot always on the move, but the acceptance of it is not easy. A fact difficult to explain is that although on 16 May we find ourselves face to face with an archimandrite in Nicosia, in the massacres of July not only do we hear nothing of an archimandrite of the archdiocese, but no archimandrite in general is commemorated among the victims.

At all events, even if these conjectures are correct, our encyclical did not produce any result. On 25 May, that is, nine days after it was issued, Küçük Mehmed executed in Nicosia five clerics and prominent laymen from the Paphian village of Giolou, the birthplace of the choroepiscopus of the archdiocese, Spyridon of Trimythous.[52] A little while later there followed the beheading of the parish priest of Phaneromeni, Hieromonk Leontios.[53]

On 28 May the French consul mentioned that in Larnaca there were demonstrations against the Russian consul, and the governor

> "became more and more enraged. Every day he hangs, strangles or butchers unfortunate people in Nicosia, against whom he has old accusations repeated, the cases of which were heard many years ago by his predecessor. He succeeds in this way in a double aim. To enrich himself and to persuade the Porte that there was in Cyprus a conspiracy for a revolution which he had succeeded in quashing. If this bloodthirsty

---

[52] I.P. Tsiknopoullos, "Παφιακά", *KS* 31 (1967), pp. 99–118, esp. p. 118; L. Ph[ilippou], "Διάφορα", *KX* 3 (1925), p. 276; ῎Ασμα τῶν ἀρχιερέων, p. 21, lines 98–101; p. 26, lines 15–16; p. 30, line 17; p. 37, lines 13–14. Cf. *Notizie del Giorno*, p. 251. On the origins of the bishop of Trimythous see L. Philippou, Ἡ Ἐκκλησία τῆς Κύπρου ἐπὶ Τουρκοκρατίας, Nicosia, 1975, pp. 131, 210.

[53] See B. Englezakis, "Περὶ τῶν κατὰ τὸ κυπριακὸν 1821 Λεοντίων", *KS* 42–44, (1978), pp. 59–74; "Καὶ πάλιν περὶ τῶν κατὰ τὸ κυπριακὸν 1821 Λεοντίων", *KS* 44 (1980), pp. 117–18 (both of which are translated below, Ch. XVII and XVIII). The enigma of this Leontios has not been finally laid to rest. If we accept as accurate the evidence of his sister that he was beheaded 40 days before 9 July, his execution must be assigned to 30 May 1821, that is to say, after the execution of the people from Yiolou, which folk memory held to have been the first to have taken place (῎Ασμα). According to the *Notizie*, however, (p. 251) the first to be executed was Leontios. I am inclined to accept the family tradition (a) because it agrees with the folk evidence; (b) because the French consul in a letter of 28 May/9 June (see below) gives no hint of Leontios, although he clearly alludes to the inhabitants of Yiolou and to Paspallas of Nicosia (the former in connection with an older matter involving a Greek woman and a Turk: *codex H-8 of the Diocese of Paphos*, the latter accused of breaking into a Turkish house, "῎Ασμα ", p. 21, lines 102–3, cf. *Notizie*); (c) because if Leontios really was the first martyr and if that had already been forgotten by the people, it would not have been forgotten by his sister, who does not refer to him as such.

madman continues to hold authority for a few more months he will bankrupt the island...".[54]

An attempt to delate him to the Porte by the bishops and leading citizens ended in failure, their emissary having been arrested at Pogazion.[55] The ninth of July was approaching.

From the morphological point of view I stress only the simplicity which is a permanent feature in the documents of Archbishop Kyprianos.[56] If we take away the articles, particles, prefixes and pronouns, the document contains about 380 words, of which 9 or about 2.5 per cent (if repetitions are included) are foreign. Except for one, διαφένδευσις, which is of medieval Western origin, the rest, regardless of their original provenance, came into Greek from Turkish after the Middle Ages. Three of these, ἀγᾶς, καδῆς and ραγιᾶς, are by their nature current even in the West, met with, for example, in the *Oxford English Dictionary*, such as *aga*, *cadi* (*-ship*) and *rayah*, while a fourth, ἐφένδης, is a corruption of the Greek αὐθέντης, and is also used in the West *(OED s.v. effendi)*. Taking these into consideration, the ratio is negligible, to a surprising degree, I would say, given that the text is in the language of the subject people and is a document of a political nature.

The flow of the speech is natural. The archbishop uses a thoroughly Greek vocabulary, neither archaizing nor excessively purist, nor, however, writing the popular Cypriot dialect. The encyclical is an example of the language spoken by learned Greeks.

---

[54] Letter of the French consul of 28 May/4 June 1821, *KX* 7 (1930), p. 51, Greek trans. N.G. Kyriazes.

[55] *Ἆσμα τῶν ἀρχιερέων*, p. 21, lines 106–15.

[56] Cf. K. Th. Demaras, "'Ἀθησαύριστο ἔγγραφο τοῦ ἀρχιεπισκόπου Κύπρου Κυπριανοῦ", *Πρακτικὰ τοῦ πρώτου διεθνοῦς κυπριολογικοῦ συνεδρίου*, Nicosia, 1973, pp. 55–61.

XVII

ON THE FOUR LEONTII MARTYRED IN CYPRUS AFTER THE EVENTS OF 1821*

The need for the study and codification of the prosopography of Cyprus is well-known. The present paper is a small contribution to this end, dealing as it does with persons and things confused by those who have written on the events in Cyprus of 1821, or in many cases unknown to them. Below are examined the cases of four clerical martyrs who bore the name Leontios, of whom three are genuine historical personages while one is the fantastic creation of the demon of the printing press and human sin.[1]

I. LEONTIOS MYRIANTHEUS, ARCHIMANDRITE OF KITION.
Writing in 1879, D.L. Nikolaides, former Scholarch of Limassol, says: "In Nicosia there are schools dating from 1815 in which Leontios Myriantheus used to teach. He had his own school in the palace of the Archbishop itself ... The blessed Myriantheus taught until the year 1821 ... L. Myriantheus was succeeded by the blessed Onouphrios Mikellides."[2] This was repeated without any indication of source by I.K. Peristianes[3] in 1924. In the same year the panel of judges of the first literary competition of Archbishop Kyrillos III, relying on the manuscript note in volume IV of the Property

* Translated from Περὶ τῶν κατὰ τὸ κυπριακὸν 1821 Λεοντίων, KS 42 (1978), pp. 59–74.

[1] I am very grateful to His Beatitude the Archbishop for permission to publish the document dated 8 May 1777 from the Archive of Chrysanthos, Archbishop of Cyprus.

[2] D.L. Nicolaides, "'Ολίγα περὶ τῆς νήσου Κύπρου", Νέον Κίτιον 2/28 Oct. 1878, No. 18; 3/15 Oct. 1878, No. 19.

[3] I.K. Peristianes, Ἱστορία τῶν ἑλληνικῶν γραμμάτων ἀπὸ τῆς Τουρκικῆς κατακτήσεως μέχρι τῆς Ἀγγλικῆς κατοχῆς (1571–1878), Nicosia, 1930, p. 116.

Register of the Metropolis of Kition given below, identified this Leontios in its *Report* (I.A.G. Sykoutres, pp. 75–6) with the archimandrite and subsequently successor of the *ethnomartyr*, Metropolitan Meletios of Kition.

> "1825. On 9 July Leontios was ordained prelate of the see of Larnaca. Having formerly been archimandrite of the same see, he is now its good chief pastor, originating from Myrianthousa. There have been four prelates from this region on the throne of Larnaca – of these the first was called Meletios, who lived out his days in peace; Chrysanthos his brother was sent into exile; Meletios II suffered capital punishment with the rest of his colleagues and some of the notables of this island as a result of the sovereign's anger."

The identification of the two Leontii by Sykoutres is accepted by Peristianes in the 1930 edition of his *History*, while L. Philippou[4] regards it as most probable. Nikolaides' information is also repeated by K. Spyridakis, again without any attribution. From that time, so far as I know, no one has expressed any doubts on the matter, even though the evidence on which the identification is based cannot be regarded as fully adequate.

If what is said by Nikolaides is true, namely that Leontios Myriantheus taught in the School of Nicosia until 1821, then Sykoutres' identification cannot be true because the Leontios who was the successor of Meletios was, according to the evidence, his archimandrite. The information given by Nikolaides that the School of Nicosia was founded in 1815 and that it was housed in the Archiepiscopal Palace is certainly not correct. The school was founded on 1 January 1812 and had its own building which had been given for the purpose by Archbishop Kyprianos and had belonged previously to the monastery of Machairas. I suspect that Nikolaides confused the first teacher at Kyprianos's school in Nicosia with the first teacher in Nicosia under Turkish rule, Leontios Eustratios,[5] or perhaps even with the mysterious Leontios who *succeeded* Onouphrios Mikellides.[6]

At any rate, in 1820 the archimandrite of the metropolis of Kition was the hieromonk Leontios Myriantheus, who in that year built the church of St Barbara of Stavrovouni. This is apparent from the commemorative plaque in the wall over the west door, the text of which was published in 1948 by N.G. Kyriazes:[7]

---

[4] L. Philippou, *Τὰ ἑλληνικὰ γράμματα ἐν Κύπρῳ κατὰ τὴν περίοδον τῆς Τουρκοκρατίας (1571–1878)*, Nicosia, 1930, vol. I, p. 190.

[5] Ibid., vol. II, pp. 32–41.

[6] Ibid., vol. I, p. 211.

[7] N.G. Kyriazes, *Ἱστρικαὶ εἰδήσεις ἱερᾶς μονῆς Σταυροβουνίου*, Larnaca, 1948, p. 18.

"the year † 1820
O martyr of Christ, saint Barbara receive the prayer of your servant
Leontios, the builder of your divine house, son of a village of Myrianthousa,
archimandrite of the chief priest of the Kitians, Meletios the second. Keep
him safe from every harm and be the cause of his salvation."

There can be no doubt that the cleric who composed this epigraph was
for his time a learned man. And this would lend weight to the identification
of the former Scholarch of Nicosia with the archimandrite of Kition. If it is
supposed that this was the case, we do not know when Leontios left Kyprianos's
school or for what reason. The fact, however, that he left not only the school
but also the service of the archbishop would have to be ascribed to a cooling
of relations between the two men. It is also likely that his leaving owed
something to the fact that both he and the metropolitan of Kition came from
Marathasa and had common bonds. According to Kl. Myrianthopoulos,
Meletios came from the village of Pedoulas and Leontios from Kalopanagiotes.[8]
We do not know whether Leontios was a former brother of the monastery
of Stavrovouni, even if his benefaction to the monastery makes it arguable.

What is certain is that in April 1821 the unfortunate archimandrite of
Kition was given by the Church as a hostage to the *Muhasil* of Cyprus, Esseyit Mehmed Emin, the notorious Küçük Mehmed, and was thrown into
the prisons of the administrative building. He emerged, however, on the terrible
9 July of the same year, was wrapped in the kaftan of honour and, promoted
metropolitan of Kition, was ordained on 18 December by the new archbishop,
Joachim, and Metropolitans Joannikios of Epiphaneia, Gennadios of Seleucia
and Methodios of Emessa of the patriarchate of Antioch.[9]

Of his activity as metropolitan of Kition we know very little. Kl.
Myrianthopoulos's statement that Leontios "built the larger part of St George
Kontos in Larnaca" does not seem securely based.[10] The signature of Leontios
of Kition, however, is found on the most important document of 19 August
1828, which the Cypriot hierarchy sent to the governor of Greece, John
Kapodistrias, and in which the union of Cyprus with Greece is proposed for
the first time.[11]

In the revolt of 1833 in Larnaca the role of Leontios was one of appease-
ment. On 4 March the populace, which had rebelled on account of Küçük
Mehmed's heavy burden of taxation, gathered outside the episcopal palace,

---

[8] Kl. Myrianthopoulos, Ἡ συμβολὴ τῆς Μαραθάσης εἰς τὴν Ἐκκλησίαν, Limassol,
1939, pp. 57, 86.
[9] *Codex I*, Archbishop's Palace, Nicosia, p. 190.
[10] Kl. Myrianthopoulos, Ἡ συμβολὴ τῆς Μαραθάσης, p. 88.
[11] E.G. Protopsaltes, Ἡ Κύπρος εἰς τὸν ἀγῶνα τοῦ 1821, Athens, 1971, pp. 92–4.

threatening to destroy it if the metropolitan did not protest. The leader of
the revolt, Nicholas Theseus, visited the metropolitan but unfortunately we
do not know what transpired between them. On 15 March the *muselim*
withdrew the tax and the new decree was brought to the rebels besieged in
St George Kontos by Leontios himself accompanied by leading members of
the Greek and Turkish communities. Leontios also persuaded the French
consul, Bottu, to give a guarantee that Theseus and the rebels would not be
prosecuted.[12]

The work of Leontios on behalf of education does not appear to have
been particularly outstanding. The arrival in Larnaca of the learned Scholarch
of Limassol, Demetrios Themistocleous, and his opening of a school in the
spring of 1822 owed more to his marriage to Maroudia Andreou Vontitsianou
than to Leontios. Similarly the foundation of the Gymnasium in Larnaca
was due to Archbishop Damaskenos, who appears to have judged it still
dangerous to open a school in Nicosia and chose Larnaca because of its cosmopolitan character and perhaps also on account of the presence there of
D. Themistocleous. Archbishop Damaskenos transferred this Gymnasium,
according to his own evidence, to Nicosia in 1826, where it replaced
Kyprianos's school, only to vanish itself in 1827 with the fall and exile of
Damaskenos.[13] When Panaretos reconstituted the school of Nicosia, however,
on 4 November 1830, the act was signed along with other prelates by
Leontios of Kition, who also presented the new school with 3 500 kurush.[14]

Kl. Myrianthopoulos's remarks about Leontios's wealth and power are
based on a well-known *leitmotiv* of oral tradition rather than on historical
evidence, even though it is possible that there is a genuine recollection of his
powerful relation, Fermanles H" Giorges.[15] The tradition concerning the
poisoning and robbing of the bishop is likewise of no great historical value.
No bishop in Cyprus in the last few centuries breathed his last without the
suspicion of poisoning hovering over his deathbed.

[12] G. Hill, *A History of Cyprus*, Cambridge, 1952, vol. IV, pp. 157–61.

[13] Peristianes, Ἱστορία, pp. 42–50, 194–6. The interpretation of L. Philippou (Τὰ
ἑλληνικὰ γράμματα, vol. I, pp. 97–9) is mistaken. The fact that the *Call* came from
Damaskenos and not from Panaretos is incontrovertible. How and by what justification
would Panaretos of Paphos have founded a school in Larnaca? Moreover, the person referred
to in the text as "our Archimandrite Kos Kyrillos" (which L. Philippou, under the influence
of his desire to justify what cannot be justified, changes to "the Archimandrite of Nicosia Kos
Kyrillos") is beyond any doubt Kyrillos, Damaskenos's archimandrite and nephew of the *ethnomartyr* Kyprianos, who later became Archbishop Kyrillos I (1848–1854). Accordingly, the
founders of the old school of the Pancyprian Gymnasium are Archbishop Philotheos,
Chrysanthos, Kyprianos, Damaskenos and Panaretos in that order. Damaskenos should
take his place in all the histories of the Pancyprian Gymnasium, from which he was unjusti-
fiably omitted.

[14] Peristianes, Ἱστορία, pp. 51–4.

[15] Myrianthopoulos, Ἡ συμβολὴ τῆς Μαραθάσης, pp. 87–8.

Leontios Myriantheus of Kition died at the end of 1836 or the beginning of 1837. On 17 February 1837 the supervision of the metropolis was placed under the presidency of the former archbishop of Cyprus, Damaskenos, who administered it until 1846, when he died.

Both men began their careers in April 1821 in the prisons of the Seraglio. As Pandit Nehru once said to his daughter, Indira Gandhi, "There are times when it is better to be in prison than outside."

II. LEONTIOS, PARISH PRIEST OF PHANEROMENI

In his description of the events of 10 July 1821, G.I. Kepiades says that "at a small bridge near the market called 'Pasmadjidika' the hieromonk Laurentios of the church of Phaneromeni in Nicosia was beheaded, having been condemned for having hidden some gunpowder."[16]

Two other pieces of evidence that a cleric of Phaneromeni was put to death on the same charge are preserved, one Turkish and the other Italian. The fact, then, is beyond doubt. The sources conflict, however, with regard to the cleric's name.

The Ottoman evidence is given by H.F. Alasya.[17] The official Turkish document, however, names neither the church nor the cleric. The Italian evidence comes from the Roman newspaper *Notizie del Giorno*, Thursday, 25 October and Friday, 2 November 1821, and is given in English translation by C.D. Cobham[18] and in Greek by N.G. Kyriazes.[19] The church is the Phaneromeni and its priest is referred to as "Fr. Leontios, parish priest of this church, a man beloved by all." The information is given by a correspondent from Zante on the basis of news brought from Cyprus by refugees arriving there on 16 and 22 August 1821 (n.s.). The episode, according to the correspondent, took place before the arrival in the island on 3 May 1821 of Ottoman troops from Acre. The *terminus post quem* must certainly be the day when the Greek population was disarmed, which we know from Archbishop Kyprianos's encyclical of 22 April 1821 to have been 21 April. This period, between 21 April and 3 May, agrees with the official Ottoman report that the gunpowder was discovered in 1236 *evahir Ramazan*.

Clearly what is said by Kepiades does not coincide with this. One of two things may have occurred: either a hieromonk of Phaneromeni called Laurentios was beheaded on 10 July 1821 and Kepiades or his source

---

[16] G.I. Kepiades, Ἀπομνημονεύματα τῶν κατὰ τὸ 1821 ἐν τῇ νήσῳ Κύπρῳ τραγικῶν σκηνῶν, Alexandria, 1888, pp. 16–17.

[17] H.F. Alasya, *Kıbrıs Tarihi*, Nicosia, 1939, p. 109.

[18] C.D. Cobham, *Excerpta Cypria*, Cambridge, 1908, pp. 450–3.

[19] N.G. Kyriazes, "Excerpta Cypria", *KX* 13 (1937), pp. 250–9.

ascribed to him the accusation which had been made against the parish priest of the same church, Leontios, forty or so days previously, or the Laurentios beheaded on 10 July 1821 was not a cleric of Phaneromeni but belonged to another church of Nicosia and being confused with Leontios acquired his charge and his church.

The choice between these two possibilities is difficult because of the lack of sufficient information. The first, however, as the simpler is the more likely (*entiae non sunt multiplicandae*). As Kyriazes has already rightly observed,[20] the Italian evidence is the more weighty, since it is given only a few months after the event, while Kepiades was writing sixty-seven years later.

As a solution of the problem Kyriazes accepts that the person referred to by Kepiades as Laurentios is simply the Leontios of the *Notizie* and in support of this gives a vague reference to a codex in the Archiepiscopal Palace dating from 1821 and referring to a hieromonk Laurentios in connection with Phaneromeni. Kl. Myrianthopoulos writes "the Laurentios referred to by G. Kepiades belonged to Trypiotes", but he supplies no evidence for this and his information concerning Leontios of Phaneromeni is incomplete, since he confuses him with the abbot of St George Mezere, who is discussed below.

Unfortunately, I have not been able to discover Kyriazes' reference. I note, however, that M.M. Panteliou refers to five documents of N.D. Oikonomides from the Oikonomides Archive relating to "the nobility of Sir Georgakes of Papa Leontios of Nicosia" to whom the rich Cypriot merchant owed many thousands of kurush from 1809 until 1812.[21] Does this Papa Leontios have any connection with our problem? I do not know. In any event, however, Kyriazes' Leontios is clearly referred to as a hieromonk, although the possessive case "of Papa Leontios" does not necessarily mean that Sir Georgakes was a son of Leontios. He could also have been his nephew, just as "Hadjinicolas of Laurentios the Protosyngelos" signifies that Hadjinicolas was a nephew of Laurentios, the son of his sister.[22]

It remains certain that one day in the last week of 1821 gunpowder was found on a country property belonging to the church of Phaneromeni. When its tenant, Sabbas, fled and went into hiding in Larnaca, Leontios, the popular priest of the church, was held responsible, arrested and beheaded by the governor's executioners in the middle of the market place. He was the first martyr of the events in Cyprus of 1821.

---

[20] Ibid., p. 251, n.2.

[21] M.M. Panteliou, "Οἱ Κύπριοι στὴν ἐπανάσταση τοῦ 1821", *KS* 40 (1976), p. 41, with reference to GAK, Vlach. I, fol. 249.

[22] Cf. K. Harmanta, "Χατζηνικόλας Λαυρεντίου Πρωτοσυγκέλλου", *KS* 35 (1971), pp. 51–8.

The clergy of Phaneromeni, however, were destined to undergo even worse experiences. According to the French historian L. Lacroix, on 9 July, upon the slaughter of the prelates, "the gates of the governor's palace ... were opened and their blood-stained bodies still in their death-throes were flung out into the square, which was the signal for a general massacre. The church of Phaneromeni was looted and its priests put to death. I am informed, says M. de Mas Latrie, that before they slaughtered them the Ottomans, in an unheard-of act of vengeance, saddled them like horses and breaking their teeth so as to insert bridles in their mouths drove them round in circles with spurs."[23]

III. LEONTIOS HADJI GIANNES, ABBOT OF ST GEORGE MEZERE

In his description of Kanares' visit to the little harbour of Asprovrysi near Lapithos on about 19 June 1821, G.I. Kepiades notes that "the Cypriots were not slow in gladly offering money and whole cargoes sufficient for three vessels, sheep and oxen and corn and barley and various other provisions".[24] But he does not mention the names of any Cypriots with whom the admiral came into contact.

Ch. Livas was the first to mention from oral tradition that the contribution of Cyprus to the national struggle (after a secret collection of funds on the orders of the archbishop) was conveyed by the stratagem of a mock funeral from Karavas to Lapithos and handed over to Kanares as he was leaving by Abbot Meletios and the guardian Phasoulas of the Acheiropoietos, a Sinai monk of the Kingdom (= Kosmas the Zakynthian) and Abbot Leontios of the monastery of St George Mezere of Karavas.

Concerning the last nothing is mentioned except his name and even Kyriazes has nothing to add.[25] In 1969 K. Harmanta says that this Leontios was the first abbot of St George's and provides a photograph of an icon of the saint from the monastery in which the martyr is portrayed kneeling before him.[26] But in 1971 the same author claims that the same icon portrays Abbot Meletios of the Acheiropoietos and remains silent about her earlier attribution.[27] In the same year C.P. Kyrris writes that Leontios "was the third *ethnomartyr* of Karavas whose name until now has escaped us".[28]

---

[23] L. Lacroix, Ἱστορία τῆς Νήσου Κύπρου, GT: K. Vontitsianou, Athens, 1877, p. 171.

[24] Kepiades, Ἀπομνημονεύματα, p. 13.

[25] N.G. Kyriazes, Τὰ Μοναστήρια ἐν Κύπρῳ, Larnaca, 1950, p. 43.

[26] K. Harmanta, "Λάπηθος–Λάμπουσα–Καραβᾶς", A. Stylianou and K. Harmanta, Καραβᾶς, Nicosia, 1969.

[27] K. Harmanta, "Χατζηνικόλας", p. 58.

[28] C.P. Kyrris, "Τὸ 'ἐνθύμιον' τοῦ Κωστῆ Ν. Χ" Παρασκευᾶ", Χρονικὰ τῆς Λαπήθου, I, ii, 1971, p. 235.

Already in 1940 K. Myrianthopoulos had provided further details about this Leontios, though without being aware of it. For he ascribed them to the Leontios who was the parish priest of Phaneromeni, with whom he had confused him, and thus failed to unearth the truth.

The key was provided by two things: the funerary inscription of Chrysanthos Ioannides, metropolitan of Kition (1889–1890) and the previously unpublished document which I give below.

In the epitaph of Chrysanthos of Kition, as given by M.G. Michaelides,[29] we read the following:

"Here lies

Chrysanthos, metropolitan of Kition, spreading scion of Nicosia, having from his tenderest years become an ornament of the Muses and imitator of his uncle Leontios who died a martyr's death for his country, received the monastic schema etc."

If we note that Chrysanthos died in 1890 at the age of 62, and was therefore born in about 1828, there remains no doubt that "uncle Leontios" was one of the martyrs of that name who suffered in the aftermath of the Greek revolt of 1821. But which one?

Chrysanthos of Kition was a son of Hadji Ioannes of Lapithos and Maria Theocharidou of Evrychos, daughter of the Lapithian notable, Hadji Konstantes Englezos. What is known about Chrysanthos's maternal relations precludes the possibility that Leontios belonged to that family line. On the other hand, even though the origins of the Ladas family are unknown, Leontios seems in principle excluded because he came from Karavas.

The problem was solved by the "old document" to which K. Myrianthopoulos vaguely refers and from which he gives excerpts as supposedly commemorating the hieromonk Leontios of Phaneromeni. I came across this document by chance in the Palace of the Archbishop of Cyprus.

It is a copy of a guarantee of the repayment of a loan which was deposited for safety at the Archiepiscopal Palace and today constitutes document No. 3 of the Archive of Archbishop Chrysanthos. It was written in Constantinople and bears the date 8 May 1777.

---

[29] M. G. Michaelides, "Ὁ Κυρηνείας Χρύσανθος Ἰωαννίδης καὶ ἡ ἀλληλογραφία του μὲ τὸν Ἱερώνυμο Βαρλαάμ (1877–1899)", *KS* 41 (1977), p. 175.

/¹ "Ισον τοῦ πατριαρχικοῦ γράμματος
/² † ὁ Πατριάρχης ἐπιβεβαιοῖ
/³ †Διὰ τοῦ παρόντος ἐνυπογράφου καὶ ἐμμαρτύρου γράμματος
τῆς πατριαρχικῆς /⁴ αὐλῆς γίνεται δῆλον, ὡς ὁ ἡγούμενος ἐν
Ἱερομονάχοις κὺρ Λεόντιος ἀπὸ χωρίον Λάπηθον /⁵ λεγόμενον τῆς
Κύπρου, υἱὸς τοῦ ποτὲ Χατζῆ Γιάννη, παραγενόμενος εἰς τὴν
πατριαρχικὴν /⁶ αὐλήν, μετὰ τοῦ ἐν Ἱεροδιακόνοις κὺρ Μελετίου
Κυπρίου τοὐπίκλην Μαναβέλλα Ὡρολογᾶ /⁷ ἀνήγγειλε, καὶ
ὡμολόγησεν ἰδίῳ αὐτοῦ στόματι, ὡς ἔλαβεν ἤδη δανειακῶς διὰ
χρείαν καὶ /⁸ ἀνάγκην αὐτοῦ παρὰ τοῦ εἰρημένου κὺρ Μελετίου
Ἱεροδιακόνου γρόσια τὸν ἀριθμὸν πεντακό /⁹ σια, κεφάλαιον
καθαρὸν ἄνευ τόκου, ἐπὶ ὑποσχέσει μέντοι τοιαύτῃ, πληρῶσαι ταῦτα
/¹⁰ ἀνελλιπῶς τῇ αὐτοῦ ὁσιότητι ἀπὸ τῆς σήμερον εἰς διορίαν μηνῶν
πέντε καὶ ἐξοφλῆσαι /¹¹ εὐχαρίστως. Παρελθούσης δὲ τῆς διορίας
ταύτης ἂν μὴ πληρωθῶσιν ἔχουσι τρέχειν εἰς τὸ ἑξῆς /¹² μετὰ τοῦ
συμπεφωνημένου τόκου πρὸς πέντε γρόσια τὸ πουγγεῖον καθ᾽
ἕκαστον μῆνα /¹³ δηλ: μέχρι τῆς τελείας αὐτοῦ ἐξοφλήσεως καὶ
ἀποπληρώσεως. Προυπέσχετο δὲ ὁ /¹⁴ ῥηθεὶς Ἱερομόναχος κὺρ
Λεόντιος ἐπομένως καὶ τοῦτο, ὅπως εἰ τύχοι ἀποθανεῖν αὐτὸν /¹⁵
πρὸ τῆς τούτου ἀποπληρώσεως, ὀφείλειν πληροῦσθαι ταῦτα
ἀπροφασίστως ὑπὸ τῆς /¹⁶ καταλειφθησομένης περιουσίας αὐτοῦ,
μηδενὸς τῶν συγγενῶν αὐτοῦ ἐναντιουμένου /¹⁷ ὅλως, ἢ
ἀντιπράττοντος, οὕτως ὡμολόγησε καὶ ὑπέσχετο ὁ ῥηθεὶς
Ἱερομόναχος /¹⁸ κὺρ Λεόντιος. Ὅθεν εἰς τὴν πιστὴν τούτου
ἔνδειξιν, ἐγένετο καὶ τὸ παρὸν τῆς πατριαρ /¹⁹χικῆς αὐλῆς γράμμα,
ἐπὶ βεβαιώσει τοῦ Παναγιωτάτου καὶ Σεβασμιωτάτου ἡμῶν /²⁰
Αὐθέντου καὶ Δεσπότου, τοῦ Οἰκουμενικοῦ Πατριάρχου Κ(υρί)ου
Κ(υρί)ου Σωφρονίου, καὶ μαρτυρίᾳ /²¹ τῶν τιμιωτάτων καὶ
λογιωτάτων κληρικῶν τῆς τοῦ Χ(ριστο)ῦ μεγάλης ἐκκλησίας, καὶ
κατασφαλισθὲν τῇ /²² ἰδιοχείρῳ ὑπογραφῇ καὶ σφραγίδι τοῦ κὺρ
Λεοντίου, ἐδόθη τῷ ῥηθέντι ἱεροδιακόνῳ /²³ κὺρ Μελετίῳ Ὡρολογᾶ:
— ͵αψοζʹ Μαΐου ηʹ:
/²⁴= Λεόντιος Ἱερομόναχος βεβαιῶ.
/²⁵= † ὁ Μέγας Διερμηνευτὴς μάρτυς.   †ὁ Πρωτοψάλτης Δανιὴλ
μάρτυς.   † ὁ Β: ος ὀστιάριος μάρτυς.
/²⁶ † ὁ Λαμπαδάριος μάρτυς. †ὁ Πριμμικήριος μάρτυς. † ὁ
Β᾽στι[..]ριος μάρτυς.
/²⁷ = Μπαλάσιος Γούλαινος μάρτυς.
/²⁸ Γεράσιμος Ἱερομόναχος προεστὸς εἰς τὸν Χριστὸν μάρτυς.
/²⁹ Σίλβεστρος Ἱερομ: προεστὸς μάρτυς.
/³⁰ Χ" Χρίστος Κουγιουμτζῆς μάρτυς:—

["copy of the patriarchal letter
† the patriarch confirms

By means of this signed and witnessed letter of the patriarchal court it is made known that the abbot hieromonk *kyr* Leontios from the village called Lapithos in Cyprus, son of the late Hadji Giannes, present at the patriarchal court together with the deacon *kyr* Meletios, a Cypriot surnamed Manavellas Orologas, has declared and acknowledged in person that he has received as a loan for his own use and expenditure from the said deacon *kyr* Meletios a sum of five hundred kurush, purely as capital without interest, on the promise, however, that this will be repaid in full to his reverence upon the expiry of a term of five months from today and the debt gladly discharged. If on the expiry of this term the sum has not been repaid the following will apply: the capital with the addition of an agreed interest of five kurush per month, that is, until the final repayment and discharge of the debt. The said hieromonk *kyr* Leontios has consequently also promised the following: that if he should happen to die before the repayment of the debt it must be repaid in full from his estate without any equivocation and without any of his relations opposing it or taking action against it. The said hieromonk *kyr* Leontios has made an acknowledgement and promise in accordance with the foregoing. Wherefore the present letter of the patriarchal court was drawn up as a reliable record of this agreement upon the certification of our most holy and reverend lord and master the ecumenical patriarch *Kyrios Kyrios* Sophronios and the witness of the most honourable and learned clerics of the great church of Christ, and sealed with the seal and autograph signature of *kyr* Leontios, and was given to the said deacon *kyr* Meletios Orologas:

1777, May 7:
= Leontios, hieromonk, I confirm.
= † the Grand Dragoman, witness.
= † the Chief Cantor Daniel, witness.
= † B: os, *ostiarios*, witness.
= † the *Lampadarios*, witness.
= † the *Primicerios*, witness.
= † the *V'sti[..]rios*, witness.
= Balasios Goulainos, witness.
Gerasimos, hieromonk and abbot, witness to Christ.
Sylvester, hieromonk and abbot, witness.
Hadji Christos Kouyoumdjis, witness."][30]

---

[30] Line 20. Sophronios II (1775–1780). Line 25. The Grand Dragoman, according to Constantine Oikonomos, is the "devout and magnanimous" Constantine Mourouzes

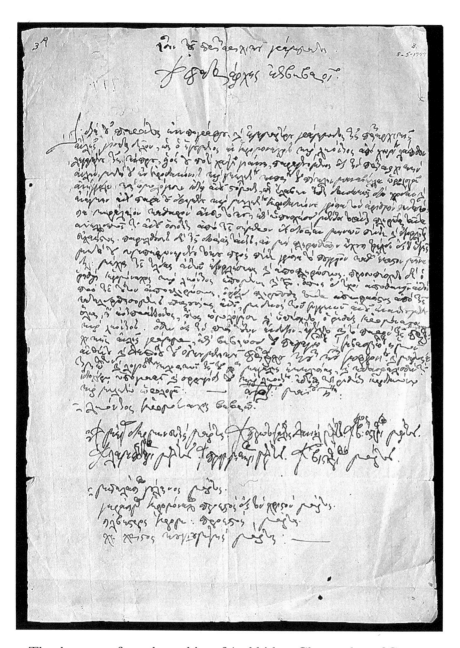

The document from the archive of Archbishop Chrysanthos of Cyprus
dated 8 May 1777

It is certain that the deacon Meletios Manavellas is the person who is known to have been steward from 1799 and abbot from 1814 of the monastery of Acheiropoietos.[31] The "abbot hieromonk *kyr* Leontios ... son of the late Hadji Giannes" is the "uncle" of Chrysanthos Ioannides of Kition who was the *ethnomartyr*. This is also confirmed by what K. Myrianthopoulos says about Leontios of Phaneromeni. He mentions that about a century after 1821 Major-General Constantine Hadjiioannou of Greece, brother of Chrysanthos, wishing to honour Leontios as his "grandfather", wrote from Patras, from the country property where he was spending his retirement, to Kyrillos III, archbishop of Cyprus, "on 13 September 1917, 6 June 1918 and 10 January 1921 saying that he was setting aside 50 bonds of the national loan of 1910 in order to found a 'Leontian asylum' for destitute children and a kind of Musicophilological School for ancient and modern drama. In addition he set aside another 10 bonds of the National Bank for 60 millions for the support of agricultural studies at the Pancyprian Gymnasium." The bonds were deposited in a trust fund but after the events of 1922 lost their value with the result that the wishes of the donor were never carried out.

The conclusion may therefore naturally be drawn that Abbot Leontios Hadji Giannes was a brother of the anonymous father of Hadji Giannes Ladas, the father of Chrysanthos Ioannides of Kition. This is also the explanation of why he was sometimes called "uncle" and sometimes "grandfather" by the children of Ladas. He was a brother of their paternal grandfather.

Of the branches of the family of the *ethnomartyr* Leontios Hadji Giannes, those of Chrysanthos, George and their brother Loizos (grandfather of G.

(1774–1777), who precisely in the summer of 1777 ascended the princely throne of Moldavia. See E.I. Stamatiades, *Βιογραφίαι τῶν Ἑλλήνων Μεγάλων Διερμηνέων τοῦ Ὀθωμανικοῦ Κράτους,* Athens, 1865.

On the brilliant Chief Cantor Daniel see Ch. Patrineles, "Πρωτοψάλται, Λαμπαδάριοι καὶ Δομέστικοι τῆς Μεγάλης Ἐκκλησίας", *Μνημοσύνη* 2 (1969), pp. 63–95, esp. pp. 78–9, 84–5, 88.

Line 26. The holder of the post of Lampadarios in 1777 was Peter Peloponnesios, the greatest musician of the third period of Byzantine composition (1650–*c*.1814), who died in the same year, 1777, of plague. See Ch. Patrineles, op. cit ., pp. 85-6, 89; G.Th. Stathes, "Η σύγχυση τῶν τριῶν Πέτρων (δηλ. Μπερεκέτη, Πελοποννησίου, Βυζαντίου), *Βυζαντινά,* 3 (1971), pp. 213–51.

V'sti[..]*rios*: perhaps Vestiarios (keeper of the wardrobe).

Line 27. The name Balasios is also borne by the important ecclesiastical hymnodist of the 17th century, Balasios priest and Nomophylax. See G.Th. Stathes, *Η δεκαπεντασύλλαβος ὑμνογραφία ἐν τῇ Βυζαντινῇ μελοποιΐᾳ,* Athens, 1977, pp. 119–20. The word, however, can also be read as Mitelasios (cf. the Cypriot Mitellas). The surname Goulainos is borne in the 18th century by the well-known family of noble Greeks from Leonidion in Kynouria. See the *Μεγάλη Ἑλληνικὴ Ἐγκυκλοπαιδεία* VIII, p. 646.

[31] K. Harmanta, "Χατζηνικόλας", p. 54, n. 17.

Theocharides of Nicosia) later hellenised their surname to "Ioannides", and that of Constantine to "Hadjiioannou". All of them, however, were also known by their father's additional name "Ladas" (oil merchant), while George was also called Moumdjis from his former occupation (*mumcu* = candle-maker).

During the nineteenth and twentieth centuries this family became one of the most important of the island, including amongst its descendants a whole galaxy of great benefactors of the community, the Church and education and becoming connected in Greece through the daughter of General K. Hadjiioannou, Evanthia, with the Phanariot princely family of the Soutsoi.[32]

The most notable achievement of the family, however, was the help which the abbot of St George Mezere gave to Kanares and his fire-ships and for which he paid for his life in the bloody July of 1821. We must suppose that this took place in his ripe old age, for he was already an abbot in 1777.

That Küçük Mehmed had knowledge of the help given to Kanares is proved by a number of testimonies. Chief of these is the note by J. Carne that during his audience with the governor the Ottoman

> "bitterly menaced a Greek monastery on the sea-shore, a few leagues from the city; it would make an excellent post, he said, for his soldiers, and those dogs should not possess it long. This convent, in a noble situation, was inhabited by a few poor monks, and during our stay in the city some soldiers entered it, and grossly insulted and beat one or two of the fathers, and plundered whatever they could lay their hands on. Not long after our departure, it was attacked and taken possession of by the troops and all the fathers were murdered."[33]

The monastery could not have been any other than the Acheiropoietos,[34] and the reason for the governor's anger was clearly the episode involving Kanares on 19 June 1821.

Leontios's old friend Meletios, abbot of the Acheiropoietos, escaped the same fate, though we do not know how. The reason usually given is that he was of an advanced age, but in view of the fact that Leontios, who was certainly older than him, did not escape martyrdom, the real reason for his survival must lie elsewhere. Perhaps he enjoyed the protection of a powerful Turk (Mehmed Aga, the *muteveli* of the pious foundations of Lapithos and Karavas?)

---

[32] M.G. Michaelides, "Συμπλήρωμα εἰς τὴν ἀλληλογραφίαν Χρυσάνθου Ἰωαννίδη καὶ Ἱερωνύμου Βαρλαάμ", *KS* 42 (1978), p. 108.

[33] J. Carne, *Letters from the East*, 3rd edn, London, 1830, pp. 173-4.

[34] J. Koumoulides, *Cyprus and the War of Greek Independence 1821-1829*, London, 1974, p. 51, I do not know why, identifies this monastery with one "tou Stavrou, the Cross" without any further explanation.

or else the role of Leontios in relation to the Kanares affair was more important? Unfortunately we do not know and we shall not know.

With the death of its abbot the monastery of St George Mezere seems to have fallen into extreme poverty. A few years later Charalambos, metropolitan of Kyrenia, turned it into a parish of Karavas and in 1843–44 its church was replaced by the present building.[35] Perhaps it was unable to recover from the pillaging and massacres of 1821. Perhaps the debtor of 1777 was not exceptionally able at managing its finances.

IV. PSEUDO-LEONTIOS THESEUS

In 1930 N.G. Kyriazes in his Greek translation of the passages in J. Carne referring to Cyprus printed a version which translated back into English reads as follows:

> "Leondias, son of the deceased Oikonomos (Vicar) was seized and severely tortured to reveal where the nephew of the Archbishop was concealed. This man, Theseus by name, bribed those sent to arrest him and escaped at great expense from Nicosia. The old man Leondias, not knowing and not wishing to reveal Theseus' place of concealment, succumbed to his tortures. The perfidious governor not long afterwards summoned the religious and other leaders of the island."[36]

This version is not only seriously flawed and in many respects incomplete, but by a transposition of the letters i and d it prints the name given by Carne as Leondias instead of Leonidas. What Carne says is:

> "Leonidas, son of the late Vicar, was seized, and suffered cruel tortures during several days, to compel him to reveal the place where the nephew of the Archbishop was concealed. This young man, Theseus by name, had bribed the executioners sent to arrest him, and, having paid large sums to some of his chief enemies, succeeded in saving himself by flight from Nicosia, into some of the remote parts of the island. Leonidas, who was an old man, either not knowing or refusing to tell the place of his concealment, expired at last, after enduring extreme tortures. The prelate was filled with anguish at the unhappy event. It was not long

---

[35] N.G. Kyriazes, *Τὰ Μοναστήρια ἐν Κύπρῳ*, p. 43; K. Harmanta, "Λάπηθος–Λάμπουσα–Καραβᾶς", p. 33.

[36] N.G. Kyriazes, "Ἡ Κυπριακὴ τραγῳδία τοῦ 1821", *ΚΧ* 7 (1930), p. 47.

afterwards that the perfidious Governor invited Cyprian to summon his chief ecclesiastics ..."[37]

There can be no doubt about the name Leonidas, as the running title in the upper margin of p.117 is: DEATH OF LEONIDAS. The passage refers to a martyr unknown to us, a victim of what G.I. Kepiades has called "the ill-conceived coup of Archimandrite Theophylact Theseus".[38] The priest who was his father also remains unknown to us, just as he was unknown even to Carne, as the vagueness of his reference indicates .

Kyriazes' mistake, however, was taken up by C.P. Kyrris,[39] who also took this Leonidas to be Leontios and indeed regarded him as a son of the grand *oikonomos* Papa Sabbas, whom he supposes to be a brother of Archbishop Kyprianos.

This interpretation was also embraced by A. Koudounares,[40] who, writing about the Theseus family, notes as its first member "Leontios Theseus", a brother supposedly of Kyprianos, Nicholas and Theophylact (whom he writes as Theophilos, as he was known to the French by assimilation to Théophile), sons of the brother of the grand *oikonomos* of the *ethnomartyr* Kyprianos.

This is certainly an imaginary person who cannot possibly have any historical value.

In the first place the word "vicar" in English usage signifies a parish priest and not an *oikonomos* (= steward). Next, how would it have been possible for the memory of such a famous man to have perished? And in the many documents of the Theseus family which we possess is it possible that none of them would have referred to "Leontios"?

At all events, Kyprianos's grand *oikonomos*, Papa Sabbas, not only did not have a son called Leontios or Leonidas but was not even a brother of the archbishop, even though the latter refers to Sabbas' children in some documents in an honorary way as "my nephews".[41] Here on account of the rarity of the periodical in which it was first published by O.I. Iasonides I simply reproduce in translation the text of an autograph declaration of Archbishop Kyprianos on the inheritance of the grand *oikonomos*. The original was discovered in 1910 amongst the documents of Iasonides' great-uncle, Nicholas Theseus. The declaration is dated 23 November 1820.

---

[37] J. Carne, *Letters from the East*, pp. 116–17.

[38] G.I. Kepiades, Ἀπομνημονεύματα, p. 11.

[39] C.P. Kyrris, "Δεδομένα ἐπὶ τῶν κοινωνικῶν θεσμῶν τῆς Κύπρου κατὰ τὰς ἀρχὰς τοῦ ΙΘ′ αἰ.", ΕΚΕΕΚ 6 (1972-3), pp. 379–80.

[40] A.L. Koudounares, "Ἡ οἰκογένεια τῶν Θησέων", KS 38–39 (1975), p. 79.

[41] C.P. Kyrris, "Δεδομένα", p. 378.

"Having given our opinion we declare that after the death of our cousin of blessed memory, the Grand *Oikonomos* of our most holy Archdiocese of Cyprus, Papa Sabbas, his property in cash has been recorded (which was found in the strong-box of the deceased amounting to so much metal coin, namely in various currencies) in the presence of ourselves, of the most reverend presbytera of the deceased, *kyria* Kornelia, and of his dearest children, the most noble *kyrios* Kyprianos Theseus and *kyria* Marina, and it amounted to six hundred and seventeen thousand and seventy-five kurush and thirty paras, from which, by the common agreement of the said most noble heirs, we have taken for the use and need of our most holy throne the six hundred thousand kurush only on the following agreed terms: First we shall be obliged upon the return to the country of the remaining two heirs, the most noble *kyrios* Nicholas Theseus and the most holy Archimandrite *kyrios* Theophylact Theseus, to repay the sum in full, if it is requested of us, and we also promise that we shall continue without fail to pay interest on this sum for as long as it is left with us at a rate of eight per cent. Secondly, for its complete security and protection we give as a surety or pledge to their nobilities first our country estate outside Nicosia with all its dependencies, secondly our other estate of 'Tymvos' in like manner, thirdly the monastery of Avgasis with all its property movable and immovable, fourthly our other estate of Strovolos, and in addition to these our two mills in Kythrea, one of which is called 'Iatros' and the other 'Koromylos'.

All these things, then, in any contrary circumstances, or upon failure of repayment on our part if any disaster should befall us or if death should supervene (God forbid) shall fall under the authority of the afore-mentioned noble heirs and shall be considered their personal property and chattels, without objection from anyone, when it shall be a criterion of justice. Wherefore in proof and confirmation of these things we validate and confirm our present declaration by our autograph signature in red ink and give it into the hands of their nobility.

In the year 1820, November 23."

The document proves that when in 1820 Kyprianos's cousin, the grand *oikonomos*, Papa Sabbas, died he left only four children born to him by the *oikonomissa* Kornelia Synglitiki, Kyprianos, Nicholas, Theophylact and Marina, the grandmother of the deputy Onouphrios Iasonides. An *ethnomartyr* called "Leontios Theseus" never existed except in the printing press.

XVIII

THE FOUR LEONTII REVISITED*

*'Day unto day uttereth speech
and night unto night sheweth knowledge'
(Ps. 18:18)*

Further study of the *Great Codex* of the Archiepiscopal Palace, Cyprus, has led me to correct some conjectures which I made on the basis of insufficient evidence in my earlier paper *On the Four Leontii Martyred in Cyprus after the Events of 1821*.[1]

On pp. 388–9 of the *Codex* there is a copy of the following letter from Major-General Constantine Hadjiioannou to Archbishop Kyrillos III of Cyprus which sheds new light on the second Leontios studied by me:

"To His Beatitude Kyrillos, Archbishop of All Cyprus, Nicosia.
Through my nephew, Dr Antony Theodotou, and in the absence of his wife Eugenia, I am sending via the Limassol branch of the Bank of Athens one thousand eight hundred francs (1800) that through the collaboration of Your Eminence with my nephew and niece this sum may be invested by the church council with a secure and consolidated return on behalf of the parish priests and the deacon of my parish of Phaneromeni, so that every Maundy Thursday the corresponding interest should be paid to them for the purchase of necessary provisions for the Easter period. My purpose is that they should commemorate the names successively of deceased members of my family beginning with the brother of my mother Maria Hadji Ioannou, Leontios, parish priest

---

* Translated from "Καὶ πάλιν περὶ τῶν κατὰ τὸ κυπριακὸν 1821 Λεοντίων", *KS* 44 (1980), pp. 117–118.

[1] "Περὶ τῶν κατὰ τὸ κυπριακὸν 1821 Λεοντίων", *KS* 42 (1978), pp. 59–74, translated above as Chapter XVII.

of the church, who was beheaded by the bloodthirsty Küçük Mehmed forty days before the hanging of the four prelates together with the chief church officials and leading members of the island's communities as members of the *Philiki Etaireia* of the Greek Revolution of 1821 for the liberation of Greece.

I trust that Your Beatitude will be happy to assist me with this sacred if inconvenient undertaking and will bless it with your prayers.

Vernardeika railway station (Patras) 12 September 1917.

I remain Your Eminence's most humble servant.

(Signed) K. Hadji Ioannou, major-general".

Further information about the *ethnomartyr* and hieromonk Leontios, parish priest of Phaneromeni, is contained in a passage from another letter of the major-general to Kyrillos III dated 6 January 1918 copied and confirmed with the red signature of the archbishop on pp.401–2 of the *Great Codex:*

"For the present, Your Beatitude, my concern is to immortalise the name of my learned uncle through the foundation of the Leontian Asylum. He was the brother of my mother, whom he educated and provided with a dowry. It was in the library of this martyr that both I and my late brother the Metropolitan of Kition pursued our studies in Cyprus.

I should like this asylum for destitute children to be founded in my parish and by the rooms of the church's courtyard which abut on my ancestral home, which is now owned by my niece Eugenia ..."

Further on the writer of the letter says that in the absence of the archbishop in England he had sent to the *locum tenens*, Metropolitan James of Paphos, 50 bonds of the national loan of 1910 for the Leontian Asylum and was now sending to His Beatitude 10 bonds of the National Bank bearing interest by lot for 60 millions for the foundation of an Agricultural Department at the Pancyprian Gymnasium.

In his third letter of 10 January 1921 the major-general sent Kyrillos III 25 new shares of 1910 for the Leontian Asylum which was to be founded and another 5 bonds of 60 millions for agricultural studies at the Pancyprian Gymnasium (*Great Codex*, pp. 402–3).

The facts speak for themselves. While sections I and IV of my 1978 study remain as they are, sections II and III need to be corrected as follows:

1. The *ethnomartyr* from Lapithos who was abbot of the monastery of St George Mezere of Karavas is certainly the person referred to in the patri-

archal document of 8 May 1777 but he is not the uncle of Chrysanthos Ioannides of Kition and his brothers, Major-General Constantine Hadjiioannou, Loizos Ioannides and George Moumdjis, father of the national benefactor, Eugenia Theodotou.

2. The uncle of these four, the brother of their mother Maria, was the *ethnomartyr* Leontios who was a hieromonk and parish priest of Phaneromeni and was put to death, according to his nephew, Major-General Hadjiioannou, forty days before the massacre of 9 July 1821.

The details concerning these two *ethnomartyrs* remain unaffected but should be assigned to them in accordance with the present correction.

XIX

THE ANTIOCHENE QUESTION
OF 1897–1899
AN UNPUBLISHED JOURNAL OF
CONSTANTINE I. MYRIANTHOPOULOS*

Dedicated to the Patriarch of Antioch,
His Beatitude Ignatius IV Hazim,
as a token of filial devotion

The relations between Cypriots and the Church of Antioch date from the earliest years of Christianity since it was to Cypriot Hellenists that Antioch owed the first preaching of the Gospel in about AD 37 (Acts 11:20). It would not be an exaggeration to say that the preservation of the Orthodox character itself of the Church of Antioch was owed in modern times to a cleric of Cypriot origin, the Patriarch Silvester (1724–66) whom the last of the eighteenth-century Arab patriarchs, Athanasios al-Dabbās (1720–24) named on his deathbed as his successor.

It was destined, however, that the last of the Greek patriarchs of Antioch, Spyridon, formerly archbishop of Tabor (1891–98), should also be a Cypriot. It is to his patriarchate, canonical resignation and succession by an Arab that the documents published below refer. They belong to the archive of Constantine I. Myrianthopoulos (1874–1962), a kinsman and ward of the patriarch, who was successively Secretary to the Greek prelates of Antioch and Archivist of the Archiepiscopal Palace of Cyprus. I have added an introduction, which has as its aim not a detailed history of the question, but a better understanding of these historic documents which are now published here for the first time.

---

* Translated from "Τὸ Ἀντιοχικὸν ζήτημα κατὰ τὰ ἔτη 1897–1899. Ἀνέκδοτον ἡμερολόγιον Κ.Ι. Μυριανθοπούλου", KS 47 (1983), pp. 109–202.

C.I. Myrianthopoulos (1874–1962)

Patriarch Spyridon of Antioch (1891–98). A portrait hanging in the
Little Chapter House of the old Archiepiscopal Palace of Cyprus
(By permission of His Beatitude the Archbishop.)

The author

Constantine I. Myrianthopoulos, on his father's side a nephew of Archbishop
Kyrillos II of Cyprus (1910–16) and a cousin of Archbishop Makarios II
(1948–50), was born in Prodromos in 1874. In 1890, at the age of fifteen,
he went to live with Archbishop Spyridon of Tabor, a childhood friend of
his father and relation by marriage. He was enrolled at the archbishop's expense
in the Franco-Arab School in Bethlehem, where the archbishop served as
patriarchal commissioner.

The following year, when Spyridon was elected patriarch of Antioch,
his Cypriot ward was sent as a boarder to the Maronite school in Beirut which
had been founded by Mgr Joseph Dibs, where there were other students on
scholarships from the patriarchate of Jerusalem. In 1892, when Spyridon
withdrew his wards from non-Orthodox schools, Constantine I.
Myrianthopoulos came to the Theological School of Halki. After its destruction by an earthquake in 1894 he left the school unwillingly at the invitation
of Gerasimos, patriarch of Jerusalem – a friend and former teacher of his
uncle Kyrillos – and at the insistence of Spyridon he came to the Theological
School of the Precious Cross in Jerusalem.

Falling shortly afterwards under the displeasure of the principal, Gerasimos
Vasilakes, he was reported by him to the patriarch of Antioch as a troublemaker with the result that not only was his scholarship suspended but his
studies came to an end, for no one else would undertake to become his patron,
not even his Cypriot cousin, who was also a cousin of the patriarch, the learned
archbishop of Jordan, Epiphanios Matteos (1837–1908).

On visiting Patriarch Spyridon in Damascus with his father, he refused
to stay with him, preferring to return to Cyprus. Thus he remained in
Larnaca with his uncle Kyrillos Papadopoulos – then metropolitan of Kition
– for two years until October 1897, when he began to keep his journal.

It was natural that the foregoing should have influenced the author's
judgment, since he was in any case an immature twenty-three-year-old.
There is no doubt, for example, that Spyridon of Antioch, like a good
Myriantheus, showed no tendency at all to profligacy but was drawn to thrift.
He was not, however, such a miser as he is portrayed by his former benefi-
ciary (who complains, moreover, that the patriarch never sent him the least
gratuity, nor did he ever send him enough money, obliging him constantly
to borrow from more fortunate fellow-students such as Polykarpos, a student
from Kykkos at Halki). Moreover, his bitter experience at Jerusalem made
the author critical of the clergy of the Holy Sepulchre, while his youth
accounts for the absence of an adequate conception of the historical circumstances or structures which determine a question, and, conversely, for

his biographical idea of history, which he regards as subject to the individual will of rulers or their servants.

The environment and the lack of broader contacts and horizons are other reasons for the narrowness of outlook and short-sightedness which are characteristic of most Greeks of that time, burdened as they were by an immature nationalism. The reader enters the atmosphere of the Hellenism of 1897, from which, in the famous phrase of the Russian foreign minister, "le sentiment de la réalité" was lacking.

Thus according to the young Myrianthopoulos, the Greeks are not racist but have unwritten rights in Syria, whereas the Syrians, in trying to administer their own house, are racists and violators of the laws and the canons. The proconsuls and employees of the little Helladic courts have the right to do as they will in Syria and Palestine, while the great empire of Orthodox Russia has only the obligation to pay millions of roubles each year to the Orthodox patriarchates and to have no other say there, leaving the various Samians, Cypriots and Euboeans to do what they wish according to their lights.

We meet here an aspect of Hellenism's difficulty in accepting that it had been transformed from the imperial race of the Romans and restricted to a modern national state. The author belongs wholly to a Helladic nationalism and not to the broad theatre of Hellenism where we encounter such figures as Joachim III of Constantinople, Damian of Jerusalem and Manuel Gedeon, who described the disordered state of the Church of Antioch as "born of clerical empty-headedness and wrapped in swaddling clothes by megalomaniac politicians (!!) of Athens and Constantinople".[1]

With regard to the subsequent career of Constantine I. Myrianthopoulos we note here simply that in 1900 he was enrolled in the Faculty of Law of the University of Athens and while also pursuing studies in the Faculty of Philosophy heard the lectures of Paul Karolides, whose theories on the ethnic origin of the Syrian Orthodox he made his own.[2] Attaching himself later to Ion Dragoumes, he became a follower of the latter's Greek Idea.[3] In 1910, sent by him to Icaria, he developed a programme of educational and nationalist work and played an energetic role in the revolutions of that island and of Samos in 1912. Having served in an administrative capacity in free Icaria he left Greece in 1915 and, arriving in Cyprus, assumed the duties of Secretary, Librarian and Archivist of the Archiepiscopal Palace. From 1920

---

[1] M.I. Gedeon, " Ἐκκλησιαστικὴ γραμματολογία 1821–1921", Πανελλήνιον λεύκωμα ἐθνικῆς ἑκατονταετηρίδος 1821–1921, III, Athens, 1925, pp. 101-16, esp. p. 106.

[2] See bibliography, p. 463.

[3] See especially I. Dragoumes, ῞Οσοι ζωντανοί, Athens, 1911; Ὁ ἑλληνισμός μου καὶ οἱ ῞Ελληνες, 1903–1909 – Ἑλληνικὸς πολιτισμός, 1913, Athens, 1927.

BENEDICT ENGLEZAKIS

he also served as a teacher at the Pancyprian Gymnasium and in 1921 also
became Secretary of the National Council. Scion of a famous priestly family,
he had the good fortune in 1948 to see a third member of his galaxy of episcopal
relations ascend the senior throne of the East as Makarios II, archbishop of
Cyprus.

Having occupied himself with the general and ecclesiastical history of
Cyprus, Myrianthopoulos published several studies, amongst which the chief
place is held by his work on Hadjigeorgakis Kornesios. He has left a manuscript
index and multivolume descriptive catalogue of 11 825 documents in the
Archive of the Archbishops of Cyprus, which is housed today in the
Archiepiscopal Palace in Nicosia.[4]

For the purposes of this introduction we note, finally, that Myrianthopoulos
had relations from the time of his stay in Jerusalem with Gregory Papamichael
and Chrysostomos Papadopoulos, professors subsequently at the University
of Athens, the latter later becoming archbishop of Greece, with whose
approach to the subject of relations between Greeks, Arabs and Russians in
the Middle East Myrianthopoulos identified himself.[5]

The journal

In spite of the weaknesses which we have noted, Myrianthopoulos's journal
is an important source for the events which unfolded in Damascus in 1897–99.
The author is thoroughly immersed in the affair, has direct knowledge of the
principals and the behind-the-scenes activities, lives the story and moves within
it. He is an intelligent person, naturally observant and, as one would expect
at his age, curious.

His youth, to which I referred earlier as a weakness, is from another point
of view a strong point. His youthful enthusiasm, given to lively sympathies
and antipathies and sweeping judgments characteristic of a robust barbarian,

---

[4] Constantine I. Myrianthopoulos, *Εὑρετήριον τῶν ἐγγράφων τοῦ Ἀρχείου τῆς
Ἀρχιεπισκοπῆς Κύπρου, 1767–1853*, Nicosia, 1941; *Ἀρχεῖον τῆς Ἀρχιεπισκοπῆς
Κύπρου. Ἀναγραφὴ ἐγγράφων, 1767–1853*, 48 vols., Nicosia, 1941–1953. There is a
table of published works in K. Chrysanthes, *KS* 45 (1981), p. 311. Publications in the press
of Constantinople, Athens, Alexandria and Cyprus and in the ecclesiastical journal, *Ἀπόστολος
Βαρνάβας*.

[5] See the bibliography, p. 463 and the decisive intervention of the then head of the
Theological School of Jerusalem, Ch. A. Papadopoulos, in the deposition of Patriarch Damian
for conducting himself in a pro-Arab and pro-Russian manner. Cf. G. Papamichael,
Ἀποκαλύψεις περὶ τῆς ρωσικῆς πολιτικῆς ἐν τῇ ὀρθοδόξῳ Ἀνατολῇ, Alexandria,
1910, and *Ἐκκλησιαστικὸς Φάρος* and *Πάνταινον* in the decade 1908–1918 (editor: G.
Papamichael).

underlines persons and situations in such an unrepeatable manner that they appear before our eyes today as vividly as in Damascus in 1898.

Beyond the monolithic formulations of historians, this journal shows how fluid and unclear were the boundaries of the two sides, how confused the battle-lines, how fragile the fronts, how many-sided the forces and multiple the phases through which the struggle between Greeks and Arabs passed for the throne of Antioch. It proves unwittingly that the revolt of the Arabs, however much it was trumpeted in Damascus by the Russian consul, was not the creation of Russian policy but a national product of an awakened Arab nationalism, which took on the character of a popular movement terrifying the notables and the hierarchy, who had been dragged – with some exceptions – into the arena by the laity. The journal reveals in a generous measure the inadequacy and incapacity of the Greek bishops, the sufferings of their native brethren, the opposition of Muslim Arabs to the aspirations of their Christian fellows, whom they regarded as Russian agents, the enduring deep philhellenism of educated Orthodox Arabs in spite of the conflict, the role of Greek education in the arousal of their nationalism, their exasperation with neo-Greek nationalism, their being pushed into anti-Christian extremes and the grievous outcome in the rupture of the bonds of love between the Eastern patriarchs until 1909.

The memoirs of Constantine I. Myrianthopoulos, together with the work of Archimandrite Gabriel Karapatakes, also a Cypriot, which is mentioned in the bibliography, and the unpublished diary of yet another Cypriot, Metropolitan Nektarios of Aleppo, which is in the Library of the Metochion of the Holy Sepulchre in Constantinople, have the value of eye-witness evidence which, although not history, can, however, be an irreplaceable source for history.

The historical background

The linguistic Arabisation of the Orthodox of Syria through the abandonment of Greek and Syriac, which began from the eleventh century, was completed in the centuries of Mameluke rule (1260–1516), when the Church of Antioch was isolated to some extent from the Church of Constantinople, which was itself from 1453 subject to the Ottomans. The capture of Syria by them in 1516 brought the two Churches close to one another again, but the process of Arabisation did not cease of course, seeing that the Orthodox community continued to live as a minority in the midst of an Arabic-speaking Muslim majority and in a land in which the last traces of Byzantine cultural influence were daily disappearing.

Thus already before the seventeenth century Arabic prevailed even as the main liturgical language of the Melkites (= Imperial = Roman Orthodox), who, in contrast with the mountain-dwelling Maronites of Lebanon and the country-dwelling Jacobites, lived for the most part in the cities, where they engaged in trade and therefore came into constant contact with the Muslims.

At about the beginning of the eighteenth century the constant internal disturbances in Syria, the wars of the Ottomans with Persia, and the opening up of new routes for seaborne trade, reduced the importance of the Syrian ports of Sidon and Tripoli. Indeed the city of Aleppo with its port of Alexandretta, the first port in the East for trade with Europe, was replaced from that time by Smyrna. The Syrian merchants, having need of direct protection, turned to France and, under the tireless instigation of the missionaries of the Vatican, to Roman Catholicism.

This pro-Uniate apostasy of the Melkite upper classes – upper, that is, with regard to money and education – reached such limits that in 1724, after a series of flirtations of the last three Arabic-speaking patriarchs with Rome, an avowedly Uniate patriarch of Antioch, Kyrillos al-Tānas, was elected by the Orthodox bishops. The Church of Antioch appeared now separated from the East, which endured under Rome the more powerful blow resulting from schism.

The Greek patriarchs of Antioch from 1724 to Spyridon

It was just at that time that the intervention of the ecumenical patriarchate saved the situation through the election in Constantinople of a successor to al-Dabbās. At first Joachim, bishop of Drama, was elected as such. When it became known, however, that the dying patriarch had indicated as his successor his Cypriot *protosyngellos* in Damascus, Silvester, the act of election of Joachim was declared null and, at the request of the Syrian Orthodox, Silvester was elected.

This man, a "second Athanasios", as Eustratios Argenti called him, began a gigantic struggle on behalf of Orthodoxy and, although not succeeding in healing the split in the Church of Antioch, nevertheless succeeded in stemming the general apostasy of the Arabic-speaking Orthodox, and – showing himself to be one of the more effective Greek clerics under Turkish rule – saved what could still be saved from the popes and the French. This was, fundamentally, the Orthodox populations of the villages, who were utterly poor and illiterate.

In the following century the Church of Antioch, suffering severely from Latin propaganda, remained under the supervision of Constantinople, from which the Orthodox of Syria sought the choice of each of their patriarchs. Coming from Byzantium, these brought with them, besides the classic

Ottoman bias against the Arabs, the spirit and the aims of Phanariot policy, which consisted, it seems, of co-existence with and adaptation to the Ottoman reality, the furthering of the ethnic interests of the Greek nation, and a resolute insistence on Orthodoxy.

The first of these aims appeared as natural in Damascus or Aleppo as it did in Constantinople; the third was equally acceptable in theory; the second aim, however, became in time objectionable to the new educated class of Orthodox. Deprived of the protection of embassies, consuls and agents of foreign powers, they began to identify themselves as a group opposed to the Turkish civil authorities on the one hand and to the Greek religious hierarchy on the other. This attitude was intensified with the appearance from the time of Napoleon's arrival of in Egypt of the Arab question. Indeed, they were the first of all the Arabs – Muslim or Christian – to acquire and thereafter to cultivate in every possible way an Arab, as distinct from a religious, self-awareness. This was based on the new European ideas about nationhood, on a common language and on common political and social goals, in which, it should be said, the Orthodox always granted the leading place to Islam, not assuredly as a religion but as a culture. This new movement was helped by the fact that the Arabs did not constitute a race (much less a state) but a nation or people, a distinctive characteristic of whom was the use of the language of the Koran.

Although the Orthodox Arabs produced thinkers of the calibre of As'ad Khayyāt, the Greek patriarch and his fellow-Greek bishops were usually ignorant even of the Arabic language. In thrall for the most part to the leading landowners and their interest, they could do little for the education of their flock, spending themselves on the struggles with the Jesuits and expecting all their resources from the Greeks and those subject to them.

The predominant crises of the Ottoman Empire and the anarchy that was always threatened by its centrifugal tendencies did not favour the non-Muslims and left them little room for positive action. Towards the end of the eighteenth century the governor of Damascus and Acre, Ahmet Jezzar Pasha, used to roast Christians in ovens, while at the beginning of the nineteenth century the liberal administration of Syria from 1831 to 1840 by the son of Muhammad 'Alī, Ibrāhīm Pasha, and the sultanic reforms of 1839 and 1856, far from improving the position of the Christians, as was intended, provoked Islamic wrath and ended in the terrible massacres of 1860.

During this time, however, the feudal nature of society in Syria was breaking down, the Arabic press was introduced from Egypt, European languages and ideas were gaining currency, roads were being opened up and communications created. In general, economic and social changes encouraged the spiritual awakening of the Arabs, while at the same time the Church of

Antioch experienced a new humiliation, falling from 1850 under the supervision of Jerusalem instead of Constantinople. In the end, through the translation in 1891 of Gerasimos (1885–91) of Antioch, formerly of Scythopolis, to Jerusalem, even the throne of Antioch itself seemed to have become, in the phrase of P. Karolides, "simply a springboard for the fought-over throne of Jerusalem".[6]

That translation was destined to act as a catalyst to the Arab Orthodox reaction which had been building up for years to the state of ecclesiastical affairs. Arab nationalism, strengthened by the British seizure of Egypt in 1882, felt the offence to the Church of the Arabs very deeply. Its representatives in Syria decided that they would never again accept a cleric from the Holy Places as their patriarch and began a campaign for the election of a native-born primate of the Church of Antioch.

The time, however, was not ripe. The notables continued to favour the choice of a Greek patriarch, the native-born bishops were not sure if they wanted one of themselves to be elected as their primate, all the Arabs in positions of authority were short of money, the ever-strong customary right of the Ottomans did not favour a change of regime, and the Sublime Porte, after the about-turn on behalf of the Bulgars the previous year, was not willing to take any new anti-Greek step.

Spyridon, patriarch of Antioch (1891–98)

Finally, these conditions, the Greek consul Marinakis in Beirut, the Cypriot grand vizier in Constantinople, Mehmet Kâmil Pasha (surnamed Ingiliz on account of his Anglophile sentiments),[7] the favour of the patriarch of Jerusalem, Gerasimos, and money, without which nothing could be done in the Ottoman Empire, imposed on the Arabs the election of the Jerusalem candidate, Spyridon, archbishop of Tabor. As objections were raised of a breach of the

---

[6] P.Karolides, "Πατριαρχείον Ἀντιοχείας", p. 139 (by an oversight the author repeatedly says Hierotheos instead of Gerasimos).

[7] His memoirs: Kâmil Pasha, *Hâtiratī Sadrī Esbak Kâmil Paşa*, Istanbul, [2]1329/1913. Cf. *Kâmil Paşanin Ayan Reisi Sait Paşa'ya Cevaplari*, Istanbul, [2]1328/1912 and *Sait Paşanin Kâmil Paşa Hâtiratina Cevaplari. Şarki Rumeli, Misir ve Ermeni Meseleleri*, Istanbul, 1327/1911; Hilmi Kâmil Bayur, *Sadrazam Kâmil Paşa-Siyasî Hayati*, Ankara, 1954: Constantine I. Myrianthopoulos, "Κιαμὴλ Πασᾶς, ὁ Κύπριος Βεζύρης, μαθητὴς τῆς Ἑλληνικῆς Σχολῆς Λευκωσίας", Ἑλληνικὴ Κύπρος 2, 1950, p. 310. The frequently expressed praised of H.C. Luke for the man (e.g. *Cyprus under the Turks, 1571–1878*, Oxford, 1921, pp. 210–11) amounts almost to adulation ("perhaps the greatest Cypriote since Zeno of Citium, the Founder of the Stoics"). On the other hand Sir Edwin Pears, *Life of Abd ul-Hamid*, London, 1917, presents a much darker picture of the Hebrew Turk from Nicosia.

canons, the election was repeated, as a consequence of which, with the exclusion of Gabriel of Beirut on account of poor health, and the transfer to the Greek side of two native-born bishops, Gerasimos of Seleucia and Misael of Tyre and Sidon, the electoral Synod of the patriarchate of Antioch elected at the beginning of October 1891 as patriarch once again Spyridon, archbishop of Tabor, and a committee of notables (Jibrān Isper, Rūf'āīl Shāmyeh and Salīm and Niqūlā Shāhīn) was sent to Jerusalem to receive him.

Spyridon I of Antioch, in the world Anastasios Euthymiou, was the third of the Cypriot patriarchs of Antioch in modern times, after Silvester and Anthemios, formerly bishop of Helenopolis (1791–1813), a cousin of Gerasimos III of Constantinople (1794–97) and of the historian of Cyprus, Archimandrite Kyprianos. Born to Mark and Katherine in the Paphian village of Agios Nikolaos Praitorios (which ceased to be Greek in the twentieth century) on 26 March 1839, which was Easter Day, he was given the name Anastasios, and in 1845, when his family was called to Palestine by the famous metropolitan of Petra, Meletios (1785–1867), who was his maternal uncle from Lemythos, he entered the Greek School of Jerusalem, which was then under the direction of the great Dionysios Kleopas.[8]

Having become a monk and taken the name of Spyridon in honour of his island saint, he was ordained deacon in 1859 and served in the central church of Constantine and Helen. In 1861 he was promoted archdeacon of the Council and Master of Ceremonies and in the meantime became fluent in the Arabic and Russian languages. In the same year his older brother Gabriel was also ordained deacon, having studied in Jerusalem and Russia at the

---

[8] The dates of birth, emigration and first ordination of Spyridon are given differently by Constantine I. Myrianthopoulos (p. 101) and the obituary "Σπυρίδων πρώην 'Αντιοχείας" in Νέα Σιών 16 (1921), pp. 223–4. According to Νέα Σιών the patriarch was born in 1840, moved to Jerusalem in 1846 and was ordained deacon in 1859. According to Myrianthopoulos the patriarch was born in 1838 on Easter Day – hence his name Anastasios – moved to Jerusalem in 1845 and was ordained deacon on 5 April 1858. With regard to the ordination, I have accepted the year given by Νέα Σιών in the hope that it was taken from the archives of the Brotherhood. With regard to the move to Jerusalem, I have adopted the year given by Myrianthopoulos, chiefly because he subsequently writes correctly that the metropolitan of Petra invited Spyridon's whole family to Jerusalem, where they were domiciled from that time, and not just Spyridon, as Νέα Σιών mentions. With regard to the year of birth, however, I have calculated it to be 1839 because (a) Easter could not have fallen within the period in which Spyridon could have been born; (b) the Easter that stayed in the memory of the family – from whom Myrianthopoulos seems to have drawn his information – could only have been the Easter of 1839, which fell on 26 March, Holy Saturday coinciding with the Annunciation. The biographical details of the patriarch given by Kl. Myrianthopoulos, Ἡ συμβολὴ τῆς Μαραθάσης εἰς τὴν Ἐκκλησίαν, Limassol, 1939, p. 32 follow those of Νέα Σιών and cannot therefore be considered independent evidence. On Meletios of Petra see Constantine I. Myrianthopoulos, "Ὁ Μητροπολίτης Πέτρας Μελέτιος", Ἐκκλησιαστικὸν βῆμα, I, No. 1 (14 January 1954), p. 2; No. 2 (28 January 1954), p. 2.

expense of his uncle, who on his death in 1867 left to Spyridon the chief portion of his enormous wealth. I note this in view of the accusations which were later made by Arabs and Russians – and most recently by D. Hopwood – about the source of the funds which Spyridon spent on behalf of the Church of Antioch and the education of the Arabs. Spyridon dedicated to the service of his flock the wealth which he had legally inherited from his uncle who had been Permanent Patriarchal Commissioner from 1840 to 1867 of the famous Mutrān al-Nūr, Archpriest of Light as the Arabs called him, one of the most eminent prelates of Jerusalem of the nineteenth century, through whom began the last era of Cypriot influence on the thrones of the East.

In 1872 Spyridon accompanied Patriarch Kyrillos II (1845–72) to Constantinople in connection with the Bulgarian question. I stress this too because, like his uncle, Spyridon belonged to the moderate pro-Russian party, another of the grounds on which Gerasimos would propose him for the throne of Antioch, from which, however, he was destined to be ejected with Russian help. (It may be mentioned that the hardline anti-Russian party in Palestine was also led by a Cypriot, Daniel Ioannides, bishop of Kyriakoupolis, a friend of the grand vizier Kibrisli Kâmil Pasha.)

After the fall of the aged Kyrillos II because of his refusal to sign the condemnation of the Bulgarians, Spyridon, on his return to Jerusalem, was ordained priest by Prokopios II (1873–75) and, promoted archimandrite, was appointed abbot of Gaza and sent away from Jerusalem. On his return after the election of the Patriarch Hierotheos (1875–82), he bought out of his own means the historic village of Bethany, built there an elegant little monastery for seven thousand pounds and installed his brother Gabriel as abbot, who from 1886 became abbot for life, member of the Synod and Inspector of Schools of the Sacred Council in Jerusalem. Spyridon also became a member of the Synod in 1881 while he was serving as Emin Hadji.

Finally on 12 February 1884 Patriarch Nikodemos (1883–90) consecrated him archbishop of Tabor in the church of the Anastasis. Having been allotted Tabor, Spyridon restored and extended the monastery on its summit, decorated the church and, at his own expense as always, bought for the support of the monastery a great expanse of land at the foot of the mountain.

On the death of Agapios of Ptolemais (1874–84) he was sent to Acre and worked among the Arabs as a preacher, restoring many churches, again at his own expense, and endowing them with vestments with his usual generosity. When the inhabitants asked for him as their metropolitan (and Ptolemais was then the largest metropolis of the region and the centre of the Palestinian Arabs), Spyridon refused, returning to Jerusalem where in 1885 he was appointed Member of the Ecclesiastical Court and the financial committee, until in 1886 he was sent as Patriarchal Commissioner to

Bethlehem. His experience as a preacher and spiritual father beloved of the Arabs would count later towards his selection for Antioch.

Spyridon was also active in Bethlehem, building a new wing onto the monastery, decorating the basilica and raising its great bell-tower, the foundations of which had been laid by Anthimos of Bethlehem (1876–86, later of Ptolemais). He fought so strongly against Latin demands for new rights in the place of veneration that he was in danger finally of being murdered in the bloody clashes of 11 May 1891, when, shot at by a Jerusalem friar carrying a pistol, he was only just saved in time by the intervention of his deacon, Gregory Peloponnesios. That courageous stand against the Latins also ensured that he was destined to be chosen for Antioch, a Church pillaged by papal propaganda and Uniatism.

I have narrated the life of Spyridon before his election as patriarch because in nearly all the literature on the Antiochene Question he is presented as incapable, insignificant and uneducated. D. Hopwood even goes so far as to accuse him of not having had pastoral experience, on the grounds that he had not previously had episcopal experience but had been elected from among the abbots of Bethlehem! Spyridon was certainly not a man of great academic background, since he had not even studied in a theological school. But neither had Joachim III nor Damian of Jerusalem passed any kind of degree in theology, nor had Spyridon's two immediate Arab successors, nor had Arsenios of Laodicea who from 1930 to 1933 contested the see as an alternative candidate. But Spyridon of Tabor was an experienced bishop who had served in a number of posts with success, moderate in his views but at the same time decisive, able, generous, public-spirited, dedicated to the Church, a man who strictly observed the fasts and canonical rules, dignified and with an extremely good voice, a pleasing celebrant who knew the entire liturgy by heart. With regard to his moral life, he was – by general consent and in contrast to many of his contemporary Greek and Arab bishops – a model of a devout and ascetic ecclesiastic. Above all, he was a simple man, affable and, as bitter experience would show in Damascus, kind to the point of naivety.

Setting out from Jerusalem on 10 January 1892 and passing through Beirut (where he silently endured the contempt and insults of the metropolitan, Gabriel Shaūla, who together with other higher clerics did not acknowledge him as their superior), the new patriarch reached Damascus on 31 January, accompanied from Jerusalem by two clerics of that city, the *Geron* Stephen Dragomanos and the *Geron* Parthenios Kamarases. He was received with ceremony, was preceded by a band and detachment of the Ottoman army to the residence of the *vali* to pay his respects, and then led to the decorated patriarchal church where in the presence of a dense crowd he delivered his enthronement speech in Greek, with Gerasimos of Seleucia translating into Arabic. In the evening there was a fireworks display at the patriarchate, and with these celebrations the patriarch embarked on his work. His opponents, however, also immediately began their campaign against him.

The first thing he did was to fill the vacant episcopal sees, choosing the Jerusalem Archimandrite Benjamin from Kassandra in Macedonia as metropolitan of Amida (Diyārbakīr) and Archdeacon Nektarios also of Jerusalem, an Anatolian Greek of Cypriot origin and a distant relation of his, as metropolitan of Beroea (Aleppo). He also filled the vacant abbatial posts, which were also given to Greeks. He later appointed as archdeacon the Cypriot Basil Topharides, a dark character who was later to cause mortal harm to Spyridon. Arab displeasure reached boiling-point with these appointments both because Greeks were promoted everywhere and because, apart from the metropolitan of Aleppo, they were not learned men. The lay Arabs thirsted for a cultural grounding and expected from their hierarchy above all action in the field of education. On the other hand it must also be said that Spyridon, in electing two Greek metropolitans, was trying in a natural way to balance the situation that existed at that time in his patriarchate. In his dioceses in Asia Minor and in Alexandretta, the second city of the diocese of Aleppo, there were sizable Greek populations, but his predecessor, Gerasimos, had not consecrated a single Greek bishop. Besides, of the two Greek abbots whom Spyridon had appointed, Kyrillos Grammatikakis of Ma'lūla, a Cretan, afterwards served the throne of Antioch under native-born patriarchs for fifty consecutive years. Spyridon also consecrated an Arab bishop, his suffragan of Edessa (Urfa), Athanasios, formerly archimandrite of Beirut, who gratefully remained loyal to him until the end. Moreover, during the seven years of his patriarchate he did not cease to take care to staff his Church with educated clergy.

Thus he frequently turned to Jerusalem and to the ecumenical throne, though without securing any help however critical the occasion. On the one hand Gerasimos of Jerusalem refused all assistance, although he was asked to send well-educated clergy trained in Arabic, and even forbade the deacon Joseph Anastasiades of Trebizond, whose philological studies he was supporting in Beirut, to help Spyridon, while on the other, the ecumenical patriarch sent only one cleric, Christodoulos Melissenos, who did not remain in Damascus. Moreover, having organised with his brother Gabriel, the abbot of Bethany, a plan for providing Arab and Greek scholarships in the Catholic and Protestant schools of Syria and Lebanon (with the intention of producing Greek Arabists and Arab clergy equipped with foreign languages), Spyridon was prevented from putting this into practice by his legal counsellor, Hippokrates Tavlarios of Kalymnos, former General Chief Secretary of the

Archipelago and commissioner, as it were, of the Phanar at the side of the patriarch. An arrogant man, this former Ottoman civil servant had studied law in Athens and Germany (1861–66) and had also formerly served Joachim III of Constantinople and Nikodemos of Jerusalem before becoming Damian's procurator in the imperial capital. He imposed a very strict line on the patriarch, harming him at the outset of his patriarchate and alienating from him even the leader of the Orthodox, Jibrān Isper, with whom Tavlarios communicated in Turkish with the result that the patriarch could not understand their exchanges.

With regard to the more immediate needs of Arab education Spyridon did not remain idle. First he appointed the very able Arab archimandrite, Paul, Scholarch of Damascus and also Chief Secretary of the Synod. Paul, a graduate of the Great National School of Constantinople and of the Theological School of Halki, was a devotee of the Greek tragedies from which he used to say, characteristically, that he had been taught everything he knew: "what freedom is and what fatherland is". Having remained loyal to the patriarch until his resignation, he crossed over to the party of his fellow Arab bishops, was elected after their victory metropolitan of Byblos and Botrys (first bishop of Mount Lebanon) and achieved much in the few years of his episcopate. In the meantime Spyridon appointed a new, well-educated teacher of Greek, Gabriel Karapatakes, a Cypriot from Kalopanagiotes who had studied at the Theological School of the Cross at the expense of the patriarch, as Deputy Scholarch. Karapatakes later published, as we have already noted, a very valuable history of the Antiochene question in which the point of view of Patriarch Spyridon on these events seems to be expressed. Besides, those Syrians who were not interested in the priesthood since they had their eye on emigration to Latin America, were interested neither in Arabic nor in Greek, but sought for their children instruction in French and especially in English.

Within two years Spyridon had dismissed Hippokrates Tavlarios and embarked on two new gestures on behalf of Arab education in Syria. In 1893 he set aside for this 10 000 pounds, a sum representing a substantial portion of his property, and in 1895 he invited the Russian Orthodox Palestinian Society to extend its activity to Syria, giving it the Patriarchal Girls' School of Damascus, which had been founded in 1868 by Patriarch Hierotheos, and the direction of fifteen other schools in Syria. From one point of view these two bold pro-Arab initiatives of Spyridon sealed his fall. For they opened the door to Russia, which until then had shown no interest in Syria (its chief ulterior motive being the places of pilgrimage in Jerusalem and not so much the native Orthodox), and at the same time provoked the anger of the Greeks against

Spyridon, without attracting the slightest gratitude from the Arabs, but rather arousing expectations amongst them which could not be satisfied.

The patriarch evidently did what he could but without succeeding in anything besides worsening his own position. Surrounded of necessity by uneducated colleagues for the most part, he looked forward to the future arrival in Damascus of students whose studies he had supported in Jerusalem and Halki, which, however, he was not destined to be allowed to see. The most distinguished of these proved later to be the Cretan Meletios Metaxakes, a subject of Benjamin of Amida, who subsequently occupied the sees of Kition, Athens, Constantinople and Alexandria. His experience as a young man of the anguished fall of his guardian through the collaboration of Arabs and Russians was something he would never forget. Of the Cypriots under the protection of Spyridon of Antioch the most famous was Meletios Kronides (1851–1918) from Omorphita, who was to become archbishop of Kyriakoupolis and then of Jordan and Commissioner of Damian of Jerusalem after Epiphanios Matteos, dying on 4 December 1918 in the patriarchate at Damascus, where, in exile with Damian, he had been given hospitality by the one-time enemy of Spyridon and then patriarch of Antioch, Gregory Haddād.

The occasion for open rebellion against Patriarch Spyridon in 1897 was provided by those who had been involved in the drawing up of the divorce of the secretary of the administration of Damascus, Yūsuf Tannūs, and also by the subsequent scandal of Archdeacon Basil Topharides.

The first trouble happened as follows: the Orthodox secretary of the civil administration of Damascus, Yūsuf Tannūs, married during the patriarchate of Gerasimos the daughter of a powerful Syrian family, to which the superior of the patriarchal church, a priest called Ailianos, also belonged. The marriage, however, was found to be barren. The husband resorted to the ecclesiastical courts and received from Patriarch Gerasimos the imposition of a seven-year trial period of separation from bed and board. When this period expired, Tannūs asked for a full divorce, to which he was entitled, since he wished to enter into a new marriage and beget legal heirs. The patriarch Spyridon, however, hesitated to implement the decision made by the court under Gerasimos, foreseeing the conflict that would be stirred up by the wife's family. Finally, and with the passage of time, he was persuaded by a Chiote friend of the similarly powerful Tannūs, a Damascus merchant called Stamatios Kontogiannis, and the patriarchal court gave a unanimous decision in favour of the husband, with the dissent only of the priest Ailianos, as was to be expected, who as a reprisal provoked a rebellion against Spyridon, hanging up opposite the court a demand for a retrial.

Metropolitan Nektarios of Aleppo (1892–99) (Ἐκκλησιαστικὸς Φάρος 2,
1909, pp. 376–7.)

The Deacon Meletios Metaxakes (1892) shortly after his ordination
to the diaconate in Damascus. This photograph is inscribed to his
dear friend Constantine I. Myrianthopoulos in his own hand and is
dated Damascus, 3 May 1892. It is possibly the earliest photograph
of him. Meletios Metaxakes was subsequently metropolitan of Kition
and patriarch of Constantinople and Alexandria.
('Εκκλησιαστικὸς Φάρος 34, 1935, pp. 494–5.)

It was 28 June 1897, the eve of the feast of St Peter and St Paul, the patronal feast of the throne of Antioch. The patriarchal church, recently equipped with new furniture and luxurious vestments by Spyridon, boasted from 1892 for the first time in the midst of an Islamic sacred capital a proud bell-tower. This too was the work of the hated patriarch. With the strengthening of Orthodoxy in Syria through the purchase of properties and estates of vast extent (to which in the meantime he had dedicated another 5000 pounds from his own resources for the building of a number of churches and the personal support of several teachers) he regarded the Christian bell-tower of Damascus as one of his finest achievements.

Towards midnight, however, before the official day, this bell began to toll mournfully and an angry crowd of Christian Arabs, men, women and children, poured into the area around the patriarchal buildings intent on an unprecedented abuse of the patriarch as supposedly having issued an uncanonical divorce, but in reality intending to extort more money from Spyridon. Therefore they sought from him a financial audit. Entering finally even into the patriarchal church under the leadership of Ailianos, they broke the steps of the patriarchal throne, and finally threatened the life of the patriarch, who, surrounded in his residence, was obliged to seek help from the *vali*, who had been prevented until then from intervening by the Russian consul. Finally, on the despatch of a detachment of Ottoman troops, most of the crowd dispersed, but a part of it under Ailianos took refuge in the church to seek asylum.

Then the evil spirit of the patriarchate, Archdeacon Basil, intervened, pouring oil on the fire. For, seeking revenge, he took with him one of the bailiffs of the patriarchate called Athanasios (whose paternal grandfather was a Greek from Adrianople) and with a hammer broke open the door of the sanctuary. With the asylum thus violated, the police entered and arrested Ailianos and his companions, taking them all to jail. This event not only aroused the crowd's religious feelings towards the Church, but also displeased those who were opposed to any violent disturbance. Greek and Arab community leaders came to the patriarch and recommended that Basil should be removed from the city. While the indecisive Spyridon still hesitated, the crowd took matters into their own hands.

A few days later the Cypriot archdeacon was caught by the Arabs coming out at night from the house of his Greek mistress and was driven in a procession with cudgels to the patriarchate. On 6 July Spyridon exiled him to the monastery of St George in Homeira (Mār Jirjis), where the abbot was a Greek from Mytilene called Gerasimos.

To make the affair easier to understand – if not easier to interpret – I would mention briefly that Basil Topharides, who after the departure of Tavlarios directed the patriarchate and the patriarch on his own, was originally from Nicosia. In early life he emigrated to Egypt where he had relations, and came to be a verger in Bethlehem and then in Jerusalem. There he attached himself to the archbishop of Tabor and accompanied him to Damascus. A kleptomaniac and a gambler and living a dissolute life, he had relations with several women in Damascus, amongst whom was a nun at Saydnāya. From her he appropriated money and votive offerings and finally burned the ledgers of the monastery in order to hide his deeds. Returning after the fall of Spyridon to Jerusalem, he was ordained to the priesthood with the support of another Cypriot bishop in the Church of Jerusalem and was appointed custodian of Ramla. He soon eloped from there with the head-mistress of the Girls' School in Jerusalem, Aglaia Veikou, whom he married and divorced in Athens. After that he became a monk on Mount Athos and a drunkard and ended his days as an old man in the monastery of Pendeli.

I mention these things not with any pleasure but out of necessity because they go some way towards explaining or justifying the fall of Spyridon and the election of an Arab patriarch. They also accord with the point of view of Myrianthopoulos's journal. The significance of these events and persons in the downfall of the power of the Greeks in Damascus should not be underestimated, but neither should they be exaggerated at the expense of deeper forces and more important factors. For with regard to the Tannūs affair it is clear that we are dealing with a vengeful inter-Arab conflict between powerful lay elements and families (a situation which any of the succeeding Arab patriarchs could have encountered). With regard to Basil, the Arab clergy presented many similar or even worse cases. To mention only one in this critical period, on 15 August 1897 at the festival on that day at the most revered place of pilgrimage in Syria, the monastery of the Theotokos at Saydnāya, the second priest of the monastery clashed with the nun who had charge of the financial affairs of the community and in revenge trans-ferred to Catholicism, where he was made welcome. It is characteristic of the mental atmosphere and commercial spirit of the Church of Antioch at this time that the patriarch sent his chief secretary Paul, who persuaded the good abba to return to Orthodoxy by offering him money and the privilege of henceforth wearing the *epigonation* when celebrating the liturgy. A large number of Orthodox Arabs went over to Uniatism over the next two years, supposedly out of hatred for the Greeks.

In the summer of 1897, however, the situation deteriorated in the Syrian capital just when Spyridon, on becoming aware of the role of the Russian consul in the exploitation of the Tannūs affair, demanded the return of the Patriarchal Girls' School to his own control. The consul persuaded the *vali* to feign ignorance of the fact that, on the instructions of the lay National Council which had been set up by Patriarch Gerasimos, the later notorious

Epiphanios Petrou (Gatas (K)andilaft) was touring the villages stirring up the country people against the patriarch. Spyridon protested to the Sublime Porte, which sent instructions to the *vali* to arrest the Council's emissary, but by then he had almost completed his work.

Andilaft was an old protégé of Patriarch Gerasimos, who had paid for his studies at the Rizareion School in Athens. Later he became the first principal of the theological school of Balament.

Towards the autumn the atmosphere in Damascus had become so oppressive and abnormal that Spyridon, despairing of the machinations against him, abandoned the city and withdrew with his entourage – including his other Cypriot deacon Niphon – to the nearby monastery of Saydnāya. From 29 June his name ceased to be commemorated in more and more parish churches. He himself was obliged to confine himself unwillingly in the end to the patriarchal residences. What would have prevented his return to Damascus was not so much the Tannūs and the Basils, or at least the activities of the lay Arab Council, as the root cause of the way the rebellion against him was allowed to develop in that year: ecclesiastical problems in both Constantinople and Sion, the Greco-Turkish war and the coalescence of opposition forces in Damascus.

In Constantinople the Greeks had been locked for years in a fanatical struggle between the Joachimites and the anti-Joachimites. The energies of the Synod and the National Council were exhausted by this controversy. When on 28 January 1897 Anthimos VII resigned – he had appeared at first to be a Joachimite and had succeeded the supposedly anti-Joachimite Neophytos VIII on 20 January 1895 – a new patriarch was not elected until 8 April 1897, when Constantine V was named. He ascended the throne in the midst of mutual recriminations on both sides and his first task was to consolidate his position. It was only with difficulty that he managed to reign until 26 March 1901. Under such conditions the affair of Spyridon of Antioch seemed of secondary importance in Constantinople and there was not the disposition or sufficient time to give the matter serious study and take effective action on his behalf. For constant support by the Sublime Porte and the Palace in the imperial capital was an inviolable rule in the Ottoman Empire, where nobody could feel secure or permanent in his office.

From 1850 onwards it was equally important for the Greek patriarch of Antioch to have the support of the Brotherhood of the Holy Sepulchre in Jerusalem, where, however, in 1897 the situation was worse than that of Constantinople. For at the end of 1896 the sudden illness and death of Patriarch Gerasimos not only deprived Spyridon unexpectedly of his chief support against the circle of the Chief Secretary, Photios Peroglu, who from 1895, when the patriarch had entrusted the education of the Arabs to the

Palestine Society, had worked unceasingly to bring about his fall, but created a more general void in Jerusalem which did not allow the election of a new patriarch for more than six months, until on 10 July 1897 Damian of Philadelphia managed to attain the required votes. This was, it was thought, simply a temporary appointment which would give time for the powerful warring factions to marshal their forces. And although Damian, a widower from Samos and former secretary of a magistrates' court, had only come in 1872, still grieving, to the Brotherhood and had been taken on as an assistant verger in the Church of the Holy Sepulchre, he was destined to achieve the impossible: he remained on the throne until his death, which did not take place until 1931. What was of importance to Spyridon of Antioch in 1897, however, was that in the months when the rebellion against him was raging in Damascus the throne of the Church of Sion was vacant and its most powerful bishops had their minds on other things. The fact that in exploiting the death of Gerasimos, the six-month suspension of authority and the internal fighting of the Brotherhood the Arabs had decided that the time had come to rebel, proves the reality of the attempt of the Russian consul in Damascus at the beginning of 1897 to persuade Spyridon to submit his candidature for the throne of Jerusalem by promising him the support of Russia. This proposal was an attempt on the part of the consul either through the successful translation or through the complete demoralisation of the Greek patriarch to bring about a change of regime in Damascus. He came up against the stubborn resistance of Spyridon, however, who rejected any idea of abandoning Antioch for the sake of Jerusalem.

A third situation that favoured the Arab revolt and its success in 1897 was of course, more than anything, the war between Greece and the Ottoman Empire in the spring of that year, the defeat of Greece, the unexpected humiliation of Turkey by the Powers in the summer and autumn, and the consequent anger of the Ottomans against the Greeks. With the intensification of clashes between Muslims and Greeks in Crete from the end of 1896, the island rose in revolt against the sultan in the last days of January 1897 and proclaimed union with Greece. A force of 10 000 Greeks under Prince George disembarked on 3 February and occupied the island, which had been plunged into a chaos of mutual slaughter, sieges and famine. On 10 April 1897 another Greek force under Prince Constantine invaded Thessaly, only to be defeated by a powerful Ottoman army, which on 5 May 1897 stood poised at the pass of Thermopylae ready to descend and take Athens.

With the Greek state saved at the last moment by the intervention of Russia and England, the sultan was unexpectedly in the following months, although the victor, forced to cede Thessaly to Greece and recognise Crete as autonomous under the government of Prince George. The fury of the

Ottoman Empire at this unprecedented, as she thought, humiliation which she had suffered at the hands of the Powers and the sight of wretched lines of Muslim refugees leaving Thessaly and Crete did not inspire any especially philhellene tendencies in Constantinople, although it did create in Athens a profound respect for Russian aims. These things were carefully followed in Damascus, where from 1893 Russia had established a consulate-general with the former secretary of the consulate of Jerusalem, Alexis P. Belyaev, as its first consul.

That this person made it his aim that a native-born patriarch should ascend the throne of Antioch there can be no doubt. Neither can there be any doubt (a) that he did not "create" Arab nationalism but on his arrival in Damascus found it already well-developed from some decades previously; (b) that he did not favour this nationalism of the indigenous Orthodox, regarding it as dangerous and revolutionary; or (c) that he himself wished to replace Arab nationalism with a local patriotism based on the idea of Syrian identity. It should be said that he acted as a servant of the Russian Foreign Ministry in conjunction with the Imperial Orthodox Palestine Society, but not as an agent of the Russian Church. That the Holy Synod of Russia recognised the Arab patriarch in 1899 does not mean that it had previously been involved in any way in the resignation of his predecessor or in the election of Meletios II. The Church of Russia, which rarely resisted the will of the government in this kind of affair, simply preceded Constantinople by ten years in the path of justice and canon law.

The tsar's ministry, at all events, took care to have a much more suitable instrument for the attainment of its goals in Syria in the person of the governor of Damascus, from whose attitude would be judged for the most part both the success of the revolt of the Arab Orthodox against Spyridon and the change of regime in the patriarchate. It is extraordinary that the various authors who have written on these matters seem to say nothing about the identity of the *vali* of Damascus, Hüseyin Nazim Pasha, considering that in reality he determined the turn of events at the most critical moments. This man was none other than the notorious Minister of Police under Abdulhamit II (1876–1909) who had massacred the Armenians. A protégé of the sultan, he served as a tax collector and secret policeman (*hafiye*) in the Constantinopolitan suburb of Pera (Beyoglu) before becoming in 1890 minister in the newly-founded Zaptiye Nezareti, where he received an order to punish the Armenians. In 1896 he fulfilled his task so successfully in organising the first genocide that Great Britain demanded his exile to Jedda in Arabia, from which he was saved through the support of Russia, which a little later co-operated in his summons from Beirut to be governor of Damascus.[9]

Owing his escape, after the sultan, to Russia in this way, Hüseyin Nazim Pasha was not of course, immediately on his arrival in Damascus in 1897, going to oppose the Russian consul, certainly not for the sake of the Greeks or to the detriment of the Arabs, towards whom the favour of his master, Abdulhamit, was well-known, even if his governments at various times did not care for them. We are in the period when Abdulhamit II imposed the teaching of Arabic in Ottoman state schools, encouraged its use as a cultivated language in the Empire, and attempted, in spite of the opposition of Sait Pasha, to have it raised to equal status with Ottoman Turkish as an official language of the state. Arabs from Syria and Lebanon filled government posts in Constantinople in large numbers in preference to their colleagues from the Balkans.

All these things – these political and ecclesiastical factors which coincided in 1897 – explain better than the Tannūs divorce or Basil Topharides, I believe, the timing of the outbreak and the successful outcome of the Arab nationalist movement against Spyridon of Antioch. The *coup de grâce* against the patriarch, however, was given by his own people.

Writing to the four Greek metropolitans of the throne from 25 November 1897, the patriarch of Jerusalem's commissioner in Constantinople, Archimandrite Germanos Apostolatos, confidentially informs them that their patriarch, Spyridon, having lost all support from the Porte, could not remain on the throne for much longer. Assuring them that the imperial government favoured the continuation of the regime in Antioch, he advised them to appeal to the ecumenical patriarchate for consultations for the proposal of a candidate from among the Constantinopolitan bishops, and put himself at their disposal. In fact he succeeded in bringing about precisely the opposite of what he proposed. For he unwittingly aroused the ambition of two of them, who in no way had grasped the critical nature of the situation, on account of which Constantinople judged that a Holy Sepulchre candidate should not be proposed again but the older custom of 1850 should be restored (a decision which in the following two years would provoke crises between Constantinople and Jerusalem, where the powerful Photios – previously elected patriarch of Jerusalem (1882) and from 1900 patriarch of Alexandria – had, it seems, coveted, the throne of Antioch for years).

---

[9] In the archives of the palace of Yildiz (BVA, Istanbul, K.36/Z131/No. 139 [80]) there is an unpublished manuscript of Nazim Pasha on the "Armenian terrorism" and his activities, under the title *Ermeni Tarihi Vukuati*.

The first to make a move, then, was the metropolitan of Arcadia, Nikodemos Zographopoulos from Chrysoupolis on the Bosphorus, who in December 1897 showed Apostolatos's letter to his Arab friend and neighbour, Gregory Haddād, metropolitan of Tripoli (later the second native-born patriarch), who was one of his supporters. They agreed to keep the letter secret until they could put into operation a plan for the election of a patriarch from one of the bishops of the region. The plan was that the metropolitan of Arcadia should be elected and then on his resignation after two years the metropolitan of Tripoli should be elected in his place – according to Gerasimos's letter Tripoli was at that time out of favour with the government along with the bishops of Beirut and Laodicea, on account of his previous coolness towards it. They did not reckon, however, with the greater ambition of the metropolitan of Tarsus and Adana, Germanos Hourmouzes.

Hourmouzes, of Patmian origin, was educated at the Theological School of Halki and called to the patriarchate of Antioch by Patriarch Hierotheos (1850–85). After serving in various posts he was finally appointed to the metropolis of Tarsus and Adana, which had its seat at Mersin and a population which was largely Greek. In no way distinguished, except in raising livestock, he was sent by Spyridon to Moscow in 1894 as his representative at the coronation of Tsar Nicholas II (1894–1917) and from that time formed a very exalted opinion of himself, cultivating friendships where needed with the ultimate goal of patriarchal office. When he read Apostolatos's letter, he thought that the moment had arrived and began to intrigue against his patriarch.

First he sent letters to all the prelates of the throne of Antioch suggesting that they should declare Patriarch Spyridon deposed and proceed to the election of a successor from amongst the prelates of the throne. On receiving a mixed response, however, and indeed a number of refusals, he left his diocese and came to Beirut, so that with certain others he could intensify his efforts there. Not only was he resisted strongly by the metropolitans of Tripoli and Arcadia, but the governor of Beirut, seeing the unseemliness of these conspiracies against the lawful patriarch, prevented any meeting or synod of bishops in Beirut. At the same time the patriarch, on learning of these plots, sent a written invitation to all the bishops to a canonical synod at the monastery of Balament, far from every influence.

The view of the Greek metropolitans of Aleppo and Amida and of the moderate and disinterested Arab prelates – and indeed of the most eminent of them, Gerasimos, metropolitan of Seleucia – was that nothing could be done before the calling of a canonical council presided over by Patriarch Spyridon. The Russian consul, Alexis Belyaev, however, thought otherwise and persuaded Nazim Pasha to allow the Beirut conspirators to meet in Damascus, in the canonical see of the patriarch itself. It should be noted that of the thirteen prelates of the throne only six met at that synod, each of whom hoped, of course, that he himself would become patriarch.

A few days before the Christmas festivities these six deserted their flocks and began to descend on Damascus. The first to arrive was Athanasios 'Atallah, metropolitan of Emessa, a man who did not simply champion his people but was hostile to the Greeks and unscrupulous. With him came Germanos of Tarsus, who on coming into the patriarchate, where a crowd of townspeople was awaiting them, said to them "I shall free you from the tyranny of Spyridon". Immediately afterwards he invited the rest of the bishops in writing to come to this synod that he had thus called in Damascus.

In the absence of the arrival of any others, those present met on 20 December and decided that the patriarch should be summoned to make his defence. When the patriarch refused, on the grounds of both the uncanonical nature of the gathering and the absence of participants, the metropolitan of Tarsus – the Arab prelates having come to an understanding with Belyaev without his knowledge – called a second meeting, on Christmas Day itself, at which it was decided to seek the resignation of the patriarch and in the event of his refusal to declare him deposed.

On the night of 26 December 1897 there arrived at Saydnāya, after a long journey on horseback, Nikodemos of Arcadia and two Arab laymen as representatives of the six: Athanasios of Emessa, Meletios of Laodicea, Germanos of Tarsus, Gregory of Tripoli, Misael of Tyre and Sidon and the metropolitan of Arcadia himself. They brought with them two letters: the first sought the resignation of the patriarch, the second proclaimed him deposed from his throne. In spite of the lateness of the hour the party presented themselves at once to the patriarch, gave him the first letter and, on receiving the same reply as before, presented themselves again after two hours and delivered the second letter, through which the patriarch was declared deposed from his throne. But the patriarch responded again as before, pronouncing the meeting of the six bishops a schismatic conventicle and its acts invalid.

The next day the metropolitans of Tarsus, Tripoli and Emessa went to the *vali* and delivered to him the documents deposing the patriarch and electing the metropolitan of Tarsus as *locum tenens* of the throne. At the same time the patriarch protested to the Sublime Porte and to the patriarchates. The Porte declared that it did not recognise the events that had taken place in Damascus, while the ecumenical patriarch replied to Spyridon in very favourable terms and to the others that their acts were contrary to the canons. The events that succeeded are related in detail in the journal published below.

Having endured misery for months, the patriarch found himself at an impasse and under great psychological pressure. Two of the four Greek bishops had betrayed him, leaving him only with the metropolitans of Aleppo and Amida and his Arab friends who remained faithful to the end, and he was kept almost as a prisoner at Saydnāya by the conspirators and unworthy subordinates. Declining the offer of the metropolitan of Seleucia to buy the votes of the Arab metropolitans among the six for 1 000 pounds, he decided to escape from the monastery and make his way to free Lebanon, where, he hoped, far from the shadow of Belyaev and Nazim, he could put his Church in order. All it needed was the fall of snow on the night of 30/31 January 1898 to bring about the collapse of resistance on the part of the unfortunate Spyridon. Regarding the snow in his despair as a divine obstacle, on the following morning, Saturday 31 January 1898, he signed the act of his canonical resignation from the throne of Antioch, hoping that in this way the hatred of both Greeks and Arabs against him would be appeased and he would be free at last to retire to the monastic peace of his beloved Bethany.

He remained for another six months at Saydnāya, trying in vain to persuade Damian of Jerusalem to respect the synodical decisions of 1891 and allow him to take up the monastic life in the monastery he had built himself at Bethany. The place appointed for his residence was a *metochion* of the Holy Sepulchre at Neohori on the Bosphorus, to which he was compelled to go in the summer of 1898 by the Reverend Dragoman of Jerusalem, Archimandrite Glykerios.

Spyridon took none of his own things with him from the patriarchate but on the contrary sent all the bishops who had harmed him valuable mementos. With great dignity and Christian fortitude he sailed from Beirut into exile in August 1898. Only one comparison need be made between him and those left in Damascus. While the bishops plundered the patriarchal apartments, the lay people denounced the patriarch to Nazim Pasha on 28 July for still owing them 1 000 pounds in settlement of a previously announced gift. In Jerusalem the learned chief secretary, Photios, who a little before had been defeated by the "uneducated" Damian – by whom as a consolation he was promoted on 6 December 1897 to the archbishopric of Philadelphia – was now about to be outflanked even by the cowherd bishop of Tarsus and Adana and receive as a further consolation the metropolis of Nazareth. On the death in August of the same year of the patriarch of Alexandria, Sophronios, and the withdrawal, on the grounds of the state of the clergy prevailing in the Church, of the candidature of the people's choice, Nektarios of Pentapolis, who was later recognised as a saint, the chief cause of the undermining of Spyridon of Antioch with the Greeks was elected patriarch of Alexandria on 10 January 1900, as Photios I.

At the beginning of July 1908, when the eight-year-old struggle in Cyprus, over the vacant archiepiscopal throne had reached its climax, Greece proposed as a solution the election of the Cypriot former patriarch of Antioch,

Spyridon. But this thought met with the refusal of the adherents of the bishop of Kition, for whom Spyridon had been too willing to make concessions in Damascus and had worked on behalf of the Russians.[10] It is an irony of history – indicative, however, of a certain modern Greek mentality – that this same accusation was repeated in 1928 by Philaretos Vapheides of Didymoteicho, metropolitan of Heracleia (one of the Constantinopolitan candidates for Antioch after the departure of Spyridon), in the third volume of his *Ecclesiastical History* where he says that Spyridon "gave proof of his unfitness by working for Russian interests".[11] It would have been interesting to have known the reaction of Alexis Belyaev if it had been possible for him to read these judgments. Perhaps he would have repeated the words of the foreign minister of his country to which I have already referred.

After twenty-two years by the Bosphorus, patriarch Spyridon died in extreme old age on Tuesday 16 February 1921, at the end of a long illness. His funeral took place the following day with great honours in the presence of eight metropolitans of the ecumenical patriarchate (the patriarchal throne being vacant and the *locum tenens* absent in London), many priests and deacons, leading figures of the Greek nation and large crowds of lay people in the *catholicon* of the monastery of St George Kremnos on Halki, which was also a *metochion* of the Holy Sepulchre, to which he had moved some time previously. The curtain falls on him there, by the tomb of Nikodemos, Patriarch of Jerusalem, who in 1884 had bestowed episcopal ordination upon him in the church of the Anastasis.

The Church of Cyprus – in spite of the fact that Constantinople along with the other patriarchates had from 1909 recognised the canonically elected second Arab patriarch – was never in communion with the Church of Antioch for as long as Spyridon was alive. Kyrillos III (1916–33) first wrote to Gregory of Antioch, formerly of Tripoli, on 10 April 1922, receiving replies from Beirut on the twenty-first of the same month and 13 May.[12]

The chief faults of the last Cypriot patriarch of Antioch were that he was born a Greek, that not appreciating the changing times he was ambitious to be elected patriarch of a fellow-Orthodox but not fellow-Greek Church, that he interested himself in Arab education, that he trusted Russian policy with regard to his own person and that he was unwilling to be always buying the Greek press to stop its croaking, buying the Damascus mob to prevent

---

[10] See G.S. Frangoudis, Ἱστορία τοῦ Ἀρχιεπισκοπικοῦ ζητήματος Κύπρου *(1900–1910)*, Alexandria, 1911, p. 427.

[11] Ph. Vaphidis, Ἐκκλησιαστικὴ ἱστορία, III, 2, Alexandria, 1928, p. 275. The account is based on the memoir by K. Delikanes noted in the Bibliography, and has no special historical value.

[12] Ἀπόστολος Βαρνάβας 4 (1922), pp. 305–10, 341–2.

it from throwing stones and buying the bishops to keep them from splitting into factions. More particularly Spyridon of Antioch seems to have been weak in his judgment of character, hesitant in adopting a course of action, excessively lenient towards all and over-parsimonious towards ecclesiastics, whom he expected to live, it seems, the frugal life of the Jerusalem clergy of his youth. He demonstrated an eagerness to undertake building works in Palestine but did not show the same interest in building up an educated clergy, with the result that he did not have suitable helpers in Syria. Above all, although he loved the Arabs sincerely, he never grasped the nature of their new nationalism, regarding the action taken against him as envy against the Greeks. The collapse came when a combination of internal betrayal and years of active undermining from Jerusalem made the strength of external aid to those who were hostile to his nationality disproportionately greater than his own material and spiritual powers. When the Greeks woke up and grasped the fact that the withdrawal of the Cypriot patriarch signalled the definitive fall of the Greeks in Antioch, it was already too late. Perhaps that was best for everybody concerned.

On 25 November 1921, nine months after the death of Patriarch Spyridon, there came to the ecumenical throne his old protégé Emmanuel Metaxakes. The name Meletios had been given to him in Damascus in memory of the patriarch's uncle, Meletios, metropolitan of Petra.[13]

Epilogue

From the moment Patriarch Spyridon submitted his canonical resignation from the throne of Antioch, the Arabs excluded any possibility of the election of another Greek, and this was a most natural thing. The Greeks had saved Orthodoxy in Syria in the eighteenth century, but by 1898 they had long ago fulfilled their mission and there was no reason for their presence to continue there, while there was every reason, such as the need to counter Latin and Protestant propaganda, for the defence of Orthodoxy to be undertaken by the local Orthodox. The victory was won by the Arabs fundamentally because history and justice were on their side.

There is no reason to repeat the matters related in the journal. Under the political and moral protection of Russia (whose minister of education had visited Damascus in March 1899) the Arabs proceeded boldly on 15 April 1899 to a canonical election and, with the majority of votes cast for the met-

---

[13] See Ἐκκλησιαστικὸς Φάρος 34 (1935). pp. 494–5: photograph of M. Metaxakis as deacon in Damascus with a dedication to Constantine I. Myrianthopoulos of 3 May 1892. After the resignation of Spyridon, Metaxakes was protected by the Cypriots, Epiphanios of Jordan and Meletios of Kyriakoupolis until his election to the throne of Kition.

ropolitans of Laodicea, Seleucia and Emessa, elected as patriarch of Antioch by seven votes to one Meletios Dumānī, metropolitan of Laodicea, who had given his own vote to Gerasimos, metropolitan of Seleucia, the one truly scholarly Arab theologian, who had been educated by the Russians. The enthronement, however, of the patriarch-elect could not take place, on account of the fall on 23 April of that year of the Ottoman imperial government. The Russian Mediterranean fleet, however, sailed into Beirut and the admiral went up to Damascus to pay his respects to the patriarch-elect. After a series of annulments by the Porte, there was a new election on 6 October 1899 (according to the civil authority) or a confirmation of the election (according to the Arabs), which with the death of the metropolitan of Seleucia and the absence in their dioceses of the other bishops was carried out by the metropolitans of Emessa, Tripoli and Arcadia without a formal meeting or a quorum, in Meletios's private apartment. They "elected" him a second time and he was enthroned by a *berat* of the sultan on 31 October 1899, the first Arab patriarch of Antioch since 1724. The first *antidoron* was received at the liturgy of the day by the Russian consul, Alexis Belyaev, who attended an official banquet that evening given in his honour by the patriarch and the holy synod. The arrival of Meletios II (1899–1906) was irregular but not uncanonical.

The following postscript was written in 1922 by the Great Chartophylax of the Great Church of Christ and Secretary of the Holy City, Manuel I. Gedeon:

"Although on the one hand Constantine V was working for closer relations between our Church and the Anglican Church, on the other, in ignorance of the sacred canons and led astray for 'nationalist reasons' he cut off the patriarchate's brotherly relations with the autocephalous patriarchal Church of Antioch, the interests of which were looked after by three metropolitans in Constantinople, and was in breach of relations with the canonical patriarch of Antioch because the latter was an Arab Orthodox and not a Greek.".[14]

It is worth noting that within a short time the Antiochene question became linked with the problem of Cyprus. A severe reprimand, for example, coming from the circle of the ecumenical patriarch Joachim III (1878–84, 1901–13) – if not from the patriarch himself – and dating from November 1902, makes the following caustic but accurate remarks on those Cypriots who refused to

---

[14] M.I. Gedeon, "Οἱ πατριάρχαι τῆς τελευταίας ἑκατονταετίας (1821–1921)" *Πανελλήνιον λεύκωμα ἐθνικῆς ἑκατονταετηρίδος 1821–1921*, VI, Athens, 1922, p. 40.

accept the arbitration of Constantinople and Jerusalem and fell under the guardianship of Photios, patriarch of Alexandria, who came from Nazareth:

> "The foolishness and ignorance of the Greeks not to say their perversion and unscrupulousness on the general questions is most strange and remarkable.
>
> The synod, the entire clergy of the Antiochene throne and all the laity do not have the right according to the canons to elect their patriarch and their bishops from among themselves, but the good Cypriots do have such a right.
>
> The Orthodox Syrians do not have the right to defend their Church and throne, yet the Cypriots do have it, since they trace their nation back to the Apostle Barnabas, which they deny to the Syrians on the basis of an apostolic principle that derives from the Chief of the Apostles himself.
>
> The Antiochene Church as a whole does not have the right to reject patriarchal and episcopal candidates originating from Jerusalem and Constantinople, but the Cypriot Church of the Apostle Barnabas does have such a right.
>
> The decisions of the patriarchs must be respected by the Syrians without the slightest objection, yet the Cypriots have the right to mock them and insult them in a vulgar way."[15]

But the ecumenical throne had already for some time distanced itself from identification with the modern Greek nationalism of the nineteenth century. The Russian ambassador to the Porte assured the grand vizier that "a system of autocephalous patriarchates independent of Constantinople would render most difficult any combination on the part of the Orthodox Church to obtain political privileges."[16] And all persons and all things without exception in the Orthodox world tended to impart to the Church an image of a Protestant type of federation of independent Churches which has characterised her external appearance in the twentieth century.

Biographical notes

Here I give a number of supplementary details about the main ecclesiastical personages who are mentioned below, or who have already been mentioned in the introduction.

---

[15] G.S. Frangoudis, Ἱστορία τοῦ ... ζητήματος Κύπρου, pp. 190–4, esp. p. 191.

[16] D. Hopwood, *The Russian Presence in Syria and Palestine, 1843–1914: Church and Politics in the Near East*, Oxford, 1969, p. 168 and n. 1. Hopwood wrongly thinks Ahmet Tewfik Pasha grand vizier in 1899. The grand vizier from 7 November 1895 to 9 November 1901 was Halil Rifat Pasha.

Meletios II Dumānī, of Antioch (1899–1906), the successor of Patriarch Spyridon, was born in Damascus in 1839. He was taken as a child into the patriarchate, where he learned excellent Greek, which was also spoken by the other members of his family. He became secretary of Hierotheos of Antioch, who came from Ganochorion in Thrace (1850–85), archdeacon of the throne, and metropolitan of Laodicea (al-Lādhiqiyā) from 1865. Not having had any higher education, he was called to the patriarchal throne as a mild man of a malleable character and indeed as a native of Damascus. Immediately after his election he ordered the strict maintenance of the rights of the Greek language in worship, as also the teaching of Greek in the theological school founded at Balament. He sent students to the Rizareion School in Athens and to the Greek schools of Constantinople. "But Meletios", writes Paul Karolides, "was not recognised by the Great Church of Christ and by the other patriarchates under the control of the ignorant embassy in Constantinople, Patriarch Constantine V knowing what was right and just but not daring to put it into effect."[17]

Gerasimos of Seleucia was born in 1840 in the Lebanese city of Hasbayyā. One day when Patriarch Hierotheos came there, the little Gerasimos approached him and taking hold of the hem of his *rason* pleaded: "Father, I want to learn Greek!" On his return from Palestine the patriarch brought the outspoken child back with him to Damascus, where he sent him with a scholarship to the Patriarchal School. Later Gerasimos went to Russia to study at the Theological Academy of St Petersburg. He published a noteworthy dissertation on Photios the Great, and became Director of the Seminary of Pskov and later of that of Riga. In 1883, on being invited to Palestine by Nikodemos, the patriarch of Jerusalem, he was appointed preacher to the Arab-speaking Palestinians and subsequently was chosen under Gerasimos of Antioch to be metropolitan of Seleucia (Zahlah). Speaking and writing perfect Greek, he was a great admirer of Greece, and boasted that he had read the multivolume *History of the Greek Nation* by C. Paparrhegopoulos more than once. On the election of Spyridon he sided with him at all the most critical moments, giving him every help and sharing in his sufferings at the hands of the people of Damascus, who never seem to have forgiven him, even though after the resignation of Spyridon he led the campaign for the election of an Arab patriarch. Being neither pro-Russian, as the Russians imagined, nor anti-Greek, he acted as an Arab, judging that the time had come for his people to take charge of their own affairs. Even though he was the most highly educated cleric of the throne, he did not wish to become patriarch – which

---

[17] P. Karolides, "Πατριαρχεῖον Ἀντιοχείας", p.140. The "ignorant embassy in Constantinople" is the embassy of the kingdom of Greece.

is not surprising – nor was he supported by the Arab prelates, which is revealing.

Athanasios of Emessa came from the Lebanese village of Shuwayfāt, where he was born in 1853. At the age of seventeen he was taken by Patriarch Hierotheos into the patriarchate, and having studied at the Patriarchal School he taught Greek there until 1879, when he was sent to Halki for theological studies. On his return after three years he became the patriarch's archdeacon and then abbot of the monastery of Prophet Elijah in Lebanon until in the patriarchate of Gerasimos he was allotted the metropolis of Emessa (Hims). An extremist, he became a tool of the Russians in the expectation that with their help he would be elected patriarch. Often censured by the other Arab prelates for his unwarrantable anti-Greek activities and speeches and his efforts to inflame the mob, he was finally excluded by them from the patriarchal office in spite of his enjoying the sympathy of the fanatical lay party and the support of the Palestine Society.

Gregory of Tripoli was a Lebanese, born in 1859 in the village of 'Abayh. Accepted in 1879 into the service of Gabriel, metropolitan of Beirut, he later became his secretary and afterwards a teacher in the school founded by him, subsequently being called to the metropolis of Tripoli under Patriarch Gerasimos. Famous for his ascetic life, he was a serious and studious man, profound even though self-taught, familiar with Arabic philology and a lover of Greek literature and moreover a collector of ancient Greek inscriptions. In 1906 he was elected to the office of patriarch in succession to Meletios, with Athanasios of Emessa once again gaining the second-largest number of votes. He served as a most distinguished patriarch until his death in 1918.

Misael of Tyre and Sidon had as his paternal grandfather a Greek priest from Zakynthos called Samuel Stavrides. He too was sent by Patriarch Hierotheos to Halki and was promoted to the metropolis of Tyre and Sidon in 1867. At first a supporter of Spyridon, he sided later with the local prelates although always remaining a philhellene.

Gregory of Epiphaneia, the most pious of all the prelates of the throne, was formerly a teacher and preacher in Laodicea. Consecrated metropolitan of Epiphaneia (Hamāh) in 1867 by Gerasimos of Antioch, he spent his life in continuous prayer.

We come now to the Greek prelates, amongst whom brief biographical details have already been given above of Germanos of Cilicia and Benjamin of Amida, who became a monk of Mount Athos and later abbot of St Nicholas in Jerusalem.

Nikodemos of Arcadia came to Jerusalem in 1854 and was accepted into the patriarchate of Antioch in 1866. Having become metropolitan of Amida

in 1885, he was translated to the metropolis of Arcadia ('Akkār) in 1889. He
was the only Greek prelate to side with the Arabs. We have already noted
his agreement with the metropolitan of Tripoli. He had no higher education.

Nektarios of Aleppo, the best educated and most able of the Greek prelates,
was born in 1862 in the village of Syllai in the district of Iconium. On his
father's side he came from Lemythos in Cyprus and was a relation of Patriarch
Spyridon. Having studied at the Theological School of the Cross, he graduated
in 1888 and followed Spyridon of Tabor to Damascus as his deacon. He was
ordained priest on Saturday 16 May 1892 and promoted the next day to the
metropolis of Beroea (Aleppo), being then in his thirtieth year. A patriotic
man of great integrity and spiritual strength, he spoke (apart from Greek)
Turkish, Arabic and French. After his return from exile (described below),
he took refuge in Constantinople and was sent to Egypt by Patriarch Photios,
whom he served as Patriarchal Commissioner in Cairo. In 1909 he presided
in Nicosia at the Holy Synod which elected Kyrillos II archbishop of Cyprus,
and in the same year, on the recognition of Gregory of Antioch by the patriarchates of the East, he received the title of Memphis. He died in 1924, having
twice visited Cyprus in 1920 and 1923.

Seraphim of Eirenoupolis, a titular bishop, was the living history of the
patriarchate in Damascus. Born on the island of Patmos, but of Kephallonian
origin, he was a nephew of Paisios, exarch of the throne of Jerusalem at Jassy
in Moldavia. He was administrator of the patriarchate for fifty years, twice
having been *locum tenens* of the throne. A good and holy man, he never once
in all his fifty years missed celebrating the daily office in the chapel of the
patriarchate.

Historical conclusion

However great the abilities or deficiencies of individuals, and however intense
or conflicting the interests of the Powers in the Syrian region, the current of
history which wanted the Arabs once again to be masters in their own homes
was even stronger. The boastful declarations in 1900 of V.N. Khitrovo,
Secretary of the Palestine Society, concerning the election "of a local Syrian"
to the patriarchate of Antioch as "the most notable political victory" of his
organisation,[18] are as short-sighted a judgment as the superficial view
expressed by him on another occasion, forgetting the services of lasting value
rendered by the Greeks in saving the Orthodoxy of Syria and Palestine, that
it would be in the Russian interest if the Greeks of the East were converted
to Islam. In his more sober moments the same writer admits that "[the

---

[18] D. Hopwood, *The Russian Presence in Syria and Palestine*, p. 159.

Election] passed unnoticed by the whole of Russian society and thereby proved that the whole [Arab] affair is important merely in my imagination or that society does not understand this question or has no sympathy for it".[19]

The modern Muslim Arab historian Sāti Al-Husrī has expressed a judgment of these events closer to the truth. "The election of an Arab patriarch of Antioch was the first real victory for Arab nationalism."[20]

From a purely ecclesiastical point of view, it can easily be established that the various secularised forms of nationalism, which nineteenth-century Orthodoxy undoubtedly inherited from the Western enlightenment, only distorted the structures of the Church, overturning every spiritual priority and burying the catholicity of the Body of Christ in its external appearance under a pile of provincial concerns. The Russian Revolution of 1917, the Asia Minor catastrophe of 1922 and the rise of the Islamic Arab states would change the situation completely. If they taught anyone anything, it is not within the scope of the present work to evaluate it.

The manuscript

The journal published below is contained on pp. 169–261 of the manuscript notebook of 202 leaves, 28 x 22cm in dimension. After the title, dedication, etc., the notebook contains 355 pages of text, numbered α′–ιγ′ (α–ν′) and 1–315 (some of these are wrongly numbered, which accounts for the difference between the number of pages and the number of leaves) and again α′– στ′ (written in reverse). There is a title on the outer cover: *The Question of the Patriarchate of Antioch in the years 1887–89 by Constantine I. Myrianthopoulos the Cypriot,* and another on the inside: *Constantine I. Myrianthopoulos, The Patriarchate of Antioch and the Antiochene Question in the years 1897–99.*

After the first four leaves the contents of the notebook are as follows:

α′–στ′(ζ′)	Introduction.
ζ′–ια′ (η′–λ′)	Alexander the Great.
ιβ′–ιγ′ (μ′–ν′)	Seleucids.
1–73	Items from the history of the Church of Antioch from the beginning to 1850.

---

[19] Ibid., pp. 171–2.
[20] Ibid., p. 159.

74–100	Patriarchs Hierotheos (1850–85) and Gerasimos (1885–91).
101–168	Spyridon (1891–98).
169–261	The narrative of the years 1897–99 translated below.
262–276	On Nektarios of Aleppo.
276–284	The patriarchates of Meletios (1899–1906), Gregory (1906–28) and Alexander (1931–59).
285–288	Chronological table of the patriarchs of Antioch.
289–292	Blank.
293–315	The patriarchate of Jerusalem.

There follow 41 blank pages and then pp. α'–στ': *Prologue*, bearing at the end the date: April 1960.

These, then, were all copied two years before the author's death when he was in his eighty-sixth year. Copying in a shaky elderly hand the journal of the years spent in his youth in Damascus, the author, as the reader will easily appreciate, added certain elements which have been retained both because we do not have the original (the survival of which is doubtful) and because they usually make the sense clearer, since they refer to later developments.

I am also inclined to believe that certain errors (very few) were in fact made as a result of the changes introduced during the copying of the text in 1960. The British ambassador in Constantinople, for example, in the period 1897–99 was not Sir Henry Elliot but Sir Nicholas O'Conor, and the Russian ambassador was not A.I. Nelidov but I.A. Zinoviev. Similarly, Belyaev's first name was Alexis, as it is usually correctly written, and not Vasili as it is sometimes noted. Mistakes were also made in the transcription of certain Arabic names and in the copying of some dates (e.g. 1887 instead of 1897). Those which I have been able to ascertain beyond any doubt, as well as certain orthographical oversights, I have corrected silently.

Words which I have not been able to read, as well as pages which have been omitted, have been marked with five dots. I have omitted only pp. 180–3, because they relate the details of the life of the archdeacon after 1899 which

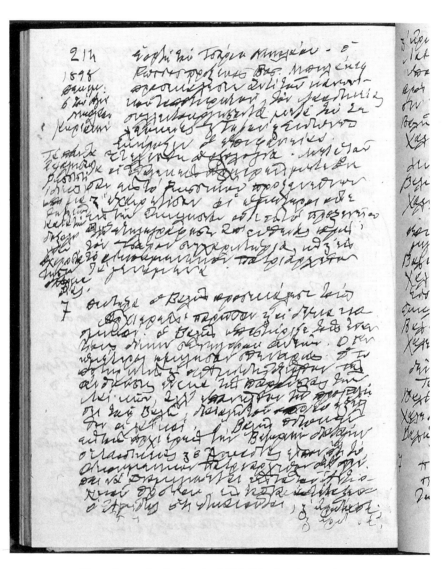

Page from the journal of C.I. Myrianthopoulos

I have abbreviated and incorporated into my introduction, and pp. 192–4 and 217–18, since they repeat the immediately preceding material either word for word or with small differences.

I have not published the work in its entirety because the events of pp. 1–100 may be found treated in a more detailed and more scholarly way in the general histories of the patriarchate of Antioch. Whatever I have judged to be important of the material on pp. 101–68 I have included in my introduction. The letters of pp. 262–72 I give from the originals, which (unlike the journal) are preserved in the author's archive. The material which follows them is easily found in many sources. The chief reason for my not undertaking a full publication is that the elderly author does not just tell the story of the patriarchate of Antioch but includes reminiscences of his private life which in spite of their intrinsic interest have no place here. The reader can be sure that the introduction has included everything of real historical significance given by Myrianthopoulos even though my perspective is completely different from his. This is in any case most natural a century after the events. What is self-evident is that without his work his editor would never have occupied himself with this subject or would have produced a much poorer result.

The labour of copying more than three hundred large pages at the age of eighty-six is in itself proof of the undying love which that old man had for the venerable Church of Antioch, to which he dedicates his book and with which he never broke off relations. In 1954 it gave him great pleasure to take part in the fiftieth anniversary celebrations of Patriarch Alexander Tahhan-Michaelides, an old fellow-student and friend of his from Halki.

The five documents in the appendix have also been taken from the archive of Constantine I. Myrianthopoulos and are as follows:

1. A translation of the *Berat* of Spyridon of Cyprus, patriarch of Antioch.[21]

2. A letter of the Cypriot deacon, Basil Topharides, from 12 July 1892, describing the installation of Nektarios, metropolitan of Aleppo, who was of Cypriot origin, in his see, which is published as illustrating the relations between Greeks and Arabs on the level of ordinary people at the beginning of Spyridon's patriarchate, and also the presence of Cypriots in the Greek communities of Asia Minor at the end of the nineteenth century.

---

[21] This document strangely makes reference to "Romans" and "Greeks". Either this is a mistranslation into Greek or, less probably, it reflects such a distinction in the Ottoman original.

3.   A letter of Nektarios, metropolitan of Aleppo, of 4 January 1900, presenting a true picture of the short-sighted ideology but also the spiritual nobility and virtue of the chief actor in the drama on the Greek side.

4.   A letter of the deacon Ignatios of Caesarea of 18 January 1900 describing the sufferings endured by Nektarios, metropolitan of Aleppo, on account of his non-recognition of Meletios of Antioch. It is published because of the lively picture it gives of events of that time, mirroring as it does the opinion of the minor heroes of the Greek party.

5.   Five of the Greek epigrams of the patriarchate of Antioch in Damascus as copied by Constantine I. Myrianthopoulos. Monuments of the last of the Seleucids, the last of whom is described proudly as "scion of Cyprus".

The bibliography (on pp. 462–464) is restricted to the absolutely essential items (leaving aside general ecclesiastical histories and encyclopaedia articles, etc.) which can serve as a basis for further study.

Thanks are due to D. Christes, who laboured over a first copy of the journal for the Society of Cypriot Studies. I am especially grateful to the son of Constantine I. Myrianthopoulos, Kimon Myrianthopoulos, for making available to the Society his father's archive relating to Antioch and for undertaking part of the expenses of the present publication.

This work is dedicated respectfully to the present occupant of the throne of the Church of Antioch, His Beatitude Patriarch Ignatius IV Hazim.

ADDENDUM

1. The present study had already gone to press when I found that my
    hypothesis in note 8 about 1839 as the year of birth of Spyridon of Antioch
    has been confirmed by Timothy P. Themeles of Jerusalem, ῾Αγιοταφικοὶ
    πίνακες, Jerusalem, 1935, p. 88, cf. 84,21 and p. 110, who draws his infor-
    mation from the registers of the Sacred Community. The year 1840 is
    repeated as a result of a mechanical copying of the details in the obituary
    in *Νέα Σιών*. The question can now be considered closed, the year 1839
    being now judged as certain. *Nobis et ratio et res ipsa centum codicibus potiores
    sunt ...*

2. On Epiphanios Matteos of Jordan see primarily, in addition to Kl.
    Myrianthopoulos, ῾Η συμβολὴ τῆς Μαραθάσης, pp. 30–31, L. Philippou,
    Τὰ ἑλληνικὰ γράμματα ἐν Κύπρῳ κατὰ τὴν περίοδον τῆς
    Τουρκοκρατίας (1571–1878), II, Nicosia, 1930, pp. 134–5, and above
    all Philaret, metropolitan of Moscow, Λόγοι καὶ ὁμιλίαι εἰς τὴν
    ἀνάστασιν καὶ τὴν ἀνάληψιν τοῦ Κυρίου, Greek trans. by Epiphanios,
    archbishop of Jordan, ed. K. Karnapas, Jerusalem, 1906, pp. α΄–ζ΄,
    56–82, cf. K. Karnapas, ῾Η ἐπὶ τοῦ ῎Ορους τῶν ῾Ελαιῶν Σταυροπηγιακὴ
    Μονὴ τῆς ᾿Αναλήψεως, Jerusalem, 1908; obituary in Νέα Σιών 7 (1908),
    pp. 638–40.
    On Meletios Kronides of Jordan see Νέα Σιών 15 (1920), pp. 147–8.

TEXT

MY MOVE TO DAMASCUS IN OCTOBER 1897

I was in the metropolis of Kition (Larnaca), when I met Mr Christophoros, an important Greek merchant from Beirut, from whom I learned about the events that had taken place in Damascus on 28 June against Patriarch Spyridon.

On hearing this, I made my way swiftly to Damascus, and from there to the monastery of Saydnāya, where I found Patriarch Spyridon. After an exchange of news with him, I received instructions and returned to the patriarchate in Damascus, where all the prelates had already gathered.

The majority sided with the view that the patriarch should resign or be deposed. The metropolitans of Amida and Aleppo opposed this, proposing that the patriarch should first be invited to attend and preside over a canonical synod, and he was invited to do this.

Matters thus became complicated. But the metropolitan of Seleucia, his mind set on another task, thought that he would find a solution. He was staying outside the main enclosure of the patriarchate, above and behind the bell-tower, in the extension of the court of the narthex of the patriarchal church, where the tombs of the patriarchs are situated. These I had visited on another occasion and copied the inscriptions on them, correcting some of the errors in earlier copies. One day I met the metropolitan of Seleucia there, and found him to be distressed at the state of the patriarchate. And I said that it depended on him whether a solution was to be found that day, just as he had found a solution at the time of the election of Spyridon, whom he had also supported later. He said in reply:

"This depends rather on Spyridon. If he wishes it we shall find a solution. All he need do is make some money available. Let him send me a thousand pounds, which I shall give to certain prelates so that they will return to their dioceses."

Then I said: "Write about this to the patriarch."

"I will write to him, but you must go to him yourself to give him the letter and convey some additional things verbally about the situation here."

Accordingly, he prepared the letter, which he gave to me and added that if he did not send him money he should send him his resignation. And although I did not agree with this, I nevertheless went off to Saydnāya on Saturday, 17 October, gave the patriarch the metropolitan's letter and told him about what had happened in Damascus, the machinations of the prelates, the activities of the Russian consul and the mood of the mob.

But the patriarch rejected both of the metropolitan's proposals and I communicated this to him. The metropolitan of Seleucia, however, did not lose heart. Taking with him the metropolitan of Aleppo he went up to Saydnāya even though there was deep snow. They communicated with the patriarch, who remained unyielding. But the metropolitan of Seleucia insisted, representing the gravity of the situation, the thoughts and ambitions of the prelates – especially of Germanos of Tarsus – and of the people of Damascus, and added that if he did not comply, he would bear a heavy responsibility as a Greek patriarch for the future of the throne, allowing it to be assumed that he would be the last Greek patriarch. Spyridon replied: "You better than anyone else know how much I have accomplished on behalf of the throne and how much I have endured."

The prelates replied: "We know all this and that is why we insist, that we may do what is good and act in time to avert evil."

But the patriarch remained inflexible, saying that he had no money. The prelates told him to think it over and give them a definitive answer before their departure.

And they came to the apartment where the patriarch was staying. The metropolitan of Seleucia was exasperated and said many things criticising Spyridon for his attitude and regarding him and Germanos of Tarsus responsible for the destruction of the throne from the Greek point of view. Turning to the metropolitan of Aleppo and me he said:

"Note the place and the day on which I tell you these things, which I have also told Spyridon, that he will be the last Greek patriarch, and if, as Greeks, you are upset, at least you will have the consolation that you were not responsible for this, but this Patriarch Spyridon and the foolish Metropolitan Germanos of Tarsus."

Finally, after they had communicated with Spyridon, who once again refused, they advised me to stay and try to persuade the patriarch to do as the prelates had suggested, and returned to Damascus. I myself remained at the monastery.

When I next saw the patriarch, he asked me about the impressions of the prelates as they left and I replied that they left in a depressed state. And I added my own opinion, that I agreed with them, because otherwise things would turn out to the detriment of the Greeks.

I repeated the same views as often as I visited him. But I found a contrary opinion expressed by the deacon Niphon, who served him as a secretary and indeed adviser. When I suggested anything to the patriarch, Niphon objected and there followed a long discussion which one day degenerated into a quarrel. For he said that the patriarch was not going to hand out any money and was going to remain patriarch. And I replied that according to the Cypriot proverb they wanted "to have the dog satisfied and not be short of a loaf". And Niphon replied that nothing would be needed because he had a plan by which they would be delivered from everything. And I replied: "Be careful that you do not escape Scylla only to fall into Charybdis", going from bad to worse.

What was Niphon's grandiose plan? To escape to Lebanon and a free territory. To this end they prepared their bags, their drivers and their animals intending to depart during the night. The following circumstances were of assistance to them: one of the patriarchal clerks from Maloula called George, who remained faithful to the patriarch, used to close the gates at night only with the bars and not with the iron bolts, which he gave to the metropolitan of Arcadia, supposedly for safety. It was decided to escape from the monastery on the night of 30 to 31 January 1898.

But unexpectedly there was a heavy fall of snow that night, which covered everything and cut off the monastery from the outside world. When Spyridon saw this in the morning and that even the natural elements were against him, he decided to resign. Accordingly, he summoned the metropolitans of Arcadia and Amida and Archimandrite Paul, who drew up the act of resignation, which Spyridon signed. It was Saturday, 31 January 1898. Thus the sufferings of Spyridon came to an end and a new age began for the patriarchate of Antioch.

Spyridon remained at the monastery for quite a long time afterwards. Some days later he visited the abbess. They both wept at what had happened.

One day, in the early evening, I was going up to the apartments when the patriarch suddenly appeared. He came up to me and said: "This is what one can expect from the world." "Yes, indeed, Your Beatitude," I replied, "and man is obliged to bear them." I added that he himself had done much for the throne and for the maintenance of Greek rights and had endured much and had already been delivered from his sufferings and had the right to be proud of his patriotism, and I added further that he had failed under necessity because he did not have morally sound and educated men around him but had been at the mercy of evil and harmful people, such as Basil, the former Bethlehem verger, whom he had promoted to be archdeacon and who had committed such vile acts in the patriarchate to the great harm of the Greeks and was the cause "of such bitterness both to Your Beatitude and myself". Patriarch Spyridon was moved at this and said to me: "Do not remind me of these things, my child", and tears came to his eyes. And I wept too and we parted for the last time.

We remained in the monastery for Cheese Week and then all left for Damascus, where a new struggle was about to begin which would end as the metropolitan of Seleucia had foreseen.

MY MEMOIRS FROM MY JOURNAL

December 1897

Most of the prelates arrived in Damascus in December. The first was Athanasios of Emessa on the thirteenth and the other four on the eighteenth.

On their arrival they went to the *vali* and the indigenous bishops went to the Russian consulate. After supper they all deliberated until midnight.

20, Saturday. The prelates wrote to Patriarch Spyridon to come to Damascus. He refused, suggesting Balament.

20, pm. The *vali* summoned Germanos of Cilicia and Meletios of Laodicea and said to them: "It is forbidden for a native Christian to be elected patriarch."

21. They telegraphed the metropolitans of Amida and Aleppo asking for their vote. They also followed this up with a letter. The metropolitan of Aleppo replied that when a *locum tenens* or president of the synod is elected, he would then come or appoint a representative. The prelates wrote a third time inviting the patriarch to come. The patriarch replied that he would come on Saturday (27) and that out of his pastoral care he was freeing the priests held in prison who had been the ringleaders of the unlawful revolt of 28 June.

22. The Damascus laity submitted to the prelates a long report against Patriarch Spyridon.

25, Thursday. The prelates proclaimed Patriarch Spyridon deposed at the instigation of the Russian consul, Alexis Belyaev, who hastened to Saydnāya to visit the patriarch and trick him, but the patriarch refused to receive him.

26. The metropolitan of Arcadia with the deacon of the metropolitan of Cilicia were sent to Saydnāya to hand Spyridon the decision of the prelates, according to which he was declared deposed from the throne.

Germanos of Tarsus and Adana was elected *locum tenens.*

27. The Damascus laity came to the patriarchate and thanked the prelates for pardoning the priests and releasing them from prison.

The metropolitans of Cilicia, Tripoli and Emessa went to the *vali* and gave him the documents deposing Spyridon and electing the metropolitan of Tarsus as *locum tenens.*

27. The Russian consul was in the patriarchate, where he remained for two hours.

1898

31 January, Saturday. The resignation of Patriarch Spyridon. After his resignation Spyridon remained some months at the monastery. In the meantime some thought was given as to where he should go. At first it was decided he should go to Jerusalem. Accordingly an official document of the Brotherhood was drawn up and ratified by Patriarch Gerasimos which would entitle him to go to Jerusalem. It was said that he would go to the monastery at Bethany which he himself had founded. But it seems that Patriarch Damian objected. Constantinople was therefore suggested.

The Departure of Spyridon from Saydnāya

On Friday 31 July 1898 he reached Coele Syria accompanied by an officer and four soldiers and arrived at the station of Amin Fik, where he was met by the Greek prelates and certain other friends from Damascus, such as Joseph Tānnūs, who came down in order to see him off. The meeting and departure took place with much emotion and many tears. The next day he left a valuable memento as a gift for each of the prelates. These divided Spyridon's raiment, not by lot, but rather seized them, the more precious items going to the first to grab them.

As for the gifts which he left to the prelates, he had brought them with him from Jerusalem and had kept them intact for six years, although if he had distributed them at the beginning he would have ensured that the prelates remained favourably disposed towards him.

Spyridon in Beirut bound for Constantinople

While Spyridon was still in Beirut, the former Archdeacon Basil arrived there. He, as I have said, was at the monastery of St George at Homeira as an exile. In the meantime, the *locum tenens* had written to the abbot to watch Basil in case he escaped, for he was being summoned to Damascus to appear before the synodical court. But as I have said, the letters to the abbot fell into Basil's hands. When he read what was in store for him, he fled from the monastery and went down to Tripoli. From there he went to Beirut, where he met Spyridon and asked if he could accompany him. But the patriarchal commissioner in Beirut, Christos Papadopoulos, pleaded with Spyridon, showing him clearly that it did not reflect well on him to have anything to do with a man who had committed such crimes. Spyridon was persuaded and set sail alone.

At first he remained at Neohori on the Bosphorus and then on the island of Halki at the *metochion* of St George surnamed Kremnos belonging to the Holy Sepulchre. He lived there recollecting the sufferings which he had endured at the hands of the people of Damascus, and also from Archdeacon Basil who had attached himself to him and had caused others such bitterness and brought shame on the Greeks. At all events, Spyridon would have been consoled because he was extremely patriotic, a true Hellene, which is why he has been forgiven by us. He died in 1921. May the earth rest lightly upon him and may his memory be eternal ...

... I return to the events that took place in Damascus between the prelates and the *vali*.

1898, 1 August, Saturday.[*] The *vali* summoned the prelates and obliged the Greeks to sign a list of candidates, since those opposed had accepted the metropolitans of Amida and Aleppo. But they protested and wired the ecumenical patriarchate, seeking protection and guidance.

2, Sunday. An appropriately coded telegram was received in which it was announced that the *vali* had arranged to summon the native-born prelates and compel them to accept the candidates of the ecumenical patriarchate.

4, Tuesday. The *vali* summoned the Greek prelates to sign the list, but they objected and announced this to the patriarchate.

10, Monday. The Russian consul was at the patriarchate, where he had conversations with the native-born prelates. He received a copy of the telegram to the Sublime Porte in which it was maintained that the act of 6 May was canonical.

15 August, Saturday. The feast of the Dormition of the Theotokos and the dedication of the patriarchal church. The *locum tenens* wanted to celebrate but the opponents objected on the grounds that it would arouse the people and have other undesirable results, and the *locum tenens* withdrew. The metropolitan of Emessa celebrated instead of him. The metropolitan of Aleppo celebrated in the suburb of Meitan, where he had been sent, and the metropolitan of Seleucia preached.

16, Sunday. The metropolitan of Tyre and Sidon presided and in the right choir, where they always sang in Greek, the metropolitan of Emessa sang in Arabic.

---

[*] The month of August , which is placed here after the patriarch's July departure from Syria, should of course be placed after p. 378 of the present tranlation (Ed.)

17. The *locum tenens* went to the *vali* and asked him to send a representative to the Church's ceremony on the feast of the accession of the sultan.

18. At vespers the metropolitan of Laodicea presided, intending to celebrate the liturgy the next day. The *locum tenens* protested to the *vali*, who sent to the patriarchate the Director of his Office, Veli *effendi*, who asked for the metropolitan of Seleucia, who promised that the matter would be regularised, which it was. Veli *effendi* said to the metropolitan of Seleucia that the *locum tenens* had been elected canonically and was recognised by the sultan and as such had precedence, "and he should commemorate first in Greek and then you in Arabic". A representative of the *vali* came and was present at both the ceremonies in Greek and Arabic.

22. The metropolitan of Aleppo went to the *vali*, who repeated that he would look after the lay interests.

30, Sunday. The metropolitan of Edessa presided. The Russian consul came to the patriarchate, where he spoke with the native-born prelates. The *locum tenens*, whom I accompanied myself, celebrated at Meitan.

31. The native-born prelates met together and deliberated for some time. Then the metropolitan of Seleucia went to the *vali* and said that they had been put under pressure to accept external candidates, and inclined towards Arsenios (representative in Russia of the patriarchate of Jerusalem). A meeting of all the native-born prelates with whom the interpreter of the Russian consulate, Joseph Sapaa (a Damascene), spent the whole day.

4 May. The *vali* summoned the prelates and said to them: "According to the latest decree of the vizier, the election must be conducted freely, according to the example of the other Churches, with either internal or external candidates being put forward. You are free to go." And he added: "I believe that this is the only time that you leave me satisfied. Make haste, however, to hold the election before the patriarchates take action against you." And all of them returned exceedingly happy, especially Germanos, the *locum tenens*, who thus thought that his election as patriarch was certain.

On the return of the prelates, I went up to the metropolitan of Aleppo's room in order to learn what the summons of the prelates by the *vali* had been about. But I found him locked in his room. He told me that he regarded it superfluous to go because it was known beforehand what the *vali* would announce to the prelates.

The same thing had been announced previously to them by the Russian consul, and the metropolitan of Aleppo had heard it from a certain Greek pharmacist in the Turkish army, called Demetrios, who, coming from Constantinople, had visited the patriarchates, where he had heard that the patriarch of Antioch would be elected from among the prelates of the throne and indeed would be a Greek, not Germanos of Tarsus, however, but the metropolitan of Aleppo. From the metropolitan of Aleppo I went to the metropolitan of Amida, whom I found angry especially towards the *locum tenens* Germanos, who had made no protest to the *vali*. He was also angry with the metropolitan of Aleppo for not having gone to the palace. I encouraged him and said: "What must be done?" He replied that reliable information must be sought as to how true the *vali's* announcement was and what should be done. Beyond that, the *locum tenens* should delay the convocation of the synod.

But the *locum tenens*, Germanos of Tarsus, with his eye on the patriarchal office, moved quickly towards the election for the following reasons.

He was in the courtyard when the metropolitan of Arcadia appeared and said: "Holy brother, let me tell you that from this moment my vote is for you."

The metropolitan of Tyre and Sidon was standing opposite, and he said the same thing to him. These things took place as a result of a decision by the rest who were leading on the insanely ambitious and extremely vain Germanos. The latter, on hearing these things, immediately went to the neighbouring house of a Greek called G. Rizos, whereupon the metropolitan of Tyre, realising where he had gone, said to the metropolitan of Arcadia:

"See, the lunatic has gone to announce that we are going to give him our vote."

And, sure enough, as soon as Germanos saw the Rizos family he said excitedly:

"I have secured the patriarchate for myself."

"How is that?" asked Rizos. Germanos, in an emotional state, replied:

"Look, just now the metropolitans of Arcadia and Tyre promised me their votes. I have another three (Eirenoupolis, Amida and Aleppo) and only lack one vote. Then I sell something to my friends and buy that vote and this ensures the majority of votes. Finally I become patriarch and I shall bless you with both my hands, and my blessing will be of greater benefit to you." Then he left.

Then Rizos said to his wife:

"Amalia, you realise Germanos is off his head, quite out of his senses?"

And Amalia replied:

"And when did Germanos ever have any sense? He had little as a young man and now that he is old has even less. Don't you know that the Damascenes call him *Harfas* – senile old man?"

I would add that when Rizos heard that the prelates had promised him votes, he was very suspicious and put Germanos on his guard in case they tricked him, and tried to persuade him not to pursue the patriarchal office because it would make things worse for Spyridon, and if the latter had managed to hold on to the throne for six years, he himself would not last for six months because the Russian consul and the Damascus populace would drive him out.

But everything that was said was like water off a duck's back because his only desire was to be elected patriarch.

As soon as Germanos left Rizos, I quickly went to see the couple, made notes of what they said and talked at length with them about the future, which we did not expect to be very agreeable, as events proved.

1898, May, Wednesday. The *locum tenens* hurriedly called a council, at which a vote took place. After this the metropolitans of Amida and Aleppo registered a protest and left the council. They went to a fellow-Greek, Demetrios Vasileiades, who was Government Civil Engineer. Finally, the *locum tenens* left and went to his room. I quickly followed him myself and in a tone of angry complaint said to him:

"Father, what have you done and brought the other prelates down on your head? You were the one who at Spyridon's election defended Hellenism's rights over the Church of Antioch, but now that you have authority as *locum tenens* you are contributing to their extinction."

He thought for a moment and said to me:

"My child, I have fears that the native-born Orthodox will intrigue against me with the Sublime Porte and my name will be crossed off the list of candidates for the patriarchal throne."

"The opposite will happen", I replied. "The Porte will remove your name if you collaborate with the native-born Orthodox against the regime. I have heard that it has already excluded the metropolitans of Arcadia and Seleucia."

"I have seen it", he replied. "Where are the metropolitans of Amida and Aleppo?"

On hearing that they had gone to see Vasileiades, he said to me: "Go and ask them if they want me to come myself." When the prelates heard this they smiled bitterly and said: "If he wants to come, let him." I went back to him and accompanied him to Vasileiades' house which was near the patriarchate. After the visit it was decided that they should make a protest to the government and report what had taken place to the ecumenical patriarchate. With this in view, I was entrusted with the task of drawing up a brief letter setting out what had happened. I therefore went to the house of G. Rizos, wrote the letter and returned. This was signed by the prelates and posted.

In the meantime the native-born Orthodox photographed the synodical documents and voting-papers and sent them to the ecumenical patriarchate. For my part, I drew up my own account of the events and sent them with a letter to the editor of *Constantinoupolis,* Mr D. Nikolaides – as usual – who used to pass these on to the ecumenical patriarchate.

The evolution of the question

But that which the *locum tenens* and the others did not do immediately at the outset, which was to protest immediately at the outset in writing and in person, the *vali* did on his own initiative. He telegraphed the Sublime Porte that he had announced to all the decision of the Porte but that the *locum tenens* and those around him had objected and protested because thus the *status quo* would be overturned. The *vali* not only did this but also summoned Mr Vasileiades to see him, announced to him what he had done and at the same time advised that the *locum tenens* and those around him should draw up a *takrir* of protest. On his return Mr Vasileiades called me and we worked together deep into the night. We drew up a resumé of the *status quo* and the external intrigues, that is, of Russia, whose interests were thus served by the native-born Orthodox. This was put in writing for the first time, but since it was true, notice of it was taken by the Turkish government. This *takrir*, signed by the *locum tenens* and the rest, was delivered at night to the *vali* who, as was to be expected, telegraphed first to say that he had received it.

7, Thursday. The prelates of the opposition party and the laymen met together and invited the *locum tenens* to join them. When he refused they wanted, in accordance with established practice, to sound the church bell in order to summon the crowd for a public demonstration, but the metropolitan of Seleucia prevented them.

All this happened because the *locum tenens*, instead of protesting, hastened to call a council ...

8 May, Friday. The native-born prelates and laymen, on coming together on their own initiative, invited the *locum tenens* to join them and sign the minutes of the preceding session. But as he refused, they drew up a *takrir* against him, which they delivered to the *vali*.

9, Saturday. The *vali* summoned all the prelates, who had many complaints to make against each other and even descended to recriminations. The *vali* proposed a reconciliation. The *locum tenens* declared that it was impossible for him to sign if the dissenters do not conform to the *status quo*.

10, Sunday. The native-born clerics and laity came to the *locum tenens* and began to flatter him to make him sign the minutes, but he refused.

11, Monday. The same again, but the *locum tenens* refused.

12, Tuesday. They came together again and also invited the *locum tenens*, supposedly for deliberations with him. When he did not come they proceeded to depose him, replacing him with Meletios of Laodicea. The metropolitans of Arcadia and Seleucia went to the palace and delivered to the *vali* the document deposing the *locum tenens*. They also delivered a copy to Germanos, who refused to accept it and went to the *vali*, who placated him.

1898, 13 May, Wednesday. The native-born Orthodox commemorated Meletios of Laodicea as the new *locum tenens.* Germanos delivered a protest to the *vali,* and they telegraphed the ecumenical patriarchate about this too.

14, Thursday. The metropolitan of Seleucia celebrated the liturgy and commemorated the metropolitan of Laodicea as *locum tenens,* also celebrating a doxology for the crowning of the tsar. The Russian consul came to the patriarchate and congratulated the metropolitan of Laodicea as *locum tenens.*

17, Sunday. The metropolitan of Emessa was chief celebrant. The priests commemorated the metropolitan of Laodicea as the new *locum tenens.*

20. Name-day of the Russian consul. The prelates called on him and gave him their greetings, but separately. The native-born prelates came in the morning, our people in the afternoon.

21 May. Feast of St Constantine. The native-born prelates telegraphed the ecumenical patriarch to congratulate him on his name-day. The metropolitan of Seleucia said in his telegram: "May you flourish and enjoy long life, may you champion the independence of the Churches." He also sent a letter via Epiphanios Petrou (Gatas Antilaft). The metropolitan of Laodicea also sent a telegram as *locum tenens* but he did not receive a reply.

24, Sunday. The metropolitan of Emessa celebrated, commemorating the metropolitan of Laodicea.

30, Saturday. The interpreter of the Russian consulate, Joseph Sapaa, came to the patriarchate, called the native-born prelates to the metropolitan of Seleucia's room and spoke with them for a long time.

1898, 6 June, Saturday. Seraphim, the titular bishop of Eirenoupolis, handed a document to the *locum tenens* Germanos in which he protested that he had been denied the right of the canonical vote although he had twice been *locum tenens* and always a patriarchal commissioner. The *locum tenens* sent the document to the *vali,* who upheld the right of the bishop of Eirenoupolis.

The sermon of Gerasimos of Seleucia on the evening of Saturday, 23 June

The Russian consul, A. Belyaev, visited the metropolitan of Seleucia on his own and stayed with him a long time, drinking raki together. The consul indicated, as if enjoining it, that something should be done to enlighten the people and stir them up against the Greeks. Accordingly the following Sunday, the seventh of the month, when the metropolitan of Tyre and Sidon was presiding, the metropolitan of Seleucia, at the prompting of the Russian consul, delivered a sermon in the church. He ignored the Gospel, basing himself on the Epistle for the day. There in the Epistle of Paul to the Romans was the following text: "But glory and honour and peace for everyone who does good, the Jew first and also the Greek" (2:10). The sermon was long and historical rather than exegetical. It began first with the Jews, telling the story of their faith, their monotheism, their life and sufferings, their going into Egypt, and the circumstances of their return under Moses. It told of the temple of Solomon and about Christianity, which was first received by the Jews.

On the Greeks. He spoke at great length on this subject, saying that the Greeks were a great and historic nation which had developed literature and the sciences, had brought forth many philosophers and in general developed a great civilisation and that they had done a great deal for liberty. He praised the work of Alexander the Great and his successors, the Seleucids in Syria and the Ptolemies in Egypt. He spoke of the spread of the Greek language which facilitated the spread of Christianity. He spoke of the empire of Byzantium and of Byzantine, that is, Christian, civilisation. And he ended by saying that because of all this, the Greeks are addicted to glory, power and privilege. They prefer nationalism to the Church and therefore do not allow us to administer our own house but want to administer us themselves.

The simple folk in the congregation said that the metropolitan of Seleucia had done well in blaming the Greeks, but the more educated said: "If the Greeks were and still are as he says, it is right that they should be in charge and administer the Church."

As it was, the sermon was not successful and the Russian consul himself was not satisfied. On meeting the metropolitan the next day, I congratulated him on his sermon.

"I spoke the truth," he replied.

"And you wish to put this into practice, Your Eminence", I said.

And he replied: "I am too deeply committed and cannot go astern. And those responsible for this were Patriarch Spyridon and Germanos of Tarsus."

16 June, Tuesday. The *vali* summoned the prelates and repeated to them all that he had said on 1 June, that is, that they should make haste to hold the election under the presidency of the *locum tenens* (Germanos). The native-born prelates said that they would only recognise him if he signed the document which excluded the candidature of the metropolitans of Amida and Aleppo and everyone who was not a prelate of the throne of Antioch. This claim was rejected by the *vali,* just as it had been rejected previously by the Sublime Porte.

17. The metropolitan of Emessa stirred up the crowd to protest and demonstrate that they did not want a patriarch from outside.

20, Saturday. The *vali* summoned the prelates again and showed them a document (addressed to the dissenters) to which they had to reply in consequence of a protest from the ecumenical patriarchate. In the document the following questions were posed:

(a) whether patriarchs of Antioch from Constantinople had ever been elected;
(b) why laymen had been introduced into the sessions of the synod;
(c) that the metropolitan of Beirut, as a sick man, was excluded from the synod;
(d) that the titular bishops have the right to vote.

1898, 22 June, Monday. The prelates, summoned to a meeting by the *locum tenens*, absented themselves for various reasons.

22, Monday. Feast of St Peter and St Paul. The metropolitans of Seleucia and Tripoli celebrated, the second of whom commemorated the bishops in Greek in the following way:

"Ἐν πρώτοις μνήσθητι, Κύριε, πάσης ἐπισκοπῆς τῶν ὀρθοτομούντων τὸν λόγον τῆς σῆς ἀληθείας" ("First be mindful, Lord, of every diocese of Orthodox who express in an Orthodox way the word of Thy truth.")

1 July, Wednesday. The native-born prelates telegraphed the ecumenical patriarch that they rejected his intervention as uncanonical and held him responsible for the consequences.

A priest called Abraham arrived from Adana so that, as a Turkish speaker, he could be used in the drawing up of documents addressed to the government (after the feast).

3, Friday. Native-born prelates visited the Supervisor of the Russian Schools in the company of the Russian consul.

5, Sunday. Anniversary of the Russian Palestine Society. Athanasios of Emessa celebrated, saying most things in Russian. Schoolgirls sang from a manuscript in Russian the Creed, the "Our Father", the "Save, Lord, Thy people" and the acclamations. The metropolitan of Emessa commemorated the Holy Synod of the Church of the Antiochenes. There was a doxology for the Russians. The Russian consul came in dress uniform to the patriarchate.

10 July, Friday. The reply of the ecumenical patriarch to the eight prelates: "I have received your telegram. We are grieved at the misunderstanding of the brotherly activity of the Church of Constantinople, which looks only to the interests of the Antiochene throne and is in accord with the other patriarchates. We advise you all in a brotherly way to come together in the name of Christ and proceed in unison to whatever duty indicates in conformity with the *status quo.*"

14, Tuesday. The eight telegraphed the Sublime Porte that they did not accept the intervention of the ecumenical patriarch and protested against it.

They beg that the election should be restricted to the throne of Antioch, since it was endowed with able and worthy prelates and because the foreigners did not know Arabic. They also telegraphed the same message to the ecumenical patriarch.

17, Friday. The *locum tenens* and his circle telegraphed the Sublime Porte that the native-born prelates were working for a self-interested and nationalistic goal. They beg that "an election should be held in conformity with the *status quo*".

18, Saturday. There arrived from Jerusalem the Dragoman of the Patriarchate, Archimandrite Glykerios, and the deacon Meletios Metaxakes, a student at the Theological School of Jerusalem on a scholarship from the patriarchate of Antioch.

1898, 19 July, Sunday. At the end of the examinations at the Boy's School, the headmaster, Epiphanios Petrou (Gatas Antilaft), a graduate of the Rizareion School of Athens, gave a speech not on the work of the school year but against the recent Greek patriarchs of Antioch, on the grounds that they only served narrow nationalist interests.

In the afternoon at the dinner the metropolitan of Seleucia criticised Gatas.

22, Wednesday. Glykerios returned from Saydnāya, having persuaded Spyridon to leave for Constantinople and stay at Neohori on the Bosphorus.

There was a doxology in honour of the tsar's mother in which only the native-born prelates took part. Of these, the metropolitans of Laodicea and Tripoli visited Glykerios in the afternoon.

26, Sunday. The metropolitans of Seleucia, Tyre and Sidon and Tripoli went to the *vali* and handed him a petition signed by the eight prelates and many lay-people in which they sought the recognition of the metropolitan of Laodicea as *locum tenens*, the involvement of the laity and the election of a native-born patriarch, since he would know the language and the customs. They criticised the Greeks, whom they blamed for proposing things for the solution of the question which should not depend on them, who were destructive to the throne, as the recent Greek patriarchs had also been. They begged that an end should be put to this long drawn-out affair because their dioceses were suffering as a result.

27. The *locum tenens* received information from abroad that the matter was going well. They praised their *takrir* and advised him to remain firm.

27, Monday. The *vali* summoned the native-born prelates before noon, and after noon the foreign ones, and said to them that the prolongation of the matter arose from the acceptance of the metropolitans of Amida and Aleppo as candidates, who were also acceptable according to a recent decree of the vizier. He advised them to proceed rapidly to an election. The *locum tenens* and his circle insisted on the *status quo*; they were working on behalf of it and wanted a decision on the matter.

28, Tuesday. Glykerios received a telegram that Spyridon had come down to the monastery of Prophet Elijah (in Lebanon). The native-born prelates told the *vali* that they had received £1 000 from him. Glykerios, as an educated man who knew Turkish, spoke vigorously and the native-born prelates retreated.

What was Glykerios's main purpose in Damascus?

This man came to Damascus ostensibly to visit Spyridon on the matter of the next stage of his life but in fact to introduce himself so that he would be preferred as a candidate for the patriarchal throne of Antioch from among the clergy of Jerusalem. At the same time he expressed a complaint to the metropolitan of Aleppo (formerly of the Jerusalem clergy) because, as he said, the ecumenical patriarchate had sent them a report from a person in the patriarchate in Damascus which criticised the last three patriarchs from Jerusalem for having damaged Greek interests and said that accordingly the new patriarch of Antioch should be elected from among the prelates of the ecumenical patriarchate. The metropolitan of Aleppo replied that he knew nothing at all about this and was telling the truth. He added only this: "I do not know if Constantine Myrianthopoulos did this", meaning me. Later when asked about it by the metropolitan of Aleppo, I said that this had most likely been written by a journalist who had come as a correspondent for *Constantinoupolis*.

But in fact it was I who had sent the report. Its chief purpose, however, was not to attack the Jerusalem patriarchs. It was a general and historical survey. For it explained the reasons for the events of the time. It referred to the general situation of the Church of Antioch and Syria, to Islam, the Crusades, Turkish rule, Latin propaganda, the Roman Catholics, the Russian Palestine Society and the nationalism of the native Orthodox.

On the last three patriarchs in particular who had come from the Jerusalem clergy, I wrote that from the Greek point of view they had made many errors. Thus Hierotheos (1850–85), after contributing to the abolition of the regime by which the patriarch of Antioch was sent from Constantinople, sent native-born students with scholarships to the Theological School of Halki, which was good, but no Greeks, not even an Arabist. Gerasimos (1885–91) raised four native-born priests to the episcopate and sent another four with scholarships to Halki, but not a single Greek, nor did he choose an Arabist although he was one himself, and finally he left the throne of Antioch when he was elected patriarch of Jerusalem, which is what he wanted from the beginning! Gerasimos, a very egoistical and ambitious man, wanted to become patriarch of Jerusalem on the destruction of the patriarchate of Antioch. He acted like the figure from antiquity who said "When I die, let the earth be consumed by fire", or as the French say, "Après moi le déluge."

The third was Spyridon. A nationalist but uneducated and miserly, he sent Greek students to the Theological School of Jerusalem but did not use them at all in the patriarchate of Antioch because he resigned in the meantime while they were still completing their studies. And he did not send a single Arabist. When he went to Damascus as patriarch he took with him from Bethlehem his coffee-maker and his verger in order to form a Greek clergy from them. And so he promoted the one to be abbot of the monastery of Prophet Elijah on Mount Lebanon – and nearly consecrated him metropolitan of Theodosiopolis (Erzerum in Armenia) where the Russians had sent a prince as consul – and the other to be archdeacon, the notorious Basil, who brought shame on the Church and the Greek community. He was even promoting the latter to be metropolitan of Lebanon, a new diocese he was detaching from Beirut. But independently of the above, from the Greek point of view, the Syrians would in no way consent to a cleric from Jerusalem. The Jerusalem Brotherhood should ask why. Perhaps they misunderstand their life, as the others misunderstood the institution of deaconesses.

1898, 29 July. The *locum tenens*, Germanos, invited the prelates to draw up a list of candidates. The eight replied that there was no need for another session, it would have been sufficient for him simply to sign the list of 6 May and that they did not recognise him as *locum tenens*. In consequence of this, the four telegraphed the ecumenical patriarch and the patriarch of Jerusalem, requesting a declaration of support, and also to the Sublime Porte thanking it for acknowledging the metropolitans of Amida and Aleppo as candidates. They also denounced the dissenters for not coming to the meeting for disreputable and nationalistic reasons and begged that a strict order should be given for the election to be expedited on the basis of the *status quo*.

They also sent a *takrir* to the *vali* on the revolt of the dissenters. They drew his attention to the conduct of those laymen they had described who, coming now freely into the patriarchate as if into their own house, behaved very provocatively towards the *locum tenens* and the others and stirred up the mob who openly intimidated our prelates.[*]

1898, September. An official letter arrived from Egypt from the native-born prelates addressed to the patriarchates and the other autocephalous Churches. The contents of this letter were offensive towards the Greek patriarchs of Antioch. .....

---

[*] See the note on p. 368 (Ed.).

1898, September. The indigenous Orthodox invited some people from the suburb of Meitan, to whom the Interpreter of the Russian consulate, Joseph Sapaa, gave £20. The metropolitan of Tripoli wanted to celebrate in Meitan but the inhabitants objected and made him responsible for anything untoward that might happen. (It should be known that Meitan remained until the end on the side of the *status quo.*)

12, Saturday. The Russian consul met with the metropolitan of Seleucia at the palace. At about the hour of vespers he came to the patriarchate and, meeting with the native-born prelates, conversed with them for a long time.

15, Tuesday. The prelates left to visit the Russian consulate in Beirut. The native-born metropolitans went in the morning and the foreign-born ones in the afternoon. At about sunset, the consul came to the patriarchate and returned the visit to all the prelates, who received him as a body.

16, Wednesday. The metropolitans of Seleucia, Arcadia and Epiphaneia went to see the Russian consul. After supper the Interpreter of the Russian consulate, Selim Schat, came to the patriarchate to bid farewell to our prelates. Leaving the others, he went up to the *locum tenens,* who was standing on his own. He said to him flatteringly and as if in confidence that an indigenous Orthodox will not become patriarch. Accordingly a new list should be drawn up containing candidates only from the throne of Antioch and not from outside, "whereupon a Greek will be elected, either you or the metropolitan of Arcadia. On the whole they want you, but because you are rather sharp-tempered a small party has formed around the metropolitan of Arcadia." The *locum tenens* said to the rest of our prelates that he objected to such proposals.

17, Thursday. The *vali* summoned the prelates, but separately, the native-born at 8 o'clock, the rest at 9. He announced to them a new vizierial decree accompanied by an imperial rescript, according to which they were required to include the metropolitans of Amida and Aleppo and draw up a new list without restrictions.

There was a long discussion during which the *vali* grew angry. The *locum tenens* wrote to the *vali* saying that he would summon the prelates but if they did not agree he would not be responsible and he asked for a copy of the vizierial decree. But only a part of it was sent and this was very condensed and difficult to understand. The prelates met for three hours but they still did not agree. The *locum tenens* announced this to the *vali.*

21, Monday. The prelates met again but did not agree, the indigenous metropolitans insisting that the list of 6 May should be signed. Some of them told the *vali,* who ordered that the list should be signed, but the *locum tenens* objected.

The newspaper *Lebanon* (published in Lebanon by Abraham-Pei-Asuat, an Orthodox) came out against the indigenous prelates in a series of three articles and infuriated them. Abraham-Pei-Asuat no doubt did this out of conviction. He only said that if the dissenters sent the issues back to him they should pay him compensation.

The *vali* replied that they should sign the lists, putting down as candidates whoever they wished in conformity with the Church's *status quo*.

23. The *locum tenens* summoned the prelates who had asked for the vizierial decree in order to study it.

The leading layman Jibran-Isper asked for a sum of £2000 from our people supposedly to buy the support of some of the dissenters, but nothing was done.

Visits, correspondence with the *vali*, and telegrams to the patriarchates and the Sublime Porte.

Candidates

The arrival in Damascus of the Dragoman of the Jerusalem patriarchate, Archimandrite Glykerios, had as its chief aim the engagement in activities which would result in the inclusion of clerics from Jerusalem as candidates. Our people replied that this was something which could only be done by the patriarchates acting in common. Those in Jerusalem made many attempts to achieve this. They proposed secretly that Archimandrite Photios, Arsenios in Russia, and Anthimos of Bethlehem should be included as candidates. Patriarch Damian himself asked the *vali* of Damascus, Nazim Pasha, who was then in Jerusalem, to help him discreetly and he promised to do so.

But in the meantime Arsenios was refused and Anthimos was passed over as too old. There remained, then, the two Photii, the metropolitan of Philippopolis of the ecumenical patriarchate and Chief Secretary Photios from the Jerusalem patriarchate. The other two from the ecumenical throne, Basil of Anchialos and Philaretos Vapheides, were judged to be teachers rather than administrators.

1898, 26 October, Monday. The arrival in Damascus of the German Emperor (Kaiser) Wilhelm. He arrived at about sunset. His reception was most imposing. His entrance into Damascus along a route parallel to the permanently-flowing Chrysorrhoes river was a wonderful sight, surpassing any description. A procession of thousands flowed along the route, soldiers, infantry and especially cavalry, the officers in uniforms of cloth of gold.

The official pashas and leaders of the various religions, first the leaders of the Orthodox.

27, Tuesday. The next day the emperor on horseback rode down the great street (Straight Street) to go to the house of Gabriel Shamyeh, an Orthodox. Here and there there were soldiers in the street, indigenous troops preceding him and crying out *"Allah in suru"*, which means "May God grant him many years." When he passed by our patriarchate, where a number of clerics were standing who shouted in Greek *"Zeto"*, the emperor smiled and waved with his right hand. At night there was an official dinner at the city hall. There were toasts at which many speeches were made, which were variously reported by the journalists, amongst whom was Mr Chr. Christovasiles of the *Acropolis* of Athens, who was put up at the patriarchate.

22, Sunday. The metropolitan of Aleppo issued a document in which he declared that he was resigning his candidacy for the patriarchate.

1898, 24 November. Abraham-Pei-Asuat asked our people if there was sufficient confidence in him for him to mediate between the opposing parties.

The *locum tenens* visited the *vali*, who read him the new orders concerning the observance of the *status quo*, and advised confidentially that some of the dissenters should be persuaded to change sides. The *locum tenens* replied that attempts had been made to bring this about but had failed and added: "There is need for pressure." The *vali* replied: "I cannot do that."

Field-Marshal Jevat Pasha visited the Greek prelates. On leaving he took the beard of the aged Seraphim of Eirenoupolis and kissed it out of respect.

1898, 6 December. Feast of St Nicholas, Sunday. Name-day of Tsar Nicholas. The Russian consul, A. Belyaev, invited the metropolitan of Laodicea instead of the canonical *locum tenens* to concelebrate with the metropolitans of Seleucia and Tyre and Sidon. The metropolitan of Epiphaneia preached. A doxology was sung. Everything was sung in Russian by schoolgirls. The metropolitan of Arcadia presided at the doxology. After this the indigenous prelates went to the Russian consulate and paid their respects. Our people went neither to the church nor to the consulate but telegraphed their congratulations directly to the tsar. They also telegraphed an account of these events to the ecumenical patriarchate.

7, Monday. The *vali* summoned the prelates. Ten lay people were also present. The *vali* supported the dissenters as if he were their advocate. Our people made a vigorous speech. The *locum tenens* and the metropolitan of Amida left the audience hall on account of the presence of the laymen but returned at the summons of the *vali*, the laymen having been ordered to leave. The *vali* gave to the prelates the vizierial decree. The metropolitans of Laodicea and Arcadia said that the ecumenical patriarchate should not interfere in the affairs of the Antiochene throne. The metropolitan of Amida objected that such interference was justified and asked: "Why are there laymen here?"

They replied: "So that we might support our rights", and in addition showed the written summons of the *locum tenens*.

Vali: Have you not issued voting papers?

Aleppo: Yes, but that election took place under deception and was exploited by the dissenters as you yourself have said.

Vali: I did not say that. Look, they are making me out a liar to my face.

Aleppo: They are the ones who have done everything. And I told you earlier so that you would forbid them to interfere in such matters.

Vali: You told me after the election.

Aleppo: And before. They are the ones who put the people out of the church on the feast day of the sultan.

Vali: They went out because they did not know the language.

Aleppo: They knew Greek until 1898 and today they do not know it? Yesterday they heard everything in Russian, and how did they understand that?

Vali: I am not interested in such things.

Aleppo: They prevent us from celebrating.

Vali: Of course, if you behave towards them in this way.

7. All the prelates at the *vali*. The metropolitan of Aleppo opens the discussion, asking about his health and the *vali* thanks him, for he had been ill for a number of days. And he adds: "During this time two telegrams arrived on the patriarchal question, and I beseech you, Your Eminences, to contribute yourselves to the satisfactory solution of the question." On saying this he showed the telegrams and added: "These were sent following the note of the three patriarchates to the Sublime Porte."

Aleppo: We shall gladly contribute when our just demands are met. And what you have said is better addressed to our opponents that they might conform to the new decree.

Seleucia: We have carried out our election in full accord with the canons on 6 May, having abolished what you call the *status quo* by a majority vote.

Aleppo: It has in no way been abolished. A majority vote would have validity where there proves to be a parity of votes at the last ballot. Now on the subject of the proposal of candidates. Everyone is free to propose whoever he wishes as a candidate, as long as there is no canonical impediment barring him from our throne. All the more since such from of old is the regime of our Church.

The *vali* is exasperated, groans and says: "*Uf yaman yarapi*"– O my God!
. . . . .
Then the *locum tenens* began to express himself sharply and illogically and threatened to resign.

Vali: Pull yourselves together and come to an agreement.

Aleppo: We will pull ourselves together and we will come to an agreement when the list is signed in accordance with your decree.

When the *locum tenens* and his companions had gone out the *vali* said to the indigenous prelates who remained: "Flatter the metropolitan of Aleppo by promising him the patriarchate."

18. The *locum tenens* and his circle celebrated a doxology for the sultan in the patriarchal hall, the indigenous prelates in the church.

25, Friday. Christmas. The metropolitan of Epiphaneia celebrated and the metropolitan of Seleucia preached. The *locum tenens* with the metropolitan of Amida celebrated the liturgy in Meitan, from where they returned early to look after their guests.

1899

During the festivities the professor of philology at the Theological School of Jerusalem, Mr Constantine Iliades, arrived in Damascus on a mission. The meetings with him took place in the house of the Greek expatriate, G. Rizos.

1 January, Friday. The metropolitan of Emessa celebrated and the metropolitan of Seleucia preached. The metropolitan of Aleppo celebrated in Meitan. The remaining native-born prelates went to see the Russian consul and paid him their respects.

2, Saturday. The Russian consul repaid the visit.

The Muslim Ramadan. On this occasion the prelates went to the administrative offices and paid their respects to the *vali* and then to military headquarters where they did the same to the field-marshal, Jevat Pasha. The latter, turning to the metropolitan of Aleppo, said: "Have you been here many years?" "Yes, indeed." And joking, he added: "Your beard will grow white before the Antiochene question is solved."

5, Tuesday. Epiphany Eve carols. The metropolitan of Emessa presided and Archimandrite Paul performed the blessing of the water. The Russian consul was also present.

16. The metropolitan of Seleucia came down to Beirut to borrow money from the rich Neguib Soursok for the maintenance of the patriarchate, but he was unsuccessful.

21, Thursday. Peter Kantilaft came to the patriarchate and insulted the Greek prelates.

When the metropolitan of Aleppo was coming out of the house of a lawyer called Nasif, Peter Kantilaft who was in the house insulted him disgracefully saying:

> "Are you not ashamed of going round houses and spending hours with women? *Melesin* [= infernal creature], accursed man, you bring disgrace on the clergy. You are *rezil* [= a scoundrel] and if you come a second time we shall give you a good beating which you will remember as long as you live."

Then, many of the crowd bursting in violently, one of them raised a revolver against Nasif, which they brought to the patriarchate and then to the government building, saying that Nasif had threatened them with it.

23, Saturday. The metropolitan of Aleppo went to the *vali* and complained about these things. The *vali* said that Peter was an honourable man! He promised, however, to punish him.

From the above and much else anyone can understand the loutish behaviour of the Damascene populace. History through the ages also witnesses to this. They set traps for the patriarchs whom they defame disgracefully. And since I am on the subject I shall add the following. Our own prelates, on account of the situation, went about paying visits. The Damascenes not only lay in wait for them and insulted them but they wrote anonymous letters to the community leaders, whom they threatened because they received Greek prelates and even called them pimps of their own wives.

25, Monday. The metropolitan of Epiphaneia preached.

1899, 10 February, Wednesday. The metropolitan of Seleucia learned from the *vali* that a ready-made patriarch would be sent in from outside, and the metropolitan replied that they would not accept him. On this announcement, the native-born clerics and lay-people drew up a petition through which they requested the deposition of Germanos of Tarsus as *locum tenens* and the recognition of the metropolitan of Laodicea as such, and they rejected the interference of the other patriarchates.

12, Friday. Feast of St Meletios. On this day Meletios of Laodicea celebrated his name-day in a grand manner. The metropolitan of Tripoli celebrated the liturgy. The Russian consul was present along with a large crowd. There were speeches and the schoolchildren sang songs.

15, Monday. The metropolitans of Seleucia and Tripoli went to see the *vali* and made a report to him. They returned at 10 o'clock and issued a statement that the *locum tenens* was being deposed within ten days.

20, Saturday. All Souls Day. Seraphim of Eirenoupolis was not permitted to go to the cemetery and say prayers.

22, Monday. About fifty Damascenes came together under the presidency of the metropolitan of Seleucia to elect *azas*. When the *locum tenens* protested, the *vali* placated him, saying that others would be elected the next day.

23, Tuesday. A crowd of people entered the patriarchate to prevent the dissenters from electing *azas*. The *locum tenens* spoke to the *vali* and appealed to his compassion. When the metropolitan of Aleppo asked the *vali* why the first decrees which concerned the *status quo* had not been published, the *vali* replied: "Because of your faults."

24, Wednesday. The *vali* summoned the prelates and the *locum tenens*, whom he wanted in order to make representations. But he suddenly heard from the *vali* that the metropolitan of Laodicea was appointed in his place. And he added: "I am very sorry for this, but you are much at fault." And on saying this he summoned the metropolitan of Laodicea, saying: "Come and sit here", and indicated a place to him above that of Germanos of Tarsus.

The metropolitans of Amida and Aleppo and the bishop of Eirenoupolis sent a document to the *vali* in which they protested at the dismissal of Germanos of Tarsus as *locum tenens* and the appointment of the metropolitan of Laodicea, whom they did not recognise. The document was sent by the metropolitan of Aleppo's deacon, especially as he knew Turkish. He found the Russian consul was also with the *vali*.

Since the metropolitan of Laodicea was ill with rheumatism the rest of the indigenous prelates went to the *vali*, whom they thanked for the appointment of the metropolitan as *locum tenens*, and then went to the Russian consulate. The Greek prelates telegraphed these events to the patriarchs.

The new *locum tenens* took over the maintenance of the patriarchate. The metropolitan of Arcadia was appointed supervisor of finances.

1899, 24 February, Wednesday. Invitation to a session of the synod. This was written in Greek and read as follows:

"To the venerable members of the Holy Synod of the Antiochene Throne.

You are invited to a meeting of a canonical session for the completion and sealing of the electoral list, without excepting anyone from the list of candidates of 6 May 1898, in conformity with the latest imperial *Irade* issued on this matter, tomorrow Thursday 25 February 1899 at 7 o'clock in Turkish.

The patriarchate, 24 February 1899."

Signature in Greek: "The *locum tenens* of the throne of Antioch, Meletios of Laodicea."

Reply:
"Since we regard the invitation of the unilaterally and unlawfully elected metropolitan of Laodicea as uncanonical and as an infringement and violation of the sacred institutions of our holy Church, we do not deign to accept the invitation to sit in council and sign the unlawful and unilateral act of 6 May of last year."

Signatures:

"The *locum tenens* Germanos
Benjamin of Amida
Nektarios of Aleppo
Seraphim of Eirenoupolis."

25, Thursday. The indigenous clerics and lay-people gathered at the patriarchate at 4 p.m. and held a meeting. The *vali* also came and greeted them.

The metropolitan of Laodicea as new *locum tenens* summoned the minority to come tomorrow (26) for the same purpose.
Reply:
"That which we wrote in reply to yesterday's invitation we still hold to and repeat in this letter."

26, Friday. The metropolitan of Laodicea summoned the minority a third time on the following Saturday at about 3 o'clock in Turkish.

They replied as follows:

"That which we wrote in reply to the first and second invitations we still hold to and repeat in the present letter, adding in sincerity and love, and not as a display or threat, that the unilateral and unlawful acts and decisions of the uncanonically elected metropolitan of Laodicea as *locum tenens* recognised by the august Government in breach of etiquette and approved by the seven metropolitans, will, as a high-handed infringement and violation of the sacred customs and institutions of our holy Church and of the unity of its body of prelates on account of racism and self-interest, bring about a disturbance and rupture of peace and harmony between the holy churches of God and an abuse of privileges, the responsibility for which and the regrettable consequences of which will be borne solely by the metropolitans mentioned above."

27, Saturday. Those who met together with the metropolitan of Laodicea elected a three-member committee consisting of the metropolitans of Arcadia, Tyre and Sidon and Epiphaneia, who went to see the minority and tried to make them change their mind and recognise the metropolitan of Laodicea as *locum tenens*. But they refused. Those around the metropolitan of Laodicea drew up a list of candidates, amongst whom they included all the prelates of the throne and, going to the government building, delivered it to the *vali,* who promised that he would send it to Constantinople and expressed the hope that it would prove acceptable and all the names would be returned.

At about sunset the Russian consul came to the patriarchate with two other people.

28, Sunday. The metropolitan of Arcadia celebrated the liturgy on the passing of the year. It seems as if he has sworn not to commemorate Germanos as *locum tenens*.

1 March, Monday. The minority telegraphed the grand vizier in French begging that the list of candidates sent by the majority should not be approved.

The majority sent a telegram to the ecumenical patriarch by the metropolitan of Seleucia as follows:

"The interests of Orthodoxy demand that you should not intervene and take action against us. Rather you should give moral support to a local and independent Church, and not accede in any way to the proposal of the minority. The question is not one of nationalism as the others represent it out of self-interest and perversity."

1899, 7 March, Sunday of Orthodoxy. The *Anathemas* were read. The metropolitan of Emessa celebrated, the metropolitan of Seleucia commemorated Russia, Greece and the three patriarchs and then preached.

8, Monday. The *vali* sent his equerry to summon the new *locum tenens*. Because he had a pain in his legs, the metropolitans of Emessa, Epiphaneia, Arcadia, Tripoli, Seleucia and Tyre and Sidon went instead. The *vali*, in the presence also of Field-Marshal Jevat Pasha, announced that their list of candidates had not been accepted by the Sublime Porte and, following protests from the patriarchates, the minority must be left free to put down external candidates and that their one-sided practices are against the privileges of the Church. And if they elect a patriarch on their own, he will not be recognised by the patriarchs. The prelates objected, saying that they did not recognise the intervention of the patriarchates. The *vali* added that the government demanded that the *status quo* should be maintained. Then the *vali* sent the decree to the metropolitan of Laodicea.

The prelates gathered in the apartment of the metropolitan of Emessa, and the laymen at the house of Jibran Louis, and deliberated about what should be done.

11, Thursday. The Russian consul visited the metropolitan of Laodicea.

12, Friday. Russian pilgrims went to Saydnāya, where, as was customary, they were received on behalf of the inhabitants. Food was sent for them from the patriarchate.

14, Sunday. The metropolitan of Epiphaneia celebrated. The Russian pilgrims were at the patriarchate.

22, Monday. The Russian Minister of Education arrived. He was met at the station by the metropolitan of Seleucia, Peter Kantilaft and others, who presented a bouquet.

1899, 25, Thursday. The Annunciation. The metropolitan of Seleucia celebrated. The whole of the liturgy was in Russian. Twenty-five schoolgirls sang, one of whom recited the Epistle in Russian from a manuscript. Likewise the Cherubic hymn, the Creed and the "Our Father", which were also sung, as the Russians are accustomed to do.

March 27, Saturday. The *vali* summoned the metropolitans of Laodicea and Seleucia and communicated to them the vizierial decree, in which an election was advised in accordance with the regimen of the Antiochene Church, with the inclusion of candidates from the two thrones, the ecumenical and that of Jerusalem. The prelates objected. And the *vali* said to them: "You labour in vain." The circle of the metropolitan of Laodicea telegraphed Constantinople to express their objections. At a conference in the patriarchate it was proposed to the metropolitan of Laodicea that he should receive the patriarchal office even by force, but he objected, foreseeing that he would not be recognised by the patriarchates.

The Russian Minister visited the Boys' School on Monday (29) and left for Saydnāya.

1899, April. Some of the prelates sought permission from the *vali* to go to their own dioceses because Easter was approaching, but the *vali* would not allow this.

The Muslim Bairam. The prelates visited the higher government officials separately.

At about dusk the Russian consul came to the patriarchate. There were also some laymen and they quarrelled with the prelates deep into the night.

(Note: The Antiochene Question has become the subject of newspaper articles. *Amaltheia* of Smyrna, 1 April. *Times* of Paris and London.)

12, Monday. The metropolitan of Aleppo visited the *vali* at home and revealed to him that the indigenous prelates were making a move to elect the metropolitan of Laodicea as patriarch and the *vali* replied: "It is impossible for them to do this. I am putting pressure on them but they are resisting. I do not know what to do." In the afternoon he sent his equerry and summoned the metropolitan of Laodicea. At about sunset the metropolitans of Emessa, Arcadia and Seleucia, Archimandrite Paul, Symeon Latkani, Boutros Antilaft and the Chief Secretary of the Administration, Joseph Tannūs, went to Germanos, whom they reminded of their letter to him of yesterday, which he had not received. In this they demanded that he should show them the accounts for his administration. But, as we have said, the patriarchate of Jerusalem used to send funds for the upkeep of the patriarchate. They also demanded that he should pack his bags and leave the patriarchal apartment.

In the meantime, the metropolitans of Amida and Aleppo came up. Then Tannūs said that the *vali* was ordering that Germanos should hand things over and abandon the apartment to the metropolitan of Laodicea. The metropolitans of Amida and Aleppo replied that this was not the work of the *vali*. Tannūs went to the *vali* and on returning said that the *vali* says that if Germanos is persuaded and leaves the apartment voluntarily, then that would be good, otherwise let them not resort to violence, for they will be held responsible. But before Tannūs returned Germanos lost his nerve and handed everything over. He said that he would have handed them over earlier but the metropolitans of Amida and Aleppo had prevented him from doing so. In the meantime a threatening crowd gathered and the well-known George Awas rushed in as if he would come up and bring down Germanos by force. He insulted him in a vulgar way, calling him *kelp* [= dog and monster]. Many others called him *hafra* [= senile old man]. Germanos came down to the metropolitan of Emessa's room, and the latter went up just for one evening to the patriarchal apartment, since he had not succeeded in being elected patriarch, as he would have wished. The metropolitan of Aleppo blamed the metropolitan of Seleucia for having stirred up the mob and for doing such things without respect for his office. And the metropolitan of Seleucia, smiling bitterly, said "My turn has often come."

There was a quarrel between the metropolitan of Aleppo and Latkani.

1899, 13 April, Tuesday. The minority addressed a protest to the *vali* at what had taken place.

15, Holy Thursday. The election of the metropolitan of Laodicea as patriarch. The metropolitan of Epiphaneia was celebrant. In the afternoon the *vali* summoned the metropolitan of Seleucia and said to him that according to the most recent order from the Sublime Porte the election of a patriarch must take place in conformity with the *status quo* with the addition of candidates from outside and that if they proceed to an election in which only one side participates they will be responsible for rebelling against the patriarchates, with whom the government is also in agreement.

The metropolitan of Seleucia on returning to the patriarchate called a conference of the prelates and the laymen. He also invited the minority to come and put forward three candidates from the list which had been sent to the Sublime Porte. But the latter did not come. Then the majority held a conference on their own. At first each person expressed his own opinion. The majority of prelates and some of the laymen expressed fears about this very risky line of action on which they were about to embark. Finally the opinion of the laymen prevailed, since they had also been encouraged by the Russian consul.

So it was that the ballot took place, each one casting three votes. The metropolitan of Arcadia, forgetting, only cast one, and then remembering demanded that he should cast the other two. Because the others would not accept this he got angry and went out, but the metropolitan of Tripoli brought him back in again.

The larger share of the votes fell to three candidates: the metropolitans of Laodicea, Seleucia and Emessa. After a session of about four hours, at about the first hour of the night, what had taken place having been announced to the *vali*, they went up into the church, where a secret ballot was held in the sanctuary. After the ballot the metropolitan of Laodicea was declared patriarch of Antioch with seven votes, the metropolitan of Seleucia coming second with one vote which had been given to him by the metropolitan of Laodicea. After this the service of the Passion of Christ began with the metropolitan of Tripoli presiding.

Archimandrite Paul, as Secretary of the Synod, came at once to the royal gates of the iconostasis and announced the result of the election. The people then started shouting "*Zeto*". At the end of the service of the Passion they went into the patriarchal hall, accompanied by the Russian consul, Belyaev. They spoke at some length and then there were cries of "*Zeto*" and "Hurrah". It was about midnight. "Long live Patriarch Meletios." "Long live Tsar Nicholas." "Long live the sultan." A large unruly crowd, some of whom were armed, called on every Greek to come up to the church for fear of attack! A trick.

16, Friday. The metropolitans of Amida and Aleppo went to the *vali*, who was very disturbed. He had not expected the dissenters, he said, to have gone so far as to hold an election, especially as he had summoned the metropolitan of Seleucia and drawn his attention to this, announcing it to him and leaving an order during the night. "But have patience. I will do what is necessary. My government and I have taken a serious view of this coup. I know what you have endured, who the demagogues are, and what the Russian consul is up to. I have advised them and they did not listen to me. They have only harmed themselves."

The majority sent the document recording the election of the metropolitan of Laodicea as patriarch to the *vali* by the hand of Archimandrite Paul, for him to forward to the Sublime Porte. The minority protested by telegram to the Sublime Porte and the patriarchates.

(The newspapers *Neologos* and the London *Times* carried reports of these events.)

18, Easter Sunday. The metropolitan of Laodicea (already elected) celebrated the liturgy with the metropolitans of Tyre and Sidon, Epiphaneia and Emessa, who commemorated him as follows: "Amongst the first be mindful, O Lord, of our elected archbishop, Meletios."

After the end of the liturgy the Russian consul went down to the patriarchal hall with some Russian women teachers, who sang in Russian. Easter greetings were exchanged. At midday the prelates went up with the Russian consul to the courtyard of the church, where they posed for photographs. Both sides waited for reactions to what had been done, but there was no news. Somebody heard that the cable from Beirut had been cut.

Meanwhile in Constantinople everything was in uproar, ministries, embassies. Démarches of the Commissioner in Constantinople of the patriarchate of Jerusalem, Archimandrite Germanos Apostolatos.

After what had been done in Damascus through the scandalous activities of the Russian consul, Apostolatos went to the embassies to denounce these actions. First he went to the German embassy. But the German ambassador pretended ignorance, and not conducting himself in an honourable fashion, reported what had been said to the Russian ambassador, Nelidov. He got angry and declared that in future he would have nothing to do with Apostolatos. Indeed later on he obliged Patriarch Damian to recall him.

Secondly, Apostolatos went to Caustan, the French ambassador, who strangely, although he had such an interest in Syria, pretended complete ignorance of the question.

Thirdly, Apostolatos went to the British ambassador, Sir Elliot, from whom he had a very favourable reception and audience. When asked if he could remain a little while until the ambassador could communicate by telegram with the Foreign Office in London, Apostolatos waited. The Foreign Office gave Elliot instructions to intervene actively as a result of which he sought an audience with the sultan. When this was granted, Elliot said to Abdul Hamit that it was in his empire's interest that the *status quo* with regard to the throne of Antioch should be maintained and that a Greek patriarch from outside should be elected. The sultan agreed with this, saying that he was awaiting fresh news from the *vali* of Damascus. (The Athenian newspaper *Neologos* published an article on this.)

1899 April 23, Friday. The government, the *vali* and the native-born prelates. An emissary of the *vali* brought to the patriarchate an official letter addressed to the President of Tyre and Sidon, and through him to those who had taken part in the election. In this letter it was announced to them that their act, since they had proceeded unilaterally to the election of the patriarch, is contrary to the regimen of the Antiochene Church and to the requirements of the law, and that the government, not accepting such an election, orders that they should proceed to a new election in conformity with the *status quo*.

During the night the Russian consul went to the patriarchate, where he gave encouragement to the indigenous prelates. The latter came together after supper and proposed that they should enthrone the metropolitan whom they had elected. But the metropolitan of Tyre and Sidon objected.

23, Feast of St George. Name-day of the heir to the Russian Throne. The metropolitan of Seleucia celebrated in Russian. Archimandrite Paul sang the *polychronismos*, wishing the tsarevich long life.

The Press

15 April. Embros of Athens: "The question of the patriarchate of Antioch." An article on the patriarchate of Antioch by an Orthodox cleric.

"Undeclared war", *Constantinoupolis*, 12 April 1899.

1899, 28 April, Wednesday. The Russian admiral Skydlov came up from Beirut with three officers. They were received at the station by the consul Belyaev and the metropolitan of Seleucia and were put up at the Russian consulate. As soon as the admiral arrived he went for a carriage ride and drove up "Straight Street" where the patriarchate was.

29, Thursday. Feast-day of Grand Duke Sergei, President of the Palestine Society. The metropolitan of Seleucia celebrated. Schoolgirls sang in Russian.

A doxology and three cheers for Skydlov, who was not present in an official capacity. The consul was in his official uniform.

They came down to the patriarchal hall and drank coffee. Then they went with the native-born prelates to the Girls' School (next to the patriarchal church). In the afternoon the indigenous prelates visited the admiral at the consulate, where they were photographed together. Then the bishop of Eirenoupolis and the metropolitan of Aleppo visited the admiral. The headmaster of the school invited the native-born prelates to dinner.

30, Friday. Skydlov departed.

30. Those who had elected the metropolitan of Laodicea as patriarch wrote to the ecumenical patriarch announcing the election and advising that he should cease opposing them. They also wrote to the other patriarchates. The letter was published in Arabic in *Manar* [= Lighthouse].

1899, 1 May, Saturday. The metropolitan of Aleppo saw the *vali*, who spoke in vague terms. He only said that in Constantinople there were many intrigues (using the English word).

2, Sunday of the Myrrh-bearers. The metropolitan of Epiphaneia celebrated. It was the metropolitan of Arcadia's name-day. Towards the evening he was visited by the Russian Director of the Schools with the women teachers.

Some of the prelates departed for their dioceses. Others travelled round various villages inciting the inhabitants to draw up petitions asking for a native-born patriarch and indeed for the confirmation of the election of the metropolitan of Laodicea.

10, Monday. At about noon the Russian consul visited the metropolitan of Laodicea. The metropolitan of Seleucia was with the *vali* for a long time. The *vali* sent the Chief Secretary, Joseph Tannūs, to the patiarchate to announce a new order. Tannūs said it would be better if others were sent with him, especially the leader of the Orthodox community, Jibran Isper, to add to the official nature of his visit.

11, Tuesday. There was an order but the *vali* announced some minor new point from one day to the next until he published an imperial decree which required that the patriarch to be elected should be a Greek and said that the metropolitan of Laodicea was regarded by the government as a traitor and as such was to be expelled even from his own diocese and Germanos of Tarsus was to return as *locum tenens*.

Jibran Isper said that he wished to work on behalf of a Greek patriarch but he needed money and indeed a lot of it.

13. The metropolitan of Aleppo went to see the *vali*, who said to him: "The news I am receiving is true and rather more pleasing than you were expecting and it will be published tomorrow." He advised them to keep their wits about them but also to take care not to fall into the same errors as before.

14. The photographer Habib Howini photographed all the buildings which were used as schools by the Palestine Society.

18, Tuesday. The metropolitan of Aleppo called on the *vali* at home, who told him that he was awaiting supplementary orders. He advised patience and calm.

20, Thursday. Feast of St Alexios. Name-day of the Russian consul. The indigenous prelates went to the consulate to convey their greetings.

The *vali* also visited him. The indigenous prelates gave out that in drinking a toast to Belyaev he said: "I hope soon to be in the happy position of being able to announce some very pleasing news to you from Constantinople, that is to say, the speedy issue of an *Irade* confirming the election of the metropolitan of Laodicea as patriarch to your great joy, Mr Belyaev, for you have laboured like no other person on this issue."

25, Tuesday. The British consul, then the Russian and finally the metropolitan of Aleppo, went to see the *vali*. He denied what had been reported about the toast to Belyaev and said that he was awaiting supplementary instructions on the punishment of the recalcitrant native-born prelates. He counselled patience and calm and said that the matter would be resolved in accordance with our wishes.

28, Friday. The Russian consul departed and was seen off by the metropolitan of Seleucia. Likewise the British consul Mr William Richard and the Russian consul in Beirut. All three were bound for Constantinople.

Note: Just as the two consuls were entering the railway carriage in Damascus, the Englishman said in French to the *vali's* emissary, Joseph Tannūs: "I thank His Excellency the *Vali* for sending you to see us off; and I thank you too and hope that before I return you will have a good patriarch." When Joseph said: "We already have one", the Englishman smiled and said: "Pay attention to what I have said to you." Then the Russian chancellor said: "Strange, what does he mean by that?"

1899, 1 June, Tuesday. The British chancellor visited all the prelates separately.

2. The latter returned the visit separately.

3. The metropolitan of Seleucia departed for his diocese.

6. Pentecost Sunday. The metropolitan of Tripoli celebrated, reading the Gospel in Greek.

The Egyptian newspaper *Ahram* wrote that the Sublime Porte had issued a decree deposing the metropolitan of Laodicea. But that the *vali* had indicated to the government that if such a decree is implemented the people will rise in revolt.

7, Monday. Communiqué with a new decree. The Russian Prince Boris was with the *vali* for a long time.

8, Tuesday. The metropolitan of Aleppo went to see the *vali*, who said that he is awaiting a new decree the day after tomorrow. He denied what had been written in *Ahram*.

15, Tuesday. Prince Boris was photographed outside the church with the metropolitan of Arcadia and the schoolchildren.

The Russian chancellor was at the patriarchate with the indigenous prelates for a long time.

30, Wednesday. Four of the native-born prelates went to the *vali*, to his residence, where he announced the new decree to them.

1899, 1 July, Thursday. The metropolitan of Aleppo went to the *vali*, who was getting ready to go out.

"What news have you?"

"You already have the news."

He recommended patience and calm.

2, Friday. Feast-day of the French Republic. The officials called on the French consul. The patriarch-elect, the metropolitan of Laodicea, was there with the metropolitan of Epiphaneia. The *vali* said that the government insisted on its earlier decision, that the patriarchates were threatening resignations in the event of the recognition of the metropolitan of Laodicea as patriarch. Accordingly, the government required that a new list of candidates should be drawn up in conformity with the *status quo*, under the presidency of the former *locum tenens* Germanos, but that it was a matter of indifference who should be elected.

In the afternoon the bishop of Eirenoupolis and the metropolitan of Aleppo went to call on the consul, who told them what the *vali* had said, adding that he was very disturbed inwardly and his ideas very confused. Finally he said that the matter would drag on but that it would finally be resolved in our favour.

There is a rumour that England has been insisting with the sultan that the question must be resolved quickly and in accordance with the *status quo*.

1899 4 July, Sunday. The metropolitans of Laodicea, Arcadia and Epiphaneia celebrated. All vested in the sanctuary and wore mitres. (There was nothing to distinguish the metropolitan of Laodicea as patriarch-elect.)

5, Monday. Feast-day of Grand Duke Sergei. Four prelates celebrated. The schoolgirls sang in Russian.

6, Tuesday. The *vali*, on summoning the metropolitans of Seleucia and Emessa, advised them to comply with the decree, but they refused, saying if force was needed that was something else.

15. Our own Demetrios Vasileiades while on a visit to Baalbek (Helioupolis) met there the biggest and richest merchant of Beirut and leader of the Orthodox community, Neguib Soursok, and had two meals with him. He was the only one of the official native-born Orthodox who helped the indigenous prelates. He said that he preferred the metropolitan of Emessa. On mention of the Russians, Neguib said: "Let the Russians give us money and they can do what they like!" Vasileiades then said to him: "I never expected to hear anything like this. But since Mr Neguib, who has an annual income of thirty thousand pounds, expresses himself in this way, what will the rest of the world, the poorer people, say?"

Neguib Soursok also said the following to Mr Vasileiades, namely, that Mr Nelidov (the Russian ambassador in Constantinople) had said to him: "The people of Moscow have protested to the Russian government and the Synod, asking that the ecumenical patriarchate should not be offended, because it was from the latter that the Russians had received Christianity."

1899, 18 July, Sunday. All the native-born prelates celebrated.

The newspaper *Mochrousa* wrote against the teacher Epiphanios Petrou (Gatas Antilaft).

23, Friday. The editor of *Manar* arrived in Damascus from Beirut.

14, Saturday. The *vali* summoned Germanos of Tarsus and received him warmly, saying that he had not seen him for a long time. The main point of summoning him was to ask him which jurisdiction Salt (in Transjordan) belonged to, whether it was to the throne of Antioch or that of Jerusalem. This would have been in connection with the rumour that the native-born prelates of the throne of Antioch were planning to detach Salt, along with the dioceses of Nazareth and Ptolemais (Acre) and Joppa, from the throne of Jerusalem and attach them to the throne of Antioch. I later wrote about this to *Tachydromos* of Alexandria.

1899, 25 July, Sunday. The metropolitan of Seleucia celebrated. At night the marriage of the Interpreter of the Russian consulate, Joseph Sapaa, was celebrated very magnificently. The *vali*, the *musir*, the consuls and seven indigenous prelates were present. The crowning was performed by the metropolitan of Laodicea in vestments. Since he had a good voice, Athanasios of Emessa took the opportunity to sing the following Greek song as a musical interlude: "Rise to receive your glory, rise Queen of cities, see from the west your heroic emperor approaches covered in glory." This song was composed and sung by the famous cantor George Gevelis, in the year in which the Sultan Abdul-Aziz (1830–76) disembarked in Constantinople on his return from Paris, where he had gone for the International Exhibition of 1858. He was so pleased with this song that he sent Gevelis a gift of a hundred pounds.

1899, August. The native-born prelates, with the metropolitan of Seleucia presiding, occupied themselves with the question of the elected community leaders. The metropolitan paid several visits to the palace on this matter.

11. The people of Damascus handed the metropolitan of Laodicea a petition against the teacher Epiphanios Petrou (Gatas Antilaft), whom they did not want as a teacher any more.

1899, 13 August. There was a meeting of the Council of Community Leaders, which lasted a long time, on the question of the teacher Gatas. But it remained unresolved. It should be noted that Jibran Isper is always absent from these meetings.

15. A telegram was received by Pogianich the Director of the Russian Schools, asking for the photographs of various schools, monasteries and other places, amounting to 106, to be sent to St Petersburg.

18–19. On the feast-day of the sultan an invitation to an evening function. Congratulatory telegrams. Calls on government officials.

23. Telegram from Alexandria received by Archdeacon Pagones, announcing the death of Sophronios, the aged patriarch of Alexandria. Condolences were sent.

24. The native-born prelates celebrated an official memorial service for Sophronios.

My move to Jerusalem

During my absence I entrusted the keeping of my journal to the metropolitan of Aleppo's deacon, Ignatios .....

First I visited Patriarch Damian, to whom I gave a letter of introduction from the three prelates of Amida, Aleppo and Eirenoupolis, which was very flattering towards myself. Patriarch Damian kept saying repeatedly: "What has Germanos of Tarsus done to us!" This was why he did not wish to add his signature to my letter of introduction, saying: "Let the oil of the sinner not anoint my head." What the three prelates said about me .....

I waited especially for Photios of Nazareth, who, when he came and learned of my arrival, invited me to stay with him and we exchanged news. With regard to the Antiochene question he said the following:

"There would not be a problem today if the patriarch of Antioch were elected from outside, either from Constantinople or from Jerusalem. The question turns on whether it is a Greek who is elected. This is something which I very much fear will not happen. But this should not disappoint us provided we secure our rights to the Antiochene throne. Many mistakes have been made, the chief culprit being Germanos of Tarsus. But what has happened has happened. Today is the day of the final attempt to rectify the mistakes in some measure."

This is what we talked about and I reported our conversation to the metropolitan of Aleppo in Damascus.

He told me nothing about himself of a personal nature, although I broached the subject in an indirect way. On the contrary, he refused to be drawn, especially as Patriarch Sophronios had died in the meantime and Photios was rumoured to be his successor – which is finally how it turned out although after many objections from the Russian Palestine Society.

Moreover I can reveal the following: the Jerusalem professor, Nicholas Christodoulou, a Cypriot and close friend of Photios, told me in confidence that the Russian Palestine Society, after trying various ways of thwarting Photios's candidature for the throne of Alexandria without success, resorted to the following scarcely honourable course of action. The Society appealed for help to Queen Olga of Greece, who was Russian. But King George opposed this and Crown Prince Constantine grew angry and called the Russians by a suitable name.

With regard to the policy of the Powers towards Greece, and especially that of Russia on the one hand and England on the other, a deputy called G. Philaretos wrote a revealing work entitled Ξενοκρατία καὶ βασιλεία (Foreign Control and Royal Power) for which he was prosecuted.

Finally, in spite of all resistance, Photios was elected chief pastor of the Church of Alexandria and was a credit to it and the other Orthodox Churches and the whole Greek world for twenty-five years. He was invited to Cyprus and resolved the Archiepiscopal Question. He represented the Orthodox Church at Stockholm, where he recited the Creed in Greek. He was a consummate diplomat and a very able writer of memoranda. He wrote classical Greek fluently and was an excellent ecclesiastical orator. He died in Switzerland. His remains were brought to Egypt and buried in Cairo.

I now return to the events in Damascus.

The *vali* of Damascus, Nazim Pasha, had obligations towards Russia, which exercised an influence on him in some measure. But fundamentally he was a Turk and as such defended the interests of his government.

On one occasion when the former *locum tenens*, Germanos of Tarsus, was visiting the *vali*, the latter asked him about his relations with the native-born prelates. Germanos replied in confidence that there was hope of winning over the metropolitan of Seleucia and when this was done some of the others might return to their dioceses. The *vali* was surprised and said to him: "The metropolitan of Seleucia! But he is a Russian from head to toe." And he added: "Do not trust him because he will probably set you a trap."

On another occasion the metropolitan of Aleppo's deacon, Ignatios, was sent to the *vali*. As a Greek from Asia Minor he spoke Turkish. After a brief exchange the *vali* said to him: "Why did your people force Spyridon to resign before making sure of the election of a Greek patriarch?" Ignatios replied: "Germanos of Tarsus was responsible for this." And the *vali* added: "It is true that he is primarily responsible."

On another occasion the Chief Secretary of the Administration, Joseph Tannūs, an Orthodox and native of Damascus (who had written before all this, as we have seen, seeking a divorce), sought leave from the *vali* to speak with him. When he met him he said: "I too am native-born and as such I would have liked a native-born patriarch to be elected. But I foresee that he will be under the thumb of the Russians." The *vali* remained silent because he did not trust him.

The metropolitan of Seleucia meets the President of the Muslim Community

Although they had not had any previous relations, the metropolitan of Seleucia visited him and asked him to help the indigenous Orthodox.

"We are of the same race," he said, "and must work together."

"It is too late", said the President, "to recall that we are of the same race, for this is not something you have ever made anything of. On the contrary, you lean towards Russia and thus create many difficulties for the government. Without wishing to get involved in this question of yours, I would say that the Greeks have rights over the Antiochene Church because the patriarchs of Antioch have been Greeks. When our ancestors captured Syria from the Greek Empire of Constantinople, they respected the Christian religion and later, under Turkish rule, the patriarchs of Antioch were Greeks sent in from outside. Today you wish to abolish the *status quo* because that is what Russia wants for her own purposes with you as her proxies."

On the following day the President invited the metropolitan of Aleppo and communicated the above to him, advising him to place no trust in the native-born Orthodox.

The sufferings of the metropolitan of Laodicea as patriarch-elect

The metropolitan of Laodicea was not recognised either by the minority prelates or by the rest of the patriarchates and the Sublime Porte, and his position deteriorated in accordance with the displeasure of the people, some of whom were against him, such as the community of the suburb of Meitan, under the leadership of their priests, who still recognised as *locum tenens* the previous holder of the office, Germanos of Tarsus. And when one day the priest in charge at the church of Meitan was summoned, he said in the presence of the metropolitan of Laodicea that he did not recognise him and sharp words were exchanged. When he came down he started shouting and condemning everybody and criticising what they had done and their ingratitude towards the Greek patriarchs, who had been benefactors of the throne.

Another problem which the metropolitan of Laodicea encountered as *locum tenens* was the following. One day an old priest, lean, pale and dressed in rags, came to the patriarchate from one of the villages seeking help because he was destitute. But he did not receive any. In his disappointment he did not do what others usually did, which was to go over to Catholicism, but something worse and unprecedented. He went over to Islam! When the *vali* heard this he called the metropolitan of Seleucia and observed with regret and embarrassment that this act of the poor priest did not reflect any credit on them at all who had a duty to help him. In the end he handed the priest over to the metropolitan of Seleucia who took him to the patriarchate to deal with the matter.

Another day a well-known troublemaker in the pay of the native-born prelates, George Awas, who used to insult the Greek prelates, came to the patriarchate seeking money from the metropolitan of Laodicea. When he was refused, Awas came out shouting and swearing that he had no respect for him but despised him and had him under the sole of his shoe (*Taht-es-sourmei*).

And what was even more wretched was the press. A journalist from Aleppo wrote some telling articles against the Greek clergy of Antioch and Jerusalem. But by now, because of the serious turn of events, independent newspapers were censuring the aberrations of the native-born clergy and laity, | who were being egged on by the Russian consul. Among those who mounted bitter attacks was the former headmistress of the Patriarchal Girls' School, called Selma. She was an educated young woman, modest and able, who gave a good education to many young girls to the general good of Damascus, but she was dismissed and replaced by a Russian woman. Selma wrote to an Arabic newspaper in Egypt castigating the people in Damascus and pitying the metropolitan of Laodicea as *locum tenens* and supposedly patriarch-elect without being recognised by the authorities. These hostile articles not only upset the metropolitan of Laodicea but cheapened him. The attacks in the press ceased when the metropolitan of Laodicea was recognised as patriarch-elect and shortly afterwards was enthroned as patriarch. But history remains as a witness and judge.

1899, 6 August. Continuation of the account of the question of the patriarchate. In the morning the metropolitan of Seleucia left for his diocese. He did not return again to Damascus.

In Damascus there were repeated meetings of the Council of Community Leaders on various matters, especially the question of the teacher Gatas, whom the community spurned. There was a violent quarrel with oaths between his cousin Boutros Antilaft and Symeon Latkani.

1899, 12 August. The metropolitan of Seleucia's servant, Joseph, departed for the village of Aaroun to convey news about the health of the metropolitan, who was suffering from anthrax.

13. The death of the metropolitan of Seleucia was announced by telegram.

14. The metropolitans of Amida and Emessa and Archimandrite Paul and some leading lay members of the community went to Zahlah for the funeral of the metropolitan of Seleucia. I have written earlier on Gerasimos of Seleucia of blessed memory at some length, and especially that loving Greek from childhood he was educated at the patriarchal school of Damascus and later at a Russian academy. He spoke and wrote Greek well and had studied Greek history. He was a philhellene by conviction and a Russophile for tactical reasons.

15. The *vali* sent representatives to the patriarchate to express his condolences to the prelates at the death of the metropolitan of Seleucia.

Some prelates and laymen opened up the room of the metropolitan of Seleucia, where they found his private papers. He did not leave any property; he lived as a poor man.

26 September. The appointment of Prince Boris, formerly chancellor of the Russian consulate in Beirut, was announced officially as consul-general in Erzerum, which is the seat of the metropolitan of Theodosioupolis, which was then vacant. Spyridon had wished to appoint Matthew, his former coffee-maker in Bethlehem, to this see because he was a Greek. But subsequent events prevented this disgrace from being put into effect, as they did the promotion of his archdeacon, Basil, to be metropolitan of Lebanon.

1899, 4 October, Monday. The *vali* summoned the prelates and announced to them that the list of candidates had been returned with the metropolitan of Arcadia crossed out (the metropolitan of Seleucia had already been crossed out). He advised them to meet in the church under the presidency of the metropolitan of Laodicea and to elect their patriarch by a majority, the results of the election being conveyed to him for him to send to Constantinople so that an *Irade* could be issued recognising the patriarch. When the metropolitan of Aleppo said that they had spent nearly two years in Damascus and had suffered much and done much on behalf of the regimen and external candidates, the *vali* made some excuse. The metropolitan of Arcadia flared up and said: "We have already elected a patriarch and we are not going to proceed to a second election." The *vali* grew angry and said: "I do not permit you to speak in this way in my presence. The candidate you have elected is recognised neither by the government nor by myself. Since you submitted a list then, you are obliged to accept its return now and not proceed unilaterally to an election."

The minority protested to the Sublime Porte and reported these events to the ecumenical patriarchate.

6, Wednesday. The Russian consul arrived and was received by the metropolitan of Arcadia.

1899, 6 October. In the evening Archimandrite Paul, as Secretary of the Synod, conveyed to the minority the following invitation in Greek:

"You are invited to a canonical meeting of the Synod tomorrow at 5 o'clock to complete the business concerning the election of a patriarch that needs to be transacted in conformity with the latest high decrees of the government."

Signed: Your beloved brother in Christ, Meletios", without any title being indicated.

Verbal reply: "We refer you to our replies to your earlier invitations."

7, Thursday. Paul came again.

Reply: "We repeat what we have said before, and add that we will not take part in unlawful acts."

Paul came again a third time. The minority repeated what they had said before, adding the following verbal statement which Paul, however, took down:

"In the absence of a canonical president of a regular and full Synod, in accordance with the sacred institutions of our Holy Church, we were not permitted to take part in the earlier coups, from which we abstained, nor are we now permitted to take part in a new irregularity and uncanonical act, that of a false synod, supposedly rendering canonical the earlier uncanonical election which is confirmed by this repetition. We sincerely and with all our heart wish peace to the Church of Antioch."

The recognition of the metropolitan of Laodicea as the elected patriarch of Antioch

In the last few months a lot has happened in Constantinople. A kind of tug-of-war has been played between the policies of Russia and England as to which of them will have the most influence over Sultan Abdul Hamit. I do not say over the Turkish government because from the beginning the government had declared itself on the side of the *status quo* and the election of a Greek patriarch from the ecumenical patriarchate. But finally Russia prevailed, since it is a dangerous neighbour of Turkey. In a letter to Sultan Hamit, Tsar Nicholas asked as a personal favour that a patriarch of Antioch should be chosen from the local clergy. So it was that the election of the metropolitan of Laodicea prevailed even though it was uncanonical. This was announced towards the end of October (1899) and thus the preparations were made for his enthronement.

In the meantime, the four Greeks who constituted the minority packed their bags in preparation for leaving Damascus for Beirut and thence for their own homes.

Their invitation and refusal

Although the four prelates were preparing to go, some of the mob broke into their rooms and subjected them to a final insult. They forced open their bags and undid their bundles as if looking for objects taken from the patriarchate. The truth was that the prelates left things for the poor patriarchate, which the mob removed. Thus the four prelates with their secretary (myself) went down to Beirut, from where the bishop of Eirenoupolis went to Jerusalem where he was looked after by the Brotherhood until his death in 1906. The metropolitan of Amida went to Constantinople, where he too died. The metropolitan of Tarsus went to his see, which was at Mersin. But because of the displeasure of the government with him, he was exiled to Bursa. On falling ill, however, he moved to Constantinople, where he suffered much. He died a monument of ignominy to all.

The enthronement of the metropolitan of Laodicea as patriarch

This took place on 31 October (13 November) in the patriarchal church with all the official trappings. Or rather, mob rule prevailed. The Russian consul, Alexis Belyaev, was particularly prominent. It may be said in passing that as a reward for all he had done for the election of a native-born patriarch he was promoted to the post of General Secretary of the Central Palestine Society in Russia.

The insults directed at the Greeks by the people of Damascus. Time does not permit me to describe these. Apart from the formal addresses and replies of the patriarch, others spoke to the people such as Jibran Louis, a lawyer, who, among other things, said that the Orthodox Syrian people had been delivered from the Greek tyranny. Somebody else said the same thing in verse, making Meletios Dumani (his surname) rhyme with *Yunani* (= Greek). And so the ceremony of the enthronement was brought to a close.

When the prelates went down to Beirut, Ignatios, the metropolitan of Aleppo's deacon, remained in Damascus. He succeeded in persuading the metropolitan of Arcadia to hand over to him some things which had previously belonged to Seraphim of Eirenoupolis.

Epiphanios Petrou (Gatas Antilaft) met him in the street and begged him to kiss the hand of the holy prelates on his behalf and ask their forgiveness if in any way he had harmed them or upset them. "The individual is one thing", he said, "and the general another", and having married in the meantime, he was particularly anxious not to burden his family with the curses of the prelates. And at the beginning he was supported and, as a Hellenist and theologian, became Director of the Seminary at Balament. Later, however, dismissed and abandoned, he suffered misfortune and paid for his ingratitude to the Greeks in this way.

APPENDIX

1

THE IMPERIAL *BERAT* OF HIS BEATITUDE SPYRIDON, PATRIARCH OF ANTIOCH

According to information received from the prefecture of Syria, the former patriarch of the Greeks of Antioch, Damascus, and the other places under him having been elected and appointed patriarch of Jerusalem, there has been elected in his place, in conformity with the rules and customs, from among intelligent and able candidates, the bearer of this my imperial *Berat,* the former Metropolitan Spyridon of Tabor. The certificate of election having been conveyed to the special council of my highest ministers and submitted to it, the appointment of the said Spyridon to the patriarchate in question has been judged suitable. This ministerial judgment having been submitted to my resplendent imperial throne, I have issued a high imperial decree confirming the imperial judgment. On this authority the present imperial *Berat* is issued which puts into effect the appointment of the said patriarch.

I therefore command that the said Spyridon, formerly metropolitan of Tabor, should govern the patriarchate of the Romans in Antioch, Damascus and the remaining places. Let those of the Greeks, the weak and the powerful, who live in those parts which have always been subject to his throne recognise him as their patriarch and not transgress his orthodox judgment in religious matters.

Let no *kasemis,* servants of the *peitulmal,* or *mutevelis* obstruct or hinder him or his metropolitans, according to ancient custom, from receiving the remains of metropolitans, monks and nuns who die within his jurisdiction.

Let no one alienate from him without a high decree any church or monastery under his throne and in his possession, nor let anyone interfere with their repair in conformity with the ancient regimen and the permission of his sacred judgment confirmed by my high decree.

Let him punish according to their crime, priests and commissioners who celebrate an illicit marriage without his knowledge. His cases which come under the ecclesiastical courts are to be reviewed in my capital city.

If any of the Romans wishes to be joined in matrimony or to divorce his spouse, no one other than the patriarch or his commissioner is to intervene or concern himself in the matter.

If any monks and lay Romans make any disposition, according to their religious customs, for the poor of the churches and for their patriarch, let this be proved in the sacred court by Roman witnesses.

If any bishop or abbot or hieromonk who is a subject of the patriarch is caught in the act of some crime, let no one prevent the patriarch from punishing him, cutting his hair and replacing him.

If the dismissal and replacement of any metropolitan of the Antiochene throne, or abbot, or priest is deemed necessary, let no one intervene with the patriarch as he dismisses him in accordance with religious practice and replaces him.

The dismissal and appointment of metropolitans by him is to be carried out by charter bearing the seal of the said patriarch and no metropolitan or bishop is ever to be appointed in his jurisdiction by the charter of any other person.

The appeals of the patriarch are to be heard and any petition on religious matters submitted by him is to be taken into consideration.

He is to return any monastic *vagrantes* found contrary to religious practice in the region subject to his throne to the monasteries wherein they originally dwelt.

When the patriarch travels with his retinue guides are to be provided for him and when he is passing through dangerous places a uniformed and armed detachment is to be assigned to him to protect him and his retinue. The *padjidars, akardjis* and other officers appointed to guard the bridges, passes and other places are not to hinder him contrary to the law and ancient custom, nor are they to importune him for gratuities contrary to the sacred law.

The *kadis* and *naipas* are never to demand money from him in matrimonial matters or in any other dispute between two Christians when the patriarch by mutual agreement between the parties concerned brings about their reconciliation, or when he imposes an oath on them in church or punishes them in accordance with their religion by excommunication.

Priests who are subject to the patriarch or to his metropolitans are never to celebrate an illicit marriage without his knowledge, nor are the rich to annoy them or put pressure on them to join a particular person with another in marriage or to dismiss a particular priest and appoint another in his place.

In circumstances in which the patriarch finds himself obliged to punish Christians subject to his throne and issue an order of excommunication in conformity with religious custom, let no one intervene.

If the imprisonment of a priest or hieromonk is judged to be necessary by the sacred law, he should be imprisoned by the patriarch.

The patriarch is to receive into his possession all the churches which have always belonged to the Roman nation along with their sacred vessels without the intervention of any other nation.

He is to receive from the metropolitans subject to him the annual sums which are given to him by established custom.

No one is to hinder him from bearing his patriarchal staff according to ancient custom or from mounting his horse.

If monks not subject to a church or monastery belong to the regions covered by the patriarchal *berat* and, living as *vagrantes,* disturb the peace and are the occasion of scandal, they are to be hindered by the patriarch and ejected.

Soldiers or others are not to be despatched to enter into his lodgings nor is anyone to annoy or distress him, demanding against his will to enter into his service.

Officers are not to oppose the patriarch when at the invitation of Christians he visits them in their houses, nor is anyone to interfere with the ancient custom by which the patriarch reviews the accounts of monasteries which in the previous patriarchate were administered by Commissioners who plundered their revenues.

Officers are never to annoy him or cause him distress by demanding money contrary to religious and civil law when on certain days he celebrates religious rites according to ancient custom.

Since there are some who, for the sake of extracting money without any real debt or guarantee of the patriarch, claim that they made a loan to him or to others on his guarantee, such people are not to disturb the patriarch contrary to the sacred law without submitting proof.

The vineyards, gardens, nurseries, mills, pastures, arable lands, houses, shops, fruit-trees, forest-trees and springs which according to religious custom have always been the property of his churches, and all his monasteries and movable property dedicated to the Church, and flocks which have to date been held and administered by his predecessors, the Roman patriarchs of the see of Antioch, are to be held and administered by the said former Metropolitan Spyridon of Tabor.

Provincial governors and police personnel in general are not to put any hindrance in the way of these matters nor are they to intervene for any cause or on any pretext whatsoever.

Given in Constantinople, the fifteenth of the month of *Rebiyül Ahir* 1309.

2

LETTER OF ARCHDEACON BASIL TOPHARIDES
TO CONSTANTINE MYRIANTHOPOULOS

ALEPPO 12 JULY 1892

ON THE ENTHRONEMENT OF NEKTARIOS OF ALEPPO

To Damascus

My dear friends Constantine and Gabriel, greetings.

By this letter I am letting you know that thanks be to God we have arrived safely in Aleppo.

We sailed from Beirut on Saturday the 27th at 6 o'clock on the Egyptian vessel, passed the whole of Lebanon and reached Tripoli at 10. I stayed on board, only Gabriel went ashore. We departed from Tripoli at 12 o'clock and, passing the mountains of Arcadia, reached Mersin on Sunday at 5 o'clock. Gabriel and I at once went ashore because the bishop did not wish to disembark.

As soon as we reached Mersin scala we met some Cypriots, who asked us to take them to the metropolis. As soon as we entered the metropolis we saw some Cypriots in the courtyard of the church playing cards, for the metropolis is inside the church, which was built by Mavromatis. They took us to the metropolis, which is nothing but two or three rooms with bare boards. A Rhodian hieromonk lives there, the duty priest, who received us warmly and asked us all our news.

We then left the metropolis and went to a hotel, where they gave us a room so that we could rest a while. Afterwards we went to the dining room to eat. They brought us roast meat, macaroni, tinned sardines, a cool Cypriot wine and pears. We thought it would cost us three medjidies but when we asked how much we should pay they told us that the whole meal was 9 kurush. Imagine how cheap it is! And it is a good hotel, not like the hotel where we ate for 20 paras and I drank water to dull the hunger.

We then left the hotel and went to the Arab church where the priest's wife was a Cypriot. He received us very well and we stayed at his house for about an hour, but as he had vespers of the Holy Apostles, he invited us to go to the church and I was immediately brought Greek books and asked to sing. I got Gabriel to sing in Greek in the right choir.

With the end of vespers the day came to an end and we returned to the steamship. On leaving Mersin at one o'clock at night and passing by the mountains of Mersin and Taurus, we arrived at Alexandretta on Monday morning (the feast of the Holy Apostles). The priests and some singers came at once to the steamship (the Greek *Spetzai*) and received the bishop with great joy. They waited until the bishop came to the church and the divine liturgy began.

When the bishop disembarked at Alexandretta all the Orthodox were at the quayside, together with the Greek consul and a detachment of soldiers, who escorted him to the church, where he stood outside the sanctuary and the divine liturgy began immediately. But unfortunately they did not have a cantor and so the bishop acted as cantor. When the liturgy was over an Antiochene Arab called George took us to his house, where we stayed until the next day.

We did not meet with Germanos even in Iskenderun because he was in the mountains at a village called Arsous.

When we set out from Alexandretta on Tuesday afternoon (that is, the 30th) up to 30 people accompanied us for a period of three hours. On crossing the whole of that plain we reached Aleppo on Friday morning at 2 o'clock, 3 July. We were met at one hour's travel from the city by all the Orthodox and the commissioners of the other communities. All the consulates sent their kavasses. And in the city the carriages could not pass because of the crowds.

When the bishop entered the church he stood at the throne and at once they began to sing a doxology. When the doxology finished, the bishop made a speech in Arabic and said: "I thank you, Your Beatitude, for having made me a bishop." When it was over we came out of the church and entered the metropolis, where music was played (not military music but music provided by the Catholic school in honour of the prelate).

And if you want to know about Aleppo, it is a beautiful city with clean air and the Orthodox are very polite and very fond of the Greek language, of which the majority have some knowledge. And the metropolis is handsome and lofty with a pool within it.

And that son of Mappuros, that splendid young man, that bright flame (I mean Gabriel), tell me what he is up to.

Give my respects to His Beatitude and kiss his right hand on my behalf. Do the same with the bishop of Eirenoupolis. Greetings to Paul and Emmanuel, to Mark, to my dear friend Emmanuel and similarly to all by name. And you have many greetings from Gabriel the secretary, who reminds you of "Kaorilafok fok".

Your friend,
Deacon Basil

Aleppo, 12 July 1892.

3

LETTER OF NEKTARIOS OF ALEPPO TO CONSTANTINE MYRIANTHOPOULOS KEFERT KHAIRIN, 4 JANUARY 1900, ON HIS NON-RECOGNITION OF MELETIOS DUMANI OF ANTIOCH

[4 January 1900]

My dear child Constantine,

I received your letter of 22nd of the last month and year and read it with pleasure.

Your love and devotion towards me and your concern for my future restoration have given me the greatest consolation, relief and encouragement in the vicissitudes and injustices I have encountered at the hands of the dissidents. I am a true soldier of the Church and nation and a loyal subject of the imperial government, and as such I am obliged to obey the orders of the government and endure all things, whether hardships, suffering, deprivations, persecutions and exile, in order to defend to the best of my ability the rights of the Church which have been violated in an arbitrary fashion. I am also obliged to assist the activities of interested parties and to hand over to them unblemished and intact the sacred deposit which I have received from the Church and the nation.

I am not anxious on account of any of this, nor am I distressed at my being sent away, which has taken place rather for prudential reasons, as a period of rest for me and for the avoidance of possible scandals and anxieties as a consequence of the division of my flock, until the final solution of this unfortunate affair. On the contrary, I am bearing my removal with every satisfaction even though endurance, patience and courage are needed, trusting firmly in God that in the end justice and truth will prevail, for the latter have been set aside and misrepresented by those who are opposing ecclesiastical order, peace, sacred institutions and established regimens, on account of a love of power, on account of an anti-Christian nationalism and on account of the service of political interests harmful to the Church and the state.

News has reached me of the injustices done to me and attributed to me at the instigation and with the support of the unlawful patriarch by a section of my flock who have been slandering me, representing me to the unlawful patriarch and to the government as a rebel and instigator of revolt who hinders the people from paying their taxes to the government and as an immoral person. I have heard this without distress and have prayed that these terrible intrigues should be cast aside for the good of the Church and that the Almighty should forgive all my enemies and enlighten their minds, for "they know not what they do".

Germanos is pursuing the ascetic life. He is loved and supported enthusiastically by his flock and by the *vali* of Adana. At the moment of writing he has not been dismissed but remains in his diocese, celebrating the liturgy and governing as the canonical metropolitan of his church. He has not recognised the unlawful patriarch but commemorates the name of the ecumenical patriarch in the divine liturgy. The metropolitan of Amida has similarly not been dismissed to date and remains at the Phanar.

The vindictiveness of the North, of the unlawful patriarch and his circle and of the entire people of Syria has been directed against me alone, having dismissed me from my diocese and having frequently demanded my ejection from the see of Antioch. But the government, to which I have protested on account of my uncanonical and unjust dismissal, has not recognised it to date, nor has it permitted me to leave this place. I am completely ignorant of the government's aim and of the programme of the parties concerned, who, apart from their advice to me to remain firm in my position out of reverence for the sacred canons, I gather are working energetically on my behalf and on behalf of the whole affair and are resisting the influence of the North. Consequently I have no idea how long I shall be staying here. I am obliged to bear and endure all things for the sake of our sacred struggle, and the lot has fallen on me alone to pursue it.

As for myself, by a judgment known to the Lord I have been condemned to spend the recent celebrations far from my flock in isolation in a Turkish village without a church, without a Christian community, in difficulty and distress for the defence of the sacred canons and prerogatives of our holy Church which have been violated and set aside by her adversaries. On account of these and all things with a heart full of emotion I utter the cry of St John Chysostom: "Glory to God for all things."

I have taken note of your proposal. When the need arises I shall send you the appropriate reply, because if the government puts pressure on me to abandon my diocese permanently I shall necessarily be obliged to have recourse to higher authority in Constantinople.

I can always receive your letters safely through Mr Valassopoulos.

Finally, I embrace you in a fatherly way and await news from you about the events in Damascus.

† Nektarios, metropolitan of Aleppo and Alexandretta.

Our deacon Ignatios also greets you.

4

LETTER OF DEACON IGNATIOS OF CAESAREA TO CONSTANTINE MYRIANTHOPOULOS KEFERT KHAIRIN, 18 JANUARY 1900, ON THE SUFFERINGS OF NEKTARIOS OF ALEPPO

1900 January 18 from Kefert Khairin
To my very dear friend Mr Constantine Myrianthopoulos.

Greetings and joy in the Lord

Dear friend,

First I must ask you about your health, and if you inquire about me, I am well to date, thanks be to God, but not as well as I could be on account of the constrictions imposed on us by the turbulent and crooked Arab nation.

Secondly, I shall make a start on telling you about our experiences from 5 November, when we sailed from Beirut, to the present moment.

We reached Alexandretta on an Egyptian steamship but 18 hours after our departure the bishop suffered terribly from seasickness. There was a rough sea the whole time, for even the elements were against us.

Two priests, a Greek and an Arab, together with five leading Greeks from among the most distinguished members of the community, came to meet the ship. We went down onto the quayside together with the metropolitan of Cilicia. About sixty Christians were gathered on the quayside, only eight of them Arabs but Greco-Arab in their sympathies. We went down to the house of the Greek priest, Papa George Anagnostiades.

In the evening the metropolitan of Cilicia left for Mersin on the same steamship, and they received him as we would have hoped, but there was no Arab reception committee. Whatever complaints his diocese may have had against him, now with the Antiochene question they have all been forgotten and all is milk and honey. The only one who has suffered and still suffers is my *geron*.

As for me, when I reached Alexandretta I went to Aleppo immediately the next day to bring back the bishop's episcopal vestments, but there too we drew a blank and the same at Alexandretta because in Aleppo too the telegrams and letters of the unlawful and uncanonical patriarch and his followers had been at work. They refused to give the sacred things on the pretext that they did not belong to Nektarios but were gifts from Russia, and if Nektarios had brought the episcopal vestments from Damascus, they were not his own but belonged to Agapios, the late metropolitan of Edessa. Finally, so as not to make a fuss without achieving anything, I left for Alexandretta without taking the vestments.

But what do you think? How much did it cost the Arabs of Aleppo and Alexandretta? For if I had stayed one more day in Aleppo, the unlawful patriarch would have spent another thousand kurush. For the telegrams went back and forth from Damascus and Alexandretta to Aleppo ten times a day.

One telegram was certainly from Alexandretta to the priests of Aleppo and the telegraph operator, without realising what he was doing, handed it to me. I opened the telegram at once and this is what it said: "Nektarios has sent his deacon to collect his episcopal vestments. Do not hand them over to him because he is no longer one of our prelates. We have informed Damascus. Date: 8 November." And there were many others of a similar nature.

When I returned to Alexandretta the Arabs started asking me why I had not brought the vestments and I know not what. Then I really let fly and came out with all the invective I knew and went right through the lot. It was Saturday. They ran up and down so as either to force the prelate to sing a doxology on Sunday and commemorate Meletios or else to prevent him from coming to the church. The Greek priest did not have permission from the bishop to commemorate the unlawfully elected and uncanonical patriarch.

From the other side, as soon as Sunday dawned all the Greeks with their wives and children came to church and the previous evening the *kaimakam* had advised the Arabs: "You do not have the right to celebrate a doxology on behalf of Meletios." Then the leading Arabs, black in soul and body, were disappointed. These were instructions from Damascus, because the Damascenes thought that that which they had done to the four Greek prelates they could also do in Alexandretta to Nektarios.

But they received no satisfaction. For when Sunday dawned we went at once to the church and heard our liturgy (we sang of course in Greek in both the left and the right choirs). The persecutors of the Greeks did not even dare to come into the church but kept going round the building in a circle. As the prophet David says: "The ungodly walk round in a circle." Those who had prepared to sing a doxology, those who had prepared to hold a celebration and rejoice over the uncanonical and unlawful Meletios did not even set foot in the church, and instead of wiring the unlawful patriarch that they had held a celebration on his behalf telegraphed dejectedly: "As long as Nektarios remains in Alexandretta that which you desire will not come about. Only if you remove him from Alexandretta can we, the people, sing a doxology on behalf of Your Beatitude. Date: 14 November."

Thereafter telegrams began arriving from the unlawful patriarch to Nektarios of Aleppo. The first telegram ordered Nektarios to recognise him as his patriarch. We did not send a reply. A day later a second telegram came again ordering him to recognise Meletios. Again no reply. Two days later a third telegram in which the unlawful patriarch harped on the same theme. We again made no reply to the third telegram.

At the same time he sent a letter apart from the telegrams. But the letter did not come directly to my *geron*. It was sent to the leading local Arabs for them to hand to Nektarios. On Saturday morning, 20 November, about twelve of the notables came to the bishop, bringing the Arab priest with them, in order to deliver the letter of their unlawful patriarch, but the bishop did not even glance at their letter. He said that he would not accept it and they should send it back. He neither recognised Meletios as patriarch nor would he receive his letter. The leading Arabs went away with long faces and returned the letter themselves.

Two days before this incident the *kaimakam* had summoned the bishop and read him the following telegram from the Sublime Porte: "Whatever Meletios decides against you, the government will say nothing." The bishop replied to the government as follows: "I respect and revere the *Irade* of the Sublime Porte and the Royal Decree, but I cannot recognise Meletios as patriarch of Antioch because his election has not taken place in accordance with the canons of the Church."

On 20 November the *kaimakam* again summoned the bishop and said to him that the governor of Aleppo, Raoul Pasha, wanted him "to go to see him because he had some things to say to him". This was a trick, but who was to know? But all these were incitements originating from Damascus to slander the bishop to the governor of Aleppo and to the *kaimakam* of Alexandretta to the effect that the Arabs were afraid of the Greeks, that they would be ill-treated by them and as long as Nektarios was in Alexandretta they could not even go to church. Then in Aleppo this same lot claimed that if the bishop came to Aleppo he would cause a great disturbance in the place (The wretches! Are they the ones who wish to bring peace to the Church?) while in Alexandretta the bishop counselled the Greeks day and night not to give the slightest cause for scandal, because they would be punished by the government and gave other similar advice, "because I do not wish you to have enmities amongst yourselves". But the Arabs on the contrary stirred up the people telling them that the bishop wished to cause a scandal in the Church. And the unlawful patriarch telegraphed the governor of Aleppo from Damascus, saying: "Remove Metropolitan Nektarios from the diocese of Aleppo and from the province of Aleppo." At the same time there were as many other scandalous things as you could wish.

It appears that on top of this the *vali* also telegraphed Constantinople for instructions on how to deal with Metropolitan Nektarios. It appears that the governor of Aleppo was ordered from Constantinople to arrange our removal from Alexandretta, for the governor did not act off his own bat.

Anyway, we finally left Alexandretta on Saturday, 20 November, in the afternoon. We thought we were going to Aleppo and were accompanied by a second-lieutenant and escorted, as we supposed, by two gendarmes.

After we had travelled for about sixteen hours we came to the halfway point on the road to Aleppo, where there was a khan with a telegraph office. After we had rested there for half an hour the officer presented us with a telegram from the governor of Aleppo which read as follows: "Until further notice, instead of coming to Aleppo you must go to the administrative district of Kharem and remain there quietly." Well, Mr Constantine, if you were in the bishop's place what would you have done?

In that deserted place there was not a soul except for seven soldiers and they had orders to receive the prelate and take him to the said town of Kharem. But the bishop accepted this decision without visible distress, and we continued our journey with a single gendarme and after four hours reached our destination.

Instead of Aleppo we arrived at Kharem, numbering 400 houses and inhabited entirely by Turks. We went to the house of an important and rich man in the village called Ahmet Aga Permeri Zade. He received us very politely and indeed lavishly (for the governor had given orders that we were to be well looked after). We stayed at his patriarchal house all evening in complete comfort and the next day, 22 November, which was a Monday morning, a second-lieutenant from Aleppo presented himself to us, accompanied by four gendarmes and bearing a letter from the governor of Aleppo to the administrator of Kefert Khairin asking him to receive the prelate and deliver the letter into the hands of the *kaimakam*. The letter contained nothing but a request from the governor to the *kaimakam* to take care of the bishop and see that everything he needed was at his disposal.

We set out again accompanied by the officer, a sergeant and four gendarmes and after travelling for three hours we reached the town of Kefert Khairin. We suffered much on the road from the cold and rain and a strong wind was blowing. The bishop was cold and lashed by the rain but he remained silent. I kept contemplating in my mind those who were responsible until we reached the village.

We stopped at a house called Arif Aga Kegiali Zade. We have been staying there until today and have had no news from any quarter. We do not know how long we shall have to stay here.

Eight days after we arrived at Kefert Khairin, that is to say, on 29th November, a telegram arrived via the governor of Aleppo from the unlawful Meletios addressed to the administrator of the village where we are living. He asked the bishop for the last time whether he would recognise him as his patriarch. We replied to the unlawful patriarch as follows: "Since the three patriarchates are cognisant of this affair, I cannot give you a reply without receiving instructions from them."

Since this reply was unsatisfactory to the unlawful patriarch he immediately decided on the dismissal of the metropolitan of Aleppo. Without delay another telegram reached us on 4 December, again via the governor of Aleppo, which read as follows: "I have invited the metropolitan of Aleppo [to acknowledge me as his patriarch] five times by telegram and once by letter but he has not even replied. Because he does not recognise the royal *Irade* and for many other reasons we are dismissing him by decision of the synod and ask Your Excellency to order the metropolitan to quit both his diocese and the province of Aleppo."

The next day we wired the governor of Aleppo asking him to give us leave to go either to Aleppo or Alexandretta and report from there to Constantinople. Three days later a reply came from the governor of Aleppo, saying: "I received your telegram and forwarded your request to Constantinople. When I receive a reply I shall inform you immediately." It is now 52 days and we have still had no news.

We have learned that the unlawful patriarch wrote a letter to Germanos of Cilicia, saying: "You do not recognise me as your patriarch, but I recognise you as metropolitan of Cilicia." We do not know what is behind this. Germanos, however, sang a doxology of St Nicholas on behalf of the North. If Meletios wrote in this way as a result of instructions coming from the North, perhaps he will draw Germanos to his side.

But the tastiest bit of news is a telegram to the priests and one to the laity of the diocese of Cilicia sent by the unlawful patriarch asking them not to recognise Germanos as their metropolitan on the grounds that he does not recognise him as his patriarch or else to force him to recognise him. This is the reply of the priests: "We are not in a position to do that which you ask." The laity replied as follows: "As long as the ecumenical patriarch does not recognise you as patriarch of Antioch neither do we. If the ecumenical patriarch instructs us to recognise you, we shall comply at once. Of course we do not want the diocese of Cilicia to be transferred to the patriarchate of Constantinople." What a nice reply for the unlawful patriarch!

He also wired the metropolitan of Amida, saying: "I order you at once to go to your diocese." The metropolitan put the telegram in an envelope and wrote on the envelope: "To the Patriarchate of the Orthodox at

Damascus." Inside he wrote as follows: "I return your telegram in the way it came." Again he received from the metropolitan of Amida what was right.

On the first of January the unlawful patriarch telegraphed the inhabitants of Aleppo, asking them to elect one of three candidates for him to ordain as metropolitan of Aleppo. The candidates were Gerasimos Moussaras, Raphael Khavavini and Christopher Jeppara. You know Christopher – he is the brother of Khama, who turned Turk. The people of Aleppo did not elect any of them but only said: "Let Your Beatitude ordain whomever Your Beatitude wishes and send him to us. We shall accept him."

On 10 January my *geron* telegraphed the patriarchate of Constantinople on this matter as follows: "Uncanonical patriarch disregarding sacred canons and ecclesiastical order has decided to go ahead with ordination of metropolitan of Aleppo and my replacement, having already proposed three candidates to flock for election. Protesting at this, I urgently beseech Your All-Holiness to make representations to central government and put definitive end to irregularities and innovations and deliver me from difficult situation, allowing me to proceed to Aleppo or Constantinople. Residence here has become unbearable."

Three days later we wired Jerusalem as follows: "The unlawful patriarch is ordaining Gerasimos Moussaras for Aleppo. What should I do?"

For we have received a letter from Aleppo telling us that the inhabitants of Aleppo have telegraphed Meletios leaving it to him to choose whom he wishes to ordain from the three candidates, and Meletios has favoured Gerasimos Moussaras for Aleppo and we still do not know whether he has ordained him or not.

In Antioch too the Christians are divided. Many of them do not want Meletios, and the same at Itlip.

There is still another thing which is something to make one laugh. On 20 December the unlawful and uncanonical patriarch wired the Minister for Religious Affairs as follows: "It is a shame for Metropolitan Nektarios to remain in Turkish villages without churches when feast days are approaching. We therefore ask that he should be given leave to go to Jerusalem, because he has been dismissed from the diocese of Aleppo and has no business to be staying at the Turkish village." But the unlawful patriarch has received no reply to his telegram. Not that he is sorry for Nektarios, but he wants him to leave the diocese so that the Arabs will quieten down.

I await a reply to my letter.

Stay in good health,

Your friend, Deacon Ignatios.

5

FROM THE GREEK EPIGRAMS
OF THE PATRIARCHATE OF ANTIOCH AT DAMASCUS

I

From a plaque on the wall of the courtyard:

Σεραφεὶμ πατριάρχης ἐμὸς ποιμάντωρ ἀνῆλθεν
Ἔνθα Μοναί τε Ἁγίων καὶ δικαίων Σκηνώσεις
Βιώσας περ ἔτη δύο πρὸς ἑβδομήκοντα
Δέκα δ᾽ ἐγγύς που μόνον ἐνταῦθα πατριαρχεύσας
Τὸ Γένος ἕλκων ἐκ Βυζαντίδος τὸ κλέος κόσμου.

Patriarch Seraphim my pastor has ascended
to the abodes of the saints and the tabernacles of the just,
having lived two years short of seventy,
nearly ten of these alone as patriarch here,
drawing his nationality from Byzantium and his fame from the world.

II

An epigram on the tomb of Methodios, patriarch of Antioch:

Ὧδε Θεουπόλεως κύδιστος κεῖται Πατριάρχης
Λῆξιν τὴν πραέων γήραϊ εὑράμενος
Πραότατος Μεθόδιος ὃν ὑμνεῖ πᾶσα Σύρων γῆ
Ναοῖς γαννυμένη μουσοτρόφοις τε δόμοις
Οὔτι θάνες ἐν δὲ τεοῖς ζῇς ὄλβιε τέκνοις
Ἔργμασιν ἀθανάτοις ἀθάνατος τελέθων.

Ἔτει ͵αωνε´ Ἰουνίου ΚΔ´.

Here lies a patriarch most renowned in the City of God,
who has come to the end of his gentle life in old age,

the most gentle Methodios whom the whole land of the Syrians hymns,
a land made happy with churches, schools and houses.
Nor have you died but live on, blessed one, in your children,
becoming immortal in immortal deeds.
In the year 1855, June 24.

III

An epigraph in a lunette in the patriarchal church:

Θεσπέσιος ὅδε ναὸς τῇ Κοιμήσει τῆς Θεοτόκου τιμώμενος ἐκ βάθρων
ᾠκοδόμηται Ἱεροθέου τοῦ πάνυ πατριαρχεύοντος. Ἐν ἔτει 1867.

This holy church honouring the Dormition of the Theotokos was built
in its entirety in the patriarchate of the famous Hierotheos. In the year
1867.

IV

On the entrance to the Girls' School, which Spyridon gave to the Russians,
above the gates on a square marble plaque is found the following incription
in small letters:

Φυτώριον ἐν ᾧ ὥσπερ ἔλαφοι διψῶσαι τὴν ψυχὴν
ἀρδεύονται αἱ τῶν ὀρθοδόξων παρθένοι
ἁδραῖς δαπάναις ὁ τῆς παιδείας ὑπέρμαχος
Ἱερόθεος ὁ πάνυ ὁ τὰς ἡνίας τῆς τῶν Ἀντιοχέων
Ἐκκλησίας διέπων δείματο. ἐν ἔτει αωξη′.

This nursery in which, like thirsting harts,
the young girls of the Orthodox are spiritually watered
was built with substantial sums by that stout defender of education,
the famous Hierotheos, who managed the reins of the Church of the
Antiochenes. In the year 1868.

V

On the bell-tower:

> Τόδε κωδονοστάσιον τοῦ τῆς Κοιμήσεως ναοῦ
> παρὰ τὰ ῥεῖθρα ἤγειρε τοῦ Χρυσορρόα ποταμοῦ
> Σπυρίδων Κύπριος βλαστὸς Ἀντιοχέων ὁ Ποιμὴν
> ἰδίοις ἀναλώμασι πρὸς Θεομήτορος τιμήν.

> This bell-tower of the Church of the Dormition
> was erected by the waters of the Chrysorrhoes river
> by Spyridon, scion of Cyprus, pastor of the Antiochenes
> at his own expense to the honour of the Mother of God.

(Note: This bell-tower was erected in the summer of 1892 by the narthex of the church where the tombs of the patriarchs are situated. It lies to the left as you come out of the patriarchate and enter the church. He also installed a bell, which the ungrateful Damascenes used to summon the mob which with its shouting and abuse drove out Patriarch Spyridon on 28 July, 1897.)

XX

THE CHURCH OF CYPRUS FROM 1878 TO 1955[*]

I

In last year's lecture on the Church of Cyprus in the eighteenth and nineteenth centuries I treated the subject from the point of view of the religious sensibility of the period and I examined successively the religion of ordinary people, the religion of the monasteries and lastly the religion of the more prominent members of this world.

The scheme of this series of lectures precludes me from referring even this year to the Church's activity in the national and educational spheres, which will be the subject of special addresses. It is evident that without taking into consideration the contribution of the Church in these areas it is impossible to present an all-round view of its life and work. Within the framework that remains I have chosen for this evening's lecture a broader angle of view than I did last year, with the natural consequence that the generalisations and the oversights will also be broader. The reasons which have led me to this choice are two: the narrower chronological band from 1878 to 1955 and above all the absence of a necessary perspective. An impartial and definitive interpretation with supportive evidence is impossible without a perspective and without the healing passage of time.

This does not mean that I shall give in to the temptation to turn history into a justification of that which has been. The sincere historian knows that history is full of possibilities which have been aborted, events which did not happen, equipotential events, things which might have been different. He views all these things in a critical but compassionate spirit without any desire to supplant divine justice. He is aware that he knows neither the deeds of darkness nor the secret counsels of the heart. If he is a Christian he knows that the Church essentially is not the blind people who run it but its divine

---

[*] Translated from "Ἡ Ἐκκλησία Κύπρου ἀπὸ τὸ 1878 μέχρι τὸ 1955", Διαλέξεις Λαϊκοῦ Πανεπιστημίου 2, Nicosia, 1986, pp. 31–62.

Founder. The Christian historian trusts in the providence of that Founder, certain that the most terrible judgment and punishment of a particular past embraces within it an unfading promise of a new future.

II

The change of regime of 1878 constitutes both an end and a beginning in the political history of Cyprus. The period which we are examining, however, 1878–1955, could very aptly be characterised by Marx's historic saying as "the revenge of society as it is on the illusion of politics".

It is well-known that the chronological periods of political history do not coincide with those of social history or, even more, with those of the history of mental outlooks. Politically Cyprus may have passed in 1878 from Turkey to England, but Cypriot society began to pass from its Ottoman to its English period only in the second decade of this century, while from the point of view of the anonymous, deep and silent history of their mental outlook it is questionable whether the Cypriots have even now been delivered from the Ottoman yoke.

Living and realising the Gospel on the personal level transcends the levels and limitations of a particular society and spiritual atmosphere. The history of the realisation of the work of the Gospel within a group of people, however, is necessarily connected not so much with the political history of these people as with their social history and the history of their mental outlook or their culture and spiritual development. From this point of view the Church of the Cypriots until the end of our period, 1955, is inevitably dominated by Ottoman attitudes in the same degree that the whole of Cypriot society and the Cypriot mentality are dominated by Ottoman attitudes – whatever this degree might be, and on that there could be much debate. I shall give just two examples to illustrate what I mean. One refers to the Cypriot generally (insofar as such a being exists) and the other to the Cypriot as an Orthodox Christian (and we are speaking of a period in which Greek Cypriot and Orthodox Christian were identical, not only in the Constitution but in 99.9 per cent of Cypriot hearts and minds).

The first example of what I mean when I say that with regard to Cypriot society and outlook the change of regime in 1878 was as if it had never happened is *rayahism*. *Rayahism* – one of the most poisonous fruits of the experience of long servitude – is a lack of principles and a repulsive combination of deference to strength and oppression of anything weak. It is connected with a historical "imprisonment of long duration" as Braudel would have said, which marked the whole era of British rule and the subsequent independent life of the Cypriot state. More particularly, in the history of the

Church *rayahism* constantly appears, for example, in the relations of the lay element with the hierarchy, or of the bishops and their courts with the presbyters. In this dimension of reality Cyprus has never completely freed itself from the Ottoman Empire.

The second example refers to the concept of religion which the Greeks of Cyprus, lay and clerical, had in 1878 and which was roughly the same as that of all the Christian subjects of the later Ottoman Empire, Greeks, Bulgars and Arabs. In spite of the political changes, the concept of religion held by Ottoman Christians was not purely Christian or Byzantine but in a large degree that of the Ottoman Turks, which traditionally identified religion with nationality or ethnic identity. According to this understanding every infidel – that is, non-Muslim – religious community which lived in the lands of Islam constituted an ethnic or racial group for which the religious primate, and by extension the clergy, were administratively responsible. The religious primate was elected by his community but as leader of his Nation was confirmed by the sultan, who for his own reasons accorded him not rights but his favour in the form of privileges.

When the English came to Cyprus in 1878 the only model they had for comparison, conveniently similar externally but in essence very different, was the position of the Roman Catholic Church in Ireland, where the bishops, being more than prelates, symbolised and represented a national idea. They at once made it abundantly clear (in matters, for example, of the taxation of Church property or of the inviolability of the monasteries) that they were ready to discuss natural and legal rights but not favours and privileges. The ecclesiastical hierarchy, experienced as it was, showed that it understood this within a few months. The underground stream, however, like another Cycloborus, watered the roots of a forest with its torrent, a forest in no danger of dying which was throwing up hybrid forms bred from Byzantine exclusivity, Eastern perceptions of religion and race and modern Greek nationalism of the nineteenth-century Balkan type. Until 1955 the Ottoman understanding of religion not only failed to leave the Greeks and hindered the Church's missionary work among the crypto-Christians (the *Linovamvakes*) but it became slowly but surely the religious understanding of the English themselves. It was thus that Field-Marshal Sir John Harding discussed very naturally with the Christian "caliph" of Cyprus not Orthodoxy but politics, a sight which in 1878 was highly repellent to Sir Garnet Wolseley. In 1983, however, it does not surprise the historian, who knows the strength of effective ideas and recalls Chaunu's dictum that with regard to history "in the beginning was the economy but at the centre was man".

This introduction has seemed to me indispensable on account of the present tendency of some Cypriots to judge the English period of their

history in biographical rather than historical terms, that is to say, overlooking the deep tendencies which in reality have worked for generations so as
to help make Cypriot history of the twentieth century that which it has been
up to the present day. If, however, they had read their history correctly in
this way – studying the workings behind the events and the structures together
with the coincidences – they would have abandoned their uncritical and for
the most part deferential attitude towards persons, groups, classes, institutions and communities and in the end would have felt pity for all: they are
tragic because we know what was unknown to them – the future. History
carried out on a scientific basis is the only possible means of reconciling the
different generations and experiences.

III

The activities of Christians may be described on three distinct but not
separate levels: the spiritual, the worldly and an intermediate level which links
the spiritual and worldly levels.

On the spiritual level the faithful act as members of the mystical body
of Christ. Whether this refers to the liturgical and sacramental life, the
practice of the virtues or contemplation, apostolic work or service in deeds
of love, the definitive object of the activity of the faithful is eternal life, God
and the things of God, and the redemptive work of Christ which they must
serve within themselves and in other people. On this level Christians act *as
Christians qua Christians* and their activity binds the Church.

On the worldly level Christians act as members of an earthly city. Their
activity on the intellectual and moral, the scientific and artistic, or the social
and political levels, in spite of the fact that if it is carried out correctly it is
referred to God as the final end, has as its definitive object goods which do
not belong to the eternal life but refer to this world and its culture. On this
level Christians act not *as Christians but in a Christian way*, binding only their
own selves, which are "in the world" even if they are not "from the world".

The third level falls into two bands. In the first, which looks to the
worldly level, the Church teaches its members a Christian wisdom with
regard to the state, society and the economy, providing a theological support
without descending to specific precepts for concrete realities. In the second
band, which looks to the spiritual level, the activity of Christians covers an
area of "mixed" matters (questions of marriage, for example, or education)
which although of concern to the earthly city also concern the supernatural
goods of the human person and the common good of the Church of Christ.

A full treatment of the history of the Church of Cyprus from 1878 to
1955 should include the life and activity of the Church and its members on

all three of these levels, the spiritual, the worldly and the mixed. Naturally to attempt such comprehensiveness in the course of a single lecture is impossible.

IV

I shall begin with an illustrative analysis on the third level.

In the first band – that of social teaching – the deficiencies of the Church from 1878 to 1955 are severe. The reasons are various. A permanent one was the constant concentration on the national problem. At the beginning of the period it was the lack of a strong stimulus from the environment and the ten-year duration of the Archiepiscopal Question. Later it was the dissolution of the hierarchy by Britain in the socially important period between 1931 and 1947. The more deep-seated reasons appear to be the following: (a) the classic weakness of Greek theological thought (which has never entered the industrial age) in the social sector; (b) the almost complete absence of theological reflection in Cyprus; (c) the fact that, in contrast with the West, Orthodoxy avoids issuing official teaching on any subject that is not doctrinal. In the long term this reluctance is one of the strong points of Orthodoxy. But in the short term it inevitably constitutes a weakness.

In the case we are examining people's perception of the Cypriot hierarchy (and I repeat that for one-third of this period Cyprus did not have a full hierarchy and remained without an archbishop) was adversely affected by the fact that the hierarchy was the greatest political, social and economic force in Cyprus after the government. In practice teaching was given continuously and the period of independence showed that the Cypriots were superior in social morality and conscience not only to their neighbours in the Middle East but even in relation to the Greeks of the mainland. In the village the priest did not cease even in this period to constitute a fundamental source of justice and peace, although until 1931 the bishops spent months every year perambulating their dioceses and, amongst other things, resolving differences of a purely social character and imposing peace through justice. The social wisdom of the Church thus flowed constantly and was conveyed from the base and not from on high. We shall look at the struggles of the Church to bring about structural changes in the relevant section on social action. Here I only stress that if the Church was backward in its teaching it was not so backward in practice – in contrast with other Churches which in these years developed very beautiful social teachings but hardly put them into effect.

The lack of systematic teaching, however, did not go without evil consequences for the laity. The Christians of Cyprus remained without theoretical bearings, a prey to emotionalism, doubts, amateurism and deceptive propaganda. The religious morality which the Church gave them in the catechism was mostly individualistic without a clear social reference and significance.

The only older cleric who worked in this field was Nikodemos Mylonas, beginning with his important article in Ἐκκλησιαστικὸς Κῆρυξ of 15 October 1917, "The state of the laity", which has rightly been said to mark the appearance of a new generation in Cyprus.

Time unfortunately does not allow me to read the passages which refer to the problems of agricultural workers, of women, or of money-lenders. I shall only give a passage concerning education. Criticising a form of teaching which was not in touch with the realities of life, but "wandered on clouds of ideas", concerned for the most part "with the dative plural of the third declension, with dissyllables ending in *ra* and verbs ending in *mi*", the young twenty-eight-year-old bishop noted:

"Elsewhere teachers are the social levers which give a lift to the masses. Here teachers hold themselves aloof from life and if they do involve themselves in it, it is with the permission of local party bosses and after first enslaving their being to the octopus of the community leader, who is prompt to exile the unfortunate teacher to the other end of the island as soon as he perceives that he is teaching revolutionary ideas (savings banks, co-operatives, agricultural banks, etc.) to the fortunate serfs of his domain."

Regretfully few similarly clear and positive pieces of social analysis and direction have been bequeathed to us by the bishops of this period. The absence of Christian thought, however, even when accompanied by Christian practice, is not a healthy phenomenon. Nor is it sufficient for Christian teaching to censure the fault without saying how it should be corrected, not in a general way but in relation to the specific society and historical circumstances which it is addressing.

By contrast, in its nationalist role the Church developed at certain times a nationalist preaching, if not teaching, which the Christian conscience could only with difficulty not describe as ambiguous. In these circumstances a concession may be discerned to the tendency for religion to be used as a kind of social tonic in times of special national need. It helped to raise morale without increasing the sources of spiritual vitality and without resolving the spiritual conflicts from which Cypriot society suffered. If we add to this the mistaken impression which most people had that the ultimate aim of the Cypriot's life was a restoration of a political nature, the colouring given to this nationalist preaching as well as the crisis which was being prepared for the succeeding period become more intelligible.

From the activity of Christians in the area of "mixed" themes – the second band of the third level – I shall take as an example the question of the continuation of the legal standing and the reality of the autocephalous Church of Cyprus. This is a sector in which the Church, for all the oversights and mistakes of the clergy and the laity, fought fierce battles, both internally and externally, and achieved a total victory.

In 1878 the British found in their new possession a most ancient Orthodox autocephalous Church. The Cypriot autocephaly had been reconstituted in the aftermath of the Turkish capture in 1572 and had been preserved intact until 1878 not only because it had been recognised by an Ecumenical Council but chiefly because it was not only Roman but Greek. (And this is of the greatest importance which to date has escaped the various ambiguities of the identity and national self-awareness of Cypriot Christians. Why did Constantinople restore the Cypriot autocephaly and not abolish it, as it abolished the Bulgarian patriarchate and the Bulgarian autocephalous archdiocese of Justiniana Prima, Ochrid or the patriarchate of the Serbs? Or why did it not colonise the Cypriot throne as it did, when the opportunity arose, the Arab patriarchates of Jerusalem and Antioch with the aim of Hellenising them? Simply because the Sublime Porte and the Phanar in Constantinople knew that the Christians of Cyprus were Greeks.)

The autocephaly, however, which was easily preserved under the sceptre of the sultan and the experienced eye of the Phanar, was threatened when the Cypriots won their independence in this sector under the legally-minded English administration and undertook for themselves the work of continuing it. The problem arose at various times and in various forms.

The first period began with the *Memorandum of the prelates* to the first High Commissioner in February 1879, that is to say, seven months after the change of regime. The prelates, amongst other things, sought legal recognition of the Church's constitution. The same thing was repeated in the *Pancypriot memorandum of the Christian inhabitants* which was handed over a little later. The new administration was not disposed to recognise the Ottoman privileges but respected the sultanic *berats* with which the bishops had been provided (and which Archbishop Sophronios invoked in anger for the first time in 1879 on the occasion of the notorious scandal of the punishment of the priests of Rizokarpasos and Xylophagos by the English administrator of Famagusta by shaving their beards. The unfortunate septuagenarian priests protested loudly and swore that they preferred to have their heads cut off rather than their hair, their beard, and even their mustache! Such serious demonstrations broke out in all the cities and such exasperation was expressed in the entire Middle East that Queen Victoria herself and the Marquess of Salisbury intervened in the affair.)

The British, however, were not opposed to investing a *Settlement* agreed by the Christians, clergy and laity, with the authority of law. In spite of Sophronios's efforts, this simple matter – as one would have thought – was not possible until his death on account of the internal divisions of the Greek community. The prelates were permanently suspicious of each other; the politicians were only concerned with getting their hands on Church property; the laity, of course, were still completely apathetic. Archbishop Sophronios died on 9 May 1900 without having succeeded in twenty-two years in persuading the Cypriots to unite for a while so as to win legal security for this greatest and unique institution – as they had united with such enthusiasm for trifles – this institution which they had inherited from history, which was their Church. The result was that until 1960 the Church never managed to regularise its relations with the civil power (as the ecumenical patriarch, Joachim III, had urged it to do, as Kyrillos II had promised and as Kyrillos III had desired but as Meletios Metaxakes had opposed as metropolitan of Kition and later as patriarch of Alexandria, fearing the intervention of the government and worse – rightly – of the Greek Cypriot deputies). This situation gave the customary Ottoman mentality of the Cypriots the illusion of independence but in real political terms meant that the civil power could intervene with greater ease at the moment it chose, either to preserve the Church, as in 1908, or to punish it, as from 1931 to 1946.

The divisions and lack of leadership on account of the advanced age of the archbishop came to such a pitch by 1899 that it was impossible to elect a new metropolitan of Paphos. When the archbishop died in the following year the Church of Cyprus found itself without a full electoral synod – which must consist of at least three bishops – and shortly afterwards, after treading the crooked paths of the Ottoman Greek synodical system, found itself without a *locum tenens* either, frequently needed the help of other Churches and finally provoked their intervention. An inquorate electoral synod occurred again in 1947 and 1948, that is to say, more times than in the three centuries of Turkish rule. The disturbance was such that in 1947 the presidency of the electoral synod was given to the foreign metropolitan rather than the *locum tenens* as if moral reasons – to do with impartiality – could abolish the order of precedence of the autocephaly.

The Archiepiscopal Question, which caused an upheaval in Cyprus from 1900 to 1910, was brought about by the Cypriots themselves both directly and indirectly. The conflict between the Kyrenians and the Kitians, however, extended beyond the principles or the obstinacies of the two Kyrilloses. Beyond the war between two great medieval princes was the conflict between two orders, the old and the new, two ideologies, the liberal conservatism of Nicosia which had its roots in the Cyprus of the Turkish period and the conservative liberalism of Limassol and Larnaca which came into being with the new generation –which essentially had not known Turkish rule – with the freemasons and with the Greeks of the "Helladic" type such as Katalanos and Zanettos. This was automatically a clash between two attitudes and programmes on the one hand and England on the other. The Kitian majority chose radicalism and had the bold Achilles as its hero; the Kyrenian minority favoured a more flexible and realistic diplomacy and had as its hero the wily Odysseus, through whom the Trojan War was finally won. On the purely ecclesiastical level the roles, as often happens in the comedy of life, were reversed. The politically liberal metropolitan of Kition was in favour of archiepiscopal absolutism, while the conservative metropolitan of Kyrenia supported the synodical administration of the Church and its modernisation. The weapons with which the battle was fought – denunciations, abuse, fists and knives – belonged to the period of Turkish rule. With regard to its ideological content, however, this division belonged to the new era and prefigured in a fateful way the period of English rule, when the permanent drama played out on the Cypriot stage would be the clash between an Odysseus and an Achilles, who would frequently change roles and masks.

The undeclared war broke out in the middle of 1900. After eight years of civil strife and upon the failure of all the attempts to mediate a peace by the neighbouring patriarchates (a new phenomenon, since under Turkish rule the right of final arbitration belonged exclusively to the Ethnarch of the Orthodox at the Phanar), the Ecumenical Patriarch Joachim III (perhaps the greatest Greek of modern times along with Trikoupes and Venizelos), persuaded that the Cypriots were incurably foolish and unreasonable, proceeded to take drastic measures and by a unanimous synodical vote in Constantinople elected Kyrillos of Kyrenia archbishop of Cyprus – even though Kyrillos was "a political boss in clerical clothing" and a friend of his enemy Photios of Alexandria. The election was "wholly irregular and exceptional, in no way ... damaging the continuing autocephaly of your Church", as Joachim III wrote to the Cypriots.

The Kitian deputies reacted immediately. After they had wired Joachim III: "The blood of the Cypriot people be upon your head", such battles broke out in Nicosia that on 28 March 1908 the High Commissioner imposed a kind of martial law (on reading a proclamation which ended "God save the King"), banned the enthronement of the newly-elected archbishop and took possession of the Archiepiscopal Palace, placing it under lock and key. On 25 May he enacted a law through the Legislative Council on the subject of archiepiscopal elections, on the basis of a draft drawn up by the archimandrite of Jerusalem, Meletios Metaxakes – who was later to be so opposed to the legal regulation of relations between Church and State. Rather than obey Joachim III or Theokletos of Athens the Cypriots preferred to hand their Church over to the English, claiming, of course, that they were doing this in order to preserve their autocephaly. In September, through the efforts of each side to prevent an opponent from being elected mayor of Nicosia, they allowed a Turk to be elected to the post.

On 8 April 1909 Kyrillos of Kition was elected archbishop on the basis of the government act, the Kyrenians not voting because they regarded Kyrillos of Kyrenia as the canonical archbishop, while Joachim wrote from Constantinople with bitter irony: "Long live the patriarch of the Cypriots, Zamberlei, and the grey-haired guardians of the masonic lodges!" On 18 February 1910 Kyrillos of Kyrenia submitted his resignation from the archiepiscopal throne of Cyprus to the Great Church and Kyrillos of Kition accorded him the title "His Beatitude the President of Kyrenia", thus recognising indirectly the election of 1908, even though he refused to add "formerly archbishop of Cyprus" or give him precedence over the other metropolitans.

The third period of tribulation for the autocephaly was the period from 1931 to 1946, when the government, hypocritically observing dogmatic and canonical pretexts, tried by every means (even attempting to buy the support of Patriarch Christophoros of Alexandria) to leave the Church without a head until the election of a pro-British or moderate archbishop could be brought about. In 1937 the British government under Chamberlain voted three bills in one night in order to manipulate the archiepiscopal election of that year, excluding not only the remaining metropolitans but also the metropolitan of Trebizond (later archbishop of Athens), Chrysanthos, a great ecclesiastic and diplomatist – as he is referred to in confidential documents at the Foreign Office – whom England feared in Cyprus.

In these years the preservation of the autonomy of the Church of Cyprus was owed externally to the tireless support of the ecumenical patriarchate (now remembered by the Cypriots) and Greece, and internally in the first place to the *locum tenens,* Leontios, a man who while alive was represented by the British as hated by the Greek Cypriots, an exploiter of people, a disturber of the peace, a rogue and a sheep-stealer, but upon his death was described by the *Economist* as "a distinguished man of great culture". The contests of that irenic and sickly cleric, who had been destined for a professorial chair after studies at Columbia University and found himself unwillingly in the arena, were directed not only against the English but also against certain "base flatterers and hunters after honours", as he called them, who belonged to the right-wing upper classes of Nicosia. After the war the government surrendered to him unconditionally and he reigned as archbishop for thirty-six days, dying exhausted on 26 July 1947 at the premature age of fifty-one.

The last unexpected trial in the period 1878–1955 which the Cypriot autocephaly underwent was on 1 March 1949 with the action brought in the Provincial Court of Nicosia against the Holy Synod of Cyprus by the lawyers John Klerides, Pygmalion Ioannides and George Ladas, who sought a ban by the civil court on the Holy Synod (on which also sat two metropolitans of the ecumenical throne) from proceeding to the election of General Representatives for the electoral subdivision of Kelokedaroi. These members of the now left-wing upper classes supported the demand that the legislature of the colonial regime should fundamentally abolish the autocephaly of the Church of Cyprus for the sake of the Kelokedarians.

The Provincial Court of Nicosia defended and confirmed the autocephaly with the historic judgment of 13 March 1948, which was announced by the court's president, the Turkish Cypriot Mehmet Zekya, who gave the Greek Cypriots the following lesson:

> "It would be exceedingly deceptive and unseemly for the Holy Synod ... of Cyprus to be compared to any Organisation or Body or to any Supervisory Council ... Consequently the application of English Common Law does not stand, seeing that there is provision for this in Ottoman Law, which constitutes a part of the legislation in force in Cyprus which regulates the questions raised in this matter."

I have dedicated an excessively large part of this lecture to the manipulation of the autonomy of the Church by the Greek Cypriots, because the Church was the most important independent institution over which the Greek Cypriots had control in the period before the founding of an independent state. Comparisons between how they manipulated their Church and how they later manipulated their state would, I am sure, demonstrate the points I raised at the beginning concerning social history and the history of mental outlooks.

V

The second level of Christian activity, the worldly level, on which the faithful act individually as members of the earthly city, but are obliged to act in a Christian way, is a level on which I shall not dwell in such detail. For we are speaking of a pre-pluralistic society in which all the citizens assert that they are Christians, or pass themselves off as Christians, deceiving themselves that they are such or keeping quiet about the fact that they are not.

I have already noted the *lacunae* in the systematic social teaching of the Church, especially the official teaching. Nevertheless, every sphere of Cypriot society in the period 1878–1955 produced exceptional Christians, particularly the educational and cultural spheres. I shall not give detailed examples because this would take me beyond my allotted time. I mention in passing that Haralambos Papadopoulos, the most famous teacher in Nicosia in this period, was a deeply religious person who also rendered great service to the Church, that journalism was served in a significant way by the Chief Cantor Stylianos Hourmouzios – whose artistic work and legacy is well-known – that Cypriot dance was taught for the first time and saved from oblivion by Hourmouzios's successor at the archiepiscopal lectern, Theodoulos Kallinikos, that one of the founders of Cypriot studies was Metropolitan Nikodemos of Kition (who has left 200 pages of studies and editions of texts and documents, comprising 4.8 per cent of the material in the 13 volumes of Κυπριακά Χρονικά, of which he was the founder). The introduction and development of athletics in Cyprus, even the creation of stadiums, was also due to ecclesiastics in a great degree, such as James of Paphos, while philanthropical work and national benefaction can show great Christian humanists or repentant sinners.

I hope I may be permitted a brief reference to the struggle for social change.

Until 1931 politics – like society in general even later – was monopolised by the Church and leading laymen, usually lawyers, doctors, merchants and money-lenders. The co-operation of these two groups was anything but calm and harmonious, as a superficial reading of history, or even of the ecclesiastical and lay press, can confirm.

Already from the earliest elections of deputies in 1883 the local press unanimously opposed the candidature of clerics, maintaining that the laity did not want the prelates as members of the Legislative Council. "The election of the metropolitan of Kition in two divisions", wrote Chrysanthos of Kyrenia on 8 June 1883 to his friend Ieronymos Varlaam, "proved that both the urban and the rural classes wanted the prelates to represent them in the Legislative Council. I ... have been invited by the country people to accept their representation ... My reply to them was that I have not been included in the electoral lists."

That his judgment of the hostile newspapers was impartial appears from the rest of his letter, which also demonstrates the plurality of views within the ecclesiastical hierarchy in 1883: "As far as I am concerned I regard it as fortunate that I am not involved in politics. A cleric should confine himself to his spiritual duties." And the following graphic piece of gossip follows:

"I do not believe that what has been said about the metropolitan of Kition is true, namely that he prefers to throw off his clerical dress rather than be excluded from the ballot box. This would do him a great injustice, making out that he regards the *schema* as superfluous. All that I have written is in the strictest confidence."

In the Legislative Council, from its foundation until its dissolution in 1931, the best experts on the problems of the people and the strongest defenders of their rights and the need for reform were, by common consent, the elected clerical deputies, Kyprianos Oikonomides, metropolitan of Kition, Kyrillos Papadopoulos, first metropolitan of Kition and later archbishop, and Nikodemos Mylonas, metropolitan of Kition. It was they who also held the leadership of the political opposition on the national question. For the Church the two issues were inseparable, even if it correctly believed that education and social development should serve the cause of political change in the future. Without the clerical deputies the Legislative Council would have been very little more than a debating club of the upper-middle class. After the Second World War the Church opposed the liberal constitutional reforms under British sovereignty and, seeking nothing less than self-determination or *enosis*, broke the reformism of this class, which was also supported by the communists – a novel situation, if nothing else, in the modern history of revolution against the West. As the struggle for liberation of 1955–59 showed, the only institution in Cyprus which without a class base could really mobilise the masses and destroy imperialism was the Church.

That all the clerical deputies were or had been metropolitans of Kition was not simply a matter of chance. Cosmopolitan Larnaca and the new commercial centre of Limassol were – as I have already said – cities with the most social unrest. It was therefore not at all strange that the first cleric to become aware of the problems of the industrial workers, a new class which had begun to appear chiefly in his see of Limassol, was again Nikodemos of Kition.

In the 1930s, however, when the working-class movement and trade unionism were beginning, all the episcopal sees in Cyprus except one were kept vacant by the English and in this most important social epoch a Church administration did not exist. The damage done to Cyprus – which was left wide open to a polarisation between plutocrats and workers – was very deep and as long-term in its consequences as the exile of the archbishop by the English again in 1956, which left the field clear once more for polarisation, violence and national disaster.

The restoration of the hierarchy in 1948 in its first phase under Makarios II saved the working-class movement from political totalitarianism, while after

1950, under Makarios III, it secured, slowly but surely, the free organisation and progress of working-class people within a framework of democratic polycentrism and solidarity.

For an agricultural community, as Cyprus was for the most part in the period we are examining, the chief need was for co-operatives, for only in this way could the agricultural worker be freed from borrowing from money-lenders and the island make progress towards a productive and creative economy. In Cyprus the co-operative movement did not spring from the English legislation on labour in the period of "mukhtar" rule (1931 onwards) –as Sir George Hill, Sir Harry Luke or Lukach and their followers have maintained – but was inspired by the Christianity of the people and the place. The father of the Cypriot co-operative movement was the nephew and ward of Metropolitan Kyprianos of Kition, John D. Oikonomides, who in 1909 founded at Lefkonoiko, with the help of the teacher Mark Haralambous, the first co-operative in Cyprus, on German lines. Also before 1930 the first co-operative in the vital winegrowing district was founded by the schoolmaster priest, Solomon Panagides, to whom I shall return later.

On the legislative side, if the development of the movement was due to a single person it was to the clerical deputy, Nikodemos Mylonas, metropolitan of Kition. We have already looked at his ideas on co-operatives, agricultural banks and savings banks in 1917, when he was still chorepiscopus of Salamis, the English were quiet, and Marxism did not yet exist for Cyprus. The student of the Church's contribution to the change of social structures in the island would have to dwell at least on the speeches on Nikodemos in the Legislative Council. And the 39 pages of his address to the session of 30 March 1926 would suffice. I regret that I do not have the time here to analyse the economic policy which the Church promoted in Cyprus through that clerical deputy (a nephew of Archbishop Kyrillos III and, in these questions, a close collaborator of the metropolitan of Kyrenia, later Archbishop Makarios II). This together with the Church's firm national policy would explain better than the demonstrations of 1931 and Sir Ronald Storrs' *Orientations* (Storrs had been the haughty companion of Lawrence of Arabia) Great Britain's undying hatred for the Church of Cyprus in the second period of colonial rule and until the end.

In Cyprus the Church was the Church of the people, not of an elite, as in England and more generally in the official world of the West. Let us not forget that from 1878 to 1955 not one of the nineteen Cypriot bishops belonged to the urban middle class, which – and this is also an unprecedented phenomenon – never sought to take possession of the five most powerful posts which were then open to the Greeks of the island, that is to say, the four episcopal thrones and the abbacy of Kykkos. To say that Cyprus did not have an urban middle class is an exaggerated generalisation deriving from the importation of foreign models into the study of our own society (in other words, deriving from historical ignorance). When in September, 1879 Onouphrios Iasonides discussed the Cypriot question with Sir Charles Dilke at the Randolph Hotel in Oxford, his family had belonged to the urban middle class for more than a century and indeed had provided Cyprus with bishops. Middle-class Cypriots were either newly-arrived with a *nouveau riche* mentality or else opportunist immigrants from the Mediterranean ports and islands with a Levantine outlook.

The Christian inspiration of the authentic mentality of Cypriot Hellenism, from which sprang the demand for social justice, may manifest itself in many forms. One – a very modern one – would be the study of the dreams of the period. Dreams are a basic source for history as understood and studied today: they are expressions of collective archetypes. As an example I would mention the dream which the well-known folklorist, Nearchos Klerides, said that he saw on the night of 21/22 December 1935 on the eve of his election as secretary of the newly-established Teachers' Savings Bank. He dreamed, he wrote thirty or so years later, that he was a deacon and was officiating in a church dressed entirely in white. The interpretation was given to him, he says, when the following morning his colleagues entrusted to him the important post which he would continue to hold for twenty years until 1955.

The study of the spiritual tools, the conceptual frameworks, the scale of values and the type of sensibility of the period – that is to say the history of its mental outlook – reveals the historical error of those who use Marxist principles to explain the struggle for social justice. They are led astray by the superficial aspects and overlook the deeper reality: the centuries-old longing of the enslaved Greek Orthodox soul to attain social justice and equality. The fortuitous and the transient cannot destroy the common and the mainstream. The historian later remembers the warning of Claude Lévi-Strauss. According to the most distinguished anthropologist of our time, Marxism in the twentieth century is nothing but the greatest Hegelian distortion of history: it is the way in which the planet is westernised in the guise of Eastern dress ... In last year's lecture I stressed that in supporting education (and now I can add social and national emancipation) the Church supported the march towards westernisation independently of the degree in which it succeeded in confronting the new situation.

It cannot be maintained that in the period 1878–1955 the Christian world of Cyprus did as much in the social sphere as theoretically it should have done. "How are so many Christians content simply to be baptised Romans?" wondered the popular poet Paul Liasides in 1946. In the face of real evil and effective injustice the Christian world of Cyprus often did not advance beyond conventional schemes and did not produce outstanding lay trade unionists or socialists as did, for example, the Churches of England and Germany. But this is not a serious criticism, nor should it be overlooked that the spiritual sobriety and cultural traditions of this world preserved the island from the mythical eschatologies or the immobility and inertia which hindered the healthy development of so many communities of the surrounding Middle Eastern countries and the Third World.

VI

I come now to the first level of Christian activity, the spiritual. The heart of this level is of course inaccessible to the historian, who bases his study on the observation of behaviour. He does this although he knows that conduct is not a safe criterion of religious life, since the human person transcends not only its outward behaviour but also its psychological make-up.

In the period 1878–1955 the most basic problem of the inner life of the Church in Cyprus concerned the care and education of the clergy. This was the source of the Church's constant difficulty in responding to the new opportunities which were offered by the environment within which it was called upon to make its presence felt, a presence of witness and service.

At the beginning of the twentieth century the situation in Cyprus was essentially no different from that which Constantine Oikonomos described in relation to Greece at the beginning of the nineteenth century. The ability to read from ecclesiastical books, and often very badly, was the only qualification needed for the post of a priest or deacon, provided he could do it in a melodious voice. In practice the Church did not recognise the need for a special education until 1910, when Meletios Metaxakes, as soon as he was elected metropolitan of Kition, opened a seminary in Larnaca. The idea of a seminary seemed to promise much both for the Church and for education. The fact that it belonged to Metaxakes, however, was not pleasing to the Church of Kyrillos II, while the fact that it belonged to the Church was not pleasing to the Cyprus of the leading laymen. The project thus did not receive any help but was resisted even though it flourished because Metaxakes was not a man to give in. Wholehearted support came with Kyrillos III, and in 1918 the Holy Synod gave official recognition to the seminary which was kept open until 1932. From 1915 it was housed in the beautiful residence of the administrator Claud Cobham, which had been bought by Metaxakes as a result of a generous gift from the Athonite monastery of Vatopedi. The directors were all Ottoman Greeks and among the teachers John Sykoutres was particularly distinguished. In spite of its high level and general contribution to Cyprus, it failed to convince because most of its students did not go on to the priesthood.

After 1931 the climate was not favourable. The Church, now without a head on account of the English, did not succeed in founding a basic seminary until 1949, as soon as the hierarchy was restored under Makarios II, a prelate who during his episcopate in Kyrenia showed a special interest in the education of his clergy. Until 1955, the end of the period we are studying, this seminary held out splendid hopes. Even in 1983, however, the problem of the education of the clergy has not found its final solution. The clergy who once educated the whole of Cyprus under English rule have been turned into a professional body which lacks not only education but even culture.

On the level of wider service I have already referred to several instances in detail. This level is naturally served in the first place by the hierarchy, whose educational level under English rule was high for the period (of the six archbishops of this period four had completed post-graduate studies – three in the West and Sophronios in Greece – while the fifth had two degrees). I shall dwell on one point only, which I have already touched on here, that of the *Linovamvakes*, those 10 000 people who in 1878 were neither Christian nor Muslim in their duties and in terms of privileges were both Greeks and Turks.

This wretched grey area could only arouse the contempt of the people and the castigation of the prelates. A people who, grouped in a theocratic community round their priests, had maintained their faith and national identity for three centuries at the cost of their blood could not be expected to open their arms to such worthless scoundrels as soon as things changed in 1878. Something of this kind could only have been the last word in *rayahism*, or the highest act of politics, or the most superlative act of virtue. History rarely presents authentic criminals, born politicians or genuine saints *en masse*. The closed Ottoman concept of religion and race hindered the evangelisation of the *Linovamvakes*, until they were discovered by Latin propaganda, which aroused the nationalist cunning of Kyrillos II, then metropolitan of Kyrenia. Unfortunately, the imprisonment of mental outlook was severe, missionary zeal was low, the quarrels over the Archiepiscopal Question were long, Islam was active, the foreign Christian administration sided with the latter rather than with Orthodoxy for self-interested reasons, and as a result the *Linovamvakes,* did not all finally return to Christianity. This had a significant effect on the relative proportions of the communities in Cyprus and in the long term would prove to be one of the greater services of the Church to the nation. To give a taste of the period before 1900 I note that the credit for saving ten villages of *Linovamvakes* in the Limassol district from Latin propaganda and securing them for Hellenism belongs to the Limassol moneylenders at 40 and 50 per cent, who, at the Church's instigation, immediately ceased to lend to their formerly Turkish and now Maronite customers until they had forced them to become Orthodox.

Without a suitably educated priesthood it is clear that little could be done on the level of local service, that is to say, on the level of the parish, which constitutes the basic cell of the Church. As if this were not enough, three cities until 1916 (when Kyrillos III moved the see of Kyrenia from Myrtou to Kyrenia) and two until 1955, Famagusta and Limassol, remained without bishops. This was because the hierarchy – for the age-old reasons of finance and privileges – could not decide on a restructuring of the administrative organisation which it had inherited from the papal bull of 1261 and the lay element had no active and responsible part in the administration of the Church. Collectivity and responsibility were concepts which, in spite of the progress which had been made after the Charter of 1914, were weak until 1955 on account of the reluctance of the bishops on the one hand and the fragmentation of the laity concerned on the other. Moreover, the ecclesiological awareness of the followers of the catechetical movements does not seem to have transcended the boundaries of their lecture halls and summer camps or their moral casuistry.

In the meantime the piety of the laity remained rooted in the Orthodox liturgy. A liturgical movement, however, never took place in Cyprus. The disfigurements which the newspapers of the years before 1900 constantly castigated – the lack of care in the services, the lack of cleanliness in the churches, the inattentive attitude of the congregation, the absence of good music and liturgical beauty and order – were put right to a great degree but were still in evidence up to 1955. The iconostases of the period of Turkish rule were not lowered, the heavy Russian vestments were not replaced by lighter ones of Byzantine form, and there was scarcely any discussion of a more active participation of the laity in the liturgy or singing. Devotional art was not reborn within the Orthodox tradition of the icon, but musical standards were raised thanks to Hourmouzios, Kallinikos and the school promoted by the Patmian metropolitan of Paphos, James Andjoulatos. The vernacular architecture and the stone-carving of Kaimakli have raised beautiful churches – like those of Vasa or Petra – but more traditional Byzantine churches of great beauty were built only by the Cretan metropolitan of Kition, Meletios Metaxakes, who brought over from Greece a sheaf of architectural plans. He was responsible for churches of unique dignity and sanctity, such as Agia Napa of Limassol in its original form.

In spite of the apathy of the *nouveau riche* critics of the past, the genuineness of popular piety should not be underestimated, whatever its shortcomings. I dedicated my first lecture last year to that piety. To the well-disposed student that piety – which continued uninterruptedly until 1955 – will always seem like another zone of spiritual geography where plants came to flower which had no need of our man-made fertilisers, irrigation, grafting and containers. The hothouse piety of the educated has much to envy in those plants. Many of those who worshipped in bright, clean churches could never rise beyond the ugly, worm-eaten beams of a Cypriot country church of 1878–1955, in which the simple priest and his parishioner prayed a wholly Christian prayer to the moving strains of their cantor. The meanness of the church building, the books, the candles, the vestments, the oils, did not imply for them the meanness of their religion: all these things were for them a blessing from God. Besides, the period after 1960 proved that the fancy ideas of the pseudo-educated (in Spengler's sense) classes did not transcend the vulgarity of the by-products of the West: nylon altar-cloths, fluorescent lights for the iconostasis and whatever was cheap and artificial, "κεραμεοῦν καὶ φαῦλον".

As the old-calendar controversy and other questions showed after 1924, however, popular piety no longer sufficed for the new vocation of the Church and the more successful accomplishment of its work. Educated clerics were an indisputable necessity and of course they were not entirely lacking. The first seems to have been the *oikonomos* of Larnaca, John Makoules, grandfather of the well-known singer, Jimmy Makoules. A former pupil of the Rizareion School of Athens, he opened two bookshops in Larnaca and Nicosia, published the first Christian periodical of Cyprus, Ἀπόστολος Βαρνάβας (the first issue of which appeared on 25 March 1901 and the last on 23 March 1902), was a noted preacher, taught divinity, French and drawing in secondary schools, published in 1910 one of the first theological works in Cyprus on modern scholarly lines, Χρονολογικὴ ἀκτίνα, wrote newspaper articles, served as a prison chaplain, and died young in 1913. His obituary records that "he was the one and only married priest in the diocese ... or rather in the whole of Cyprus who had benefited from a systematic education".

Father Makoules came from Eastern Roumelia. The more progressive clerics of Cyprus from 1878 to 1955 were mainly Ottoman Greeks such as Metropolitan James of Paphos, Archimandrite Dionysios Haralambous, a former inmate of Dachau and first director of the Seminary – later a distinguished metropolitan of Trikkala – and above all Meletios Metaxakes, metropolitan of Kition. A serious impediment in this area was the excessive local patriotism of the Cypriot islanders. Bishops from the Turkish Empire were not elected again after 1910, not even Dionysios Haralambous, who was not proposed when Makarios III chose Photios of Paphos and Anthimos of Kition (whom he was later obliged to dismiss, a phenomenon which had not happened previously since the end of Turkish rule). The capable metropolitan of Kition, Meletios, who from 1913 was already a candidate for

Constantinople and became archbishop of Athens in 1918 and ecumenical patriarch in 1921, only received one vote in the Cypriot archiepiscopal election of 1916, while the abbot of Kykkos, Kleopas, who was also unsuccessful, received twenty-three votes. It should be noted, however, that apart from Metaxakes' non-Cypriot origins, a decisive part in his failure of 1916 was played by his being suspected of modernism, his unconcealed admiration for Venizelos, and his authoritarian character.

Another example of a distinguished married cleric of the period was the *oikonomos* of Limassol, Solomon Panagides, whose activity extends from 1933 to 1953, an admirer of Metaxakes and a product of his seminary. An exceptional teacher, he founded the first catechetical school of Cyprus in the Limassol parish of Agia Triada in 1933. In 1937 he introduced into Cyprus the institution of Christian summer camps, with the first at Ai-Gianni of Agros, while in 1939 he founded the first Christian organisation for young people in Cyprus – the Limassol OXEN. An ardent preacher, a confessor and a teacher at the Gymnasium, he also supported the theatre, pursued agricultural studies and succeeded in discovering two unknown Cypriot wild flowers. An old student of Marxism in Greece, he tried to inspire a movement of Christian socialism. He organised charitable works on new lines and founded, in spite of the opposition of freemasons and communists, a night school for working children in Limassol, where lessons were given in Greek, arithmetic, history, religious studies and English (a bold move for the time). The Solomon Panagides Foundation perpetuates his memory and at the same time indicates what the state of the Church of Cyprus could have been if the celibate clergy had been more conscious of their duties towards their married colleagues, who bore the brunt of the Church's work and yet were only fed crumbs from its wealth.

In spite of shining examples, since the work of evangelisation could not be undertaken by the parishes it was always lame and lacking in impulse. Preaching is an example. Coming from above rather than from the life of the parish, it was carried out chiefly by laymen, who having no pastoral gifts or responsibilities channelled it into moralising sermons in the pompous rhetoric of the period. "Even though the pulpit speaks very rarely," complained Nikodemos of Salamis in 1917, "it dissipates itself on themes reeking of medieval tombs."

With regard to the press, in the period 1878–1955 about 38 printed periodicals were in circulation, the most important of which were the Ἐκκλησιαστικὸς κῆρυξ of Meletios Metaxakes (1910–1918), Ἀπόστολος Βαρνάβας in its first two phases (1918–1924 and 1929–1936) and the newspaper Ἐκκλησιαστικὴ Ζωή, which was published by Archbishop

Makarios III, while on the purely catechetical side there was Ἀπόστολος Παῦλος of Larnaca and Φωνή of the Limassol OXEN.

Noteworthy for its missionary zeal was the contribution of the Athenian community of preachers, Zoe, in the 1920s and 30s when it was still in its prime and before it hardened, as happened later, into a system of *petit bourgeois* piety.

If Christian perfection consists in purity of heart, without which there is no salvation and there are no true pastors, an authentic spirituality beyond moral virtue cannot be developed in a Church without a genuine monasticism. The period 1878–1955 is a period of decadence of the stavropegial monasteries. Strictly speaking, they cannot really be called monasteries since they ceased to clothe the brethren in the monastic *schema*. Already in 1897 the French visitor Deschamps noted that before novices learn to use a pen they must learn to use a broom and this feudal system of education hardly improved before 1955.

For the Church the regime of these places of pilgrimage was an obstacle, because they controlled the greater part of ecclesiastical revenues. A permanent policy of all the archbishops of the period was by one means or another to reduce this exempt regime to obedience to the Synod, as was the case in the other Orthodox Churches and had been expressly requested by the ecumenical patriarchate before the crisis which lasted from May to September 1931 and led to the fall and permanent suspension of the abbot of Kykkos.

Within this atmosphere of hostility between the hierarchy and laity on the one hand and the stavropegial monasteries on the other, and with the internal monastic divisions and intrigues which were always undermining the power of the monasteries, only one monk between 1878 and 1948 was allowed to ascend an episcopal throne, Epiphanios of Paphos in 1890. In the first third of the century Abbots Gerasimos and Kleopas of Kykkou in spite of their university background were always runners-up in the episcopal elections. After failing four times as an episcopal candidate and once as a candidate for the Legislative Council, Kleopas finally lost his own post and the practice of his priesthood. The situation was changed in 1948 by Makarios II, who favoured the fallen Kleopas for the throne of Paphos, while the strong man of the archiepiscopate, Polykarpos Ioannides, favoured another monk of Kykkos for the throne of Kition (who later became Makarios III), in order to block the election of the Cypriot archimandrite of Egypt, Andronikos Vryonides, whom he suspected of being a moderate or even pro-British. When in 1950 Makarios, now to the chagrin of Ioannides, ascended the archiepiscopal throne, he was the first archbishop from a monastic background since 1840, during which one hundred and ten years celibate secular clergy were preferred for the archiepiscopate, chiefly former teachers, such as Sophronios, Kyrillos II, Kyrillos III and Leontios. Makarios III would show that the dynamic energy of the stavropegial monasteries, far from having been exhausted, could still raise up individuals of exceptional spiritual stature.

Genuine traditional monasticism, however, was preserved only at Stavrovouni, the renaissance of which began in 1875 with the then superior, Dionysios, a Cypriot Athonite monk of the Skete of Kafsokalyvia. The new period of brilliance was given official recognition in 1910 with the installation of the first abbot, Barnabas, by Meletios Metaxakes of Kition. During the abbacy of Barnabas, a former member of the Athonite monastery of Karakallou, the austere *coenobium* grew to sixty members. Photographs show him as an old man with a youthful face. Meek and guileless, he rejected every mark of honour and did not even ever become a priest, but lived dedicated to prayer and asceticism, inspiring others in word and deed with the non-possessiveness, virginity and obedience of the monastic life.

Stavrovouni shone in this period with the purest Christian light, even though the world did not always have eyes with which to see it. Simple men from humble backgrounds reached there the heights of virtue of the early desert Church. Such were the brothers Barnabas, Kallinikos and Gregory from Kaimakli, Paisios and Damaskenos from Aradippou, Dionysios, a former teacher who dedicated his life to the pursuit of noetic prayer, Stephen, Makarios and Theodosios, and the great spiritual father of the Church of Cyprus at that time, Hieromonk Kyprianos. He had learned from the great Athonite hesychasts Kallinikos and Gerasimos and directed the spiritual lives of thousands of ordinary people in Cyprus. He used to celebrate the divine Liturgy with his eyes shut and an expression of mourning, shedding tears before the Sacrament.

The *locum tenens*, Leontios, a sick and tormented man who had always loved the monastic life, frequently used to stay with these people, provoking the ironic comments of the ecclesiastical establishment. In 1939 Leontios invited Paisios and Damaskenos, together with some others, to transplant Stavrovouni to Trooditissa, and later brought from Khartoum an old fellow-monk of his at St George Alamanos, the devout Cypriot archimandrite Pankratios, who came from Assia in the province of Famagusta, to be its abbot. Trooditissa thus became the second *coenobium* of the period, an oasis of inspiration and enlightenment for the faithful. According to worldly criteria the life of these *coenobia* did not achieve any startling success. But when it is studied according to the criteria of the Gospel it shows that within the mysterious power of the holiness, which is the power of God, the Church of the desert attained for its people something which should make the Church of the world feel very humble about its plans, programmes and works.

The third *coenobium*, from which later began the renewal of women's monasticism after its disappearance in the period of Turkish rule, was St George Alamanos, which was dedicated as a women's monastery by the metropolitan of Kition, later Archbishop Makarios III, an admirer of simple lay monasticism and Cypriot hagiology – to which he had applied himself since 1948. In 1968 he completed his work with the publication of his well-known lexicon of Cypriot saints, *Κύπρος, ἡ ἁγία νῆσος*.

In the period, however, until 1955 the greatest archbishop of Cyprus was still Kyrillos III (1916–1933). This outstanding personage was born in Prasteio in the Mesaoria in 1859 and was the last archbishop who had known Ottoman rule. In his face all the virtues of the great archbishops of the Turkish period shone in perfect harmony: prudence, good sense, the dignified recognition of compelling necessity and the avoidance of extremes, united with persistent work for a predetermined end, the love of learning and an antipathy to ostentation and vainglory. The years of his archiepiscopate, 1916–1933, were the golden age of the Church of Cyprus in the period 1878–1955, and were marked by a more dynamic and more efficacious Synod, with James and later Leontios of Paphos, Metaxakes and later Mylonas of Kition and Makarios of Kyrenia, who subsequently became the heroic Makarios II. In spite of his having led the so-called "old caste" in the period of the Archiepiscopal Question, Kyrillos proved to be one of the more progressive archbishops, Venizelist in his personal political views and in religious matters, according to his sycophantic opponents, a Makrakist, that is to say, a supporter of change in the ecclesiastical situation.

He expressed his opinion about the bishops of the period before 1900 in a letter dated 31 May 1895 to his brother Jago Vasileiades, who lived in Alexandretta. Justifying his hesitation before accepting the metropolitanate of Kyrenia, he notes:

"With regard to the conditions under which the prelates live, I thought and believed that I should never have been able to satisfy the myriad demands of one person or another with imaginary favours on my part. I judged myself unable to pretend, as many of the present-day bishops do, saying one thing and thinking another. Intrigues and machinations are very frequent amongst our clergy and indeed are praised by people of our era and described as intelligent and apt but in no way will I resort to them even in thought. In short, I disapprove of acting in a political fashion."

It could be said that this was the programme of his archiepiscopacy, which was to begin twenty-one years later. As soon as he became archbishop in 1916 he applied himself energetically to the work of renewing the life of the Church, supported by Meletios Metaxakes and supporting him in turn without adopting his methods or extreme positions.

With regard to the administrative organisation of the Church he proposed drastic changes which even seventy years later have still not been adopted. In 1916, having already moved his former see during Nikodemos's period as *locum tenens* from Myrtou to Kyrenia, he announced to the Synod that he judged the creation of new metropolitanates of Limassol and Famagusta to be a matter of necessity. He also announced this to the laity but opposition was strong for the same reasons that prevented the creation of a metropolitanate of Famagusta until 1974. Similarly he was prevented from creating protopresbyters, as he had proposed and keenly desired, so that the administration could be centralised and local co-operation could be more easily developed (an idea completely up-to-date but already the system in the Early Church).

Although others for decades both before and after him did not succeed in issuing a single canon, Kyrillos III, apart from a host of encyclicals which did not leave a single theme in Cypriot society or the Cypriot Church untouched, issued twelve *Special Canons, Decrees and Statutes* with a total of 569 articles and the *Statutory Charter* of 1929 with another 231 articles, making him the greatest legislator of the Church of Cyprus of all time.

His concern for the clergy was unfailing. Apart from officially adopting the Seminary and giving it his constant support, already in 1916 he was encouraging the foundation of an Association of Priests, which he helped develop, although his successors allowed it to lapse and did not allow its reconstitution in case it should threaten their monarchical rule. At the same time he sent clerics abroad for their studies, to Halki, Athens and even Oxford (where Kyrillos II had also sent his nephew for higher studies, who subsequently became Makarios II). His expectations, however, were not fulfilled in every case.

With regard to preaching, Kyrillos III constantly invited preachers from Greece, and he himself perambulated his two dioceses, Nicosia and Famagusta, alternately every year, celebrating the Liturgy, preaching and resolving differences in every village without exception. These perambulations began, as in the nineteenth century, on 27 June and lasted until 7 September, when the archbishop returned to Nicosia. Kyrillos III used a landau drawn by horses which he used to buy from the stables of the government villa of Athalassa. He was the last archbishop of Cyprus who perambulated his dioceses in this manner, away from his seat for two-and-a-half months every year.

As for his philanthropic work, it suffices for me to say that nothing happened in Cyprus during his archiepiscopate without his aid. He showed a special personal interest in the Foundlings Home and the Orphanage, that is, in supporting the unprotected child.

Above all, Kyrillos III was the model of a learned bishop. He took care that the manuscripts of the Archiepiscopate should be catalogued and preserved, he appointed Kyrillos II's nephew, Constantine Myrianthopoulos, to put the Archive in order, and he was in reality the founder of the library of the archiepiscopal palace, which owes whatever of value it still contains to the scholarly Kyrillos III. He published the Greek version of J. Hackett, translated and supplemented by Ch. Papaioannou. At the suggestion of S. Menardos he invited the academician G. Soteriou to come from Athens and study, catalogue and photograph the Byzantine monuments of Cyprus at the expense of the Church. This resulted finally in the publication of Soteriou's imposing work under that title. With an inheritance of £500 Kyrillos III founded his important *Literary Competition,* and dedicated his entire wealth to the advancement of Cypriot literature, founding in 1929 the Κληροδότημα Ἐκδόσεων, for funding publications, with a capital of £1 000, an enormous sum for that time. At the expense of the bequest of Kyrillos III the monographs on Cypriot themes of L. Philippou, I. Peristianes, K.I. Myrianthopoulos, K. Georgiades, Kl. Myrianthopoulos and others were published, that is to say the fundamental works of native Cypriot historical research and still the most important tools at the disposal of the modern student.

The broad spirit of the old archbishop (in spite of his contempt for the affair of the *Linovamvakes*) was also responsible for the introduction to Cyprus of the new ecumenical movement. The Church of Cyprus was represented at the Lausanne Congress in 1927 and at the Dialogues with the Old Catholics and the Anglicans in 1930 and 1931. The "branch theory" of the Church had nevertheless already been definitively rejected by Cyprus in 1898, with the painstaking printed response of the theologian of the Pancyprian Gymnasium, S. Spyridakis, to the theories of the Anglican chaplain in Nicosia, J. Duckworth. In the periodical Ἀπόστολος Βαρνάβας during the archiepiscopacy of Kyrillos III one may read accounts of the celebrations on the eleventh centenary of St Ansgar in Sweden, of the scholarly work of Harnack, or of the latest encyclicals of the archbishop of Canterbury, accompanied at the same time by a constant flow of articles against Millenarianism or against Latin and Protestant propaganda in Cyprus.

On the national question the influence of Kyrillos III was irenic and unwaveringly unionist, but without fulminations and nationalist exaggerations. He was the only archbishop who won the respect and admiration of the British, in spite of the fact that he clashed with them just as frequently as anyone else. In relation to the political divisions of Greece, which had such a profound effect on Cyprus that the royalists and the Venizelists wanted to fight for Union with Greece in accordance with who was in power in Athens, Kyrillos III summarised his policy – of course in vain many times – with the slogan: "Country before politicians."

With regard to his family and those around him his attitude was austere. I mention as an example that when Archbishop Kyrillos II died in 1916 he left £600 for the building of a new residence for the archbishop and twice in 1919 and 1920 the Throne Committee decided on the erection of a new Archiepiscopal Palace to enhance the authority of the Ethnarch. Kyrillos III, however, refused to agree to it, declaring that he was not going to put the Church in debt so as to raise up palaces for himself. His instinct to save and preserve was so strong that in the sixteen years of his primacy he did not sell one inch of ecclesiastical land. His donations for the common good and the fact that on his death he left nothing to his relations prove that his attitude sprang not from avarice but from his religious convictions.

In his personal life he was a man of study, asceticism and prayer. He was the last archbishop who celebrated all the services daily in his private apartment, in accordance with the system that prevailed under Turkish rule. He fasted most severely and his servants observed him at night making constant prostrations full-length on the ground and when he became tired praying kneeling by his bed. This asceticism, which was betrayed only by the keyholes, was pursued by him steadfastly into extreme old age even in periods of exhaustion. The people, in spite of regarding him as comically thin and sallow, venerated him as a saint and wonder-worker (an affirmation which I heard from his servant at that time who was sure that he saw the Apostle Andrew helping Kyrillos). In cases of prolonged death agony the people of Nicosia used to sprinkle the dying person with water which they had previously sent to be blessed by the aged archbishop. The absolution of the archbishop signified divine forgiveness and the finding of longed-for peace.

In 1920 the whole of Cyprus celebrated his twenty-five years as a bishop. The celebrations reached their apogee in 1931, when he carried out official ceremonies at the monastery of the Apostle Barnabas in Salamis to mark the 1500 years of the Cypriot autocephaly, published a commemorative volume and received as a final honour the Grand Cross of the Romanian Crown. On 13 March 1929 the newspaper Ἐλευθερία was already writing:

"Within the last hundred years Cyprus has perhaps not seen a finer episcopate ... Preaching is constantly becoming more widespread. A not inconsiderable impulse is being given to education. Whenever funds are being collected the Church is in the forefront ... All the evidence shows that ecclesiastical activity is being rationalised and organised in an ever more effective way."

The violent outburst of October 1931 and the inexorable vengeance of England against the Church after that crisis destroyed the work of Kyrillos III, who died in 1933 full of anxiety for Cyprus, which he was leaving in the hands of an inexperienced young bishop of thirty-six years of age.

In 1950 another young archbishop would take up the succession, Makarios III, who like Leontios was thirty-six years old. His ideal was his predecessor on the throne of Kition, Nikodemos Mylonas.

VII

This in broad outline is a history of the Church of Cyprus in the period from 1878 to 1955. I have said *a* history and not *the* history of the Church of Cyprus in this period because the full, precise and unique understanding of history belongs only to God, who will reveal it to us finally at the Judgment.

Knowing that pure objectivity is inaccessible to a human being (without accepting that history is inevitably relativistic, since I believe in the existence of an absolute truth), I have tried to be "sublimely subjective", in Paul Ricoeur's phrase, that is to say, methodically to go beyond the simple subjectivity of everyday opinion.

My reader must remember that I was speaking in the Cyprus of 1983 and especially for an audience of the Popular University. In another country at some other time in the past or the future I would surely have addressed my audience differently. I thus acknowledge that I was speaking from a particular viewpoint, making it clear to my audience, however, that no one can write history from all viewpoints and for everyone.

The fact that I am a Christian means simply that I see in the history of the Church a special significance, that is to say, I interpret it from a certain perspective and from within a certain existential commitment. If I were not a Christian that does not mean I would have been less bound by commitment. I could have been a liberal, a Marxist, a Buddhist or a capitalist. Such people also have their commitments or attachments and interpret events giving them a certain colouring in accordance with these. On the contrary, my own emotional involvement with the object of my study, the Church, far from narrowing my perspective, affords it greater possibilities of comprehensiveness. My belief that a purely objective historical perspective is impossible, belonging only to God, is something I have already acknowledged.

I would draw the following conclusions from the history I have narrated this evening:

1. The study of the period 1878–1955 requires some care. The sources, in the first place, are rather difficult, not easily accessible, not classified and not gathered together in a single centre. The secondary literature is no less problematic. The English have expressed a series of colonial and neo-colonial points of view. The Ottoman Greek politicians have left their memoirs in the form of apologias. The products of Cypriot party politics are "political programmes for the past" rather than history. Modern monographs, written mostly in English, usually belong to the sociological, political or legal disciplines and not to the historical. The older aids –N. Katalanos, Ph. Zannetos, G. Frangoudes – in spite of their continuing basic value are written on the whole from one side of the Greek political divide. A more methodical perspective is indispensable if a modern historical account is to be written. And the student must above all examine and judge *problems* and not simply set out a chronological succession of external (and often unimportant) events.

2. The society and mentality of Cyprus show that the period of English rule cannot constitute for historical research a Toynbeean self-contained field. For it to be understood it needs to be approached like a promontory of the deep Ottoman hinterland. Nothing else will enable it to be interpreted correctly.

3. In the period 1878–1955 the Church of Cyprus managed in spite of the difficult conditions of the times to transcend the collapse of the Hellenism of Asia Minor and the Orthodoxy of the Middle East, the collapse, that is to say, of its vital environment. A Church which at the beginning of the century was almost an insignificant province which gazed in awe at the patriarchal thrones around it was by 1955 the strongest bastion of Hellenism and of Orthodoxy in the East.

Immediately after the change of regime the Church, which was already prepared from the previous era, was able through its economic strength, its reasonably good administration and its identification with its people to organise and offer to the Greeks of Cyprus the new education and social concerns which were of vital importance. It thus excluded the possibility of self-interested foreign assistance and education, either from its political masters or, chiefly, from the heterodox Protestant or Latin propagandas which at that time were decimating the Orthodox Middle East. A mixture of Hellenistic benefaction and Christian philanthropy, the solidarity with which the Church inspired society from 1878 to 1955, if not entirely ideal, was, however, in practice a unique phenomenon in both the Balkans and the Middle East.

If Britain ensured the physical survival of the Greeks of Cyprus at a time when genocide and mass expulsion of Christians was the general rule in the

Middle East, the preaching, the pastoral care and the cultural and social service of the Church drove out of the land of Cyprus the possibility of any kind of ethno-religious change or social polarisation, thus ensuring the continuity of the existence and the identity of Cyprus, not for the sake of survival in itself but for the sake of witness, the witness of the Gospel and of Hellenism in its historical cradle, the Eastern Mediterranean. Existence without witness is pointless and therefore useless, a prolongation not of a life, or even of survival, but of a mortal anxiety.

4. Cypriot society in the period 1878–1955 was rural, almost of the medieval type, for the most part. The fact that the Church was not that which the "smart sophists" of that time or today would have wished was not necessarily an impediment. The Church in its interior structures was conservative because it was the Church of the people and therefore of the village communities.

Rural societies are everywhere rather conservative. In its teaching the Church spoke the language of the farmers and in its liturgical life followed their rhythms, for Cyprus was a land of agriculturalists. The Church belonged to the cultivators of the soil, because they were the poor and the place of Christ was there with them. If the present-day Christian is more interested in interpersonal relationships and social justice, the urban Cypriot of that time was no doubt interested in his individual salvation in the next life, while the religion of the country-dweller was attached, as always, to the shrines of the saints, from whom he sought protection from the adversities of everyday life. Just as the Church today has the duty to humanise the folklore of comic strips and the pace of city life, so then it had to humanise country folklore. Which of the two is more ridiculous or more dangerous it is not difficult to judge.

In the measure with which Jesus identified himself with "the least of this world" the real history of the Church is not the history of the great and powerful but of the weak and insignificant. Theological historical thought – which I have hardly touched upon this evening – is not interested in what the great men of the world have done, even if they are called archbishops, or what the respectable middle classes have done, but it finds out, like God, who were the poor of a particular system, that is, outside it, without value, useless and therefore disposable, and asks what the disciples of Christ did for them. For salvation belongs to those who see Jesus in the faces of the poor and serve him. This, according to the twenty-fifth chapter of Matthew's Gospel, is the essential criterion of the true history of the Church. It is on this basis that Christian Cyprus of 1878–1955 will be judged at the ultimate tribunal of metahistory.

5. In external affairs the Church of Cyprus in the period 1878-1955 can be called neither particularly conservative nor liberal. Its attitude was pastoral and catholic, that is to say, not hostile to other faiths. In a period of change, when Cypriot society was in some ferment, the Church did not remain cool or indifferent. It was rather in ferment itself and favoured contacts with the new culture in the form introduced by the Greece or England of that time, avoiding, however, both the Scylla of deracinated levantinism and the Charybdis of the old Ottoman mentality. It thus remained the still centre of a process of exchange, being at the same time the chief factor of internal cultural contact between town and country, the past and the present, the island and the wider Greek world, the spiritual tradition of the East and the material wealth of the West.

6. From 1878 to 1955 the Church continued to give the Cypriot people as a whole a moral framework, thus making it a nation. There is nothing especially Christian in the natural virtues, of which one of the more attractive is basically patriotism (in spite of the fact that it can evidently easily pass into the pathological forms of nationalism or imperialism, of collective pride or collective rapacity). Religion and politics merge into a unity only in the City of God. In plunging into the fire of political activity Cypriot Christianity was often threatened with destruction. Not to have taken part, however, in the work of building a human society for the Cypriots would not have meant the preservation of its odour of sanctity. It would have meant a frozen state of isolation, which is the consequence of indifference to the elemental needs of human beings.

For the people of Cyprus their liberation from the immoral regime of colonial rule was a question of the life or death of their human identity if not of their Greek identity (if the two could be separated). Confronted with an arrogant occupying power, which based its right to be there on its financial and military strength, the Church inspired its subject people with faith in the spirit and with confidence in itself, in its dignity, its history, its calling, and in the power of Justice. A proof of the grandeur of Cyprus and its dynamism, of what it once was in civilised society and what, if it wished, it could again become, was its autocephalous Church. Without this living historical institution of continuity and performance, what would modern Cyprus have been but, in the worse case, a military base or at best yet another grocer's shop in the Middle East?

A firm rock rooted in its soil (but with its head well above ground), the Church of the period 1878–1955 remains, for all its exaggerations and defects, fundamental. That is why it refuses to compromise and obligingly go wherever the wind blows. It travels along the road not of change but of necessity. Its eyes only seek out suffering. It taught the Cypriots not the modern desperate heroism of egocentric revolution but the Christian asceticism of redeemed mankind, the heroism of a person's dedication and self-offering for the sake of a world.

7. In the period 1878–1955 the Church kept Greek Cyprus a *Christian* community even if the "community of Christians" was, in this period as always, a "little flock". Without a lot of words or showy gestures this Church, although humble in worldly terms, achieved what other great, well-organised and learned Churches failed to achieve. It remained a national Church when they remained confined to a social class or else were marginalised. From 1878 to 1955 Christianity in Cyprus did not lose the workers, while keeping the peasants and middle classes. This fact constitutes the most eloquent apologia for the work of that Church.

After the Second World War, however, the gulf between the values that were presumed and those that were actually experienced became evident. The period 1955–59 was an armistice, a prelude to a struggle for liberation which was led by the Church.

Cyprus, one of the most ancient Christian countries, would upon acquiring independence change gradually into a country in need of missionaries. It is still too early to judge the outcome of this work. Cyprus could take the path either of spiritual renewal or of dechristianisation, both spiritual and physical. In the period 1878–1955 the Church was for Cyprus an inspiration and a blessing. For the Church of today to turn back, however, in nostalgia to this Church would only help it to turn into a pillar of salt. The Lord is calling it to climb new mountains.

BIBLIOGRAPHIES

I BYZANTINE AND FRANKISH CYPRUS

AHRWEILER, H., *Byzance et la mer*, Paris, 1966.

— Λιμάνια στὸ Βυζάντιο, Piraeus, 1990.

BECK, H.-G., *Kirche und theologische Literatur im byzantinische Reich*, Munich, 1959.

BROOKS, E.W., "Byzantines and Arabs in the Time of the Early Abbasids", *The English Historical Review* 15 (1900), pp. 728–47.

BROWNING, R., "Byzantium and Islam in Cyprus in the Early Middle Ages", *EKEEK* 9 (1977–79), pp. 101–16.

CALEPIO, A., *Vera et fidelissima Narratione del successo dell'espugnatione & defensione del Regno de Cipro*, in Estienne de Lusignan, *Chorograffia et breve historia universale dell'isola de Cipro ... per in sino al 1572*, Bologna, 1573.

CAPPUYNS, N., "Le Synodicon de Chypre au XIIe siècle", *Βυζάντιον* 10 (1935), pp. 489–504.

CHARANIS, N., "Ethnic Changes in the Byzantine Empire in the Seventh Century", *DOP* 13 (1959), pp. 23–44.

— "The Transfer of Population as a Policy in the Byzantine Empire", *Comparative Studies in Society and History* 3 (1960–61), pp. 140–54.

COBHAM, C.D., *Excerpta Cypria*, Cambridge, 1908.

CONSTANTINE PORPHYROGENITUS, *De administrando imperio* (eds, G. Moravcsik & R.J.H. Jenkins), Washington, DC, 1967.

DAGRON, D., "Minorités ethniques et religieuses dans l'Orient byzantin à la fin du Xe et au XIe siècle: l'immigration syrienne", *Travaux et mémoires* 6 (1976), pp. 177–216.

DARROUZÈS, J., "Les documents byzantins du VIIe siècle sur la primauté romaine", *REB* 23 (1965), pp. 42–88.

— *Les Regestes des Actes du Patriarcat de Constantinople*, Paris, 1977.

— "Listes épiscopales au concile de Nicée II (787)", *REB* 33 (1975), pp. 5–76.

— *Notitiae episcopatuum Ecclesiae Constantinopolitanae*, Paris, 1981.

— "Textes synodaux Chypriotes", *REB* 37 (1979), pp. 5–122.

DELEHAYE, H., "Saints de Chypre", *AB* 26 (1907), pp. 161–297.

DIKIGOROPOULOS, A.I., *Cyprus "Betwixt Greek and Saracens"* A.D. 647–965, D.Phil. Diss., Oxford, 1961.

— "The Church of Cyprus during the Period of the Arab Wars, A.D. 649–965", *GOTR* 11 (1965-66), pp. 237–79.

— "The Political Status of Cyprus A.D. 648–965", *Report of the Department of Antiquities, Cyprus 1940–1948*, Nicosia, 1958, pp. 94–114.

DOANIDES, S.I., "Ἡ παραίτησις Νικολάου τοῦ Μουζάλωνος ἀπὸ τῆς ἀρχιεπισκοπῆς Κύπρου. Ἀνέκδοτον ἀπολογητικὸν ποίημα", *Ἑλληνικά* 7 (1934), pp. 109–50.

DVORNIK, F., *The Idea of Apostolicity in Byzantium and the Legend of the Apostle Andrew*, Cambridge, Mass., 1958.

DYOVOUNIOTES, K., "Νεφύτου Ἐγκλείστου ἀνέκδοτα ἔργα", *EEBS* 13 (1937), pp. 40–9.

— "Νεφύτου Ἐγκλείστου ἀνέκδοτον ἐγκώμιον εἰς Ἰωάννην τὸν Χρυσόστομον", *EEThSA* 1 (1926), pp. 329–45.

EHRHARD, A., *Uberlieferung und Bestand d. hagiogr. und homilet. Lt. d. griech. Kirche*, III. I, Leipzig, 1943.

EICKHOFF, E., *Seekrieg und Seepolitik zwischen Islam und Abendland. Das Mittelmeer unter byzantinischer und arabischer Hegemonie (650–1040)*, Berlin, 1966.

GENNADIOS, Metropolitan of Heliopolis and Thera, Ἱστορία τοῦ Οἰκουμενικοῦ Πατριαρχείου, Athens, 1953.

GEORGIOU, Ph., Εἰδήσεις ἱστορικαὶ περὶ τῆς Ἐκκλησίας Κύπρου, Athens, 1875.

GERMANOS, Metropolitan of Sardis and Pisidia, "Ἱστορικὴ μελέτη περὶ τῆς Ἐκκλησίας τῶν Σάρδεων καὶ τῶν ἐπισκόπων αὐτῆς", Ὀρθοδοξία 4 (1929), pp. 16–18.

GILL, J., "The Tribulations of the Greek Church in Cyprus 1196–c.1280", *Byzantinische Forschungen* 5 (1977), pp. 73–93.

GOUILLARD, J., "Le Synodikon de l'Orthodoxie", *Travaux et mémoires* 2 (1967), pp. 1–316.

HACKETT, J., *A History of the Orthodox Church of Cyprus*, London, 1901.

HADJIIOANNOU, I., Ἱστορία καὶ ἔργα Νεοφύτου πρεσβυτέρου μοναχοῦ καὶ ἐγκλείστου, Alexandria, 1914.

— Νεοφύτου πρεσβυτέρου μοναχοῦ καὶ ἐγκλείστου, Ἑρμηνεία εἰς τοὺς Ψαλμούς, Athens, 1935.

HADJIPSALTES, K., "Ἡ Ἐκκλησία Κύπρου καὶ τὸ ἐν Νικαίᾳ Οἰκουμενικὸν Πατριαρχεῖον ἀρχομένου τοῦ 13ου μ.Χ. αἰῶνος", *KS* 28 (1964), pp. 137–68.

— "Νεοφύτου πρεσβυτέρου μοναχοῦ καὶ ἐγκλείστου βιβλιογραφικὸν σημείωμα", *EKEEK* 6 (1972–3), pp. 125–32.

— "Συμβολαὶ εἰς τὴν ἱστορίαν τῆς Ἐκκλησίας Κύπρου κατὰ τὴν βυζαντινὴν περίοδον", *KS* 18 (1954), pp. xxvii–clv.

HANSON, C., "Epiphanius of Constantia and the Defense of the Cypriot Orthodoxy and Ecclesiastical Independence", *Seventh Annual Byzantine Studies Conference, November 13–15, Abstracts of Papers*, Boston, 1981, pp. 50–1.

HEAD, C., *Justinian II of Byzantium*, Madison, Milwaukee & London, 1972.

HILL, G., *A History of Cyprus*, Cambridge, 1940–52 (IV vols).

HORNA, K., "Das *Hodoiporikon* des Konstantin Manasses", *BZ* 13 (1904), pp. 313–55.

HUSSEY, J.M., *Church and Learning in the Byzantine Empire, 867-1185*, London, 1937.

— *The Orthodox Church in the Byzantine Empire*, Oxford, 1986.

IOANNOU, P.-P., *Discipline générale antique*, I, 1, Rome, 1962 (Pontificia commissione per la redazione del codice di diritto canonico orientale, *Fonti*, IX).

IORGA, N., *France de Chypre*, Paris, 1966.

JEHEL, G., *La Méditerranée médievale de 350 à 1450*, Paris, 1992.

JENKINS, R.J.H., "Cyprus between Byzantium and Islam, A.D. 688-965", *Studies presented to D.M. Robinson* (eds G.E. Mylonas & D. Raymond), St Louis, Mo., 1953, pp. 1006–1014.

JUGIE, M., "Le témoinage de Néophyte le Reclus sur l'Immaculée Conception", *Bessarione* 35 (1919), pp. 7–20.

— "Néophyte le Reclus (1134–1220?), "Homélies sur la Nativité de la Sainte Vièrge et sa Presentation au Temple", *Homélies mariales byzantines* in *PO* 16, Paris, 1922, pp. 526–38.

— "Un opuscule inédit de Néophyte le Reclus sur l'incorruptibilité du corps du Christ dans l'Eucharistie", *REB* 7 (1949), pp. 1–11.

KONIDARES, G.I., "Ἡ θέσις τῆς αὐτοκεφάλου Ἐκκλησίας τῆς Κύπρου ἔναντι τοῦ Οἰκουμενικοῦ πατριαρχείου κατὰ τὸν Θ' καὶ Ι' αἰῶνα", Akadimia Athinon, *Πρακτικά*, XVIII, 1943, pp.135–46.

— "Ἡ θέσις τῆς Ἐκκλησίας τῆς Κύπρου εἰς τὰ Ἐκκλησιαστικὰ Τακτικά (Notitia Episcopatuum) ἀπὸ τὸ Η' μέχρι τοῦ ΙΓ' αἰῶνος (Συμβολὴ εἰς τὴν ἱστορίαν τοῦ αὐτοκεφάλου)", University of Athens, *Ἐπετηρὶς Ἐπιστημονικῶν Ἐρευνῶν*, II, Athens, 1970, pp. 139–72, also published in A. Papageorgiou (ed.), *Πρακτικὰ Α' Διεθνοῦς Κυπριολογικοῦ Συνεδρίου*, II, Nicosia, 1972, pp. 81–120.

— "Τὸ αὐτοκέφαλον τῆς Ἐκκλησίας Κύπρου", *XVe Congrès International d'Études Byzantines, Rapports et Co-Raports*, V, ii, Athens, 1976, pp. 3–29.

KYPRIANOS, Archimandrite, Ἱστορία χρονολογικὴ τῆς νήσου Κύπρου, Venice, 1788.

KYRRIS, C.P., "Ἡ Κύπρος καὶ τὸ ἡσυχαστικὸν ζήτημα κατὰ τὸν ΙΔ´ αἰῶνα", KS 26 (1962), pp. 19–31.

— "Ὁ Κύπριος Ἀρχιεπίσκοπος Θεσσαλονίκης Ὑάκινθος (1345–6) καὶ ὁ ῥόλος του εἰς τὸν ἀντιπαλαμικὸν ἀγῶνα", KS 25 (1961), pp. 89–122.

— "The Nature of the Arab-Byzantine Relations in Cyprus from the Middle of the 7th to the Middle of the 10th Century", Graeco-Arabica 3 (1984), pp. 151–6.

LA MEERE, W., La tradition manuscrite de la correspondence de Gregoire de Chypre, Bruxelles–Rome, 1937.

LA MONTE, J.L., "A Register of the Cartulary of the Cathedral of Santa Sophia of Nicosia", Βυζάντιον 5 (1929–30), pp. 441–522.

LAURENT, V., "La succession épiscopale des derniers archêveques grecs de Chypre, de Jean le Crétois (1152) à Germain Pésimandros (1260)", REB 7 (1949), pp. 33–41.

LEMERLE, P., Le premier humanisme byzantin, Paris, 1971.

LILIE, R.-J., Byzanz und die Kreuzfahrerstaaten, Munich, 1981.

LOKIN, J.H.A., "Administration and Jurisdiction in Cyprus in the 6th Century AD", Subseciva Groningana 2 (1985), pp. 35–46.

LOMBARD, M., "Arsenaux et bois de marine dans la Méditerranée musulmane (VIIIe-XIe siècles)" in Le navire et l'économie maritime du moyen-âge au XVIIIe siècle principalement en Méditerranée (ed. M. Mollat), Paris, 1958, pp. 53–99 (106).

MAGOULIAS, H.J., "A Study in Roman Catholic and Greek Orthodox Church Relations on the Island of Cyprus between the years A.D. 1196 and 1360", Byzantinische Forschungen 5 (1977), pp. 73–93.

MANGO, C. and E.J.W. HAWKINS, "The Hermitage of St. Neophytus and its Wall-Paintings", DOP 20 (1966), pp. 119–206.

MANSI, J.D., Sacrorum conciliorum nova et amplissima collectio, XI, Florence, 1765.

MAS LATRIE, L. de, Histoire de l'île de Chypre sous le règne des princes de la Maison de Lusignan, Paris, 1855.

MEYENDORFF, J., "St Peter in Byzantine Theology" in The Primacy of Peter in the Orthodox Church (ed. J. Meyendorff et al.), London, 1963, pp. 7–29.

MICHAELIDES, H., "Περὶ τὸ αὐτοκέφαλον τῆς Ἐκκλησίας Κύπρου", Ἀπόστολος Βαρνάβας, Ser. II, 3, 1931, pp. 797–801.

MITSIDES, A.N., "Τὸ αὐτοκέφαλον τῆς Ἐκκλησίας Κύπρου", XVe Congrès international d'Etudes Byzantines, Rapports et Co-rapports, V, ii, Athens, 1976.

MORINI, E., "Apostolicità ed autocefalia in una chiesa orientale: La leggenda di S. Barnaba e l'autonomia dell'Arcivescovato di Cipro nelle fonti dei secoli V e VI", *Studi e ricerche sull'Oriente Cristiano* 2 (1979), pp. 23–45.

— "Richiami alle tradizioni di apostolicità ed organizzazione ecclesiastica nelle sedi patriarcali d'Oriente", *Bulletino dell'Istituto Storico Italiano per il Medio Evo e Archivio Muratoriano* 89 (1980-81), pp. 1–69.

MUNITIZ, J.A., "Synoptic Byzantine Chronologies of the Councils", *REB* 36 (1978), pp. 193–218.

OHME, H., *Das Concilium Quinisextum und Seine Bischofsliste*, Berlin/New York, 1991.

OIKONOMAKIS, "Ἡ Κύπρος καὶ οἱ Ἄραβες (622–965 μ. Χ.)", *Μελέται καὶ Ὑπομνήματα* 1 (1984), pp. 217–374.

OSTROGORSKY, G., "Byzantine Cities in the Early Middle Ages", *DOP* 13 (1959), pp. 45–66.

— *History of the Byzantine State* (trans. J. Hussey), Oxford, 1968.

— "The Byzantine Empire in the World of the Seventh Century", *DOP* 13 (1959), pp. 1–21.

PACE, V., "Presenze e influenze cipriote nella pittura duecentesca italiana", *XXXII Corso di Cultura sull'Arte ravennate e bizantina*, Ravenna, 1985, pp. 259–98.

PAPADOPOULLOS, Th., "Chypre: Frontière ethnique et socio-culturelle du monde byzantin", *XVe Congrès International d'Etudes Byzantines, Rapports et Co-rapports*, Athens, 1976, pp. 43–7.

— "Ἱστορικαὶ περὶ Κύπρου εἰδήσεις ἐκ τοῦ Χρονικοῦ τοῦ Ἐρνούλ καὶ Βερνάρδου τοῦ Θησαυροφύλακος", *KS* 28 (1964), pp. 39–114.

— "Μαρτύριον Κυπρίων", *Ἀναμνηστικὸς τόμος ἐπὶ τῇ πεντηκονταετηρίδι τοῦ περιοδικοῦ Ἀπόστολος Βαρνάβας*, Nicosia, 1975, pp. 307–38.

PAPAGEORGIOU, A., "Les premières incursions arabes à Chypre et leurs conséquences", *Ἀφιέρωμα εἰς τὸν Κωνσταντίνον Σπυριδάκιν*, Nicosia, 1964, pp. 152–8.

PETER, Bishop of Kherson, "Problemy svjazannye s avtokefaliej", *Messager de l'Exarchat du patriarche russe en Europe occidentale* 97-100 (1978), pp. 71–97.

PETIT, L., "Vie et ouvrages de Néophyte le Reclus", *EO* 2 (1898–9), pp. 257–68.

RAQUEZ, O., "Les confessions de foi de la chirotonie épiscopale des églises grecques", *Traditio et progressio. Studi in onore del Prof. Adrien Nocent, OSB* (ed. G. Farnesi), Rome, 1988, pp. 469–85.

RHALLES, G.A. and M. POTLES, *Σύνταγμα τῶν θείων καὶ ἱερῶν κανόνων*, Athens, 1852.

SANTA MARIA MANNINO, P., "La Vergine 'Kykkiotissa' in due icone del Duecento" in *Roma anno 1300* (ed. A.M. Romani), Rome, 1983, pp. 487–96.

SATHAS, K., Μεσαιωνική Βιβλιοθήκη, Venice, 1873.

SOTIRIOU, G.A., Τὰ βυζαντινά βιβλία τῆς Κύπρου, Athens, 1935.

SPITERIS, J., *La critica bizantina del primato romano nel saecolo XII*, Rome, 1979.

STIERNON, D., "Néophyte le Reclus", *Dictionnaire de spiritualité*, II, Paris, 1981, cols 99–110.

STRATOS, A.N., Τὸ Βυζάντιον στὸν Ζ΄ αἰῶνα, Athens, 1977.

THEOPHANES, *Theophanis Chronographia* (ed. C. de Boor), Leipzig, 1883.

TONIOLO, E.M., "Omelie e Catechesi mariane inedite di Neofito il Recluso (1134–1220c.)", *Marianum* 36 (1974), pp. 184–315.

TROITSKIJ, I.E., *Arsenij i Arsenity*, London, 1973.

— "K istorii sporov po voprosu ob ishozdenii Sviatago Duha", *Hristianskoe ctenie* 69 (1889), I, pp. 338–77; II, pp. 280–352, 520–70.

TSIKNOPOULLOS, I.P., Ἡ ἱερὰ μονὴ τοῦ Χρυσοστόμου τοῦ Κουτζουβένδη καὶ τὰ ἱερὰ αὐτῆς κτίσματα, Nicosia, 1959.

— "Ἡ ὀρθογραφικὴ ἰδιομορφία τῶν συγραφῶν τοῦ Ἐγκλείστου ἁγίου Νεοφύτου", *KS* 19 (1955), pp. 43–72.

— "Ἡ θαυμαστὴ προσωπικότης τοῦ Νεοφύτου πρεσβυτέρου, μοναχοῦ καὶ ἐγκλείστου", *Βυζάντιον* 37 (1967), pp. 311–413.

— "Κυπριακὰ τοῦ ἁγίου Νεοφύτου", *KS* 24 (1960), pp. 113–49.

— "Ἡ ὀρθογραφικὴ ἰδιομορφία τῶν συγγραφῶν τοῦ Ἐγκλείστου Ἁγίου Νεοφύτου", *KS* 19 (1955), pp. 43–72.

— Κυπριακὰ Τυπικά, Nicosia, 1969.

— "Ὁ λεξιλογικὸς πλοῦτος τοῦ Ἐγκλείστου ἁγίου Νεοφύτου", *KS* 20 (1956), pp. 97–171.

— "Συγγραφικὴ τέχνη καὶ Γραφικὸς πλοῦτος τοῦ ἁγίου Νεοφύτου", *KS* 23 (1959), pp. 57–184.

— "Τὰ ἐλάσσονα τοῦ Νεοφύτου πρεσβυτέρου μοναχοῦ καὶ ἐγκλείστου", *Βυζάντιον* 39 (1969), pp. 318–419.

— "Τὸ συγγραφικὸν ἔργον τοῦ ἁγίου Νεοφύτου", *KS* 22 (1953), pp. 67–214.

— "Τρία ἀνώνυμα βυζαντινὰ ποιήματα ἐπανευρίσκουν τὸν ποιητὴν των ἅγιον Νεόφυτον", *KS* 7 (1963), pp. 75–117.

TSOLAKES, E., "Ὁ Γεώργιος Λαπίθης καὶ ἡ ἡσυχαστικὴ ἔριδα", Ἑλληνικά 18 (1964), pp. 83–96.

VACALOPOULOS, A., "Une reine grecque de Chypre mal comprisée par les historiens, Hélène Paléologine (1442-1458)" in Πρακτικὰ τοῦ Πρώτου Διεθνοῦς Κυπριολογικοῦ Συνεδρίου (ed. A. Papageorgiou), II, Nicosia, 1972, pp. 277–80.

VRYONES, S., Βυζαντινὴ Κύπρος, Nicosia, 1990.

II TURKISH CYPRUS

ALASYA, H.F., *Kibris Tarihi*, Nicosia, 1939.

BELOBROVA, O.A., *The Cypriot Circle in Ancient Russian Literature* (in Russian), Leningrad, 1972.

CAMARIANO-CIORAN, A., "Contributions aux relations roumano-chypriotes", *Revue des études sud-est européennes* 15 (1977), pp. 493–508.

CARNE, J., *Letters from the East* (3rd ed), London, 1830.

COBHAM, C.D., *Excerpta Cypria*, Cambridge, 1908.

— *Travels in the Island of Cyprus. Translated from the Italian of Giovanni Mariti*, Cambridge, 1909.

CODEX I, Archiepiscopal Palace of Cyprus, Nicosia.

DARROUZÈS, J., "Eveques inconnus ou peu connus de Chypre", *BZ* 44 (1951).

DEMARAS, K. Th., "Ἀθησαύριστο ἔγγραφο τοῦ ἀρχιεπισκόπου Κύπρου Κυπριανοῦ", *Πρακτικὰ τοῦ Πρώτου Διεθνοῦς Κυπριολογικοῦ Συνεδρίου*, Nicosia, 1973, pp. 55-61.

EVANGELIDES, N., "Μελανοδοχεῖον τῆς Ἀρχιεπισκοπῆς Κύπρου", *Ἐκκλησιαστικὸς Φάρος* 4 (1912), pp. 58–61.

GEORGIOU, Ph., *Εἰδήσεις ἱστορικαὶ περὶ τῆς Ἐκκλησίας τῆς Κύπρου*, Athens, 1875.

HACKETT, J., *A History of the Orthodox Church of Cyprus*, London, 1901.

HADJIPSALTES, K., "Ἕλληνες ἐπίσκοποι Πάφου καὶ Κυρηνείας κατὰ τὴν περίοδον τῆς Τουρκοκρατίας (ΙϚ′ καὶ ΙΖ′ αἰών)", *KS* 24 (1960), pp. 63–71.

HARMANTA, K., "Λάπηθος–Λάμπουσα–Καραβᾶς" in A. Stylianou and K. Harmanta, *Καραβᾶς*, Nicosia, 1969.

HASIOTES, I.K., *Ἱσπανικὰ ἔγγραφα τῆς Κυπριακῆς ἱστορίας*, Nicosia, 1972.

HILL, G., *A History of Cyprus*, Cambridge, 1940.

IASONIDES, O.I., "Ἀνεύρεσις αὐτογράφου ἐθνομάρτυρος Κυπριανοῦ", *Ἑλικών* I, fasc. 20, Limassol, 1910.

KARGIOTOU, G., "Ἡ Μονὴ Παλλουριωτίσσης", *KS* 13 (1949), pp. 47–81.

KEPIADES, G.I., *Ἀπομνημονεύματα τῶν κατὰ τὸ 1821 ἐν τῇ νήσῳ Κύπρῳ τραγικῶν Σκηνῶν*, Alexandria, 1888.

KOUDOUNARES, A.L., "Ἡ οἰκογένεια τῶν Θησέων", *KS* 38–39 (1975).

KOUMOULIDES, J., *Cyprus and the War of Greek Independence 1821-1829*, London, 1974.

KYPRIANOS, Archimandrite, *Ἱστορία χρονολογικὴ τῆς νήσου Κύπρου*, Venice, 1788.

KYRIAZES, N.G., 'Αγωνιώδεις ἡμέραι τῆς ἐν Λάρνακι εὐρωπαϊκῆς παροικίας", *KX* 13 (1937), pp. 210–27.

— "Ἡ κυπριακὴ τραγωδία τοῦ 1821", *KX* 7 (1930).

— Ἱστορικαὶ εἰδήσεις ἱερᾶς Μονῆς Σταυροβουνίου, Larnaca, 1948.

— Τὰ μοναστήρια ἐν Κύπρῳ, Larnaca, 1950.

— "Τσελεπῆς Χατζηπετράκις Κυθήριος", *KX* 1 (1923), pp. 320–3.

KYRRIS, C.P., "Δεδομένα ἐπὶ τῶν κοινωνικῶν θεσμῶν τῆς Κύπρου κατὰ τὰς ἀρχὰς τοῦ 19ου αἰ.", *EKEEK* 6 (1972–3), pp. 379–80.

— Ἱστορία τῆς μέσης ἐκπαιδεύσεως Ἀμμοχώστου 1191–1955, Nicosia, 1967.

— "Νέαι ἱστορικαὶ καὶ προσωπογραφικαὶ εἰδήσεις ἐξ ἄρτι ἐκδοθέντων Κυπριακῶν ἐγγράφων. Ἐπίμετρον περὶ Ἀρχιεπισκόπων Χριστοδούλου, Παρθενίου, καὶ Νικηφόρου", *Κυπριακὸς Λόγος* 6 (1974), pp. 47–9, 96–9, 178–83.

— "Symbiotic Elements in the History of the Two Communities of Cyprus", *International Symposium on Political Geography: Proceedings*, Nicosia, 1976.

— "Τὸ 'Ἐνθύμιον' τοῦ Κωστῆ Ν.Χ. Παρασκευᾶ", *Χρονικὰ τῆς Λαπήθου*, I, ii, 1971.

LACROIX, L., Ἱστορία τῆς νήσου Κύπρου, GT: K. Vontitsianou, Athens, 1877.

LEONTIOU, L., "Ὁ Ἀρχιεπίσκοπος πάσης Κύπρου καὶ Νέας Ἰουστινιανουπόλεως, Πρόεδρος παντὸς Ἑλλησπόντου", *Παγκύπριον Λεύκωμα*, Nicosia, 1925, pp. 11–26.

LIVAS, Ch., "Ἱστορικὰ γεγονότα ἀπὸ τοὺς μάρτυρες τοῦ 1821", *Πάφος* 8 (1943), pp. 125–7.

LUKE, H.C., *Cyprus under the Turks 1571–1878*, London, 1921.

LUSIGNANO, S., *Chorograffia et breve historia universale de Cipro*, Bologna, 1573.

MARITI, G., *Viaggi Per l'Isola di Cipro*, Lucca, 1769.

MENARDOS, S., Ἡ ἐν Κύπρῳ ἱερᾷ μονῇ τῆς Παναγίας τοῦ Μαχαιρᾶ, Peiraeus, 1929.

MICHAELIDES, M.G., "Ὁ Κυρηνείας Χρύσανθος Ἰωαννίδης καὶ ἡ ἀλληλογραφία του μὲ τὸν Ἱερώνυμον Βαρλαὰμ (1877–1899), *KS* 41 (1977)", pp. 117–76.

— "Συμπλήρωμα εἰς τὴν ἀλληλογραφίαν Χρυσάνθου Ἰωαννίδη καὶ Ἱερωνύμου Βαρλαάμ", *KS* 42 (1978), pp. 107–27.

MYRANTHEUS, K., Κειμήλια τοῦ ἱεροῦ ναοῦ Χρυσελεούσης Στροβόλου, Nicosia, 1949.

— Ὁ ἅγιος Ἰωάννης ὁ Λαμπαδιστής, Nicosia, 1969.

MYRIANTHOPOULOS, Kl., Ἡ συμβολὴ τῆς Μαραθάσης εἰς τὴν Ἐκκλησίαν, Limassol, 1939.

MYRIANTHOPOULOS, K. I., 'Αρχεῖον τῆς 'Αρχιεπισκοπῆς Κύπρου. 'Αναγραφὴ ἐγγράφων ἀπὸ τοῦ 1767–1853 (MS), Nicosia, 1941.
— 'Αρχεῖον τῆς 'Αρχιεπισκοπῆς Κύπρου. Βιβλίον Μ' (MS), Nicosia, 1948/9.
— Χατζηγεωργάκης Κορνέσιος, Ὁ Διερμηνεύς τῆς Κύπρου 1779–1809, Nicosia, 1934.
— "Σπουδαῖον ἔγγραφον τοῦ ἐθνομάρτυρος 'Αρχιεπισκόπου Κυπριανοῦ", 'Απόσστολος Βαρνάβας 2, per.II (1930), pp. 440–1.

NICOLAIDES, D.L., "'Ολίγα περὶ τῆς νήσου Κύπρου", Νέον Κίτιον 2/28 Oct. 1878, No.18; 3/15 Oct. 1878, No. l9.

PANTELIOU, M.M., "Οἱ Κύπριοι στὴν ἐπανάσταση τοῦ 1821", KS 40 (1976), pp. 29–60.

PAPACHARALAMBOUS, G., "'Εγκύκλιος τοῦ ἀρχιεπισκόπου Κυπριανοῦ εἰς τὰ ἐν Κύπρῳ γεγονότα τοῦ 1821", KS 28 (1964), pp. 175–81.

PAPADOPOULLOS, Th., Social and Historical Data on Population (1570–1881), Nicosia, 1965.
— "Τὸ 'Ασμα τῶν 'Αρχιερέων", KS 35 (1971), pp. 1–50.

PATRINELES, Ch., "Πρωτοψάλται, Λαμπαδάριοι καὶ Δομέστικοι τῆς Μεγάλης 'Εκκλησίας", Μνημοσύνη 2 (1969), pp. 63–95.

PERISTIANES, I.K., Γενικὴ ἱστορία τῆς νήσου Κύπρου, Nicosia, 1910.
— 'Ισρορία τῶν ἑλληνικῶν γραμμάτων ἀπὸ τῆς Τουρκικῆς κατακτήσεως μέχρι τῆς 'Αγγλικῆς κατοχῆς (1571–1878), Nicosia, 1930.
— "Μονογραφία τῆς Μονῆς 'Αρχαγγέλου Μιχαήλ", Παγκύπριον Λεύκωμα, 1925, pp. 159–73.

PHILIPPOU, L., "Διάφορα", KX 3 (1925), p. 276.
— Ἡ 'Εκκλησία τῆς Κύπρου ἐπὶ Τουρκοκρατίας, Nicosia, 1975.
— "Νικόλαος καὶ Θεόφιλος Θησεῖς", Paphos 1 (1935), pp. 81–85.
— Τὰ ἑλληνικὰ γράμματα ἐν Κύπρῳ κατὰ τὴν περίοδον τῆς Τουρκοκρατίας (1571–1878), Nicosia, 1930.

PROTOPSALTES, E., Ἡ Κύπρος εἰς τὸν ἀγῶνα τοῦ 1821, Athens, 1971.

SPYRIDAKIS, K., "Ὁ ἐθνομάρτυς ἀρχιεπίσκοπος Κύπρου Κυπριανός", Μελέται, διαλέξεις, λόγοι, ἄρθρα, Α', Nicosia, 1972, pp. 297–317.

STAMATIADES, E.I., Βιογραφίαι τῶν 'Ελλήνων Μεγάλων Διερμηνέων τοῦ 'Οθωμανικοῦ Κράτους, Athens, 1865.

STYLIANOU, A. and J.A., The History of the Cartography of Cyprus, Nicosia, 1980.

SYKOUTRES, I.A.G. (ed.), "Εκθεσις τῆς κριτικῆς ἐπιτροπῆς τοῦ Α' Φιλολογικοῦ διαγωνισμοῦ τῆς Α. Μ. τοῦ 'Αρχιεπισκόπου κ.κ. Κυρίλλου Βασιλείου τοῦ ἀπὸ Κυρηνείας, Nicosia, 1924.

TILLYRIDES, A., "'Αγνωστα κείμενα διὰ τοὺς μητροπολίτας Κυρηνείας Τιμόθεον (1625?–1647), Πάφου καὶ Τριμυθοῦντος Νεκτάριον

(1677–1686) καὶ Ἀμαθοῦντος Γερμανῶν (1572–1600)", offprint from Θεόφιλος, Athens, 1976.

TSELIKAS, A., "Ἑπτὰ ἐπίσημα κυπριακὰ ἐκκλησιαστικὰ ἔγγραφα (1578–1771)', Θησαυρίσματα 14 (1977), pp. 251–74.

TSIKNOPOULLOS, I.P., Ἡ ἱερὰ βασιλικὴ καὶ σταυροπηγιακὴ μονὴ τῆς ὑπεραγίας Θεοτόκου τοῦ Μαχαιρᾶ, Nicosia, 1968.

— "Παφιακά", KS 31 (1967), pp. 99–118.

TSIRPANLES, Z.N. Ἀνέκδοτα ἔγγραφα ἐκ τῶν ἀρχείων τοῦ Βατικανοῦ (1625–1667), Nicosia, 1973.

WARE, T., Eustratios Argenti. A Study of the Greek Church under Turkish Rule, Oxford, 1964.

III THE ANTIOCHENE QUESTION

AL-HUSRI, S., Muhādarāt fī Nushū' al-Fikra al-Qawmīya, Cairo, 1951.

ANTONIUS, G., The Arab Awakening, London, 1939.

AZOURY, N., Le reveil de la nation arabe, Paris, 1905.

BETTS, R.B., Christians in the Arab East: A Political Study, London, 1979.

BURAYK, M, Al-Haqā'q al-Madīyah fī Ta'rikh al-Kanīsah al-Antākiyah al-Urthudhuksīyah (ed. S. Qab'in), Cairo, 1903 (see esp. pp. 73ff by the editor).

CHARLES-ROUX, F., France et chrétiens d'Orient, Paris, 1939.

CHRYSANTHES, K., "Ὁ Κωνσταντῖνος Μυριανθόπουλος καὶ ἡ Ἰκαρία", KS 45 (1981), pp. 309–33.

DELICANES, C., Ὑπομνήματα ἐπὶ Ἀντιοχικοῦ ζητήματος, Constantinople, 1900.

DMITRIEVSKI, A.A., Imperatorskoe Pravoslavnoe Palestinskoe Obshchestvo i ego deyatel'nost', 1881–1907, St Petersburg, 1907.

DURNOVO, N.A., Russkaya Panslavistskaya politika na pravoslavnom vostoke i v Rossii, Moscow, 1908.

FISHER-GALATI, S., Ottoman Imperialism and German Protestantism, Cambridge, 1959.

FRAZEE, C.A., Catholics and Sultans: The Church and the Ottoman Empire, 1453–1923, Cambridge, 1983.

GIERS, A.A., Rossiya i Blizhny Vostok, St Petersburg, 1906.

HADDAD, Rashid, "Sources (Hellènes) de la controverse dans l'Eglise melchite au XVIIIe siècle", Actes du premier congrès international des études balkaniques et sud-est européennes, IV, Sofia, 1969, pp. 499–505.

HADDAD, Robert M., Syrian Christians in Muslim Society: An Interpretation, Princeton, NJ, 1970.

HAJJAR, J., *Le Vatican, la France et le Catholicisme oriental*, Paris, 1979.

HITTI, P.K., *The Impact of the West on Syria and Lebanon in the XIXth Century*, Paris, 1955.

HOPWOOD, D., *The Russian Presence in Syria and Palestine 1843-1914: Church and Politics in the Near East*, Oxford, 1969.

HOURANI, A.H., *Arabic Thought in the Liberal Age, 1798-1939*, Oxford, 1962.

ISSAWI, C., (ed.) *The Economic History of the Middle East, 1800-1914*, Chicago, 1966.

KARAPATAKES, G., *Τὸ Ἀντιοχικὸν ζήτημα*, Constantinople, 1909.

KAROLIDES, P., *Περὶ τῆς ἐθνικῆς καταγωγῆς τῶν ὀρθοδόξων χριστιανῶν Συρίας καὶ Παλαιστίνης*, Athens, 1909 (Arabic translation, Jerusalem, 1910).

— "Πατριαρχεῖον Ἀντιοχείας", *Πανελλήνιον λεύκωμα ἐθνικῆς ἑκατονταετηρίδος 1821-1921*, VI, Athens, 1922, pp. 137–41.

KARPAT, K., *An Inquiry into the Social Foundations of Nationalism in the Ottoman State: From Social Estates to Classes, from Millets to Nations*, Princeton, NJ, 1973.

KURBAN, I., *Al-azma al-Batriyarkīyah al-Anṭākiyah al-Urthudhukṣīyah, 1891-1899*, Beirut, 1979.

LEVENQ, P.G., SJ, "Akhir Mazhar al-Siyasa Rusīya al-Dīnīya fī al-Sharq al-Adnā", *Al-Mashriq*, 1935, pp. 574–85.

LEWIS, B., *Race and Color in Islam*, New York, 1971.

MYRIANTHOPOULOS, Kl., *Ἡ συμβολὴ τῆς Μαραθάσης εἰς τὴν Ἐκκλησίαν*, Limassol, 1939.

PAPADOPOULOS, Ch. A., *Ἡ λατινικὴ προπαγάνδα ἐν Συρίᾳ*, Athens, 1949.

— *Ἱστορία τῆς Ἐκκλησίας Ἀντιοχείας*, Alexandria, 1951 (Arabic translation, Beirut, 1984).

— *Ἱστορία τῆς Ἐκκλησίας Ἱεροσολύμων*, Athens, (2nd edn) 1970.

PHOTOPOULOS, Ph., "Ἁγιοταφίται ἀναδειχθέντες Πατριάρχαι Κωνσταντινουπόλεως καὶ Ἀντιοχείας", *Νέα Σιών* 9 (1909), pp. 300–306.

POLIAK, A.N., *Feudalism in Egypt, Syria, Palestine and the Lebanon, 1250-1900*, London, 1939.

RICHTER, J.A., *A History of Protestant Missions in the Near East*, Edinburgh, 1910.

RUSTUM, A., *Kanīsah Madīnah Allāh Anṭākiyah al-'Uzmā*, III, Beirut, 1958.

SAUVAGET, J., *Alep. Essai sur le developpement d'une grande ville syrienne des origines au milieu du XIXe siècle*, Paris, 1941.

SHAW, S.J. and E.K., *History of the Ottoman Empire and Modern Turkey*, II. *Reform, Revolution and Republic: The Rise of Modern Turkey, 1808-1975*, Cambridge, 1977.

STAVROU, T., *Russian Interests in Palestine, 1882–1914,* Thessaloniki, 1963.
Tafāsil al-azma al-Batriyarkīyah al-Antākiyah al-Urthudhuksīyah, Cairo, 1899
TIBAWI, A.L., *American Interests in Syria, 1800-1901: A Study of Educational, Literary and Religious Work,* Oxford, 1966.
–   *British Interests in Palestine, 1800–1901,* Oxford, 1961.
ZEINE, Z.N., *Arab–Turkish Relations and the Emergence of Arab Nationalism,* Beirut, 1958.

INDEX

Marrou, H.-I., 44
Marseilles, 229
martyrion, 46
Mary of Antioch, second wife of Manuel I
    Komnenos, 5
Marx, Karl, 422
Mas Latrie, L. de, 164, 309
Matteos, Epiphanios, patriarchal commissioner,
    338
Matthew II, patriarch of Constantinople, 230
Matthew, abbot, former coffee-maker of
    Spyridon of Antioch, 401,
Mavrogordato, Alexander, Phanariot Greek, 18
Maximus the Confessor, Church Father, 209
Méchain, Edmond, French consul in Larnaca,
    293, 296n, 300–301
Mehmed Aga, *muteveli* of Lapithos, 315
Mehmed, Esseyit, Ottoman pasha of Cyprus,
    221
Mehmed Silahşor (= Esseyit Mehmed Emin,
    nicknamed Küçük Mehmed), Ottoman
    governor of Cyprus, 292–3, 294, 295,
    300–301, 315, 320
Meitan, suburb of Damascus, 368, 369, 379,
    383, 400
Meletios II Dumānī, patriarch of Antioch,
    formerly metropolitan of Laodicea
    (Latakia – al-Lādhiqīya)
    activities after the fall of Spyridon, 348, 366,
        369, 372, 373, 376, 381, 384
    activities as patriarch, 400–401, 402, 403–4,
        413, 414, 416–7
    biographical details, 354
    elected *locum tenens* in succession to Germanos
        of Tarsus, 372, 385, 386, 387, 388, 389
    elected patriarch, 352, 390, 391
Meletios I, metropolitan of Kition, 304
Meletios II, metropolitan of Kition, 22, 304, 305
Meletios III Metaxakes, metropolitan of Kition
    (subsequently Meletios IV of
    Constantinople, Meletios II of Alexandria)
    early career, 338, 376, 430
    as metropolitan of Kition, 428, 436, 438, 442,
        443, 444
    subsequent career, 351 439–40
Meletios, abbot of the monastery of the
    Acheiropoietos, Karavas, 309, 315
Meletios, metropolitan of Kyrenia, 250
Meletios, metropolitan of Petra, 333, 351
Meletios Kronides, archbishop of Kyriakoupolis
    (later of Jordan), 338, 351n
Meletius I, archbishop of Antioch, 34, 35
Melissenos, Christodoulos, cleric of
    Constantinople, 336
Melkite schism, 330

Memorandum of the Prelates, presented to the British
    authorities in 1879, 427
Menardos, S., 445
Mersin, town in Asia Minor, seat of the metro-
    politan of Tarsus, 347, 403, 408–9
Mesaoria, *kadilik* of, 251
Mese Street, Leucosia, 58
Metaxakes, Meletios *see* Meletios III Metaxakes,
    metropolitan of Kition
Methodios, patriarch of Antioch, 418
Methodios, metropolitan of Emessa, 305
Methodius, Church Father, 114
metochion, small monastic house and estate
    belonging to a larger monastery, 55, 202,
    247
Metrophanes II, patriarch of Constantinople, 18
Metropolitan Luke, monastery in Syria, 6
Metropolitan Museum of New York, 44
Michael I, emperor, 86
Michael Romanov, tsar of Russia, 223, 228,
    234–5
Michael I Keroularios, patriarch of
    Constantinople, 173, 175, 189, 190, 191,
    192
Michael I the Syrian, Jacobite patriarch of
    Antioch, 3, 55, 163n
Michael, archangel, 13, 225, 238
Michael, metropolitan of Russia, 157n
Michaelides, H., 85, 86, 89
Michaelides, M.G., 310
Mikellides, Onouphrios, schoolmaster, 303, 304
Mimis, renegade Christian, nephew of
    Parthenios of Kyrenia, 230
Mirror of Examples, 19th-cent. devotional work,
    240
Misael, metropolitan of Tyre and Sidon
    biographical details, 333, 355
    conduct after election of Meletios II, 391, 392
    conduct during interregnum, 368, 370, 373,
        376, 381, 387, 388
    at Saydnāya, 348
Mitrophanes, doctor and monk of Machairas,
    246
Mochrousa, Damascus newspaper, 396
monastic life in Cyprus, 243–7, 251, 442; *see also*
    Hermitage of St Neophytos the Recluse,
    Koutzouvendi, Kykkos, Lakatamia,
    Machairas, Stavrovouni
"Monks' Revolt" of 1832, 246
Monothelitism, 38
Monophysitism, 44, 47–8
Morini, E., 2
Morphou, town in Cyprus (Nicosia), 250
Morris, C.M., 11
Moumdjis, George, *see* Hadji Giannes, George

Mourouzes, Constantine, Grand Dragoman, 312n
Moyses, bishop of Famagusta, 232
Mu'awiya I, Umayyad caliph, 73
Mu'awiya, Muslim general, 66
al-Muqtadir, Abbasid caliph, 51, 52
Muhammad, prophet of Islam, 109, 115, 133, 137, 170, 254
muhasil, tax collector, 251, 305
Munitiz, J.A., 9
Murat III, Ottoman sultan, 271n, 297
muselim, Ottoman governor, 306
musir (Turkish: *müsür*), Ottoman field-marshal, 396
Muslim Community in Damascus, President of, 399
Muslims, and Iconoclasm, 50; in the eyes of Neophytos the Recluse, 198
Mustafa, renegade Christian, nephew of Parthenios of Kyrenia, 230
muteveli (Turkish: *mutevelli*), administrator of a *vakuf*, a pious Muslim foundation, 315, 405
Mutrān al-Nūr, Archpriest of Light, 334
Mylonas, Nikodemos, *see* Nikodemos Mylonas, metropolitan of Kition
Myrianthopoulos, Constantine
  his career and work as Archivist of the Archdiocese of Cyprus, 285, 310, 314, 323, 326–9, 445
  his journal, 23, 328–9, 357–61, 363–404
  his opinion of Patriarch Spyridon, 378
  his participation in the Antiochene crisis of 1897–99, 363–6, 371, 374, 377
Myrianthopoulos, Kl., 305, 306, 308
Myriantheus family, 326
Myriantheus, Leontios, *see* Leontios Myriantheus, archimandrite of Kition
Myrianthousa, district of Cyprus, 304
Myriocephalon, battle of, 56, 160
Myrtou, village in Cyprus (Kyrenia), 444

naipa, Islamic judge, 406
Naples, collection of funds for Cyprus, 227, 228
Nasif, Damascus lawyer, 384
Naxos, Aegean Island, 244
Nazim Pasha. Hüseyin, *vali* of Damascus
  allows bishops opposed to Spyridon to meet in Damascus, 347
  biographical details, 345–6
  his conduct after the election of Meletios II, 391, 393–6
  his conduct during the interregnum, 349, 366, 368, 372, 374, 379–89
Nehru, Pandit, 307
Neilos, bishop of Tamassos (Tamaseia), 53, 182, 203, 229n

Nektarios, metropolitan of Beroea (Aleppo)
  account of his enthronement in Aleppo, 360–61, 408–9
  biographical details, 336, 356
  maintains the Greek side during the interregnum, 366, 368, 369, 370, 371, 374, 381, 382–3, 384, 385
  protests at the election of Meletios of Laodicea first as *locum tenens* and then as patriarch, 386, 389, 390, 391, 393, 399, 402
  supports Patriarch Spyridon, 348, 363, 364
  his subsequent exile, 412–17
  his unpublished hournal, 329
  writes to K. Myrianthopoulos on his non-recognition of Patriarch Meletios, 410–11
Nektarios, bishop of Paphos, 229n
Nektarios, St, bishop of Pentapolis, 349
Nelidov, A.I., Russian ambassador at Constantinople, 358, 392, 396
Neohori (Yeniköy), village on the Bosphorus, 349, 368, 369
Neologos, Athenian newspaper, 391, 392
neomartyrs, *see* George, Cypriot neomartyr; George, martyred priest of Yiolou; Kantara, martyrs of; Polydore, Cypriot neomartyr; Sozon, Cypriot neomartyr; Theoteknos, Cypriot neomartyr
Neophytos II, patriarch of Constantinople, 230
Neophytos VIII, patriarch of Constantinople, 343
Neophytos I, archbishop of Cyprus, 53
Neophytos the Recluse, St, Cypriot monk
  on the *azymes*, 176–7, 190, 203
  birth and biographical details, 97–8, 100–101, 152–3, 155, 200–202, 207
  brother of Koutzouvendi, 6–7, 97, 107, 207
  his contact with Jerusalem, 14, 202
  his cultural level, 107n, 112, 118, 152, 155, 190, 210
  on the emperor, 158, 160, 182–3, 184
  founder of the Hermitage, 97, 200–202
  on the Frankish rulers of Cyprus, 197–200, 202–3, 204
  his hermeneutic method, 114–5
  on the Holy Spirit, 176, 177–81, 186, 193, 197
  on Islam, 115, 170, 171
  on the Latin Church, 116, 148, 162–3, 166–7, 170–72, 175–7, 182, 184, 188–97, 203–4
  on the lenten fast, 174–5
  his lexical characteristics, 56–7, 159–60, his library, 8, 101, 102, 108, 109, 112, 208
  his literary activity, 99–104, 106, 107, 108–9, 111–14, 147, 152, 201, 207–8, 210